Musics of Many Cultures

Musics

of Many Cultures
An Introduction • Elizabeth May, Editor

Foreword by Mantle Hood

UNIVERSITY OF CALIFORNIA PRESS

Berkeley • Los Angeles • London

University of California Press
Berkeley and Los Angeles, California
University of California Press, Ltd.
London, England

Library of Congress Cataloging in Publication Data
Main entry under title:

Musics of many cultures.

   1. Ethnomusicology.   2. Music–History and criticism.
3. Music and society.   I. May, Elizabeth, writer on
music.
ML3798.M87   781.7   76-50251

Copyright © 1980 by The Regents of the University of California
First Paperback Printing 1983
ISBN 0–520–04778–8
Printed in the United States of America
        6   7   8   9

The paper used in this publication meets the minimum
requirements of American National Standard for Information
Sciences—Permanence of Paper for Printed Library Materials,
ANSI Z39.48-1984. ∞

To Kurt Stone

Contents

Foreword

by Mantle Hood

In considering the authors of this volume a familiar adage comes to mind: "If you want a job well done, ask a busy man." To make the saying even more pertinent we might alter it as follows: "If you really want to know and understand, ask the person who's been there and done it."

The sense of these words is essential to a field such as ethnomusicology. Some senior scholars have repeatedly resisted publishers' pleas to write a "music-of-the-world" book. And wisely. The difficulty in such a commission is not in finding information about some remote musical culture of the world. Chances are, if it is known at all, it is known through publications. For some musical cultures, of course, publications and even unpublished music manuscripts are available in great number. In sum the total of volumes and articles devoted to the musical cultures of the world and original manuscripts in some kind of music notation is truly staggering. Many musical cultures are also represented by commercial recordings and films. Multitudes more can be included among the random recordings and photographic collections of tourists, anthropologists, linguists, and other fieldworkers. The plethora of secondary sources of all kinds is patent. Then why can't one person write a music-of-the-world book?

In the course of a lifetime, the scholar-researcher can hardly be expected to master more than two or three musical cultures, including closely related ones. The problem in extending beyond these in response to a publisher's wish is not the availability of secondary sources or of understanding them; the problem is knowing what to include and what to leave out. The person with years of accumulated knowledge and with actual experience in the *performance* of a given music *knows* what to include and what to omit, for example, within the restricted space of a dictionary entry, an encyclopedic article, or a condensed introduction like those appearing in this volume. The person who's been there and done it can tell you reliably what it is and how it works.

The first modest attempt at corporate authorship based on this recognition was a booklet published in 1960 by the Department of Music at UCLA under the title *Festival of Oriental Music and the Related Arts*. The present volume appears twenty years later. Time has allowed unmistakable signs of maturity in a relatively young field like ethnomusicology. Expectations of high standards in scholarship and a range of essential methodologies, including training in musical performance and performance practice in the field, have nearly stabilized the maverick directions typical of a few years ago. Sporadic imitation of methods germane only to other disciplines sometimes attracts the novice momentarily; but the mainstream of investigation has achieved an identity. Rather than the cluster of individual approaches it may have been a decade ago ethnomusicology is fast becoming a discipline.

Appearing twenty years after the first UCLA publication, *Musics of Many Cultures* is much more satisfying, much broader in coverage, and much more thorough in treatment.

It is satisfying to me, personally, because I am familiar with the writings of every one of its authors. It is particularly satisfying, because many of the contributors are former students of mine. From the beginning of their studies, however, they have been regarded as colleagues, "fellow workers" in a field largely unknown to most Western musicians, who claim unabashed ignorance of all except the European art tradition of music. It is rare to find an artist or architect or philosopher or some other humanist who is totally ignorant of the culture of the non-Western world in his or her respective field.

Late in the twentieth century, no serious musician of whatever professional commitment can any longer afford to remain ignorant of the music, for example, of China (about one fourth of the world's population) or of Korea and Japan, which it strongly influenced. As we near the twenty-first century, an admission of ignorance of the primary cultural features (and music is one of them) of India, Southeast Asia, the North and South American continents is an embarrassing confession for anyone claiming to be educated. With daily reminders of an energy crisis, it is at our own imminent peril that we remain ignorant of cultural values in the Middle East. In this day of shrunken continents and Third World nations bristling with new identities in Africa and elsewhere, each introduction in this volume should be regarded as one means of relieving, at long last, our ignorance of the values and sanctions, of the very identity of peoples and their cultures, which until now have not been readily accessible or not reliably accessible.

Essential foreign terms and their concepts are listed as a glossary at the end of each article, and a highly selective bibliography is added to take the reader as far beyond these introductions as he may wish to go.

The subject matter of ethnomusicology is both aural and visual. What a pleasure to read a discography prepared by an expert and a filmography by someone who's been there.

Several years ago, the first "giant leap for mankind" was taken in the name of technology and science. In the name of the humanities this book is a modest but significant first step in alleviating mankind's ignorance of its cultural self.

Honolulu   Mantle Hood
December, 1979

Editor's Preface

Ethnomusicologists are concerned with music anywhere in the world and with almost as many approaches to this music as there are scholars.
McALLESTER 1972:xii

My goal in assembling this book has been to present a series of introductory essays on the musics of several cultures, countries, and continents around the world, each written by a specialist. It is intended for readers with a serious interest in enlarging their musical horizons. For even a scholar to know the music of another culture in addition to his own is a lifetime task. To the best of my knowledge there has been no such compilation. The essays are arranged by continent beginning with Asia. I have omitted Europe and North America (with the exception of Eskimos and "Native Americans") for the reason that there is a vast amount of material available on the many facets of European music and on the musics of the many peoples who have produced the kaleidoscope of "American music."

The essays vary greatly in both approach and scope, as ethnomusicologists come from many disciplines. In this collection most of the contributors are musicologically oriented and trained; some are anthropologists; a few are at home in both fields; two are primarily performing artists. Their writing of course reflects their orientation. Wherever feasible, an author writes about *his own* music. He relates to that into which he was born in a way that no outsider can; however, the outsider occasionally perceives musical structures and relationships that the native-born takes for granted without conscious analysis. The scope of the essays varies from a description of the music and dance in a village in Ghana written by two brothers who are master drummers in that village, to two essays on the music of South America by a North American. This range, from a small village to an entire continent, illustrates the fact that although one may expect to find certain general recognizable traits in the music of South America or of sub-Saharan Africa, yet in every small area within a large expanse the music has certain characteristics unique to itself.[1]

In the sections on Africa, Asia, and Oceania there are regrettable omissions. Again consideration of space necessitated arbitrary decisions. Another factor was the availability of writers when this book was conceived. The choices do not necessarily reflect the interest of one music over that of another. All musics are interesting for one reason or another and there are many distinguished ethnomusicologists not represented herein.

As in every scholarly field, ethnomusicologists must absorb a common core of knowledge that in time becomes a sort of framework for their thinking. To avoid duplication in the glossaries accompanying each essay and in the essays themselves, I have appended here a brief list of concepts and terms known to every ethnomusicologist.

Those most often referred to by this group of writers are the Hornbostel-Sachs system of instrument classification and the *cents* system of interval measurement.

---

1. Nettl's statements that "Today, after a period in which the particular character of a music was stressed above all else, the search for universals is again important" and that ethnomusicology is in "a state of ferment" were underscored by the call for papers to be read at the 1978 annual conference of the Society for Ethnomusicology. "Broad Awareness and World Musics" was the general theme. Papers were invited on the following subjects: "Musical changes, applications of ethnomusicology in diverse settings, current issues, and future directions in ethnomusicology, urban ethnomusicology, and analytical aspects of the social context of music" (S.E.M. Newsletter March-April, 1978:1). This fermentation has swept through the discipline since the writing of most of these papers though the implications are apparent.

The Hornbostel-Sachs (Erich von Hornbostel, 1877-1935; Curt Sachs, 1881-1959) system was developed following the discovery that the sounds of much non-Western music do not fit into the well-known grouping of Western orchestral and band instruments: strings, woodwinds, brass, and percussion. The Hornbostel-Sachs classification groups instruments as follows: idiophone, any instrument "whose material itself produces the sound, without being previously stretched in any way whatever" (Kunst (1969:58); aerophone, a wind instrument, any instrument whose sound is caused by the vibrations of a column of air (with a few exceptions such as the bull-roarer); membranophone, "made to sound by means of a skin or membrane stretched over the instrument" (ibid.); chordophone, a stringed instrument; electrophone (added after 1914), an instrument dependent on an electrical current for sound production.

In 1884 Alexander John Ellis (1814-1890) a reportedly tone-deaf English mathematician and philologist, was inspired to divide a half step (the distance from any note in Western equal temperament to the nearest note above or below it) into one hundred equidistant parts, which he called "cents." He also devised a system for the conversion of Western tempered intervals into cents with the aid of logarithms. This cents system has made possible the almost completely accurate measurement of any interval in any of the extremely disparate tonal systems around the world. To aid in notation the symbol ↑ *or* + is often used to indicate that a tone is a little higher than written; ↓ *or* − to indicate that it is lower. Ellis's article "On the Musical Scales of Various Nations" (1885) earned him the title of "Father of ethno-musicology" (Kunst 1969:2-12).

A few more concepts basic to ethnomusicological thinking include the following terms.

Acculturation—The continuous process by which one culture assimilates and adapts certain aspects of another culture or cultures. A striking example is the interweaving of Western popular music and instruments with musics around the world.

Diffusion vs. Polygenesis—A much discussed and not satisfactorily answered question is whether similar instruments appear in widely separated parts of the world as a result of migration or do they simply emerge? The diffusion theory seems the obvious answer in neighboring cultures.

Ethnic Music—This term is wrongly used as an umbrella to cover all non-Western music. *All* music, including Western music, is ethnic in that it is a part of the culture from which it emanates.

"High" vs. "Primitive" Music Cultures— These two snobbish terms should be abolished, although they are difficult to replace. "High" in general connotes music with an ancient and well-known theoretical system, a form of notation, and at least some intricate instruments. "Primitive" refers to the music of nonliterate societies. Such music is not necessarily primitive at all. Its makers simply live by a set of values different from those of the literate societies. Their music can be intricate indeed (see the music examples in the Jones essay on the music of Australian aborigines). Perhaps *aural* or *oral* can be substituted for *primitive*.

Male-Female Concept—prevalent in many societies, including Western—for example, Western masculine and feminine cadences. In some societies women are not permitted access to certain rites or instruments.

Recording and Transcription—With the advent of the portable tape recorder, the obtaining of completely accurate field recordings is no longer a problem, but the transcription of them still is. There have been a number of attempts to solve this stumbling block; the best known is Charles Seeger's melograph.

Tonal Framework—The music of any society, except the purely rhythmic (i.e., drum music), is based on some kind of tonal system called scale, mode, and by many other names, as evidenced in this volume. These frameworks vary greatly in both concept and construction. In some aural societies the use of them may be instinctive rather than rationalized (deliberate).

Acknowledgments

First, foremost, and over a long period, to the scholars who have made this volume. They have stood by through vicissitudes, rewritten, lengthened, abridged, and taken care of tiresome details ad infinitum. This book is theirs.

I am also deeply indebted to the following: James Kubeck, University of California Press, who saw the potential of this volume and who, from his perceptiveness and vast experience provided guidance and support, encouragement and discouragement, in innumerable ways; Shirley Warren, also of the University of California Press, who took hold of this huge compendium at the eleventh hour and made it ready for publication; Michael Moore, rerecording engineer and tape editor, the best; David Dexter, who, in addition to copy editing, provided illuminating suggestions as to content and organization; my excellent typists, Annette Morgan, Diana Spears, and Antonia Turman.

Elizabeth May

Los Angeles
June 1979

Glossary
A Brief Glossary of Ethnomusicological Terms in Common Use[*]

aerophone-see under Hornbostel-Sachs above

anhemitonic-without half steps, usually refers to scales

chordophone-see under Hornbostel-Sachs above

conjunct-successive degrees of a mode or melody not more than a modal degree apart

disjunct-successive degrees of a mode or melody separated by more than a modal degree

electrophone-see under Hornbostel-Sachs above

gapped scale-omits one or more pitches of a tuning system in creating a mode or scale

heptatonic-six note, usually refers to a tonal framework or scale

heterophony-the paralleling of a musical line, usually vocal, by another voice or instrument with almost, but not quite, the same tones. The second melodic line may slightly embroider the first, anticipate it, follow it by a beat or so, or move with it, often slightly distuned to it

hexatonic-seven note, usually refers to a tonal framework or scale

hocket-consists of the rapid alternation of two (or more) voices or instruments with single notes or short groups of notes

idiophone-see under Hornbostel-Sachs above

membranophone-see under Hornbostel-Sachs above

microtone-an interval smaller than a half step or semitone

music notation-may consist of notes or neumes, a graph or graphs, tablature, numbers, letters or, in some cases, symbols unique to a culture

[*]With a few exceptions, terms to be found in the Harvard Dictionary are not included here.

organology-"the science of musical instruments—should include not only the history and description of instruments but also equally important but neglected aspects of 'the science' of musical instruments, such as particular techniques of performance, musical function, decoration (as distinct from construction), and a variety of socio-cultural considerations (Hood 1971:124)"

rhythm (in those definitions dependent on types of meter-pulse groupings

-additive: a metrical unit made up of subdivisions used successively in a cyclic manner

-asymmetrical: metrical units not divisible by 2 or 3. May be in the time signature or in rhythmic accents or subdivisions of measures, i.e., $\frac{12}{8} - 3 + 2 + 3 + 4$ or $5 + 7$

-divisive: evenly subdivided measures as in much Western music

A few more points may facilitate reading:

A word foreign to the English language is italicized on its first appearance only and not then if it has been admitted to Webster's Third International Dictionary.

A map accompanies an essay when it is needed for clarification of discussion.

An annotated list of ethnographic films has been appended to most of the essays. Almost all contain music. Such films are an excellent introduction to a music, especially if one looks at ethnomusicology as "the study of music in culture" (Merriam 1964:6).

Bibliography

A Selective Bibliography of Publications Relevant to the General Field of Ethnomusicology

GENERAL REFERENCES

Baker's Biographical Dictionary of Music and Musicians and Supplement.
    1958, 1971. Edited by Nicolas Slonimsky. New York: G. Schirmer.
    Basically a dictionary of Western musicians. Includes a few ethnomusicologists.

Directory of Ethnomusicological Sound Recording Collections in the United States and Canada. Special Series No. 2.
    1971. Ann Arbor, Mich.: Society for Ethnomusicology, Inc.

Harvard Dictionary of Music.
    1969. 2d ed. Edited by Willi Apel. Cambridge, Mass.: Harvard University Press.
    Deals primarily with Western music. Some ethnomusicological entries.

Kunst, Jaap.
    1955. *Ethno-musicology. A study of its nature, its problems, methods and representative personalities to which is added a bibliography.* The Hague: Nijhoff.
    1969*a*. 3d edition. "Much enlarged."
    1969*b*. Supplement to the third edition.
    The first and second editions are out of print. The third is indispensable to any serious ethnomusicologist.

The New Encyclopaedia Britannica in 30 Volumes: Macropaedia.
    1974. Chicago: Encyclopaedia Britannica. 19 Vols.
    Contains numerous articles on ethnomusicological subjects.

The New Grove Dictionary of Music and Musicians.
    1980. Washington, D.C.: Grove's Dictionaries of Music Inc.
    Twenty volumes. In the field of ethnomusicology "there are contributors from over 50 countries in every part of the world" as well as an "ethnomusicological index with over 9000 entries . . . listing all the references to instruments and terms in the entries on non-Western and folk music and directing the reader to the article section where they are defined or mentioned." A number of the writers contributed to this volume.

GENERAL

Collaer, Paul.
    1971. *Music of the Americas.* New York: Praeger.
    About the Eskimos and Indians in North America, the non-Hispanic peoples of some South American countries. Profusely illustrated.

Festival of Oriental Music and the Related Arts.
    1960. Los Angeles: University of California.
    Essays on Bali, Java, Japan, India, Persia, and Brecht's *Good Woman of Setzuan.*

Haywood, Charles, ed.
    1966. *Folk Songs of the World.* New York: John Day.
    With each culture introduced there is a brief description of salient features of its folk songs.

Hood, Mantle.
    1963. "Music the Unknown." In F. Harrison, M. Hood, V. Palisca, *Musicology.* Pp. 215–326. Englewood Cliffs, N.J.: Prentice-Hall.
    A summary of the early history of ethnomusicology.
    1971. *The Ethnomusicologist.* New York: McGraw-Hill.
    Drawing on his own experience Hood discusses, among other topics, the problems of transcription and notation; organology, including a proposal for a new system of instrument classification, the organogram; and field methods, with a section on the making of ethnographic film.

Lomax, Alan.
    1968. *Folk Song Style and Culture: A Staff Report on Cantometrics.* Washington, D.C.: Association for the Advancement of Science.
    Propounds Lomax's theory that analysis of the singing style of a people, including voice quality, form, and a number of other elements will show analogies with the total social structure of that people.

1971. "Song Structure and Social Structure." In *Readings in Ethnomusicology.* Pp. 227-252. Edited by David P. McAllester. New York: Johnson Reprint Corporation.

Malm, William P.
1977. *Music Cultures of the Pacific, the Near East, and Asia.* 2d ed. Englewood Cliffs, N.J.: Prentice Hall. An introductory book. Includes sections on Oceania; the Philippines, Borneo, and Indonesia; Moslem Africa, Ethiopia, and the Near East; Central and Southern Asia; Southeast Asia; East Asia; and Northeast Asia and the Island Countries. In addition to selective bibliographies and discographies, Malm defines many terms relevant to the areas discussed.

McAllester, David P.
1971. "Some Thoughts on 'Universals' in World Music," *Ethnomusicology,* XV, 3, 379-380.

McAllester, David P., ed.
1971. *Readings in Ethnomusicology.* New York: Johnson Reprint Corporation.
A series of twenty-three essays by distinguished ethnomusicologists grouped under the following rubrics: The Field, Notation and Classification, History, Functionalism, and Regional Studies. Includes an annotated bibliography.

Merriam, Alan P.
1964. *The Anthropology of Music.* Evanston, Ill.: Northwestern University Press.
Many approaches, concepts, and attitudes to the study of music as a part of culture are introduced and thoroughly reviewed.

Moorhead, Gladys Evelyn, and Donald Pond.
1942. *Music of Young Children. II. General Observations.* Santa Barbara, Calif.: Pillsbury Foundation Studies.
A study of the uninhibited chant of young children and of their free use of a group of non-Western instruments. Other booklets in this series include *Chant I* (1941), *Musical Notation III* (1944), and *Free Use of Instruments for Musical Growth IV* (1951).

"Music in World Cultures"
1972. *Music Educators Journal,* 59, 2.
Entire issue.

Nettl, Bruno.
1956. *Music In Primitive Culture.* Cambridge, Mass.: Harvard University Press.
1964. *Theory and Method in Ethnomusicology.* London: Free Press of Glencoe.
A comprehensive introduction to the field.
1973. *Folk and Traditional Music of the Western Continents.* With chapters on the music of Lat-

in America by Gérard Béhague. 2d ed. Englewood Cliffs, N.J.: Prentice Hall.
A companion volume to Malm's *Music Cultures of the Pacific, the Near East, and Asia.*
1975. "The State of Research in Orally Transmitted Music." *International Folk Music Council, Working Papers of the Twenty-third Conference.* Regensburg, West Germany.

Reck, David.
1977. *Music of the Whole Earth.* New York: Charles Scribner's Sons.
A personal and original approach. Profusely illustrated with photographs; also maps, drawings, and diagrams, most of them hand drawn.

Sachs, Curt.
1943. *The Rise of Music in the Ancient World East and West.* New York: Norton.
1953. *Rhythm and Tempo. A Study in Music History.* New York: Norton.
1962. *The Wellsprings of Music.* The Hague: Nijhoff. Edited by Jaap Kunst.

Selected Reports, Volume 1, No. 1.
1966. Edited by Mantle Hood and others. Los Angeles: Institute of Ethnomusicology, University of California.
Essays by Chianis, Hood, Hutchinson, Knopoff, Kremenliev, Lui, Moore, Seeger, Wachsmann.
1968. *Volume 1, No. 2.*
Essays by Briegleb, Garfias, Harrison, Lui, Williamson.
1970. *Volume 1, No. 3.*
Essays by Crossley-Holland, Hood, Koetting, Powers, Seeger.
1974. *Volume 2, No. 1.*
Essays by Moore, A. Moyle, Pacholczyk, Caton, Walcott, Liu, Morton, Woodson, Addison, Flora, Giles, Owens. With particular emphasis on the melograph, its functions and failings.
1975. *Volume 2, No. 2.*
David Morton, special editor for this issue on the musics of Southeast Asia. Essays by Silapabaleng, Morton, Mendenhall, Hood, Trân Văn Khê, Cadar, Toth, Harrell, Williamson, U Khin Zaw, Sheppard, Dyck.
1978. *Volume 3, No. 1.*
Edited by James Porter. Essays by Porter, Marcel-Dubois, Burman-Hall, Erdely, Koskoff, Fory, C. Niles.

INSTRUMENTS

Baines, Anthony, ed.
1966. *Musical Instruments through the Ages.* London: Faber.

Buchner, A.
  1972. *Folk Music Instruments of the World.* New York: Crown.
    Profusely illustrated.
Diagram Group.
  1976. *Musical Instruments of the World: An Illustrated Encyclopaedia.* New York: Paddington Press.
Jenkins, Jean.
  1970. *Ethnic Musical Instruments: Identification, Conservation.* London: M. Evelyn for the International Council of Museums.
    Parallel texts in English and French.
  1970. *Musical Instruments: Handbook to the [Horniman] Museum's Collection.* 2d ed. London: Inner London Education Authority.
    Contains distribution maps of the incidence around the world of jew's-harps, single membrane drums, pan-pipes, bagpipes, bullroarers, and bow-harps.
Marcuse, Sybil.
  1964. *Musical Instruments. A Comprehensive Dictionary.* New York: Doubleday.
Montagu, Jeremy, and John Burton.
  1971. "A Proposed New Classification System for Musical Instruments." *Ethnomusicology,* XV, 1, 49–70.
    Indebted in part to the Linnaean system of botanical classification.
Sachs, Curt.
  1940. *The History of Musical Instruments.* New York: Norton.
    Covers the history of both Western and non-Western instruments. Divided into four parts and an epilogue: "The Primitive and Prehistoric Epoch," "Antiquity," "The Middle Ages," "The Modern Occident," and "The Twentieth Century." Contains a detailed exposition of the Hornbostel-Sachs system of instrument classification.

JOURNALS
Ethnomusicology (Journal of the Society for Ethnomusicology). Published three times yearly, sent to members.
Yearbook (formerly Journal) of the International Folk Music Council. Published annually, sent to members.

IMPORTANT FILM CATALOGS AND SOURCES
Catalog of Dance Films.
  1974. New York: Dance Films Association, Inc.
Catalogues of Macmillan-Audio Brandon and Contemporary Films/McGraw-Hill.
A Filmography for American Indian Education.
  1973. Prepared by Carroll Warner Williams and Gloria Bird. Sante Fe: Zia Cine, Inc.
    "With the support of the Research and Cultural Studies Development Section, Santa Fe, Bureau of Indian Affairs, Department of the Interior."
Films for Anthropological Teaching. 5th ed.
  1972. Prepared by Karl Heider. Washington, D.C.: American Anthropological Association.
Films on Traditional Music and Dance.
  1970. Edited by Peter Kennedy. Paris: UNESCO.
Heider, Karl G.
  1976. *Ethnographic Film.* Austin and London: University of Texas Press.
    Contains chapters on the history, attributes, making, and use of ethnographic films in teaching, as well as a brief annotated filmography.
University Film Collections, especially Universities of California (Berkeley and Los Angeles), Indiana, and Washington.
Embassies and Consulates.
Airlines.

Abbreviations

Abbreviations of Film and Record Companies Used in Text

(Addresses are not included because of the frequency of change. Since this book went into production a number of interesting ethnographic films have come on the market. For reviews of these, see recent issues of *Ethnomusicology* and related journals.)

FILM COMPANIES

ACFU	Australian Commonwealth Film Unit
AIAS	Australian Institute of Aboriginal Studies
AP	Audience Planners, Inc., New York
ASEA	American Society for Eastern Arts
BBC	British Broadcasting Corporation
CF/MH	Contemporary Films McGraw-Hill
CGJ	Consulate General of Japan
CMC	Center for Mass Communication
DER	Documentary Educational Resources
DF and DFA	Dance Films Association, Inc.
EDC	Education Development Center
FCE	Film Classic Exchange
FI	Film Images. A division of Radim Films, Inc.
FSC	Film Study Center
GI	Government of India Information Service
GITB	Government of India Tourist Bureau
HP	Hartley Productions, Inc.
IE	Institute of Ethnomusicology, UCLA
IFF	International Film Foundation
IR	Image Resources
IU	Indiana University, Audiovisual Center
LAC	Latin American Center, UCLA
ML	Meyer Levin
MOMA	Museum of Modern Art
NFBC	National Film Board of Canada
NGS	National Geographic Society
NYF	New Yorker Films
NYU	New York University
NZ	New Zealand Government Travel Commission
PSU (PCR)	Pennsylvania State University (Psychological Cinema Register)
SAM	Society for Asian Arts, New York
TODD	Todd Film Collection, New York
UC	University of California
UCB	University of California, Berkeley
UCEMC	University of California Extension Media Center
UWF	United World Films
UWP	University of Washington Press
WAAC	Western Affiliated Arts Company
WFD	Westinghouse Film Division

RECORD COMPANIES

(In a few instances it was impossible to obtain full names.)

AAFS	Archive of American Folk Song (Library of Congress)
AHM	Asch Records
AIAS	Australian Institute of Aboriginal Studies
BAM	La Boîte a Musique
CBS	Columbia Broadcasting System
Col.	Columbia
CRI	Composer's Recording
CS	Connoisseur Society
EMI	EMI Company

FE	Ethnic Folkways	LDX	Le Chant du monde
FW	Folkways	LLST	Lyrichord
GALP		OCR	Ocora
and GE	Gallotone	PHLP	Philips
HMV	His Master's Voice	S and R	S & R Recording Company
IER	Institute of Ethnomusicology, UCLA	SRLP	Sheikh
		TR	Instrumental Library of African Music, Music of African Series
IFF	International Film Foundation		
KKL	Jewish National Fund	W and G	W & G Record Company

The Contributors

John Blacking, Department of Social Anthropology, The Queen's University of Belfast. Formerly chairman of the African Studies Programme at the University of the Witwatersrand, Johannesburg, South Africa.

Kuo-huang Han, Department of Music, Northern Illinois University, DeKalb.

Mantle Hood, Senior Distinguished Professor of Ethnomusicology, University of Maryland, Baltimore.

Trevor A. Jones, Department of Music, Monash University, Clayton, Victoria, Australia.

Adrienne L. Kaeppler, Anthropologist at the Smithsonian Institution, Washington, D.C.

Margaret J. Kartomi, Department of Music, Monash University, Clayton, Victoria, Australia.

Cynthia Tse Kimberlin, formerly School of Ethnic Studies, San Francisco State University, Fulbright Fellow in Ethiopia, Department of Music, University of Ife, Nigeria.

Lorraine D. Koranda, formerly on the staff of the University of Alaska, is currently teaching in Saratoga, California.

Alfred Kwashie Ladzekpo and Kobla Ladzekpo, School of Music, California Institute of the Arts, Valencia. Kwashie: Dance Department, University of California, Los Angeles. Kobla: Department of Music, University of California, Los Angeles.

Kang-sook Lee, College of Music, Seoul National University, South Korea.

William P. Malm, School of Music, University of Michigan, Ann Arbor.

Lindy Li Mark, Department of Anthropology, California State University, Hayward.

Elizabeth May, writer and editor, has taught ethnomusicology and Western music at American and Australian universities and in American public schools.

David P. McAllester, Department of Anthropology and Music, Wesleyan University, Middletown, Connecticut.

Atta Annan Mensah, formerly Head of the Department of Music, Dance, and Drama, Makerere University, Kampala, Uganda, is now on the Faculty of Education, University of Cape Coast, Cape Coast, Ghana.

David Morton, Department of Music, University of California, Los Angeles.

Bruno Nettl, School of Music, Division of Ethnomusicology, University of Illinois, Urbana.

Dale A. Olsen, Department of Music, Florida State University, Tallahassee.

Josef M. Pacholczyk, Department of Music, University of Maryland, Baltimore.

Abraham A. Schwadron, Department of Music, University of California, Berkeley.

Bonnie C. Wade, Department of Music, University of California, Berkeley.

Ella Zonis Mahler, author of *Classical Persian Music* (Harvard University Press, 1973) has lectured and taught widely.

1. Ethnomusicology: Definitions, Directions, and Problems

Bruno Nettl

Ethnomusicology has been defined in many ways, none of them completely satisfactory. It has often simply been called the scholarly study of non-Western music, probably a poor definition because there are certainly no differences between Western and non-Western music greater than the differences among the non-Western musics themselves. It has been defined as the study of music that exists in oral tradition, but we also know that oral tradition is an important component of the many musical cultures that use notation. The transmission of Western concert music, for instance, despite its formidable notation system, includes many aural components, among them timbre and vibrato. And again, many cultures primarily dependent on oral tradition nevertheless use music notational and other mnemonic devices. For example, in Indian classical music drummers employ syllables to indicate types of strokes and sounds and as an aid in the memorization of rhythmic patterns. Indian singers also use a syllabic system analogous to the solfège of Western music. Iranian folk singers use written texts that give only the words of songs. These inevitably play a role in the realization of the music.

Ethnomusicology is sometimes defined as the study of a music foreign to one's own, but we also find scholars who call themselves ethnomusicologists and who study the music of their own native culture, usually the music of a group outside the framework of Western, educationally élite social strata. We also find other definitions, among them that ethnomusicology is the study of contemporary musical systems, an idea perhaps acceptable in practical terms to all scholars working in the field except for those (and there are quite a few) who are interested in traditional historical research in the musics of Asia and, to a lesser extent, other areas of the world. Many anthropologists favor a definition of ethnomusicology as the study of music *in* and *as* culture; the study of how people use, perform, compose, and think about music; and of their general attitudes toward it. The emphasis of this definition is at the other end of the continuum from that of the musicologically oriented researchers whose primary concern is in the structure of the music itself. The best results and insights can be obtained by combining and fusing these two approaches, but this ideal balance has not often been achieved.

A final definition is that ethnomusicology is the comparative study of musical systems and cultures. This definition may be controversial in that some scholars think that we do not know enough about the musical cultures of the world to carry out meaningful comparisons. Others are of the opinion that musics are intrinsically not comparable, that they cannot be translated into a set of common denominators; however supporters of this definition would be inclined to say that only from comparison can insight be gained, that one can learn something new only by comparing it with what one already knows.

It is evident, then, that there is no completely acceptable definition of ethnomusicology. It is equally uncertain whether ethnomusicology is a separate discipline, requiring its own rationale, methodology, apparatus, courses, curricula, and learned societies, or whether it is indeed simply a field of interest and an activity that draws its adherents from a number of recognized disciplines—musicology, anthropology, folklore, linguistics, psychology, and others. Or yet whether it is simply a subdivision of musicology, or of anthropology. Most individuals who consider themselves ethnomusicologists began as musicians, some as students of musicology in the more traditional sense, and some as anthropologists. It is not my purpose here to solve this problem of the identity of ethnomusicology; it may never be solved, but the reader should be aware of just where this field stands in academe in the United States and elsewhere.

Even the term *ethnomusicology* has been in existence for only about twenty-five years, although activity in the field began much earlier. It had immediate predecessors–comparative musicology, musical ethnology, foreign terms such as *Musikethnologic* or *ethnographie musicale*. In a sense the field is new, for it has changed constantly and is now moving rapidly in many directions; but in another sense it is old, its roots go far back to the rather simple, not always reliable, yet valuable descriptions of Asian, African, and Latin American native musics by missionaries, travelers, and civil and military officials who were often highly educated and perceptive. The individuals who began making musicology into a formal discipline in the last part of the nineteenth century, mainly Germans and Austrians, but also some Englishmen and Americans, included in their purview the kinds of things that ethnomusicologists do today. These scholars were aware of the existence of many musics throughout the world and were also becoming acquainted with theories of biological and cultural evolution. They began to look for universals in world music and also to try to comprehend the vast variety of musical phenomena found in the cultures developed by mankind.

The reason for discussing the identity and hinting at the history of ethnomusicology, however briefly, is that we have in this volume a number of essays treating various and enormously different musics of the world, and treating them from many points of view. In some instances these differences are derived from the differences among the cultures themselves. For example, Native Americans do not have written music theory, thus this aspect of their music cannot be discussed; but this is not true of the classical music of India. Moreover, the differences among the essays derive also from the differences in the kinds of information available for the various cultures of the world. For some, much musical material has been recorded, but information about its cultural context is spotty and has been gathered unsystematically; for others the opposite is true. But most important, the differences of approach that the reader will find here derive from the fact that among the authors are represented a number of views of what the field of ethnomusicology really comprises. Here are authors who worked initially as musicians, some whose background is in musicology, some who actually began their studies in non-Western music (among them Americans and Europeans as well as natives of non-Western nations), and there is of course the anthropologist. Therefore, the volume at hand presents not only a large variety of musical cultures but also provides the reader with a panorama of approaches to the field of ethnomusicology.

The fact that ethnomusicology is defined in a number of different ways and is populated by individuals coming from a number of disciplines does not mean that we do not have a rather substantial core of agreement. There are indeed a number of things to which ethnomusicologists, on the whole, would probably subscribe. I should like to mention a few and to discuss them very briefly.

1. *Ethnomusicologists seem to have been torn between two ideals: the basic unity of mankind as exhibited in music and musical behavior, and the infinite variety of musical phenomena found in the world.* On the one hand, we have been seeking universals. This was certainly true of the early scholars in our field who tried to characterize broad areas of musical culture such as "primitive music," folk music, and tribal music; who tried to say very general things about the way in which scales everywhere are built, the general direction of melodic movement, and the way in which music throughout the world may have developed, from simple to complex, from vocal to instrumental, from exclusively religious to diverse in use and function, from simple universal structures to a considerable variety of phenomena, yet united by such characteristics

as the usual existence of meter, and the overriding importance of melodic intervals close to the major second. Today, after a period in which the particular character of a music was stressed above all else, the search for universals is again important. Ethnomusicologists are aware that musical phenomena in different cultures may seem identical to an outsider, but can be interpreted quite contrastively by the members of these cultures. For instance, surface similarities between African and East Indian rhythms may obscure the totally different ways in which these structures are perceived in their cultural contexts—but they are beginning to feel that there is a kind of deep structure that identifies the phenomenon of music.

At the same time, ethnomusicologists are still interested in presenting the vast diversity of musical sounds and modes of musical behavior. The ethnomusicologist is typically a person who, when confronted with a general statement about music, will say: "But in this or that culture or on this or that island, we do not find the phenomenon, things are different." He has acted as the debunker of generalizations based essentially on experience with Western art music. So in the heart of the ethnomusicologist there are two strings: one that attests to the universal character of music, to the fact that music is indeed something that all cultures have or appear to have, whether they themselves have a definition of the concept or not, and one responsive to the enormous variety of existing cultures.

2. *Ethnomusicologists agree that in order to carry out research it is necessary to work in the field.* Theoretical information, logically derived, is not the core of what we provide. Ethnomusicologists engage in field research in order to gather information. This fieldwork is also experientially transferable. Fieldwork in a culture outside a researcher's own will in a certain sense give him some understanding of other cultures that he has not visited, or at least give him an idea of the problems that he may encounter in carrying out research in other regions. Also the tendency of ethnomusicologists has been to work intensively rather than extensively in the field. This means that one concentrates on

working with a small number of informants or teachers, does not usually survey large populations but, instead, emphasizes study in depth of small numbers of people.

The concept of "the field" has of course changed greatly over the past few decades. At one time, ethnomusicologists did research only in what were considered highly exotic venues, but today many of them work in neighborhoods in their own cities, with members of racial, national, often non-English speaking minorities and, indeed, with members of their own culture, at home. Certain special techniques for field research have been developed, from sophisticated recording and filming devices to contemplation of various approaches to gathering information from people who have not been used to thinking or talking about music in the way in which the researcher phrases his questions, or perhaps have hardly thought or talked about music at all.

Ethnomusicologists are very much concerned not only with going into the field but also with the kind of work that must be done, with methods and techniques.

Field techniques vary greatly. They are intensely personal, they involve the specific relationship between an investigator, with his own cultural and personal background, and his informant or teacher. Field research has changed a great deal in the last half century. It began essentially as a gathering of raw material, with concentration on the music—songs, instruments, and instrumental pieces—with secondary attention to the cultural context. For example, a researcher would ask an informant to sing a number of songs. He would record them and ask, for each song, information about its origin, function, means of transmission, and other pertinent matters. From this sort of technique, ethnomusicologists moved on to more sophisticated approaches—the practical study of an instrument, development of questionnaires, inquiries about attitudes toward music, investigation of taxonomies used to classify musical phenomena in the culture, and so on. These inevitably necessitated spending much longer periods in the field. Today most ethnomusicologists devote at least a year to carrying out any kind of major field project, and many of them return again and again to the area in which they work, passing perhaps half a dozen or more years in nations such as Japan, India, Iran, or Ghana.

Within this discussion of field techniques one should mention two recent developments. One is the establishment of the fieldworker as primarily a student within the cultural context of his "field." In earlier times, he regarded himself mainly as a collector, a figure of authority who had to persuade a group of informants to work with him, to deliver, so to speak, the goods. Later it became evident that it is more productive, satisfying, and perhaps ethically more defensible to approach another culture as a student, to be taken in hand by a master who will teach him as he teaches students in his own culture. This approach is of course extremely valuable in many ways. One learns much about a musical system from the learning process itself and finds out how members of the culture internalize their own music. One gains some of the same kinds of insights that members of the culture acquire in the course of their lives. At the same time, it is possible that one may not, using this kind of technique, learn some of the kinds of things that an outsider, observing the culture from his special vantage point, may gain. For example, some of the intricacies of the *radif*, the repertory of Persian music memorized by students of the classical tradition as a basis for improvisation, are not evident to Iranian musicians; or, at least, they are not conscious of them, until an outsider points them out.

There has also been increasing concern with the kinds of obligation that a fieldworker incurs toward the people from whom he has been learning. This concern involves such things as the sharing of earnings from commercial recordings, but it goes much farther, including perhaps such considerations as the recording of music that members of the culture investigated consider should not be recorded at all, often for religious reasons, and the treatment of informants as dignified individuals. In any event, the most important hallmark of ethnomusicological research is the concept of fieldwork with its many ramifications. And, of course, ethnomusicological studies must be evaluated to some extent in relation to the quality of the fieldwork on which they are based.

3. *Ethnomusicologists agree, on the whole, that music can be written down and analyzed from visible format.* We might not take this so much for granted were not we ourselves, in Western culture, visually oriented, and had we not, as a result, suffered considerably in our ability to hear and retain music without the intervention of music writing. The notation provided by Western art music has often been found inadequate for ethnomusicological purposes. From the beginning of their history, ethnomusicologists have found various means of transcribing non-Western music into a notation of some sort, usually that of Western music to which have been added certain symbols that make it possible to record phenomena that either do not appear or are not important in conventional Western music. Three particularly interesting approaches to notation are discussed in Mantle Hood's book, *The Ethnomusicologist*. One of them, the "Seeger Solution," involves the development of complex machinery to notate music automatically by means of computer logic circuitry to produce a three-part photographic display consisting of pitch, loudness, and timbre. The best known apparatus developed for this purpose is the melograph at UCLA. There are others as well. Not too many publications have resulted from work done with this approach. This paucity makes me feel, first of all, that we are still on the threshold of learning how to use the apparatus, and second, that there is somehow here a lack of appeal to the scholar who prefers to work directly with the musical material, and who objects to relying on machinery to do what is essentially an initial processing of raw data.

Another approach described by Hood is the "Hipkins Solution." The approach (I am giving my own interpretation, not Hood's) is based essentially on the notation systems found in various non-Western cultures, on the assumption that one cannot notate everything about a music anyway, that there are too many significant and insignificant phenomena, and that if we are to look for the really essential, we may well look to the culture's own statement as exhibited in its notation. This is a valuable approach.

The third approach is named by Hood the "Laban Solution," after Rudolph von Laban, inventor of the most widely used notation for dance. Hood proposes the use of a kind of notation for music that would indicate the sound as well as the stance, movements, and interrelationships of the musicians, in enormous detail. This seems highly desirable but may not be practical at this stage. The relationship of sound and behavior in notation is an ideal for which we should strive.

In the end, an examination of ethnomusicological publications shows that scholars in earlier times transcribed music simply for the sake of preserving it, thinking that their main task was indeed to transcribe and not necessarily to analyze. Today we have moved to a different sort of approach. Realizing the futility of notating everything about all musics of the world, we now tend to use transcription as a device for solving specific analytical problems, and the kind of method of transcription that we select is related to the particular problem confronting us, such as comparison of section lengths in an extended improvisation, types of ornaments, identification of a tone system.

Following transcription—in many cases preceding it—is analysis. As a scholar transcribes music, he must first have in mind the characteristics of the musical system, which means that he must analyze the music aurally to some extent before he can transcribe. Having transcribed a body of music into notation, however, he may then proceed to further analysis. A large number of procedures have been devised. Indeed, it is difficult to survey them, but I should like to point out that there are publications (e.g., B. Nettl, *Theory and Method in Ethnomusicology;* Marcia Herndon, "Analysis: the herding of sacred cows?" in *Ethnomusicology,* 18:219-62) that provide overviews. There are really two types of systems in use. One attempts to provide a framework for all musical phenomena of the world, or for all imaginable kinds of music, and to make it possible within this framework to describe and compare musics. The other comprises approaches that are culture-specific, derived in each case from the music under study and, if possible, based on the theoretical system developed by the culture that has produced the music.

There are many approaches that fall between these extremes, and one of the unfortunate characteristics of ethnomusicology is that there has been no standardization of analytical procedures. At one time there was widespread adherence to the approaches derived from the work of Erich M. von Hornbostel and Béla Bartók, but as time has gone by we have become more and more interested in providing for each scholarly problem a particular way of analyzing the music. In that sense, the history of analysis parallels the history of transcription. We devise analytical and notational methods to fit what we wish to find out about the music.

It is important to realize that in recent years elements from the discipline of linguistics and from French anthropological structuralism have been found useful by certain ethnomusicologists for musical analysis. Moreover, concepts developed in cognitive studies have had an impact, as have other approaches derived from the social sciences.

4. *Ethnomusicologists are always interested in music as a phenomenon produced by a culture.* Whether they come from the field of anthropology or not, to some extent they are all interested in the study of music in its cultural context. They may carry out the study of this relationship very systematically or in a rather haphazard fashion, but even those among us who regard ourselves primarily as musicians find that it is impossible to understand very much about a music without knowing something about its cultural and historical background. Of course, many musicologists also share this view. At the same time, we feel that the contrary is true, that one cannot really understand a culture without taking into account the almost inevitably great importance of its music.

The types of approach that ethnomusicologists have taken to study the relationship of music to its culture vary greatly. There have been attempts to encapsulate entire cultures;

there have also been efforts to establish frameworks for comparative study. There have been efforts to show correlations between musical types and culture types and to single out the cultural determinants of music, which would mean that certain types of culture inevitably produce particular kinds of musical style. Curt Sachs, an early scholar in the field of ethnomusicology, and Alan Lomax today have addressed themselves to some of these approaches. There have been attempts to show that certain aspects of human experience and behavior, types of early childhood training, kinds of relationships among social and economic classes and between sexes, and relative freedom of movement or restriction thereof are particularly important in determining the type of music that a culture produces. Some have noted that music in a culture can be studied either as a microcosm of the culture, the musical system replicating in detail the total cultural and social system that a people have adopted; or that music can also be considered a commentary on a culture, existing somehow outside the culture itself and reacting to what goes on in the society either by reflecting it or even by denouncing it through exhibiting opposite characteristics and tendencies; and finally that music can be regarded as one among the various other activities of man, carrying out in each culture a task, having, as it were, a special niche in each society. It must be pointed out that ethnomusicologists have made much more progress in the study of musical sound, in the analysis of transcribed music, than in the study of music as culture; but this is surely due simply to the relatively greater difficulty of the latter pursuit.

5. *Whether or not they really consider themselves historians, ethnomusicologists are always interested in the processes through which music changes, remains stable, grows, and disappears, and they have this interest for a culture as a whole, in the individual song or piece, and in the life of an individual or group.* Understanding music requires an understanding of some of these processes and, using the concept of history very broadly, it is fair to say that ethnomusicologists are interested in history. A number of approaches to historical study have been taken, of which we can mention only a few.

The first stirrings of interest in the history of world music, the growth of some present musics with all their complexity from some kind of earlier, simple stratum is one such interest. Comparison of cultures throughout the world, the search for universals, lead one almost automatically to a consideration of the possibility that those phenomena that are most widespread in the world are also likely to be among the oldest, and that the simplest may also exhibit an archaic layer. This is true of music with few tones and brief one- or two-phrase forms, and of certain simple instruments such as the musical bow, flutes without fingerholes, and rattles. In general, the extrapolation of historical strata from a repertory presently extant has been a characteristic of ethnomusicological research. There are a good many scholars who think that this approach is not fruitful, that the chances of our knowing whether we are right in such extrapolations are too small to make this kind of study worthwhile. Critics assert that this view places a kind of special value on complexity and denigrates relatively simple music. It should certainly not be assumed that what we consider qualitatively simple in a musical culture is necessarily, in all cases, old; nor that a culture with an archaic repertory is automatically archaic in other respects; nor, indeed, that this is a value judgment. Some cultures have what we might regard as extremely simple musical styles—very few tones in their scales, very short repetitive songs, very simple forms. This is true of some Australian aboriginal music (by no means all) and of some Native American songs.

Ethnomusicologists have also taken great interest in the history of individual compositions. On the assumption that oral tradition produces variants, that we do not, in most cases, have the originally composed form of a piece, ethnomusicologists study the many different ways in which one particular piece, or song, may be performed. Sometimes this involves literally hundreds of variants of one tune, as in the case of studies made by students of Hungarian and other Eastern European folk music, or of the 120 or so tunes found to be sung with the ballads of "Barbara Allen" or "Lord Randall" or "Lord Bateman." From a comparative study of these variants, one may be able to gain some insight into the history of the tune as it has unfolded into its many different versions, variants, and forms.

Another way in which ethnomusicologists pursue an interest in processes is of course the conventional study of history. The civilizations of Asia have for centuries had documents that give information on history in general, and on the history of music, and one can study these more or less as one studies theoretical and biographical documents in the history of European music. Many treatises, for example, exist in the literary, historical, or philosophical annals of Japan, China, Indonesia, India, and the Middle East. Moreover, as historians in recent times have begun to make increasing use of oral tradition, musicologists have begun to use it as a source for standard historical research. The histories of the musics of African and Native American cultures have been studied in part from the use of information current in oral tradition.

More characteristic of ethnomusicology, however, is the attempt to observe processes as they occur, to assess them, and to see whether from a particular set of evolving cultural conditions one may be able to predict certain types of musical changes. Ethnomusicologists have therefore been concerned with recent phenomena in world history—Westernization, modernization, urbanization, all types of culture contact subsumed under the general term *acculturation*. After all, one of the main characteristics of the twentieth century in music and in other areas of life is the coming together of many cultures, their interactions, their conflicts, and the ultimate resolution of these conflicts through conquests or accommodation. Musical conquests have certainly taken place; some cultures have simply abandoned their traditional music and taken up the Western counterpart. Accommodation has also taken place and is perhaps a more typical phenomenon of the twentieth century. The musics of the world have

changed, influenced by Western products such as the mass media, amplification, notation, the value placed on large ensembles, Western harmony, the idea of concert performance, the concept of the professional musician. But traditional music retains its identity, modified by compatible (and sometimes not so compatible) elements imported from Western musical culture.

There was a time when ethnomusicologists thought that they could find pristine, unpolluted, uncontaminated musics around the world. They assumed that musics in other cultures had remained static until, under the impact of Westernization, they had begun to change rapidly and drastically. Today we have come to feel that all musics have probably undergone substantial change at all times. Sometimes the change was snail-paced; this may have been true of Gagaku, the music of the Japanese court orchestra, or of Indian classical music. Elsewhere the change may have been rapid, as in certain periods in the history of Indonesia and the Middle East. It depends on the amount of contact with other cultures, on the structure of the society itself, on the values placed on stability and on novelty. Therefore, while it is generally assumed that there is a polarity between the typical musicologist, who is interested in history, and the ethnomusicologist, who is not, it is indeed the ethnomusicologist who is especially interested in what has happened in world music at large, who takes a broad view of the concept of change, and who wishes to know what types of things happen under various conditions in which cultures find themselves in the twentieth century, and particularly in the ways in which various types of intercultural relationships affect music.

If, then, there is a methodology in the field of ethnomusicology, it must, it seems to me, revolve around these five characteristics of the field: the interest in universals balanced by appreciation of infinite variety; the emphasis on fieldwork; the possibility of notating and analyzing music visually and verbally; the insistence that music can be understood only in its cultural context; and the interest in processes. This configuration of approaches seems to me to constitute the essence of ethnomusicology.

At the time of this writing, there are scholars who believe that ethnomusicology is in a state of crisis. There are panels and publications that discuss the future of this field, that ask whether it has legitimacy among the various academic disciplines, and that deal with its possible political, racial, and economic overtones. We who work in ethnomusicology are still constantly trying to define ourselves, and we feel that we have identity problems. But indeed, ethnomusicological research has shed a great deal of light on issues facing the musician, the music teacher, and the scholar. It is ethnomusicologists who have made it clear that it is impossible to gain a perspective of music at large without taking into consideration the enormous diversity of the musics of the world and of the cultural contexts in which they exist. It is the ethnomusicologists who have called the attention of composers to the multitude of phenomena around the world on which they might draw for inspiration. It is they who have, in the long run, made the various ethnic groups in the West, and also the various downtrodden peoples of the world, proud of their musical heritage in a modern cultural context and aware of the fact that their music is an important symbol of their ethnic or national identity. Among scholars, it is ethnomusicologists who have drawn attention to certain central issues of musicology, who have pointed out the enormous importance of the arts in human life to the anthropologist and psychologist. Ethnomusicology has rendered valuable services to the world, to the arena of artistic and intellectual concerns.

Nevertheless, we face problems, and one can well consider these in relationship to the five areas that have been mentioned as constituting the methodological and theoretical core of our field.

With all our interest in diversity and in universals, we still do not have data on all the world's musics and thus cannot make definitive statements about the range of diversity, or pinpoint the universals. We still have not established what constitutes *a* music, a concept analogous to a language, so that we can scientifically define the units that might serve as a basis for an understanding of this diversity.

We agree that fieldwork is essential, but we have difficulty in teaching anyone how to do it. There are not many courses on ethnomusicological fieldwork, and not very much has really been written on how it should be done or how it was carried out in particular instances. We don't know very well how to deal with this curious phenomenon of recent decades, the scholar using his own backyard as "the field."

Although we accept the usefulness of transcription and analysis, we find ourselves constantly working with two sides of the coin, trying to balance the outsider's observations against those of the person who has been brought up within the culture being studied and who can provide immediately the kind of information that may take an outsider years to obtain. We wonder whether the outsider's view is at all valid and we struggle to comprehend and codify the insider's understanding of his culture. As outsiders, we are sometimes discouraged with the idea that in a sense most of us will never understand some of the most fundamental things about the musics that we study.

We have not yet figured out just how best to study music as a part of culture. There are a few techniques, a few sample approaches, but we are barely beginning to scratch the surface. We do not know whether to treat music as a truly component part of culture or as something that somehow resides outside culture itself but comments on it and describes or reflects it, and we have difficulty in balancing the ways in which people with whom we are working tell us how music affects them with the observations that we can make of their behavior.

And finally, we are still frustrated by the fact that while we are enormously interested in processes, in the development of music as a whole or as the product of one culture, and as an individual song or piece, over a period of time, and we wish to know how music is created, taught, learned, changed, and perpetuated, we realize that we are a long way from knowing the answers and that we may never have sufficient data to find the answers. We fear that we will never come to the kinds of definitive conclusions expected by students of the natural sciences.

Therefore, ethnomusicology is a field that has contributed much, but which must contribute a great deal more because its approaches are essential to an understanding of music as a product of mankind. But it is also a field struggling to establish itself, not so much among the scholars in other disciplines (they have, on the whole, accepted us with little reservation), but in our own minds, with concrete questions, goals, methods, and some certainty of being able to reach reliable conclusions. It is a field in a state of ferment. I believe that the reader of the essays in this book will gain, from their diversity, from the great variety of cultures, musics, and approaches, some sense of this ferment, a sense that will impart to him the excitement as well as the frustrations but also ultimately the love that the scholars who are writing here have developed, a love for the music they have heard and recorded and learned, for the activities that lead them laboriously to understand this music, and for the peoples who in the end have produced all that they have studied.

2. Evolution and Revolution in Chinese Music

Kuo-huang Han and Lindy Li Mark

The notion that music making can be treated as separate and distinct from other forms of human behavior is a narrow one. Modern industrial society may demand an extreme division of labor and the compartmentalization of social life. But the degree of specialization in music, the conceptual separation of music from concomitant media of expression, vary from one society to the next, and from one genre to another. In traditional China music was imbedded in social and ideological contexts. Music was mostly programmatic or symbolic: programmatic in that it evoked other sensory forms; symbolic in that it expressed philosophical ideas, ritual, and social behavior. The notion of "absolute music" created and performed explicitly and purely for the aesthetic enjoyment of tonal patterning, rhythm, timbre, and dynamics did not exist. In general these concepts apply to modern Chinese music also. In describing Chinese music, then, we emphasize the integration of music with the social and cultural life of the people.

We also emphasize the generic diversity and dynamic change in the history and development of Chinese music. According to the eminent musicologist Yang Yin-liu[1] the evolution of Chinese music resulted from four kinds of conflict: between popular and ritual music, between musicians and politicians, between mysticism and empiricism, and between nationalism and internationalism (1952:332-34). Over and beyond his revolutionary rhetoric, Yang has summed up succinctly the social and cultural forces that precluded uniformity and stagna-

tion. Varied social contexts and functional demands generated diverse musical styles. These styles in time interpenetrated and created new styles. Music that lost appeal to popular taste became extinct. Foreign music and instruments were assimilated or modified to suit native appetites.

To present a dynamic view of Chinese music in a brief essay, we shall limit ourselves to three areas. First, we shall review recent researches into the history of Chinese acoustic theory by music historians such as Yang Yin-liu, F. Kuttner, and J. Needham and K. Robinson. Next, we shall present a brief survey of the major developments in various historical periods. Last, we shall describe the major extant genres including traditional forms as well as twentieth-century creative trends. With great reluctance and regret, musics of ethnic minority peoples in China and Taiwan will be omitted. We must, however, point out that these musics have mingled with and influenced Chinese music significantly in both the past and present.

Since we find verbal and notational delineation of Chinese musical styles cumbersome, they are kept to a minimum. Instead, we have made extensive discographic and up-to-date pictorial references in the text for aural elucidation and enjoyment.

It may be appropriate at this point to clarify what we mean by *China* and *Chinese music*. *Chinese music* will be an overall designation for the various traditional[2] modern, classical, popular, and folk musics found within the Republic of China (Taiwan) and the People's Republic of

1. Authors of Chinese language publications are cited in the native manner of surname first, unless they have appeared otherwise in Western language publications.

2. By traditional music we mean folk music and composed forms that are relatively free of nineteenth-twentieth century European harmonic and contrapuntal influence.

China (socialist China). Where needed, we shall use *Taiwan* to indicate republican China and *China* to designate socialist China. Despite their political bifurcation, these two territorial entities share the same musical and cultural heritage. We will point out divergent transformations that took place within each area in recent decades.

ACOUSTIC THEORY
IN CHINESE HISTORY

Music is a cultural universal. Every society, simple or complex, has some form of musical activity. Some of the complex civilizations, however, developed metaphysical notions about the relationship between music and cosmos which, in some cases, led to mathematical computations of acoustics. Ancient China and Greece were two such societies. Although there were parallel discoveries in both civilizations, the ideological contexts were vastly different. In ancient Greece, Pythagoras's acoustic discoveries were part of a mystical metaphysics. In ancient China, music was from the beginning unmistakably linked to politics. This linkage, while not true of all genres, is the most consistent theme in the history of Chinese music. Ancient treatises on music and acoustics were always found as parts of political documents, court chronicles, and state protocols (see below). From a practical standpoint, acoustic calculations must have stemmed from the need to determine the dimensions of fixed pitch instruments used in state ceremonies, such as panpipes, stone chimes, and bronze bells. Other musical uses of the elaborate pitch series which followed from such calculations were less apparent.

The earliest reference to scale intervals is found in the *Chou Li* (Rites of the Chou Dynasty, compiled c. 400 B.C). The names of the five scale tones are *kung, shang, chiao, chih,* and *yü* (Yang Y-l. 1952:76). It is generally accepted that the intervals among them correspond to those of do, re, mi, sol, la in the Western scale. According to another source, the *Kuo Yü* (Discourses on the State, compiled c. 400 B.C.), two additional tones appeared during the latter part of the Chou dynasty (c. 400 B.C.): *pien kung* and *pien chih,*

corresponding to si and fa respectively. Although the precise dating of ancient sources is notoriously difficult, there is little doubt that a seven-tone scale existed from antiquity.

The *Kuo Yü* also contains the earliest reference to a twelve tone chromatic gamut (Yang Y-l. 1952:73). The name for each pitch is symbolic and richly connotative. For example the fundamental or lowest pitch was called the *huang-chung*, or "yellow bell": it symbolized the emperor and yellow was the imperial color. Other pitches were *ta-lü*, or "great tone"; *lin-chung*, or "forest bell"; and *ying-chung*, or "resonating bell." (For a scientific interpretation of such names see Kuttner 1965.) Theoretically, pentatonic scales could be constructed upon any of the twelve pitches or *lü* as the fundamental. Needham and Robinson cite evidence from the *Li Chi* (Book of Rites) that modal changes were employed in ritual music (1962:217–18), but to what extent all twelve modes were in use is not known.

The earliest record giving mathematical ratios of musical intervals is the *Lü Shih Ch'un Ch'iu* (Chronicles of the House of Lü, c. 239 B.C.). This work described the construction of a set of twelve pitch pipes by the method of the cycle of fifths[3] and tuned to the love song of a pair of phoenixes. This event was retrodated to the time of the legendary emperor Huang-ti and his musical minister Ling-lun in the year calculated as 2698 B.C (Needham and Robinson 1962:176–79).

There is no way to authenticate the date of the legendary event itself. However we do know that by the third century B.C. the practice of

3. The cycle of fifths is based upon the fact that a simple ratio of 3:2 exists between the length of a vibrating body producing a given pitch and of that producing the fifth above. For example, if a pipe of X length produces the tone middle C, then a pipe of 2X/3 will produce G above it. If the same ratio is applied to the pipe producing G, D above will be produced. All twelve semitones within an octave can be generated by this ratio providing that each successive shorter length is doubled or quadrupled to place it within octave range. However, if one adheres to the mathematical values, the thirteenth pitch produced by this ratio is perceptibly sharper than the true octave. Therefore, the cycle of fifths spirals on to a new twelve tone series, with a slightly higher fundamental. For the mathematical details of this phenomenon the reader should consult a music dictionary or calculate it for himself.

tuning court instruments to standard pitch pipes was well established. The ascription of this practice to Huang-ti in all likelihood set the precedent for restandardization of pitches, weights, and measures for each succeeding dynasty. From the third century B.C. onward, an important element of the state ideology was that music could influence the cosmic and social order. Peace and prosperity could be brought about by exhaustively locating all possible pitches by mathematical calculations and by performing music in tonalities appropriate to seasonal cycles. Like Pythagoras, the ancient Chinese metaphysical musicians discovered that pitches derived from the cycle of fifths did not form a closed system. Thus Ching Fang (77-35 B.C.), a court diviner, calculated pitches up and down the cycle of fifths to the sixtieth interval, and Chien Lo-Chih (c. A.D. 450) continued calculating to the 360th interval (Kuttner 1975a:172).

The effects of these acoustical calculations upon musical performance is largely unknown. There is evidence, however, that ancient acousticians were aware of intonational problems. The *Hou Han Shu* (Book of the Latter Han Dynasty, compiled c. A.D. 450) refers to a discourse of Ching Fang on the necessity of tuning strings by pitch pipe because tension might cause the string to be sharp or flat (Yang Y-l. 1952:154).

William P. Malm has perceptively pointed out that Chinese acoustic calculations were always based on the cyclical principle, whereas in Western Europe they were based on dividing the octave (1967:108). Could it be that the cyclical principle derived from and was more consistent with Chinese views of dynastic cycles, seasonal and diurnal changes, and other recurrent patterns in life?

Two historical items confuse our understanding of ancient Chinese pitch-mode systems. We have alluded to the restandardization of measurements with each new dynasty (for further discussion see Pian 1967:1-11). Although the same names and terminologies were used, obviously they denoted different things. Second, the gradual introduction of foreign scales and instruments caused changes in the indigenous music. During the Sui dynasty (seventh century), Cheng I learned to play the *p'i-p'a* (four-

stringed lute) from the Turkestan master Su-shi-po, and made concordances between Su's heptatonic scales and Chinese scales. He proposed that eighty-four modes were possible by using each of the seven tones as tonic (kung) and transposing them to the twelve lü (Yang Y-l. 1952:172). Here again, as in other points in history, it is difficult to bridge the gap between theory and practice.

The publication of a method of equal temperament by prince Chu Tsai-yü in 1584 is one of the widely discussed issues in Chinese acoustic history. According to Kuttner, Chu arrived at his method by adopting a slightly diminished divisor in the 2:3 and 4:3 ratios for the pipe lengths of the fifth and fourth respectively. Thus, by altering the ratio of the fifth from 500/750 to 500/749, Chu arrived at a nearly tempered fifth of 699.69 cents (tempered fifth = 700 cents) as compared with the theoretical perfect fifth of 702 cents (Kuttner 1975b:180-85).[4] Chu, writing in the sixteenth century, attributed this method to the venerable *Book of Huai Nan Tzu* (c. 123 B.C.). However, Kuttner could find no such method in extant editions of this book. Instead he found the use of the 749 divisor in the correction of certain intervals in the *Chin Shu* (Book of Chin, completed during the seventh century), and in the *Sung Shu* (Book of Liu-Sung, completed during the sixth century). If we accept Kuttner's findings, Chu would be credited as the reviver and general applicator of the method rather than as its originator.

The earliest known writing in Europe concerning equal temperament was by Mersenne in 1636. Could the theoretical tempered scale have been introduced to Europe from China sometime in the late 1500s? Needham and Robinson give considerable evidence for trade and cultural contact between China and Europe in the sixteenth century, and for the fact that Europeans were apparently interested in Chinese music (1962:216-17, 224-28). Kuttner, how-

---

4. The cumulation of 2 cents through the cycle of fifths leads to an octave tone that is 24 cents, or almost a quarter tone sharper than a normal octave. This is a numerically distinct as well as audible discrepancy. It was this discrepancy that led ancient Chinese musicologists to believe that an infinite series of natural pitches existed and that they can be mathematically located.

ever, argues that it is a moot question as to who was first. The tempered scale was widely used by J. S. Bach and others within a century of its conception. In China, the tempered scale remained theoretical and dormant. Music continued to be performed in untempered scales.

The practical consequences of Chu Tsai-yu's work on acoustics were negligible in his day—for example, the court did not adopt his system—nevertheless, his efforts to overcome the mystical morass in music with empirical observation and good musical sense were impressive. Little was written about his abilities as a musician, but his great compendium, the *Yüeh Lü Ch'üan Shu* (Complete Book of Rules for Music, 1584), testified to his deep interest in music. This work included more than acoustic considerations. Treatises on instruments, choreography, musical compositions, and orchestration were detailed and richly illustrated. He was a meticulous mathematician who carried all calculations to the seventh decimal point, but his discriminating ear told him something was amiss with traditional calculations. In the treatise "On the Rejection of Uniform Diameters" he wrote:

> ... the ancient sages thought that only the lengths (of pitch pipes) should be different. The diameters were kept constant. This was their mistaken view. If you do not believe it, take two bamboo tubes or writing brush tubes and tune them to the YELLOW BELL. Then cut one of them in half and blow the full length tube and the half length tube together. They will not be in tune. ... Generally, in longer tubes, the air is constricted ... and the tone is sharp (*ch'ing*). In the shorter tube the air is broad, thus the tube is shorter but the tone is flat (*shu*). (from the *Lü Lü Ching Yi*, in vol. 91:645 of *Ku Chin T'u Shu Chi Ch'eng*). [Italics ours]

Chu then went on to propose a method for determining length-diameter ratios of pitch pipes that would yield perfect intonation.

Chu was apparently not the only skeptic of his day. Another writer, in the *Ching Chou Pi Pien* (circa sixteenth century), proposed an alternate explanation for the origin of the nine-inch YELLOW BELL (pitch pipe):

> The *Lü Shu* (Book of Pitches) says that the volume of the YELLOW BELL is 177, 147 [unit unnamed]. The length is 9 inches. The *kung* of the YELLOW BELL mode is the longest and is therefore called the fundamental tone, also, the first tone. However, the so-called 9 inches was not of the ordinary foot measure. *It was derived from the human voice.* The method for obtaining it was to let a person sing and make note of the lowest pitch. Then a tube of about 9 inches long and 0.9 inches in diameter was blown to match the voice. If the tube (tone) was higher than that of the voice, it was lengthened; if lower, then shortened. After alternating up and down, cutting the tube until it matched the human voice perfectly, that tube was designated the *9 inch Yellow Bell kung*. [*Ching Chou Pi Pien*, in *Ku Chin T'u Shu Chi Ch'eng*, vol. 91:620. Italics ours.]

Here in one stroke he disposed of the enchanting legend of the singing phoenixes.

To end Chinese acoustical history at the sixteenth century may seem somewhat abrupt, but in fact there was no progress thereafter. The achievement of Chu Tsai-yü represented the triumph of empiricism over mysticism, even though his system of tempered scales was not put into practice. In the following centuries, court musicologists were preoccupied with cataloguing and reconciling popular scales and modes with the current court system. The contribution of collaborating musicians and instrument makers was probably considerable, but was only fragmentarily documented. Professional musicians and actors were considered lowly and unworthy of mention in historical literature. The fact that many scholars wrote librettos for musical dramas during the Yuan, Ming, and Ch'ing dynasties suggests that there was a close working relationship between the scholarly elite and the musical proletariat.

HISTORICAL SURVEY

In this survey we shall adopt Yang Yin-liu's division of Chinese music history into three major periods: *ancient*, from the neolithic to 246 B.C.; *middle ancient*, from 246 B.C. to A.D. 907; and the *late historical*, from A.D. 907 to 1911 (Yang Y-l. 1952). Later developments, including the recent Westernization of Chinese music, will be discussed separately.

The Ancient Period

Reconstructing the actual sounds of ancient music is of course impossible. However, archeological specimens, graphic arts, and historical records give us some idea of the musical life. Musical instruments such as pottery ocarinas, *hsün*, and tuned sets of stone chimes, *pien-ch'ing*, were found in late neolithic and Shang dynasty sites dating from 1600 to 1066 B.C. (Chuang 1968; 1972). Tuned sets of bronze bells, *pien-chung*, were found in Chou dynasty sites (*Arts of China* I, 1969: pl. 44; Needham and Robinson 1962: pl. 109; Sullivan 1973: pl. 23). By the middle of the third century B.C. instruments had been classified into eight categories according to the materials from which they were made: metal, stone, silk (strings), bamboo, gourd, pottery, leather, and wood. This classification indicates that a wide variety of instruments—aerophones, chordophones, idiophones, and membranophones—were in use. Each instrumental category was associated with the seasons, months, cardinal points, and metaphysical substances (for a list, see Sachs 1940:164, in Elizabeth May's bibliography).

During the sixth century B.C., the age of Confucius and Lao-tzu, music was divided into many functional categories as well. There was music for the chanting of poetry, worshiping ancestors, worshiping heaven and earth, royal banquets, rural feasts, archery contests, and battles (Yang Y-l. 1952:30–38). Musical art was a necessary part of the education of a gentleman, for he had to participate properly in all these functions. Moreover, music was thought to be an instrument of government. According to the *Li Chi* (Book of Rites):

> . . . we must discriminate sounds in order to know the airs; the airs in order to know the music; and the music in order to know [the character of] the government. Having attained to this, we are fully provided with the methods of good order. [Legge 1967:95]

For political reasons, chronicles of the period contain many references to folk songs and festivals, and the ruling princes apparently favored secular music and popular entertainment. Confucius alone lamented the decline of ceremonial music and the neglect of ritual.

The Middle Ancient Period
During the empire of the Han dynasty from 206 B.C. to A.D. 220, the establishment of a ministry of music (*yüeh-fu*) indicated governmental emphasis on music. This agency was responsible for

CHRONOLOGY OF CHINESE DYNASTIES

Predynastic	Neolithic	circa 8,000 B.C.
Dynastic	Shang	1523–1027
	Chou	1027– 250
	Ch'in	256– 206
	Han	206 B.C.–A.D. 220
	Three Kingdoms	220– 265
	Chin	265– 420
	Southern and Northern Dynasties	420– 618
	T'ang	618– 906
	Five Dynasties	906– 960
	Sung	960–1279
	Yuan	1260–1368
	Ming	1368–1644
	Ch'ing (Manchu)	1644–1911
	Republic of China	1911–1949 mainland
		1949–present Taiwan
	People's Republic of China	1949–present

recruiting and training over a thousand dancers and musicians for state functions. Standard pitch was enforced, at least in court music. Three major divisions of music were recognized: ritual music (*ya-yüeh*), secular music (*su-yüeh*), and regional or folk music (known by various names). The popularity of musical entertainment was evidenced in several archeological finds depicting singing minstrels (*Arts of China I*, 1969:pl. 287) and acrobatic performances with musical accompaniments (*New Archeological Finds 1974*: unpaged; Sullivan 1973: pl. 69). Excavations within the last decade also yielded real instruments over a thousand years old: a twenty-two-pipe mouth organ, *shêng*, a set of twelve pitch pipes marked with pitch names, a twenty-five-string zither, *se* (*New Archeological Finds 1974*), and the earliest seven-string zither, *ch'in*, without the fret studs found on all later instruments (Institute of Archeology 1975, 1:56).

Music from central Asia began to penetrate China during the Han dynasty, but from the sixth century A.D. on, the popularity of foreign music engulfed China (*Arts of China I*, 1969:pl. 251). The pear-shaped lute, *p'i-p'a*, the harp, *k'ung-hou*, cymbals, horns, and oboes were introduced and later assimilated into Chinese instrumental ensembles (*The Chinese Exhibition* 1975:pl. 265-272). Trade and cultural exchanges seemed to stimulate Chinese appetite for exotic clothing, goods, religion, music, dance, and art (Schafer 1963). During the Sui and T'ang dynasties (seventh through tenth centuries), the court maintained nine or ten ensembles, including ensembles from India, Turkestan, Turfan, Samarkand, and Bukhara (Yang Y-l. 1952:109-13). Secular music all but eclipsed ritual music in the literature of T'ang times. In 714 the emperor T'ang Ming-huang established an academy, the Pear Garden (*Li-yuan*), for training musicians and dancers. Court performers numbered 11,307 at one time (Kishibe 1960-61:22; 1965). Orchestras were divided into standing and sitting ensembles, possibly analogous to present day marching and concert bands. The liveliness of musical performance of this time has been preserved for us in a number of paintings in which a dozen or more ladies in flowing gowns, with hairdos askew, play various instruments (Kishibe 1965:pls. 1 and 2; Rowley 1969:pl. 13). The glory of this period in Chinese music is still felt today. In Taiwan, T'ang Ming-huang is venerated as the patron deity of musicians and actors, and actor-musicians are referred to as "brothers of the Pear Garden." (T'ang Ming-huang is no longer so worshiped in socialist China.)

The Late Historical Period
Three major developments took place during this period: the revival of Confucian musicology after the T'ang dynasty, the rise of musical dramas, and the popularization of regional dramas.

During the Sung dynasty (960-1279), neo-Confucianism gained court support and scholars attempted to expunge foreign elements from Chinese music. The ch'in, the favorite of ancient sages, was revived to become the sine qua non of the proper scholar-gentleman. It became a popular subject in paintings: the emperor Hui-tsung was depicted playing a ch'in under a tree (Fourcade 1965:21); a page carried one behind his strolling master (Cahill 1960:82; Sullivan 1973:pl. 135); and a sage meditated with a ch'in in front of him (Fourcade 1965:28). Odes and poems praised the instrument. The following poem, although written by a T'ang poet, Wang Wei (699-756), conveys the mood and aesthetics of ch'in playing:

> Sitting alone among the quiet bamboos,
> I strum the ch'in and burst into song.
> No one notices me in the lush green,
> But for the moon that shines bright above me.
> [Translated by K.-h. Han]

Despite the efforts of Confucian scholars, ch'in music probably appealed only to a relatively small circle of urban elite. It is a very soft and contemplative instrument, comparable in sonority to the clavichord. The p'i-p'a, with its greater dynamic range and versatility, appealed to a much wider popular audience. Apparently attempts were made to adapt the twenty-eight p'i-p'a modes for compositions for the ch'in (Pian 1967), but notations of the pieces were so skeletal that the actual melodic realizations would be hard to reconstruct.

The Sung dynasty also saw the beginnings of

musical dramas, *hsi-wen*, which rose to great literary heights during the ensuing Yuan and Ming dynasties (1260-1644). The Italian priest Matteo Ricci made a revealing remark about the great interest in theater in sixteenth-century China: "I believe this people is too much interested in dramatic representations and shows" (Ricci; trans. Gallagher 1953:23). As we shall see later, the theater has been not only an important form of entertainment for the Chinese people but a powerful educational tool used by the governments.

As far as we know, Chinese drama always included musical arias, spoken dialogue, dance and mime, and instrumental accompaniments. Yuan drama consisted of two styles. In the northern style, *pei-ch'u*, the p'i-p'a was the main accompanying instrument and there were seven-tone modes. The singing was done by one central character. In the southern style, *nan-ch'u*, the transverse flute (*ti*) was the main accompanying instrument and there were five-tone scales. Almost all of the characters sang. Yuan drama was a very popular form of urban entertainment. Hundreds of plays were written about the lives and adventures of common folk, incorruptible as well as corrupt officials, heroes, and genteel lovers. *The Romance of the Western Pavilion* by Wang Shih-fu, a love story, and *P'i-p'a Story* by Kao Che-ch'eng, a saga of wifely loyalty, have long attracted the attention of Western scholars. The latter was even made into a Broadway musical, "Lute Song," in the 1940s, starring Mary Martin. After 1949, the People's Republic of China promoted the translation of plays dealing with peasant life in order to counterbalance the romanticism and Confucian outlook of the former (Yang and Yang 1958).

The direct descendant of the Yuan drama is the *k'un-ch'ü* (K'un opera) which evolved in Kiangsu province, central China, during the middle of the Ming dynasty (1500s). The northern and southern styles merged during this time and seven- and five-tone modes were used in different acts of the same play. The major accompanying instrument was the transverse flute, but the p'i-p'a was also sometimes used. The elegant poetic texts, the complex plot—sometimes running to forty acts—and the highly melismatic style of singing made K'un opera an elitist art form. It is still performed by small groups of devotees in Taiwan, Hong Kong, and the United States. Despite limited appeal, it had tremendous impact on the development and refinement of popular regional operas during the nineteenth century, especially the Peking opera.

As we mentioned earlier, the Ming dynasty was a period of much contact with Europe. Matteo Ricci was the first to introduce Western music to China. He brought a clavichord as a gift to the emperor Shen-tsung in 1600 and wrote a number of pieces for his Chinese audience. Royal eunuch musicians were ordered to study the instrument with him, but the results were unsatisfactory (Cameron 1970:183). The influence of Western music would not be felt until a later period.

During the Ch'ing dynasty (1644-1911), ancient court music was revived for a time under the emperor K'ang-hsi (1662-1722). It was decreed that only pre-Han instruments were to be used and that writings on music and literature were to be collected. The Ch'ing government was energetic in the promotion of traditional Chinese learning and arts and crafts despite the fact that the ruling dynasty was a foreign one. Musically speaking, the introduction of regional theaters to the court, and the royal patronage they enjoyed, were by far the most important developments. The undisputed favorite among all classes during the nineteenth century was Peking opera, *Ching-hsi*, a refined version of regional operas from northern central China. By the first decades of the twentieth century it had become so popular throughout China that the name *kuo-chü* (national drama) was coined.

We should mention finally that localized traditions of narrative song, minstrel music, and folk songs developed alongside the great traditions of court and urban music. The natural rustic appeal of these genres is being recognized today and nationally promoted in China and Taiwan, as we show in the following section.

TRADITIONAL MUSIC TODAY

This section is devoted to the description of major traditional musical genres still being performed today. Numbered references to recordings listed at the end of this essay are included in the text for the reader's use and enjoyment. Two features are immediately noticeable in modern arrangements of traditional Chinese music: the incorporation of Western instruments into traditional ensembles and the employment of Western compositional techniques such as counterpoint, bass lines, triadic arpeggios, and sequential motifs.

Ritual Music

The only music resembling ancient court ritual music to some degree is performed for the celebration of Confucius's birthday (September 28) in Taiwan and is supported by the government. The music and dance follow the Ming dynasty tradition; the rhythm follows the Ch'ing dynasty; the idiophones are modeled after the Chou dynasty; and the costumes are in the style of the Sung dynasty. This is the only occasion on which such ancient instruments as tuned stone chimes, bronze bells, and panpipes are heard in ensemble with flutes (*ti*), mouth organ (*shêng*), sixteen-stringed zither (*chêng*), and drums (*ku*). All the instruments play in unison or octaves and the melody is strictly pentatonic (disc 19).

Buddhist and Taoist ritual music is performed in Taiwan and Hong Kong. The most common instruments used for Buddhist rites are the temple block (*mu-yü*), cup gong (*ch'ing*), bell (*chung*), handbell (*yun-ch'ing*), and drums.

Taoist music in Taiwan also uses these instruments in addition to the harmonium, coconut fiddle (*ye-hu*), oboe (*sona*), and various drums (discs 9, 17, 43).

Modern Classical Music

The distinction between classical, folk, and popular music has become blurred in recent decades. A concert of "classical" Chinese music today may include pieces performed on instruments such as ch'in, chêng, shêng, *hsiao* (vertical flute), as well as formerly folk and theater instruments such as p'i-p'a and ti. The modern classical repertoire also includes folk songs arranged for concert performances by solo or ensemble instruments.

Music for the ch'in, the seven-stringed zither with thirteen-fret studs, has survived among a small group of scholar-musicians. The revival of the art before the Cultural Revolution by Kuan P'ing-hu and Cha Fu-hsi (disc 44) as well as modern research (Gulik 1940; Pian 1967; Lui 1968; Liang 1972) have made this highly refined music more accessible. The strings may be tuned to several pentatonic modes. The left hand stops the strings while the right hand plucks (discs 5, 8, 11, 21, 26, 44).

The cheng, a sixteen-stringed (some have thirteen) zither with movable bridges, is another traditional classical instrument. Pleasantly resonant and easy to learn, this instrument has been successfully promoted by Liang Tsai-

EXAMPLE 2-1. Sixteen bars from "Greeting the Divine Spirit of Confucius." Notation by Chuang Pen-li. From *Chi K'ung Li-yueh chih Kai-chin* (The Improvement of Ritual and Music in the Confucian Ceremony), p. 12. See disc 19.

FIGURE 2-1. Chinese chamber music featuring (from left) cheng, p'i-p'a, kao-hu (a variant of erh-hu) and yun-ch'ing. Performed by students of Northern Illinois University.

p'ing, the Chinese musicologist. Its popularity among young ladies in Taiwan today is comparable to that of the virginal among sixteenth- and seventeenth-century European ladies. The strings are also tuned to the pentatonic scale and are plucked with the fingers of the right hand. Vibrato is produced by pressing down on the string to the left of the bridge (discs 4, 5, 6, 7, 14, 26). In socialist China, chromatic mechanisms have been added and new techniques of performance developed (discs 1, 32, 37).

The p'i-p'a has occupied a central place in Chinese music since it was introduced to China during the T'ang dynasty (Kishibe 1940). The Chinese have long discarded the plectrum in favor of the right-hand fingernails. An instrument of great flexibility and dynamic range, its sound resembles that of a mandolin. Percussive sound

and microtones can be produced for depicting battle scenes (discs 1, 21) and many other programmatic effects. It is used in solo or ensemble and in accompanying narrative song. The Lui brothers, Lui Tsun-yuen and Lui Pui-yuen, have taught and concertized widely with this instrument (along with the ch'in) in Hong Kong and the United States (discs 8, 11, 21, 26, 35).

One of the most popular folk instruments, the *erh-hu* (or *nan-hu*), is now used in both classical and folk music. *Erh* means "two" and *hu* means "barbarian"; thus, "double (stringed) barbarian (fiddle)." (*Nan* means "south"; the instrument first became popular in central southern China.) It is made in a number of sizes and registers and is used for solo, in ensemble, and in theater orchestras. Ancient pictorial sources of the erh-hu are rare, an indication of its recent introduction,

FIGURE 2-2. Kin-woon Tong plays the ch'in.

"Southern Silk and Bamboo." Traditionally they play in unison with some heterophonic effects, but nowadays Western influence can be heard in the use of triadic chords and sequential melodies. The use of low register instruments is another sign of Western influence; sometimes cellos or double basses are used instead of Chinese instruments (discs 15, 30).

Different styles of folk-popular ensembles are represented by northern Shantung style (disc 6), which is strident and loud because of the use of the sona and percussion, and by the southern Cantonese style (disc 15), which is soft and lyrical because of the dominance of strings. The hammer dulcimer (*yang-ch'in*), or butterfly

or lowly status. The two strings are usually tuned in fifths and the bow passes between them. Its capacity ranges from lyricism to dazzling displays, including programmatic imitation of birdcalls (disc 15). The composer-performer Liu Tien-hua (1895-1932) adapted Western violin techniques for this instrument and wrote a number of solo pieces demonstrating their effects (discs 6, 30). Many concert pieces have been created in China for this instrument and its variants (discs 1, 22, 32, 37, 42).

Various types of transverse flute (ti or *ti-tzû*) are used as the solo or lead instrument in local theater orchestras and in modern folk ensembles. The ti has seven holes, one covered with a reed membrane to produce the buzzing sound characteristic of this instrument. Again, many virtuoso pieces have been written for it in recent years (discs 22, 32, 42) and master performers such as Lai Siu-hang are making it an important concert instrument in Hong Kong and the United States (disc 12).

Other folk-popular instruments that have appeared in concert are the oboe sona (discs 6, 22, 32, 42), which is also famous for its imitation of birdcalls (discs 1, 33), and the mouth organ shêng, one of the few wind instruments that can play more than one melodic line simultaneously (discs 1, 7, 26, 37, 42).

The modern Chinese classical orchestra evolved from the traditional southern Chinese instrumental ensemble known formerly as

FIGURE 2-3. Chinese p'i-p'a master, Lui Pui-yuen.

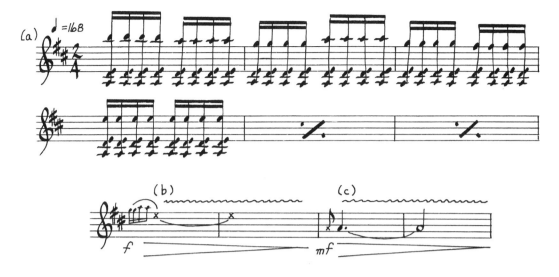

EXAMPLE 2-2. Instrumental depiction of a battle scene in the p'i-p'a piece "Ambush from Ten Sides." Notation by K-h Han. (a) melody against chord drone; (b) indeterminate pitch produced by twisting two strings together while plucking; (c) snapping string against soundboard for cracking sound.

harp, an eighteenth-century import from Persia, is essential to the southern style. Many modern orchestral works have been composed recently in the northern style in China, featuring display passages for solo instruments such as ti, sheng, sona, and erh-hu. Again, these reflect Western influence (discs 22, 37, 42).

In the 1950s a number of films made in China used melodies from *Huang-mei* opera, a local genre from Anhui province. These melodies were taken up by Hong Kong moviemakers and the music created a sensation, setting the standard for film music in Hong Kong and Taiwan for many years (disc 37). Since then, the use of Huang-mei tunes has disappeared from films made in China.

Folk Song and Minstrel Music
Research in Chinese folk music is a most difficult area today. Modern published folk songs are usually "modernized," that is, harmonized by Western-minded Chinese who took Stephen Foster or nineteenth-century European Romantic composers' arrangements of European folk songs as models. Consequently their indigenous characteristics are obscured. In recordings and concerts, the high-pitched and nasal voices indigenous to many regions are replaced by lieder or Western operatic styles of singing. Piano accompaniment is almost universal in this kind of performance. Genuine folk songs sung in native style and accompanied by folk instruments in heterophony are rare (discs 24, 25).

The treatment of texts also presents a problem. Traditional melodies have been set with new verses to fit modern ideology. This practice has been especially prevalent in China since the 1950s. However, songs newly created for the revolutionary ideology do follow the general folk-popular style and may survive as the folk songs of the new society. Typical examples of the latter are the "Five Revolutionary Folk Songs of the Shensi-Kansu-Ningsia Border Region" (disc 23). The credits on the record cover read: "Words written or rewritten and music composed by the literary and art workers of Shensi Province." Triadic harmony and Western orchestration are used, but the native vocal style is preserved.

The situation in Taiwan and Hong Kong is different. There is no restriction by the government regarding folk music. However, the survival of folk songs is threatened by Western and Japanese popular songs whose influence either alter or destroy the originals.

In traditional China, where the majority of

the people were illiterate, the transmission of moral teaching and history through theater or minstrel performances was very effective. Although local variants are numerous, two major styles of minstrel music are: northern *ta-ku* (Peking area), accompanied by the three-stringed lute, *san-hsien*, and percussion; and, southern *t'an-tz'û* (Soochou area), accompanied by the p'i-p'a and san-hsien (disc 34). The intricate alternation of heightened speech with singing and instrumental interludes creates a distinctive narrative music. In Taiwan and Hong Kong this art is almost extinct; in China effort has been made to preserve the musical style but the texts have contemporary revolutionary themes.

Theater Music

Many regional types of Chinese opera existed in the past; some provinces had several sub-genres. Their stories were drawn generally from history and folktales, although in the course of evolution old stories dropped out and new ones were adopted. The singing was accompanied by a small onstage orchestra. The acting featured stylized gestures and colorful costumes. In the first decade of the People's Re-

public, systematic studies of regional operas were undertaken. Over twenty genres have been issued on recordings to date.

As stated earlier, the Peking opera is most widely known. Its acting and gestures are highly stylized. For instance, there are twenty-six ways to laugh, twenty types of beard, and thirty-nine ways of manipulating the beard (Chi 1962:137–42, 313–41). There are four major role classifications: *shêng* ("male"), *tan* ("female"), *ching* ("painted-face male") and *ch'ou* ("clown"). The shêng role class is subdivided into *lao-shêng* ("old man") and *hsiao-shêng* ("young man without beard"). Tan is subdivided into *hua-tan*, which can be roughly glossed as "flirtatious female," and *ch'ing-i* or "lady of propriety." Until the first half of this century, men performed both male and female roles. In the case of tan roles and hsiao-shêng roles they sang in falsetto with a nasal quality (discs 2, 16, 31, 33, 39). The other male voices were quite natural except that certain kinds of timbre were thought to be appropriate for certain characters—for instance, for a bearded martial role, a broad gutteral quality was cultivated. The most famous singer of female roles was Mei Lang-fang (disc 31), who visited the United States in

EXAMPLE 2-3. "Kung Yuan," a T'an-tz'û excerpt showing heterophony between voice and instruments. From Li Yin-hai: *Han-tsu Tiao-shih chi Ch'i Ho-sheng* (Han Peoples' Modes and Their Harmonization, p. 106). See disc 23.

the 1930s. Because of the dramatic content of Peking opera, it has attracted much scholarly attention (Scott 1957; Halson 1966; Yang D. 1967; Mackerras 1972 and 1975), although these scholars are primarily interested in the literary aspects of this genre.

The stage performance of Peking opera combines singing, heightened speech, mime, dancing, and acrobatics. The stage is almost propless. The orchestra consists of two sections: the percussion section of gongs and drums plays preludes and punctuates the singing and action, and the melodic section of strings and winds accompanies the singing and plays instrumental interludes. The music for Peking opera is arranged from a traditional repertoire of stock arias. Original compositions are not particularly valued, but fresh interpretations and original embellishments of familiar tunes are highly prized. In general, we might say that the combination of familiarity and originality, virtuosity, tension of plot, emotional states symbolized by specific melodies, and voice timbre associated with personality characteristics makes Peking opera a multidimensional experience. However, it does take study to appreciate it.

The government of the Republic of China in Taiwan supports and promotes traditional Peking opera by sponsoring one opera school, Fu Hsing (disc 16) and several troupes managed by the military. A group of players has been sent abroad annually since 1973. Taiwanese folk operas are still performed on open air stages and in temples on festival occasions. Cantonese opera maintains its popularity in Hong Kong and among overseas Cantonese.

CONTEMPORARY CHINESE MUSIC

When the Republican Revolution brought down the Ch'ing dynasty in 1911, it ended the long history of court music tradition as well. The educational system of republican China was modeled after that of the West, and Western music or Westernized Chinese music was taught in schools. After the initial introduction of a program in both Chinese and Western music in 1920, a music department was established at Peking University in 1923. The first conserva-

tory of music in Western style was founded in Shanghai in 1927 (Hsu 1970:13–14) where Chinese students studied everything their Western counterparts did. Before long, to study Western music became a fashion among young intellectuals; traditional music and instruments were denigrated as old-fashioned and primitive. Since many teachers were Westerners, especially Russians or Western-trained Chinese, compositions with Western harmony, counterpoint, and instruments were the inevitable result. At the same time, nationalism swept the nation. The search for a synthesis in musical expression between the West and China became the major concern of young composers. The result was a Chinese nationalism comparable to the nationalistic trend of late nineteenth-century Europe. The following quotation written by Lieu Da-kun, a graduate of the University of Michigan, reveals the attitude of that generation:

> So, in one word, Chinese music lacks a standard in every respect. It has no standard scale, no standard pitch, no standard instrument, no standard music composition. And the problem cannot be solved by borrowing all these things from foreign sources. [1919:110]

Western compositional techniques were first used in the early 1930s and have continued in practice to the present in socialist China. Musicians began to think and hear in Western ways and became less tolerant of high-pitched music, untempered melodies, and native styles of performance:

> The majority [of our instruments] have no fixed pitch and their compass is narrow. We possess no bass instruments like the cello and the double-bass. In these respects we are behind the West. If we refuse to learn from it, we shall be the losers. [Ho 1956:7]

> The high-pitched notes in the Szechuan songs in some passages are really too high. When you hear it you feel that the singer is making superhuman efforts and the sound is very much forced. *The public may like it, but this is not scientific.* [*China News Analysis*, July 21, 1961, p. 4. Italics ours.][5]

5. These two statements were made after 1949. Since the overall attitude toward music was the same after this date as before, we think that it is appropriate to quote them as evidence.

Mao Tse-tung's speech in May 1942, "Talk at the Yenan Forum on Literature and Art," outlined the purpose of the arts in a socialist country:

> Literature and art fit well into the whole revolutionary machine as a component part; they operate as powerful weapons for unity and educating the people and for attacking and destroying the enemy. [1967:2]

With the founding of the People's Republic in 1949, this promise was realized. Four trends were apparent and continue today: the return to folk tradition, the emphasis on rigorous training in performance, the infusion of political content in program music, and the combination of Western and Chinese elements to a great extent. We have discussed politics and music, the third trend, earlier.

For the first time a conscious effort to encourage folk-musical culture has been instituted from the top. Large-scale research, collecting, and editing of folk material have been carried on side by side with rigorous training in performance. Thousands of books and recordings of folk and traditional music and drama have been published. For example, between 1949 and 1959, 2,428 music books and 3,533 recordings were issued ("Shih n'ien-lai" 1959:32–35). Compositions with messages about revolution, socialism, peasants, workers, and soldiers are strongly promoted, whereas music devoid of revolutionary message is discouraged. The purpose is to create a "socialist-realism" based on folk tradition. Creativity is seldom credited to individuals; most works, especially recent ones, are created by committees of composers. There is always the question of whom the art serves. Since music and the other arts are to be understood by the masses, works of abstract, avant-garde nature and the electronic medium are not allowed. The following quotation regarding modern Western music in general expresses this view:

> Most of their music uses dissonances or even all noise as sources. Therefore, it is not possible to hear any normal human emotion and personality in their music. In essence they are advocating mysticism, insanity and extreme individualism. If the modern reactionary music is not thoroughly criticized and is let free, it can bring the art of music into total disaster. [Wang 1959:38]

With this attitude, the compositional technique after 1949 has been, of course, a continuation of the nationalism mentioned above. Many traditional pieces have been abandoned or modified and many new works have been composed. Only selected Western music of the eighteenth and nineteenth centuries has been allowed public performance.

Ever since the 1930s Western forms have been adopted in compositions regardless of the purposes for which they were written. Lieder (disc 13), sonatas, concertos, symphonies, and choral works have poured out by the scores. Huang Tzû (1904-1938), an Oberlin and Yale graduate, is still remembered for his lieder, and Hsien Hsing-hai (1905-1949), the Paris-trained composer, is still respected for his cantata, "The Yellow River" (1939: disc 27), which is also the source of the recent piano concerto with the same name. The first version of the much publicized "folk" opera "The White-Haired Girl" was completed in 1945 by several composers. Since then, composition by group effort without credit to individual composers has become the norm rather than the exception. More recent notable examples of such communal creation are the piano concerto "Youth" (1960: disc 10) and the violin concerto "Butterfly Lovers" (1961: disc 10).

During the Cultural Revolution (1966–69) just about everything in the arts, old or new, Chinese or Western, was banned for carrying "feudal" and "bourgeois" ideas. For several years only eight revolutionary works—including the Peking opera "The Red Lantern" (disc 41)—and the two ballets "The Red Detachment of Women" (discs 36, 41) and the "The White-Haired Girl," a dance version of the earlier opera (disc 41) were allowed.[6] Since the Cultural Revolution, new works must conform to a rigid guideline. The most popular one is the piano concerto "The Yellow River" (1971: disc 45). These newly created revolutionary compositions are revisions of the "old revolutionary" works with even heavier political messages.

6. The other five works allowed were the operas "Taking the Tiger Mountain by Strategy," "On the Docks," "Raid on the White Tiger Regiment," "Shachiapang," and a symphonic oratorio based on the last.

The modern revolutionary Peking opera, which was promoted by Chiang Ching in 1964, employs contemporary themes and costumes and Western realistic staging (Ching 1968). The heightened speech is replaced by ordinary Mandarin and the facial paintings and designs are replaced by bright and dark faces only. Not only are the traditional four divisions of roles abandoned, but many stylized and symbolic gestures have been abolished or altered. Traditional fixed tunes are now mingled with Red Army songs, "The East is Red" and the "Internationale." The orchestra has been greatly expanded by the addition of Western instruments to increase dramatic tension, although traditional Chinese percussion retains its prominent position. Western harmony and modulation are common features. Traditional acrobatics, on the other hand, are greatly emphasized, excellently executed, and combined with Western ballet elements. One attempt to accompany the Peking opera with the piano in concert form was introduced in "The Red Lantern" (disc 39) during the Cultural Revolution. In this version, traditional percussion is kept but all other instruments except the piano are eliminated. The rationale behind this is the interpretation of Mao's concept: "Make the past serve the present and foreign things serve China." A statement from an Anhui newspaper emphasizes this point:

> In the past we thought that the piano could not serve workers-peasants-soldiers, that the workers-peasants-soldiers would not stand it and could not enjoy it, that the piano could only perform foreign, bourgeois music. Now we know that if the piano is employed by a person armed with the Thoughts of Mao Tse-tung, then it is welcome to the masses and can serve workers-peasants-soldiers and proletarian politics. [*China News Analysis*, July 12, 1968, p. 3]

Another innovation was to perform the Peking opera "Shachiapang" as an oratorio (disc 40). In this work Peking opera melodies are sung by soloists and chorus in harmony and accompanied by a full Western orchestra.

Since 1969, control over the performing arts has relaxed somewhat. Local operas banned during the Cultural Revolution have been reintroduced after grafting the themes from the above-mentioned models. Some ancient instru-

EXAMPLE 2-4. "Ta Nan-Kou-Chou," a modern northern Shensi folk song, harmonized as the opening theme of the piano concerto "Youth." See disc 10.

mental works, such as the famous p'i-p'a piece "Ambush from Ten Sides," have been newly recorded (disc 1) and Western symphony orchestras such as the London, the Vienna, and the Philadelphia Philharmonics have been invited to perform in China. However, this does not necessarily mean a return to the pre-1949 scene. As long as the seemingly endless discussion on the value of the arts from a class-conscious viewpoint continues, traditional music will be denounced for its feudal and bourgeois content and Western absolute music will be rejected for its lack of social function.

As for performance technique on Chinese and Western instruments, as well as in opera and ballet, a high degree of excellence is vigorously cultivated. In international competitions, Fu Ts'ung won third place at the Chopin Festival in 1955 and Liu Shin-k'un won third at the Liszt Festival in 1956 and second at the Tschaikovsky Festival in 1958 (*China News Analysis*, July 21, 1961, p. 2.). Excellent performances of all varieties are also available on recordings and films.

In Taiwan and Hong Kong the musical culture is very diverse. In general people prefer popular music, Western or Westernized. Those who study music usually take up Western music, and academic musicians generally subscribe to the Western idea that new music must be innovative. Appeals for music that is both Chinese and modern are heard repeatedly:

> We cannot deny that the so-called "new music" in China, from the viewpoint of world music trend, is nothing but Western "old music." At least in structure, it is modeled after eighteenth- and nineteenth-century Western music, not twentieth-century music. [Hsu 1970:49]

> Chinese music, traditional or Westernized, cannot remain in the past.... Traditional Chinese music is excellent material for study, but is obsolete for creativity ... no one is writing Gregorian chant anymore. We also have music in the Romantic style ... which is not appropriate for expression in the modern age. Therefore, we must use modern compositional techniques. [Han 1972:11]

Since composers are relatively free in Taiwan and Hong Kong, many write avant-garde music. But some of them also use new techniques to express nationalism. Hsu Ts'ang-houei, another Paris-trained composer, was the first to intro-

duce new ideas to Taiwan in the 1950s. His choral work "The Burial of Flowers" (1962) is an example of blending tradition with new idioms (disc 28). In this work the soprano solo sings a pentatonic melody over a quasi-atonal choral line which is punctuated by two Buddhist ritual instruments. Chou Wen-chung, now in the United States, uses fragments of pentatonic melody in an impressionistic setting to suggest the mood of Chinese paintings in his "Landscapes" (1949; disc 18).

* * *

In conclusion, we may sum up the present state of Chinese music as follows. Traditional music and drama are being preserved in Taiwan, Hong Kong, and overseas Chinese communities. They are being "revolutionized" in the People's Republic of China. Among overseas Chinese, in major cities of Southeast Asia and North America, there are amateur music groups and drama clubs that carry on the music and drama of their ancestral land. Moreover, some Western academic institutions support research and performance in traditional Chinese musical art. In the People's Republic of China, many formerly neglected folk genres are being resurrected and promoted and folk musicians are being accorded the respect and esteem that they have long deserved. On the other hand, the arts are strictly monitored by the state to conform to political ideology.

As for modern composition, the People's Republic continues in the nationalistic style begun in the 1930s. Chinese musical themes and instruments are combined with Western orchestration, using largely nineteenth-century harmony. The emphasis is on programmatic presentations of revolutionary themes. In Taiwan, Hong Kong, and Chinese communities overseas, Chinese musicians have kept pace with international trends. Classical Western music and popular music, sometimes not the best, are widely cultivated. Intellectual composers are writing original and modernistic pieces while selectively and eclectically using Chinese stylistic elements.

In retrospect, the evolution of Chinese music is a history of conflict and compromise among

FIGURE 2-4. Chinese instrumental ensemble of Northern Illinois University. From left, first row: willow-leaf lute, p'i-p'a, butterfly harp, erh-hu. Second row: yueh ch'in, chung-ruan, sheng, ti, erh-hu, kao-hu. Third row: percussion.

diverse elements. Musical elements from abroad have been continuously absorbed and synthesized. The enduring feature, however, seems to be the central role of political ideology. The use of music and drama to promote and reinforce social values has always been as important as aesthetic expression.

Glossary

Anhui-a province in north central China, original home of the Peking opera and Huang-mei opera.

chêng-13- or 16-stringed zither.

ch'in-a 7-stringed zither, usually with 13 studs set into the soundboard.

ch'ing-a stone chime or bowl gong (the Chinese characters are different, but homophonous).

Ching hsi-Peking Opera, literally "drama of the capital."

chung-bronze bell.

Cultural Revolution-a political movement in China, 1966 to 1969, during which a general purging of elements considered undesirable took place.

erh-hu-2-stringed fiddle.

hsiao-vertical flute with 6 finger holes.

hsün-pottery ocarina shaped like a squat bottle and blown across the opening at the top.

K'un ch'ü-musical drama from central China of the Ming and Ch'ing dynasties, still surviving today.

k'ung-hou-an archaic harp, no longer in use.

kung, shang, chiao, chih, yü-names of the five scale tones, corresponding to the Western scale tones of do, re, mi, sol, la, respectively.

lü-the Chinese term for "pitch" or "tone."

mu-yü-wooden block shaped like a fish's head, a percussion idiophone.

nan-chü-southern style of musical drama of the Yuan dynasty, which used five-tone modes.

nan-hu-2-stringed fiddle, southern style.

neo-Confucianism-a revival of Confucianism during the Sung dynasty, in which secular ethics were integrated with metaphysics.

pei-chü-northern style of musical drama of the Yuan dynasty, which used seven-tone modes.

pien-ch'ing-sets of tuned stone chimes.

pien-chung-sets of tuned bells.

p'i-p'a-pear-shaped lute with 4 strings.

san-hsien-a 3-stringed, long-necked lute with an octagonal, square, or cylindrical head of which the top and bottom are covered with snakeskin. Played with a small plectrum or with fingernails.

se-an archaic zither with 25 strings.

shêng-a mouth organ with 12 or more reed pipes set in a bowl.

sona-belled oboe, double reed instrument.

su-yüeh-ancient secular music.

Szechuan-a province in southwestern China.

ta-ku-literally "great drum," a type of narrative song popular in northern China.

t'an-tz'û-a style of narrative song popular in central China.

ti or *ti-tzû*-transverse flute with 7 finger holes of which one is covered with a reed membrane, giving the instrument a reedy timbre.

ya-yüeh-ancient court ritual music.

yeh-hu-2-stringed coconut fiddle.

Yüeh Fu-ministry of music during the 3d century B.C.

yün-ch'ing-small cup gong attached to a rod and struck with a small mallet; a Buddhist ritual instrument.

Bibliography

Alley, Rewi, and Eva Siao.
  1957. *Peking Opera: An Introduction Through Pictures*. Peking: New World Press.

Arts of China, Vol I.
  1969. Tokyo and Palo Alto, Calif.: Kodansha International Ltd.

Cahill, James.
  1960. *Chinese Painting*. Geneva: Skira.

Cameron, Nigel.
  1970. *Barbarians and Mandarins; Thirteen Centuries of Western Travelers in China*. New York: Walker/Weatherhill.

Chao Hua.
  1974. "Do Musical Works Without Titles Have No Class Character?" *Chinese Literature* (April), pp. 89–94.

Chao Tsung.
  1969. *Chung-kuo Ta-lu te Hsi-chü Kai-ke, 1942–67* (Drama Reform in Mainland China, 1942-67). Hong Kong: Chinese University.

Chi Ju-shan.
  1962. *Kuo-chü I-shu Hui-k'ao* (A Study of the Art of the National Opera). Taipei: Ch'ung-kuang Publishing Co.

Chiang Ching.
  1968. *On the Revolution of Peking Opera*. Peking: Foreign Languages Press.

Chi K'ung Li-yüeh chih Kai'chin (The Improvement of Ritual and Music in the Confucian Ceremony).
  1970. n.p. Chi K'ung Li-yüeh Kung-cho Committee.

China News Analysis.
  1961 and 1968. Hong Kong. No. 381 (July 21, 1961) and No. 716 (July 12, 1968).

Chu Tsai-yü.
  1584. *Yüeh Lü Ch'üan Shu*. (Complete Book of Rules for Music).

Chuang Pen-li.
  1968. *A Study of the Chime Stones*. Taipei: National Museum of History.
  1972. "A Historical and Comparative Study of Hsün, the Chinese Ocarina." *The Bulletin of the Institute of Ethnology, Academia Sinica, Taipei* no. 33 (Spring), 177-253.

Deza, Sophia.
  1973. "The Dance-Arts in the People's Republic of China: The Contemporary Scene." *Asian Music* 5:28–39.

Fourcade, François.
  1969. *Art Treasures of the Peking Museum*. Translated by N. Guterman. New York: Harry N. Abrams, Inc.

Gulik, Robert H. van.
  1951. "Brief Note on the Cheng, the Chinese Small Zither." *Toyo Ongaku Kenkyu* 9:10-25.
  1969. *The Lore of the Chinese Lute: An Essay in the Ideology of the Ch'in*. Tokyo: Sophia University, 1940. Reprint, Rutland, Vermont: Tuttle.

Halson, Elizabeth.
  1966. *Peking Opera: A Short Guide*. Hong Kong, London: Oxford University Press.

Han Kuo-huang.
  1972. *Yin-yüeh te Chung-kuo* (A Musical China). Taipei: Chih-wen Ch'u-pan She.

Ho Lu-ting.
  1956. "What Kind of Music for China?" *China Reconstructs* (December), pp. 5-8.

Hsu Ts'ang-houei.
  1970. *Chin-tai Chung-kuo Yin-yüeh Shih-hua* (A History of Modern Chinese Music). Taipei: Morning Bell Publishing Co.

Institute of Archaeology, Academia Sinica and the Hunan Provincial Museum.
  1975. "Significance of the Excavation of Han Tombs Nos. 2 and 3 at Mawangtui in Changsha" (in Chinese). *Kaogu*, nos. 1, 47-57, 61.

Kagan, Alan L.
  1963. "Music and the Hundred Flowers Movement." *Musical Quarterly* 49 (October), 417-30.
Kishibe Shigeo.
  1940. "The Origin of the P'i-p'a, with Particular Reference to the Five-stringed P'i-p'a Preserved in the Shosoin." *Transactions of the Asiatic Society of Japan* no. 19, 2d ser., 259-304.
  1960-61. *A Historical Study of the Music in the T'ang Dynasty* (English summary). Tokyo: University of Tokyo Press.
  1965. "A Chinese Painting of the T'ang Court Women's Orchestra." In *The Commonwealth of Music*, edited by G. Reese and R. Brandel, 104-17. New York: The Free Press.
Ku Chin T'u Shu Chi Ch'eng (Compendium of Ancient and Modern Books).
  n. d. 91 vols. Taipei.
Kuttner, Fritz.
  1964. "The Music of China: A Short Historical Synopsis Incorporating the Results of Recent Musical Investigations." *Ethnomusicology* 8 (May), 121-27.
  1965. "A Musicological Interpretation of the Twelve Lüs in China's Traditional Tone System." *Ethnomusicology* 9 (January), 22-38.
  1975a. "Prince Chu Tsai-Yü's Life and Works: A Re-evaluation of His Contribution to Equal Temperament Theory." *Ethnomusicology* 19 (May), 163-206.
  1975b. "The 749-temperament of Huai Nan Tzu (123 B.C.)." *Asian Music* 4, nos. 1 and 2, 88-105.
Legge, James, trans.
  1967. *Li Chi: Book of Rites: An Encyclopedia of Ancient Ceremonial Usages, Religious Creeds, and Social Institutions.* 2 vols. New Hyde Park, N.Y.: University Press.
Li Yin-hai.
  1959. *Han-tzu Tiao-shih chi Ch'i Ho-sheng* (Han People's Modes and Their Harmonization). Shanghai: Shang-hai Wen-i Ch'u-pan-she.
Liang, David Ming-yueh.
  1972. *The Chinese Ch'in: Its History and Music.* San Francisco: Chinese National Music Association, San Francisco Conservatory of Music.
Lieberman, Fredric.
  1970. *Chinese Music: An Annotated Bibliography.* New York: Society for Asian Music. First supplement in *Asian Music* 5 (1973), 56-85.
Lieu Da-kun.
  1919. "Chinese Music." In *Peking Leader Special Anniversary Supplement—China in 1918.* Peking (February 12).

Lin Ch'un-kuang.
  1960. "Fu Yu Ch'uan-chao Chin-shen ti 'Ch'in-nien Kang-ch'in Hsieh-ts'ou-ch'u'" (The Piano Concerto "Youth" Is Full of Creative Spirit). *Renmin Yinyüeh* (February 4-5, 7).
Lin Fei-hsiung and Chou Jun-hua.
  1971. *Cheng-yang T'an P'i-p'a* (How to Play the P'i-p'a). Hong Kong: Hsing-ch'en Book Store.
Lui Tsun-yuen.
  1968. "A Short Guide to Ch'in." *Selected Reports, Institute of Ethnomusicology, UCLA* 1:179-204.
Mackerras, Colin.
  1972. *The Rise of the Peking Opera, 1770-1870; Social Aspects of the Theatre in Manchu China.* Oxford: Clarendon Press.
  1975. *The Chinese Theatre in Modern Times: From 1840 to the Present Day.* Amherst: University of Massachusetts Press.
Mao Tse-tung.
  1967. *On Literature and Art.* Peking: Foreign Languages Press.
Mitchell, John D., compiler.
  1973. *The Red Pear Garden: Three Great Dramas of Revolutionary China.* Boston: D. R. Godine.
Moule, A. C.
  1908. "A List of the Musical and Other Sound Producing Instruments of the Chinese." *Journal of the North China Branch of the Royal Asiatic Society* 39:1-160.
Needham, Joseph, and Kenneth Robinson.
  1962. "Sound." In *Physics and Physical Technology. Science and Civilization in China*, 4:126-228. Cambridge: The University Press.
New Archaeological Finds in China: Discoveries During the Cultural Revolution.
  1974. Rev. ed. Peking: Foreign Languages Press.
Pian, Rulan Chao.
  1967. *Sung Dynasty Musical Sources and Their Interpretation.* Cambridge, Mass.: Harvard University Press.
Picken, Laurence.
  1957. "The Music of Far Eastern Asia, 1: China." In *The New Oxford History of Music, I: Ancient and Oriental Music*, edited by Egon Wellesz, 83-134. London: Oxford University Press.
  1969. "T'ang Music and Musical Instruments." *T'oung Pao, Leiden* 55, nos. 1/3, 74-122.
Ricci, Matthew.
  1953. *China in the Sixteenth Century: The Journals of Matthew Ricci, 1583-1610.* Translated from the Latin of Trigaut (1615) by Louis J. Gallagher. New York: Random House.

Rowley, George A.

 1969. "A Chinese Scroll of the Ming Dynasty: Ming Huang and Yang Kuei-fei." *Artibus Asiae* 31:1–31.

Schafer, Edward H.

 1963. *The Golden Peaches of Samarkand: A Study of T'ang Exotics*. Berkeley and Los Angeles: University of California Press.

Scott, Adolphe C.

 1957. *The Classical Theatre of China*. London: Allen and Unwin.

 1963. *Literature and the Arts in Twentieth Century China*. New York: Doubleday.

 "Shih-nieh-lai Wo-kuo Yin-yüeh Shi-yeh te Fa-chan" (The Development of Musical Activities in Our Country in the Past Ten Years).

 1959. *Renmin Yinyüeh* nos. 10/11, 32–35.

Snow, Lois Wheeler.

 1972. *China on Stage; an American Actress in the People's Republic*. New York: Random House.

Sullivan, Michael.

 1973. *The Arts of China*. Berkeley, Los Angeles, London: University of California Press.

Wang Shu-ho.

 1959. "Hsien-tai Tsu-ch'an Chieh-chi Fan-tung Yin-yüeh Liu-p'ai Ch'ien-chieh" (A Short Introduction to the Modern Capitalistic Reactionary Musical Trends). *Renmin Yinyüeh* no. 2, 37–38.

Yang, Daniel S. P.

 1967. *An Annotated Bibliography of Materials for the Study of the Peking Theatre*. Madison: University of Wisconsin.

 1968. "The Peking Theatre Under Communism." *The Theatre Annual* 24:32–46.

Yang, Hsien-yi, and Gladys Yang, trans.

 1958. *Selected Plays of Kuan Han-ching*. Shanghai: New Art and Literature Publishing House.

Yang Yin-liu.

 1952. *Chung-kuo Yin-yüeh Shi-kang* (Outline History of Chinese Music). Shanghai: Wan-yeh Book Co.

Discography

Western-made discs are listed as much as possible although they may not necessarily be the best in each genre. Art Tune Record Company in Hong Kong reprinted a large number of pre-Cultural Revolution recordings that are now collector's items. New recordings made by China Record Company are available in most bookstores selling Chinese books and periodicals. Other Hong Kong discs can be found in Chinatowns.

1. *Ambush from All Sides*. China Record M 2037. Includes old pieces for p'i-p'a and sona and new pieces for cheng, erh-hu, and sheng.

2. *Beating the Dragon Robe*. Folkways FW 8883. Complete Peking opera sung by masters trained in the old tradition.

3. *Beyond the Great Wall*. Original Chinese sound track recording from the motion picture. Capitol T 10401.

4. *The Cheng: Two Masters Play the Chinese Zither (Louis Chen and Liang Tsai-p'ing)*. Lyrichord LLST 7262.

5. *China I—Instruments*. Anthology AST 4000. Reprint of Chinese recordings featuring masters playing on ch'in, cheng, yang-ch'in, san-hsien, and other instruments. With notes by Fredric Lieberman.

6. *China: Shantung Folk Music and Traditional Instrumental Pieces*. Lu-sheng Ensemble of Taiwan. Nonesuch H 72051. Sona, sheng, cheng, ti, ann-hu, and others.

7. *China's Instrumental Heritage: Liang Tsai-p'ing and His Group*. Lyrichord LLST 792. Sheng, hsiao, hsün, cheng, nan-hu.

8. *China's Treasures: Lui Tsun-yuan on P'i-p'a and Ch'in*. Lyrichord LLST 7227.

9. *Chinese Buddhist Music*. Lyrichord LLST 7222.

10. *Chinese Classical Masterpieces: "Youth," Concerto for Piano and Orchestra," and "The Butterfly Lovers," Concerto for Violin and Orchestra*. Everest 3212.

11. *Chinese Classical Masterpieces for the P'i-p'a and Ch'in: Lui Tsun-yuen*. Lyrichord LLST 7182.

12. *Chinese Classical Music: Pipe (Ti-tzu) Solo by Lai Siu-hang*. Fung Hang (Hong Kong) PHLP 225.

13. *Chinese Lied, Vols. 1 & 2*. Lucky Record (Taiwan) LY 154 & 157. Works by Huang Tze and others.

14. *Chinese Masterpieces for the Cheng: Liang Tsai-ping and David Liang*. Lyrichord LLST 7142.

15. *Chinese Masterpieces for the Erh-hu: Lui Man-sing and His Group*. Lyrichord LLST 7132. The first piece is a programmatic depiction of birds; most of the others are not erh-hu, but orchestral pieces in the southern style.

16. *The Chinese Opera: Arias from Eight Peking Operas*. Lyrichord LLST 7212. Performers of the Fu Hsing Opera Academy, Taiwan. One example each of K'un opera and folk opera; the rest are Peking opera selections.

17. *Chinese Taoist Music*. Lyrichord LLST 7223.

18. *Chou Wen-chung: Landscapes.* Composers Recording CRI 122.
19. *Confucian Chants, with English Translations.* Sheikh SRLP 006.
20. *The East Is Red.* Paredon P 1007 (3 discs).
21. *Exotic Music of Ancient China.* Lyrichord LLST 7122. Lui Tsun-yuen on p'i-p'a and ch'in. Includes "The Great Ambush."
22. *Fishermen's Triumphant Song.* China Record M 2036. Wind and percussion, cheng, ti, erh-hu, sona, and others.
23. *Five Revolutionary Folk Songs of the Shensi-Kansu-Ningsia Border Region.* China Record M 917.
24. *Folksongs—Bidding Farewell to My Lover.* Art Tune COL 3150.
25. *Hakka Mountain Songs—Brother and Sister with the Same Heart.* Art Tune COL 5079.
26. *Hong Kong: Instrumental Music.* EMI CO64-1798. P'i-p'a, yang-ch'in, hsiao, ti, ch'in, shêng, erh-hu, chêng.
27. *Hsien Hsin-hai: The Yellow River Cantata.* Oriental (Hong Kong) ORB 3.
28. *Hsu Ts'ang-houei: Works, Vol. I.* Four Seas Record (Taiwan). Includes his "Burial of Flowers."
29. *Li-Chen-tung Nan-hu Solo Album (Ten Masterpieces by Liu Tien-hua).* Four Seas Record (Taiwan).
30. *Lotus Lantern: Chinese Classical Orchestra.* Lui Pui-yuen. Lyrichord LLST 7202. Modern orchestral ensemble.
31. *Mei Lang-fan Recordings.* Art Tune COL 3167, 3183, 3184.
32. *New Song of the Herdsmen.* China Record M 2064. Cheng, ti, p'i-p'a, sona, erh-hu, and others.
33. *Peking Opera: Official Ensemble of the Chinese People's Republic from the Peking Opera (recorded at the Paris International Festival of Dramatic Art, 1955).* Seraphim 60201. A reprint of Opéra chinois. Pathe FCX 429. Only three excerpts of Peking opera; others are instrumental pieces and a folk song.
34. *Ping-t'an: Tu Shih Liang.* Art Tune ATC 27.
35. *Pi-p'a Solo: Lui Pui-yuen.* Four Seas Record (Taiwan).
36. *The Red Detachment of Women: Highlights from the Modern Chinese Revolutionary Ballet.* Everest 3338.
37. *The Red Flower of Tachai Blossoms Everywhere.* China Record M 1019. Sheng, erh-hu, cheng, liu-yeh-ch'in, and orchestral pieces.
38. *The Red Lantern, with Piano Accompaniment.* China Record M 916.
39. *The Ruse of the Empty City, a Peking Opera.* Folkways FW 8882. Complete Peking opera sung by masters trained in the old tradition.
40. *Shachiapang: Revolutionary Symphonic Music.* China Record M 935 (2 discs).
41. *Selected Scenes from the Modern Revolutionary Theatrical Works.* China Record M 964–967 (4 discs). Includes selections from Peking operas "On the Docks," "The Red Lantern," "Taking the Tiger Mountain by Strategy," "Shachiapang," and ballets "The Red Detachment of Women," and "The White-Haired Girl." Complete or highlight recordings for each work are available separately.
42. *Spring Comes Early to the Commune.* China Record M 972. Pan-hu, ti, p'i-p'a, and sona.
43. *Taoist Chants, with English Translations.* Sheikh SRLP 007.
44. *Yu Lan, Ku-ch'in Solo by Kuan Ping-hu, Cha Fu-hsi and Fu Hsueh-tsai.* Art Tune ATC 73.
45. *The Yellow River, Concerto for Piano and Orchestra.* China Record M 905. The same piece is recorded by RCA: Epstein and the Philadelphia Orchestra under Eugene Ormandy. RCA ARL 1-0415.

Films

The Beautiful Bait. Chinese Information Service. Col. 20 min.

An abridged version of a Peking opera performed by students of the Fu Hsing Drama School in Taiwan. Features singing, dancing, and acrobatics. Note Western influences in the use of spotlight and scenery.

Chinese, Korean and Japanese Dance. SAM. Col. 25 min.

Shows the likenesses and dissimilarities in the dance styles of the three countries.

Chinese Music and Musical Instruments. AP, #956. Col. 25 min.

Pictures of traditional instruments, both photographs and old paintings. Scarf dance, young boys with shaved heads doing ceremonial dance, lovely scenery.

The East Is Red. CF/MH. Col. 130 min.

A pageant of song and dance on the revolutionary history of the People's Republic. Soundtrack in disc 20.

Music in China. Chinese Information Service. Col. 28 min.

Introduces the function and history of music in

ancient China and the various kinds of Chinese musical instruments. Concludes with a modern Chinese classical orchestral performance (Broadcasting Corporation of China in Taipei).

A Night at the Peking Opera. Film Images. Col. 20 min.

Originally produced by Claude Jaeger in France. Includes a short introduction and four excerpts from "The White Snake," "The Monkey King," "Meeting at the Crossroads," and "The Autumn River," the last one being a Szech'uan opera. Emphasis on acrobatics and dancing movements, no singing.

The Traditional Chinese Opera. Leo Seltzer Associates for China Art Films, Ltd. Col. 15 min.

Introduces the training of actors and actresses at the Fu Hsing Drama School in Taiwan. Presents short excerpts from Peking operas; orchestra clearly shown on stage.

Two Chinese Dances. CF/MH. Col. 10 min.

Folk dancing. Marriage and funeral drum dances "among an aboriginal tribe in China's southwest."

Revolutionary Ballets. Not available commercially.
The Red Detachment of Women.
The White-Haired Girl.

Revolutionary Peking Operas. Not available commercially.
The Azalea Mountain.
Fighting on the Plain.
On the Docks.
Taking the Tiger Mountain by Strategy.

The last six films have been shown here and there by people who have connection with Mainland China. NBC showed some of them in 1972.

3. Certain Experiences in Korean Music

Kang-sook Lee

The most crucial step toward understanding Korean music is to realize that Korean tonal materials and their interaction must be viewed only in terms of Korean music-grammar, which is totally different from that of any other country. Indeed, the differences are so great that Westerners might initially reject the validity of the system. Thus, even a sympathetic Westerner needs a step-by-step orientation to Korean music.

Geographically located between gigantic China and busy Japan, Korea, about the size of Minnesota, is vast in terms of music culture. Korean music is also unique, despite tremendous influences from China, as is Japanese music despite the influence of Korea. Evidence of these influences can be presently found in both Korea and Japan, namely, in the existence of Koreanized Chinese music called *t'angak* in Korea and of Japanized Korean music called *komagaku* in Japan. The Korean term t'angak literally means music from T'ang Dynasty China, *ak* being the Korean word for music. Similarly the Japanese term komagaku signifies music from the *Koryŏ* Dynasty (937–1392) in Korea. A study of these influences, though not pertinent for this essay, would provide an important view of East Asian music as a whole.

Korean traditional music can be roughly divided into two major categories, *chŏngak* and *sokak*, music for the ruling class and for the common man, respectively. Within these two major types are various subcategories that

make up the whole of Korean music. Thus, in chŏngak there are two different, but somewhat related meanings. In its broader sense the term refers to the elegant musical style that was "right" for the Korean ruling class in terms of Confucian philosophy (the word *chŏng* literally means "right"), and within this broader meaning it also refers to ensemble music for men of high social status outside of the court. In this context the reader should become familiar with three terms: *aak*, t'angak, and *hyangak*. Chŏngak and aak can be used interchangeably in their broader sense, both referring to music for the ruling class, which includes t'angak, hyangak, and Confucian ritual music. In its narrower sense aak refers to this ritual temple music, of which at the present time only one example remains, "Munmyoak." "Munmyoak" is music performed at *munmyo*, which is the shrine where Confucius and his disciples are honored. T'angak refers to secular music of both the Chinese T'ang and Sung dynasties, which was altered to become court music after its introduction to Korea. Hyangak simply means native Korean music, a famous example of which is "Sujech'ŏn," a piece of instrumental music often claimed to be at least 1300 years old, existing, therefore, before the first compilation of Gregorian chant.

Court music, a subcategory of chŏngak, includes three types: ritual, banquet, and military music. Ritual music includes Confucian music and Imperial shrine music, while banquet music is of course music for courtly banquets. The above mentioned "Sujech'ŏn" is one of the most famous pieces of banquet music.

The music for the upper class consists of a type of ensemble music, *pungnyu*, the most so-

This essay is developed from ideas essential to the author's dissertation, "The Development and Trial of Korean-based Musical Activities for the Classroom" (The University of Michigan, 1975), and partly taken from it.

phisticated Korean lyric song genre, *kagok*, and the indigenous Korean popular song, *sijo*. Pungnyu is an archaic word that formerly meant music in general, but its present literal meaning denotes the state of being in which a man at leisure physically and mentally removes himself from the everyday world into a harmonious mood suitable for the appreciation of poetry, music, and female companionship. When the term is used in the context of Korean classical music, however, it refers to a type of ensemble music for the nobility. One variety of this music, called *chul-pungnyu*, consists mainly of stringed instruments; a second variety, *tae-pungnyu*, consists mainly of wind instruments; and a third is a combination of the first two. Kagok uses a rhythmic pattern of either a 16-beat *changdan* (which literally means "long-short") or its varied form, a 10-beat chang-dan. Any kagok selection is based on the *ujo* or *kyemyŏnjo* mode, or sometimes on both. Instruments used for accompaniment are the *kŏmungo*, *kayagŭm*, *yanggŭm*, *haegŭm*, *p'iri*, and *changgo*. Sijo is to be discussed in detail later in this essay.

Sokak, music for the common man, includes shaman music, Buddhist music, folk songs, farmers' music called *nong'ak*, a form of dramatic song called *p'ansori*, and an instrumental solo music called *sanjo*. In shaman music the role of an inspired female priest called a *mudang* is very important. The mudang plays the role of a medium between the visible world and the supernatural; singing, dancing, and instrument playing are always involved. One of the most important types of Buddhist music is called *pŏmp'ae*, a song of praise to Buddha, today preserved by only a few priests. To promote this music, the government has designated pŏmp'ae as a national cultural treasure and is taking steps to encourage new devotees of the art.

Since Korea has been traditionally an agricultural nation, a majority of the population has been associated with farming, and the life of the farmer has always had significant influence on the musical history of the country. The most fascinating characteristic of farmers' music is its twelve different rhythmic patterns called *si-pyich'ae*, which are played on a small gong called *kkwaenggwari*. One of the more appealing genres of sokak is the sanjo, an instrumental solo piece originally in improvisational style for various instruments: the kayagŭm, kŏmungo, *taegŭm*, haegŭm, *tanso*, and p'iri. P'ansori is another musical treasure of the highest importance in Korea and can be defined as song in drama, an indigenous Korean operalike production. Within the p'ansori, *aniri* is the spoken description of the dramatic content between songs, and *pallim* is the physical motion of the drama.

INSTRUMENTS

There are more than sixty different Korean musical instruments in existence today. Of these, I have selected five of the more popular instruments for discussion, giving particular attention to the most popular, the kayagŭm.

The kayagŭm has twelve strings stretched between the two ends of a soundboard made of paulownia wood. Twelve movable, inverted, Y-

FIGURE 3-1. *Kayagŭm.*

total length-147 cm   width at center-20 cm
width at ends-10 cm   height-9 cm
number of strings-12

shaped bridges support the strings and modify the pitch and tonal quality as they move. The kayagŭm is sometimes played by plucking with thumb, index, and/or middle finger of the right hand, or by springing the index and/or middle finger from the thumb to the string, or by quick alternation between plucking and springing, while the index and the middle fingers of the left hand press and release the strings in a technique, *nonghyŏn*, that produces the unique Korean vibrating sound phenomenon. The correct playing position is sitting cross-legged on the floor. There are two types of kayagŭm: the pungnyu-kayagŭm and the sanjo-kayagŭm, for use in the pungnyu and sanjo respectively.

One instrument always associated with Korean music is the *changgo*, an hourglass-shaped drum. Used as an accompanying instrument, the right side of it is struck with a stick, while the left side is hit by the fingers held together. The tone qualities produced by the right and left sides are of course different.

The haegŭm is a two-stringed bowed instrument. To play it the musician sits cross-legged on the floor, holds the long neck in his left hand, and rests the sound box on his left leg. The bow is held with the right hand and moved between the two strings in a horizontal back and forth motion. Pitch is modified by squeezing the strings with the fingers of the left hand in vertical up and down movements.

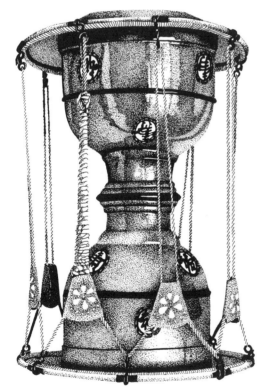

height–62 cm
diameter of heads–44 cm
diameter of center–14 cm

FIGURE 3-2. *Changgo.*

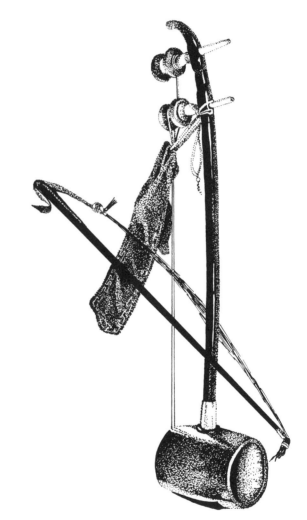

length–69 cm
depth of chamber–10 cm
width of chamber–9 cm

FIGURE 3-3. *Haegŭm.*

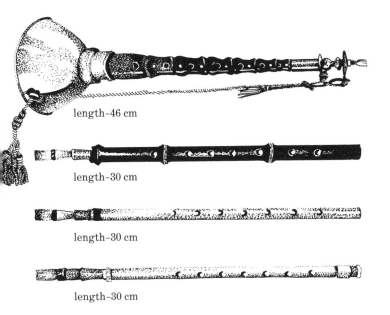

length-46 cm

length-30 cm

length-30 cm

length-30 cm

FIGURE 3-4. 1. T'aep'yŏngso. 2. T'ang-p'iri. 3. Hyang-p'iri. 4. Sae-p'iri.

The p'iri is a double reed aerophone that can be effectively used in both ensembles and solos. There are four p'iri: *hyang-p'iri*, *sae-p'iri*, *t'ang-p'iri*, and *t'aep'yŏngso*. The hyang-p'iri and sae-p'iri (the same as the hyang-p'iri except a smaller size) are used in the performance of a hyangak while the t'ang-p'iri is used with a t'angak. The bell instrument, t'aep'yŏngso, is played with old military music and nong'ak.

The taegŭm (large size) is one of the three bamboo flutes of the *samjuk* category; the other two are the *chunggŭm* (middle size) and *sogŭm* (small size). The taegŭm is approximately thirty inches in length and one inch in diameter, and the position for playing is about the same as for the Western flute. However, because of the relatively great distance between the finger holes and the fact that the hole for the mouth and the finger holes are directly in line, the playing position for the beginner could seem awkward.

MODES AND MELODY

Although there are a number of important modes in Korean music, I shall limit myself to a discussion of two.[1] An approximation of these

1. For further information regarding Korean modes, see Appendix A: "Korean Modes" in my dissertation (1975).

primary modes, ujo and kyemyŏnjo, in Western notation is given in example 3-1. The most crucial point to understand here is that these modes should not be understood in terms of Western pitch relationships. If one tries to view them in terms of an equal-tempered scale system he will fail to comprehend genuine Korean music,[2] which has nothing to do with intervals based on this scale system. The interval of a major second in Western music, for example, contains 200 cents. The corresponding interval in Korean terms could contain 135 cents (Rockwell 1972:81) which is neither a major nor a minor second. In other words, Westerners could often think Korean melodies are out of tune.

The problem is, then, how Westerners can possibly appreciate a melody which seems out of tune. Is not aesthetic sensitivity to a certain type of music, as Leonard Meyer says, essentially a learned behavior (1956:60)? Why do Koreans accept, for example, several tones in a nonghyŏn technique as a single tone while

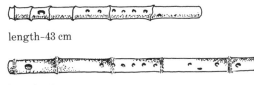

length-43 cm

length-56 cm

length-76 cm

FIGURE 3-5. 1. *Sogŭm*. 2. *Chunggŭm*. 3. *Taegŭm*.

Westerners might consider them as several tones? The answer is rather simple: Koreans have learned to appreciate and hear the several tones in nonghyŏn as an entity of one tone. Nonghyŏn refers to the method of depressing and releasing a string on a kayagŭm or kŏmungo (a six-stringed instrument similar to the kayagŭm) with the index and middle fingers of the left hand, thereby producing many subtle nuances that color and enrich the melody. Of course, a similar sound phenomenon exists in

2. For a detailed discussion on genuine and quasi-Korean music, see my article, "Korean Music Culture: Genuine and Quasi-Korean Music" (forthcoming).

EXAMPLE 3-1.

EXAMPLE 3-2. The first half of the initial phrase of "Ch'ŏngsalli"[3]

EXAMPLE 3-3.

Korean singing too. It is often said to be a vibrato, which is in one sense true, because when nonghyŏn is used the sound wavers, involving more than one note around the essential tone. However, if one simply says, for the sake of easy translation, that nonghyŏn is a vibrato, he is in great danger of distorting his understanding of the genuine quality of Korean music. Vibrato, although it has an expressive quality, might imply a kind of decorative embellishment; in nonghyŏn the additional wavering pitches around the central tone are essential to the sound phenomenon denoted by the term.

To illustrate the nature of Korean melody further, I have selected the initial phrase of a famous sijo, "Ch'ŏngsalli." This piece clearly illustrates the sung nonghyŏn technique, called *yosŏng,* which literally means "wavering tone."

3. "Ch'ŏngsalli" means "the heart of the green mountain." The straight line visually indicates a straight A♭ tone that increases dynamically until shortly before the start of the waver when it weakens slightly. The waver is constant through part of the pronunciation of *li,* when the pitch drops a perfect fourth, the waver becomes a straight tone for a moment, and then begins to waver again.

An approximation in Western notation is provided in example 3-2. Initially, all the listener hears is one long sustained note, later with a waver tone, followed by another long sustained tone at a different pitch level, in other words, nothing but two simple long sustained notes. Casual listeners might say that this is not a true musical event, but what actually *is* a musical event? In this context consider the following two musical examples.

In both Bach's "Air for the G string" (ex. 3-3) and the excerpt from the sijo, the first note of each phrase is greatly extended. Anyone familiar with the Bach piece would say there are many musical events in the first note because he can feel the implied harmonic changes within this one tone; he knows that this tone is moving toward an expected point. In this situation the events occur in the movement from tonic to dominant as shown in example 3-4. Now look at the sijo phrase. In it the tonic and dominant are not physically present but the feeling of movement between two points is created with the use of the straight tone and waver, through which the culturally conditioned individual can sense the mentally implied dramatic changes, including the feeling of tension and release. In short, there are musical events significant enough in the single tone of both the Bach and the sijo examples. In Bach we move from tonic to dominant through a harmonic progression, while in sijo we move from a toniclike to a dominant-like position through a straight/waver progression.

RHYTHM

The same phrase could also serve as an excellent musical example of Korean nonmetrical rhythm. Example 3-5 is a notation of this phrase showing the referential points in Korean elastic rhythm. Of the two rhythm patterns in sijo, the five-beat line and the eight-beat line, this example represents the former. (Here, we are dealing with *p'yŏng-sijo*.) The important point is that the distance between each two beat-refer-

ential-point is different. This is nonmetric or elastic rhythm:

> Nonmeter can be viewed in two contexts—the succession of metronomic beats freed from the necessity of constant division into regular small groupings, and a fluctuating distance between the beats themselves, as in a parlando or elastic style, that negates the power of any notational divisions into temporal units. [Malm 1972:97]

This definition applies perfectly to the Korean case too. The question here: Is this rhythm "musical?" To a Korean musician the answer will be an emphatic "Yes." In his mind there is absolutely no question about the aesthetic validity of nonmetric rhythm. Probably those who love Mozart would argue, but even conservative performers of Mozart deal with the music in terms of artistic or psychological meter rather than metronome meter. Here metronome meter refers, of course, to "constant division into regular small groupings," whereas psychological meter refers to a little adjustment in rhythmic

EXAMPLE 3-4.

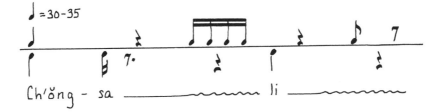

EXAMPLE 3-5. Rhythmic structure of sijo.

execution to enhance the flow and effect of the music. For example, any great performance of a Mozart piano work will not match absolutely with the metronome from beginning to end. There are always some delays or anticipations during the course of an actual performance. That is why some of the great masters allow the use of the metronome only in practice and not in actual musical or artistic performance. This is particularly true with Chopin's music, which deviates a great deal from metronome meter in what is called rubato.

The first difficulty in dealing with elastic rhythm in Korean music is that the unit of referential beat is much greater than the Western norm. The function of metronome meter in Western music is that of a reference for dealing with psychological meter, the basis for musical rhythm. When the underlying pulse of the music is fast, the deviation between metronome meter and psychological meter is at a minimum. However, when the underlying pulse is slow, the deviation may be greater. In dealing with Korean elastic rhythm, the same principle applies, except that, as mentioned, the pulse unit is much greater than the Western norm. The sijo pulse unit is $\downarrow = 30\text{-}35$, whereas the metronome's slowest pulse unit is only $\downarrow = 40$.

The second difficulty of elastic rhythm is that the Korean musician approaches psychological meter in a different fashion from that of a Western performer. Using example 3-5 as the reference point, Korean masters teach psychological rhythm in the following manner. The student sits cross-legged like Buddha, faces the instructor, and slowly beats the palms of his hands on his thighs. The student measures the length of time it takes to exhale, about the same duration it might take to sing one phrase of a song, and he is told that this breath represents the length of the five-beat pattern. With the initial thrust of exhaled air, the downbeat is hit with both palms on the insides of the knees. His eyes are closed in order to improve his concentration. Then after about two seconds, hands still resting in the same place on his legs, the second beat is tapped on the left leg with the index finger of the left hand. After another two seconds, when the breath is weakening, the third

beat is hit with the right palm on the right thigh, the voice at this point starting a wavering tone. The beginning waver is usually a sign of the third beat in the sijo rhythm. The fourth beat is once again struck with the left palm on the left thigh after two seconds, followed at nearly the same interval by the right palm on the right thigh for the fifth beat. After this beat the pattern is concluded by raising both hands up in front of the chest in a position like that for holding a basketball; this is followed by a quick downward jerk, giving a sense of finality to the line. This concluding motion often confuses Westerners who lose the beat context because it seems to indicate the beginning of the next phrase. The student may be asked to repeat the movements of the line as many times as necessary for him to gain a sense of confidence and conviction in this rhythmic execution. The crucial point to remember is that it is not important to strike a given beat at an exactly specific time, but to feel in one's mind the "rightness" of the divisions of the time continuum with the limitations of the pattern. In other words, within the referential frame given in example 3-5 the student should obtain psychological confidence through practice. The reason for the existence of so many different sijo singing styles lies in the fact that each individual performer's conception of "psychological rightness" is unique to him.[4]

HARMONIC TEXTURE

To understand harmonic texture in Korean music one should not think in a chordal sense, but in the literal sense; that is, Korean harmony is any simultaneous combination of tones that results in a pleasing sound to a listener. As in the musics of other world cultures, the role of heterophony in Korean music is great in creating a characteristic harmonic texture. The *Harvard Dictionary of Music* defines the term heterophony as "... the simultaneous use of slightly or elaborately modified versions of the same melody by two (or more) performers" (Apel 1969: 383). This definition can, of course, be applied to Korean heterophony, but my concern here is

4. This account of the method and purpose of teaching Korean rhythm appears in one of my articles, "Providing Korean Rhythmic Experiences in the Classroom" (1975).

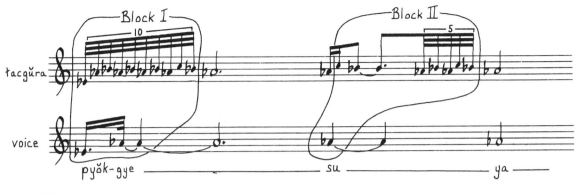

EXAMPLE 3-6.

not merely to describe but to explain its musical operation.

Korean heterophony exists only if there is an intended conscious interaction between performers who fully realize the musical principle of variety within unity. In order to understand this conception of heterophonic sound, it is helpful to look at a specific piece of Korean music. Take for example the initial phrase of the sijo, "Ch'ŏngsalli" (ex. 3-2). A transcription of the second half of the initial phrase is provided in example 3-6. Three instruments are involved: the changgo, taegŭm, and voice. The heterophony occurs between the voice and taegŭm as shown in the transcription, with the taegŭm modifying the vocal melody. However, the intended heterophony and its aesthetic effects are far greater than this simple description can suggest. The long sustained vocal line is operating aesthetically within itself as discussed earlier, but the taegŭm part in heterophony strongly reinforces the inner musical coherence; the instrument and voice complement each other. Consider the first appearance of heterophony in the taegŭm part (Block I of ex. 3-6). While the vocal line maintains a constant tone, the taegŭm enters, initially in unison, but it soon deviates and, to a degree, fights against the voice so as to cause a kind of musical tension before it reaches a point of relaxation by which a temporal release is achieved. At this point of release the two parts are again in unison.

As mentioned earlier this piece is nonmetri-cal, so the beat is not easily perceived. However, the heterophonic taegŭm part clearly aids in the anticipation of the elastic beat. In other words, the second beat falls when the two parts are in unison again after the first deviation. The casual listener should keep in mind that the heterophonic moment in Block I occurs in a matter of a few seconds, though it substantially contributes to the total effect of the piece as a whole.

In Block II the B♭ creates an appoggiatura-like effect—at which point the greatest tension is reached—before falling back to the consonant tone once again. The taegŭm part moves to a line of greater tightness, although less tense than in Block I because of the already strong conflict between B♭ and A♭, the main melodic line. The basic function of heterophony in this situation is, therefore, to create a satisfactory resolution from a feeling of dissonance to a resultant release.

To summarize this phrase, there are two structural notes, each of which is held in a seemingly monotonous manner. In fact, it is very difficult to create vitality in music while dealing with only two long-sustained notes; however, because of the use of heterophony, the phrase operates well aesthetically, especially in terms of the foreground level.[5] One describes a Western classical piece as being in C major, for

5. For a complete discussion of foreground, middle ground, and background in the context of Schenker's theory, see *Structural Hearing: Tonal Coherence in Music* by Felix Salzer (1952).

example, and in Schenkerian terms this means that the C tone is prolonged. In this sijo, similarly, one note, *chungnyŏ* (A♭), is prolonged in the background level. At the middle-ground level, the piece operates through a straight tone/waver progression, and the foreground level is characterized by heterophonic manifestations.

FORM

Limitations of space prevent a complete discussion here of form in Korean music, but by looking closely at one important instrument genre, kayagŭm sanjo, one can make a significant beginning. In this way one of the most important concepts of Korean form can be grasped, that of having several musical movements without pauses between them. After an initial acquaintance with the writings of Korean scholars one might argue that the terms, *hwanip* or *hwandu* for example, should be discussed for their uniquely Korean qualities. (In a musical piece such as "Pohŏja," the second half is an identical repetition of the first with the exception of the beginning which is varied. This varied beginning of the second half is called hwandu, "changed head," and the remainder of the second half is called hwanip.) However, to do so would be incorrect because the various repetitions of certain sections can easily be found in Western as well as in Korean music.

Before getting into the main topic one point should be made clear: to understand Korean music a piece should be heard in its entirety. The kayagŭm sanjo in its original form usually lasts more than thirty minutes, but occasionally in performance the movements are shortened; perhaps only a single movement is played. There are six movements, of which *chinyangjo, chungmori,* and *chajinmori* are the most representative of the sanjo form. Often when a recording is produced for foreign markets, the most important movement in terms of representative Korean tone systems, chinyangjo, is omitted, or in a performance each of the six movements is presented in very abbreviated form. These abridgments are made because a piece may seem to be overly long and boring to the casual listener or to provide an introduction for the beginner. However, this practice of shortening could lead

the beginner to misunderstand the essence of the original sanjo and especially the significance of the first movement, chinyangjo.

To discuss or analyze the form of a piece means, in a certain important sense, to explain the placement of punctuation in various levels (both molar and molecular) and to determine how they are logically connected (Berry 1966:1). One obvious place for musical punctuation is just prior to the appearance of a reversion—sometimes exactly the same, sometimes modified—to material that has appeared before, although punctuation can, of course, be used in areas other than a reversion situation. Example 3-7, an abridgment of the first movement of a kayagŭm sanjo, can be punctuated with a musical comma between measures 12 and 13. This punctuation is also based on learned behavior, but the rule itself was formulated from the way Korean musicians have traditionally performed the piece, placing a temporary closure at this particular point.

The most striking difference between the sanjo form and the Western classical form is the lack of a pause between movements. The player of a sanjo piece seldom stops between movements throughout its entire thirty-minute duration. Therefore only the trained musician can determine where divisions occur and he does this by sensing the presence of a pivotal rhythm that bridges the movements, a change that the average listener can only perceive after it has occurred, when he can feel a dramatic change in tempo. Unlike Western classical pieces in which the tempo often alternates between slow and fast, the sanjo tempo begins slowly with the first movement and gradually increases throughout the piece, culminating with a sudden, abrupt terminal gesture. The attentive listener could, of course, sense a slight tempo relaxation just prior to the final gesture, which serves to anticipate the approaching finale. The slowest movement, chinyangjo (this term indicates both the name of the movement and the rhythmic pattern), flows into the chungmori movement without pause, and each succeeding movement follows in the same manner. Not only do the tempi of all the movements differ from one another but also the rhythmic patterns vary.

The trained musician knows that each movement, and the divisions within it, is organized according to the principle of *tchoeŏtta-p'urŏtta*, which literally means "tightening and loosening" (H. Lee 1957:76) and can be directly compared to the principle of an alternating tension-release relationship. For my purpose here it is not actually necessary to examine an entire thirty-minute piece to learn the essence of sanjo; however, the most important first movement, chinyangjo, should be examined in some detail.

The first movement of this sanjo (part of which is shown in ex. 3-7) can be divided into three sections by their characteristic modes, ujo, *p'yŏngjo*, and kyemyonjo, respectively. The first section in ujo consists of five changdan and 18 beats. (Here changdan refers to a unit of 24 beats.) Ujo can be further subdivided into five parts, the first of which consists of two changdan; the second part, 12 beats; the third, one changdan and 18 beats; the fourth, 18 beats; and the fifth, 18 beats. Of course, different schools have different lengths and numbers of subdivisions. The section in p'yŏngjo is the shortest one of the three, consisting of only 18 beats. Between ujo and p'yŏngjo is a short bridge called *toljang*, consisting of 12 beats. The section in kyemyŏnjo is the longest, consisting of 13 changdan and 18 beats (C. Lee 1969:135–151).

As an initial experience, I suggest that the reader listen to an American recording that includes a simplified version of sanjo.[6] For recording purposes the piece was reduced from its original thirty-minute length to seven minutes, not by actually omitting any of the six movements but merely by shortening them. The first movement, chinyangjo, is extremely simplified, the section in ujo having been completely left out. The recording starts from the section in p'yŏngjo and moves into the kyemyŏnjo section in a slightly modified way. The long original kyemyŏnjo section is again very much simplified. However, on this recording, one can notice the obvious difference between the characteristics of p'yŏngjo and kyemyŏnjo, the predominant interval of the fourth in kyemyŏnjo, and the third and second in p'yŏngjo. Another advantage of this recording is that even though it is very much simplified, each of the six movement changes can be easily recognized, allowing the beginner to sense the uniquely Korean concept of musical movements without pauses between them.

A transcription of part of this recording (ex. 3-7) makes clear how the movement changes from the first to the second, without stopping, by means of a rhythmic modulation that is more expressive than an actual pause. The beginner probably would not hear six different movements within a seven-minute piece without formal training.

The reader should focus attention on measure 37, in which the first movement ends and the second movement begins. The dual staffs of measure 37 are used solely for ease of explanation; in actuality only the bottom staff is used. At this point the student is encouraged to listen to the recording several times to locate this measure. It would be very difficult to comprehend the following explanation unless one listens to the recording many times.

Each measure of the first movement has one long beat and three subbeats within it. In the second movement, each measure has three beats only, each of which is of shorter durational value than the one beat of a first-movement measure but of longer durational value than one of the first-movement subbeats. Because measure 37 acts as a rhythmic pivot between movements it has the characteristics of both the first and second movements at the same time. Therefore the durational value of the three subbeats of the first movement is equal to the durational value of two beats of the second movement within this measure. However, in the second movement a third beat is added, thereby lengthening the durational value of the measure. In other words, the dotted quarter note of the first movement has the same durational value as the quarter note of the second movement, although it is notated differently. At this pivotal point the same durational value that has been divided by three —in terms of the first movement—is divided by

6. The performance is by Mme. Keum-yŏn Sŭng, who is a virtuoso in her own right but who usually prefers to play in the manner of Sanggŭn Pak. *P'ansori, Korea's Epic Vocal Art and Instrument Music* (Nonesuch-72015) includes other excerpts from Korean traditional pieces played by leading performers in their fields.

two—in terms of the second movement—to create a new unit of pulsation. But measure 37 alone does not provide a firm establishment of the new second movement rhythmic unit, which must be reconfirmed, and this is done in measure 38. This pivotal measure 37 is thus a good example of how one movement moves into another without a pause. The reader should know, however, that movements can sometimes change without having specific pivotal measures, but with other signallike phrases which serve as cues to the next rhythmic pattern.

I want to mention two crucial points for appreciating the *seemingly* monotonous kayagŭm sanjo. The first is that a particular pitch or tone can be produced by different techniques. For instance, g in measures 3 and 4, produced by plucking, is different from g in measure 5, which is produced by nonghyŏn. An important function of this is to give the music tension and

EXAMPLE 3-7.

release, which creates a sense of vitality—the most obvious observable mechanism is the press-and-release string handling process. According to the context of the music, the degree of nong-hyŏn differs, or it may be omitted altogether, adjusting to the overall balance of the piece at both molar and molecular levels.

The second crucial point concerns the claim that the kayagŭm sanjo is monotonous, having little variety or activity within it. Could not this same claim be made about Bach's music by the uncultured Westerner? It is as incorrect to think this way in the case of the kayagŭm sanjo. Many subtle musical nuances are continually in operation, and the listener can perceive them if he is familiar with the tchoeŏtta-p'urŏtta principle. In addition, to develop his appreciation further the listener must gain a sensitivity to and appreciation of the tone quality of the kayagŭm itself and to that produced by the nonghyŏn technique. However, to overcome the claim of monotony within the kayagŭm sanjo it is necessary to comprehend thoroughly the relationships among the structural components of the piece. Example 3-7 illustrates the following features that make up the organization of this first movement: (1) the predominance of the fourth interval in the kyemyŏnjo section versus the second and third intervals in the p'yŏngjo section as a basis for melodic motion; (2) the greater use of the nonghyŏn technique in p'yŏngjo than in kyemyŏnjo; (3) a wider second interval in p'yŏngjo—for instance, c to d in measure 8 is wider than d to c in measures 27–28; and, finally, (4) the presence of five versus three structural tones in p'yŏngjo and kyemyŏnjo, respectively (Kim 1969:16).[7] These characteristic features indicate that there is a temporary pause at the end of measure 12, and a complete closure at measure 37.

In this essay I have discussed Korean music, focusing on rhythm, melody, texture, and form. Rhythm is the fundamental driving and shaping force, either metric or nonmetric, and the term *melody* signifies a series of tones, which may be repeated or move up and down in equal tempered or nonequal-tempered intervals. Form is "the sum of those qualities in a piece of music that bind together its parts and animate the whole" (Berry 1966:Preface), and harmony in its literal sense denotes a pleasing simultaneous combination of sounds. It is important to note that criteria for determining "a pleasing combination of sounds" differ with each music culture as well as within any given culture at different periods in history. My exposition of the elements of Korean music bears this out.

Glossary

aak (雅樂)-*a* = grace or elegance; *ak* = music. Confucian ritual music, music for the ruling class; used interchangeably with chŏngak.

aniri (白)-Verbal description of dramatic content between songs in a p'ansori performance.

chajinmori (자진모리)-1) A specific 12-beat rhythmic unit with a fast tempo used for p'ansori or sanjo pieces; 2) A piece based on this rhythmic pattern.

changdan (長短)-*chang* = long; *dan* = short. A term denoting a specific rhythmic pattern repeated throughout a piece.

changgo (杖皷)-Hourglass-shaped drum.

chinyangjo (진양조)-1) A specific slow, 24-beat rhythmic unit used for a p'ansori or sanjo piece; 2) a piece such as the first movement of a sanjo based on this rhythmic pattern.

cho (調)-Mode.

chŏngak (正樂)-*chŏng* = right; in its broader sense the elegant style that was "right" for the ruling class.

chul (줄)-A string.

chung or *chungnyŏ* (仲 or 仲呂)-A Korean pitch name normally corresponding to A♭.

chunggŭm (中琴)-A medium-size flute of the samjuk category. See *samjuk*.

chungmori (중모리)-1) A specific 12-beat rhythmic unit with a moderate tempo slightly faster than chinyangjo used for p'ansori or sanjo pieces; 2) A piece based on this rhythmic pattern.

haegŭm (奚琴)-A two-stringed, bowed instrument.

hwandu (환두)-Literally "changed head," the first and varied part of a repetition. See "Forms" in essay.

hwang or *hwangjong* (황 황종)-A Korean pitch name normally corresponding to E♭.

---

7. The structural tones of p'yŏngjo in example 3-7 are c, d, f, g, and a; those of kyemyŏnjo are G, c, and d, which are used in the nonghyŏn technique. The flexible nonghyŏn tone d thus carries extra tones, such as f and e♭.

hwanip (환입)-Follows hwandu. See "Forms."

hyangak (鄕樂)-Native Korean music.

jo (調)-See *cho*.

jung or *jungnyŏ* (仲呂)-See *chung*.

kagok (歌曲)-A traditional Korean vocal form.

kayagŭm (伽倻琴)-A twelve-stringed zither.

kkwaenggwari (쟁과리)-A small gong used in nong' ak. See *nong'ak*.

kŏmungo (거문고)-Six-stringed zither.

kyemyŏnjo (界面調)-One of the primary Korean modes.

mudang (巫堂)-An inspired female priest in shamanistic ritual.

munmyo (文廟)-Shrine where Confucius and his disciples are honored.

nong'ak (農樂)-Music for the farmer, one of the oldest forms in Korea.

nonghyŏn (弄絃)-A press-and-release technique for playing zithers, through which the uniquely Korean wavering quality is produced in varying degrees.

pallim (科)-Physical motion to describe dramatic action in a p'ansori performance.

p'ansori (판소리)-An indigenous Korean operalike production.

p'iri (피리)-A double-reed aerophone.

pŏmp'ae (梵唄)-A chant in praise of Buddha.

pungnyu (風流)-Ensemble music. See Introduction in essay.

p'yŏngjo (平調)-One of the primary Korean modes.

p'yŏng-sijo (平時調)-One of the sijo types.

samjuk (三竹)-*sam* = three; *juk* = bamboo. A three-item category of bamboo flutes.

sanjo (散調)-An instrumental solo piece originally in improvisational style, but more recently conforming to relatively fixed styles of individual sanjo schools.

sijo (時調)-One of the indigenous Korean vocal genres.

sipyich'ae (십이채)-Twelve different rhythmic patterns used in nong'ak.

sogŭm (小琴)-A small flute of the samjuk category.

sokak (俗樂)-*sok* = mundane, earthly. Music for the common man.

taegŭm (大琴)-A large bamboo flute.

t'aep'yŏngso (태평소)-One type of p'iri.

t'angak (唐樂)-Secular music of both the Chinese T'ang and Sung dynasties, which was altered to become court music after its introduction to Korea.

tanso (단소)-An end-blown flute.

tchoeŏtta-p'urŏtta (풀었다)-*tchoeŏtta* = to tense;

p'urŏtta = to relax. A tension and release process in various dimensions, usually associated with sanjo, contributing to the total musical coherence of a piece.

toljang (돌장)-A short bridge between the ujo and p'yŏngjo sections in chinyangjo.

ujo (羽調)-One of the primary Korean modes.

ŭmak (音樂)-Music.

yanggŭm (양금)-A Korean dulcimer.

yosŏng (요성)-Wavering sound.

aak	아악
aniri	아니리
chajinmori	자진모리
changdan	장단
changgo	장고
chinyangjo	진양조
cho	조
chŏngak	정악
chul	줄
chung or *chungnyŏ*	중 중려
chunggŭm	중금
chungmori	중모리
haegŭm	해금
hwandu	환두
hwang or *hwangjong*	황 황종
hwanip	환입
hyangak	향악
jo	조
jung or *jungnyŏ*	중 중려
kagok	가곡
kayagŭm	가야금
kkwaenggwari	쟁과리
kŏmungo	거문고
kyemyŏnjo	계면조
mudang	무당
munmyo	문묘
nong'ak	농악
nongnyŏn	농현
pallim	발림
p'ansori	판소리
p'iri	피리
pŏmp'ae	범패
pungnyu	풍류
p'yŏngjo	평조

p'yŏng-sijo	평시조
samjuk	삼국
sanjo	산조
sijo	시조
sipyich'ae	십이채
sogŭm	소금
sokak	속악
taegŭm	대금
t'aep'yŏngso	태평소
t'angak	당악
tanso	단소
tchoeŏtta-p'urŏtta	쬐었다 풀었다
toljang	돌장
ujo	우조
ŭmak	음악
yanggŭm	양금
yosŏng	요성

Bibliography

Berry, Wallace.
   1966. *Form in Music*. Englewood Cliffs, N.J.: Prentice-Hall.
Chang, Sa-hun.
   1966. *Kukak Non'go* 國樂論攷 ("Studies of Korean Music"). Seoul: Seoul National University Press.
   1969. *Han'guk Akki Taegwan* 韓國樂器大觀 ("Korean Musical Instruments"). Seoul: Korean Musicological Society.
   1972. *Glossary of Korean Music*. 2d ed. Seoul: Korean Musicological Society.
Hahn, Man-young.
   1973. "Theory." In *Survey of Korean Arts: Traditional Music*, pp. 91-106. Seoul: Information Service Center, National Academy of Arts.
Kim, Chong-ja.
   1969. "On U-mode and Kemyon-mode Used in Sanjo (Solo Music) for Kayako." In *Essays in Ethnomusicology: A Birthday Offering for Lee Hye-ku*, edited by the Korean Musicological Society, pp. 1-33. Seoul: Seoul National University Press.
Kim, Ki-su.
   1972. *Kukak Yipmun* 國樂入門 ("Introduction to Korean Music"). Seoul: Han'guk Kojŏn Ŭmak Ch'ulpansa.

Korean Musicological Society.
   1969. *Yi Hye-gu Paksa Songsu Kinyŏm Ŭmakhak Nonch'ong* 李惠求博士頌壽紀念音樂學論叢 ("Essays in Ethnomusicology: A Birthday Offering for Lee Hye-ku"). Seoul: Seoul National University Press.
Lee, Chae-suk.
   1969. "Diverse Styles of Kayako Sanjo (Solo Music for Kayako)." In *Essays in Ethnomusicology: A Birthday Offering for Lee Hye-ku*, edited by the Korean Musicological Society, pp. 135-168. Seoul: Seoul National University Press.
Lee, Hye-ku.
   1957. *Han'guk Ŭmak Yŏn'gu* 韓國音樂研究 ("Studies in Korean Music"). Seoul: National Music Research Society of Korea.
   1967. *Han'guk Ŭmak Sosol* 韓國音樂序說 ("Topics in Korean Music"). Seoul: Seoul National University Press.
   1970. *A History of Korean Music*. Seoul: Ministry of Culture and Information.
Lee, Kang-sook.
   1975. "The Development and Trial of Korean-based Musical Activities for the Classroom." Ph.D. dissertation, University of Michigan (University Microfilms, Ann Arbor, Michigan).
   1975. "Providing Korean Rhythmic Experiences in the Classroom." *Korea Journal* (December), 25-30. Seoul, Korean National Commission for UNESCO.
   Forthcoming. "Korean Music Culture: Genuine and Quasi-Korean Music." In *A Birthday Offering for Professor Chang Sa-hun*.
Malm, William.
   1972. "Teaching Rhythmic Concepts in Ethnic Music." *Music Educators Journal*, 59, 4 (October), 95-99.
Meyer, Leonard.
   1956. *Emotion and Meaning in Music*. Chicago: The University of Chicago Press.
Rockwell, Coralie.
   1972. *Kagok: a traditional Korean vocal form*. Providence, R.I.: Asian Music Publications.
Salzer, Felix.
   1952. *Structural Hearing: Tonal Coherence in Music*. New York: Dover.
Song, Bang-song.
   1971. *An Annotated Bibliography of Korean Music*. Asian Music Publications, series A, no. 2. Providence, R.I.: Brown University.
Standifer, James.
   1976. *A Study of Folk Songs and Related Music*

Activities in the Kyeongsang-Do Province. Rackham Research Project. Ann Arbor: The University of Michigan.

Survey of Korean Arts: Traditional Music. 1973. Seoul: Information Service Center, National Academy of Arts.

Chang, Sa-Hun	장사훈
Hahn, Man-Young	한만영
Han'guk Akki Taegwan	한국악기대관
Han'guk Ŭmak Sŏsŏl	한국음악서설
Han'guk Ŭmak Yŏn'gu	한국음악연구
Kim, Chong-Ja	김정자
Kim, Ki-Su	김기수
Kukak Non'go	국악논고
Kukak Yipmun	국악입문
Lee, Chae-Suk	이재숙
Lee, Hye-Ku (Yi, Hye-Gu)	이혜구
Lee, Kang-Sook	이강숙
Song, Bang-Song	송방송

Yi Hye-gu Paksa Songsu Kinyŏm Ŭmakhak Non-ch'ong 이혜구박사 송수기념음악학 논총

Discography

Han'guk Kukak Chŏngsŏn 韓國國樂精選 : *The Selection of Korean Classical Music.* Kŭm Sŏng Publishing Co., Seoul.

A collection of Korean traditional music performed by members of the National Classical Music Institute. Selections include examples of aak, sanjo, hyangak, kagok, sijo, kasa, p'ansori, and folk songs. There are other recordings with the same title which can only be distinguished by the publishing and recording company.

Han'guk Ŭmak Sŏnjip 韓國音樂選集 : *The Selection of Korean Classical Music.* Sets I & II. National Classical Music Institute, Seoul.

A collection of Korean traditional music performed by members of the National Classical Music Institute, made up of three volumes for each set. Selections include examples of aak, sanjo, hyangak, kagok, sijo, kasa, p'ansori, and folk songs. Hye-ku Lee gives a brief introduction to Korean music in English and comments on the selections in both Korean and English.

Kukak Taejŏnjip 國樂大全集 : *Anthology of Korean Traditional Music.* Three Volumes. Sinsegi Recording Co., Seoul.

One of the most comprehensive recordings of Korean traditional music. There are 3 volumes containing 30 discs, including aak and sokak. Most of the pieces are performed in their original manner, with a few exceptions that use Western-style accompaniment for Korean folk songs. These recordings are accompanied by the book, *Anthology of Korean Traditional Music* by Hye-ku Lee, Kyŏng-nin Sŏng, and Ch'ang-bae Lee.

Folk and Classical Music of Korea: Folkways FE 4424.

Korean Court Music: Lyrichord LL-7206.

Korean Social and Folk Music: Lyrichord LL-7211.

Korea: Vocal and Instrumental Music: Folkways FE 4325.

P'ansori, Korea's Epic Vocal Art and Instrument Music. Nonesuch-72015.

Han'guk Kukak Chŏngsŏn	한국 국악 정선
Han'guk Ŭmak Sŏnjip	한국 음악 선집
Kukak Taejŏnjip	국악 대전집

Films

Korean Court Music. UWP. 16mm, color, 15 min.

Musical examples of the ruling class performed by members of the National Classical Music Institute. Traditional musicians' customs and the physical appearance of various aak instruments are portrayed.

Korean Vocal Music. UWP. 16mm, color, 14 min.

As a main feature, an excerpt from "Hŭngbu-ga," one of the famous p'ansori, is performed by Miss Kim So-hi. The handkerchief and fan held by her are a familiar feature of the genre. No examples from the other vocal genres such as kagok and sijo.

Korean Folk Dances. UWP. 16mm, color, 25 min.

Primarily excerpts from nongak, farmers' music and dance. Rhythmic intricacy in the nongak music was delineated by the body movements with typical nongak instruments such as kkwaenggwari and changgo.

Sanjo: Korean Improvisational Music. UWP. 16mm, b&w, 31 min.

Excerpts of kayagŭm sanjo as the main feature. Two of the most important techniques in kayagŭm sanjo playing, the plucking and springing and nonghyŏn, are demonstrated both visually and aurally by the leading native performers.

Other films on Korean music issued by the University of Washington Press include the following:

Five Korean Court Dances. 16mm, color, 33 min.

Buddhist Dances of Korea. 16mm, color, 18 min.

Yangju Sandae Nori: Masked Drama of Korea. 16mm, color, 33 min.

Pong San T'al Ch'um: Northern Korean Masked Drama. 16mm, color, 32 min.

Salp'uri: Korean Improvisation Dance. 16mm, b&w, 15 min.

Three Dances from Chŏlla-do, Korea. 16mm, color, 23 min.

4. Some of Japan's Musics and Musical Principles

William P. Malm

Archaeological materials and Chinese sources reveal the presence of music in Japan at least as far back as the third century B.C., but surviving music traditions have their origins in the Nara Period (A.D. 552-794). Japanese written records do not appear until the eighth century, however, so one could say that the chronicled lengths of Western and Japanese music history are about the same.

To carry this rough analogy further, note that both cultures derived much of their early music nomenclature, theory, and practice from a dominant religion: Christianity in the West and, since the sixth century, Buddhism in Japan. Both also incorporated other music sources from foreign, "overseas" cultures. The mysteries of the ancient "hypothetical" Greek music theory and, later, through the crusades, the living Islamic traditions influenced the West. In comparison, Japan was able to turn to the dazzling world of the Chinese T'ang dynasty (618-907) and the equally viable Korean kingdoms for inspiration and importation. This comparison must end with the important note that both the Western and the Japanese musical traditions, over the past twelve hundred years, have gone through many different periods and created many different styles and genres. Thus generalities are not easily applied to all musics in either of these cultures. For example, what is true about sixteenth-century Renaissance music in Italy is not necessarily correct for nineteenth-century Italian opera, much less for Wagnerian works in the same period. By the same token, the imperial court music of eleventh-century Kyōto differs greatly from that of nineteenth-century theater music in Edo (now Tokyo). With such comparisons and a warning in mind, let us now look in a general chronological order at some of the better-known Japanese musics and glean from them a few aphorisms that can sometimes be applied to other Japanese forms.

ANCIENT JAPANESE COURT MUSIC

The first importation of court orchestra music (*gagaku*) is traditionally dated in 453, when eighty musicians were sent from the Korean Silla (in Japanese, "Shiragi") kingdom to participate in an imperial funeral. Another Korean, Mimashi, is said to have brought other entertainments in 612, some of which survive in the dance of the imperial court. Traditions from other parts of Asia also entered into the culturally hungry courts of Japan in the Nara and Heian (794-1185) periods. Today music in such ancient traditions is still played. It is called *kangen* when it is purely instrumental and *bugaku* when it accompanies dance. The repertoire and performance ensembles can be divided into two basic types: *tōgaku* (fig. 4-1), which contains Chinese and Indian musics, and *komagaku*, in which are both Korean and Manchurian materials. Of course, Japanese original pieces are found in both repertoires. Melodically, both types use the double-reed *hichiriki* aerophones and flutes (the *ryūteki* in tōgaku and the *komabue* in komagaku). A third aerophone, used in tōgaku, is the *shō*, a mouth organ consisting of thirteen bamboo pipes set in a wind-chest. The pipes of the shō have free metal reeds which sound when a finger hole on a pipe is closed. Today the shō primarily plays harmonic clusters, though its original function may have been quite different since similar mouth organs in

FIGURE 4-1. A bugaku dancer enters to the accompaniment of togaku wind and percussion. Instruments from left to right: two shōs, kakko, hichiriki, gakudaiko, shoko.

East and Southeast Asia are generally used melodically with a harmonic fourth or fifth sounded only occasionally. Such a distinct difference in performance practice may be the result of gradual misinterpretations of ancient shō part books which were, like most Japanese notations, in the form of memory aids rather than detailed markings. Whatever the cause, the resulting series of nontriadic harmonic backdrops for gagaku pieces have become a special feature of such music today. [For descriptions, photographs, and drawings of Japanese musical instruments, see Malm 1959—ed.]

The gagaku string section consists of a four-stringed, pear-shaped *biwa* lute and a thirteen-stringed board zither with movable bridges called the *gakusō* or koto. They are not used when a piece accompanies dance (bugaku, fig. 4-1). Both are capable of playing melodies and are noted as doing so in early novels such as the eleventh-century *Tale of Genji* by Murasaki.[1] However, surviving part books only show the names of stereotyped patterns which today are played primarily as time markers between phrases.

The lead drum of tōgaku is the two-headed, barrel-shaped *kakko*, whereas komagaku uses an hourglass-shaped *san no tsuzumi*. Both employ a hanging, tacked-headed barrel drum (*tsuridaiko*) and a small hanging gong (*shōko*). Several ancient secular vocal forms survive in the court tradition, as well as special Shinto re-

1. For quotations from such sources see Harich-Schneider 1973:242–51.

EXAMPLE 4-1.

ligious compositions which are called collectively *kagura*. When either is sung, the accompaniment often includes the hichiriki and/or a flute plus a six-stringed *wagon* board zither and *shakubyōshi* wooden clappers. The clappers are used by the lead singer to signal entrances of the unison chorus and other formal divisions.

The tone system of gagaku is heavily based on ancient Chinese and Buddhist sources. As in the ancient Western tradition, these are founded on a set of twelve untempered divisions to the octave which are used for the creation of heptatonic scales. The basic *ryo* and *ritsu* scales of gagaku are shown in example 4-1. Note that they each have a pentatonic core. In theory the ryo scale can be transposed to the pitches D, G, and E (*ichikotsu, sōjō,* and *taishiki*); the ritsu scale appears on E, A, and B (*hyōjō, ōshiki,* and *banshiki*).[2] These six transpositions are called *chō* and the part books[3] are arranged with all the pieces in the same chō in sequence. The term chō is normally translated as a mode but at first glance it seems merely to imply a transposition of one of the two basic scales. However, a study of certain pieces that are performed in more than one chō (a technique called *watashimono*) shows that such a change does involve a change of pitch center within the scale itself which thus could be called a mode.[4] Before performing a composition in a chō, it is customary to play a *netori* (introduction) in which each melodic instrument enters in order to identify the pitches of the chō and evoke its "mood." The lack of clarity on this point in East Asian theory books has caused considerable confusion. Fortunately for the listener, however, the overall sound of gagaku has a special appeal which bypasses its academic problems. It also titillates the histor-

ian's mind, for gagaku, along with its counterpart in Korea (*aak*), must be the oldest continuous, documented orchestral music in the world. Gagaku is also one of the very few living clues as to what the East Asian music world must have been like some twelve hundred years ago.

MEDIEVAL NARRATIVES AND THEATRICALS

Blind bards and epic storytellers were as much a part of old Japan as they were of the ancient West. Japanese balladeers accompanied themselves on the biwa, in a traditional style of which several schools are found to this day. But the best-known narrative idiom of earlier times is the noh drama. In the same manner as ancient European theater, the noh drama grew out of a host of earlier forms connected with religious events.[5] Outdoor, raised stages (*kagura-den*) were part of most Shintō shrines and Buddhist temples and it is from the various kinds of plays and dances performed on them that the performer and writer, Kannami Kiyotsugu (1333-1384) and his son, Zeami Motokiyo (1363-1444), developed the maturer form eventually called noh, literally "an accomplishment." As performed today (fig. 4-2), the music of noh consists of the dialogue and songs of the main actors plus other music sung by a unison chorus (*ji*). The accompanying instrumental ensemble is known collectively as the *hayashi*. It consists of a flute (*nōkan*), an hourglass drum held on the left hip (*ō-tsuzumi*), a smaller one held on

2. Two names are given to E to distinguish which scale is intended.

3. Full scores did not exist in ancient times.

4. For an example see the article "Music, East Asian" in the 1974 *Encyclopaedia Britannica*.

5. A good summary of the background of noh is found in P. G. O'Neill's *Early Nō Drama* (London: Humphries, 1958).

FIGURE 4-2. The actors, chorus, and instrumental accompaniment of the noh drama. Instruments from left to right: taiko, ō-tsuzumi, ko-tsuzumi, nōkan.

the right shoulder (*ko-tsuzumi*), and a stick drum (*taiko*) set on a stand.

The theory and nomenclature of noh are based on writings like Zeami's *Kadensho*, plus some five hundred years of performance practice. Simply stated, noh theory divides the actor's part into basically recitative sections (*kotoba* or *serifu*) and actual songs (*fushi*). The melodies of the songs are categorized as primarily lyrical (*yowagin*) or strong (*tsuyogin*), these terms musically referring to the placement of basic pillar tones. In noh theory there are three basic pitches called *jō*, *chu*, and *ge* around which one may move through upper and lower tones by rules analogous to those of Western sixteenth-century counterpoint, though the sound is very different. In the lyrical style the three pitches tend to be fourths apart (for example, D, G, and C), whereas in the strong style the major reciting tones are often reduced to pitches as close as

a minor third (for example A and C). The Western listener hearing the fluid movement of noh singing from one point of emphasis to the next sometimes senses an improvisatory spirit in the music. If that occurs the listener has been misled, for one of the few aphorisms that can be applied to Japanese music is that improvisation plays almost no role in any of its genres. In noh, the various notations of the different schools of singing tell one exactly what to do, but only to a point. Like most Japanese notations they stop short for two reasons: first, notation in Japan serves as a memory aid for a sonic event and is not a necessary adjunct to performance, and second, the musical secrets of each school's tradition are stored only in the mind and voice of authorized teachers. The importance of this secret music tradition is a reflection of a general guildlike tendency in most surviving Japanese traditional musics.

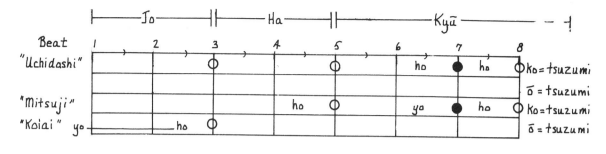

EXAMPLE 4-2.

Since I have just dared to present a few generalizations concerning Japanese music, let me go a step farther by looking at the hayashi music of noh in terms of three more aphorisms which apply to many forms of Japanese music.[6] They are: (1) a general ideal in Japan is to achieve a distinct chamber music sound rather than a coalescing orchestral one; (2) the concern is for not only what one does but also physically how one does it; and (3) a maximum effect is desired from a minimum amount of sonic material. The first ideal is evident to anyone who has heard the actual sound of the noh drama ensemble. The flute, for example, does not necessarily play in the same tonality as that of the singer and it never plays the singer's tune. The three drums, likewise, have very different tones and tend to play on different beats in different but related stereotyped patterns. This kind of chamber-music separation of parts is clearly appreciated in most Japanese music, but of course there are many Japanese who personally prefer the thick, congealed texture of some Western orchestral music. The goal of the modern listener of any nationality, however, should be towards the kind of aural flexibility which will allow him to enjoy such things as the distinctive Japanese traditional sound ideal without losing a sensitivity to other very different sonic textures.

For the second generalization, note that the hayashi ensemble is in full view on stage (fig. 4-2). Every movement, whether of playing an instrument or picking it up, is choreographed so that it will contribute to the theatrical whole of the stage movement. A clear example of the third generalization is found in the use and construction of the taiko. It normally plays only in the final dance of an act so that its sounds are fresh and not overused. A small patch of deer-skin is placed in the center of the drumhead so that its potential brightness is deliberately muffled. In the same spirit only one major sound occurs on the ō-tsuzumi and four on the ko-tsuzumi. Much more could be done on any of these drums, but the Japanese have chosen to perfect just a few meaningful sounds rather than to indulge in the excesses of all-combinatorial possibilities sometimes found elsewhere in the world. To enhance the power of these "limited" sounds the noh drum music includes calls that are at first rather puzzling to Western listeners, until one remembers that music exists in a time continuum and that a sense of anticipation and prediction is essential if a listener is to become involved in the music. This point can best be made if the reader will try out for himself an opening ko-tsuzumi pattern called *uchidashi*, shown in example 4-2.[7]

If one claps the hands on beats 3, 5, and 7, 8, where the actual sounds of the drum occur, the resultant rhythm is hardly compelling. The two vocal interjections of "ho" add a dynamic feature to the sound but their function seems more related to the fact that a characteristic of noh drum music is that it consists of a series of

6. Most of the aphorisms of this article are discussed in more detail in Malm 1971.

7. This pattern can be heard when the drums first enter in the performance of *Hagaromo* in *Japan, VI* in the UNESCO collection recording listed in the discography.

named, stereotyped patterns which must be aurally perceivable. Without the drum calls one hears four sounds from the ko-tsuzumi, but with them one hears the pattern uchidashi. A maximum effect has also been achieved from relatively little action on the drum itself. At the same time we should note that often in noh music the tempo is extremely elastic and thus the drum calls serve as means of signaling and controlling the entire ensemble rhythmically in a fluid situation where visual contact with a conductor would be impossible.

The next patterns in example 4-2 (and in the opening of the play *Hagaromo*) are *koiai* on the ō-tsuzumi and *mitsuji* on the ko-tsuzumi. The first "yo" and "ho" of the ō-tsuzumi produce a sense of anticipation in a culturally conditioned listener which would be as powerful as a tympani crescendo roll in Western music. In both cases one anticipates that something soon has to happen. One distinction is that the Japanese formula is able to create this atmosphere before the drum is actually hit! Of course not all listeners will react to this pattern in such a dramatic way, because music is *not* an international language. One cannot approach this sonic event with the same set of rules used to follow a piano sonata. In the same way one cannot apply the equally logical but very different system of noh music to the understanding of a symphonic movement. Fortunately musical styles, like languages, are so logically structured that one can learn to understand many different musical as well as linguistic idioms. In that spirit let us look further at the koiai and mitsuji patterns that link the two tsuzumi together.

The hayashi music may be used merely to accompany dance. However, in noh much of the time the two tsuzumi are involved in accompanying the vocal parts. At present we are viewing one pattern combination, which is like saying in Western music that we know one major chord such as a C-major triad. Neither case gives the whole story of the music but each can teach a few additional things as long as we recognize the limitations of the frame of reference. To enrich koiai-mitsuji note that whereas some Japanese music and sections of pieces use the two-part (arsis and thesis) division familiar in the West, there are many cases in Japan which employ a three-part division called *jo*, the "introduction," *ha*, the "scattering," and *kyū*, the "rushing toward the end." As in Western divisional terms, jo ha kyū may be applied to an entire piece or its subsections, but I have placed it at this moment over one combination as shown in example 4-2. A vocal line accompanied by this pattern quite commonly divides its syllables in a similar tripartite manner. Thus we can see that beat 3 is clearly marked by the drum pattern as the end of the jo section, beat 5 as the end of the ha, and kyū is set with the most rhythmic activity. Other drum patterns will not be as cooperative nor will vocal parts behave "correctly." Therefore this brief insight into one microscopic moment of musical logic in Japanese music must be viewed with the same attitude that should be taken when looking at Beethoven's handling of a sonata-allegro form. Both cases are guides to musical logic, but both are open to highly varied applications.

The form of noh dramas in general is often described in terms of the jo ha kyū division, but each of these sections may contain smaller units called *dan*. In their turn, the dan will have a variety of subsections characteristic of the particular situation or formal spot in a play. Details on such sophistications can be read in other studies.[8] What is more vital in the context of this much broader assessment is an understanding of the fact that an "ancient" Japanese drama form is no more simple, improvised, or arbitrary than a Bartók string quartet, although the means by which each of these establishes its musical logic may be very different.

EDO PERIOD INSTRUMENTAL AND THEATRICAL MUSIC

The best-known Japanese instrumental music is that of the thirteen-stringed koto zither shown in figure 4-3. We have seen already that

8. See Malm 1959:112 or Yokomichi 1973. These readings remind us of the important fact that noh is a complete theatrical event and can become equally powerful as a dramatic experience. This fact should be applied as well to other Japanese theatricals such as kabuki and bunraku discussed later.

FIGURE 4-3. In this dance recital accompaniment a singer is joined by a sankyoku ensemble of koto, shamisen, and shakuhachi.

such an instrument was found in the gagaku ensemble. Solo and chamber music for the koto existed in ancient times as well, but the most played literature comes from the Edo period (1615-1868). One distinctive feature of such music is the use of the *in* scale with transpositions and modes as well as the *yō* scale with its pen-

tatonic core, as shown in example 4-3.

The basic surviving schools of the so-called vulgar (*zokugaku*) or noncourtly music are the Ikuta, founded by Ikuta Kengyō in 1695, and that of Yamada Kengyō (1757-1817). There are important differences in the instruments and playing methods but the general style of their

EXAMPLE 4-3.

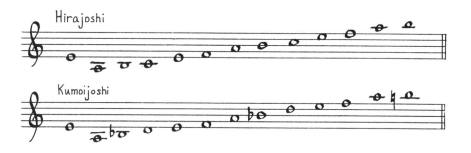

EXAMPLE 4-4.

EXAMPLE 4-5.

repertoires is the same. Example 4-4 shows two of their several standard, common tunings. Many pieces alternate vocal sections with instrumental interludes in what can be called a *jiuta* or *kumiuta* style, whereas other pieces are purely instrumental (*shirabemono*). The most common instrumental ensemble is the *sankyoku* (fig. 4-3), which consists of koto, a three-stringed plucked shamisen lute, and an end-blown *shakuhachi* flute or, less frequently today, a bowed *kokyū* (spiked fiddle). Solo koto music often consists of a series of sections (dan), each usually one hundred and four beats long. The degree to which the internal structures of the dan are similar is quite striking,[9] but this is another example of obtaining maximum effect from minimum material. As in many schools of East Asian painting, the artistic goal in koto music is not hampered by a continual search for "originality." Thus in hearing such music one listens for the skill and beauty with which traditional materials are manipulated rather than for new ideas.

The solo music for the shakuhachi is perhaps an even more powerful example of artistic restraint. Like a Japanese garden, this end-blown flute looks deceptively simple and natural but its entire construction is carefully controlled by the skill of its maker. Its music defies all standard notation systems with the use of continual nuances in pitch and color although, as in other Japanese traditions, each school of shakuhachi has its particular system of written memory aids.[10]

The basic source of Edo-period theater music is the shamisen, known in the Osaka-Kyoto area

9. For details see Adriaansz 1973.
10. A description of one such system is found in Elliott Weisgarber's "The Honkyoku of the Kinko-Ryu."

as the samisen. Imported into Japan in the mid-sixteenth century from the Ryukyu Islands, its ancestry goes back to the Chinese *san hsien*. The construction of the Japanese instrument changed drastically under the influence of biwa lutenists who adopted it: the former Chinese oval shape was changed to a rectangular one, the snakeskin was replaced by cat or dog, and a wooden or ivory plectrum was used instead of a bone finger pick. In addition, the upper bridge was so constructed that only the upper two strings passed over it, thus creating a buzzing sound (*sawari*) on the lower string. This effect was probably an attempt to reproduce some of the sound of the older biwa. The new instrument was soon taken up by various types of narrative singers as well as performers of popular and brothel music. Today one tends to divide the many genres of shamisen music into two basic types, the lyrical (*utamono*) and the narrative (*katarimono*), which range from short popular ditties to impressive musical monuments composed by known composers. I will try to show some of the spirit and structure of these two types as they appear in Edo-period theatricals.

The best-known shamisen narrative genre is *gidayū*, created by Takemoto Gidayū (1651-1714) when he was narrating those plays of Chikamatsu Monzaemon (1653-1724) that were written for the flourishing puppet theater of Osaka known today as *bunraku*. Each genre of shamisen music has a different-sized instrument, plectrum, string gauge, and bridge, and gidayū is the largest in each case. The basic tunings of the three strings shown in example 4-5 are the same for most other genres. The actual fundamental pitch of a tuning is accommodated to the needs of a given singer.

FIGURE 4-4. The tayu narrator and shamisen accompanist.

In the puppet theater the singer and shamisen player sit on a dais to the side of the stage, as seen in figure 4-4. One narrator speaks all roles and sings all commentaries, thus making gidayū one of the most challenging musical drama idioms in the world. There are four basic elements in gidayū style: (1) instrumental interludes (*ai*), (2) spoken text (*kotoba*), (3) sung passages (ji, *jiai*, or *fushi*), and (4) parlando, or half-spoken sections (*iro, ji iro,* or *kakari*). In a given play these four styles continually interchange in a very fluid and effective manner. The overall approach is melodramatic and it often seems as if the narrator (*tayū*) by the intensity of his performance is instilling life into the puppets, whose own emotions are otherwise evident only from their skillful manipulation by three men.

Turning to basically lyrical forms of shami-sen music, the most obvious examples are the short songs (*kouta* and *hauta*) whose romantic or descriptive texts have their place in traditional entertainment settings. I have already mentioned the use of shamisen in the ensembles that play kumiuta or jiuta, but the major source of lyrical shamisen music is found, along with several narrative genres, in the kabuki theater. Kabuki, like the bunraku mentioned earlier, arose in the Edo period in response to the needs of a new urban audience. Melodramatic acting and a variety of musics and dancing have made it comparable to opera in the West in terms of its continued popularity. Its music can be divided into two basic types: that appearing onstage (*debayashi*) and that performed from a small room offstage right (*geza*). I will concentrate on one form of onstage music, *nagauta* ("long song"), the major lyrical form in kabuki and on

FIGURE 4-5. A complete nagauta ensemble on a concert stage.

the concert stage. The nagauta ensemble normally consists of the three drums and flute of the noh (the hayashi) plus a group of shamisen and of singers (fig. 4-5). The flautist may also use a bamboo flute (*takebue* or *shinobue*) derived from the festival and folk traditions. Since the repertoire of kabuki is as large and varied as that of a Western opera house, it is obviously impossible to describe fully the forms or performance practice of its music. Therefore, let us consider a typical kabuki dance accompaniment by a typical nagauta composition in the same spirit and context with which one might introduce a reader to the entire concept of symphonic form over the past two hundred years with one explanation of sonata-allegro form.

Using the tripartite division mentioned earlier, the basic sections of a so-called kabuki dance-form nagauta composition could be divided as follows:

Jo: oki michiyuki

Ha: kudoki odori-ji

Kyū: chirashi dangire

The introduction (*oki*) varies according to the needs of the piece. If the piece is derived from

an earlier noh it may contain noh-style music in the hayashi section and the singer may enter with a slight imitation of noh singing. Another composition dealing with a specific location or season may open with a shamisen interlude (*ai-kata*) in the mood of that setting. The first vocal section might be in a recitative style called *ōsatsuma*, in which a vocal line in free time is accompanied by standard shamisen patterns, or the opening vocal line may be more lyrical and metronomic. In most lyrical parts of shamisen compositions, as shown in example 4-6, one is struck by the general tendency for the vocal part to be "out of time" with the shamisen accompaniment. This might be called an example of heterophony, for both parts seem to be performing the same melody with simultaneous variations. The reason behind this style in Japanese vocal music accompanied by the shamisen seems to be that since both parts tend to perform the same melodic line, it is necessary for the singer to delay or anticipate the sound of a given tone on the shamisen in order that the text can be clearly heard.

The *michiyuki* (literally "going along the road") was originally intended for the first entrance of a dancer and is often begun by a fully

EXAMPLE 4-6.[11]

orchestrated instrumental section. The drums may use noh patterns, and the noh flute, if it is used, will perform in a noh style that is unrelated to the shamisen part both tonally and melodically. Another common style for the drums is a kabuki innovation called *chirikara byōshi* after the mnemonics by which it is learned. As seen in example 4-7, this drumming is in direct support of the shamisen line. However, when noh drumming is mixed with a shamisen melody one often gets the impression that the two units are rhythmically out of synchronization.[12] This might be called a "slide rule" effect, for each unit is internally correct but they are not set in terms of the same first beat. Such a device is used deliberately in several different kinds of music in Japan (and some other nonharmony-oriented cultures) to create a sonic tension that drives the music forward in its time continuum toward a cadence point where rhythmic agreement is reached. An analogy with the use of chords in Western classical music is appropriate, for both

methods create aurally perceivable events that color the melody and drive the music forward in progressions that cause musical tension and imply relief at some future cadence point.

Kudoki sections are the most lyrical—the percussion instruments are often not present in order that the orchestration will not interfere with the singer's soaring flights. As seen in example 4-6, there seems to be an inverse relation between the amount of activity in the shamisen part and the tonal tension of the melodic line. The basic principle shown here deals with the relatively inert feelings of the pitch center and fifth of a given tonal system and the tension of passages that stop on the upper or lower leading tones of these two "pillar" tones. Through exploiting these tensions and releases the slower section of shamisen pieces keeps the music "alive." The *odoriji* section can often be marked by a change in orchestration with, for example, perhaps the taiko and the bamboo flute entering and a change in tuning of the shamisen. The *chirashi* section normally involves the full ensemble and a quickening pace; the *dangire* is a traditional finale passage which, like much European baroque and classical music, changes lit-

11. This passage can be heard toward the end of the first lyrical section of "Echigojishi," side 1, band 1 of the UNESCO record *Japan, III* listed in the discography.

12. A detailed explanation of this is found in Malm 1963.

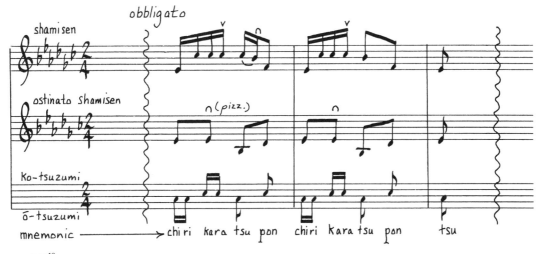

EXAMPLE 4-7.[13]

tle from composition to composition.

Experiments with Western listeners have shown that one can learn quickly to recognize various formal sections of a piece written in a form such as that outlined above. Between sections and within each one there are transitional materials and insertions, but an informed listener can feel as much at home with such music as with sonata-allegro form, even though nagauta is a through-composed tradition and does not lean on repeated first and second themes to hold it together. Both the Western and the Japanese examples are, after all, special kinds of musical languages which one learns, like a foreign tongue, through training and attentive listening. Both musics are equally logical, but different, and both include better and lesser compositions. Perhaps it should be noted as well that both derive their basic literature from composers of the eighteenth and nineteenth centuries. Although some of the Kineya Rokusaemons (for example VI, X, or XIV), who composed many famous nagauta pieces, are not found in Western music history books

13. This passage is eleven beats after the singer's solo text "temochi busatan ni hyoshi soroete wazakure" halfway through "Ninin Wankyu" on the *Azuma Kabuki Musicians* record (side 1, band 4) of the Columbia record listed in the discography.

along with Mozart or Brahms, they are by Japanese connoisseurs equally appreciated and performed. Because of the guild system performances of a given work will vary slightly in melodic nuances and hayashi accompaniments. However, these variants are played with all the strictness and finesse of the Western "one-version" symphonic tradition.

MUSIC SINCE MEIJI (1868)

The cult of the composer was minimal in Japan until Western musical ideas began to have their effect after the Meiji Restoration of 1868, when the so-called modernization of Japan began. In the 1880s a public school and a teacher training program were set up in such a way that Japanese classical music was unable to play any role in education for some eighty years. Of course it continued in its own *hōgaku* (Japanese music) world. At the same time a *seiyogaku* (Western music) world was built in Japan by eager and talented Japanese who acquired skills in the music centers of Europe and America. Symphony orchestras, operas, and ballets soon made louder sounds in Japan than traditional musics, while the radio systems, founded by German technicians, made Beethoven and Schubert part of every Japanese listener's morning life. Some sensitive traditionalists attempted to make compromises with the West by forming "new" traditional music ensembles and by toying with the Western propensity for bigger groups, louder and fancier sounds, and theme-based forms. At the same time a Western-trained Japanese would on occasion write an orchestral work or opera *à la japonaise*. Michio Miyagi (1894-1956) is the best-known talented composer on the hōgaku side; Kosaku (later Koschak) Yamada (1886-1965) was the most energetic of the early Western-trained musicians. Today one can hear many layers of music in Japan, each maintaining a viable sociological and economic base. In Tokyo one can attend kabuki and a concert of rare biwa narrative genres, or European Renaissance choirs and ensembles of lutes and recorders. A marching band, singing demonstrators, or a Buddhist evangelical parade seem equally at home on Tokyo streets. Thus all the many layers of music in Japan seem to flow synchronically, with apparently little leakage of style or life view between them.

On the surface it would seem that because the world of music consists of equally logical but different systems no musical meeting of East and West has been compositionally possible in Japan. No one composer on either side of the musical battle line understood the deeper structure of the other side's music well enough to make any more than a superficial token gesture in the other musical direction. However, in recent years the distinctions of specific nationalistic idioms have broken down in the world of so-called art music. In such fields as, for example, electronic music the surface structure of tone systems and specific instruments and forms has given way to a sensitivity to textures, timings, and musical gestures in a far deeper sense. In this context one might say that Toru Takemitsu (b. 1932) succeeded in bridging the compositional gap between two very different worlds with such pieces as "Ai" ("Love"), an electronic composition based entirely on manipulations of this one syllable. This maximum effect from minimum material is treated in many of the ways mentioned in the earlier aphorisms of this essay though the idiom is technically most modern. The unashamed eclecticism of popular music in the last third of the twentieth century may prove to be another fruitful avenue for international musical tolerance. In any event, modern times are blessed or cursed with a condition that makes any music of any period from any part of the world easily available if one can combine the correct electronic devices.

My brief comments here on a few aspects of Japanese traditional music are intended to facilitate the understanding of some of the structures and the meaning of at least a few sets of Japanese sonic events. Perhaps they will even help to make Japanese music more enjoyable to new listeners—this is, in fact, one of the fundamental goals of this introduction.

Glossary

biwa-a pear-shaped lute, usually four-stringed.
bugaku-court dances and the accompanying music.
bunraku-Japanese puppet theater.
chirikara-byōshi-a mnemonic device used by kabuki drummers.
chō-a class of tone systems.
dan-a section of music.
debayashi-onstage kabuki music.
gagaku-court orchestra music.
gakusō-the gagaku koto.
geza-offstage kabuki music.
gidayū-best-known narrative shamisen genre of bunraku.
hauta-short songs accompanied by shamisen.
hayashi-accompanying ensemble of drums and flute used in kabuki and noh.
hichiriki-double-reed aerophone.
hōgaku-Japanese music.
in-a zokugaku scale.
ji-the chorus in a noh drama; also a sung passage in gidayū. Has other meanings.
jiuta-music of the Edo period alternating vocal and instrumental sections.
jo ha kyū-a three-part division in Japanese music: *jo*—introduction; *ha*—scattering; *kyū*—rushing toward the end.
kagura-Shintō music.
kakko-two-headed, barrel-shaped drum used in tōgaku.
katarimono-narrative shamisen music.
kokyū-spiked fiddle.

komabue-flute used in komagaku.

komagaku-court music influenced by Korean and Manchurian music.

ko-tsuzumi-hourglass drum held on right shoulder.

kouta-see hauta.

kumiuta-music of the Edo period alternating vocal and instrumental sections.

nagauta-"long song," the major lyrical form in kabuki.

netori-an instrumental introduction in gagaku.

nōkan-the flute in the noh ensemble.

ō-tsuzumi-hourglass drum held on the left hip.

ritsu-one of the two basic scales used in gagaku.

ryo-one of the two basic scales used in gagaku.

ryūteki-a flute used in tōgaku.

sankyoku-instrumental ensemble consisting of koto, shamisen, and shakuhachi (or, occasionally, kokyū).

san-no-tsuzumi-hourglass-shaped drum used in komagaku.

shakubyōshi-wooden clappers.

shakuhachi-an end-blown bamboo flute.

shirabemono-the principal type of koto instrumental music.

shō-seventeen-pipe (two of them silent) aerophone which operates on the principle of a mouth organ.

shōko-small, hanging gong used in gagaku.

taiko-stick drum, used in noh.

tōgaku-court music originally derived from China and India.

tsuri-daiko-hanging, barrel-shaped drum with tacked heads used in gagaku.

tsuzumi-a generic term for drum.

utaimono-noh vocal music.

utamono-lyrical music for shamisen and voice.

wagon-six-stringed zither.

yō-a zokugaku scale.

zokugaku-"vulgar" or noncourtly music.

Bibliography

General
Harich-Schneider, Eta.
  1973. *A History of Japanese Music*. London: Oxford University Press.
Kishibe, Shigeo.
  1966. *The Traditional Music of Japan*. Tokyo: Kokusai Bunka Shinkokai.
Malm, William P.
  1959. *Japanese Music and Musical Instruments*. Tokyo: Tuttle.

  1971. "Practical Approaches to Japanese Music." In *Readings in Ethnomusicology*, edited by D. McAllester, pp. 353-70. New York: Johnson Reprint.

Gagaku
Garfias, Robert.
  1968. "The Sacred Mi-kagura of the Japanese Imperial Court." In *Selected Reports* Vol. 1, No. 2, 1:150-78. Los Angeles: Institute of Ethnomusicology, University of California.
  1975. *Music of One Thousand Autumns: The Tōgaku Style of Japanese Court Music*. Berkeley, Los Angeles, London: University of California Press.
Harich-Schneider, Eta.
  1965. *Roei. The Medieval Court Songs of Japan*. Tokyo: Sophia University Press.
Murasaki, Lady.
  1976. *The Tale of Genji*. Translated by Edward G. Seidensticker. New York: Knopf. There are many other editions.
Togi, Masataro.
  1971. *Gagaku*. Tokyo: Weatherhill.

Noh
Keene, Donald.
  1966. *Nō: The Classical Theatre of Japan*. Tokyo: Kodansha.
Malm, William P.
  1958. "The Rhythmic Orientation of Two Drums in the Japanese Nō Drama." *Ethnomusicology* 4, (Sept), 89-95.
  1960. "An Introduction to Taiko Drum Music in the Japanese Nō Drama." *Ethnomusicology* 4 (May), 75-78.
  1975. "The Musical Characteristics and Practice of the Japanese Noh Drama in an East Asian Context," in *Chinese and Japanese Music-Dramas*. Michigan Papers in Chinese Studies no. 19, J. Crump and W. Malm, eds. Ann Arbor.
Nakamura, Yasuo.
  1971. *Noh: The Classical Theater*. Tokyo: Weatherhill.
O'Neill, Patrick G.
  1958. *Early No Drama*. London: Humphries.
Yokomichi, Mario.
  1973. *The Life Structure of Noh*. Translated by F. Hoff and W. Flindt. Tokyo: Nogaku Shorin.

Koto, Shakuhachi, and Shamisen
Adriaansz, William.
  1973. *The Kumiuta and Danmono Tradition of*

Japanese Koto Music. Berkeley, Los Angeles, London: University of California Press.

Ando, Tsuruo.
1970. *Bunraku*. Tokyo: Weatherhill.

Brandon, James R., William P. Malm, and Donald H. Shively.
1978. *Studies in Kabuki: Its Acting, Music, and Historical Context*. Honolulu: University Press of Hawaii.

Ernst, Earle.
1956. *The Kabuki Theatre*. New York: Grove Press.

Gunji, Masakatsu.
1970. *Buyo: The Classical Dance*. Tokyo: Weatherhill.

Malm, William P.
1963. *Nagauta: The Heart of Kabuki Music*. Tokyo: Tuttle.
1977. "Music in the Kabuki Theater," Chapter 3 of *Studies in Kabuki*, J. Brandon, W. Malm, and D. Shively. Honolulu: University of Hawaii Press.

Toita, Yasuji.
1969. *Kabuki*. Tokyo: Kodansha.

Wade, Bonnie.
1976. *Tegotomono*. Westport, Conn.: Greenwood.

Weisgarber, Elliott.
1968. "The Honkyoku of the Kinko-Ryu." *Ethnomusicology* 12 (Sept), 33–41.

Music Since Meiji (1868)

Malm, William.
1973. "Layers of Modern Music and Japan." *Asian Music* 4:3-6.
1971. "The Modern Music of Meiji Japan." In *Tradition and Modernization in Japanese Culture*, pp. 257–304 (chap. 7). Princeton, N.J.: Princeton University Press.

May, Elizabeth.
1963. *The Influence of the Meiji Period on Japanese Children's Music*. Berkeley and Los Angeles: University of California Press.

Toyotaka, Komiya, ed.
1956. *Japanese Music and Drama in the Meiji Era*. Translated by E. Seidensticker and D. Keene. Tokyo: Ōbunsha.

Discography

The Azuma Kabuki Musicians. Columbia ML 4925.
Japan. UNESCO Collection. A Musical Anthology of the Orient. Musicaphon BM 30 L 2012-2017. Edited for the International Music Council by the International Institute for Comparative Music Studies.
I. *Sankyoku*. Hans Eckhardt.
II. *Gagaku*. Hans Eckhardt.
III. *Music of the Edo Period*. Detlaf Foljanty.
IV. *Buddhist Music*. Eta Harich-Schneider.
V. *Shinto Music*. Eta Harich-Schneider.
VI. *Nō Play/Biwa and Chanting*. *Nō*—Hans Eckhardt; *Biwa*—Detlaf Foljanty.

The Noh. Caedmon TC 2019.
Traditional Folk Songs of Japan. Folkways FE 4534 A/B. Notes by Ryutaro Hattori.
The Traditional Music of Japan. Nippon Victor JL 32-34. Notes by Shigeo Kishibe.

For the uses and limitations of Lyrichord and Nonesuch recordings, see Malm, "Recent Recordings of Japanese Music," *Ethnomusicology* 11 (January 1967), 97–105.

For an excellent list of Japanese recordings, see David Waterhouse's "Hogaku Preserved," in *Recorded Sound* 33 (January 1969), 383–402; and 57-58 (January 1975), 408-26. Shigeo Kishibe is editor of a definitive thirteen-volume series of recordings and notes, *Hogaku Taikei*, released in 1971 by the Chikuma Shobo firm, Nippon Victor UP 3006-3031.

Films

Bunraku, Japanese Doll Drama. CGJ. Col. 20 min.
A presentation of the Japanese puppet theater together with its shamisen and vocal music.

Discovering the Music of Japan. BFA. Col. 22 min. Sotirios Chianis, advisor.
Demonstrates three important instruments —the koto, shamisen, and shakuhachi. Includes traditional singing and dancing and a performance by an ensemble of the three instruments. Study guide included.

Gagaku—Court Music. CGJ. Col. 21 min.
The ancient music of the Imperial Court and Shintō shrines.

Kabuki—Classic Theater of Japan. CGJ. Col. 21 min.
Includes a great variety of song, drama, and dance.

Noh Drama. CGJ. Col. 29 min.
A presentation of this highly stylized musical and dramatic form.

5. The Music of Thailand

David Morton

Most people are first attracted to the music of a culture other than their own by the *sound* of that music—the tone quality of the solo instruments or the total sound of an ensemble. When I first became interested in Thai music, as one of the principal high-art musics of Southeast Asia, however, there were only two or three recordings of the music available —yet they were enough to intrigue me. I was intrigued in a reverse way, so to speak, because the recordings contained only excerpts; as a musician and composer I wanted to know what complete compositions consisted of and what the principles of the music system were. But the recordings contained only fragments of the music, and on investigation I found that there were no books or articles that could tell me anything technical about it, so I decided I had to go to Thailand to find these things out for myself.

The day after my arrival in Bangkok, I was invited to a Buddhist ceremony at the old summer palace some miles north of the city. While we were eating our lunch, I gradually became aware of the sound of music coming from somewhere beyond the lush tropical greenery. I made my way toward it and saw spread out at one side of the Buddhist temple a group of instruments—xylophones, sets of gong-kettles, a double-reed instrument, cymbals, a gong, and a drum—being played by Thai musicians. I was hearing traditional or classic Thai music in Thailand—an event, I was soon to discover, that was more the exception than the rule.

The sound of traditional Thai ensemble music might be likened to a stream or river: the main current, the main melody, flows relentlessly onward surrounded by secondary currents that meander in and out of the main flow; here and there little eddies and swirls come suddenly to the surface to be seen momentarily, then to dis-

appear as suddenly. There are no high points and no low points to the ear not educated to this kind of music; it flows onward in a steady non-differentiated band of sound, almost hypnotically, the various threads of seemingly independent melodies of the individual instruments bound together in a long never-ending wreath —like a Greek frieze that in a constantly repeating pattern decorates the top of a wall. But this is a subjective reaction and description. What is this music really? Let us see where it came from and how it may be discussed in an objective way.

HISTORY

The Thai people have inhabited the area of present-day Thailand only since the latter part of the thirteenth century. They trace their ancient homeland to southern China, probably the province of Canton, just west of Hong Kong. Until the Sung dynasty (ca. A.D. 900-1200) the center of Chinese culture and the capital were in the north, in Peking, and this southern area was a semitropical jungle to which exiles were sent, although a number of indigenous tribes also inhabited the region. Probably during the Han dynasty (ca. 200 B.C. to A.D. 200) peoples of this southern territory began to develop an organized culture, and one integrated group—one of the indigenous tribes, or exiles and others who migrated southward from the northern Chinese civilization, or both—became known as the *Thai*, a word that means "free." By A.D. 600, about the time of the beginning of the northern T'ang dynasty, a large Thai city called Nan-chao (literally "southern people") is known to have been flourishing in what today is the province of Yunnan. During the next six hundred years the Thai and the Chinese had considerable contact, and there was undoubtedly much exchange between the two cultures. At times

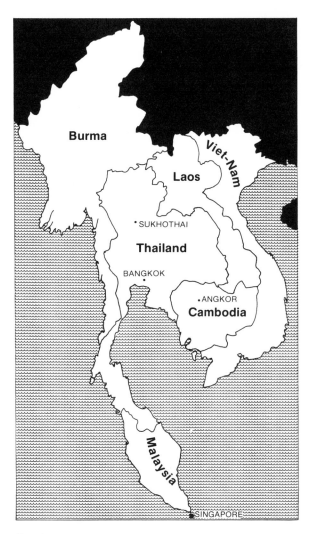

Southeast Asia

from the north, probably over a period of a generation or two—long enough for such influences to take effect. The similarities that can be seen between Thai and Chinese music today indicate that during this time, if not before, the musics of the two peoples became virtually the same.

As the southern areas became overcrowded and it became clear that the Mongols would eventually conquer all of China, as they did in the last quarter of the thirteenth century, the Thai began to migrate southward, spreading in three main directions: into Laos and north Vietnam, into northern Burma, and into what is present-day Thailand. In 1238 a group of Thai captured the city of Sukhothai from the Khmer, whose capital city was Angkor in contemporary Cambodia and who had at that time control of most of Southeast Asia. From this time on the Thai conquered more and more of the Khmer territory until about 1450, when they took Angkor and effectively put an end to the Khmer kingdom. Now the Thai controlled all the area of present-day Thailand, including the part of Cambodia in which Angkor is located. This area they were forced to cede in 1907 to France, who controlled what was then called Indochina.

The Khmer were a high civilization; the Thai at this time were concerned with conquering territory for a new homeland and were understandably not in a position to give much attention to the development of the arts. Many Khmer people and much of their culture were absorbed by the Thai, and it has been said that although the Thai conquered the Khmer, the Khmer civilized the Thai.

Very little is known of the music of the Khmer. The carvings of some instruments on the buildings of Angkor give us only a hint (fig. 5-1). Since the people and culture of Angkor were a final stage of movement inland of earlier Indian colonies along the coast, Khmer music may have contained some remnants of early Indian music. Although they cannot be traced or documented, those elements in Thai music not strictly Chinese-derived are likely to be constituted of Khmer-Indian influences that were absorbed into the music brought by the Thai from China.

the Thai were independent; during other periods they were under Chinese rule. But apparently the Chinese control was nominal, and because of royal intermarriage, treaties, and other such political arrangements, the two areas and people were frequently more or less united.

With the Mongol invasion of northern China (beginning about the tenth century), the situation changed. The ruling Sung dynasty was threatened, and royal, wealthy, highly cultivated people from the north began to flee southward. This brought the Thai even more strongly into contact with cultural elements

FIGURE 5-1. A small ensemble in a procession, using drums, gongs, woodwind instruments, and the early form of the gong-circle in a slightly curved arc.

Sukhothai was the capital of the new Thai kingdom from about 1250 to 1350 when control, through royal intermarriage, passed to Ayutthaya, a city farther to the south. Ayutthaya remained the capital for over four hundred years, during which time there was intermittent warfare between the Thai and the Burmese to the northwest. The Burmese finally destroyed Ayutthaya in 1767. Mutual cultural influences between the Thai and Burmese are probable because there is a group of Burmese songs called *Yodaya* (Ayutthaya) and because the titles of several Thai compositions have the prefix *Phamā* (the Thai word for Burma). For a brief fifteen years a general, Taksin, ruled the Thai; his capital was at Thonburi, across the river from Bangkok. In 1782 another Thai general had Taksin put to death and declared himself king, moving the capital to Bangkok. This general became known as Rama I of the Chakri dynasty; the present king is Rama IX, a direct descendant. Some of the kings and several of the princes of this dynasty have been instrumental in the development of the Thai arts, including music.

Through the Khmer, or possibly directly at a later date, influences from Javanese music have apparently also been absorbed into the music of Thailand. But a complete reconstruction of the evolution of Thai music is not really possible. Very few extant references to music in old court annals and on such objects as stone carvings exist: with the destruction of Ayutthaya, documents and artifacts that may have been related to music were lost. Since culture has changed relatively slowly in Asia in these past periods, however, the music of the Bangkok period is probably not very different from the music of the Ayutthaya period. Thai music today, then, is an amalgamation of the music with which the Thai were in contact in southern China and Burma, the music of the Khmer, which possibly contained Indian and Javanese elements, and the core of Thai music itself, which will be discussed later.

THAI MUSICAL INSTRUMENTS

Most of the instruments used in Thai music can be traced to four sources: (1) those brought by the Thai from China, (2) those adopted and adapted from Khmer models, which in turn were probably derived from Indian and Indonesian models, (3) those from other foreign sources, and (4) those the Thai themselves may have originated. The instruments from China are mostly stringed instruments and drums; from the Khmer culture and Java came mainly those of the melodic percussion type. Two instruments —a three-stringed "spike fiddle" and a goblet-shaped drum—seem to have been derived from Middle Eastern models.

The principal instruments in traditional Thai music may be conveniently discussed also under four main headings: (1) melodic percussion, (2) strings, (3) winds, and (4) rhythmic percussion.

Melodic percussion instruments are of two main types: those with bars of wood (xylophones) and of metal (metallophones), and sets of tuned horizontal gongs, often referred to as "gong chimes" or "sets of gong-kettles."

There are two xylophones: (1) *ranāt ēk*, the higher-pitched of the two, having a boat-shaped frame on a pedestal and twenty-one wooden bars of hardwood or bamboo, and with a range of three octaves; (2) *ranāt thum*, lower-pitched, having a rectangular, box-shaped frame that sits on the floor, and with a range of about two and a half octaves. The player uses two long mallets padded on the end.

There are also two sizes of gong circles, a higher-pitched, *khawng wong yai*, and a lower-pitched, *khawng wong lek*. They have an overall range of a little over two octaves and are tuned an octave apart. The tuned gong-kettles are placed horizontally in diatonic order left to right (low to high) in a circular frame stand that rests on the floor. The player sits in the center of the

stand and plays with two short mallets with hard leather discs on the end.

Two metallophones were created in the nineteenth century, adapted from the Indonesian *saron* and *gendèr*. The Thai models, which match the xylophones in pitch and range, have rectangular, box-shaped frames; the keys are rectangular and about a quarter of an inch thick. The instruments are played with two long mallets having disc heads. These two metallophones (*ranāt ēk lek* and *ranāt thum lek*) are used only in large ensembles.

Stringed instruments brought by the Thai from China are two-stringed bowed lutes between the strings of which the hair of the bow is permanently fastened. The sound box is of two types: (1) cylindrical, or approximately so, made of a section of bamboo, a piece of hollowed-out wood, or occasionally a section of ivory from an elephant tusk; (2) half a coconut shell, or occasionally some other material, such as gourd, of that general shape. The neck may be of wood or, in elegant models, of ivory. The two strings, formerly of silk or gut, are now frequently nylon and are tuned a fifth apart. The instrument with the cylindrical sound box is the higher-pitched of the two, and its lower-pitched string has the same pitch as the higher-pitched string of the instrument with the half coconut shell sound box. The two instruments are usually used together, playing a variation part in octaves. The names of this type of instrument in China usually include the word *hu*, which means "barbarian" or "foreigner" and indicates that the instrument is not indigenous to China; it is said to have come into China from the north or northwest some time in the distant past.

A three-stringed "spike fiddle" was probably derived from a Middle Eastern model, though in some ways the instrument also resembles the rebab of Java, which, however, has only two strings. The sound box of the Thai instrument is triangular in shape, formerly made from a part of a coconut shell that had three moundlike projections on it. Since this kind of deformed coconut shell was rarely found, few instruments of this type were made. The size of the instrument corresponds to the size of the coconut shell, and therefore instruments vary in size. It is used primarily solo or to accompany voice.

A three-stringed floor zither is used both as a solo instrument and in ensembles. If this instrument is not an original Thai creation, it is probably derived from a somewhat similar Burmese model, and both the Burmese and Thai instruments may be derived from zither-type instruments of southern India. Like old Thai models, the front part of old Burmese floor zithers was carved to represent the head of a crocodile, an indication that the instruments of the two cultures are related. Contemporary Thai models have been stylized and simplified, and the front part of the instrument is no longer in the shape of a crocodile head but smoothed and rounded. Further, the Thai instrument is called the *jakhē*, a shortened form of the Thai word for "crocodile." It is played with an ivory plectrum, about the size of a woman's little finger, which is tied to the index finger of the right hand of the player; the left hand fingers the strings, which are stretched over raised frets. The plectrum is moved back and forth across the strings in a fast, strumming motion.

There are a few other stringed instruments found in Thailand, but these are folk instruments of various sizes and shapes and the older instruments are now practically obsolete.

Wind instruments are of two main types: bamboo flutes and double-reed instruments. Thai bamboo flutes have a pegged mouthpiece, similar to Western recorders, and are played vertically. There are three sizes: small, medium, and large, but the medium-sized flute is the one usually played today. Large ensembles frequently will include the large model, but the small size is rarely used. The double-reed instruments are of two types. The *pī* seems to be an original Thai creation, if it was not adapted from a Khmer model. Wind instruments are represented on the stone carvings on Angkor, but the stone has weathered greatly, and it is impossible to decipher exactly what kind of wind instrument is depicted. The pī is made of wood with a conical bore, and the exterior has slight indentations between a central "bulge" and the two ends which are fluted out. The reed is actually quadruple rather than double, made of four layers of dried palm leaf fastened to a

small metal tube which in turn is inserted into the top of the instrument. The other prominent double-reed instrument (also actually a quadruple reed) has a conical-shaped wooden body. A detachable metal or wooden horn fits snugly over the lower part of the body and is tied on. This instrument is almost identical with the Chinese *sona*, although the Thai name is *pī chawā—chawā* being the Thai word for Java.

Although this discussion is concerned primarily with the traditional high-art instruments, mention should be made of the *khāēn* (fig. 5-2), probably the most important folk instrument. The khāēn is found mainly in north Thailand and in Laos, although related models of this type of instrument, such as the Chinese *shêng* and the Japanese *shō*, are found in many

FIGURE 5-2. Khāēn.

FIGURE 5-3. Large pī phāt ensemble.

places in Southeast Asia. The instrument consists of a number (usually about fourteen) of long thin bamboo tubes, often as much as four feet in length, into each of which has been put a small free-beating metal reed. These are tuned usually to a pattern of seven pitches per octave, thus giving approximately a two-octave range. Unlike the high-art system, the tuning is frequently not equidistant but often approaches Chinese tuning with large and small intervals (similar to Western whole and half steps). The bamboo pipes are put in two rows through a wooden mouthpiece, above which in each pipe a small round hole is cut. The instrument is held with the two hands cupped around the mouthpiece so that the fingers fit naturally over the holes. When a finger closes a hole, the air is forced up through the reed and a pitch is sounded; when the hole is open, the air escapes and no sound occurs. The music for the khāēn is basically monodic, though sometimes simultaneously sounded intervals, chords, or tone clusters are used. The hole of one pipe may be closed with a piece of wax, pitch, or other material to produce a drone. The sound of the khāēn is often described subjectively as mournful and plaintive.

Rhythmic percussion instruments may be divided into two categories: those of metal, and the drums with leather heads. Sets of gongs in

the National Museum in Bangkok suggest that formerly gongs of various sizes were used, but today, if a gong is used, it is only one of medium size struck with a padded mallet. Contrary to the highly developed colotomic structure of Indonesian music, the part played by the single Thai gong is very simple and the gong is not tuned to any specific pitch.

The most important metal percussion instrument in Thai ensembles is a pair of small hand cymbals called *ching*, made of rather thick metal, and probably derived from Chinese models. The metal used in these and other Thai instruments is an alloy similar to bronze. The ching are indispensable to all ensembles playing traditional high-art music; they keep the tempo, and their pattern of strokes indicates the form of the composition.

The origin of Thai drums—from China, Indonesia, or India—is easily discernible by the type and style of drum. Those from China have heads stretched tightly over the ends of the body, permanently fastened with pegs or nails. Two large barrel-shaped drums of this type are important in the large ensembles, and a small shallow frame drum of similar construction is used in ensembles with stringed instruments. The drums from India and Southeast Asia, which probably came to the Thai through the Khmer, have laced heads, and in many cases the

FIGURE 5-4. Large mahōrī ensemble.

thongs holding the heads cover the entire wooden body of the drum, which is usually barrel-shaped. Another type of drum, more like Indonesian models, has laced heads but only a few thong lacings between the heads.

A goblet-shaped drum, used in ensembles of stringed instruments along with the Chinese-derived frame drum, seems related to a similar type of drum of the Near and Middle East and probably came to the Thai through the Malayans when the latter adopted the Islamic religion. In the old days elegant models were made of Chinese ceramics or had wooden bodies inlaid with ivory, mother-of-pearl, bits of mirror, or even precious stones. The single head of these elegant instruments was of snakeskin. Contemporary models have bodies of plain wood and leather heads.

All the types of Thai instruments can be combined in three principal Thai ensembles: (1) the *pī phāt* (fig. 5-3), consisting of melodic and rhythmic percussion instruments and the pī, the instrument giving the ensemble its name; (2) the *mahōrī* (fig. 5-4), consisting of melodic and rhythmic percussion instruments, the flute, and strings; (3) the *khrฺyāng sāi* ensemble, infrequently heard today in Thailand, which consists only of stringed instruments, the flute, and rhythmic percussion (fig. 5-5). Ensembles may be of three sizes: small, including only the essential instruments; medium, including all the necessary and allowable instruments; and large, including every instrument possible, in many cases two of each.

THE FUNDAMENTALS OF THAI MUSIC

The Thai traditional music system, like the other traditional music systems of Southeast Asia, is based on a technique that Mantle Hood has termed "polyphonic stratification." In this style of music one main melody is played simultaneously with a number of versions and variants of itself. The word *polyphonic* is used here in its basic meaning of "many lines of music heard simultaneously"; the term "stratification" refers to layers of simultaneous melodies, all of which are interrelated but are not independent, and each of which proceeds in its own idiomatic way. In contrast, in Western polyphonic music the lines are relatively independent, although constrained by, or operating within, a harmonic progression.

These derived versions of the main melody might be likened to the facets of a diamond: each is a different view of the gem, but all are part of the gem, inseparable from it, and the

FIGURE 5-5. Large ensemble of stringed instruments, flutes, and rhythmic percussion.

gem consists of itself and the facets. Traditional Western harmonic music, on the other hand, is organized vertically, that is, clusters of interrelated pitches forming chords follow a systematic movement from one to another. A typical impression of Western harmonic music is of a dense texture in which many pitches sound simultaneously, yet form few identifiably independent strata. The movement from chord to chord furnishes the tension-relaxation complex—the motor power that drives the music forward. In the horizontal complex of musics using polyphonic stratification, the versions of the melody progress in slower or faster rhythmic units in relation to the main melody. Each of the several layers of sound is usually carried by one instrument only and is readily discernible to the ear educated to this type of music. There *is* a type of harmony in this linearly organized music in the basic meaning of the word, "simultaneous sounds": individual lines converge to unison or octaves at specific structural points, between which the lines follow the style idiomatic for the instruments playing them. Thus the music is regulated by this linear adherence to style. The motor power driving this type of music forward is the alternation of relative consonance at structural points of unison (or octaves) with relative dissonance between these points, through the idiomatic treatment of the lines.

Thai instruments of fixed pitch are tuned to an equidistant system of seven pitches per octave. The average distance between pitches is 171-172 cents,[1] about one-eighth of a whole tone less than that Western interval. As in Western traditional music, however, all pitches of the tuning system are not used in one mode (often referred to as "scale"); in the Thai system five of the seven are used as principal pitches in any mode, thus establishing a pattern of nonequidistant intervals for the mode.

No documentation exists as to when or where

1. For an explanation of the cents system see the Preface.

EXAMPLE 5-1.

EXAMPLE 5-2.

EXAMPLE 5-3.

the Thai seven-pitch equidistant tuning system developed. Chinese tuning is based on a series of perfect fifths: the first five are the principal pitches, modally speaking (e.g., C, D, E, G, A in Western pitches),[2] and the next two fifths are decoration pitches (B and F♯), the first functioning with the tonic pitch (i.e., C) and the second with the fifth above the tonic, often referred to as the dominant (i.e., G). The Chinese tuning is frequently described as an "anhemitonic pentatonic" system (a five-pitch system without half-steps) or a gapped pentatonic, in which the gaps are approximately equivalent to the Western minor third and in which there are no small intervals comparable to the Western

2. The first seven pitches of a series of perfect fifths beginning on C would be: C, G, D, A, E, B, and F♯. This would cover a range of many octaves. To produce this series within one octave, a simple procedure is to ascend a perfect fifth and descend a perfect fourth (the acoustical "opposite" of a fifth). When these pitches are put in diatonic order, the series is: C, D, E, (F♯), G, A, (B); C–D–E–G–A is the pentatonic series, and F♯ and B are the auxiliary pitches. See also the essay on Chinese music in this volume.

half-step. In numbers or ciphers, as they are usually called, this is indicated as 1 2 3 5 6 1.

Thai melodies characteristically have few leaps, progressing from one pitch of the pentatonic mode to a neighboring pitch. Because the gap in the pentatonic does not imply a missing pitch as the Western ear hears it, movement from pitches 3 to 5 and 6 to 1 does not constitute a leap but is stepwise in the pentatonic system (ex. 5-1). Occasionally a leap of an acoustical fourth (called a perfect fourth in Western terminology) is used, after which the melody turns in the opposite direction from the leap (e.g., pitch 1 to lower pitch 5—a leap, then turning and ascending to pitch 6), as can be seen in example 5-1. Rarely, a leap of a fifth is used; example 5-2 shows such an occurrence. When leaps larger than a fifth occur, it is generally a result of transferring the melody to a different octave register, an occurrence of which is shown in example 5-3.

Thai melodies are of two general styles. The

EXAMPLE 5-4.

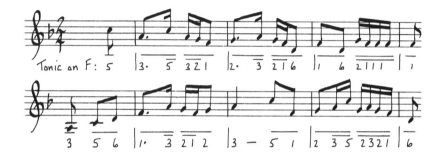

EXAMPLE 5-5.

older style may be termed "motivic" and is rhythmically simple and divisible into fairly regular small units of, in Western terms, two-measure lengths. The total effect is not of a long lyrical line of melody but of rhythmically simple, small units of a relatively neutral melodic nature strung together to make a section of music. Example 5-4 shows a typical main melody of this motivic type played by the khawng wong yai. In the newer, more lyric style, greater rhythmic diversity is found in the main melody, and the effect is much more what a Westerner considers as "melody." Example 5-5 shows the beginning of the well-known Thai composition *Khamēn Sai Yōk*, which has a melody of this type.

Thai traditional music is always in duple meter whenever a steady tempo is observed and is usually notated with a 2/4 time signature when it is shown in Western staff notation, whatever the actual tempo of the composition. The metrical pulse is outlined by the ching (the hand cymbals), which alternate open or undamped sounds and closed or damped sounds.[3] The open, ringing sounds are unaccented strokes and the damped sounds are accented strokes in the structural pattern. The pitches occurring with the accented (damped) strokes of the ching are those of the mode of the composition; the hierarchy of pitch emphasis in the mode is a result of the number of times each pitch occurs and the concurrent ching stroke.

There are three patterns of ching structure, and because the ching structure is the basis of form, it might thus be said that there are three

3. For a more detailed explanation of "damped" and "undamped," see the Glossary.

basic forms in Thai music. In the long or "extended" pattern or version, as it is called, the ching sounds once per "measure" (as it is notated in Western staff notation); in the middle version, the ching sounds twice per measure; and in the short version, four times per measure—a measure in each version being played in the same amount of clock time. It can be seen, then, that each version is twice as fast or slow as the preceding or following one, insofar as the number of ching strokes per unit of time is concerned. However, from any version a composition always proceeds to the next faster one; there is never movement from a faster tempo to a slower one in a Thai composition.

The system of emphasis is the same as that found in Indonesian music, probably the most complex in Southeast Asia: in groups of four pulses the strong pulse is on the fourth unit or beat, a secondary emphasis occurs on the second beat, and beats one and three are relatively weak. This is quite different from the procedure in Western music in which, at least in notation, the strong pulse occurs on the first beat of the measure. These ching patterns and the system of emphasis are shown in example 5-6, a diagram of four-measure units. When a gong is used, it is played on the second accented ching stroke in the extended pattern (that is, at the end of every fourth measure), and on every accented ching stroke in the other two patterns.

This pattern of emphasis—a secondary accent on the second of four strokes and a primary accent on the fourth—underlies the entire

structure of a Thai composition and occurs in several lengths, from small to large (ex. 5-7). In a sixteen-measure phrase the accents, 1 2 3 4, fall at the end of each of the four four-measure phrases.[4]

Although the modal concepts in Chinese music are relatively clear and the rāga system of India is perhaps the most highly developed modal system in the world, if, as I speculate, these two musical cultures met and combined in Thai music when the Thai began to inhabit present-day Thailand and absorbed Khmer music, the result was not a more complex system combining the elements of both the Chinese and Indian systems, but rather a diffusion and breakdown of modality. There seem to be no indications that the Indian rāga system left any appreciable marks on Thai music. What modal concepts there are in Thai music are related to the Chinese system in which each of the five principal pitches of a pentatonic arrangement can be a starting point or tonic for a mode. There are, then, five possible modes in a pentatonic arrangement starting on any pitch:

Mode 6:						6	1 2 3	5 6	
Mode 5:					5 6		1 2 3	5	
Mode 3:				3	5 6		1 2 3		
Mode 2:			2 3		5 6		1 2		
Mode 1:	1 2 3				5 6		1		

Because the distances between the pitches in the Thai tuning system are equidistant (as in the Western system), a similar modal pattern can be started on each of the seven pitches (just as in the Western system the major mode can be started on C, D, E, F, etc.—though these are generally called "scales" in the Western system). In practice, however, such is not the case in Thai music; only four pitches are commonly used as starting points for modes. Although very lit-

Extended version		1 ○		2 ⊕		3 ○		4 ⊕
Middle version	1 ○	2 ⊕	3 ○	4 ⊕	1 ○	2 ⊕	3 ○	4 ⊕
Short version	○ ⊕ ○ 1 2 3	⊕ 4	○ ⊕ ○ 1 2 3	⊕ 4	○ ⊕ ○ 1 2 3	⊕ 4	○ ⊕ ○ 1 2 3	⊕ 4

EXAMPLE 5-6. Numbers representing the pulse emphases are included. Heavy vertical lines are the ends of the units in Thai style; dashed vertical lines represent bar lines as they would occur in Western staff notation. Ching strokes: ○ and +. Ching and gong: ⊕.

4. In notating Thai music in Western notation the music is arranged so that the primary accent of the Thai phrase falls on the first beat of the Western measure, as this is more natural for readers of Western notation. It must be remembered, however, that this primary accent in Thai music comes at the *end* of a phrase of music, of whatever length, and therefore the phrase-unit of whatever length in Thai style when put into Western notation will begin on the second beat of a Western measure and will conclude on the first beat of a measure.

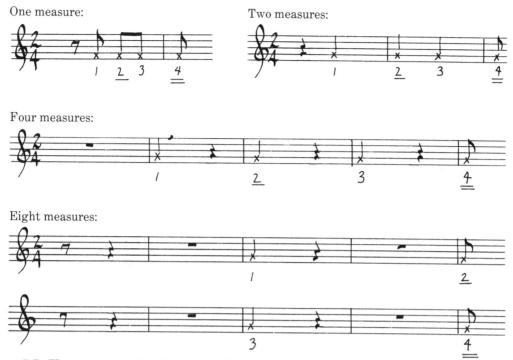

EXAMPLE 5-7. The structure of emphasis in staff notation.

tle terminology is used by the Thai themselves, there is an old set of Thai terms for the seven pitches of the tuning system. They are not, however, uniform in derivation. *Kruat* refers to the quality of sound (probably of the instrument associated with that pitch), *phiang aw* refers to the instrument itself identified with that pitch, another refers to the style of music used with that pitch, another to the position of the pitch in relation to another pitch, and so forth. A simpler system seemed in order for Western readers, not involving complicated Thai words, so I decided to label the pitch level (i.e., in Western terms, the "home key") used by the pī phāt ensemble as pitch level I and labeled the other six pitches II through VII. The four pitch levels commonly used in Thai music are I, VII, IV, and III, notated in Western notation as the keys of G, F, C, and B♭, respectively. (It must be remembered that these Western pitches are used only for convenience and for notation; they do not represent the true Thai pitches.) Pentatonic modes on any pitch level are then indicated by Arabic numerals: 1 2 3 5 6 1, in whatever

arrangement. The interrelationship of the pentatonic modes on the four basic pitch levels may be seen clearly in the following table:[5]

Pitch level I:					1	2	3		5	6	1
Pitch level VII:			1	2	3		5	6	1		
Pitch level IV:	1	2	3		5	6	1				
Pitch level III:	1	2	3		5	6	1				

There are two basic modal styles in Thai traditional music. The older and simpler I have termed "Thai" style. It is characterized by use of the five pitches of the pentatonic mode, with or without occasional use of pitches 4 and 7 as passing tones or other ornaments (exs. 5-1,

5. The pitches in Western staff notation used for these modal positions are as follows: Pitch level I: G–A–B–D–E; Pitch level VII: F–G–A–C–D; Pitch level IV: C–D–E–G–A; Pitch level III: B♭–C–D–F–G. Pitch 3 on level I is B, but pitch 1 on level III is B♭. It is the same pitch in the Thai system, and the same key on the xylophones and the same gong-kettle on the gong-chime instruments. The only reason for notating it in B♭ is that this entails only two accidentals; in B it would entail five. Also, the 172-cent interval of Thai tuning is closer to a whole step than a half-step; therefore a C–B♭ relationship represents this better. Also a perfect fifth below G is C, and a perfect fifth below F is B♭.

5-2, and 5-5 are in this style). The other style, which I term *mawn*, seems possibly to have been derived from the music of a group called Môn (as the name is usually written in Roman letters) who already inhabited part of Thailand when the Thai conquered the area. This style is characterized by the use of six or seven pitches and a composition in this style generally does not have the feeling of being in mode 1, but rather in mode 2 or 6. With the use of six or seven of the pitches in the equidistant system, the music in this style seems much more vague in its tonality than the music in Thai style, which has one clear tonal center (see ex. 5-8).

As previously shown, Thai melodies are constructed by combining a number of symmetrical phrases of two- or four-measure units, which I term *phrase units*. The pitch that falls on the fourth accented beat in any of these (refer to ex. 5-7) will also coincide with a damped, accented ching stroke. These accented pitches, those of the mode in which the composition is written, form a pattern of pitches—a skeleton of stressed pitches (which I term the *pitch outline*)—and these pitches and the way in which they are used and stressed give a composition its overall mood. One may say, then, that mode, in all its ramifications, produces mood.

Some Thai compositions remain on the same pitch level (i.e., in the Western sense, in the same key) throughout the entire composition; others may shift the same mode to another starting pitch (comparable to the movement from C major to G major in Western music, for example). This practice has been termed *metabole* by Brailoiu, who borrowed the term from the ancient Greeks, in whose music apparently a similar practice occurred. The term was used further by Trân Văn Khê, specialist in Vietnamese music, to describe the same procedure in that music. Modulation, in the strict sense of the word—change of mode (such as movement from F major to d minor in Western music)—also occurs in Thai music (as well as in other Southeast Asian musics), such as in moving from mode 1 to mode 6. Both metabole and modulation may be brought about in two ways: (1) by means of a pivotal pitch: a principal pitch in one mode may become a different principal pitch in another

mode (e.g., in Western music, C is pitch 1 in the key of C and pitch 5 in the key of F); (2) by means of a nonmodal pitch: a passing tone, pitch 4 or 7, in one mode can become a principal pitch in another mode (this is comparable to chromatic modulation in Western music where a nonmodal pitch, such as F♯ in the key of C, becomes a modal pitch in a new mode—F♯ in the key of C becoming pitch 7 in the key of G, for example). Some Thai compositions have only one or two metaboles in them; others may have several. Example 5-8 is a short Thai composition in which there is a simple metabole from the starting pitch level on B♭ to the pitch level a fifth above, F, returning to the original pitch level at phrase-unit 4 (see ex. 5-9, the pitch outline).

There are few forms in Thai music; form essentially corresponds to the ching pattern that underlies the music. The oldest compositions in the Thai traditional repertory today are probably of the Bangkok period, that is, from the nineteenth century. Long ago they were grouped into suites, and this is how they are known today. Most of them have been forgotten, however; few are played at the present time. Contemporary forms in Thai music are spoken of generally as *sām chan*, with the long or extended ching pattern, *sawng chan*, the middle pattern, and *chan dio*, the short pattern (or sometimes merely *phlēng reo*—"fast" song).

In the late nineteenth and early twentieth centuries a new Thai style or form developed called *thao*. This word means "a set of something in gradated sizes" and describes well this variation form, which is constructed as follows: a composer chooses for treatment an existing piece of music of about sixteen measures per section and usually of two or three sections. This music is often an old composition—one or part of one from a suite, sometimes a folk song, or a melody borrowed from a neighboring culture. Whatever the original tempo or ching pattern, the composer changes it to that of the middle pattern. Then he enlarges the music to twice the original length (thirty-two measures if the original is sixteen measures), retaining the same pitches at the essential structural points, and reduces the original to half its structural length (for example, sixteen to eight measures), also retaining

EXAMPLE 5-8. Phrăm Dīt Namtao.

EXAMPLE 5-8. (continued)

essential structural pitches. The enlarging and condensing must be done so as to retain the style of the original, and herein lies the need for the composer (actually, the arranger) to have talent and ability. The three divisions are then played in order: extended, middle (original), and short. Example 5-8 is a composition in mawn style with one section of two phrase-blocks (a "phrase-block" consists of a group of four phrase-units, or four lines of notation as they are shown here). In the notation the ciphers of the principal pitches have been added below the staff, and the ching and gong strokes (see fig. 5-6 for symbols) have been added above, to aid in seeing the correspondence of pitches among the three versions. The middle version (labeled 2 at the beginning of the line) and the short version (labeled 1) have been notated in a widely spaced manner to show further this correspondence of the principal

unit 3). In the first half of the last phrase-unit in the extended version (labeled 3) a tonic on F is again suggested; the last half of the unit has only one pitch—G in the notation. The tonal center of this last phrase-unit is ambiguous, and the composition, at least as far as the extended version is concerned, may be either in mode 2 or 6 (with the pitch labeled 1 on B♭). In the original version (2), however, the pitches indicate mode 6 more clearly.

The structural pitches extracted from the composition are as shown in example 5-9, called a *pitch outline*. An examination of these structural pitches will reveal other significant interrelationships, which lack of space precludes going into here.

Frequently the extended version became popular in itself; no short version was composed and the original was discarded. These composi-

Extended Version						*Middle Version*			*Short Version*	
○	+	○	⊕			⊕	⊕		⊕	⊕
III: 3	1	1	3			1	3		1	3
7	3/6	(6)	2	VII		3/6	2		3/6	2
VII: 3	1	1	6/3	III		1	6/3		1	6/3
III: 3	2	3	(3)			3	(3)		3	(3)
3	1	1	3			1	3		1	3
3	1	2	(2)			1	(2)		1	(2)
3	1	2	6			1	6		3	6
III: 6	5	6	(6)			3	(6)		3	(6)
or VII: 2	1	2	(2)							

Each line = 4 measures — *Number of measures: 32* — *Each line = 2 measures* — *Number of measures: 16* — *Each line = 1 measure* — *Number of measures: 8*

EXAMPLE 5-9. Pitch outline of *Phrām Dīt Namtao* (ex. 5-8). In each version, one line represents a phrase-unit. (Numbers in parentheses indicate pitches held over from the previous measure.)

pitches—how versions 3 and 1 have been derived from version 2. Where deviations from the original structural pitches occur, they are so indicated (in version 3 mostly). The metabole is shown by two numbers with a slash (e.g., 3/6): in the middle of phrase-unit 2, pitch 3 of the original mode on III (B♭) becomes pitch 6 of a mode on VII (F). The melody returns to the mode on III at the end of the next phrase-unit (phrase-

tions are referred to merely as sām chan. Some of these have long "developmental" sections and are used as virtuoso and exhibition pieces. Although it has not been customary for Thai composers to compose "original" music per se, and especially not in sām chan form, there are a few notable exceptions to this among compositions in sawng chan form. The chan dio pattern is not used for separate compositions.

OTHER KINDS OF THAI MUSIC

Traditional Thai theater is better described as a kind of music drama. Contemporary presentations include soloists and chorus, instrumental accompaniment, instrumental interludes, and dance; the vocal parts include spoken dialogue, chantlike sections, and solo song and chorus sections in various styles. The soloists and chorus sit at the side of the stage with the instrumental ensemble and sing for the actors on stage who mime the parts, not singing for themselves. Dialogue and comedy scenes, however, are usually performed by the actors on stage.

Thai dance, unlike the music, is almost entirely derived from the Khmer, as a comparison of costumes and postures of Thai dancers with those of the carvings at Angkor has shown. There is probably not a little Indian influence in both the contemporary Thai and Cambodian dance, which came through the Khmer; dance postures and hand positions are extremely important in the dance of Southeast Asia in general, as they are in Indian dance.

At some time in the past, vocal sections in the traditional music were separated from the instrumental sections. The tonal aspects of the language were said to have restricted the free melodic style more suitable to instruments and limited them; therefore vocal and instrumental sections began to be alternated. This is still the tradition in the entertainment repertory[6] as well as in theater music.

Vocal style is characterized by a tone quality of richness and complexity, similar to other Asian vocal styles. There is little or no vibrato, and pitches other than those of the fixed tuning system are used, particularly in the vocal ornaments, which occur at more or less fixed places in the music, such as at cadences, and are learned as fixed ornaments. Because the language restricts melody, vocables such as *oh* and *ah* in Western languages are frequently used, to which a free melody may be sung.

6. "Entertainment" music is the music written for the courts in the old days for amusement and recreation—for the private concerts of the nobility, as it were. It might also be considered all the music that is not specifically theatrical, ceremonial, or connected with some other special function.

When the standard ensembles are used for ceremonies, they play music that is specific for those occasions. But this music, like the theater music, is in the same general style and tradition as the entertainment music and cannot be distinguished from it except by a knowledgeable member of the culture or by a specialist.

Thai folk music has not been researched, but a few general comments about it may be made. Folk songs are of two types. Those in which the text predominates are more chantlike than true songs. The vocal line is more in the nature of heightened speech, following the inflection of the necessary tones of the words as regulated by the rules of the tone language. Other folk songs tend to be melodically free, generally pentatonic, and independent of linguistic control factors—in other words, true songs. Folk instrumental music seems to be based on the principles of the traditional music system but used in a much freer way.

Popular songs in Thai style are being composed. They generally have pentatonic melodies too, but are harmonized in Western style with a few simple chords.

CONCLUSION

Thai traditional music evolved in the many royal households. With the change in 1932 from an absolute monarchy to a form of democracy, these rapidly declined, and with the disintegration of the environment in which the court music flowered, the music, too, was to some degree abandoned. Since 1932 there has been an attempt on the part of the government and some private schools to maintain the traditional music and, if not to elevate it to its former high state, at least to preserve it.

In the past musicians were attached to the royal households; although in actuality they were servants, they were highly respected. Today there is little opportunity for a traditional musician to perform, and he cannot make a living through playing—he must hold another job as well. Many Thai, however, have begun to learn and practice traditional music as a hobby or avocation.

The music heard in Thailand today, aside from the folk music in the rural districts, is mostly Western and Thai popular music. Occasionally Western symphonic music and Thai traditional music are heard on recordings over the radio and on television and at public concerts given by the Department of Fine Arts. Some private schools, as well as the Department of Fine Arts, give shows for tourists of representative styles of traditional music and dance. But one cannot say that there is much musical activity in Thailand despite the efforts of these groups to make the general Thai public more music conscious.

Little is being done these days in composing in the traditional style; performances are only of the known repertory. Occasionally, new arrangements and sometimes new compositions are created for the theater dramas, principally by Montri Tramote, head musician of the Department of Fine Arts in Bangkok. The system has evolved toward narrower and narrower restrictions so that instead of evolving and developing new forms and styles, the standard procedures and techniques have been worked and reworked. It does not appear that anything new can be done in the traditional music system as it now stands, and whether any Thai musicians and composers will arise in the future to expand the system without destroying its essential "Thai-ness" remains to be seen. As it is today, the traditional music is more of an anachronistic museum piece than a vital force in contemporary Thai culture.

Glossary

ching-small hand cymbals.

damping-to put something against the sound-producing material or part of the instrument as soon as the sound has been produced in order to silence it. With drums, the drumsticks or hands may be pressed against the skin of the drumhead after it has been hit. With metallophones, the fingers of one hand may firmly grasp the metal key immediately after it has been hit with the mallet in the other hand. With two cymbals, they may be hit together and held together, producing a dull, metallic click, as opposed to the clear ringing sound produced when the two parts are struck together sharply and immediately pulled apart.

gong-kettle-a gong-shaped metal instrument with a wide flange and a boss (the raised knob in the center of the flat surface), placed horizontally in a rack, often in tuned sets (frequently called "gong-chimes"), and played on the boss with a mallet.

jakhē-floor zither.

khāēn-"mouth organ" of northern Thailand and Laos, comparable except in size and shape to the Chinese *shêng* and the Japanese *shō*.

khawng wong lek-circle of gong-kettles, the smaller in size and higher-pitched of the two Thai instruments of this type.

khawng wong yai-circle of gong-kettles, larger in size and lower-pitched than *khawng wong lek*.

kruat-a Thai mode.

mahōrī-ensemble of instruments, consisting of melodic and rhythmic percussion, stringed instruments, flute, and drums.

metabole-the transferring of a mode to another starting pitch. The term *modulation* is used in Western music to describe this procedure as well as a change in mode. *Metabole*, an ancient Greek word, has been used recently by Brailoiu and Trân Văn Khê to describe this practice in the musics of Southeast Asia. Since these music systems have no harmony in the Western sense, metabole was considered a more appropriate term because modulation has come to imply, in Western music at least, tonality and harmony, which do not exist in non-harmonic systems.

phiang aw-a Thai mode.

pī-wind instrument with wooden body, conical bore, quadruple reed, and a range of two octaves and a fourth.

pī chawā-wind instrument—wooden body with a detachable metal horn, conical in shape, quadruple reed—comparable to the Chinese *sona*.

pī phāt-ensemble of instruments—melodic and rhythmic percussion, *pī*, and drums.

ranāt ēk-xylophone, higher-pitched of the two instruments of this type, with boat-shaped stand.

ranāt ēk lek-metallophone, higher-pitched of the two instruments of this type, with rectangular metal keys suspended over a box resonator.

ranāt thum-xylophone, lower-pitched than ranāt ēk, with wooden keys suspended over a box resonator.

ranāt thum lek-metallophone, lower-pitched than ranāt ēk lek, with rectangular metal keys suspended over a box resonator.

thao-variation form in three divisions of which each is double or half the length of the adjoining division. For example: extended version (*sām chan*) —32 measures; middle version (*sawng chan*)—16 measures; and short version (*chan dio*)—8 measures; played in this order.

Bibliography

Ayer, Margaret.
 1964. *Made in Thailand*. New York: Knopf.
Bidyalankarana, Prince.
 1926. "The Pastime of Rhyme-making and Singing in Rural Siam." *Journal of the Siam Society* 20:110-13.
Blanchard, Wendell, ed.
 1958. *Thailand: Its People, Its Society, Its Culture*. New Haven: Human Relations Area Files.
Brailoiu, Constantin.
 1955. "Un problème de tonalité (la métabole pentatonique)." In *Mélanges d'histoire et d'esthétique musicales*, 1, pp. 63-75. Paris: Bibliothèque d'études musicales.
Brandon, James R.
 1967. *Theatre in Southeast Asia*. Cambridge: Harvard University Press.
Duriyanga, Phra Chen.
 1956. *Thai Music*. Thailand Culture Series, no. 8, 4th ed. Bangkok: National Culture Institute. (*Note:* Later editions of this pamphlet may exist, issued by the Department of Fine Arts.)
Dyck, Gerald P.
 1975*a*. "Lung Noi Na Kampan Makes a Drumhead for a Northern Thai Long Drum." In *Selected Reports in Ethnomusicology* 2:183-203.
 1975*b*. "They Also Serve" (Blind musicians of north Thailand). In *Selected Reports in Ethnomusicology* 2:204-16.
 1975*c*. "The Vanishing *Phia*: An Ethnomusicological Photo-Story." In *Selected Reports in Ethnomusicology* 2:217-29.
Hood, Mantle.
 1975. "Improvisation in the Stratified Ensembles of Southeast Asia." In *Selected Reports in Ethnomusicology* 2:25-33.
Hornbostel, Erich M. von.
 1919/1920. "Formanalysen an siamesischen Orchesterstücken." *Archiv für Musikwissenschaft* 2:306-33.

Kunst, Jaap.
 1929/1930. "Een overwalsche bloedverwant van den Javaanschen gamelan; geschiedenis van het Siameesche orkest." *Nederlansch Indië Oud und Nieuw* 14:79-96.
Mendenhall, Stanley T.
 1975. "Interaction of Linguistic and Musical Tone in Thai Song." In *Selected Reports in Ethnomusicology* 2:17-23.
Moore, Sidney.
 1969. "Thai Songs in 7/4 Meter." *Ethnomusicology* 13:309-12.
Morton, David.
 1968. *The Traditional Music of Thailand*. Los Angeles: Institute of Ethnomusicology, University of California at Los Angeles. (This is a booklet of commentary and analysis which accompanies the two-record album *Traditional Music of Thailand* issued by the Institute. See the Discography.)
 1969. "Thailand." In *Harvard Dictionary of Music*, 2d ed., pp. 842-43. Cambridge, Mass.: Harvard University Press.
 1970. "Thai Traditional Music: Hot-House Plant or Sturdy Stock." *Journal of the Siam Society* 58, part 2, 1-44.
 1971. "An American Discovers Thai Music." *Arts of Asia* 1:11-15.
 1971. "Polyphonic Stratification in Traditional Thai Music: A Study in Multiple Tone Color." *Asian Pacific Quarterly of Cultural and Social Affairs* 3:70-80.
 1972. "The Traditional Instrumental Music of Thailand." In *The Musics of Asia*, pp. 90-105. Manila: National Music Council of the Philippines and UNESCO National Commission of the Philippines. Paper first read at an International Music Symposium, Manila, April, 1966.
 1973. "Music in Thailand; The Traditional System and Foreign Influences." In *Musikkulturen Asiens, Afrikas und Ozeaniens im 19. Jahrhundert*, pp. 185-213. Regensburg: Bosse.
 1974. "Vocal Tones in Traditional Thai Music." In *Selected Reports in Ethnomusicology* 2:89-99.
 1975. "Instruments and Instrumental Functions in the Ensembles of Southeast Asia: A Cross-Cultural Comparison." In *Selected Reports in Ethnomusicology* 2:7-14.
 1976. *The Traditional Music of Thailand*. Berkeley, Los Angeles, London: University of California Press. (This is the published version of the Ph.D. dissertation.)

Pringsheim, Klaus.
    1944. "Music of Thailand." *Contemporary Japan* 13:745-67.
Silapabanleng, Prasidh.
    1975. "Thai Music at the Court of Cambodia." In *Selected Reports in Ethnomusicology* 2:3-4.
Stumpf, Carl.
    1901. "Tonsystem und Musik der Siamesen." In *Beiträge zur Akustik und Musikwissenschaft* 3:69-138. Reprinted in *Sammelbände fur Vergleichende Musikwissenschaft* 1:(1922) 122-77.
Thai Publications
    1954. "Tham Khwan" (Musical Suite). Bangkok: Department of Fine Arts. (A suite of music to be performed during a ceremony invoking spiritual bliss.)
    1960 (Buddhist Era 2503). *Bibliography of Material about Thailand in Western Languages.* Bangkok: Chulalongkorn University Library.
    n.d. "Homrong Yen" (Evening Prelude). Bangkok: Department of Fine Arts. (Full score and part books.)
    1961. *Thai Classical Music: Book I.* Bangkok: Department of Fine Arts.
Trân Văn Khê.
    1962. *La musique vietnamienne traditionelle.* Paris: Presse universitaire de France.
Yupho, Dhanit.
    1960. *Thai Musical Instruments.* Translated from the Thai by David Morton. Bangkok: Department of Fine Arts. (A second edition, only in Thai, has been issued.)

Discography

Music of Thailand. Ethnic Folkways FE 4463. Recorded by Howard Kaufman.
    This record contains over a dozen bands of excerpts of different kinds of Thai music.
Musique de Thailande. BAM LD-338. 7 inch.
    Several Thai compositions recorded by Jean-Claude Berrier and Louis le Bourgeois.
Traditional Music of Thailand. IER 7502.
    A two-record album of all the important genres of the traditional music, in simulated stereo made from the field tapes collected by David Morton in Thailand in 1958-1960. Accompanied by a booklet of commentary and analysis (see Bibliography, Morton 1968).

Films

Angkor, The Lost City. CF/MH. B&W. 12 min.
    About the ancient city of the Khmer. Includes a few moments of a Cambodian ensemble, comparable to the Thai pī phāt ensemble.
Bangkok. Films Inc. Col. 18 min.
    Includes material on the arts.
Thai Traditional Music and Classical Dance. IU. Col. 28 min.
    Produced by the Government of Thailand.
The Diamond Finger. NYU. Col. 25 min.
    A section of a typical Thai dance-drama. No dialogue or singing, but a musical background, performed mostly by the pī phāt ensemble.

6. Some Principles of Indian Classical Music

Bonnie C. Wade

Westerners have long been fascinated by Oriental cultures. In the music sphere, the most intense and widespread interest of Westerners has been in Indian classical music. It is not surprising that Western interest in Indian music should be accompanied by absorption in other aspects of Indian culture, particularly religion, for music and religion here form a vital link. Some scholars argue that nothing in India can be regarded as completely secular and separate from religious connotation. Social structure, eating habits, in fact every action is related to a religious philosophy, be it Hindu, Muslim, or another. So it is with Indian music. Before a musician of the classical tradition begins to practice or to perform he offers prayers, and the musical training of a child begins with worship.[1]

As in Western cultures, music in India is of various folk and classical types. The music made and enjoyed by most Indians—folk music—is as varied as folk music in any culture. It includes work songs, music and dance for festive occasions, and devotional songs for the many religious ceremonies and for personal worship. The folk music varies not only in type but also according to geographic area, for the subcontinent is large and has absorbed peoples of numerous cultures.

Music in the classical tradition has been patronized by the upper classes, performed by and for them, formerly in court centers, now in towns and cities throughout the country. Most Indian music that Westerners hear is of one part of India, the north, which was overrun and was ruled by Muslims from the thirteenth through the nineteenth centuries. As Muslims settled into the rich northern areas of the subcontinent, political divisions encouraged divergent cultural development. By the sixteenth century India had developed two distinguishable classical music cultures—Hindustānī in the north and Karnatak in the south, each based on the same ancient tradition but evolving according to different cultural vicissitudes.[2] Because Hindustānī music is most widely available in the country it will be the focus here, but comparisons will be drawn with Karnatak concepts of melody, meter, and musical milieux.

HINDUSTĀNĪ MUSIC

Ensembles and Instruments

A single line of melody, a drone, and drumming constitute the ensemble texture of Hindustānī classical vocal and instrumental music. By vocal music is meant a performance featuring a solo vocalist accompanied on one or two types of stringed instruments and a drum. By instrumental music is meant a performance featuring a solo instrumentalist frequently accompanied by a stringed instrument and always by a drum. As in Western music, the specific composition of a performance ensemble depends on the genre of music to be performed. A Schubert lied, for example, is composed for vocal soloist with piano accompaniment; songs in operas may be for solo,

---

1. See Ravi Shankar's autobiography, *My Music, My Life* (1968).

2. The Indus River, formerly called Sindhu, was called *Hindu* by the Persians who had difficulty pronouncing an initial *s*. From Persia the word passed to Greece, where it came to mean the whole of India. With the Muslim invasion the Persian name returned in the form *Hindustān* and those who followed the old religion became known as Hindus (Basham 1959:1).

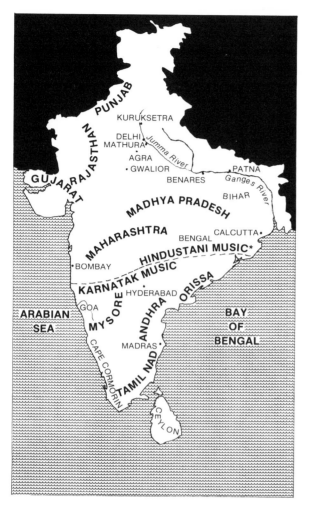

Indian Subcontinent

plucked lute. The predominant drum in North India, and one that is both a solo and an accompanying instrument, is the *tablā*, a set of two drums hand-beaten by one player. Another type of drum used in North India is the *pakhāvaj*, a double-headed wooden drum handstruck on both ends.

Accompanying vocal solos was the main traditional role of instruments in Hindustānī classical music until about the end of the nineteenth century. An oft-repeated tale in North Indian music lore concerns one Nyamat Khan, a *bīn* (an instrument rarely played today) player without rival in the court of Muhammad Shah (1719-1748), the last Mogul emperor to lavishly patronize the arts. As a bīn player, Nyamat Khan accompanied the court singers and, according to custom, had to sit behind them. Considering this an affront to his dignity, Nyamat took steps to better his position, not by trying to elevate the status of bīn players as one might expect, but rather by endorsing a style of vocal music, different from that performed by the court singers. The popularity of the new style undercut the unrivaled esteem for the traditional court singers (Gosvami 1957:273).

Bīn, sitār, and sarod came to the fore as solo instruments rather than as accompaniment, and today other melody instruments such as flute and Western violin seem to be featured more and more. One artist in particular, Ram Narayan [Narain] has been pushing to include the sāraṅgī in the solo ranks. In addition, Ustad Bismillah Khan has brought the *shehnai*, an instrument traditionally associated with outdoor performances and largely with folk music, into the arena of classical music performance.[4] Shehnai is a double reed instrument, one and one-half to two feet long with a tube that gradually widens toward a metal bell at the lower end. It usually has seven or eight finger holes.

The accompanying ensemble for sitār, sarod, flute, and violin[5] always includes a tablā; the

duet, trio, and the like with orchestral accompaniment.

The single line of melody is sung, or played on instruments such as the *sitār* and *sarod*, two plucked lute-type instruments.[3] The soloist's melody in some genres of music is supported by an additional melodic instrument. The most frequently used is the *sāraṅgī*, a bowed lute. In every performance ensemble a drone must be present. It is built into some instruments such as the sitār and sarod, but even so, an instrument specifically for producing a drone will be present. That will most likely be a *tambūr*, a

3. For a detailed explanation of the respective instruments and ensembles see the author's *Music in India: The Classical Traditions* (1979).

4. *Ustād* is the honorific address for respected Muslim artists, as *Pandit* is for the Hindu.
5. The Western violin was adopted by South Indian musicians from the British and is their primary accompanying melody instrument. Held between chest and foot, it is tuned to Sa and Pa (see Melody section). It is primarily a solo instrument in North India, where it is not widely used.

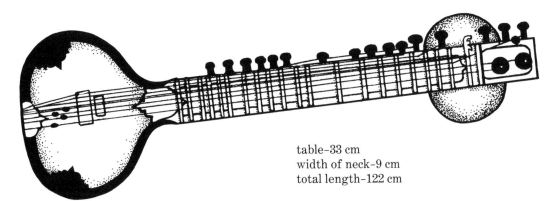

SITĀR

table-33 cm
width of neck-9 cm
total length-122 cm

shehnai ensemble might retain the *naghará*, a shallow metal, single-headed, bowl-shaped drum that comes in various sizes and is played in pairs by a single drummer. Sarod and sitār have their own drone strings, but a tāmbūr is usually there to provide continuous drone, as it does for flute and violin performances; small shehnai fulfill the role of the tāmbūr for solo shehnai, using the technique of circular breathing. Two solo in-

classical music.[6] The term refers not only to the system as a whole but also to each of several hundred melodic entities. Defining rāga is no simple matter, because a single rāga encompasses musical and extramusical ideas about melody which we in the West do not group together in quite the same way. Rāga would lie closest to tune on a theoretical continuum from random pitch to tune (fig. 6-1).

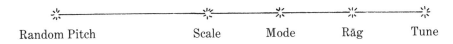

Random Pitch   Scale   Mode   Rāg   Tune

FIGURE 6-1

struments are sometimes played together (sitār and sarod, violin and sitār, etc.); they alternate or play in unison. The ensemble ideal of one melody, a drone, and a drum is maintained in all these ensembles.

Even though it is an ensemble tradition, improvisation is central to Hindustānī classical music. To improvise simultaneously, the soloist and accompanists must all be sensitive and well-trained musicians. Their improvisation is based on given elements—melody, meter, and structure.

Melody
The system that encompasses the given elements of a melodic nature is called *rāga*; rāga is the single most important element of Indian

A Hindustānī rāg includes a selection of pitches, often a distinctive melodic shape, usually a pitch hierarchy, sometimes characteristic ornamentation on certain pitches, and an association with an hour of the day, perhaps with a season of the year, and also with an emotional state of mind.

Melodies are composed in a rāg. The song in example 6-1, "Balma morī," is in Rāg Bāgeshrī, a serious rāg most suitably performed at night. (See the section on meter for an explanation of the symbols used in this example.)

Sources on Hindustānī rāg will give pitches

6. In South India rāga is pronounced as in Sanskrit with the final *a* sounding–rāga; in Hindi the final *a* is silent–rāg. It will be spelled here as pronounced in the system under discussion.

EXAMPLE 6-1.

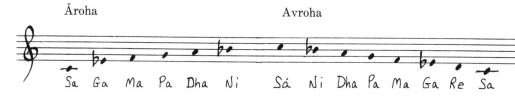

EXAMPLE 6-2.

permissible in the ascent (*āroha*) and descent (*avroha*) of Bāgeshrī, as in example 6-2. The syllables below the pitches are the Indian solfège syllables; called *sargam*, they are equivalent to the Western solfège syllables, *do re mi fa sol la ti*.[7]

If the pitches used in "Balma morī" are extracted from the melody in order of first appearance, the selection in example 6-3 is found.

7. The pitches in any rāg are from among a possible twelve in the Hindustānī system. Re, Ga, Dha, and Ni can be flat (*komal*); Ma can be sharp (*tivra*) as well as "pure."

No other pitches than these can be used for melodies in Rāg Bāgeshrī. If other pitches are added, the selection no longer will be Rāg Bāgeshrī—it might be a different rāg or there may be no rāg with such characteristics. *All of these pitches must be used* for melodies in Rāg Bāgeshrī, however. If any of these pitches are omitted, again it will no longer be Rāg Bāgeshrī.

Distinctive shape in a particular rāg is a means of achieving subtle variety in the melodic system. Found in Bāgeshrī are two of the means by which a rāg can have a distinctive melodic

High		Sà Rè Gà Mà Pà Dhà
Middle		Sa Re Ga Ma Pa Dha Ni
Low	Sạ Rẹ Gạ Mạ Pạ Dhạ Nị	

FIGURE 6-2

shape: (1) the pitches used in ascending phrases are not all the same as those used in descending melodic phrases, and (2) special treatment of one pitch or more creates short motives (*pakaḍ*) that are associated with one particular rāg.

In "Balma morī" and in all other Bāgeshrī melodies, pitch Re may not occur in ascending phrases. In the first line of "Balma morī" (ex. 6-1) Re occurs only in descent; a pivot for descent is considered descending.

Pitch Pa is given special treatment in Bāgeshrī. Although in principle Pa is permissible in all ascending phrases, it is avoided in direct ascent to high Sa (Sà). The motive (pakaḍ) that developed around the avoidance of Pa in that instance is associated specifically with Rāg Bāgeshrī and can be found in "Balma morī." These melodic characteristics are shown in example 6-4.

Another means by which a rāg can have a distinctive shape—but one which does not occur in Bāgeshrī—involves octaves (*saptak*). In theory, an artist should traverse three full octaves in the course of improvising on a rāg: low (*maṅdra*), middle (*madhya*), and high (*tār*). (Note that there is a dot below a pitch name in the low register, a dot above in the high.) This wide range is more frequently heard in instrumental performances than in vocal. Some rāgs, however, emphasize one part of the range—that is, one register—more than other parts. A distinction is drawn between two varieties of Rāg Todī, for example, partially by this means: Bahaduri-Todī melodies often begin in the low register and move gradually upward, while Gujari-Todī melodies usually start and move in the middle octave region. Rāg Bāgeshrī has no such registral associations.

The pitch of Sa of the middle octave (madhya Sa) is determined by the natural range of an individual singer's voice or by the construction of a particular instrument. No ideal of "perfect pitch" relative to a "concert pitch" exists in Indian theory. In addition, no standard exists for

EXAMPLE 6-3.

EXAMPLE 6-4.

EXAMPLE 6-5.

interval sizes; intervals can be quite different (larger or smaller) than those in Western tempered tuning.

Madhya Sa and mandra Sa are heard in the tambūr drone, along with Pa. If a rāg has no Pa, then Ma will be substituted to complement Sa in the drone. If no Pa or Ma occurs in the particular rāg being performed, another prominent pitch will be chosen. Example 6-5 gives tambūr tunings.

Although Sa is crucial in contemporary Hindustānī rāgs as a melodic base reinforced in a drone, it is not necessarily one of the most important structural pitches in a rāg. In Bāgeshrī, it does happen to be considered the most important pitch and is accordingly called *vādī*; pitch Ma is considered the second most important pitch, *samvādī*. The prominence of these two pitches is not confirmed by the melody of "Balma morī," however (see ex. 6-1). In many rāgs performed today, the labeling of a pitch hierarchy seems more theoretical than practical.

In Hindustānī classical music, ornamentation may be dictated by tradition or may be a matter of a performer's particular style. Additional pitches such as grace notes, means of connecting pitches such as slurs, and means of rendering a pitch with a slight or wide vibrato are all considered ornaments (*gamak*s). Tradition dictates that particular gamaks must be present in some rāgs. Rāg Bhairav, for example, is distinguished by a slight vibrato on pitches Re♭ and Dha♭, and by a pulling slur (called *mīnd* or *meend*) from Ga or Ma down to Re♭ after Ga or Ma has been sung in ascent.

The characteristics of a single rāg may include, then, a selection of pitches that may be different in ascent and descent or different from one octave to another, thus determining a distinctive melodic shape; pakaḍs, or melodic motives; a pitch hierarchy, and specified gamaks. That single rāg may include all of these types of characteristics, or it may consist of only a selection of pitches that are the same in ascent and descent. Rāgs with few distinctive specifications allow the greatest flexibility for improvisation.

In the West we think mood and music have a natural association. In North India the same is true, but there the associations are worked out very specifically. *Rasa*, the classical Indian theory of aesthetics, classifies human emotions into transitory feelings (*sanchārī bhāva*) and enduring moods (*sthāyī bhāva*) such as love, courage, loathing, anger, and mirth.[8] Rasa is concerned with the means by which emotions are expressed and can be aroused in a reader or listener. It is by suggestion of word and, by extension of the theory, of music, that emotions are expressed.

In Indian classical music the moods of rāgas and the suggestive content of song texts are expected to fall within the purview of the theory of rasa. Rāg Bāgeshrī is thought a serious rāg and, accordingly, the text of "Balma morī" is serious.

O my beloved, I love you. The house, the courtyard—nothing else gives me pleasure. Well-wishers and friends, come to my house to see the strange way of love. [translated by B. D. Yadav]

In Rāg Jaijaivantī, an amiable, playful, rather romantic rāg of nighttime, is sung the song "Palana gad lā re badaiyā."

Carpenter, prepare and bring a cradle. It should be adorned with jewels, for the infant Lord Krishna will swing in it. [translated by B. D. Yadav]

8. For the best single discussion of rasa, see S. K. De, *Sanskrit Poetics as a Study in Aesthetic* (1969); for a scientific approach, see B. Deva, *Psychoacoustics of Music and Speech* (1967). See also additional items in the bibliography.

According to traditional thought, certain pitch combinations create moods that are attuned to certain times of the day or seasons of the year.[9] The tritone between Ma# and Sa, for instance, manifests a feeling of uncertainty; it occurs in a group of rāgs called *Sandhi-prakash rāg*s which are performed at sunrise or sunset. More generally, rāgs are usually specified for morning, midday, late afternoon and into the evening, and night.

The time-of-day system is said to have been flexible enough for a maharajah to hear what he liked whenever he liked, and now of course we

Meter

Tāla is the term used for the Indian metric system as a whole, and also for each of many meters. In both India and the West, meters measure out specified cycles of counts. The Western meter 3/4 is a cycle of 3 counts, 2/2 of 2 counts, 12/8 a longer cycle of 12 counts. The tāls used in Hindustānī classical music generally have rather long cycles: *tīntāl* and *tilwaḍa tāl* have 16 counts (16 *mātrā*s); *ektāl* and *chautāl*, 12 counts (12 mātrās); *jhūmrā tāl*, 14 mātrās, to cite a few examples.

diameter of head–24 cm
diameter of foot–8 cm
total length–29 cm

BĀYĀN

diameter of head–18 cm
diameter of foot–10 cm
total length–30 cm

TABLĀ

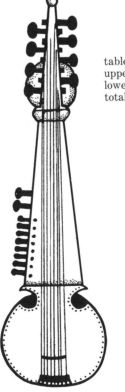

table–25 cm
upper width of neck–8 cm
lower width of neck–15 cm
total length–1.09 cm

SAROD

can command a performance of any rāg available on a recording, according to our own mood. All-India Radio schedules live broadcasts of classical music so that the artists, who perform twice during a day, will be able to include both a morning or midday rāg and an evening or night rāg. Daylong or weekendlong festivals often complement the regular season of evening concerts, but for scheduling most musical performances, modern urban life is not ideal for such time-of-day associations. The compromise seems to be to disregard the extramusical associations rather than to reduce the repertoire of rāgs.

Rasa was expounded in the *Nātya Śāstra*, the earliest treatise on dramaturgy (c. second century A.D.).

9. See Deva, *Psychoacoustics . . .* and W. Kaufmann, *The Ragas of North India* (1968), Introduction.

Tīntāl

Jhūmrā tāl

Symbols

X = Count 1 if a tālī
2 = 2
3 = 3
o = Khālī

EXAMPLE 6-6.

But the Western meter 3/4 is 3 counts of a specified value—three quarter notes, ♩♩♩; 2/2 is 2 counts each of half note value, ♩♩; 12/8 is 12 counts each of eighth note value, ♫♫ ♫♫ ♫♫ ♫♫. In the Hindustānī tāls a count is a count; the relative value of a single count is not specified in its name.

As notated above, the Western 12/8 is usually conceived as four groups of three eighth notes each; 4/4 is subdivided into 2 + 2 by an implied heavy stress on count 1 and a lighter stress on count 3, ♩♩♩♩. Similarly, tāls are subdivided so that a musician can keep track of his place in the cycle. In tīntāl the subdivision of the 16 counts is regular—4 + 4 + 4 + 4, but in jhūmrā tāl the 14 counts are grouped 3 + 4 + 3 + 4. These two tāls are notated in example 6-6. Certain important structural counts, called *tālī* (clap), are marked with Arabic numbers or, if on count 1, with *x*. The other type of structural count, *khālī* (empty), is marked with *o*. Tīntāl is so named because it has three (*tīn*) tālī, counts 1, 5, and 13. (But note that jhūmrā tāl also has three tālī.)

Westerners leave it to one individual, a conductor, to count out the meter in a performance that needs such a coordinator. A conductor has learned traditional Western motions which all participants can easily follow. In India, however, the "keeping of the tāl" is an individualized matter. It may hardly be discernible, happening in a hundred minds or being counted out discreetly by each person in the audience with small movements of fingers or hands in traditional Indian motions, but it *is* happening as an audience sits listening to a concert. The degree of personal involvement in the music making adds excitement to the performance. The hand motion for a tālī is a clap (soundless unless there is a reason for sound); for a khālī a wave to the right; for individual counts a touch of the thumb to each finger starting from the last (fig. 6-3).

A tāl is a theoretical framework that undergirds rhythmic and melodic play. Musicians may choose to delineate the details of the framework clearly during improvisation, or they may choose to obscure them by musical means, but the framework is always there.

A single measure in a Western meter does not normally encompass a complete musical idea; several measures are linked to form a phrase. The short duration of one measure is a practical reason for such a concept of phrase structure. In contrast, a melodic phrase can be

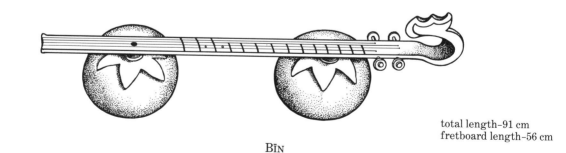

BĪN

total length—91 cm
fretboard length—56 cm

completed within the length of a single cycle of most Hindustānī tāls. Or, if the artist chooses, he may improvise through two, three, four, or more cycles before finishing a musical idea. He must know where he is within a cycle at all times, especially in order to end a "thought" at the proper place—on count 1 of the next cycle.

Count 1 is both a beginning and an end. In practical terms it functions more obviously as an end than a beginning, because all musical factors come together at a cadence point in a noticeable fashion. To create the cadence, the im-

fresh. A possible structure is shown in ex. 6-7; melodic improvisation is indicated by the phase marks. This tāl, rupak tāl, begins with khālī (o) and has two tālī (𝄐 and 2).

Drumming

It should be no surprise that the art of drumming and exploitation of rhythmic intricacies are highly cultivated in a musical culture that puts such stress on percussion accompaniment, on metric theory, and on improvisation by every performer. Though the opportunities for being

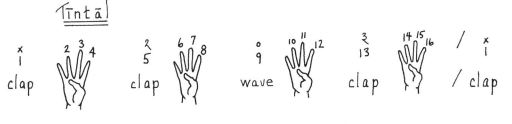

FIGURE 6-3

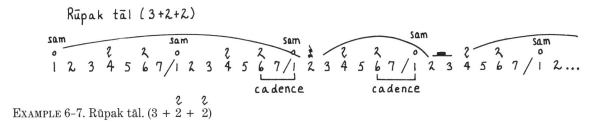

EXAMPLE 6-7. Rūpak tāl. (3 + 2 + 2)

provised melody flows into that cadential fragment mentioned in the discussion of ālāp (see section on structure); it is designed to end at count 1. As the drummer feels it coming, he and the soloist build to the cadence together, the partnership of melody and rhythm to be consummated at *sam* (together), as count 1 is called.

A few counts of rest may follow, then the music begins to flow again. The long-term types of climax found in ālāp are replaced by short-term climaxes with everyone's attention riveted to time with awareness of that tāl. Because count 1 is a beginning as well as an end, the performance is open-ended: a performer may play or sing as long as his imagination remains

diameter of heads—23 cm, 19 cm
total length—64 cm

PAKHĀVAJ

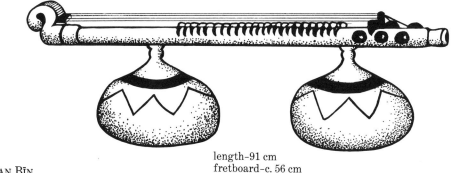

length-91 cm
fretboard-c. 56 cm

NORTH INDIAN BĪN

a featured soloist come relatively seldom to drummers in North India, they must be accomplished artists in their own right.

Drumming is not so much a matter of mastering an assortment of percussion instruments whose timbres are richly varied as it is mastery of the rhythmic and timbral possibilities offered on one instrument. It is a highly intellectualized exploration of rhythmic intricacy within the framework of a tāl, while at the same time it is cultivation of the poetry of sound.

to speak some combinations than others. In Benares tablā tradition, for example, Ta and Na refer to the same right-hand stroke. In speaking that stroke in combination with others, saying "Ta" or "Na" depends on the syllables/strokes before and after it; it is easier to say "Tin Na" than to say "Tin Ta." Furthermore, the stroke Tin can be played in two ways. One will produce a clear ringing pitch and the other an open, fuzzy sound and it is necessary for a teacher to say which is preferred in a particular pattern.

Chautāl, Pakhāvaj bols (ɣ=4, the fourth tālī)

x		o	⁊		o	⁊		ɣ		x	
Dha	Dha	Dhin	Ta	Kita	Dha	Dhin	Ta	Tita	Kata	Gadi gana /	Dha

Ektāl, Tabla bols

x		o	⁊	o	⁊		ɣ		x	
Dhin	Dhin	Dhage	tirakita	Tu	Na	Ka	Ta	Dhage	tirakita	Dhin	Na /	Dhin

EXAMPLE 6-8.

For each drum stroke there are one or more verbal syllables (generically called *bol*). The process of studying drumming involves both learning to speak drumming patterns in bols and learning to play the patterns. The choice of particular strokes in a drummed pattern is made partially for physical reasons. The choice of particular bols for those strokes in the spoken pattern is made for euphonic reasons; it is easier

Tablā bols are to be played either with one hand or with both hands, in other words on left- or right-hand drum alone or on both drums simultaneously. While Ta and Tin are played on the right drum, Dha and Dhin are produced on both drums. Ge, Ghe, and Ki are produced only on the left drum.

For different drums' strokes the bols differ, for the sounds they produce are not the same. In example 6-8 the same 12-count tāl structure is given with two sets of bols: chautāl, as played on the pakhāvaj; and ektāl, that same tāl transferred to tablā.

Bols are combined into patterns which can be used in many different contexts. The pattern *tirakita* of four bols, for instance, can be used to fill 4 counts, ♩♩♩♩, or 2 counts, ♫♫, or even 1 count, ♬, depending on the speed at which it is played. It can be combined with other patterns to form longer drumming sequences: *dha* plus *ga ti ra ki ta* as in example 6-9, or *ti ra ki ta ta ka*, or even longer, *dha ti ra ki ta ta ka*.

When put into the framework of a tāl, such sequences are combined with others and manipulated to form compositions. Compositions *khyāl*, one type of vocal performance, singers insist that the drummer restrict his playing to just the theka, or to slight variations on the theka. In accompanying an instrumental soloist, a drummer will play the theka, but he can also match the rhythm of the melody in portions of the performance. That means the contrast between playing one stroke for most counts in the tāl as in the theka and matching whatever rhythmic intricacies the soloist is creating. Also, during an instrumental performance the drummer will be given the nod to play a brief solo; at those moments he may improvise.

Improvisation means to a drummer instantaneous decisions as to which compositions to draw on in a particular musical situation. He

Tīntāl, Tablā bols

x   3   o   3   x
Dha Dhin Dhin Dha Dha Dhin Dhin Dha Dha Tin Tin Ta Ta Dhin Dhin Dha / Dha

EXAMPLE 6-9.

need not be a whole cycle of the tāl: a *mohrā*, for example, is a very brief composition written for only the last half (or less) of a cycle and is therefore used at cadences. Most tablā *gats*, on the other hand, are one or two cycles in length. Some types of compositions act as the basis of variations, so that even if the composition itself is brief, the improvisation on it can be many cycles long.

An example of a simple type of tablā composition is a *theka*. A theka encompasses one cycle (*āvarta*) of a tāl; a student will learn a tāl by learning to play a theka. The two bol sequences in example 6-9 are thekas, the first for chautāl, the second for ektāl.

Perhaps the most familiar theka to Western audiences is that for tīntāl. The most commonly used tāl in Hindustānī music at present, tīntāl can be heard on many recordings and the theka given in example 6-9 is seen spelled out on many record jackets.

Use of a theka varies according to the type of performance a drummer is accompanying. In needs, for instance, to pick a proper one for the number of counts remaining in a tāl cycle if a melodic phrase seems to be leading to a cadence, or to plan a short solo quickly if he is given the opportunity to use a number of cycles to develop one composition fully. At such a time, the soloist will play only the gat melody, providing a melodic background that delineates the tāl cycle. Subtle signals fly from soloist to drummer, as each contributes his part to the improvisation.

One important way to create a cadence is to use a *tihāī*. In tihāī a pattern is played three times in exact repetition, timed to end on sam. The tihāī in example 6-10 fills the second half of a cycle of tīntāl. The pattern is: ┐ *Dha tirakita Dha*.

Structure: Principles of Improvisation

When Westerners attend a concert of classical music, they can anticipate the type of music they will hear. An orchestra concert, for instance, may include a symphony or a tone poem, an overture, or other compositions for large ensemble. If a soloist joins the performance, a concerto probably will be offered. The music heard at a violin or piano or vocal concert will be a different selection. In India, too, different types of concerts include different types of music. In North India all of them will be largely improvisatory.

	Unmetered		*Metered*
Vocal	Ālāp→Nom-tom ālāp——→		Dhrupad
Instrumental	Ālāp→Jor——→Jhālā——→		Gat

In ālāp (more technically rāgālāp), emphasis is solely on melody; through improvisation a musician re-creates as imaginatively as possible

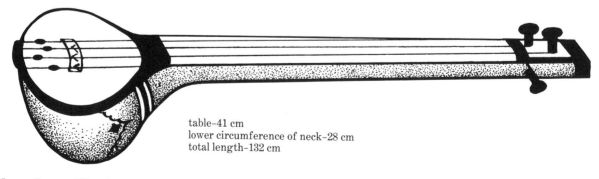

EXAMPLE 6-10.

In genres of music, whether Western or Indian, the musical factors of melody and rhythm are organized in distinctive ways. A Western symphony usually has four movements and might be regarded as a study in musical contrast. Using differing keys, meters, speeds, orchestration, and the like, a composer creates movements with quite different moods. The major selection (*ālāp-jor-jhālā-gat*) in a Hindustānī sitār concert also might be regarded as a study in musical contrast. In this case, the performer (who is at the same moment the composer) creates sections differentiated partially by the relative emphasis on melody or rhythm. An additional contrast is provided in this type of instrumental selection and in one type of vocal selection, ālāp-dhrupad, by the absence or presence of a meter (*tāl*) in the different sections of the performance.

the personality and mood of the rāg chosen. This he does in a traditional way. Singing (on Re, Ne, Ā, or other syllables) or playing very slowly and intensely but in freely floating rhythm, he presents the pitches of the rāg gradually: first those around middle Sa, then others as they fall in the low octave (see ex. 6-11). The pitches, the melodic shape, and other characteristics of the rāg are manipulated as he now begins to climb farther into the middle, up to the high octave. The intent in ālāp is to build a climax on the psychological effect of constantly rising pitch register, realized when Sa of the high octave is attained and sustained.

Further exploration in the high octave provides a release of tension as the focus of the performance is shifted from "pure rāg" in floating rhythm to rāg plus an increasingly pulsating rhythm in the faster second section,

table–41 cm
lower circumference of neck–28 cm
total length–132 cm

NORTH INDIAN TĀMBŪR

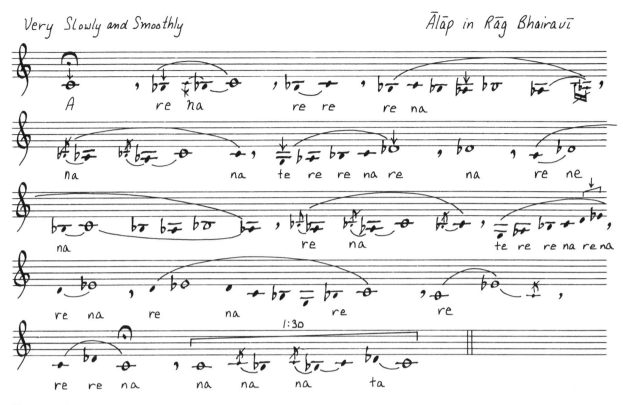

EXAMPLE 6-11.

called *nom-tom-ālāp* in a vocal context and *jor* in an instrumental context.

As nom-tom-ālāp progresses, the rhythm becomes regular, emphasized finally by rapid and constant repetition of pitch Sa. In an instrumental performance this is achieved by constant stroking on the drone strings, and a third section is designated, *jhālā*. A second climax, this one speed- and rhythm-oriented, is built in anticipation of the entrance of the drum and utilization of a meter (tāl).

When a vocal ālāp ends at the height of that climax, a *dhrupad* is begun; an instrumental ālāp will give way to a *gat*. Dhrupad and gat are each a composition in the same rāg as the preceding ālāp, and in a tāl. Improvisation that follows dhrupad and gat is discussed later in the compositions section.

In addition to the progression of focus from melody to rhythm, ālāp displays another princi-ple basic to the Hindustānī classical music tradition, whether in a metered or nonmetered portion of a performance: the use of a single recurring fragment of melody in the manner of a cadence pattern to mark the completion of a musical unit.

The fragment of melody that recurred to mark completion of musical units in one vocal performance is shown in example 6-11, the first one and one-half minutes of an ālāp in Rāg Bhairavī. Arrows indicate pitches when they were first introduced. Note how gently it was exposed that an ascent from Pa (G) that stops on Re (D) is to Reb (Db), but an ascent from Pa that continues up to Gab (Eb) goes through Reꞩ (Dꞩ); and a Sa Re Sa progression must use Reb–Sa Reb Sa. At the end of one and one-half minutes came the fragment (see bracket) that recurred again and again; fresh aspects of Rāg Bhairavī were presented before that fragment was heard again. In the metered portion of a performance such a fragment is designed to fit properly into the tāl and to end on count 1.

Speed

Performance speed (*laya*) is an important issue in Hindustānī classical music; gats, for instance, which bear no name other than their rāg, are referred to as a "slow gat" or a "fast gat." But how slow is slow? How fast is fast? Using the pulse rate as metronome, Indian musicians in ancient times set durations for tāl cycles in levels of speed—slow (*vilambit*), medium (*madhya*), and fast (*drut*). In slow speed, they said,

place in the metered portion of the performance as the rate of the tāl counts picks up. At the beginning of a slow selection, a tāl cycle may take those 29 seconds to a minute, but by the end it will take only 11 to 21 seconds.

Further acceleration takes place when a slow-speed or medium-speed composition is followed without stop by a fast-speed composition in the same rāg. In instrumental performance, for example, slow ālāp, gradually accelerating jor, and jhālā lead into a slow- or medium-speed gat, and that leads to a fast-speed gat.

The speeds stated for ancient times were based on mathematical proportion—24, 12, 6 sec-

EXAMPLE 6-12.

one cycle of 16 counts would take 24 seconds, in medium speed only half that time—12 seconds, and in fast speed 6 seconds.[10] How does this compare with contemporary practice? Slow is slower—29 seconds to a minute for one cycle—but fast is faster—4 to 5 seconds through that cycle.[11]

But slow speed performances in contemporary Hindustānī practice do not remain that slow throughout. Just as acceleration takes place within unmetered ālāp, it continues to take

onds for a cycle of 16 counts. This principle still operates as a favorite means of adding rhythmic variety within an established level of speed. In medium-speed rūpak tāl, for example, it may take 18 seconds to drum the theka through one cycle. Subdividing each count, the theka can be played through two times in those 18 seconds, at double speed (*dugun*). Further subdivision gives

10. According to Ranade (1961:122).
11. Calculations taken in a study of khyāl. Wade (1971: 264-67).

quadruple speed (*chaugun*) in which the theka is played four times in 18 seconds (see ex. 6-12.) This is done with many traditional drumming patterns besides the thekas and is an important musical practice whether drummed or done melodically.

Compositions

Amid this discussion of improvisation and speed, the names of three types of compositions have been interjected frequently—dhrupad,

in two, as is "Balma morī" (ex. 6-1); gats are for the most part even shorter, as in example 6-16. The sections of the dhrupad and khyāl are shown below.

	I	II	III	IV
Dhrupad:	Sthāī	Aṅtarā	Sańchārī	Ābhog
Khyāl:	Sthāī	Aṅtarā		

As short as dhrupads and khyāls are, performers nowadays tend to reduce them. Khyāl singers often present only the sthāī. Dhrupad singers

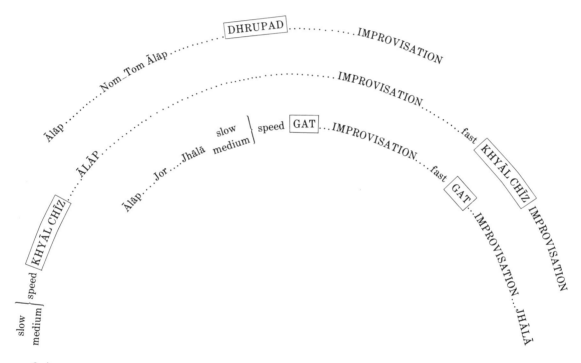

FIGURE 6-4.

khyāl, and gat: dhrupad associated with the pomp and grandeur of the Mogul courts and with the "most correct" way to sing a rāg; khyāl the more romantic and imaginative song relating the tales of Krishna, a Hindu deity, in Muslim courts; and gat, the brief melodies that serve to introduce the tāl into instrumental performances.

Each of these types of composition is a short, metered melody. Dhrupads were composed in four brief sections; khyāl compositions (*chīz*) are

have begun to sing only the sthāī and aṅtarā, as in example 6-13.

Obviously it is not sufficient to play or sing such a brief melody and have done with it. Each of these types of compositions states the rāg and tāl, and in the case of vocal music also presents the text "in a nutshell," then is followed by improvisation of a specific sort. Figure 6-4 shows the position of the metered compositions (see the boxes) within the total performance of a selection. The top arch in figure 6-4 is ālāp-

EXAMPLE 6-13. A full transcription of this dhrupad as performed is found in Wade, *Music in India.*

dhrupad; the middle is khyāl, and the bottom is ālāp-jor-jhālā-gat. The unmetered sections in each genre are in capital letters, the metered portions in small letters.

In chronological order of development, khyāl followed dhrupad and gat came last. Khyāl differs from dhrupad in one distinct way: no unmetered ālāp precedes the composition. An entire khyāl performance is metered since the metered chīz is sung first; ālāp-type improvisation then begins. The events of instrumental performances are a composite of various events

from dhrupad- and khyāl-type performances, as might be expected considering that both those vocal genres were in vogue when instrumental solo music came into its own.

Improvisation in dhrupad is largely rhythmic in orientation, featuring manipulations in double and quadruple speed and manipulations of the text. It is of primary concern in dhrupad to enunciate the text clearly and to keep strictly to the rules of the rāg.

A common complaint directed at khyāl singers, on the other hand, is that they mumble the

EXAMPLE 6-14. Arkār tāns.

EXAMPLE 6-15.

text or choose a few words and repeat them endlessly. Moreover, the improvisation within khyāl includes a type of melodic figuration, *tān*, that is sometimes "more or less true" to the specifications of the rāg as the singer moves rapidly over a series of pitches.

Tāns can be sung on a vowel sound (*akār tān*) or to text (*bol tān*). The shift within the ālāp-type improvisation in slow- or medium-speed khyāl from "rāg in floating rhythm" to "rāg plus more pulsating rhythm" is made through the use of tāns or of *bolbant* (rhythmic play with words). See examples 6-14 and 6-15. Similar types of improvisation occur in instrumental gat performance, as well.

When an instrumental soloist has finished

unmetered ālāp and is ready to begin gat, he starts right out with the melody. Upon first hearing the gat melody the drummer, who has been sitting onstage listening to the ālāp, launches into a brief, fast, virtuosic composition that ends on count 1, and the metered portion of the performance is under way. As shown in example 6-16, a gat melody is likely to be composed

melody and rhythm of the mukhṛā may vary somewhat, but the text, the placement at sam of the long syllable "ī" of "gaī," and the pitch it falls on remain the same.

The role of compositions seems to have become less and less important in Hindustānī music with the passage of time: dhrupads of four sections are reduced to two, khyāls of two sec-

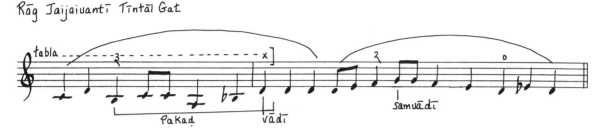

EXAMPLE 6-16.

to begin several counts before count 1, so this meeting at count 1 by melody and drum can be accomplished neatly.

The composition comes back into play during khyāl and gat improvisation either in complete restatements or, as is often the case, only at cadences. That melodic fragment mentioned previously is the beginning phrase of a khyāl chīz or of a gat—those counts leading up to and including count 1. In examples 6-14 and 6-15, "Uchata gaī," that fragment (called *mukhṛā*, "mouth" in khyāl) is marked with brackets. The

tions are reduced to one, and most gats fall into one tāl cycle. The importance of text in relation to music seems to have decreased as well, since in dhrupad the text has to be clear, but in khyāl it is all too often obscure, and it plays no part at all in instrumental music.

The contradiction to the assumptions about compositions is *ṭhumṛī*, the second most popular vocal genre of today. Ṭhumṛī compositions have sthāī and antarā; both sections are sung, repeated, and repeated amid improvisation that stresses not rāg or tāl but text, as the artist

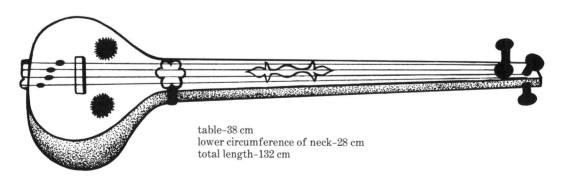

table-38 cm
lower circumference of neck-28 cm
total length-132 cm

SOUTH INDIAN TAMBŪR

seeks to express the feeling in the romantic, lyrical poetry. Ṭhumṛī reflects a popular trend to "light classical" music since its melodies very often lay no claim to being in a rāg.

In pre-Muslim India musical training apparently was widespread among upper-class citizens; because of the reverence for music as a sacred art, it was likely to be part of the education of any cultured individual. To peoples of the invading Muslim cultures, however, music was primarily a form of entertainment, performed by particular groups from lower strata of society. At the Muslim courts these conflicting ideas about music met and a compromise was reached: the practice of the art was to be isolated within families (many of whom converted to Islam)

these innovations—are taking classical music to a larger audience than ever before.

KARNATAK MUSIC

Hindustānī and Karnatak music both stem from the same ancient tradition, and many musical ideas have remained very similar across the centuries. They share the concept of rāgas with their groups of characteristics, and of tāla as a metric framework undergirding compositions and improvisation. They also share the delight in structural juxtaposition of fixed and improvised. But how they use these concepts in making music and how they organize the musical detail are quite different.

Pitch selection is a primary factor in distin-

Rāga Shrī

EXAMPLE 6-17.

who devoted themselves to performing and teaching, yet maintaining the Hindu respect for music as an act of worship. A style of playing or singing, a repertoire played or sung, became associated with a family of musicians (*gharānā*) and those few individuals accepted from outside the family to study the tradition. Thus, for centuries in North India the study of music among Muslims has been a family affair.

Later, the European attitude toward Indian culture did nothing to uplift music in the eyes of upper-class Indians over whom they ruled. Had it not been for a few princes who continued the tradition of royal courts patronizing the arts, much of India's precious musical heritage would have been lost. Not until the early decades of this century, during the Independence Movement, did wealthy Indians again begin to patronize their music, and to study it themselves.

The family traditions still remain strong. But the introduction of music courses into universities, radio broadcasts, public concerts—all of

guishing Karnatak rāgas from one another. It is less likely that two Karnatak rāgas would have the same selection of pitches as two Hindustānī rāgs. Thus, less weight is put on such aspects as special ornamentation or melodic shape for distinguishing rāgas. That is not to say that melodic shape is unimportant for some Karnatak rāgas. Ascent and descent patterns may differ, and rāgas in which pitches are to be performed in nonscalar order are designated *vakra* (crooked). Rāga Shrī in example 6-17 demonstrates both these instances. In addition, characteristic melodic motives (such as pakaḍ in Hindustānī music) occur in some Karnatak rāgas, but that idea has not been exploited in the southern system.

Other distinctions can be drawn between Hindustānī and Karnatak rāgas. Ornamentation is used more profusely in Karnatak music. It is often vital as an element of performance practice for a particular rāga rather than as a distinguishing detail in the structure of a particular rāga. In addition to specifying that two pitches in a rāga must be joined with a slur because that is part of what makes it that rāga, for example, descriptions of some rāgas state that every pitch can be performed with a certain kind of ornament. The association of pitch selection with moods and with performance time has not been carried through with as much enthusiasm in the southern tradition.

A major difference between the Karnatak and Hindustānī systems is that a great deal more attention is paid to classification in the southern tradition. In North India various systems of classifying (grouping) the hundreds of rāgs have been suggested; the prevalent but by no means universally accepted one is musicologist Bhatkhande's list (1963) of 10 *thāṭs* (melody types).[12] In contrast, the Karnatak *melakarta* system details 72 *mela*s (melody types); each possible combination of the pitches used in the melodic system becomes a mela, whether or not there are actually rāgas in use that include that selection of pitches. It is a system derived from theory rather than from performance practice.[13]

The Karnatak delight in classifying has been applied to their tāla system as well; indeed, the system is conducive to it. Cycles are subdivided as they are in Hindustānī tāls, but subdivisions are of three specific types:

(*a*) 1 count   anudruta   notated ×
(*b*) 2 counts   druta   notated 0
(*c*) 3, 4, 5   laghu   notated |³, |⁴, | ⁵, |⁷, |⁹
     7, 9 counts

The number of counts in laghu depends on the particular tāla, and that number is mentioned in the tāla name. For example,

Jhampa tāla	| × 0
	| + 1 + 2 = 4 counts
Jhampa tāla tisra (3) jāti	|³ × 0
	3 + 1 + 2 = 6 counts
Jhampa tāla khaṇḍa (5) jāti	|⁵ × 0
	5 + 1 + 2 = 8 counts.

12. See Jairazbhoy, *The Rāgs of North Indian Music* (1971) and Kaufmann, *The Ragas of North India* (1968) particularly.

13. For details of the system, see Sambamoorthy, *South Indian Music.* Information is scattered throughout all five volumes.

South Indian audiences keep the tāla much more noticeably than Hindustānī audiences. Their traditional motions are also clap, wave, and finger counts.

anudruta	X	clap
druta	0	clap, wave
laghu	|	clap plus the appropriate number of finger counts

Triputa tāla chaturasra (4) jāti, otherwise known as *Adi tāla*, is the most commonly used Karnatak tala at present; it is counted out in figure 6-5. Adi tāla 1⁴ 0 0 is 4 + 2 + 2, a cycle of 8 counts.

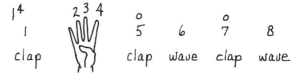

FIGURE 6-5

Use of the tāla and the approach to speed differ somewhat in Karnatak and Hindustānī music. Count 1 of a tāla cycle is not as prominent in Karnatak practice. Cadences are formed by repetition of a melodic phrase that falls consistently at the same place in the tāla cycle, but without consistent emphasis on count 1 as a point of finality. Acceleration of the rate of tāla counts *is not permissible*; increase of speed is achieved by increase in rhythmic density-doubling, tripling, quadrupling, and the like. Since the audience is keeping tāla, any acceleration will be immediately noticeable. There are three levels of speed, that is, basic rates of tāla counts: slow, medium, and fast. Table 6-1 shows comparative terminology in the rhythmic systems of the two musical cultures.

A variety of percussion instruments is used in Karnatak classical music to keep the tāla and develop rhythm, including *ghatam*, a clay pot, and *kanjīra*, a tambourine-type instrument, both of which are supplementary to the *mridangam*, a double-headed cylindrical wooden drum, with heads tuned by means of paste and by tension of the lacing that holds the head on.

Since the eighteenth century Karnatak clas-

TABLE 6-1.

	Karnatak	Hindustānī
One cycle of the tāla	āvarta	āvarta
A subdivision of the āvarta	anga	vibhāg
Types of anga:		
One count	anudruta	
Two counts	druta	
Variable finger counts	laghu	
Type of laghu	jāti	
Stressed counts marking beginning of vibhāg		tāli
Nonstressed counts marking beginning of vibhāg		khālī
A single count	akshara	mātra
Hand motions to "keep tāla"	krīya	krīya
Speed	kāla	laya
Slow	vilamba	vilambit
Medium	madhya	madhya
Fast	druta	drut

sical music has consisted of two types of performances: (1) improvisation-oriented performances such as the *rāgam tānam-pallavi*, which are similar to the Hindustānī ālāp-nom-tom-ālāp-dhrupad or ālāp-jor-jhālā-gat; and (2) traditional composition-oriented performances of *kriti* and of dance-related genres.

The close relationship between dance music and concert music is another major distinction between the Karnatak and Hindustānī cultures. In Hindu Indian thought, dancing, like music making, has been considered an act of worship. Did not Lord Shiva Nataraj create life in lifeless matter through the rhythm of his cosmic dance? The Muslim culture's idea of the servant dancing girl forced a revised attitude toward dance in the courts of Hindustan, but in South India Hindu traditions continued without much severe interference. Accordingly, much of Karnatak classical music remains prominently associated with the dance; *varnam, padam, tillānā*, and other genres accompany Bharata Natyam, the premier classical dance style of all of India, and are heard in musical concert versions, as well.[14]

14. The four primary classical dance styles of India are Bharata Natyam and Kathakali of the south, Kathak and Manipuri of the north. Bharata Natyam conforms most closely to the ancient tradition described in the *Nātya Śāstra* (Treatise on Dramaturgy).

The performance practice principle of one melody, a drone, and percussion is maintained in South India as well as in North India. The drone is kept usually by a tāmbūra, which differs slightly in construction from the northern type. For melody making the voice and vocal genres occupy the premier place. Vocal melody is usually supported by a Western violin—the playing technique and position and the tuning of the violin have been adapted to the Karnatak musical style. The primary solo instruments are flute and vīnā, the latter a plucked-type instrument.

Karnatak classical music remains a vehicle for the expression of personal religious devotion—to Krishna, to Rama, repeating the names of the Lord. The text below is a kriti, composed by South India's most revered composer, Tyagaraja.[15]

Nive Nanneda Jesita
Rāga Sourastra   Tyagaraja

Pallavi: If, knowing my mind, you yourself abandon me, to whom shall I complain?

Anu-Pallavi: I have worshipped you thinking that my desires will be fulfilled, and you harass me; it is not proper; what is my crime? You protect me, now and here.

Charana: I have been attracted to you [Lord Rama], knowing that the Lord Siva himself has been constantly praising that devotion to Rama is the best type of devotion and seeing that true devotees are all in rapture over your Sakti. I have taken a resolve always to keep the company of the good and the pious and chant Thy holy name.

[Ramanujachari and Raghavan: 234-35]

Kriti is by far the most prominent Karnatak genre today. It is a vocal style easily adapted for instrumental performance. No comparable performance genre exists within the Hindustānī tradition. But most important is its availability to amateur musicians, for some kritis can be sung singly or in a group, without improvisation or with a few learned variations. Other kritis, of course, are difficult compositions that an artist will want to sing with lengthy and imaginative improvisation. Like the dhrupad and khyāl of Hindustānī tradition, these can only be mastered by performers with extensive training.

15. Pallavi, anu-pallavi, and charana are the three sections of a kriti.

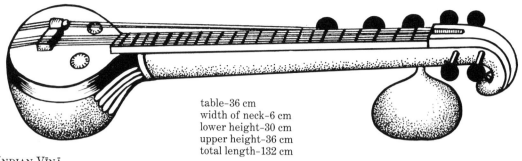

table-36 cm
width of neck-6 cm
lower height-30 cm
upper height-36 cm
total length-132 cm

SOUTH INDIAN VĪṆĀ

This brief overview of a few distinctions between Karnatak and Hindustānī musics by no means does justice to the Karnatak tradition. Nor, in fact, can so short an essay definitively describe the Hindustānī tradition. As many an Indian scholar would say, we have had but a glimpse, and I agree, for the two traditions are complex, extremely old, but vital to the present, and the treasure of their cultures.

Glossary

ālāp-improvised melody presenting the structure and mood of a particular *rāga*; see also *rāgam*.

āroha-"ascent"; ascending succession of pitches.

avroha-"descent"; descending succession of pitches.

bol-in drumming, the euphonic syllable for a particular stroke; in song, the entire text or one word.

chīz-"a thing; song" (Urdu); a song with two sections—*sthāī* and *antarā*—on which a *khyāl* performance is based (Hindustānī).

dhrupad (dhruvapada)-a song with sections—*sthāī*, *antarā*, *sanchārī*, *ābhog*—on which improvisation is based; a genre of Hindustānī vocal music; preceded by a lengthy *ālāp*.

gamak-melodic "ornament" (Hindustānī).

gat-an instrumental composition from one to sixteen *tāl* cycles long from which improvisation is done (Hindustānī).

gharānā-a group of musicians largely from one family, with a distinctive tradition (Hindustānī).

jhālā-portion in an instrumental performance when constant rapid stroking on pitch Sa creates regular rhythmic pulsation.

jor-portion of instrumental *ālāp* when rhythm becomes more regular and speed increases (Hindustānī).

khyāl-vocal genre consisting of a brief composition (*chīz*) of two sections and extensive improvisation in its *rāg* and *tāl* (Hindustānī).

kriti (kṛti)-vocal genre consisting of a composition of three sections—*pallavi*, *anu-pallavi*, and *charanam*—and usually improvisation on it.

madhya/madhyam-"middle, medium"; level of speed (Hindustānī and Karnatak).

mandra-"low"; specifies pitch register.

meend (mīnd)-a "pulling slur" (down). (Hindustānī)

mela-a melody type (Karnatak).

mukhṛā-"mouth"; the initial phrase of melody and text in *khyāl chīz* (Hindustānī).

nom-tom ālāp-the second portion of a vocal *ālāp* (usually pre-*dhrupad*), when rhythm becomes more regular, then pulsating, and speed increases (Hindustānī).

pakaḍ-a short melodic (and rhythmic) motive associated with one particular *rāg* (Hindustānī).

pallavi-vocal and instrumental genre usually of *rāgam-tānam-pallavi* succession, consisting of a line extracted from a *kriti* or other composition or newly composed, and improvisation in its *rāga* and *tāla* (Karnatak).

rāgam-unmetered *ālāp* (Karnatak); also called *ālāpana*.

rasa-the classical Indian theory of aesthetic bliss; in a shallower sense "mood," here specifically associated with *rāg* theory (Hindustānī).

sam-count 1 of a *tāl* cycle functioning as the final count of a phrase (Hindustānī).

samvādī-theoretically one of the two most important structural pitches in a *rāg* (Hindustānī).

saptak-"an aggregate of seven things"; in music commonly translated as "octave."

sargam-term for solfège syllables (Hindustānī).

svara-pitch, tone; vowel.

tān-a moderately or fast moving improvised melodic passage (Hindustānī).

tānam-the second portion of a vocal or instrumental *ālāp*, when rhythmic pulsation begins to be regular (Karnatak).

tār-string of a musical instrument; "high" pitch register.

ṭhāṭ-melody type (Hindustānī); setting for sitār frets.

theka-a simple tabla composition one cycle long that is associated with a particular tāl (Hindustānī).

ṭhumrī-light classical vocal genre featuring romantic texts; often performed instrumentally (Hindustānī).

tihāī-in drumming, a pattern of strokes repeated exactly three times in succession and calculated to end on *sam*; in vocal music also, but the repetitions are less precise (Hindustānī).

tillānā-vocal genre essentially rhythmic in nature (Karnatak); for Bharata Natyam accompaniment; drum syllables provide the text and passages correspond with footwork; in concert tillānā drum syllables, solfège, and poetry are used as text.

vādī-theoretically the most important structural pitch in a rāg (Hindustānī).

vakra-"crooked"; designation for rāgas whose pitches should not be performed in scalar order (Karnatak).

varnam-a lively vocal or instrumental genre that presents the full scope of a rāga and tāla in two speeds; for concert or dance (Karnatak).

Bibliography

Aesthetics and the Arts

Coomaraswamy, Ananda K.
1965. *History of Indian and Indonesian Art*. New York: Dover Publications.
1968. *The Dance of Shiva*. Revised ed. New Delhi: Sagar Publications.

De, S. K.
1963. *Sanskrit Poetics as a Study in Aesthetic*. Berkeley and Los Angeles: University of California Press.

Gangoly, O.C.
1935. *Ragas and Raginis: A Pictorial and Iconographic Study of Indian Musical Modes Based on Original Sources*. Vol. 1: Text. Bombay: Nalanda Publications.

Gargi, Balwant.
1962. *Theater in India*. New York: Theater Arts Books.
1966. *Folk Theater of India*. Seattle: University of Washington Press.

Ghosh, Manumohan, trans.
1967. *Nātya Śāstra*, 2 vols., 2d rev. ed. Chapters 1-27. Calcutta: Granthalaya Private.

Jones, Clifford, and Betty True.
1970. *Kathakali: An Introduction to the Dance Drama of Kerala*. Los Angeles: American Society for Eastern Arts and Theatre Arts Books.

Keith, Arthur B.
1924. *The Sanskrit Drama*. Oxford: Clarendon Press.

Kramrisch, Stella.
1954. *The Art of India Through the Ages*. New York: Phaidon Press.

Stooke, Herbert J., and Karl Khandalavala.
1953. *The Laud Ragamala Miniatures: A study in Indian Painting and Music*. Oxford: Cassirer.

Zimmer, Heinrich Robert.
1955. *The Art of Indian Asia: Its Mythology and Transformations*. 2 vols. Edited by Joseph Campbell. New York: Pantheon Books.

Anthropology

Beals, Alan.
1962. *Gopalpur: A South Indian Village*. New York: Holt, Rinehart, and Winston.

Lewis, Oscar.
1958. *Village Life in Northern India: Studies in a Delhi Village*. Urbana: University of Illinois Press.

Mandelbaum, David.
1972. *Systems of Society in India*. Vol. 1: *Change and Continuity*. Vol. 2: *Continuity and Change*. Berkeley, Los Angeles, London: University of California Press.

Nair, Kusum, ed.
1961. *Blossoms in the Dust: The Human Factor in Indian Development*. New York: Praeger.

Srinivas, M. N.
1962. *Caste in Modern India and Other Essays*. Bombay and New York: Asia Publishing House.

Wiser, William, and Charlotte Wiser.
1963. *Behind Mud Walls—With a Sequel*. 2d rev. ed. Berkeley and Los Angeles: University of California Press.

Bibliography

Barnett, Elise.
   1970. "Special Bibliography: Art Music of India." *Ethnomusicology* 14 (May), 278-312.
Mahar, J. Michael.
   1964. *India: A Critical Bibliography.* Tucson: University of Arizona Press.
Powers, Harold.
   1965. "Indian Music and the English Language: A Review Essay." *Ethnomusicology* 9 (January), 1-12.
Van Zile, Judy.
   1973. *Dance in India: An Annotated Guide to Source Materials.* Providence, R.I.: Asian Publications.

Biography

Brecher, Michael.
   1959. *Nehru: A Political Biography.* Abridged ed. Boston: Beacon Press.
Chakravarty, Amiya, ed.
   1966. *A Tagore Reader.* Boston: Beacon Press.
Gandhi, Mohandas K.
   1957. *An Autobiography: The Story of My Experiments with Truth.* Boston: Beacon Press.
Raghavan, V.
   1966. *The Great Integrators: The Saint-Singers of India.* New Delhi: Publications Division, Ministry of Information and Broadcasting, Government of India.
Ramanujachari, C., and V. Raghavan.
   1966. *The Spiritual Heritage of Tyāgarājā.* 2d ed. Madras: Sri Ramakrishna Math.
Tiwari, Parasnath.
   1967. *Kabir.* Translated by J. P. Uniyal. New Delhi: National Book Trust, India.

History

Abul Fazl-i-'Allami.
   1948. *Ain-i-Akbari.* Translated from Persian to English by Colonel H. S. Jarrett, first published in 1893-96. Revised and annotated by Jadu Nath Sarkar. Calcutta: Royal Asiatic Society of Bengal.
Ahmad, Aziz.
   1969. *An Intellectual History of Islam in India.* Edinburgh: Edinburgh University Press.
Basham, Arthur L.
   1959. *The Wonder That Was India.* New York: Grove Press.
deBary, William Theodore, ed.
   1958. *Sources of Indian Tradition.* 2 vols. New York: Columbia University Press.
Manucci, Niccolao.
   1907. *Storia do Mogor (Or Mugul India 1653-1708).* Translated and with notes by William Irvine. 4 vols. London: John Murray.
Spear, Percival.
   1972. *India, A Modern History.* Revised ed. Ann Arbor: University of Michigan Press.
Wolpert, Stanley.
   1965. *India.* Englewood Cliffs: Prentice-Hall.

Literature

Brough, John, trans.
   1968. *Poems from the Sanskrit.* Baltimore: Penguin Books.
Dimock, Edward C.
   1963. *The Thief of Love: Bengali Tales from Court and Village.* Chicago: University of Chicago Press.
   1967. *In Praise of Krishna: Songs from the Bengali.* New York: Anchor Books.
Dutt, Romesh C.
   1972. *The Ramayana and The Mahabharata.* New York: Dutton.
Gokhale, Aravind.
   1957. *The Unmarried Widow and Other Stories.* Translated by S. Pradhan. Bombay: Jaico Publishing.
Madgulkar, Vyankatesh.
   1958. *The Village Had No Walls.* Translated by Ram Deshmukh. Bombay: Asia Publishing House.
Markayanda, Kamala.
   n.d. *Nectar in a Sieve.* New York: Avon.
Narayan, R. K.
   1971. *The Vendor of Sweets.* New York: Avon Books. (And many other Narayan novels.)
Prem Chand.
   1968. *Godan.* Translated by Jai Ratan and P. Lal. 2d ed. Bombay: Jaico Publishing House.
Ryder, Arthur.
   1959. *Shakuntala and Other Writings by Kalidasa.* New York: Dutton.
Ryder, Arthur, trans.
   1964. *The Panchatantra.* Chicago: Phoenix Books.
Tagore, Rabindranath, trans., and Evelyn Underhill.
   1967. *One Hundred Poems of Kabir.* London: Macmillan.
Van Buitenen, J. A. B.
   1961. *Tales of Ancient India.* New York: Bantam Books.

Music

Bhatkhande, Vishnu Narayan.
1963. *Kramik Pustak Mālikā*. 2d ed. Edited by L. N. Garg. Hathras: Sangit Karyalaya.

Bhattacharya, Sudhi Bushan.
1968. *Ethnomusicology and India*. Calcutta: Indian Publications.

Brown, Robert E.
1965. "The Mrdanga: A Study of Drumming in South India." 2 vols. Ph.D. dissertation, University of California, Los Angeles. (Ann Arbor: University Microfilms, 1974).
1971. "India's Music." In *Readings in Ethnomusicology*, edited by David P. McAllester, pp. 293–329. New York: Johnson Reprint Corporation.

Clements, Ernest.
1960, 1967. *Introduction to the Study of Indian Music* (reprint). Allahabad: Kitab Mahal.

Daniélou, Alain.
1968. *The Ragas of Northern Indian Music*. London: Barrie & Rockliff, the Cresset Publisher.

Day, Charles Russell.
1891. *The Music and Musical Instruments of Southern India and the Deccan*. Introduction by A. J. Hipkins. Reprinted. Delhi: B. R. Publishing Corporation, 1974.

Deva, B. Chaitanya.
1967. *Psychoacoustics of Music and Speech*. Madras: The Music Academy.

Fox Strangways, A. H.
1914. *The Music of Hindostan*. Reprinted. Oxford: Clarendon Press, 1965.

Gosvami, O.
1957. *The Story of Indian Music*. Bombay: Asia Publishing House.

Jairazbhoy, Nazir.
1961. "Svaraprastara in North Indian Classical Music." *Bulletin, School of Oriental and African Studies* (London), 24, pt. 2, 307–25.
1971. *The Rāgs of North Indian Music: Their Structure and Evolution*. London: Faber and Faber. Middletown, Conn.: Wesleyan University Press.

Joshi, Baburao, and Antsher Lobo.
1965. *Introducing Indian Music*. Bombay: Bhatkal Books International. Book and four records.

Kaufmann, Walter.
1965. "Rasa, Raga-Mala, and Performance Times in North Indian Ragas." *Ethnomusicology* 9 (September), 272–91.
1968. *The Ragas of North India*. Bloomington, Indiana: Indiana University Press.

Kothari, K. S.
1968. *Indian Folk Musical Instruments*. New Delhi: Sangeet Natak Akademi.

Krishnaswamy, S.
1965. *Musical Instruments of India*. New Delhi: Publications Division, Ministry of Information and Broadcasting.

Powers, Harold.
1970. "An historical and comparative approach to the classification of ragas (with an appendix on ancient Indian tunings)." *Selected Reports* 1:12–78. Los Angeles: Institute of Ethnomusicology, University of California.

Prajnananda, A.
1965. *A Historical Study of Indian Music*. Calcutta: Anandadhara Prakasharan.

Ranade, G. H.
1961. "Some Thoughts About the Laya-Aspect of Modern Music." In *Commemoration Volume in Honour of Dr. S. N. Ratanjankar*, pp. 121–23. Bombay: K. G. Ginde.

Sambamoorthy, P.
1958–1969. *South Indian Music*. 6 vols. Madras: The Indian Music Publishing House.

Shankar, Ravi.
1968. *My Music, My Life*. New York: Simon and Schuster.

Sharma, Bhagvat Sharan, and Ravi Shankar.
1966. *Sitār Mālikā*. Hathras: Sangit Karyalaya.

Wade, Bonnie.
1971. "Khyāl: A Study in Hindustānī Classical Vocal Music." 2 vols. Ph.D. dissertation, University of California, Los Angeles. (Available from University Microfilms, Ann Arbor, Michigan.)
1973. "Chīz in Khyāl: The Traditional Composition in the Improvised Performance." *Ethnomusicology* 17 (September), 443–59.
1979. *Music in India: The Classical Traditions*. Englewood Cliffs: Prentice-Hall.
1980. "India: Folk Music." *Groves Dictionary of Music and Musicians*. 6th ed. London: Macmillan.

Willard, Captain N. Augustus.
1965. "A Treatise on the Music of Hindoostan." In *Hindu Music from Various Authors*, compiled by Raja Sir Sourindro Mohun Tagore, pp. 1–122. Benares: Chowkhamba Sanskrit Series Office.

Discography

This listing is arranged in the order in which the topics were discussed. If an item is cross-listed, the company number only is given after first mention.

HINDUSTĀNĪ MUSIC

Sitār
Khansahib Rais Khan. Odeon MOCE 1087.
Nikhil Banerjee. Odeon SMOAE 155.
Ravi Shankar: Three Ragas. World Pacific WPS 21438.
Sound of the Sitar: Ravi Shankar. World Pacific WPS 21434.
Ustad Ghulam Hussain Khan. Vogue Disques CLVLX 260.
Ustad Halim Jaffar Khan. Odeon MOCE 1056.
Ustad Vilayat Khan. Odeon MOAE 169 and MOAE 153.

Sarod
Sharan Rani. Odeon MOCE 1070, 1039.
Sharan Rani. Vogue Disques CLVLX 119.
Kālpana/Improvisations. Nonesuch H 72022. Mrinal Gupta.
Ustad Ali Akbar Khan. Odeon SMOAE 141, 168, 179. MOAE 130, 145, 146, 125.
Ustad Ali Akbar Khan: Master Musician of India. Connoisseur Society CM 462.
Ustad Ali Akbar Khan: Morning and Evening Ragas. Connoisseur Society CS 1766.
Ustad Ali Akbar Khan: Pre-dawn to Sunset Ragas. CS 1967.

Sāraṅgī
Beat and Bow: Ramnarain and Chatur Lal. Odeon MOAE 174.
Pandit Ramnarain. Odeon SMOAE 183.
Sarangi: The Voice of a Hundred Colors. Nonesuch H72030. Ram Narayan [Narain].

Shenai
Shenai Nawaz Bismillah Khan. Odeon MOAE 128, 170, 166.

Flute
Flute Recital by Hariprasad Chaurasia. Odeon SMOCE 1152.
Himangshu Biswas. Odeon SMOCE 1068.
Vijay Raghavrao. Odeon MOCE 1089.

Rāg Bāgeshrī
Indraneel Bhattacharya, Sitar. Odeon SMOCE 1170.
Shenai Nawaz Bismillah Khan. Odeon MOAE 128.

Tīntāl
Drums of North and South India. World Pacific WPS 21437. Kanai Dutta, tabla. Bols spoken and tāl clapped.
Indian Drums. Connoisseur Society CM 1466. Mahapurush Misra.

Ektāl
(see under *Tīntāl* above)
World Pacific WPS 21437. Chatur Lal.

Dhrupad
Dagar Brothers: Nasir Zahiruddin and Nasir Faiyazuddin. Odeon SMOAE 181.
India III: Dhrupad. Bärenreiter BM 30 L 2018. Mohinuddin and Aminuddin Dagar.
North India: Vocal Music Dhrupad and Khyāl. Philips 6586 003. Mohinuddin and Aminuddin Dagar.

Ālāp-jor-jhālā-gat
See sitār, sarod, flute recordings.

Rāg Bhairav
Shenai Nawaz Bismillah Khan. Odeon MOAE 151.

Khyāl
Amir Khan. Odeon MOAE 103, and SMOAE 180.
Bhimsen Joshi. Odeon MOCE 1029 and MOAE 129. Accompanied by harmonium.
Hirabai Barodekar. Odeon MOCE 1050.
Pandit Omkarnath Thakur. Odeon MOAE 139.
North India: Vocal Music Dhrupad and Khyāl. Philips 6586 003. Robin Kumar Chatterjee.
Ustad Bade Ghulam Ali Khan. Odeon MOAE 105, MOAE 137.
Ustad Niaz Ahmed Khan and Ustad Fayyaz Ahmed Khan. Odeon MOCE 1058.

Ṭhumrī
Begum Akhtar: Thumris and Dadras. Odeon SMOCE 1147.
Khan Sahib Abdul Karim Khan. Odeon MOAE 165.
Nirmala Devi and Lakshmi Shankar. Odeon MOCE 1085 and MOCE 1084.
Padma Bhooshan Ustad Bade Ghulam Ali Khan. Odeon MOAE 5005.
Ustad Faiyaz Khan Sahib. Odeon MOAE 131.

KARNATAK MUSIC

Rāga Shrī
India IV: Karnatic Music. Bärenreiter BM 30 L 2021 (A Musical Anthology of the Orient, UNESCO Collection). In pancharāgam, vīna.

Adi Tāla
Bhāvālu/Impressions: South Indian Instrumental Music. Nonesuch H 72019. Palghat Raghu.

Bharata Natyam
India II: Music of the Dance and Theater of South India. Bärenreiter BM 30 L 2007.
Vyjayanthimala: Bharata Natya Dance Music. Odeon SM CE 2005.

Rāgam-tānam-pallavi
Ramnad Krishnan: Vidwan. Nonesuch H 72023. Vocal.

Kriti
Dhyānam/Meditation. Nonesuch H 72018. K. V. Narayanaswamy. Vocal.
Bhāvālu/Impressions. Nonesuch H 72019. Instrumental. K. V. Narayanaswamy. Vocal.
Sounds of Subbalakshmi. World Pacific WPS 21440. Vocal.

Films

A Bridge in Music. CF/MH. B&W. 20 min.
    Yehudi Menuhin compares Eastern and Western music, with emphasis on the music of India.
Aparajito. AB. B&W. 108 min.
    One of *The Apu Trilogy* directed by Satyajit Ray. Music composed and played by Ravi Shankar.
Bharata Natyam. Todd. Col. 10 min.
Bismillah Khan. UC. B&W. 29 min.
    A study of the playing and lifestyle of a famous *shehnai* player, a native of Benares. Includes much music, a demonstration of learning to play by rote, and glimpses of Benares and its culture.
Classical Music of North India. UWP. Col. 33 min.
    Features Ali Akbar Khan playing sarod, Pandit Mahapurush Misra on tabla.
Discovering the Music of India. BFA. Col. 22 min.
    Made under the auspices of the American Society for Eastern Arts and Wesleyan University; T. Viswanathan, advisor. A discussion of the structure of Indian music. Presents Karnatak and Hindustānī music separately, introducing instruments and music typical of each. A dance with explanation of the hand gestures is presented. Study Guide included.
Fifty Miles from Poona [village in India]. CF/MH. B&W. 20 min.
    "A classic of its kind. Patterns of village life centering on a Marathi farmer's family. A straightforward presentation providing many insights into Indian rural life. Authentic background music. Accented narration a bit difficult to understand at times." Wallace Thompson.
God with a Green Face. ASEA. Col. 25 min.
    "India's most famous dance-drama performed by the celebrated Kerala Kalamandalam Kathakali troupe." Wallace Thompson.
Kathak. Todd. B&W. 10 min.
    "One of the major dance techniques of India, Kathak features rapid footwork and subtle rhythmic nuances, and is the product of a mingling of Hindu and Muslim cultures. . . . A number of the hand gestures, called mudras, are demonstrated." Allegra Fuller Snyder.
Kathakali. ASEA. Col. 22 min.
    "A portrayal of India's most famous theater tradition in relation to Kerala," on India's southwest coast. Begins with scenes of daily life, and portrays the vigorous training of the dancers, the intricate art of makeup, and actual performances of the dances.
Lord Shiva Danced. GI. B&W. 24 min.
    "Ram Gopal and company, with Shevanti, in one of the great ethnic dance documentaries. Six dances illustrate the major dance techniques of India. One of the highlights of the film is the appearance of Gopal's aged guru, Chandupanikar, in a Kathakali dance depicting a jungle fight between an elephant, a cobra, and a tiger." Allegra Fuller Snyder.
Martial Dances of Malabar. Petroleum Films Bureau. B&W. 21 min.
    "The film includes the 'velakali' (battle dance with swords and shields) accompanied by cymbals and drum. A village 'gurukal' (teacher) is shown teaching children this ancient art. The film culminates in the 'velakah' dance accompanied by drums and 'shehnai.'" Peter Kennedy.
Musical Instruments of India. GI. B&W. 10 min.
Music of India. GI. B&W. 11 min.
    "An introduction to the music of North India featuring Ravi Shankar, sitar; Ali Akbar Khan, sarod; Ram Nayaran, sarangi; and Mohammed Khan, vina." ASEA Film Rental List.
Music of India (drums). GI. B&W. 12 min.
The Music Room. AB. B&W. 95 min. Directed by Satyajit Ray.
    Adapted as a screenplay by Ray from the novel *Tarashankar Banerjee.* A melancholy picture "of colonial days when maharajahs and British potentates moved in an atmosphere of luxury and cultural isolation." Much use of Indian music.

Pather Panchali ("The Song of the Road") (part of the *Apu Trilogy*). AB. B&W. 112 min.

"Life in rural Bengal." Karl Heider.

The Sword and the Flute. FI. UCLA. Col. 23 min. James Ivory, producer.

A sequence of sixteenth-century Mogul and Rajput paintings depict the court life of the Mogul emperor Akbar and tell the legend of Krishna and Radha. Background music by Ali Akbar Khan, Ravi Shankar, I. Vishwanathan, and others.

Undala. CMC. Col. 28 min.

"*Undala* is the name of the hot, windy months that precede the relief of monsoon rains in India. This film portrays the varied movements and rhythms of life in a small Hindu village that borders on the Thar desert in northwest India (Rajastan) during that season. For the farmer it is a time of leisure and repair, for women endless water-bearing, and for craftsmen little change in their daily routine. The activities shown are pot-terymaking, spinning, leatherwork, ropemaking and the all-important task of drawing water. The diffuse lighting of dust-laden air, the dynamic patterns of people at work make *Undala* a unique viewing experience. There is no narration, and the original music score is in the Hindustani classical and folk styles." C.M.C.

The World of Apu (Apur Sansar) (part of the *Apu Trilogy*). AB. B&W. 103 min.

"Apu's manhood—his life as a writer in Calcutta, marriage and his relationship to his son." K.H.

K.H.-Reviewed in *Films for Anthropological Teaching* by Karl Heider.

P.K.-Reviewed in UNESCO *Film Catalogue* by Peter Kennedy.

A.F.S.-Reviewed by Allegra Fuller Snyder in *Dance Magazine*, vol. 43, no. 4 (April 1969).

W.T.-Reviewed by Wallace Thompson in *Teaching About Asia*.

7. Musical Strata in Sumatra, Java, and Bali

Margaret J. Kartomi

Among the fascinations of the Indonesian musical world are the wealth and diversity of musical styles, objects, and functions, both within and among Indonesia's many regions. Geographical, religious, and historical factors have prevented the growth of any one single homogenous Indonesian style, or even one single regional style; at first acquaintance the islands present a seemingly bewildering array of musical forms, with a large number of local variants.

This variation is partly the result of the geographical isolation of some areas, especially in the mountainous interiors, and is attributable to the fact that the musical culture of each region may be said (to use a geological metaphor) to consist of a number of strata, distinguishable from one another by the predominant religious and cultural characteristics that color the musical styles of each layer. Art forms belonging to a very old stratum coexist throughout the archipelago with more recent ones, the old forms remaining viable entities because they still have functional and aesthetic meaning in society. In some cases, the weathering of time has resulted in a mixing of certain strata, as in the case of the art forms associated with the Javanese religion (*agama Jawa*), which consists primarily of a synthesis of so-called animist, Hindu, and Buddhist layers of thought. In the case of some other art forms, the elements of one stratum are clearly much stronger than the elements of any other. This is especially true of some of the Muslim and Christian art forms in Indonesia.

Their diversity will be illustrated in this essay by examining the musical scene in a few of Indonesia's regions. I shall consider parts of three of the most populous islands in the western half of the archipelago—Sumatra, Java, and Bali—and shall attempt to pinpoint the various musical strata in each area and the traits that the areas have in common.

These common traits are not as immediately obvious as the dissimilarities, but all the regions have similar linguistic and social traditions and shared experiences in history. All have common, basic, religio-artistic attitudes at certain levels, as well as similar musical instruments, ensembles, and vocal forms. There is a common preference for communal living and music making. The traditional music, dance, theater, and religious ritual still constitute an indivisible concept of unity in some parts, especially in rural inland areas of the three islands. And the ubiquitous presence of such instruments as gongs, kettles, bamboo flutes, and two-headed drums lends a unity to the diversity.

A basic element of cultural unity among the three islands is the fact that each still preserves, to varying degrees, an animist artistic stratum[1] of spirit and ancestor worship and veneration of fertility deities, a tradition presumably predating periods of substantial foreign contact. In addition, the inhabitants of the coastal areas of the islands have possibly been in some kind of contact with one another and the outside world for more than two millennia. Similar religious and cultural influences have been brought to bear on the islands through commercial and political contact with China, mainland Southeast Asia, India, the Middle East, and, in the last five centuries, Europe. The most durable of these

1. This pre-Hindu stratum may itself consist of various substrata that we are unable to distinguish because of our comparative ignorance of ancient Indonesian history.

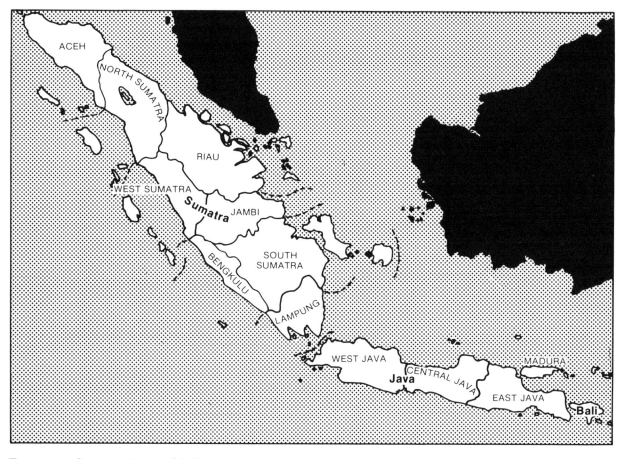

FIGURE 7-1. Sumatra, Java and Bali

early influences probably came from India.

Indian philosophies and arts, a second stratum, were introduced into the Hindu and Buddhist courts of Java and Sumatra during the first millennium A.D. Near the middle of the second millennium, they eventually reached Bali in Hindu-Javanese form, via refugees from Java.

Reliefs on the eighth-century Borobudur temple, the ninth-century Prambanan shrine, and other triumphant architectural structures of Central Java tell us that a wealth of musical instruments and dances, probably both indigenous and borrowed, were known in the Hindu-Buddhist courts of the first millennium. But Indian musical systems and instruments were probably confined even in their heyday to Indonesian courtly circles. There is little in common between Indian and Indonesian musical styles and instruments as a whole today.

This divergence may have been partly due to the fact that Indian religions did not supplant the old animist beliefs in Indonesia, but were eventually absorbed into them. An artistic example of this syncretism is the Balinese *barong* dance which, though performed in Hindu temple courtyards, is based on the ancient Indonesian concept of the benevolent, mythical barong animal. Forms of musical theater, such as Javanese and Balinese leather puppet plays (*wayang kulit*), are based on epics of Indian origin: the *Mahabharata* and the *Ramayana*. But many of the characters and most of the concepts associated with the puppet theater are indigenous, such as the belief that certain performances may induce rain, and the fact that the instruments of the accompanying gamelan (orchestra) in Java are venerated as holy objects within the context of the Javanese religion. Gamelan are still strongly associated with beliefs of the Hindu and the pre-Hindu eras, therefore many orthodox Muslims disapprove of them.

In Sumatra, some music and dance forms still practiced today are more akin to those of Hindu-Buddhist Java than to the Muslim culture with which Sumatra is mostly associated. There is no doubt, for instance, that the origins of the popular South Sumatran dance *tari inai* ("long fingernail dance"), performed by girls wearing long golden fingernails and elaborate gold-ornamented headdresses and dance costumes, belong to the pre-Muslim period. This dance, normally performed as a welcome to guests by a group of dancers, one of whom carries a box of betel nut, is accompanied by a small orchestra (*tabuhan*) of kettles, gongs, and drums, playing pieces with such ancient titles as *Lagu Sriwijaya*.[2]

A third stratum of religion and culture was superimposed on the conceptual foundations of the archipelago's peoples when Islam spread along their shores, first in Sumatra from approximately the twelfth century and later in Java, where it was especially dominant along the north coast and in parts of West Java. Islam has not been influential, however, in Hindu Bali, apart from a few small Muslim pockets.

The Muslim religion and certain foreign Muslim-influenced art forms hold sway in many coastal areas of the Indonesian-Malaysian area, including most coastal areas of Sumatra, the neighboring coast of the Malaysian peninsula, and the northern coast of Java.

Until recent decades, the northern coastal areas of Sumatra and the western Malaysian peninsula coast had many cultural elements in common, at both Muslim and pre-Muslim levels. But the Malaysian peninsula's western coast in recent years has become, as a whole, much more urbanized and "modernized" than most parts of Sumatra, with a resultant loss of some traditional forms both areas once had in common.

Foreign Muslim (Arabic, Persian, Indian, and perhaps other) artistic influences were absorbed to a certain degree in areas that accepted Islam, but European culture and religion, which

were brought to Indonesia beginning with the Portuguese in the sixteenth century, claimed relatively few adherents. A few areas eventually did adopt Christianity as a result of missionary activity, as in the Batak Toba region of North Sumatra, where Western-influenced church and folk music flourish. Some successful syncretic musical forms developed as a result of early contact between *orang Portugis* (Portuguese nationals) and Indonesians, creating a fourth artistic stratum. They include *kroncong*, a solo vocal form traditionally accompanied in Western harmonies by Western plucked strings and violin or flute but with Javanese characteristics too, which are apparent, for example, in the gamelanlike rhythmic continuity of the accompaniment. Nationalist songs, moreover, based on Western-style melodies and Indonesian texts, accompanied the growth of anticolonialism and the Indonesian nationalist movement in the twentieth century. And many young city dwellers identify today with Western pop music.

Centuries of Dutch colonial rule left their musical mark in a few small ways, for example in courtly *prajurit* (guards) corps music (Kunst 1949:239-40). More significantly, the West gradually influenced certain Indonesian artistic attitudes, including attitudes to the Indonesians' own traditional art, with the result that, especially in twentieth-century Java, the primarily foreign concepts of musical notation, conductor, composer, and virtuoso performer have begun to be fairly widely accepted, along with an increasing secularization of art in urban areas. But direct European musical influence in Indonesia to date has been, generally speaking, slight.

SUMATRA

One of the most devoutly Muslim areas in Indonesia is the Minangkabau region in the province of West Sumatra. In an area where indigenous traditions of animism, magic, and worship of deities such as the rice goddess are frowned upon by orthodox Muslims, one might well expect to find few traces of the art forms of the pre-Hindu stratum.

The Minangkabau distinguish two cultural areas: the coastal lowland or *pasisir* and the

---

2. Sriwijaya is the name of the seventh-century Buddhist court centered in South Sumatra. *Lagu* means "piece of music" or "song."

largely mountainous interior or *darat*. Music in the pasisir is strongly influenced by foreign Muslims and by neighboring peoples along the northwest and northeast Sumatran coasts and in Aceh, northern Sumatra. But the darat retains many autochthonous pre-Muslim characteristics, and it is here that one must go to find the oldest layers of Minangkabau musical culture.

It is said that skilled bronze workers may have come from Tonkin to West Sumatra a few centuries before Christ, and that Hindu and Buddhist influences from India may have been present from the first centuries A.D. Whatever the truth of the matter, the people of western Sumatra may doubtless claim a very long period of artistic history before their Muslim conversion, which possibly did not occur until the late sixteenth and seventeenth centuries A.D. Bronze kettles and gongs played today in ensemble with drums, and sometimes a wind instrument, belong to one of the oldest musical strata in western Sumatra.

There are fewer varieties of bronze instruments to be found among the Minangkabau than in Java and Bali, whose inhabitants have developed their bronze orchestras to a very complex degree. The Minangkabau equivalent of the gamelan is the so-called *talempong* ensemble. This consists primarily of small and large bronze, knobbed kettle gongs called talempong and *canang*, respectively. There is a good deal of local variation in the size, tuning, and instrumental components of the ensembles, but a common combination consists of five or six kettles, two or three canang and a pair of large and small two-headed drums (*gandang*). Musicians play fast interlocking melodies on the kettles, which may be tuned as follows:

EXAMPLE 7-1.

Each player holds one or two kettles in the left hand and an unpadded wooden stick for beating

the instrument in the right. Sometimes the kettles are arranged in a long frame, holding five to nine kettles, played by one musician. In a typical piece, such as *Ujung Bukik* ("Edge of the Hill"), canang, drums, and talempong enter one after the other, the canang establishing an unchanging pattern. The talempong and drums, however, play continually changing, interlocking rhythmic patterns, as shown in example 7-2. The larger canang kettles also interlock, creating a melodic line corporately improvised by three differently pitched kettles.

Talempong ensembles are still sometimes played at ceremonies; for example, the ceremony to become a village elder, or a rice ceremony to ensure a good harvest or to give thanks for a successful harvest. They may be heard on the local radio on weekly market days. They are used to accompany dances such as the *tari lilin* (candle dance), and as interludes in Minangkabau *randai* theater. They may also be played in accompaniment to a solo melody on one of the Minangkabau single- and double-reed wind instruments (*pupuih*), of which there are many types, or on the plucked bamboo zither (*kacapi bambu*). Alternatively, a pair of tambourinelike instruments of foreign Muslim origin—the *rabana*—may combine with the talempong and gandang.

In Minangkabau settlements in Malaysia (Negeri Sembilan) as well as in West Sumatra itself, a wind instrument (for example, a *sarune*) is occasionally used in a talempong ensemble. Ensembles consisting of kettles and/or gongs, drums, and an optional solo wind instrument are part of a very widespread, pre-Muslim musical stratum in the Malaysian-Indonesian area. Talempong ensembles may therefore be said to be typical.

Also typical are the musical principles upon which talempong ensemble playing is based. These include the aforementioned principle of interlocking parts, whereby a melodic line is corporately improvised (within the limits and stylistic rules of a given musical tradition) by two or more instruments weaving a continuous single stream of sound, with each instrument contributing a note at a time into the melodic line, either in turns or at given intervals. This technique of interlocking makes possible the performance of fast melodies without great effort on the part of each player.

Another important musical principle associated with talempong ensemble playing, also found in other parts of Indonesia, is the principle of varied tone densities, where tone density is defined in terms of the number of tones played per unit of time, either in a single part or collectively in simultaneous ensemble

mostly to be found in the interior; the Muslim art forms of the Minangkabau are widely practiced in both the coastal and interior areas.

On national holidays, at fancy fairs, and on other happy occasions in mixed darat-pasisir cultural areas such as Solok, the people may choose among a variety of art forms. A popular custom is to have a performance of *indang*, a variant of which is called *rodat* in Malaysia. In indang, a number of boys or men play tambou-

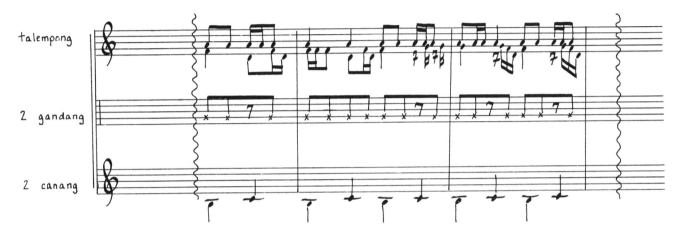

EXAMPLE 7-2. The larger canang kettles also interlock, creating a melodic line corporately improvised below three differently-pitched talempong.

EXAMPLE 7-3. Indang Melody

parts. Thus the two canang play a rhythmically unvarying two-toned melody, the drums play a varying rhythmic part at double density to the gongs, and the interlocking kettles play a rhythmically varied texture at quadruple or double density. As the density increases, so does the rhythmic interest.

Talempong ensembles and other pre-Muslim instrumental music and classical songs are

rinelike instruments called *rabana* or *indang* while they sing structurally symmetrical, sequential melodies with Arabic or Minangkabau texts (ex. 7-3). They sit close together in a long row, swaying back and forth in a wavelike fashion in various group formations and, placing their rabana on the floor, perform elegant hand movements. Songs are mostly in quatrains (*pantun*), and some deal with the social and ancestral history of the Minangkabau. Although the art form itself is pre-Muslim, many songs today deal with Muslim themes about the Prophet and morality.

Indang performers also take part in the apparently strongly Muslim art form called *dabus*, which was probably imported long ago from Aceh. A group of men sing Arabic songs to rabana accompaniment in an attempt to reach an extreme state of religious concentration. On reaching this state, they can perform astonishing feats, such as walking on broken glass or tolerating red-hot chains placed around their necks, with no ill effects. Since a traditional Minangkabau shaman sometimes takes part in this ceremony, it cannot be said to be a purely foreign Muslim importation.

Several art forms combine Muslim and pre-Muslim strata. Traditional Minangkabau theater—randai—is often based on stories with a Muslim moral, such as the need to beware of gambling or the advantages of devoting oneself to religion. It also follows the Muslim ban on female actors, allowing only men to perform both the male and female roles. However, some of the plots are based on pre-Muslim Minangkabau history and on folk stories. Talempong and other traditional Minangkabau instrumental music entertain the audience between scenes. Song and dialogue are not in Arabic but in local dialects. The circular dance characteristic of randai theater is based on movements of the art of self-defense, and is associated with the practice of welcoming guests with a bowl of betel nuts and accessories.

In Solok one may also hear a variety of songs which are disapproved of by orthodox Muslims, mainly because their texts are believed to be magically powerful in a non-Islamic way. Songs banned by Islamic law include those performed at funerals by professional women mourners, who weep uncontrollably as they work themselves into a deeply emotional state while singing the saddest of songs (*ratok*), thus ignoring the Muslim belief in heaven. Music tinged with animist beliefs includes some beautiful songs performed nocturnally by shamans in the jungle as they attempt to capture man-eating tigers. However, even these songs may be made accep-

table by preceding the tiger capturing with Muslim prayers. Such calmly sung, subtly ornamented songs as these, set to imaginative poetic texts and accompanied at times by a long bamboo flute (*saluang*), belong to the most classical of the Minangkabau musical traditions (Kartomi 1972:41). Introspective classical songs in relatively free meter, sometimes associated with shamans, magic, and trance, are also found in many parts of Sumatra, as well as in Java, Bali, and elsewhere in Indonesia.

In addition to the pre-Muslim and Muslim strata, a third musical layer is found in the Minangkabau area, especially along the coast; it incorporates the partially Westernized Malay songs called *lagu Minang moderen* ("modern Minangkabau songs"), set to poetic texts and generally accompanied by *biola* (violins), guitars, rabana, and drums. They are frequently used to accompany dances (fig. 7-2), such as the happy tari lilin, the gay *tari piring* ("plate" or "saucer dance," sometimes with candles attached to the plates), and the sad love dance *tari slendang* ("scarf dance"). Whereas classical Minangkabau vocal music is nearly always sad, subdued, and inward looking, much of the dance music is gay and extrovert in character. Thus, gay European and Arabic-influenced music was fairly easily adapted to the traditional dances of the area. Dance music may still, however, be played on traditional instruments, sometimes with choral or solo singing.

Besides the Minangkabau, many other Sumatran musical cultures may be distinguished, each associated with a particular language or dialect. For instance, the people of Aceh are well known for their traditional dances and Muslim art forms, including the aforementioned dabus.

Local musical variability in the regions of the province of North Sumatra is due partly to the strong Christian convictions of the inhabitants of some areas (as in part of the Karo area), the Muslim convictions of others (as in the Padang Lawas area), and the underlying indigenous religious beliefs everywhere. The Toba, Pak-pak Dairi, Simelungun, Mandailing, Angkola, and Sipirok areas each have their own musical identity, not one single Batak identity as is often

FIGURE 7-2. One form of the Minangkabau plate dance, *tari piring*, as performed in Lubuk Sikaping, West Sumatra.

supposed;[3] but they also have characteristics in common, such as sets of five or nine large, one-headed drums, which may be beaten in complex interlocking rhythms at a thunderous degree of intensity. The east and west coasts of this province have a somewhat related pasisir musical culture, combining Malay, Arabic, European, and other characteristics. They are known for their own variety of pantun vocal music, light string and percussion bands, and flirtation dances.

Isolated islands off the Sumatran coast can boast some of the most unusual and fascinating cultures in the world, for example the megalithic, choral-singing culture of Nias. Equally detached from their neighbors are the aboriginal Kubu, Ulu, and Lubu peoples scattered over several areas. In Palembang, near the ancient capital of the Buddhist Sriwijaya king-

dom of South Sumatra, one can hear not only the Arabic-influenced music of the *Sandiwara* (theater), but also dance music which, it is claimed, may be traced back to Sriwijaya times, accompanied by that ubiquitous Indonesian ensemble—gongs, kettles, and drums.

JAVA

Moving eastward from the southern tip of Sumatra, we reach the smaller but much more densely populated island of Java. Here the three main cultural-lingual areas are the Sundanese in the province of West Java, the Central Javanese in the province of Central Java and part of East Java, and the East Javanese in the eastern part of the province of East Java and the island of Madura.

During its Bronze-Iron age, long before Christ, the Javanese were renowned for their skills in metalworking, including the making of large bronze kettledrums, which were probably used for the mystical purpose of rainmaking (Kunst 1949, 1:105). Some of these instruments

3. *Batak* is the generic name for several groups of people living in the interior of the province of North Sumatra, including the Batak, Karo, Toba, Pak-pak Dairi, Simelungen, and Mandailing.

A TYPICAL ARRANGEMENT OF A GAMELAN SLÉNDRO-PÉLOG IN CENTRAL JAVA

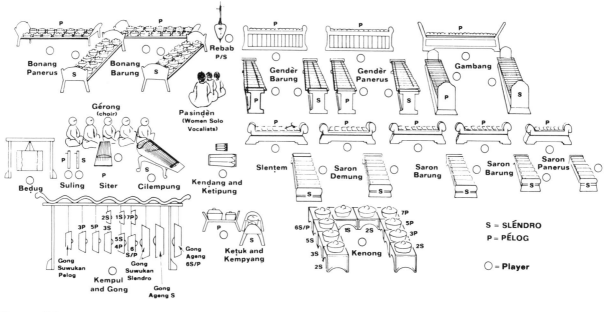

FIGURE 7-3.

have been unearthed in recent times, for example near Semarang, Central Java. Blacksmiths have always, it seems, been highly revered members of the community, not only in Java but in many parts of Southeast Asia. According to Javanese mythology, a blacksmith named Panji is the primal ancestor of the Javanese people. Similarly, another blacksmith, Pande Bosi, is believed to be the ancestor of the Mandailing people in North Sumatra.

Not surprisingly, the crowning musical achievement of the Javanese is in bronze: the great bronze gamelan orchestra of Central Java, which in its complete modern form comprises seventy to eighty instruments. With it are solo vocalists (*pasindhen*) and a choir (*gerongan*) of up to fifteen members. A complete gamelan (fig. 7-3) consists of two almost identical-looking sets of instruments with some gongs and drums common to both sets, one set tuned to the five-toned *slendro* tonality and one to the seven-toned *pelog*. No two orchestras are tuned exactly alike, because of the Javanese predilection for pitch variability and nonequidistant intervals. Several *pathet* (modes) are incorporated in the

tonal concepts of pelog and slendro,[4] but the basic scales may resemble the tones as shown in example 7-4.

The "complete" gamelan of Central Java is, in fact, a greatly enlarged version of the typical Indonesian ensemble—kettles and/or gongs, drums, and an optional solo wind instrument. At least two centuries ago, the plucked zither, the xylophone, keyed metallophones, and a bowed lute were variously added to the ensemble, to make it one of the largest orchestra types in the world.

Mythologically, the most revered instrument of the gamelan is the great gong (*gong ageng*) where, it is said, the great spirit of the orchestra resides. In the courtly center of Surakarta, it has been customary to sell the holy healing fluid in which the most sacred gongs have been washed. Often more than a meter in diameter, they are suspended from a frame and struck with a padded mallet on their central knob or boss.

4. Discussions of the instrumental concept of pelog, slendro, and their various "modes" are to be found in Hood 1954, Hood 1966, and Becker 1980. Tones 4 and 7 are less important in practice than the other five pelog tones.

Each gong has its own unique sound world.

In the talempong example (ex. 7-2), the lowest degree of tone density (per time unit) is in the canang part. A general principle in Indonesian ensembles is that the larger the gong, the lower its tone density in ensemble performance. Gongs in a complete Javanese gamelan are much larger than in Sumatran and most other rural Indonesian ensembles, including Javanese.

upright on crossed cords in wooden frames, which together perform the rhythmic subdivision patterns set for each type of piece. The end of each gongan, filled out by regular-metered melodic pacing on the metallophones, is marked by the gong ageng or, in certain pieces, by a slightly smaller suspended gong (*gong suwukan*). The main phrases are further subdivided by a set of fairly large, suspended gongs

EXAMPLE 7-4.

vanese. Large Javanese gongs are, therefore, sounded much more sparingly than in smaller ensembles, and are reserved for marking off the ends of relatively long time units called *gongan* (periods between two strokes on a great gong). These periods are comparable to the great, smooth, cyclic movements of the cosmos and the calm, controlled state of mind aimed at by many Javanese.

In a gamelan piece, the great gong enters on the last beat of the solo introduction and thereafter plays at the end of each gongan. Pieces vary from the very long and slow, with gongan of, say, 64 or 132 beats, to the short and moderately fast, with gongan of, say, 16 or 32 beats. Just before the end of a piece, it is proper for all the instruments to wait respectfully for the great kingly gong to enter before playing their final note. The seeming lateness of the final gong entry is often only a continuation of the gradual slackening of tempo, indicated by the drums, which usually occurs at the end of a gamelan piece.

A large Central Javanese gamelan today includes several bronze suspended gongs and a number of large horizontal gong kettles resting

(*kempul*), a set of high-rimmed, pot-shaped, horizontal knobbed kettle gongs (*kenong*), a pair of smaller, duller-sounding, horizontal knobbed kettle gongs (*kethuk*), and a pair of high-pitched, bell-like sounding, horizontal knobbed kettle gongs (*kempyang*). Each of these gong and kettle types has its own unique qualities of resonance, pitch, and timbre and its own highly appropriate onomatopoeic name.

The melodic instruments of the gamelan include the three sizes of bronze metallophone that make up the *saron* family (fig 7-4). They play a melodic "skeleton" (*balungan*) of a piece, which represents a medium level of note density or subdivision of the gongan.[5] Consisting of five to seven bronze slabs nailed to a resonating wooden underframe, each saron is beaten with a wooden mallet to produce a loud brilliant sound. After each key sounds, it is cleanly damped by

5. Kunst (1949:57), Hood (1954), and others referred to the saron part in a gamelan piece as a "nuclear melody." Becker (1972) does not see the saron part as having thematic importance, but as one of many levels of subdivision of the gongan. This concept is basic to my usage of the term *tone density* in Javanese music, degrees of which are measured against the gongan time unit. The latter term is also applicable to music in most parts of Southeast Asia, including areas that do not possess a concept of gongan.

FIGURE 7-4. A *saron panerus*.

shaped, knobbed kettles arranged in two parallel rows on a wooden underframe, each set struck with two padded hammers (fig. 7-5). As with the saron, there are three sizes of bonang, which characteristically play interlocking roles, together producing a fast melodic commentary on the saron melody. The two-row bonang is the Central Javanese equivalent of the handheld talempong of the Minangkabau, the variously shaped, framed sets of *renteng* kettles of West Java, and the single-row framed *reyong* kettles of Bali.

In certain contemplative pieces, a female vocalist (*pasindhen*), a two-stringed bowed lute (*rebab*, fig. 7-6), and an end-blown bamboo flute (*suling*) may perform their respective free-metered, ornamented versions of a vocal melody, performing at relatively high levels of tone density. Simultaneously, the *gender* family (metallophones with "floating" keys and bamboo resonators), the *gambang* (xylophones), the *cilempung* (a large zither), and its smaller relative the *siter* may add melodic versions applicable to the style of the respective instrument. They play at relatively high levels of tone density, like the members of the bonang family. The sarons may add their medium dense, octave distorted lines, and the vertical and horizontal gongs and gong kettles play their various subdivisions of the gongan, at a low to very low level of tone density.

In such meditative pieces, the rebab player may be regarded as the leader and dominant melodist of the instrumental ensemble. In many other pieces, however, especially in gay, loud, and cheerful pieces such as the aforementioned *Gendhing Lancaran Ricik-ricik*, the drum player is the leader. He may use four drums, namely, the large two-headed cylindrical drum called kendang (fig. 7-7), a small two-headed drum called *ketipung*, a moderately large, brilliant-sounding drum called *ciblon*, and a large, suspended barrel-shaped drum called *bedhug*. The two latter are optional, often used for special theatrical and other effects. Besides providing a varied rhythmic line at a fairly high degree of note density, the drum player establishes the tempo in the introduction to a work

the performer's left hand. The Western-notated saron melody in example 7-6 assumes that tones 6 5 3 2 1 are tuned approximately as shown above the melody.

In Java, such a melody as that in example 7-6 is normally written in the Javanese kepatihan or number notation system as follows, subdivided by the gong (○), kempul (∪), and kenong (∩):

BUKA	... 6	.356	.532	.356	
A	.3.5	.6.3	.6.5	.1.6	x 2
B	.3.2	.3.2	.3.2	.1.6	x 2

EXAMPLE 7-5.

Saron melodies in such relatively simple pieces as this, playing at a medium degree of note density, serve as the basis of semi-improvisations on other instruments playing at a relatively high degree of density. They elaborate the melodic skeleton, making minute subdivisions of the gongan. Loudest of these elaborating instruments are the *bonang*, sets of pot-

EXAMPLE 7-6. Notes with downward stems in bars 3-4 are the notes actually played in the introduction by the bonang. Notes with upward stems in bars 3-4 are transcribed from the *kepatihan* notation. Bars 5-20 are repeated many times, ending on the note in bar 20. *Gendhing lancaran* means a gamelan piece in lancaran form. *Pathet* manyura is the highest pitched of the three modes in laras slendro.

(played by a solo melody instrument and drums or by the drums alone), gives rhythmic signals during the performance to the rest of the orchestra in order to increase or slacken the pace as he sees fit, and controls the ending. In some pieces, the drum is played in a very brilliant and prominent manner; in others it assumes a subdued but nevertheless commanding role.

Gamelan are played not only for the sake of musical entertainment but also to accompany many forms of Javanese theater and dance. Little is known about the origin of the theatrical and dance forms, but some of them have clear Hindu-Javanese and pre-Hindu-Javanese, animistic characteristics. The most deeply loved and

respected of all art forms in Java is the classical, all-night puppet play (*wayang kulit*), in which hundreds of puppets depicting characters from Indonesian stories and Indonesianized epics of Indian origin (the *Mahabharata* and the *Ramayana*) may be used to cast their shadows on the screen. The two-dimensional puppets are made of carved, painted, and gilded leather and are designed and made with great artistry. Clowns have amusingly distorted fleshy proportions. Great elegant characters with spiritual power are slim and small, with beautiful fine hands, delicate long noses, almond eyes, and lowered gaze. Strong giants on the other hand are about twice as big, have bulbous eyes, fleshy

FIGURE 7-5. A *bonang barung.*

noses, and a raised gaze. The brave, manly Gathotkaca (fig. 7-8) has characteristics both of an
elegant prince and a coarse giant, being the son
of the herculean warrior Bima and the giantess
Dewi Arimbi.

The *dhalang* or puppeteer is a man highly respected for his artistic and spiritual powers.
Wayang is based on the religious syncretism of
the agama Jawa. While performing, the dhalang
not only manipulates the puppets with astonishing skill, but he also chants and sings the
story in fine poetry, plays percussion instruments with his foot on the puppet box, and controls the gamelan and singers. A good dhalang
can keep his audience enthralled the whole
night. In the comic sections he may make up-
roarious jokes; in the war scenes he may surprise the audience with the dexterity of his
puppeteering. It is believed that his great en-

durance and ability to entertain for long periods
are products of his superior spiritual powers,
which allow the Javanese, through wayang, to
explore human relationships and the relationships among man, nature, and the supernatural.
Certain wayang performances are given for
entertainment, others to celebrate a wedding or
other happy event, and yet others are to ask help
from spirits in case of adversity. The relatively
small gamelan for wayang kulit is traditionally
tuned in slendro. In the past, an almost identical-looking gamelan pelog was used for special
kinds of theater and dance. Today the two gamelan are often placed together to form a complete double gamelan slendro-pelog, in which
each slendro instrument may be placed at right
angles to its corresponding pelog instrument.
If, during a performance, the dhalang wishes to
change from a slendro to a pelog piece, each

FIGURE 7-6. A *rebab*.

FIGURE 7-7. A *kendhang* (right) and a *ketipung*.

player will be directed to move from his slendro to his nearby pelog instrument, and will thus be facing in a different direction.

Today the classical wayang kulit may be accompanied by a gamelan slendro-pelog. But the other most popular form of theater in Java—the more recent *wayang orang*—is traditionally also accompanied by a complete double gamelan. Wayang orang shows are performed by human actor-dancers, but the plots are mostly taken from the same sources as in wayang kulit. The performers wear exquisite, elaborate costumes, such as that of Gathotkaca (fig. 7-9) performing the famous love dance *Gathotkaca Gandrung*. The infatuated hero, miming his ever-growing passion for his absent beloved, Dewi Pregiwo, preens himself like a peacock, hoping she just might pass by. Then he imagines he is with her and, with exultation, falls into a state of hallucination. Swaying over legs planted wide apart,

playfully tossing his dance scarf ends which fly up at the sides, he looks into the distance, shielding his eyes, anticipating the arrival of Dewi Pregiwi. With fast restless movements and with violent, clashing accompaniment on the gamelan, he sings of his desire.

The four courts of Central Java—the Kasusuhunan and Mangkunagaran in Surakarta and the Kasultanan and Pakualaman in Yogyakarta—have each been developing their own unique music, dance, and theatrical styles since their foundation between 1742 and 1813. Distinct religious-artistic layers of Islam, Hinduism-Buddhism, and agama Jawa cannot always be isolated in the courts, and in most rural villages, a remarkable religious tolerance has allowed elements of all these faiths to combine into an artistic synthesis. Although many devout Muslims disapprove of gamelan music, which, like wayang, is strongly associated with the pre-Muslim tradition, the courts and villages have been able to adapt some pre-Muslim customs to the practice of Islam. For instance, a special archaic type of orchestra called *gamelan sekati* was long ago approved for use in Muslim celebrations during an important week of the Muslim calendar. Similarly, some classical Javanese songs (*tembang macapat*) have been set to Muslim and even (outside the courts) Christian texts, while retaining the old musical styles.

FIGURE 7-8. Gathotkaca, a Javanese leather puppet.

However, many other aspects of courtly and village culture clearly belong to the pre-Muslim tradition of Hindu and pre-Hindu Java. Both court and village may be seen as incorporating the same historical and religious layers. The philosophy of wayang in the courts and the villages belongs to this tradition. Performances of trance dances in the villages, such as the hobbyhorse dance *jaran kepang* and the *nini thowong* rain-inducing ceremony (of Banyumas), probably belong to one of the oldest pre-Hindu layers of Javanese culture. Village orchestras have the same basic instrumentation, performance principles, and philosophical connotations as courtly orchestras; but the courtly orchestras are often much bigger and more magnificent in sound and appearance. Each small type of village gamelan has its own repertoire. Each is a typical Indonesian ensemble of kettles, gongs, and drums, plus a xylophonelike instrument and an optional solo wind instrument in the villages and an additional cymballike instrument in the courts.

One must go to the north coast to find the strongest Muslim cultural layer in Central Java. A popular musical genre here is the so-called *gambusan*, with four or more veiled girls (*nu-syidah*) singing Muslim songs, mostly in Arabic, accompanied traditionally by four tambourines, a flute (suling), and a small drum (kethipung). An enlarged, modern orchestra may include, in addition, four violins, a clarinet, an accordion, and not least, a *gambus*. The gambus is a pear-shaped plucked lute said to have been brought long ago from the Persian-Arabic area to Pekalongan on the north coast, and to other strongly Muslim areas such as Minangkabau.

Another important form of Muslim music in the area is *terbangan*, usually performed with drums (*terbang*) and tambourines. The players, all male, sing Arabic songs while they accompany themselves on the terbangan ensemble. *Marhabanan*, Muslim blessing songs, are often sung in the mosques or in homes to celebrate a birth, wedding, or ceremony of cutting a child's hair.

A Muslim cultural layer may also be found in parts of East and West Java, but pre-Muslim art forms are more generally popular and widely practiced in these two provinces. East Java is famous among other things for its transvestite musical theater *ludruk* (Peacock 1968) and its high-pitched gamelan, in which plucked zithers play a prominent role.

Most of the inhabitants of mountainous West Java are Sundanese, whose language and culture differ from that of the Javanese in Central and East Java. But Banten, to the northwest, was partly settled by Central Javanese and is a meeting place for Javanese and Sundanese musical forms; the courtly center of Cirebon to the northeast has its own unique combination of Javanese, Sundanese, and other extraregional characteristics;[6] and the metropolitan city of Jakarta and its environs, a meeting place for music from abroad and from all over the archipelago, has developed its own art forms, such as the Chinese-influenced *gambang kromong*. The original music of the Sundanese is said to be practiced by the Badui people, who live in isolated jungle areas of West Java. But performances of the more elaborate and elegant music of the typical Sundanese orchestra, the *gamelan degung*, and of the kacapi-suling (zither and flute) ensemble are concentrated in the areas

6. For an introduction to Sundanese music, see section on West Java in Kunst 1949 and Harrell 1975.

FIGURE 7-9. The character Gathotkaca as played in Javanese *wayang orang* theater.

FIGURE 7-10. A *gambang*.

around Bandung and the site of the venerable old Sundanese kingdom of Pajajaran. A reduced Central Javanese style gamelan is also used in West Java, among other things for the presentation of *wayang golek* theater performances, in which the characters of Indian and Sundanese epics are played by three-dimensional wooden puppets dressed in elaborate costumes.

BALI

It has often been pointed out that the island of Bali is a paradise of the arts. Almost every villager in this rural island is a musician, singer, dalang, dancer, sculptor, painter, or actor. In many areas more gamelan per head of the population are to be found than anywhere else in Indonesia. Anyone who walks through a Balinese village in the evening is bound to hear a gamelan performing or rehearsing. The profusion of Hindu-Balinese festivals and processions held throughout the year creates an everlasting demand for music and dance all over the island, not to mention the traditionally based but abridged and relatively meaningless performances created especially for the influx of tourists over the past few decades.

Perhaps the main reason why the arts are in such a healthy state is that every aspect of traditional artistic life is felt to have some religious significance. Art, religion, and social living are integrated to an unusually high degree; the Balinese believe they are fulfilling a religious duty when they play gamelan music, dance, or engage in other artistic pursuits for a local temple or Hindu-Balinese deity.

The first people to disturb Bali's aboriginal inhabitants, about whom little is known, probably came from mainland Southeast Asia long before Christ and brought with them a tradition of spirit, nature, and ancestor worship.

Culture contact between Java and Bali has been in process for many centuries, as indicated by the fact that the first known Balinese monarch—Erlangga (the subject of many Balinese plays and dances)—ruled the island in the tenth century from his seat in Hindu-Buddhist Java. Probably in the early sixteenth century, Javanese kings fled to Bali at the onslaught of Islam, bringing their culture with them. Until the early twentieth century, however, Bali was almost totally isolated from the outside world. This isolation ended in 1906, when the Dutch gained control of the island and eventually allowed the promotion of tourism. The small Javanese-created courts of Bali, which once patronized the arts, have ceased to exist during recent decades (McPhee 1966:4–5).

Although a few Muslim pockets exist in parts of the island, the two main musical strata in Bali are the Hindu and the animist. Hindu and animist beliefs have merged in Balinese art forms over the centuries, but some art forms are more closely associated with one belief than the other. For example, the trance art phenomenon in Indonesia is generally believed to be very old indeed and presumably pre-Hindu, whereas many of Bali's gamelan types probably developed during the Hindu period, as they did in Java.

Many more art forms associated with trance are to be found in Bali today than in Java (Belo 1960). On both islands, some trance forms are accompanied by an instrumental ensemble, others by a unison choir. An example of the former is the Balinese *Calonarang* drama, based on the eternal struggle between the symbol of goodness, the mythical animal Barong (fig. 7-11), and the symbol of wickedness, the witch Rangda. During the performance some of the

Barong's assistants enter into trance and, it is believed, are possessed by demons, who force them to perform a dangerous kris (dagger) stabbing dance. Incredibly, they do not wound themselves, protected as they seem to be by their trance state. The Barong eventually saves the day. The music is usually provided by a small gamelan of drums, cymbals, metallophones, kettles, and gongs.

In one type of choral-accompanied folk trance, an entranced person believes he is possessed by a pig spirit. The unison female choral singing, with its many slightly varied repetitions, resembles quite closely the choral singing by women in the *nini thowong* trance performances of Java.

But the most famous trance choir dance of all is the *kecak*, which was originally a *sanghyang* (literally meaning "spirit") trance dance performed to appease the gods in times of drought, epidemic, and other emergencies. It is performed after sunset in a temple courtyard by men dancers sitting in a wheel of concentric circles around a flickering light. The dancers sway back and forth, raising their fluttering

FIGURE 7-11. A Balinese *barong*.

The many forms of gamelan music in Bali are more strongly associated with the Hindu-Balinese tradition than are the forms of trance music. At temple festivals, two or more gamelan usually play different pieces simultaneously, in order to make the atmosphere happy and gay. During the colorful and very frequent Hindu processions along the roads and paths of Bali, and at cremations and other ceremonies, musi-

EXAMPLE 7-7.

arms and performing with remarkable precision a fast interlocking pattern of vocal sounds, shouts, grunts, and hisses. Straightforward, five-toned kecak melodies (ex. 7-7) are very imposing and moving when sung by a surging unison mass male choir often two hundred strong. Unison melody alternates with a virtuoso choral texture achieved through the technique of fast interlocking vocal insertions on syllables such as "*Cak.*" This impressive style of execution is almost unique. The addition into kecak of the *Ramayana* drama, performed by glamorously costumed actor-dancers encircled by a male choir, is probably fairly recent.

cians carry and play instruments of the *gamelan gong* and the *gamelan angklung*.[7] The instruments of most types of Balinese gamelan basically resemble those of Javanese ensembles.

The gamelan *semar pegulingan* has a sweet, delicate sound. It consists of a few gender, gongs, drums, rebab, and a long set of kettles in frames—the *trompong*. Once a popular courtly gamelan, it is rapidly disappearing; but its life will continue through its offspring the *gamelan pelegongan*, which is really a developed, en-

7. A bamboo idiophone. It is usually played with several other single-pitch angklung in interlocking hocket fashion, with or without other gamelan instruments.

FIGURE 7-12. A Balinese *jegogan*.

larged gamelan semar pegulingan with flutes added. This gamelan accompanies the famous legong dance and its players achieve a very high standard of virtuosity and rhythmic precision through tireless nightly practice.

But the main ceremonial gamelan is the gamelan gong. In its large form it may consist of six large and small *gangsa* (saronlike instruments); three sets of four large, medium, and small *gender*like instruments; a long row of kettles called *reyong* with two to four performers; two sizes of trompong, each with one performer; two pairs of single kettles; two or three pairs of small cymbals called *cengceng*; a pair of cylindrical drums; and a set of suspended gongs called *bebende* and *kempur* with, as the largest of the gongs, the *gong lanang* and the *gong wadon*.

As in many other Indonesian ensembles, the suspended gongs and single kettles perform subdivision patterns, the gangsa, and sets of kettle gongs move melodically at different tone densities, and the pair of drums leads changes in tempo and dynamics. In most nontheatrical Javanese music, one drummer plays two or more drums in a fairly calm manner. But in the gamelan gong, two drummers play on two drums a very prominent and brilliant role in fast interlocking playing, alternating with vivid rhythmic statements separated by dramatic pauses. This brilliant effect can be achieved only after long,

painstaking rehearsal, as is the case with the other instruments. Such rehearsal precision is unusual in most parts of Southeast Asia, where music making is normally informal and only minimally rehearsed.

Another reason for the great brilliance and carrying power of the Balinese gamelan is the fact that its instruments are tuned in pairs, in such a way that one is slightly higher in pitch than the other (Hood 1966:31). When the corresponding keys of a pair of instruments are struck simultaneously, acoustical beats may be heard as a result, giving the whole ensemble its characteristic tremulous, quivering sound. Hammers used to beat those metallophones are much harder than in Java. The addition of cymbals, too, gives the Balinese ensemble a much louder, crisper sound than its Javanese counterpart.

Even more spectacular in its precision, speed of execution, and frenetic mood is the gamelan *gong kebyar*, a twentieth-century development of the gamelan gong. Its instrumentarium differs slightly from that of the gamelan gong, one major development being the extension of the reyong from four to twelve kettles. Both the Balinese reyong and the Minangkabau talempong consist of a number of kettles played in an interlocking fashion by several performers, with three reyong per player in the one case and one or two talempong in the other. The sound and performance style of the latter, however, is soft and gentle in comparison with the hard brilliance of the former.

Several other types of gamelan and a wealth of dance and theatrical forms all belong primarily to the Hindu stratum of Balinese culture. These include the dance dramas *gambuh*, wayang wong, and the recently developed but traditionally based *arja*. The island is also famous for its beautifully designed, expressive face masks which are used in some dances. Balinese puppet theater music is uniquely different from the Javanese in that it is not accompanied by a whole gamelan but by a virtuoso quartet of gender, in the case of *Mahabharata* excerpts, and a gender wayang plus a few drums and kettle gongs for stories from the *Ramayana*. Although the leather puppets are more naturalistically carved than in Java, most other elements of this form of theater in Bali closely resemble those of Java.

* * *

On all three islands, religious beliefs are expressed in myth, legend, and prayer set to music. Music is an indispensable part of family and community rituals, a form of instruction, and a means of entertainment. Music, dance, and theater not only serve to express and share thought and emotion but also are important in rituals requesting supernatural assistance.

Each of the three islands has certain religio-cultural layers in common with one or both of the others. Certain areas demonstrate one predominant religio-artistic characteristic; others show traces of several or all of them.

Thus, in many a rural village of interior Central Java, for example, one may hear not only live or recorded Western "pop," "rock," "jazz," "classical," and church music, but also Muslim *samroh* and *terbangan*, theatrical music with Hindu-Javanese characteristics, and forms of trance music with roots that probably go back to neolithic times. Mixed art forms such as Catholic masses with elements of Gregorian chant and gamelan accompaniment may also be heard. Art forms associated with a particular historical subject may be typical of a given area, such as the Prajuritan dance drama in Kopeng, south of Semarang, associated as it is with the fourteenth-century conflict between the East Javanese kingdoms of Majapahit and Balambangan (Kartomi 1973*b*:179-89).

The historical and religious strata upon which the artistic landscapes of Sumatra, Java, and Bali are based have weathered away considerably over the centuries to form a fertile mixed soil, highly favorable to further artistic developments. But the original quality of the rock in each layer may be seen still to show through.

Glossary

aguang-the Minangkabau name for suspended gong.
angklung-a bamboo instrument with mobile tubes in a frame, producing only one note (plus its octave); it is usually played in an ensemble consisting of several angklung and, in some cases, other instruments.

Barong-a mythical monster-beast of the underworld; a symbol of relative goodness.

bedhug-a large, barrel-shaped drum used in the Javanese *gamelan* orchestra and in the mosques to call people to prayer.

bonang-a set of kettle gongs resting on crossed chords in a double-row frame and beaten with two padded hammers.

buka-the short instrumental introduction in a gamelan piece.

canang-a relatively large Minangkabau kettle gong.

cengceng-a pair of Balinese cymbals.

cilempung-a plucked Javanese zither.

dabus-a Muslim art form of Acehnese origin (called *dabuih* in Minangkabau), in which performers reach a religiously induced trancelike state; they sing, dance, and carry out extraordinary feats such as wearing hot chains, with no pain or aftereffects.

gamelan-an orchestra or ensemble of the Javanese, Sundanese, and Balinese musical traditions.

gambang-the xylophone in a Javanese or Sundanese gamelan orchestra.

gandang-a Minangkabau drum.

gendhing-a gamelan piece of various possible formal structures; in the strict sense, it is a serious, soft piece omitting the use of the *kempul* in its formal construction.

gong-a large, suspended, bossed gong found in many parts of Southeast Asia; in a Javanese gamelan, the largest gong is called *gong ageng*, and the second largest is called *gong suwukan*.

indang-a Muslim-Minangkabau art form performed by a group of boys who dance, sing, and play a type of tambourine.

kecak-an ancient Balinese trance dance with choral music; in modern Bali it is often associated with a *Ramayana* dance-drama segment.

kempyang-a pair of kettles tuned to two slightly different pitch levels, struck simultaneously; sometimes only one kettle is used. The kempyang belong to the Javanese gamelan.

kempul-a fairly large suspended gong in a Javanese gamelan.

kendhang-the Javanese name for a variety of two-headed drums, two main types of which are commonly used in the Javanese gamelan. It is also the Balinese name for drum (*gendang* in West Java).

kethuk-a large kettle resting on cords in a modern frame, normally found in a modern Javanese gamelan.

klenengan-Javanese gamelan music intended for contemplative listening, played by a soft chamber ensemble.

pantun-a quatrain with rhyme in alternate lines, with a hidden meaning in the first couplet, and the second couplet explaining the first.

pasindhen-a female vocalist who sings with gamelan accompaniment.

pelog-a seven-toned Javanese tuning or tone system which, unlike the slendro tone system, features some semitone intervals. Five-tone scales are selected from the seven tones for each of three main pelog modes.

peningkah-subsidiary, less important (Minangkabau).

pokok-main, leading.

puput-a wind instrument (Minangkabau).

rabana-a tambourinelike instrument, used primarily in Muslim music, with skin stretched over a circular wooden frame tightened with rattan cord, and sometimes featuring small metal discs.

ratok-a lament, a song performed while crying (Minangkabau).

rebab-a bowed lute found in Sumatra, Java, Bali, and elsewhere; it usually possesses two strings.

renteng-a row of kettles in a frame; the name of a Sundanese gamelan ensemble, particularly popular in the Cirebon area.

reyong-a row of Balinese kettle gongs played in interlocking fashion, usually by three performers.

saluang-a long Minangkabau bamboo flute played (for comfort) on the slant.

saron-a Javanese metallophone with thick bronze slabs, beaten with a hard mallet, and occurring in four main sizes.

siter-a small, plucked Javanese zither.

slendro-a five-toned Javanese tuning system or tone system which, unlike the pelog tone system, has no semitone intervals. There are three main slendro modes.

suling-a bamboo flute of various possible sizes, found in Sumatra, Java, Bali, and elsewhere.

talempong-a small Minangkabau kettle gong; also the name of a Minangkabau ensemble, usually consisting of four or five talempong, one or two gongs, and one or two drums.

wayang-the generic name for theater in Java and Bali, including shadow puppet theater (*wayang kulit*), human dance-drama theater (*wayang orang* or *wayang wong*), and theater using three-dimensional puppets (*wayang golek*, most popular in West Java).

Bibliography

A large number of publications in Dutch and other languages are listed in Jaap Kunst's encyclopaedic *Music in Java*, vol. 2, 1949. This partial listing intended for the general reader includes, with one exception, English language publications only.

Sumatra

Adam, Boestanoel Arifin.
1970. "Seni Musik Klasik Minangkabau." In *Himpunan Presaran den Kertas Kerdja Seminar Sedjarah den Kebudajaan Minangkabau.* Batusangkar: Pemerintah Daerah Kotamadya Padang.

Goldsworthy, David.
1978. "Honey-collecting Ceremonies on the East Coast of North Sumatra," *Studies in Indonesian Music*, ed. M. Kartomi, Clayton, Australia: Centre of Southeast Asian Studies, Monash University.

Kartomi, Margaret J.
1972. "Tiger-capturing Music in Minangkabau, West Sumatra." *Sumatra Research Bulletin*, 2 (October), 24-41. Republished as "Tigers into Kittens," *Hemisphere*, vol. 20, nos. 5 and 6 (1976).
1979. "Minangkabau Musical Culture: the Contemporary Scene and Recent Attempts at Its Modernisation." *What Is Modern Indonesian Culture?* ed. Gloria Davis. Athens: Ohio University Press.

Java

Anderson, Benedict, R. O'G.
1965. *Mythology and Tolerance of the Javanese.* Ithaca, N.Y.: Cornell University Modern Indonesia Project.

Becker, Judith O.
1975. "Kroncong, Indonesian Popular Music." *Asian Music*, 7:14-19.
1980. *Traditional Music in Modern Java.* Honolulu: University of Hawaii Press.

Falk, Catherine.
1978. "The Tarawangsa—A Bowed Stringed Instrument from West Java," *Studies in Indonesian Music*, Monash University.

Geertz, Clifford.
1960. *The Religion of Java.* Glencoe, Ill.: The Free Press.

Harrell, Max.
1975. "Some Aspects of Sundanese Music," *Selected Reports in Ethnomusicology*, 2:81-102.

Hatch, Martin.
   1976. "The Song is Ended: Changes on the Use of Macapat in Central Java." *Asian Music* 7:59-71.
Heins, Ernst.
   1966. "Supplemental Note on a Recent Javanese Gamelan Record." *Indonesia* 1:22-29.
   1967. "The Music of the Serimpi 'Anglir Mendung': Some Observations Regarding the Music of Central Javanese Ceremonial Court Dances." *Indonesia* 3 (April), 135-52.
   1970. "Cueing the Gamelan in Javanese Wayang Performance." *Indonesia*, 9 (April), 101-27.
   1975. "Kroncong and Tanjidor—Two Cases of Urban Folk Music in Jakarta." *Asian Music*, 7:20-32.
Holt, Claire.
   1967. *Art in Indonesia—Continuities and Change.* Ithaca, N.Y.: Cornell University Press. Especially Parts 1 and 2.
Hood, Mantle.
   1954. *The Nuclear Theme as a Determinant of Patet in Javanese Music.* Groningen/Djakarta: J. B. Wolters.
   1963a. "The Javanese Rebab." In *Music, Libraries, and Instruments*, edited by Unity Sherrington and Guy Oldham, pp. 220-26. London and New York: Hinrichsen.
   1963b. "The Enduring Tradition: Music and Theatre in Java and Bali." In *Indonesia*. Ed. Ruth McVey, pp. 438-71, 555-60. New Haven, Conn.: Southeast Asian Studies, Yale University, by arrangement with HRAF Press.
   1966. "Sléndro and Pélog Redefined." *Selected Reports*, 1:28-48. Los Angeles: Institute of Ethnomusicology, University of California.
   1971. "Aspects of Group Improvisation in the Javanese Gamelan." In *Musics of Asia*, Ed. José Maceda. pp. 16-23. Manila: National Music Council.
Kartomi, Margaret J.
   1970. "Conflict in Javanese Music." *Studies in Music*, no. 4, 62-80.
   1973a. "Music and Trance in Central Java." *Ethnomusicology*, 17 (May), 163-208.
   1973b. "Jaran Kepang and Kuda Lumping: Trance Dancing in Java." *Hemisphere*, 17 (June), 20-27. Reprinted in *Indonesia* (Canberra: Hemisphere, 1976), 92-97.
   1973c. *Matjapat Songs in Central and West Java.* Canberra: Australian National University Press.

   1976. "Performance, Music and Meaning of Reyog Ponorogo," *Indonesia*, no. 22, 85-130.
Kornhauser, Bronia.
   1978. "In Defense of Kroncong," *Studies in Indonesian Music*, Monash University.
Kunst, Jaap.
   1949. *Music in Java (Its History, Its Theory and Its Technique).* 2d ed. 2 Vols. The Hague: Martinus Nijhoff.
   1968. *Hindu-Javanese Musical Instruments.* 2d ed. The Hague: Martinus Nijhoff.
Mellema, R. L.
   1954. *Wayang Puppets, Carving, Coloring, Symbols.* Amsterdam: Koninklijk Instituut voor de Tropen.
Peacock, James L.
   1968. *Rites of Modernization. Symbolic and Social Aspects of Indonesian Proletarian Drama.* Chicago: University of Chicago Press.
Perris, Arnold B.
   1971. "The Rebirth of the Javanese Angklung." *Ethnomusicology*, 13 (September), 403-407.
Rassers, Willem H.
   1959. *Pañji, the Culture Hero: A Structural Study of Religion in Java.* The Hague: Martinus Nijhoff.
Soedarsono.
   1969. "Classical Javanese Dance: History and Characterization." *Ethnomusicology*, 13 (September), 498-506.
Stutterheim, Willem F.
   1935. *Indian Influences in Old-Javanese Art.* London: The Indian Society.
Sumarsam.
   1975. "Inner Melody in Javanese Gamelan Music." *Asian Music*, 7-1:3-13.
Susilo, Hardja.
   1972. "Musics of Southeast Asia." In *Music in World Cultures*, Washington Music Educators National Conference, pp. 19-23, 96-100. Originally published in *Music Educators Journal*, October 1972.

Bali

Baum, Vicki.
   1938. *Tale of Bali.* Translated by Basil Creighton. New York: Literary Guild of America.
Belo, Jane.
   1950. *The Balinese Barong.* New York: J. J. Augustin.
   1953. *Bali: The Temple Festival.* New York: J. J. Augustin.

1960. *Trance in Bali*. New York: Columbia University Press.

Coast, John.
1953. *Dancers of Bali*. New York: G. P. Putnam's Sons.

Covarrubius, Miguel.
1942. *Island of Bali*. New York: Alfred A. Knopf.

McPhee, Colin.
1936a. "The 'Absolute' Music of Bali." *Modern Music* 12: 163-69.
1936b. "The Balinese Wayang Koelit and its Music." *Djåwå*, vol. 16.
1937. "Angkloeng Gamelans in Bali." *Djåwå*, vol. 17, nos. 5-6.
1938. "Children and Music in Bali." *Djåwå*, vol. 18, no. 6.
1946. *A House in Bali*. New York: John Day.
1949a. "Dance in Bali." *Dance Index*, vol. 7, nos. 7-8, 156-207.
1949b. "The Five-tone Gamelan Music of Bali." *Musical Quarterly* 37 (April), 250-81.
1966. *Music in Bali*. New Haven: Yale University Press.

Ornstein, Ruby.
1971. "The Five-tone *Gamelan Angklung* of North Bali." *Ethnomusicology*, 15 (January), 71-80.

Zoete, Beryl de, and Walter Spies.
1939. *Dance and Drama in Bali*. New York: Harper.

Other Islands in Indonesia

Holt, Claire.
1939. *Dance Quest in Celebes*. Paris: Les Archives internationales de la danse.

Kaudern, Walter, A.
1927. *Musical Instruments in Celebes*. Vol. 3 of *Ethnographical Studies in Celebes*. Göteborg: Elanders Boktryckeri, 1925-1944.

Kunst, Jaap.
1931. *A Study on Papuan Music*. Weltevreden: G. Kolff.
1939. "Music in Nias." In *Internationalarchiv für Ethnographie*, 38:1-91. Leyden: Brill.
1942. *Music in Flores*. Leyden: Brill.

Discography

Since discs pressed in Indonesia are not generally available, they have been excluded from the Discography.

Bali—divertissements musicaux et danses de transe. Ocora OCR 72. Recorded by Gilles Fresnais.

Bali—Folk Music. EMI CO64 17858. Recorded by Jacques Brunet.

Bali—Joged Bumbung. Ocora 558 501. Recorded by Jacques Brunet.

Bali—Musique et Théâtre. Ocora OCR 60. Recorded by Gilles Fresnais.

Bali—Paradis des Iles de la Sonde. Alvares LD113. Recorded by Merry Ottin.

Bali South. IER 7503. Recording and commentary by Gertrude Rivers Robinson.

Chants et danses d'Indonésie, Le Chant du Monde. LDX 74402.

Dancers of Bali. Columbia Masterworks ML4618. Recorded by the Pliatan gamelan.

Gamelan Garland. Fontana 858 614 FPY. Music from the Mangkunagaran at Surakarta, recorded by Ernst L. Heins.

Gamelan Music from Bali. Lyrichord LL7179. Recorded by Ruby Ornstein.

Gamelan Music from Java. Philips 831 209 PY. Recorded at the Court of Surakarta.

Gamelans de Bali. Alvares LD096. Musée de L'Homme, Paris. Recorded by Louis Berthe and Bernard Ijzerdraat.

Gamelan Semar Pegulingan. Nonesuch H-72046. Recorded by Robert E. Brown.

Golden Rain. Nonesuch H-72028. Recorded by David Lewiston.

Indonesia. Columbia Masterworks KL 210. Recorded by Jaap Kunst.

Indonesian Folklore—George de Fretes en zijn Krontjong-orkest. Decca 846519. Recorded in Holland.

The Jasmine Isle. Nonesuch H-72031. Recorded by Suryabrata and David Lewiston.

Java—Historic Gamelans. Philips 6586 004.

Java—Une Nuit de Wayang Kulit, Légende de Wahyu Tjakraningrat. CBS 65440. Recorded by Jacques Brunet.

Javanese Court Gamelan. Nonesuch H-72044. Recorded by Robert Brown.

Krontjong Music from Indonesia. Philips 831 229 PY.

Minang Asli, Orkes Kesenian Minang Asli. "Ganto Sori." Philips PSY 112-276.

Music for the Balinese Shadow Play: Gendèr Wayang. Nonesuch 72037. Recorded in Bali by Robert Brown.

Music from Bali. Argo RG1 and RG2. Recorded in England by Derrick de Marney.

The Music from Bali. Philips 831 210 PY stereo; 631 210 P mono. Recorded by Joachim E. Berendt.

Music of Indonesia. Ethnic Folkways Library FE 4537A/B. Edited by Henry Cowell.

Music of the Orient. Daca Album DL 9505-06. Contains recordings of Javanese and Balinese music.

Music from the Morning of the World. Nonesuch Explorer Series H-72015. Recorded by David Lewiston.

Music of Sulawesi. Ethnic Folkways Library FE 4351. Recorded by Eric and Catherine Crystal.

Musique et Chants Traditionels Soundanais—Java Ouest. Alvares LD110. Recorded by Merry Ottin.

Musiques Populaires d'Indonesie—Folk Music from West Java. Ocora OCR 46. Recorded by Ernst Heins.

Tabuh-tabuhan Bali. Request SRLP 10101.

Films

Bali Today. HP. Col. 18 min. Margaret Mead, advisor.

Background music by gamelan and temple singers accompanies the film, which shows how art permeates the daily life of the Balinese. A kecak dance and legong dancers are presented.

A Balinese Gong Orchestra. Film Australia. Col. 20 min.

"Our Asian Neighbors" series. Demonstration and explanation of the instruments of a gamelan gong.

The Buddha. FI. Col. 11 min.

The legend of Bodhisattva as depicted in the sculpture at Borobudur. Accompanied by the Gamelan Orchestra of Radio Republik Indonesia.

A House, a Wife, and a Singing Bird. U.S. Information Agency, also NYU and CG Java. Col. 30 min.

Gamelan background music throughout.

Indonesian Dances. Ministry of Information, Jakarta. Col. 10 min.

"Fishermen's dances and songs as performed in many coastal fishing villages: courting dance; formal 'Golek'; dance of Javanese Sultan's court; Candle dance from Sumatra. They are danced by a small group in traditional costume with a small gamelan orchestra supplying accompaniment and singing." Peter Kennedy.

Miracle of Bali. Xerox (BBC-TV). Col. three films, each about 1 hour. Produced and narrated by David Attenborough, supervised by John Coast:

1. *Recital of Music and Dance*. Gamelan Angklung, Jew's Harp Orchestra. Baris and Kecak Dances, gamelan performance.

2. *The Midday Sun*. Temple festival, training and performance of legong dancers. Baris dance from country.

3. *Night*. Trance in remote village. Legong dancers perform remarkable feats. Others in trance act like pigs, horses, a potlid. A scene in a holy cave, where a python lives off the innumerable bats and cockroaches.

Nias and Sumatra. FCE. B/W. 10-15 min.

"Nias is an island not reached by many people and in many ways untouched. The film shows the ceremony of manhood. A high stone tower must be leaped by the young men. An 8-foot stone. The dance of the hunters is included. Scenes on Sumatra show the contrast of village life in civilization." Karl Heider.

The Puppet Play of West Java. IE. Col. 6 min.

The Shadow Play of Bali. IE. Col. 6 min.

Taram—A Minangkabau Village. Film Australia. Col. 22 min. "Our Asian Neighbours" series.

A general introduction to Minangkabau life, including a traditional ceremony for the installation of a *datuak* (family and village leader), with talempong music.

Tari Topeng Sunda. IE. Col. 10 min.

Three Brothers. California Texas Oil and CG Java. Col. 35 min.

Trance and Dance in Bali. UC. B/W. 20 min. Produced by Dance Films Association. Gregory Bateson and Margaret Mead.

A documentary of ceremonial dance drama in a Balinese village. The performers appear in a hypnotic state.

Wayang Kulit. ASEA. Col. 15 min.

A behind- and before-the-scene study of the Javanese shadow puppets, with glimpses of the dhalang (the puppeteer), the nightlong audience, and with the almost continuous sound of the gender wayang music.

Wayang Kulit: The Shadow Puppet Theater of Java. ASEA. Col. 22 min.

Although the gamelan is glimpsed and heard, the film focuses on an actual performance by Oemartopo, one of Java's greatest dhalangs, and on a description of the puppets.

8. Polynesian Music and Dance

Adrienne L. Kaeppler

Polynesian music requires three-dimensional analysis encompassing the study of poetic text, melodic and rhythmic rendering, and visual expression in movement. Texts are the basic and most important feature in a componential analysis of generic structure; musical and movement features are more sensitive to context. Indeed, in many ways music and dance in Polynesia can be considered as secondary and tertiary "decoration" of oral literature. Not all oral literature, however, is rendered in musical or visual form and it is useful to envision a continuum of the "musicality" of oral literature which ranges from no musical decoration, on one extreme, to highly complex performances that depend on the interrelationships of poetry, music, and movement on the other. A related continuum delineates the various demands placed on performers and spectators ranging from casual instruction, or the games of children, to anxiety-laden situations, such as funerals, and finally to highly ritualized honoring of chiefs and gods. There seems to be little point in constructing generalizations about Polynesian music derived by comparing, for example, the music of a dirge with that of a ceremonial dance, especially in a cross-cultural context. Burrows has given an adequate summary of Polynesian vocal music as follows:

> Polynesian vocal music is largely either formal declamation (recitative) or little songs built on couplets. Rhythm is governed mainly by the words, and is irregular except where responsive couplets or dancing give it symmetry. Tonality is simple, with narrow compass and emphasis on one tonic. The commonest melodic lines are level and arched. Structure consists most often of simple progression, varied repetition on one motive, or alternation of two contrasting motives. Singing in two parts is found in most of the islands, usually in the form of bordun or heterophony. [1940:338]

There is considerable variety in Polynesian music both within a society and between island groups. This variety has gone largely unrecognized because important dimensions to Polynesians are not the melody and harmony, which are important to European analyzers, and the analyses have all too often resulted in simplistic categories of "indigenous" and "acculturated" based on musical elements most apparent to an outside observer. In my view it is a mistake to consider Polynesian music acculturated simply because of changes in pitch intervals and the substitution of Western harmony, for these may be only irrelevant changes in "decoration." Rather, one might consider Polynesian music to be "Polynesian" as long as the structure and sentiment have not changed or have evolved along indigenous lines. This, however, poses the problem of indigenous function, for not many genres have the same function today as in pre-European times. The dynamic interrelationship between musical and social change is a promising field for investigation, particularly if the views of Polynesians are taken into account.

Perhaps it will be meaningful to analyze Polynesian music in four categories:[1] *traditional music*, a continuation of music as it was known and performed in pre-European times; *evolved traditional music*, a continuation of traditional music, having the same structure and sentiment, but incorporating Western pitch intervals or Western harmony; *folk music* (living music of the community), which in addition to changes in pitch intervals and harmony has changes in structure—often incorporating aspects of Protestant hymns such as verse-chorus alternation; and *airport art music*, which is either consciously changed in sentiment, or in which

---

1. This framework was developed specifically for Polynesian music and is not meant to be applicable on a worldwide scale.

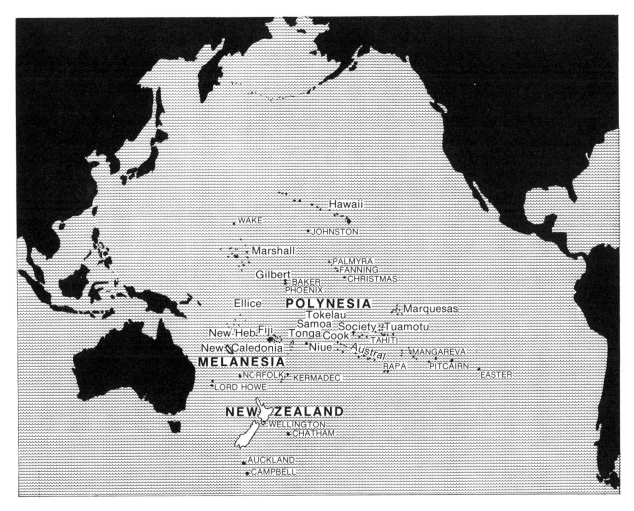

The Pacific Ocean

the performance dominates the poetry. This last may include instrumental accompaniment, danced pantomime, costume, dangerous fire or knives, iridescent properties, vocal dramatization, or other elements intended to fulfill the demands of untrained observers who do not understand the poetic text. In more usual classifications the first category would be considered indigenous while the latter three would be considered acculturated, but this dichotomy has little justification in serious study of Polynesian music today. One must be aware not only of exactly what component of the music has changed and what this means in terms of the culture itself, but also that the analytical categories employed are meaningful in terms of the total social milieu. These four potential categories

may or may not be relevant in the study of a particular Polynesian music, but they provide a useful framework for analysis.

A three-dimensional analysis of poetry, music, and movement, which takes into consideration structure, sentiment, and function for the whole of Polynesia, would not be feasible within the scope of this paper. In addition to the lack of space, comprehensive research from this perspective has not been done. A number of important descriptive studies on music and oral tradition are useful (Burrows 1933, 1945; Christensen and Koch 1964; Collocott 1928; Emerson 1909; Handy and Winne 1925; McLean 1969; Roberts 1926; and see Burrows 1934, 1940; and Smith 1968), but little information of any kind exists either on dance or on musical or poetic structure. Lacking comparable information for the several archipelagos that comprise Polynesia, in this essay I emphasize Tonga in west Polynesia and Hawaii in east Polynesia, using my own research.[2] Information on other Polynesian musics comes mainly from published sources.

The islands of Polynesia are roughly in the shape of a triangle, with Hawaii at the north, Easter Island at the southeast and New Zealand at the southwest. The ancestors of the Polynesians, who originated generations back in Asia, arrived in Tonga from eastern Melanesia at least by the twelfth century B.C. Eventually Polynesians inhabited all the major island groups. Culturally Polynesia can be divided into three subdivisions—west Polynesia, including Tonga, Samoa, Ellice Islands, Uvea, Futuna, Niue and Tokelau; east Polynesia, including the Marquesas Islands, Society Islands (Tahiti), Mangareva, Cook Islands, Austral Islands, Tuamotu Islands, Easter Island, New Zealand, and Hawaii; and the Polynesian outliers in Melanesia and Micronesia which were populated in a reverse migration westward from islands in west Polynesia, including Tikopia, Anuta, Nukuoro, Kapingamarangi, Ontong Java, and others.

Social structure and religion in Polynesia were intimately related to music. Although work songs, game songs, songs of derision, and laments were used in everyday life, highly structured, formal music was usually used to honor gods and chiefs. Genealogical rank based on descent from the gods resulted in pyramidal social structures with the highest chief at the apex and commoners at the base. Relative rank within the pyramid influenced social relationships and power resided chiefly in offices rather than in self-made men. Political regimes were long and enduring and succession to chiefly office was by genealogical rules. In these relatively stable societies specialists composed po-

etry, added music and movement, and rehearsed the performers. Drama or dramatic production had little or no place in the indigenous Polynesian repertoire—verbal and movement interpretation was that of storyteller rather than actor. Even in quotations within stories there was no attempt at realistic portrayal; instead a different quality of vocal production was used.

WEST POLYNESIA—TONGA

Many of the traditional functions or evolved traditional functions of music are still found today in Tonga, where they are primarily secular rather than religious. Tongan music is essentially poetry rendered melodically and sometimes accompanied by percussion instruments and bodily movement. Melodic rendering of poetry was often done polyphonically in two main parts—*fasi*, or melody, and a *laulalo*, a drone—both sung by men. Up to four additional parts decorated the fasi. These were two women's parts described as high and low contralto, and two men's parts sung above and below the fasi. Today, much of this polyphony has been replaced by Western harmony, in which a more melodic bass has replaced the drone and a soprano fasi, usually an octave above the men's fasi, has been added. Polyphonic decoration reaches its greatest elaboration in ceremonial dance songs.

If we construct a Tongan continuum of musical decoration of poetry, we begin at one extreme with children's game songs which accompany exercise, juggling, and hiding games. The poetry, in short rhythmic verses, is usually sung on one or a few notes. In the juggling game *hiko*, as many as six balls are juggled, and the poetic verse helps to keep the juggling in rhythm and serves as a counting device.

More musical decoration is characteristic of Tongan mourning songs, but this category is extremely varied. Dirges that were immediate expressions of grief at a wake were intoned essentially on one tone and sometimes had descending slides at the ends of phrases.[3] Such

2. Research in Tonga from 1964 to 1967 was supported by the Wenner-Gren Foundation for Anthropological Research and Public Health Service Fellowship 5-F1-MH-25984-02. To both of these agencies I wish to express my appreciation. I also wish to thank my mentors of Hawaiian music and dance, Mary Kawena Pukui and Patience Namakauahoaokawena Bacon, as well as many Polynesian friends for their more casual, but none the less important, instruction.

3. A similar vocal style is also used in intoning famous sayings and the unchanging poetic sections that are inserted in oral narrations.

dirges consisted mainly of stylized expressions of grief interspersed with kinship endearments and wailing. Laments of more thoughtful poetic creation in praise of the departed one had a more complex poetic structure and decorative melodic form. These were through-composed in several stanzas with varying numbers of lines per stanza. Often there is only one melodic contour per stanza, but each repetition may include many small variations in ornamentation. This melodic contour may change from stanza to stanza. Such poetic laments are sometimes included in ceremonial dance songs, exchanging their lament-style musical decoration for decoration appropriate to the dance genre. Today this is usually *lakalaka* (see below) which includes up to six-part polyphony and dance accompani-

boat, the poetry is simple and the music consists of a single melodic contour, slightly varied during repetitions. Many such examples are sung in two parts—fasi and drone. The same melodic contour and drone may be used for different poetic texts, such as an example given by Collocott for which he gives twenty texts (ex. 8-1; Collocott 1928:121-122). In ceremonial contexts, however, such as the presentation of a large pig to the king by an entire village, there may be two groups, each of which may sing in six parts a formal poetic creation in verse-chorus alternation or responsorial style. The musical content in the former is secondary to getting the work done, whereas in the latter a more elaborate structure and additional decoration are appropriate.

EXAMPLE 8-1. Melodic contour for tau'a'alo.

ment. Thus in the most anxiety-laden contexts there is a minimum of musical decoration, whereas a fond remembrance in the context of a ceremonial dance includes a maximum decoration of polyphony and choreographed dance movement in men's and women's parts.

McLeod (1972) has pointed out a similar context sensitivity in musical content in the Polynesian outlier of Tikopia. In the ritual music of Tikopia called *fuatanga* there are two diverse styles of musical content. The fuatanga used in funeral dirges have a "very limited number of melodic bits," whereas those songs used for religious ceremonies use a greater variety of melodic bits so that "each song is very different from every other in its class."[4]

Another Tongan musical genre in which the musical decoration of the poetry varies is *tau-'a'alo* or work songs sung during tasks requiring coordinated movements, such as rowing or dragging a food-laden sledge. In contexts requiring real physical labor, such as dragging a

Narrative songs (*fakaniua*) describe famous places, past events, and legends in rhythmic-melodic speech. These may be accompanied by handclapping, which is often syncopated to form complex rhythmic patterns. The original melodic content of these songs is unknown—those that exist today are often acculturated to Catholic church music, where they are used to relate Bible stories. It is reasonable to assume, however, that they did not have a great deal of melodic or polyphonic decoration because their function was to convey historical and mythological information primarily by text and they seem not to have been used in ceremonial contexts that would have required decorative elaboration.

In terms of musical change the four genres of Tongan music mentioned so far can be categorized as traditional music or evolved traditional

4. McLeod's hypothesis (1972) that "melodic content will become more redundant in moments of higher anxiety" appears to be as viable in Tonga as it is in Tikopia.

FIGURE 8-1. *Nafa*, Tongan slit drum. Courtesy Bishop Museum.

music; that is, the changes that have occurred are primarily in pitch intervals and Western harmonic decoration. The essential structure has not changed nor has the sentiment. Any elaboration of structure has usually been according to Tongan principles rather than Western.

Ceremonial dance songs have the greatest musical elaboration and decoration by movement. These dance songs, called *faiva*, are of six main types, one of which is obsolete and two of which are post-European. The formal ceremonial dance type in pre-European times and which is still performed is *me'etu'upaki*, a standing dance performed by men, in which dance paddles (*paki*) are used. It is accompanied by a *nafa*, a slit drum (fig. 8-1) made of a log hollowed out in various thicknesses so that when hit in the middle or near the sides different sounds are obtained. It is played with one or two wooden beaters and not only sets the rhythm for the large group of dancers (often more than a hundred) but also adds a decorative element in its own right. In former times it is said that two or three nafa were beaten and that the highest chief (Tu'i Tonga) played while lesser chiefs danced. Vocal music is provided by a group of men and women who sit with the nafa player in front of the dancers. The dignified movements are slow and graceful and are performed with

great precision. The men dance as one, two, or three groups, using the same or a different series of movements as they execute complex changes in the floor plan. Sometimes they sing a three-part canon resulting in an exciting polyphony. At other times the singing is responsorial or it may be in two parts of fasi and drone, or simply fasi alone. The melodic range is narrow, usually within a fifth except for larger drops at the ends of phrases. The fasi and the melodic range may change with each section of the text, and ornamentation may vary with each repetition and with each performer. Each stanza is sung at least twice, but occasionally six or more repetitions may be necessary to change the floor plan. Each section ends with a shout, "tu!"

Me'etu'upaki were performed on occasions of national importance such as the *'inasi*, first fruits ceremony, when quantities of food were brought to the Tu'i Tonga (highest chiefly descendant of the gods) to insure abundant harvests in the future, or to the funerals of high chiefs. Today it is performed by men of the villages of the Tu'i Tonga (who is no longer in power) or the Catholic church (the religion of the Tu'i Tonga line)[5] to demonstrate their Tu'i Tonga affiliation and their allegiance to the present ruling line. The dance leader, a ceremonial attendant to the Tu'i Tonga line, arranges a performance according to the desired duration and the number of men participating. This dance leader is not a choreographer, for there are no new compositions today within this genre. Instead, he chooses the stanzas to be used, decides on the number of repetitions, and teaches the men the dance as he learned it without conscious deviation.

Traditional dances performed by women were not strictly formal, as was the me'etu'upaki, and could take place during the day or night, whereas formal dances almost always take place during the day. The *'otuhaka*, a sitting dance, and *ula*, a standing dance, also are no longer created, but are still occasionally performed by the female counterparts of the dancers of me'etu'upaki, namely, women of the Tu'i Tonga villages or the Catholic church. The arm movements and vocal characteristics of these two

5. The dominant religion in the kingdom is Wesleyan.

dance types are similar. In former times they were accompanied by an idiophone made of lengths of bamboo wrapped in a mat and struck with two sticks, *tofua*, or *fala*. Today a skin drum, two sticks struck together, or the back of a guitar may be used to set the tempo and keep it steady. The pulse organization is usually in four or eight, and the vocal range is narrow except for descending slides. The tempo often accelerates and builds to a climax accentuated by rhythmic handclapping in which the beats are often subdivided and syncopated. These two dances are usually performed together, an ula—performed by two, four, six, or eight young women—following an 'otuhaka or series of 'otuhaka—performed by a larger number of women of any age who sit in a curved row. An 'otuhaka is usually through-composed, although verse-chorus alternation may occur. The movements

ference is that the instrumental decoration has been dropped. Me'elaufola were accompanied by bamboo stamping tubes and "sounding boards" (fig. 8-2). Stamping tubes were three to six feet in length, one end open and one end closed by a node. Striking the ground with the closed end produced low, hollow tones, the pitch depending on the length of the tube. This was offset by an acute rattling tone produced by striking a sounding board, a cylindrical staff made by loosely fastening one piece of wood to another, or by striking a longitudinally split bamboo. Me'elaufola were performed by men or women, usually separately—the movements decorating poetry of current creation which probably told of recent events. It was probably in this type of faiva that the elaborate vocal polyphony and varied dance movements developed. The poetry was not in ceremonial language and did not re-

EXAMPLE 8-2. Melodic contour for Ula. From repertoire of Sister Tu'ifua.

are sometimes minimal, consisting simply of striking the knee with an open palm during the main part of the poetry, and executing a limited number of movement motifs during a refrain. Here the text is most important and usually conveys historical or mythological information. 'Otuhaka are essentially fakaniua (see above) with the addition of decorative movements. Indeed, some poetry can be either fakaniua or 'otuhaka, depending on the context—the difference is that 'otuhaka has more decoration. The structure of an ula is based on poetry that has only one or two phrases repeated over and over and often responsorial. In ula the importance of poetry is replaced by the importance of movement motifs and the beauty of their execution.

A more informal dance type in pre-European times was the *me'elaufola*, which is no longer performed, but has evolved into the present-day lakalaka (Kaeppler 1967*b*, 1970). The main dif-

quire unchangeable vocal or movement decoration. Here the creative abilities of the *punake* (composer) had free rein. The context required aesthetic decoration which resulted in verbal, musical, and movement elaboration.[6]

These attributes have been taken over by the lakalaka, the new formal dance type. Lakalaka are performed by all the men and women of a village standing in two or more rows—the women on the left, the men on the right (from the observer's point of view). Composition of a lakalaka (which is often a half-hour in length) starts with poetry. The fasi is added by a specialist and parts are often improvised and elaborated by skillful singers of the group. Two sets of movements, for men and women, are added by a specialist. The group rehearses for as long as three months before a performance to in-

6. To use McLeod's (1972) terms, there is a minimum of anxiety and thus little redundancy.

FIGURE 8-2. Tongan dance *me'elaufola* with bamboo stamping tubes. Drawing by John Webber from the third voyage of Captain James Cook. Courtesy Bishop Museum.

sure accuracy and precision. The structure is based on formal speechmaking and includes three movements: an introductory *fakatapu*, which acknowledges the chiefly lines; the main part, called lakalaka, which relates the story; the *tatau*, or closing counterpart of the fakatapu. Each section may have one or more stanzas, but the longest section is the middle lakalaka movement. Each stanza is repeated at least once, and sometimes several times if a change in floor plan is involved. Lakalaka is a good example of evolved traditional music which has retained traditional structure and sentiment and has incorporated Western pitch intervals and harmony as part of the decoration. In addition, it is one of the important living musical genres of the community.

Another faiva, *mā'ulu'ulu*, although in its movement aspects an evolved form of 'otuhaka, is considerably changed in its musical aspects and should be considered an example of folk music. Its function is nearly the same as lakalaka, that is, it is presented on formal

occasions and pays allegiance to the rank-based sociopolitical system. Mā'ulu'ulu poetry incorporates Western ideas, based on education and Christianity, and is often performed by school or church groups rather than drawing its performers from a village as lakalaka does. Thus it cuts across traditional social institutions by taking formal notice of Western institutions and incorporates a new structure, the prototype of which are Protestant hymn tunes with verse-chorus alternation and Western harmony and pitch intervals. It is accompanied by a Western-prototype skin drum (called nafa after the slit drum of the me'etu'upaki) which plays a solo prelude accompanied by arm movements and handclapping, but without poetry. This drumming sequence doubtless evolved from the slit drum accompaniment of the me'etu'upaki, and structured as a solo prelude it is quite elaborate and adds an aesthetic element in its own right. Mā'ulu'ulu is a sitting dance which uses movements of 'otuhaka, ula, and lakalaka, but the new structure and modern music make it satisfying to old or young, Tongan or non-Tongan, and it may be considered folk music in that it has adapted parts of European music tradition to produce a phenomenon that is still unmistakably Tongan and part of the living music of the community.

The most acculturated of all Tongan music, and another example of folk music, is *hiva kakala*, or "sweet songs." The poetic sentiment is Tongan, but all else has changed. The poetry is an evolved form of *pō sipi*, informal spontaneous poems consisting mainly of metaphorical allusions to people through references to flowers, birds, and place names, which were recited during informal *kava* drinking. Sometimes melodic decoration was added and examples in traditional style consist of polyphonic through-composed poetry. Modern examples, however, are in the verse-chorus alternation of Protestant hymn tunes with Westernized pitch intervals and harmony, accompanied by stringed instruments. Indeed, Western secular songs and hymn tunes slightly adapted to Tongan tastes often form the musical basis to which the poetry is set. Although composed primarily to be sung, hiva kakala may be accompanied by a new dance form, *tau'olunga*, which is a combination of traditional ula and movements borrowed from Samoa. Tau'olunga are usually spontaneous rather than choreographed. Occasionally today, however, they are used on more formal occasions following a *mā'ulu'ulu* (just as traditionally an ula followed an *'otuhaka*) at which times they have set movements performed together by a number of women. Like its movement prototype ula, the importance of tau'olunga is in the execution of beautiful movements, especially traditional hand and arm movements.

A subtype of hiva kakala is *'upe*, usually translated as "lullaby," although the main function of 'upe appears to have been to *arouse* from sleep. Traditionally 'upe were said to have been accompanied by a nose flute or played as a nose flute solo or by an ensemble of nose flutes to awaken chiefs (an act tabu in any other way). Present-day 'upe are usually hiva kakala, composed and sung in honor of the royal children. The nose flute (*fangufangu*) is closed by nodes on both ends and, though it is possible to play it from either end, one end is usually preferred. It has six holes (five on the top and/or sides, and one central hole on the underside), but only four notes are obtained. Only the holes at the far end and the first from the nose hole are used. In playing, the left nostril is closed with the thumb of the left hand and the first hole (which may be either on the left side or on the top) is covered with one of the fingers of that hand. The other three notes are sounded by covering the far end hole with the first or second finger of the right hand, by covering both of these holes at the same time, and by playing the open tube. An example of such a scale is approximately f#-a-b-c, but the scale of each nose flute may be slightly different. Today only a few play the nose flute—usually for demonstration purposes rather than to awaken chiefs. It may be heard each day, however, as an opening sequence on A3Z, the Tongan radio station.

The only other melodic musical instrument in Tonga was the panpipe, which seems to have been used only for amusement. At the time of European contact panpipes were not reported for other Polynesian islands except on rather unreliable evidence for Samoa. I have suggested elsewhere (Kaeppler 1974) that panpipes were introduced from Fiji in fairly recent prehistoric times but died out rather quickly after the coming of Europeans.

This three-dimensional analysis has shown that music in Tonga is essentially poetry that has been decorated in various ways—specifically with melody, rhythm, and movement—and that at its greatest elaboration the decoration is polyphonic, polyrhythmic, and polykinetic (two or more simultaneous sets of movements, as in lakalaka). It has also been shown that decoration varies with context—specifically, that there is less decoration in contexts that are anxiety-laden or in which poetry serves a primarily non-musical function (such as counting or physical labor) and that there is a maximum of decoration in ceremonial and recreational contexts. Melodic decoration of the poetry was shown to have secondary decoration, in that the fasi and drone were further decorated by up to four additional vocal parts. Rhythmic decoration of the poetry, which basically sets the tempo and can be considered as a kind of rhythmic drone, can also be considered to be further decorated with complex, syncopated drumming and/or hand-clapping. Finally, movement decoration of the poetry, which is sometimes in two parts, can similarly be considered to have "drone" (i.e., relatively unchanging) leg movements that are decorated with movements of the arms and head. With Western contact, the first changes were the adoption of Western pitch intervals and harmony, which deemphasized the drone. Instrumental accompaniment sometimes disappeared completely, as in the lakalaka, or was considerably changed, as in the mā'ulu'ulu. In the most acculturated dance form, tau'olunga, traditional leg movements were replaced with Samoan variants.

WEST POLYNESIA—OTHER ISLANDS

A west Polynesian musical study useful for comparison was made by Burrows in 1932 in Uvea and Futuna (Burrows 1936, 1937, 1945).[7] Burrows, alone among ethnomusicologists specializing in Polynesian music, has acknowledged with more than just a casual passing note the integral importance of dance to Polynesian music. Comparative material from the studies of Burrows and others shows regional differences and illuminates aspects of the Tongan summary above.

According to Burrows (1945:3), "Uvea is in most respects a province of Tonga." The inventory of musical instruments—slit drums, bamboo stamping tubes, sounding boards, mat idiophones, and nose flutes—the uses of songs, the lack of serenades and true lullabies, and the types and uses of dance (1937:144–58) demonstrate that his assessment is essentially correct. Musical accompaniment for a javelin-throwing game was mentioned by Burrows for Uvea (ibid., 157–58) and, although this game was also known in Tonga, both the game and the songs are no longer practiced. In Samoa such songs are still known, and Moyle has analyzed six exam-

ples. The stylistic features, including melodies based on the interval of a perfect fourth, are characteristic of Samoan game and children's songs and stylistically help to separate them from other Samoan song types (Moyle 1970:244). This is only one example of adult games accompanied by music. Often, as in some Hawaiian string games, these songs had erotic overtones. An interesting variation on this theme is the use of music for sexual aggression in Tikopia, where evenings of song and dance conclude with improvised song duels and vicious taunts. Songs contain "direct reference to genitalia and the sexual act" as well as "aggressive solo dancing, done as a challenge to the opposite sex" (McLeod 1972).

A specialty of Uvea is *kailao*, a dance performed with clubs and accompanied only by percussion (traditionally a sounding board, or today an empty kerosene tin). Kailao is also known in Tonga, but is recognized as an import from Uvea. The absence of poetry in this and other Uvean implement dances, as well as in the Samoan *sasa* (slap dance), is intriguing because this appears to be a non-Polynesian characteristic. Further research may indicate that the Samoan sasa is of post-European origin, but kailao is more difficult to explain. A logical, but so far unsupportable, explanation may be that it is a creative combination of Fijian implement dances and the Tongan me'etu'upaki, both of which were known to Uveans.

Although Fiji is variously included in either Polynesia or Melanesia, there is little question that Fijian music is closely related to Tongan (for a discussion of Fijian music see Thompson 1971). The importance of the human voice, vocal polyphony, musical instruments used in conjunction with dance (slit drum, bamboo stamping tubes and handclapping), melodic musical instruments (nose flute and panpipe), and similar kinds of dance, especially the *vakamalolo* sitting dance and the *seasea* standing dance, all point to common ancestral forms. The importance of poetic narratives as the basis of musical and movement decoration is entirely in keeping with other Polynesian musics. On the other hand, Tonga shares its word for some

---

7. The reader is also referred to Christensen's musical analysis of recordings collected in the Ellice Islands by Koch (Christensen 1964; Christensen and Koch 1964; and see Christensen and Kaeppler 1974) and the field study of Samoan music by Moyle (Ph.D. diss. 1971).

kinds of dance (*me'e*) mainly with Fiji (*meke*),[8] as well as its elaborate polyphonic singing—in Fiji it has as many as eight parts. In other parts of Polynesia (see, for example, the characterizations of traditional musical polyphony by Zemp for Ontong Java (1972), Christensen for the Ellice Islands (Christensen and Koch 1964), and Burrows (1945) for Uvea and Futuna) polyphony is usually in the form of bordun (i.e., a monotone drone and one or more melodic lines that rise and fall above it).[9] It might be reasonable to assume that some aspects of Tongan music were introduced from Fiji in comparatively late prehistoric times after the initial migrations from Tonga to Samoa, and from there to east Polynesia. Modern compositions of Fijian meke use Western triadic harmony and pitch intervals, and, like Tongan lakalaka music, should be considered evolved traditional rather than simply "acculturated," because the rhythm, movement, structure, and sentiment have remained essentially unchanged.

The relative unimportance of melody and inconsistencies in pitch appear to be widespread in Polynesia. An Uvean informant of Burrows sang successive performances of the same song with variations in pitch of as much as a fourth, but although pitch varied widely, consistent rhythm was an essential part of the music (Burrows 1945:3, 86). Meter is usually duple and change in tempo within a song is nearly always acceleration. Songs often end in a glissandolike downward trailing off of the voice. In traditional music intensity or loudness is not varied for effect, no doubt because this would inhibit understanding of the poetry. This underscores the lack of dramatization in the storytelling process that is also absent in dance movement—vocal and movement dramatization being another index of acculturation.

We have seen that pitch intervals change first and most easily in Polynesian music because melodic consistency is relatively unimportant —melodic rendering being a variable element of poetic decoration. Music collected in any Polynesian area today is almost certain to have been influenced by European scales. Burrows did the first systematic work in analyzing music in west Polynesia and his analysis of tonality will be used here. He found that the predominance of a single tone made it possible to regard this tone as a tonic and that often whole songs were sung essentially on this tone. The tone next in importance was a dominant, a fourth below the tonic, usually quite accurately pitched. A variable cluster of tones a second below the tonic (or a third above the dominant) often completed the scale, or there might be one or two tones above the tonic. Melodic or polyphonic intervals were usually a major second, a variable third, or a fourth. The most usual scales had two to four tones, a range of less than a fifth, and a level melodic movement with a prevailing monotone.[10]

How these musical elements, pieces of movement, and poetic phrases are combined into whole compositions gives the distinctive character to each Polynesian music. Structure, however, is probably the most elusive element in an analysis (except for aesthetics, an aspect that is simply disregarded by most researchers). Burrows (1940:337) in a general context characterized Polynesian musical structure as basically of three main types: (1) simple progression from one motive to another; (2) repetition, varied by expansion, contraction, or addition of a polyphonic part; and (3) repetition of two alternate motives. The larger compositions can also be divided into sections or movements as in lakalaka. These four features are general enough to be used for all Polynesian music and yet are useful for analyzing specific Polynesian musics into genres. Although analyses of structure usually have been made from the observer's point of view, the point of view of the people of the society studied should also be considered, for only this can reveal the "crucial turning points in the course of action that give formal significance to the whole" (Sapir 1949:547). Unfortunately, such information is not yet available.

---

8. Although Uvea also used the term *me'e*, it is probable that these dances are Tongan or Fijian in origin, *e.g.*, the Uveans took part in the Tongan 'inasi ceremony where the me'etu'upaki was performed.

9. Burrows, however, gives native names for other vocal parts for Uvea (Burrows 1945:102).

10. For further information see Burrows 1945:79–106.

FIGURE 8-3. Hawaiian mouth bow (*'ūkēkē*) from the collection of Bishop Museum, played by Pele Pukui Suganuma.

EAST POLYNESIA—HAWAII

Moving to east Polynesia, we find that the musical instrument inventory varies greatly from that of west Polynesia—membranophones of different sizes, each made of a hollowed cylinder of wood covered with sharkskin, replaced the slit drum in many areas; mouth bows were found in the Marquesas, Australs, and Hawaii (fig. 8-3), and mouth flutes in the Marquesas; rhythm sticks were used at least in the Marquesas and Hawaii; a variety of idiophones were especially characteristic of Hawaii; and, strangely enough, only Hawaii appears to share bamboo stamping tubes with west Polynesia. The Maori of New Zealand had a surprising lack of musical instruments, except for an elaboration of

mouth flutes (McLean 1972) (fig. 8-4, top) and poi balls, which create an audible rhythm as they strike the body. In other musical elements, however, east and west Polynesia are much alike.

The last major area of Polynesia to be settled was Hawaii, and, although geographically separated by nearly 2,000 miles from the closest large island groups, its music, in its concepts, contexts, and characteristics, was remarkably similar to other Polynesian musics, except for the absence of polyphony—a characteristic shared with the Maori. Hawaiian music is a useful contrast to Tongan music because these were the last and first major island groups to be populated; geographically they are quite distant and geologically they are dissimilar—Tonga consists mainly of flat raised coral islands, the Hawaiian Islands are high, rugged, and volcanic. Hawaii not only has some of the most acculturated music but also has retained many examples of the most traditional music (unlike many east Polynesian groups).

As in other parts of Polynesia, music in Hawaii was a complex integrated system of poetry, rhythm, melody, and movement which served many functions, from prayer to entertainment. Performers were either priests in service of the gods or professionals trained under religious restrictions imposed in the name of Laka, patron god of the hula. Training took place in specially built schools under the tutelage of a teacher who was also a priest (*kahuna*). Schools, teachers, and performers were subsidized by chiefs who maintained them as part of their retinue for their own entertainment, to sing their praises, and for the enhancement of their prestige. This specialization appears to be an outgrowth of the *arioi* and *ka'ioi* of the Society and Marquesas islands. The arioi were groups of professional traveling entertainers accomplished in music and dancing who practiced compulsory infanticide and led uninhibited sex lives. They were not subsidized by a particular chief and in their performances they sometimes satirized and ridiculed chiefs and priests with impunity, using improvised words suitable for the occasion. In addition to long recitals of historic events, there were songs accompanied by drums, nose flutes, and risqué dance movements. The ka'ioi of the Marquesas were not so highly organized, but they also devoted themselves to pleasure and self-adornment. They erected special structures for feasts and ceremonies and prepared and performed eulogistic as well as recreational songs (Handy and Winne 1925:13). In the slightly different social milieu of Hawaii, performers were more restrained and their function was to honor the gods and to praise the chiefs and their ancestors. In contrast to their southern counterparts who criticized social institutions, Hawaiian music specialists paid homage to the sociopolitical system.

Music was classified by Hawaiians according to style and function. All poetry is known as *mele* and there are several ways of rendering it. Mele is divided into two main types: *oli*, all kinds of mele not intended for dancing, and *mele hula*, all mele with dance accompaniment. Stylistically, oli can be divided into four main styles distinguished by vocal quality, of which important dimensions are enunciation and the amount of guttural tremor of some vowels called *'i'i*. *Kepakepa*, the least "musical" of the four styles, which can be described as rhythmic speech, was used for reciting *ko'ihonua* (historical-genealogical recitations). Often performed on one pitch and without regular meter, the words are clearly enunciated without prolonged vowels or use of 'i'i. The most important style, oli (or "plain oli"), was used for prayers and name chants. It is characterized by moderate use of 'i'i and easily understood enunciation. Usually there were from two to four principal pitches. Although the succession of these pitches was not absolute and might vary with each performance, the melodic line was relatively more fixed than in other styles. *Ho'aeae*, used for love chants, were less clearly enunciated and had more 'i'i, which, according to the Hawaiian view, made them more emotional. Most emotional of all was *ho'ouwē uwē*, which had even more 'i'i and often included outbursts of wailing. This vocal style was used for dirges and in selected parts of oral narrations. Enunciation varied when singing dirges but was quite clear when ho'ouwē'uwē style was used in singing selected parts of oral narrations. Unlike Tongan music however, in which the dirge vocal quality is distinguished partly by pitch register, in Hawaii, dirge vocal quality is distinguished mainly by the amount of 'i'i. A New Zealand comparison is also illuminating. A large category of Maori songs called *waiata* can be divided into two main types, *waiata aroha*, or love songs; and *waiata tangi*, or laments. McLean categorizes these according to musical style (1969:53-57) and this categorization, along with the Hawaiian example, may indicate a more widespread east Polynesian idea of the emotional similarity between love and mourning and their musical expression.

Performance styles appear to be more explicit in Hawaiian than in other Polynesian musics,

EXAMPLE 8-3. Melodic contour for hula. From the repertoire of Mary Kawena Pukui.

yet if one looks at the literature as a whole from this perspective, comparable examples occur. Indeed, Burrows (1933:58) recognized this when he compared the rapid enunciation of the Tuamotuan *patakutaku* to the Hawaiian kepakepa. He also noted that Tuamotuans distinguished *tarava*, or steady tone, from *fakatukutuku*, or quavering of the voice.[11] These two styles are comparable to the even vocal quality used in oli and the elaboration of 'i'i used in love chants and laments.

The Hawaiian classification of music by function distinguishes four main types. *Pule* were religious chants used to call upon the gods. These prayers were rendered oli-style and were usually through-composed. Pule were intoned by priests as a part of the worship of the major gods (*akua*) at temples and ceremonies of national importance. The function of pule was to worship the gods and to give power to the wood, stone,

or feather images which were their dwelling places. Comparable religious chants in the Marquesas, *pu'e*, were accompanied by great and small drums (Handy and Winne 1925:25, 44-45), and it is reasonable to assume that Hawaiian pule were accompanied by the large *pahu* drums said to have been used in temple ceremonies.

Ko'ihonua and *mele inoa*, historical-genealogical epics and name songs, were used to honor (not worship) the chiefs and to demonstrate their relationships to the gods and to nature. Ko'ihonua, such as the *Kumulipo*, a long genealogical narrative which tells of the relationships of Kalākaua (Hawaii's last king) to his great ancestor Lono-i-ka-makahiki, were probably rendered kepakepa style. These long through-composed chants (sometimes more than 2,000 lines) were probably remembered by rhythm and, although performed quite rapidly, were easy to understand because of clear enunciation and absence of 'i'i. Mele inoa honored *'aumakua* (gods of a family or personal nature) and chiefs

11. Burrows's Hawaiian comparison here, however, seems to be confused (1933:58).

and were often accompanied by dance. Koʻiho-nua (like pule) were probably performed by kahuna who specialized in learning extensive epic narratives. Mele inoa were performed by individuals trained in the *halau* (school) after being accepted from the general populace, and who were tabu[12] while learning. After *ʻuniki* (graduation) the tabu was lifted; however, performers continued under the patronage of the god Laka. Mele inoa were rendered oli-style and sometimes further decorated by musical instruments and movement. While mele inoa were sometimes through-composed (see, for example, the mele inoa "Kaulilua" in Kaeppler 1976:211), they were usually composed in couplets with an even number of beats, especially those meant to be accompanied by dance. A special type of mele inoa was *mele maʻi*, composed in honor of an individual's genitals—usually those of a chief. Sometimes, mele maʻi likened a chief's sexual parts to the beauties of nature, thus honoring the physical attributes necessary to perpetuate the royal line.

Mele hoʻoipoipo, songs of a topical or endearing nature, were secular and could be performed by anyone. They might be extemporaneous or could be composed for a particular occasion. At least some were sung hoʻaeae style, which was considered appropriate for endearment. A subtype of this category was *mele hoʻala*, an awakening song for a chief or favorite child, much like ʻupe in Tonga. Like the nose flute in Tonga, in Hawaii bamboo stamping tubes were said to be suitable for awakening. Probably of recent origin are songs to soothe children or put them to sleep which are also categorized as mele hoʻoipoipo. Lovemaking songs played on musical instruments also belong to this category. A mouth bow (*ʻūkēkē*), nose flute (*ʻohe hano ihu*) (fig. 8-4, lower), and nose whistle (*ipu hōkiokio*) were used by lovers to entertain each other and to send messages. These instruments were not tuned to absolute pitches, but the intervals were approximately the same as those used in singing and the player used the instrument as a re-

placement for the voice—the player of the ʻūkēkē actually chanting without using the vocal cords. The Hawaiian nose flute, unlike its Tongan counterpart, had only one end closed by a node and had two finger holes drilled farther down

FIGURE 8-4. Maori wind instrument (*putorino*); Hawaiian nose flute (*ʻohe hano ihu*). Bishop Museum Collection.

the flute. A whirring rattle (*ʻūlili*) was also used for accompanying poetry used in lovemaking games.[13] Mele hoʻoipoipo vary in structure from through-composed to couplets.

The fourth functional category of Hawaiian music was *kanikau*, dirges and laments. Kanikau extolled the virtues of the deceased in hoʻouwēuwē style which provided an appropriate medium for stylized wailing.

Mele inoa and mele hoʻoipoipo were decorated with musical instruments and dance movements, instruments and movements often being integrally related. Instruments were membranophones and idiophones of indefinite pitch, and, as in west Polynesia, two different instruments were often used together to create subtle differences in sound. The function of these musical instruments was rhythmic rather than melodic, but they did not simply set the tempo and assist the performers. Instrumental rhythm was a significant element in its own right in addition to the poetry and movement and gave another dimension to the Hawaiian musical aesthetic. Membranophones included a large sharkskin-covered drum, pahu, and a small drum made of a coconut shell covered with fish skin, *pūniu*. These could be used separately or together (fig. 8-5 and ex. 8-4). Other instruments included a

---

12. The hula tabu is sometimes interpreted today to mean that specific hula were tabu, but I think there is little doubt that it was the performer that was tabu rather than the repertoire.

13. For more information on these instruments see Roberts 1967:17-56; Hiroa 1957:387-416; and Kaeppler 1973*b*.

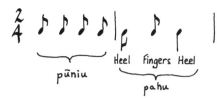

EXAMPLE 8-4. Hawaiian drum rhythm from repertoire of Mary Kawena Pukui.

large gourd that was struck with the hand or on the ground, gourd rattles, rhythm sticks, treadleboards, stone clappers, slit bamboo rattles, bamboo stamping tubes, and the striking of the human body.[14] The kind of accompanying musical instrument was determined by the seriousness of the composition and the elevation of the poetry; for example, the most serious formal compositions in honor of a high chief's genealogy would be accompanied by a pahu. The melodic contour, the choice of musical instruments, and the movements that decorated a specific composition could vary from school to school, from individual to individual, or from performance to performance.

With Western contact, the first musical element to change was pitch intervals; most of the old compositions of mele inoa and mele ho'oipoipo extant today should be considered evolved traditional music. Even pule and ko'ihonua might be slightly changed in this respect. Perhaps a few old laments that still exist retain traditional pitch intervals, but many nineteenth-century laments were written in the acculturated style based on Protestant hymn tunes. More extreme acculturation is characteristic of mele ho'oipoipo. These are now invariably accompanied by stringed instruments based on Spanish and Portuguese prototypes altered to suit contemporary Hawaiian tastes for such forms as the "Hawaiian" guitar and 'ukulele. Most of the compositions in this genre are best considered as folk music. They have incorporated Western pitch intervals and harmony, Western musical instrument accompaniment, and a changed structure to verse-chorus alternation. As in other Polynesian musics, entire melodies of Western songs have been used and Hawai-

14. See n. 13 for more on these instruments.

ian texts composed for them (see Kahananui 1965:123-30). A creative combination of Western and Hawaiian music, often thought to have a Hawaiian prototype, is *leo ki'eki'e*, or singing in falsetto. However, this method of vocal production may have been introduced near the end of the nineteenth century by a New Yorker, Theodore Richards, who used falsetto and yodeling in his teaching at the Kamehameha schools (Peters 1973).

This analysis has shown that Hawaiian music, like other Polynesian musics, is essentially poetry that has been decorated in various ways—specifically with melody, rhythm, movement, and a variety of instruments. In contrast to Tongan music, in which decoration was elaborated by adding more parts, Hawaiian decorative elaboration was achieved by variation of the parts. That is, instead of adding polyphony, the melodic line was varied by addition of 'i'i, and instead of additional movement parts, the dancers use more variation in leg and arm movement and the whole additional dimension of hip movement. Rhythmic elaboration usually was not achieved polyrhythmically but rather by varying the percussive instruments from one short composition to another. Though the means of achieving an integrated composition aesthetically satisfying to performer and spectator was different, the end result was much the same. The Tongan musical aesthetic aimed at elaboration by addition. Large groups of performers who were not specialists sang, danced, and played instruments. Each part was simple enough in itself, but in ensemble created a complex performance in which precision in simultaneous variety engaged the spectator and challenged him to interpret and understand the relationships among the parts and the poetry and to compare them with abstract qualities of precision and individuality (Kaeppler 1971). The Hawaiian musical aesthetic seems to place more value on elaboration by variation. Smaller groups of intensively trained performers sang in an acquired vocal style, played a variety of instruments, and performed difficult movements. The performance of each individual was complex—one performer sometimes simultaneously played two musical instruments, sang,

FIGURE 8-5. *Pahu* and *pūniu* from the collection of Bishop Museum, played by Pele Pukui Suganuma.

and even danced, or moved three different sections of the body. Here it was not the precision of a large group that was important, but individual precision. The spectator again was engaged in understanding the relationships between the parts and the poetry and was challenged to compare the performance with an abstract aesthetic ideal.

The importance of poetry cannot be overemphasized as the basis for Polynesian music and dance. The context in which this poetry is performed influences the kind and complexity of decoration with melody, rhythm, and movement, while the volition for performance is a function of the social structure. Thus, Polynesian music and dance cannot be fully understood or appreciated by examining or analyzing only its sound or movement. Rather, its content must be consistently related to its context, and to its social and aesthetic values in a variety of situations. Polynesian musics can then be appreciated, not only for their apparent beauty and function but also as examples of literary and aesthetic philosophy.

Glossary

arioi-professional traveling entertainers (Society Islands).
faiva-inclusive term for ceremonial dance songs (Tonga).
fakaniua-narrative song (Tonga).
fakatukutuku-quavering vocal quality (Tuamotu Islands).
fangufangu-nose flute (Tonga).
fasi-melody (Tonga).
hiva kakala-sweet songs, a musical genre (Tonga).
ho'aeae-vocal style used for love chants (Hawaii).
ho'ouwēuwē-vocal style used for laments (Hawaii).
'i'i-guttural tremor of vowels (Hawaii).
'ipu hōkiokio-nose whistle (Hawaii).
kailao-dance performed with clubs (Uvea, Tonga).
kanikau-dirges or laments (Hawaii).
kepakepa-rhythmic recitation (Hawaii).
ko'ihonua-historical-genealogical recitation (Hawaii).
Kumulipo-genealogical narrative in honor of Lono-i-ka-makahiki, an ancestor of King Kalākaua (Hawaii).

lakalaka-contemporary formal dance type (Tonga).
laulalo-drone (Tonga).
leo ki'eki'e-falsetto (Hawaii).
mā'ulu'ulu-post-European sitting dance (Tonga).
me'e-inclusive term for some kinds of dance (Tonga).
me'elaufola-pre-European informal dance type (Tonga).
me'etu'upaki-pre-European formal dance type (Tonga).
nafa-slit drum (traditional usage), skin drum (modern usage) (Tonga).
'ohe hano ihu-nose flute (Hawaii).
oli-sung poetry without dance accompaniment (Hawaii).
'otuhaka-traditional women's sitting dance (Tonga).
pahu-skin drum (Hawaii, Marquesas, Society Islands).
paki-dance paddle used in *me'etu'upaki* (Tonga).
patakutaku-rapid enunciation (Tuamotu Islands).
pō sipi-spontaneous poems (Tonga).
pu'e-religious chants (Marquesas Islands).
pule-religious chants (Hawaii).
punake-composer (Tonga).
pūniu-small membranophone with coconut shell body and fish-skin membrane (Hawaii).
sasa-dance with much striking of the body (Samoa).
seasea-standing dance (Fiji).
tarava-steady vocal quality (Tuamotu Islands).
tau'a'alo-work song (Tonga).
tau'olunga-post-European informal dance type (Tonga).
tofua-mat idiophone (Tonga).
'ūkēkē-mouth bow (Hawaii).
ula-traditional women's standing dance (Tonga).
'upe-"lullaby" or song to arouse from sleep (Tonga).
vakamalolo-sitting dance (Fiji).

Bibliography

Andersen, Johannes C.
1933. *Maori Music with Its Polynesian Background*. Polynesian Society Memoir 10.
Armstrong, Alan.
1964. *Maori Games and Hakas*. Wellington: A. H. and A. W. Reed.
Armstrong, Alan, and Reupena Ngata.
1960. *Maori Action Songs*. Wellington: A. H. and A. W. Reed.
Burrows, Edwin G.
1933. *Native Music of the Tuamotus*. Honolulu: Bishop Museum Bulletin 109.

1934. "Polynesian Part Singing." *Zeitschrift für vergleichende Musikwissenschaft*, 2:69–76.

1936. *Ethnology of Futuna.* Honolulu: Bishop Museum Bulletin 138.

1937. *Ethnology of Uvea.* Honolulu: Bishop Museum Bulletin 145.

1940. "Polynesian Music and Dancing." *Journal of the Polynesian Society* 49 (September):331–46.

1945. *Songs of Uvea and Futuna.* Honolulu: Bishop Museum Bulletin 183.

Christensen, Dieter.
1964. "Old Musical Styles in the Ellice Islands, Western Polynesia." *Ethnomusicology* 8 (January), 34–40.

Christensen, Dieter, and Gerd Koch.
1964. *Die Musik de Ellice-Inseln.* Berlin: Museum für Völkerkunde.

Christensen, Dieter, and Adrienne L. Kaeppler.
1974. "Oceania, Arts of (Music and Dance)." *Encyclopaedia Britannica, 15th ed.* 13:456–61.

Collocott, E. E. V.
1928. *Tales and Poems of Tonga.* Honolulu: Bishop Museum Bulletin 46.

Elbert, Samuel H.
1941. "Chants and Love Songs of the Marquesas Islands, French Oceania." *Journal of the Polynesian Society* 50 (March), 53–91.

Emerson, Nathaniel B.
1909. *Unwritten Literature of Hawaii. The Sacred Songs of the Hula.* Washington: Bureau of American Ethnology Bulletin 38.

Fischer, Hans.
1956. *Schallgeräte in Ozeanien: Bau und Spieltechnik, Verbreitung und Funktion.* Hamburg: Collection d'études musicologiques 36.

1961. "Polynesische Musikinstrumente: Innerpolynesische Gliederung—Ausserpolynesische Parallelen," *Zeitschrift für Ethnologie*, 86(2): 282–302.

Handy, E. S. C., and J. L. Winne.
1925. *Music in the Marquesas Islands.* Honolulu: Bishop Museum Bulletin 17.

Hiroa, Te Rangi (Peter H. Buck).
1957. *Arts and Crafts of Hawaii.* Honolulu: Bishop Museum Press.

Kaeppler, Adrienne L.
1967a. "Folklore as Expressed in the Dance in Tonga." *Journal of American Folklore* 80 (April-June), 160–68.

1967b. "Preservation and Evolution of Form and Function in Two Types of Tongan Dance." In *Polynesian Culture History*, edited by G. A. Highland et al., pp. 503–36. Honolulu: Bishop Museum.

1970. "Tongan Dance: A Study in Cultural Change." *Ethnomusicology* 14 (May), 266–77.

1971. "Aesthetics of Tongan Dance." *Ethnomusicology* 15 (May), 174–93.

1972a. "Method and Theory in Analyzing Dance Structure with an Analysis of Tongan Dance." *Ethnomusicology* 16 (May), 173–217.

1972b. "Tongan Musical Genres in Ethnoscientific and Ethnohistoric Perspective." Paper presented at the annual meeting of the Society for Ethnomusicology, Toronto.

1973a. "Acculturation in Hawaiian Dance." *Yearbook of the International Folk Music Council 1972*, 4:38–46.

1973b. "Music in Hawaii in the Nineteenth Century." In *Musikkulturen Asiens, Afrikas und Ozeaniens im 19. Jahrhundert*, edited by Robert Günther, pp. 331–38. Regensburg: Gustav Bosse Verlag.

1974. "A Study of Tongan Panpipes with a Speculative Interpretation." *Ethnos.* 39 (1–4): 102–28.

1976. "Dance and the Interpretation of Pacific Traditional Literature." In *Directions in Pacific Traditional Literature*, edited by A. L. Kaeppler and H. A. Nimmo, pp. 195–216. Honolulu: Bishop Museum Special Publication 62.

Kahananui, Dorothy.
1965. "Influences on Hawaiian Music." In *The Kamehameha Schools 75th Anniversary Lectures*, pp. 117–37. Honolulu: The Kamehameha Schools Press.

McLean, Mervyn.
1969a. "An Analysis of 651 Maori Scales." *Yearbook of the International Folk Music Council* 1:123–64.

1969b. "Song Types of the New Zealand Maori." *Studies in Music* 3:53–69. Nedlands: University of Western Australia Press.

1972. *The New Zealand Nose Flute: Fact or Fallacy. Galpin Society Journal* 27:79–94.

McLeod, Norma.
1972. "Redundancy, Boredom and Survival." Paper presented at the annual meeting of the Society for Ethnomusicology, Toronto.

Moyle, Richard.
1970. "An Account of the Game of Tāgāti'a." *Journal of the Polynesian Society* 79 (June), 233–44.

1971. "Samoan Traditional Music." Ph.D. dissertation, University of Auckland.

1972. "Samoan Song Types." *Studies in Music* 6:55–67. Nedlands: University of Western Australia Press.

Peters, Robert E.
1973. "Leo Ki'eki'e." *Honolulu Star-Bulletin*, editorial page, May 12.
Roberts, Helen H.
1967. *Ancient Hawaiian Music*. Honolulu: Bishop Museum Bulletin 29, 1926. New York: Dover (reprint, 1967).
Sapir, Edward.
1949. *Selected Writings of Edward Sapir in Language, Culture and Personality*. Edited by David G. Mandelbalm. Berkeley and Los Angeles: University of California Press.
Smith, Barbara B.
1968. "Music of Polynesia." In P. Crossley-Holland, ed., *Proceedings of the Centennial Workshop in Ethnomusicology*, pp. 94–101. Government of the Province of British Columbia.
Smith, Barbara B., and Peter Platt.
1962. "Ozeanien." In *Die Musik in Geschichte und Gegenwart*, edited by Friedrich Blume, pp. 520–32. Kassel: Bärenreiter-Verlag.
Thompson, Chris.
1971. "Fijian Music and Dance." *The Fiji Society Transactions and Proceedings* 11:14–21.
Wong, Kaupena.
1965. "Ancient Hawaiian Music." In *The Kamehameha Schools 75th Anniversary Lectures*, pp. 9–15. Honolulu: The Kamehameha Schools Press.
Zemp, Hugo.
1972. "Musique de Luangiua, Atoll d'Ontong Java." In *La Découverte de la Polynésie*, 3 unnumbered pages. Paris: Musée de l'Homme.

Discography

Cook Islands
Cook Islands Spectacular. Viking VP 361.

Ellice Islands
Die Musik der Ellice Inseln, Christensen and Koch 1964 (see Bibliography). 7-inch disc included in book.
An Evening in the Ellice Islands. Salem XP 5033. Salem Record Co., Ltd., Wellington, New Zealand.
Gilbert and Ellice Spectacular. Viking VP 365.

Fiji
Fiji Calls. Viking VP 47.
Fiji Spectacular. Viking VP 363.

Hawaii
Bill Kaiwa Sings at Maunalahilahi. Hula Records H-519.
Hawaiian Chant, Hula and Music. Folkways 8750.
Hawaiian Chants, Hula and Love-Dance Songs. Ethnic Folkways FE 4271.
Hawaiian Musical Instruments (Tape and Slides). Bishop Museum, Department of Anthropology.
Mele Inoa, Authentic Hawaiian Chants. Poki SP 900B. Poki Records, Honolulu.

New Zealand
Authentic Maori Chants. Three 45 rpm records. EC-8, EC-9, EC-10. Kiwi Records, A. H. and A. W. Reed, Wellington, New Zealand.
The Maori Girls of Turakina. Viking VP 255.
Maori Songs of New Zealand. Ethnic Folkways P 433.
Meet the Maori. Viking VPX257.

Niue
Niue Island Spectacular. Viking VP 354.

Ontong Java
Musique polynésienne traditionelle d'Ontong Java. Vols. 1 and 2. Vogue-L.D.785 and L.D.M.30.109, Collection Musée de l'Homme.

Samoa
American Samoa Spectacular. Viking VP 360.
Songs and Dances of Samoa. Viking VP 134.

Society Islands
Aparima et Otea. Tahiti Records. EL 1017, Papeete. Tahiti.
The Gauguin Years, Songs and Dances of Tahiti. Nonesuch H-72017.

Tonga
The Music of Tonga. A Sounds of the World Recording. National Geographic Society.
Tonga Spectacular. Viking VP 353. Viking Record Company, New Zealand.
Tongan Festival Contingent, Vols. 1 and 2. Hibiscus HLS 39 and 40. Hibiscus Records, New Zealand.

Tuamotu Islands
Ua Reka Mariterangi (Music of the Tuamotu Islands). Tahiti Records. EL 1018.

Films

Dorfleben im Tonga-Archipel (Village Life in the Tonga Archipelago). Institut für den Wissenschaftlichen Film, Göttingen. B/W. 15 min. Silent. Photographed and directed by G. Koch.

"Authentic documentation on village life in the Tonga islands, including *lakalaka* (standing dance) *ma'ulu'ulu* (sitting dance), and *tau'olunga* (sitting dance), all accompanied by barrel drums." Peter Kennedy.

Easter Island. 1934. MOMA. B/W. 25 min.

"It grew out of the Franco-Belgian Expedition to Easter Island undertaken jointly by the Trocadéro Museum, Paris, and the Musée Royale of Brussels . . . a record not only of the work of the expedition but also of the present-day life of the inhabitants. . . . Anthropological information is the burden of the commentary; the visuals and music combine to create an impressionistic picture of relapse and decay which finds culminating poignance in the sequence depicting the island leper colony. . . . Commentary in French, no English titles." MOMA.

Fa'a Samoa. The Samoan Way. DF. Col. (?). 17 min. Lowell D. Holmes, director.

"Documents the technological ceremonial and social events associated with the construction of a traditional Samoan guest house on the island of Ta'u (the locale of Margaret Mead's famous work, *Coming of Age in Samoa*)." DFA.

The Honourable Out-of-step. BBC. Col. 50 min. Michael Macintyre, director. Adrienne Kaeppler, consultant.

Documents the musical life of the Tongans, especially their dance and its relationship to poetry and social structure. Filmed at the Centennial celebration of the Tongan constitution, November 1975.

Ho'olaulea: The Traditional Dances of Hawaii. DFA. Col. 33 min.

"Seven traditional hulas performed by Iolani Luahini, granddaughter of dancers at the royal Hawaiian court." Allegra Fuller Snyder and Monica Moseley.

Maori Arts and Culture. NZ. Col. 29 min.

Emphasis is on carving and its symbolisms. Also shows the *toetoe* (pampas) grass used by women in weaving and explains the old techniques used in dying it.

Songs of the Maori. NZ. Col. 18½ min.

Begins with a Western-type choir sequence. What follows resembles a Rotorua "Concert Party": a poi ball song, a canoe song, and a haka. Performers wear native dress in this section.

Ula Nōweo. Bishop Museum, Honolulu. Col. 30 min. Prepared by the Committee for Preservation of Hawaiian Language, Art, and Culture.

An instructional film for the hula "Ula Nōweo" by Eleanor Hiram. A 7-inch, 45 rpm "Record for Practice and Performance" is included.

9. The Traditional Music of the Australian Aborigines

Trevor A. Jones

There are many features of the music of the Australian Aborigines[1] that are probably unique in the world today. To understand this music, however, it is necessary to know something of the Aborigine's traditional way of life—its social and religious structures and its expression in other art forms such as painting and the dance.

The Aborigines are believed to have inhabited Australia, the whole of the mainland as well as many of the offshore islands, for at least forty thousand years and to have lived in extreme isolation from the rest of the world (except for some contact with Indonesian and Melanesian traders in the north coastal areas). Only in the late eighteenth century did the first European settlers begin to arrive, with disastrous results for Aboriginal culture. Although it is likely that several waves of Aboriginal migration from southern Asia to Australia took place, it is generally held that the Aborigines constitute a recognizable and reasonably homogeneous ethnic group known as Australoids, possibly related to the Veddas of Ceylon, certain south Indian hill tribes, and some Malayan groups. Thus, though hundreds of Aboriginal languages are either still in use or exist in vestigial form all are identifiably "Australian," and though many substyles of music can still be found all are much more closely related to one another than to any other type of music. Even considering the fact that we know much more about northern and central than about southern, western, and eastern Aboriginal cultures, it is

commonly accepted that some generalizations apply to the cultures as a whole.

Probably the clearest and most concise recent picture of traditional Aboriginal religion and society is found in Kenneth Maddock's *The Australian Aborigines. A Portrait of Their Society* (1972). Some of his findings will be helpful toward explaining the essential background of Aboriginal music and providing a framework for specifically musical observations. It is important to note, however, that few Aborigines still live the traditional life, owing to the influence of Christian missionaries and Western civilization in general, and that only the oldest of them still remember and preserve much of their traditional beliefs and, consequently, their traditional music.

The Aborigines were traditionally hunters and gatherers, never farmers and graziers. They were therefore to a large extent nomadic, their existence depending on regional and seasonal variation; this does not imply a lack of territorial identification or geographical stability, however, especially in coastal areas where fish and edible plants and animals are plentiful. The division of labor was clearly and rigidly based on sex: men were the hunters and fishermen, women the gatherers (who incidentally contributed most of the normal diet). Women were essentially the "menials," men were the "aristocrats" concentrating on art, ritual, and fighting. Thus, though the sexes filled complementary economic roles, religion and the arts, including music, were almost entirely male activities.

The basic belief sustaining this way of life was that the cosmic order of things included the social order, but the latter affected and shaped the total cosmic order—a "mutual dependence of

---

1. The words *Aborigine* and *Aboriginal* are customarily capitalized in Australia to identify the aboriginal people of Australia.

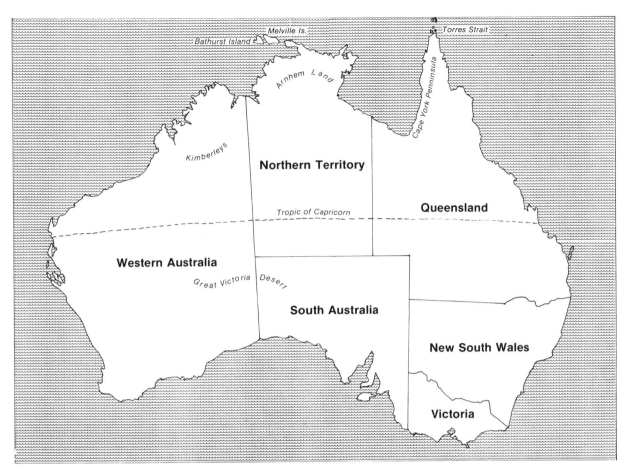

Australia

society and nature." Nature had to be stimulated by means of ritual, in which music, dance, and art were of fundamental importance. An elaborate but highly consistent "plan of life" formed the basis of this rich ritual activity, centering on the concept of The Dreaming.

The events that took place in The Dreaming are recorded in myths. The Dreaming was a time when the earth was featureless landscape or water. Life was in a state of structureless flux until self-existent, world-creative "powers" moved about the surface, creating topographical features (which can still be seen), species of living creatures (which gave rise to the myths and rites still performed), and a structured society (whose codes are still observed ceremonially and in daily behavior), after which these powers either sank into the earth or water or rose into the sky to form stars or constellations.

The powers are imaginatively conceived of as not merely having human or animal form, but also as being able to fluctuate between the two or from male to female (or to be both at once), and their portrayal in sung stories and in pictures is therefore distorted in many ways. An essential dualism in Aboriginal belief embraces both the timeless *then* of The Dreaming and the ongoing *now* of the present, both the extraordinary existence of the powers and the ordinary existence of men and their environment. The "mutual dependence" rests on the belief that communication between the powers of The Dreaming and men of the present can and does take place by signs (such as a rainbow, which gave rise to the all-important Rainbow Serpent entity) and by the paranormal experiences of dream and trance, during which "new" songs, dances, and rites may be received or magical abilities acquired. In addition, the codes of everyday living honor the events of The Dreaming, which are dramatically commemorated at appropriate times and places with ceremonial cult performances.

Creativity is therefore an attribute of the powers only. Men, by strict fidelity to tradition, "follow up The Dreaming"; they do not create forms, but receive and reproduce them.

In creating a structured society, the powers gave rise to one of the most complex and all-embracing social systems known to man. In Aboriginal society, people are related, by an extremely elaborate kinship system, to one another, to places, and to animal, bird, or insect species. (The relationship to natural species is known as totemism.) The kinship system operates in exogamous clans, but in addition most Aboriginal groups recognize a system of classes, in which clans, persons, places, powers, and species have fixed locations in a total order. Five kinds of class are normally found: matrimoieties, patrimoieties, sections, semi-moieties, and subsections (the last three probably being uniquely Australian classes). An idea of the complexity resulting from such a system can be gained by noting that matrimoieties and patrimoieties divide things into two types, sections and semimoieties into four, and subsections into eight.

The totemic powers themselves fall within this system of clan, class, and kinship, but the transcendental or "superpowers" (commonly the All-Father in the southeast of the continent, or the All-Mother in the north) are world-creative and stand in equal relation to all things, including men. Transcendental powers may be depicted only in ground and rock art, but totemic powers are represented by human actors in ritual performances and by body paintings and are associated with particular localities such as waterholes.

The particular relevance for music of this involved religious and social system is the existence and organization of ritual practices that fall into two equally important and in some cases identical types: the rites of life and the rites of death. Aspects of both may be in effect "rites of passage", or rites associated with "ages and stages", since the "passage" from life to death, for a people who believe as do the Aborigines in the reincarnation of a spiritual essence, is not markedly different from a "passage" from one age or stage of life to another. An Aborigine's life is seen as essentially consisting of a succession of clearly differentiated stages.

The rites of life are of two kinds: initiatory and fertility rites. The former cover the often highly traumatic initiation of a boy into manhood and many subsequent stages in a man's lifelong progress from degree to degree of religious knowledge. In many of these rites, ceremonial objects and art are particularly important and diverse, ranging from elaborate body painting, decoration, and headdresses, through carved and painted objects, to ground designs, earthworks, stone layouts, poles, models, and fires. Fertility rites (sometimes called "increase" rites) involve the ritual actors in acts of cooperation with, rather than coercion of, nature in perpetuating animal and plant species, each clan being responsible for its own particular totemic species. The rituals of certain major cults combine initiatory and fertility functions.

Rites of death occupy a major position in Aboriginal culture, not only because of the belief in reincarnation, but also because death is considered to be the result of sorcery (often brought about by "singing" a person, that is, performing a "poison song" against him). These rites may have one or more of three functions: to separate a spirit reluctant to leave its body or surroundings, to dispose of the body after spiritual separation, and to "settle" the spirit and dispatch it to its "spirit home." Death rites may therefore have both mourning and mortuary functions.

It is fundamental to nearly all Aboriginal rites that women are excluded both from the myths and the rituals of the major cults. They do have their own cults, of a more personal (such as love) rather than cosmic concern, but these are far less extensive and important than the men's cults.

In addition to the religious beliefs and social systems mentioned, the basic principle of "exchange" that permeates many facets of Aboriginal life is significant when considering their music, as are the varying applications of "mutuality" and "exclusion" in general. These concepts help to explain matters such as *why* some songs can be sung by certain men only while other songs are traded freely, *how* extended series of songs can cover many places and linguistic groups, and *when* and *where* particular songs may or may not be performed. The concepts also underline the fact that music is considered to be a most highly valued property and a powerful asset in Aboriginal society, and any conclusions we may draw about its structure, considered purely as *sound*, must never lose sight of its immense social and spiritual significance to its custodians.

Mention has already been made of various kinds of art, such as painting, carving, and ground designs. Of special importance in the present context are rock art and body and bark painting, for they are closely associated with, and often accompanied by, appropriate music. Rock and cave paintings are widespread, a particularly interesting type being the *Wandjina* cave paintings of spirit beings in northwest Australia (Crawford 1968). These are retouched from time to time, and the accompanying chants refer in detail to the various parts of the spirit being's body, as the artist paints them, and assert his kinship with the subject of the painting. Similarly, as elaborate designs are painted on the bodies of dancers and musicians before a ritual, each portion of the design will be executed to the correct chanted verse. In Arnhem Land (central north Australia), the art of painting on rectangles of bark (measuring from quite small to two or more meters in length and half a meter wide) has reached a very high level of artistry, both in its highly stylized depiction of birds, fish, animals, objects, and spirits, and in its use of symbols to relate a mythological story that is also celebrated in song. The materials used for colors are found in the earth and are ground to powder form: gypsum, white pipe-clay, black charcoal, and yellow and red ochre. Mixed with water (or sometimes blood) to form a paste, they are applied with twigs chewed to form a brush and then fixed with beeswax, tree sap, or the yolk of turtles' eggs. At its best, bark painting displays the finest sense of design and skilled draftsmanship allied to a remarkable economy of forms and constitutes an art form uniquely and unmistakably Australian Aboriginal (R. M. Berndt 1964).

Very closely linked with music in Aboriginal ceremonies is dancing, frequently of a powerfully evocative nature, in which the minutely observed movements of birds (such as the emu and brolga), animals (such as the kangaroo), and reptiles are most vividly emulated. Distinctive and stylized individual steps and gestures and elaborately choreographed group actions are precisely synchronized with the rhythms of the music, and many differing styles can be identified in different areas. A rich field of study still awaits the expert attention of trained investigators of dance in Aboriginal Australia.

Aboriginal music is primarily vocal, but instruments (most of them mapped by Alice Moyle in 1967) are not lacking, though almost all are percussive. Among those idiophones known to us through sound recordings or through references in earlier anthropological literature are short, rounded hardwood sticks (struck together, or one struck either on the ground or on another stick laid on the ground), pairs of boomerangs (struck or rattled together), bark or skin pads or bundles struck on the palm of the hand, hollow log drums struck with one or more sticks or with pieces of pandanus palm, single-headed skin drums struck with the palm of the hand or with a stick (imported from Melanesia and found only in northern Queensland and the Torres Strait Islands), wooden "gongs" struck with a stick, and a stone or wooden shield beaten on a mound of earth. A rarely found friction device consists of a small stick rubbed along the serrated edge of a wooden spear-thrower. Percussive sounds produced by the body alone include hand clapping, thigh and lap slapping, and foot stamping, and further "unaided" sounds such as hissing, high-pitched ululating and ritual "calling," growling, grunting, shouting, and wailing add to the variety of sounds apart from singing. The bull-roarer, a short wooden mega-

FIGURE 9-1. Didjeridu player and songman with clapping sticks. Goulburn Island, western Arnhem Land, 1963. Copyright Ronald M. Berndt, reprinted with permission.

phone (*ulbura* or *ilpirra*), a folded-leaf whistle, and a bone or reed pipe have also been found, though only the first of these is at all common. The most distinctive and, from the point of view of technique, advanced instrument, however, is the *didjeridu* (Jones 1974).

The origin of the name didjeridu is not known for certain, though it seems likely to be an onomatopoeic description of some of the instrument's sounds and has gained wide currency. (In different areas of Australia it is known by various names, such as *kanbi*, *mago*, *lhambilbilg*, *yiraki*, *yiraga*, and the possibly Western derived *bambu*.) It is found right across the northern coastal areas of Australia from west to east, but not very far inland. The didjeridu (fig. 9-1) is a trumpet, made of a tree branch that has been hollowed principally by termites, or of bamboo (in northeastern tropical areas where that plant grows) with the nodal membranes burnt through, or nowadays from virtually any hollow tubular material, including metal or plastic piping. Its length varies from area to area but averages a meter and a half, with the internal diameter usually around three centimeters at the mouth end, widening to perhaps twice this at the far end in the case of conical specimens made from branches. A gum or beeswax mouthpiece is sometimes added, and the tube may be decorated with carved or painted designs, but no other modifications are made. It is therefore an exceedingly crude instrument in itself. What make the didjeridu so outstandingly interesting are its extraordinarily elaborate playing techniques and the resultant musical patterns. Although detailed discussion of these techniques and styles, necessary to a full understanding of the art, cannot be given here, some basic points can be made.

The instrument is both blown and sung into.

The blowing technique involves the production of a low-pitched basic tone (the fundamental) by loosely buzzing the lips, and, in some styles, the production of a higher tone (the first available overtone), pitched from a ninth to an eleventh above, with tighter lips. The fundamental's pitch is sometimes raised momentarily by one or two semitones through heavily accented blowing, and the overtone is produced sometimes as a long "hoot," sometimes as a briefer "toot," and sometimes as a very lightly tongued, almost inaudible "poot." Since the main function of the fundamental tone is to act as a continuous drone interrupted by the various kinds of overtone (in styles where the latter is used), a method of continuous or "cyclic" respiration is used whereby frequent breaths are snatched through the nose while a small but sufficient amount of air, stored in the mouth, is expelled into the tube to keep the air column vibrating. In addition to the lip-blown tones, however, vocalized tones are simultaneously superimposed over them from time to time. These produce different kinds of "beating" or interference waves, varying from smooth, rich chordal effects (when a major tenth above the fundamental is gently sung), through explosive "blurts" of reinforced sound (when a major ninth is sung loudly with a very open throat), to very raucous "squawks" or "squeals" (usually imitative of particular bird calls) which result from distorted falsetto screaming at much higher pitches. An exceptionally large didjeridu, measuring up to three meters in length and seven centimeters in internal diameter at the mouth end, is used for certain secret ceremonies in Arnhem Land, in which it represents *Yulunggul*, a great snake. It is impossible to maintain a continuous note when so large a column of air and so wide a bore are involved. Consequently, long, separate blasts of the very low fundamental tone are produced, creating a most awe-inspiring sound.

Using these and other techniques, the didjeridu player is able to produce an astonishing variety of rhythms and timbres while maintaining the continuous drone function of the instrument. The extremely complex patterns produced, varying greatly from place to place and from style to style, supply introductions, interludes, and conclusions as well as accompaniments to the singing of one or more songmen and their accompanying clapping sticks, and provide intricate aural counterparts to the foot movements of the dancers who usually perform simultaneously (ex. 9-1).

Recent (and as yet unpublished) research seems to indicate that there may be a further aspect of this complex art of didjeridu playing-singing, namely the possibility that a secret "language" is mouthed into the instrument, since the vibrations of the lips and vocal cords are essentially secondary, and to some extent incidental, manifestations of this basically "verbal" exposition. The existence of half-spoken, half-sung patterns of consonants and vowels that serve both to identify specific didjeridu patterns among songmen and players and to emulate the blowing-singing techniques involved in the actual execution of these patterns tends to reinforce the notion that a specific and pseudoverbal communication is inherent in at least some styles of didjeridu performance, and that we should perhaps in future speak of didjeridu playing-singing-*speaking*!

Comparison with the use of similar instruments in many other cultures throughout the world indicates that although most of the separable aspects of didjeridu technique are found in isolation elsewhere, the total combination of these aspects and the stylistic results of their extensive exploitation by expert Aboriginal performers is unique to Australia and musically most remarkable (Jones 1967). It is not surprising, therefore, that although most Aboriginal men in northern Australia learn to play the instrument, virtuosi are rare and much admired.

Despite the considerable variety of percussive devices and the very highly developed techniques of didjeridu playing, it must again be emphasized that Aboriginal music is preeminently vocal. The primary function of the didjeridu (never more than one at a time) is to accompany the singers and dancers. Besides, it is found only in the northerly regions. There are certain "songless sacred performances" in which the beating of percussive instruments is the only music present, but these are rare.

Many different kinds of vocal production are

EXAMPLE 9-1. Djerag: didjeridu and sticks accompaniment only (northeastern Arnhem Land). Reprinted with permission from *Studies in Music*, no. 1 (1967), University of Western Australia Press.

Notes:

♪ = "spot" staccato overtone

⌢ = "hooted" overtone

× = "croaked" note

⊘ = "hummed" overtone (second bar only)

= "pulsated" note (i.e., second note is accented but not tongued.)

EXAMPLE 9-1. (continued)

found in different parts of Aboriginal Australia, ranging from soft, "inward" singing to loud, throaty, and energetic vocalizing. Unusual effects found occasionally include continuous singing (that is, maintaining vocal cord vibration even during breath intakes) and deliberate "croaking" of two or more pitches at once by allowing the vocal cords to divide into more than one section. A very important aspect of Aboriginal singing is *polyvocality*: a singer cultivates several different voice qualities, and an essential aspect of correctly performing a particular song is to use the appropriate voice (or manner of vocal production) for that song. In some areas a special practice consisting of the cultivation of a pulsating vibrato called "shaky voice" is found.

In examining the broad features of Aboriginal music it is convenient to make a rough division between north and south, taking the Tropic of Capricorn as a kind of dividing line. Research to date tends to indicate that, very generally speaking, most of the features of the south are also found in the north, but that the north contains a number of additional elements that may be the result of more cultural contact with Macassans and of European influences

FIGURE 9-2. Men resting after singing sacred songs, beating sticks on sand. Warburton Range, 1961. Copyright Ronald M. Berndt, reprinted with permission.

(though this is still highly conjectural). The most important remaining major groups in the south are the Aranda-speaking people of Central Australia and the Pitjantjatjara-[2]speaking people of the Western Desert; in the north the large areas of interest are the Kimberleys in Western Australia, the Arnhem Land peninsula of the Northern Territory, and the Cape York peninsula area of Queensland.

The most fruitful recent work on Pitjantjatjara and Aranda music has been carried out by Catherine J. Ellis (1966, 1967a, 1967b, 1969, 1970, and with A. M. Ellis 1970).[3] Ellis has reported that song is held by these peoples to be of great power in influencing nonmusical events and that if performed correctly in all essential details it will enable performers to draw on supernatural power left within the soil by the powers during

The Dreaming. This power may be used for evil as well as good, for which reason the teaching of the songs is very strictly controlled. Only the oldest and wisest men know the most potent songs. Song thus is used as a means of social control, in that miscreants are sung about as well as talented hunters and the like, for legal and moral codes are perpetuated in the songs and they also serve to educate children morally and socially.

The Pitjantjatjara peoples have a concept that they call *inma*, which not only embraces music as sound but also includes behavioral responses and mythical associations, together with *mayu*, meaning "flavor" or "sound." *Inma mayu* then refers to a particular melodic shape that permanently records the "flavor" or personality of a specific ancestral power. Other terms refer to aspects of singing, stick beating, dancing, body painting, and so on, but Ellis attempts to supply, by means of musical analysis, the details of the actual musical techniques for which no Aboriginal terms have been found, and in this she has provided what must be regarded as a first major breakthrough into comprehending the processes involved. The operative feature, she shows, is an intricate overlay of patterns of design, dance, song text, melodic structure, and rhythm. During the performance of a long series of totemic "history" songs, constant cross-references occur, whereby several of these patterns may simultaneously refer to different segments of the story concerned. The more "powerful" a song is, the more intricate the overlay of interlocking patterning.

As an example of how one of these patterning processes appears to work, Ellis considers that a melody begins with a basic series of culturally accepted intervals, from which is constructed a melodic framework associated with a particular sacred being. This framework is determined and identified by the pitch distance between the main pivot points of the terraced descents of the melody, together with the length of time spent within the ambit of these pivot points. The actual elaboration and decoration of this melodic framework are variable and depend on separate rules discerned by the other singers from the song leader's opening solo. There is thus con-

2. Also spelled Pitjantjara. [Ed.]
3. Conveniently summarized in Catherine J. Ellis, "Australia, Folkmusic of: Aboriginal Music and Dance (south of the Tropic of Capricorn)," *Grove's Dictionary of Music and Musicians*, 6th ed. (London: Macmillan, 1980).

siderable melodic flexibility from one performance to another, yet remarkable unanimity among the singers in any one performance. (All the melodies descend in pitch and are much more syllabic than melismatic.)

A second example of patterning, rhythm, involves an equally intricate process. The accompanying beating (fast or slow, and emphasizing triplet groupings of syllables) may be rhythmically opposed to the sung accents which in themselves may deliberately distort the "normal" spoken rhythm wherein the accent always falls on the first syllable of a word. The established song rhythm is repeated to the same text, and in the same accentual relationship to it, until the full melodic descent is completed. Certain identifiable primary rhythmic patterns are used to interrelate and develop successive verses in a long series (which may have hundreds of verses) and by recurring serve to divide them into large sections or subseries of verses. Although differences in musical structure occur in various linguistic areas, certain myths (and therefore song series) may cross linguistic boundaries and some of Ellis's studies indicate that in such cases the rhythm encodes this specific information.

Texts are also subjected to the patterning process. In addition to the distortion of natural accentuation, vowels may be changed, syllables "turned" (or transposed), and deliberate grammatical ambiguities introduced to obscure or conceal secret meanings. Texts may have many levels of meaning, specificity, and allusion, varying from place to place and from person to person (according to the singer's age, status, and degree of initiation).

In short, then, these songs consist of an intensely elaborate encoding of information, of many kinds and levels of experience, by means of interlocking layers of melodic, rhythmic, and textual patterning. In revealing to us for the first time (by eliciting the indigenous concepts held by the Aborigines themselves about their music and by penetrating musical analysis) the complex processes underlying these structures, Ellis has made an outstanding contribution to our understanding of these sacred performances in southern Australia. There seems little reason to doubt that the same processes will be found to operate in performances of at least some similar sacred rituals in the north.

The Arnhem Land area in the central north, however, possesses secret ceremonies whose melodic style is quite different from that of the south. Thus, though the chanting in such cults as the *Kunapipi* and *Waranggan* is syllabic and rhythmically regular, melodies associated with the *Maraian* ceremonies, for example, are highly melismatic, intricately ornamented, and rhythmically very free against even stick beating. It seems likely that these and certain other Arnhem Land ceremonial chants make use of specific melodic "key figures" or "germinal motives" that clearly identify them. A musically interesting feature of Maraian singing occurs when groups representing the two moieties, called *Yirritja* and *Dhuwa*, perform their own Maraian chants simultaneously while seated about ten yards apart. The melodies sung by the two groups have different scale structures, different compasses, and different rates of stick beating (three against five), but they are coordinated to the extent that both end their phrases on the same "tonic" or sustained final pitch at approximately the same time. Also, after a slight pause, both groups sing a short "amen"-like concluding phrase simultaneously, although these phrases too, like the chants, are quite different from each other melodically. There thus arises a kind of halfway situation between total independence and planned polyphony (ex. 9-2).

In addition to this great body of secret melismatic chants, the north has several other kinds of music, which have been extensively recorded and analyzed (Elkin and Jones 1958; Jones 1965; Moyle 1967). As in the south, the sacred ceremonial cult chants are normally accompanied solely by one or more of the various percussive devices listed earlier, but the north has the didjeridu and uses it extensively to accompany an immense body of traditional clan totemic songs of a sacred but not secret nature, songs openly performed before (though not fully understood by) women and children. There are also many kinds of recently "found" or "dreamed" songs dealing with recent or contemporary events, songs that may be individually owned and exchanged, such as the *Djed-*

EXAMPLE 9-2. Simultaneous Yirritja and Dhuwa Maraian singing (eastern Arnhem Land).

bangari "fun" songs sung by young bachelors in eastern Arnhem Land and the nondanced *Djabi* songs of northwest Western Australia. Arnhem Land has various kinds of "gossip" or "sweetheart" songs that refer in indirect ways to scandals and affairs of a very personal nature without naming specific people, and thus serve the very useful social purposes of entertainment and harmless relief of interpersonal tensions.

Many different musical regions exist in the north and can be clearly differentiated with ref-erence to these nonsecret songs, both sacred and secular. For example, Moyle identified four such regions within the northerly sector of the Northern Territory alone (taking in adjacent islands and the Arnhem Land area) by listing such factors as the style of didjeridu playing (when present), the durations of songs, the ratio of verbal to melodic repetition, the compass of melodies and number of descending phrases used, and the translatable or untranslatable texts (1967). Further, within each area, each one

EXAMPLE 9-3. Wongga (western Arnhem Land).

of many clans has its own distinctive songs that conform to the general characteristics of the musical region, yet have undeniably individual traits. The resulting richness and profuse variety of musical styles are remarkable.

The compass or range of melodies, for example, varies from the monotone chanting on Bathurst and Melville Islands to nearly two octaves in western Arnhem Land. At one extreme are melodies exclusively concerned with the enunciation and repetition of a short or long text and hence highly syllabic; at the other extreme are elaborately melismatic songs of great melodic beauty and balance, involving no words at all but simply nonsense syllables of vowels and occasional consonants. In the latter, represented by the *Wongga* of western Arnhem Land, the voice becomes virtually an instrument, its free-

dom unimpeded by considerations of verbal meaning (ex. 9-3).

Although the vocal style of most traditional Aboriginal music is characterized by minute fluctuations of pitch, intricate ornamentation by means of short glides and trills, and a persistent blurring of clear melodic outlines, quite a lot of Arnhem Land singing of clan songs and contemporary event songs shows a simpler and more stable approach to what we would call "scale." Very frequently full seven-note scales (akin to our major and minor scales) are used, but also common are gapped scales using only three or four notes within the compass of an octave or more.

Probably the most fascinating attributes of this northern nonsecret music, however, at least for most non-Aboriginal listeners, are its rhyth-

EXAMPLE 9-4. Djedbangari (northeastern Arnhem Land).

EXAMPLE 9-5. Gunborg (north central Arnhem Land).

mic subtleties and variety. Syncopation, a basic feature of jazz and Western popular music, is very prevalent both in the vocal lines and the didjeridu accompaniments. The stick beating is often by no means confined to simple time-keeping, but may generate further rhythmic patterns conflicting with voice or didjeridu rhythms. A popular example of this is the simultaneous use of duple (or march) rhythm by the sticks against triple (or waltz) rhythm by the didjeridu (ex. 9-4). Another example involves singers (with their sticks) performing in patterns based on six, divided into two groups of three, while other players strike sticks on the ground in groups of three beats, each beat being twice the length of that of the singers, and the didjeridu at the same time divides each six-beat measure into four equal parts. Needless to say, considerable polyrhythmic intricacy results (ex. 9-5).

The basic meters of this music are not restricted to multiples of two and three, but may be additive, giving rise to regularly recurring "measures" of five, seven, ten, and even thirteen beats. When such meters are further enlivened by syncopation and polyrhythm among the participants, a feeling of boundless yet strictly controlled vitality is produced and fully conveyed to the dancers, whose foot movements accurately reflect almost every rhythmic subtlety of the music.

Rhythmic variation within a song ranges from a comparatively simple repetition many times of a basic pattern (which may in itself be quite complex) to the insertion by the didjeridu of "breaks" in the pattern, of changes to quite different meters, or of different patterns within the same meter. In some extreme instances rhythmic patterns may change constantly throughout a song, and some sections of songs may abandon meter altogether in a kind of free-rhythm rhapsody. Although a song may last only half a minute (though some extend to two or more minutes), it may be divided by means of rhythmic changes into several sections, frequently involving recurring refrains, interludes, and a concluding coda.

On the whole there are no wide variations of dynamic level, accentuation depending more on length than on stress. In other words, relative durations are far more important than relative volume of sound in creating this music's highly developed rhythmic life.

Where individual songs are grouped in sequences to produce extended series, a well organized variation principle can often be observed. Tempi may be changed, the compass of the melody reduced or expanded, new notes added to the basic scale within the same compass, fresh melodic curves or "reciting" points incorporated, sections omitted or juxtaposed differently, the overall pitch level or "tonic" moved up or down, and so on. The sense of plan, structure, order, and control of all the elements that create a recognizable musical entity is very strongly present in the most highly developed music found especially in northeast Arnhem Land.

An institution of great importance in Arnhem Land is the specialist songman who owns, trades, and "dreams" songs and controls performances of them, including the dancing and didjeridu playing. The existence of the songman in the north probably accounts for the variety and ingenuity of nonsecret music found there, for unlike the situation that applies elsewhere (as well as in Arnhem Land) for ceremonial cult music—in which a headman of the cult is responsible for musical leadership—here a semiprofessional approach that encourages innovation and individual expression to a considerable degree adds a further dimension to Aboriginal culture. The songman may have several assistant singers, or may join with songmen of other groups, and both of these situations may sometimes produce polyphony. Canonic imitation, countermelodies in two or three parts, and singing in parallel intervals (including thirds) are not infrequent in central and northeast Arnhem Land.

Two exceptional areas that fall neither into the southern nor the northern musical practice are the island of Tasmania, south of the Australian mainland, and the Torres Strait islands that lie between Cape York Peninsula and New Guinea to the north. Since it is more than a century since the Tasmanian native peoples became extinct, virtually nothing is known of their music, though conjectural attempts to reconstruct it, based on a few surviving descriptions, notations, and wax cylinder recordings, have been made by Moyle (1960 and 1968). In her view there are indications that in addition to some similarities with mainland Aboriginal music, a connection with Melanesian music seems likely. This connection is so strong in the case of Torres Strait music that it is better considered belonging with Papua-New Guinea than with Australian Aboriginal culture (Jones 1972).

Finally, brief mention must be made of women's and children's music in Aboriginal Australia. Women's ceremonies exist and some have been studied (Ellis 1970), but they are very minor compared with those of men. Women also have functional songs such as lullabies and very characteristic ritual "wailing" at deaths and initiations. Furthermore it has been observed that women perform stylized "wailing" versions of some of the men's chants, in which the same texts are said to be involved. Children too have their own songs and ceremonies (as well as the expected imitations of adult performances), which play an important role in their lives not only for their pleasure and creativity but for their gradual enculturation (Kartomi 1970).

As the traditional way of life of the Australian Aborigines gives way before the inroads of Western man, most of the secret and sacred music here described disappears, and there seems little doubt that before long all ceremonial life will have ceased in the north, west, and center, as it long since has in the east and south. It is of some comfort, therefore, to note that the nonsecret music of the north continues to exist and even to evolve, that didjeridu playing remains a valued achievement and is spreading into areas formerly ignorant of it, and that at long last real efforts are being made to preserve at least something of this great cultural heritage as a living process for future generations. The world can ill afford to lose so distinctive a music and so well adapted a people.

Glossary

didjeridu-long wooden or bamboo trumpet found among the north Australian Aborigines. Synonyms: *bambu, kanbi, lhambilbilg, mago, yiraga, yiraki.*

Djabi-recently composed, individually owned, nondanced songs of the Aborigines of northwest Australia.

Djedbangari-an individually owned "fun" song, of comparatively recent origin, performed by young bachelor Australian Aborigines of eastern Arnhem Land.

Djerag-a northeast Arnhem Land type of clan song; the word means "seagull."

Gunborg-a north-central Arnhem Land type of dance-song.

inma mayu-a complex concept of the Pitjantjatjara (southern Australian Aboriginal) people, referring to a particular melodic shape that conveys the "flavor" or personality of an ancestral power.

ulbura-short wooden megaphone sung into in some central Australian Aboriginal ceremonies. Synonym: *ilpirra*.

Wongga-a western Arnhem Land type of dance-song.

Bibliography

Berndt, Ronald M., ed.
   1964. *Australian Aboriginal Art*. Sydney: Ure Smith.

Berndt, Ronald M., and Catherine H. Berndt.
   1964. *The World of the First Australians*. Sydney: Ure Smith.

Berndt, Ronald M., and E. S. Phillips, eds.
   1973. *The Australian Aboriginal Heritage: An Introduction through the Arts*. Sydney: Australian Society for Education through the Arts, in association with Ure Smith. Includes two 33⅓ LP records and 25 slides (see Discography).

Brandl, E. J.
   1973. *Australian Aboriginal Paintings in Western and Central Arnhem Land*. Canberra: Australian Institute of Aboriginal Studies.

Crawford, Ian M.
   1968. *The Art of the Wandjina*. Melbourne: Oxford University Press.

Elkin, A. P.
   1964. *The Australian Aborigines*. 4th ed. Sydney: Angus and Robertson.

Elkin, A. P., and Trevor A. Jones.
   1958. *Arnhem Land Music (North Australia)*. The Oceania Monographs, No. 9. Sydney: The University of Sydney.

Ellis, Catherine J.
   1963. "Ornamentation in Australian Vocal Music." *Ethnomusicology* 7 (May), 88-95.
   1964. *Aboriginal Music Making. A Study of Central Australian Music*. Adelaide: Libraries Board of South Australia.
   1965. "Pre-Instrumental Scales." *Ethnomusicology* 9, no. 2 (May), pp. 126-44.
   1966. "Aboriginal Songs of South Australia." *Miscellanea Musicologica*, no. 1, 137-90.
   1967a. "Folk Song Migration in Aboriginal South Australia." *Journal of the International Folk Music Council* 15:11-16.
   1967b. "The Pitjantjara Kangaroo Song from Karlga." *Miscellanea Musicologica*, no. 2, 171-267.
   1968. "Rhythmic Analysis of Aboriginal Syllabic Songs." *Miscellanea Musicologica*, no. 3, 21-49.
   1969a. "Structure and Significance in Aboriginal Song." *Mankind*, no. 7 (June), 3-14.
   1969b. "Aboriginal Music and the Specialist Music Teacher." *Australian Journal of Music Education*, no. 5 (October), 19-24.
   1970. "The Role of the Ethnomusicologist in the Study of Andagarinja Women's Ceremonies." *Miscellanea Musicologica*, no. 5, 76-208.
   1980. "Australia, Folkmusic of: Aboriginal Music and Dance (south of the Tropic of Capricorn)," *Grove's Dictionary of Music and Musicians*, 6th ed. London: Macmillan.

Ellis, Catherine J., and A. M. Ellis.
   1970. *Andagarinja Children's Bullock Corroboree*. Port Moresby: Papua Pocket Poets.

Gould, Richard A.
   1969. *Yiwara: Foragers of the Australian Desert*. Sydney: Collins.

Jones, Trevor A.
   1963. "A Brief Survey of Ethnomusicological Research in the Music of Aboriginal Australia." In *Australian Aboriginal Studies, a Symposium of Papers Presented at the 1961 Research Conference*, edited by H. Sheils, pp. 281-304. Melbourne: Oxford University Press.
   1965. "Australian Aboriginal Music: The Elkin Collection's Contribution toward an Overall Picture." In *Aboriginal Man in Australia*, edited by R. M. and C. H. Berndt, pp. 283-374. Sydney: Angus and Robertson.
   1967. "The Didjeridu. Some Comparisons of Its Typology and Musical Functions with Similar Instruments Throughout the World." *Studies in Music*, no. 1, 23-55.
   1968. "The Nature of Australian Aboriginal Music." *Australian Journal of Music Education*, no. 2 (April), 9-13.
   1972. *Traditional Music of Torres Strait*. Companion booklet for LP disc AIAS/11, pp. 8-24. Canberra: Australia Institute of Aboriginal Studies. Musical analysis, fifteen transcriptions and examples.
   1974. "The Yiraki (Didjeridu) of North-East Arnhem Land: Techniques and Styles." In *The Australian Aboriginal Heritage*, edited by R. M. Berndt and E. S. Phillips. Sydney: Ure Smith. With accompanying discs and color slides.

Kartomi, Margaret J.
1970. "Tjitji Inma at Yalata." *Hemisphere* 14 (June), 33-37.
Maddock, Kenneth.
1972. *The Australian Aborigines. A Portrait of Their Society.* London: Allen Lane, The Penguin Press.
May, Elizabeth, and Stephen Wild.
1967. "Aboriginal Music on the Laverton Reservation." *Ethnomusicology* 11 (May), 207-17.
Moyle, Alice M.
1959. "Sir Baldwin Spencer's Recordings of Australian Aboriginal Singing." *Memoirs of the National Museum of Victoria*, no. 24, 7-36.
1960. "Two Native Song-styles Recorded in Tasmania." *Papers and Proceedings of the Royal Society of Tasmania*, no. 94, 73-77.
1964. "Bara and Mamariga Songs on Groote Eylandt." *Musicology* 1:15-24.
1966. *A Handlist of Field Collections of Recorded Music in Australia and Torres Strait.* Occasional Papers in Aboriginal Studies, No. 6 (Ethnomusicology Series No. 1). Canberra: Australian Institute of Aboriginal Studies.
1967. *Songs from the Northern Territory.* Companion booklet for five LP discs I.A.S. M-001/5. Canberra: Australian Institute of Aboriginal Studies.
1968. "Tasmanian Music, an Impasse?" *Records of the Queen Victoria Museum, Launceston*, no. 26 (May), 1-10.
1969. "Aboriginal Music on Cape York." *Musicology* 3:3-20.
1971. "Source Materials: Aboriginal Music of Australia and New Guinea." *Ethnomusicology* 15 (January), 81-93.
1974. "North Australian Music. A Taxonomic Approach to the Study of Aboriginal Song Performances." Ph.D. dissertation, Monash University.
Strehlow, Theodore G. H.
1971. *Songs of Central Australia.* Sydney: Angus and Robertson.
Waterman, Richard A.
1968. "Aboriginal Songs from Groote Eylandt, Australia." In *Proceedings of the Centennial Workshop on Ethnomusicology*, edited by Peter Crossley-Holland, pp. 102-16. Vancouver: The University of British Columbia. Reprinted 1970.
1971. "Music in Australian Aboriginal Culture—Some Sociological and Psychological Implications." *Music Therapy* (Kansas), no. 5 (1955), 40-49. Reprinted in *Readings in Ethnomusicology*, edited by David P. McAllester, pp. 167-74. New York: Johnson Reprint Corporation.
Wild, Stephen.
1975. "Walbiri Music and Dance in Their Cultural Nexus." Ph.D. dissertation, University of Indiana.

Discography

Arnhem Land—Authentic Australian Aboriginal Songs and Dances. HMV (Aust.) OALP 7504-5 and OALP 7516. Three discs. A. P. Elkin.
Arnhem Land Popular Classics. Wattle Ethnic Series (Aust.), No. 3. La Mont West.
The Art of the Didjeridu. Wattle Ethnic Series (Aust.), No. 2, D4. Trevor A. Jones.
The Australian Aboriginal Heritage. The following records are included with this text edited by R. M. Berndt and E. S. Phillips:
Learning Aboriginal Music. E1-a. C. J. and A. M. Ellis.
Yiraki (Didjeridu) Playing in Northeastern Arnhem Land, N.T. E1-b. Trevor A. Jones.
Six Aboriginal Songs. E1-b. Ronald M. Berndt.
Songs by Young Aborigines. E2-a&b. Alice M. Moyle.
The Land of the Morning Star. Songs and Music of Arnhem Land. HMV (Aust.), OCLP 7610. Sandra Le Brun Holmes.
Mornington Island Corroboree Songs. W. & G. Records (Aust.), WG-B 5007. George Kansky.
Music from Australia and New Guinea. Columbia (U.S.) SL 208. A. P. Elkin.
Songs from Arnhem Land. Australian Institute of Aboriginal Studies, AIAS/6. Lester R. Hiatt.
Songs from the Northern Territory. Australian Institute of Aboriginal Studies, I.A.S. M-001/5. Five discs. Alice M. Moyle.
Songs from Yarrabah. Australian Institute of Aboriginal Studies, AIAS/7. Alice M. Moyle.
Songs of Aboriginal Australia and Torres Strait. Ethnic Folkways (U.S.), FE 4102. Geoffrey N. O'Grady and Alix O'Grady.
Songs of the Western Australian Desert Aborigines. ASCH Mankind Series (U.S.), AHM 4210. Richard A. Gould.
Traditional Music of Torres Strait. Australian Institute of Aboriginal Studies, AIAS/11. Jeremy Beckett.
Tribal Music of Australia. Ethnic Folkways (U.S.), FE 4439. A. P. Elkin.

Films

Most of these films are available through the Australian Institute of Aboriginal Studies, though they are not all produced by them. They include some of the greatest ethnographic films yet made. [Ed.]

Aboriginal Arnhem Land. AIAS. B/W. 45 min. Directed by Robert Edwards.

Anthropologists, guided by Aboriginals, make a long and difficult trip by landrover from a reservation to the Aboriginals' ancient ceremonial sites in Arnhem Land in the far north of Australia. We are shown a site marked by ceremonial stones, watch and listen to a young didjeridu player. Background music of didjeridu and clapping sticks almost throughout.

Camels and the Pitjantjara. AIAS. Col. 57 min. Directed by Roger Sandall.

Scenes from the life of the Pitjantjara tribe on a reservation in Central Australia. Shows their use of camels, originally introduced from Afghanistan. Considerable section on men's ceremonies and clapping sticks.

Dances at Aurukun. AIAS. Col. 29 min. Directed by Ian Dunlop.

Camp dances with wooden carvings of creatures familiar to the Aborigines. Singing, handclapping, two boomerangs.

Dance of the Buffalo Hunt. ACFU. B/W. 4½ min. Directed by J. Rogers.

The hunting and killing of a water buffalo: one man carrying the horns of a buffalo mimes the part of the hunted animal, while ten other dancers mime the hunters.

Desert People. CF/MH. B/W. 51 min. Directed by Ian Dunlop.

Abridged version of *People of the Australian Western Desert*.

Djalambu. AIAS. Col. 55 min. Directed by Cecil Holmes.

Mourning ceremony of the Emu Clan in Arnhem Land, with singing, clapping sticks, and didjeridu. The making of a *djalambu* (a hollow gravepost) is shown.

Eight Aboriginal Songs. AIAS. Col. 21½ min. Directed by Alice M. Moyle.

Singing and didjeridu playing by Waṉindilyaugwa and Nunggubuyu linguistic groups on Groote Eylandt east of Arnhem Land. Songs describe the brolga bird, stingray, dolphin, curlew, and west wind.

Emu Ritual at Ruguri. AIAS. Col. 16 min. Directed by Roger Sandall.

"Preparation of a spectacular ground painting; initiation of a young man to the secret designs on cave walls and a ritual dance associated with both the caves and the painting.... Calling and singing to the accompaniment of boomerang, clapping and tapping of a single boomerang against a shield." Peter Kennedy.

Five Aboriginal Dances from Cape York. AIAS. Col. 8 min. Directed by Ian Dunlop.

Dances from Queensland.

The Mulga Seed Ceremony. AIAS. Col. 25 min. Directed by Roger Sandall.

Rites "to promote the fertility and growth of the Mulga bush." [Stanley Hawes] Dancing and chanting. Shows body decoration with paint and feathers.

Ngoora-A Camping Place. AIAS. Col. 50 min. Directed by T. D. Campbell.

A record of the centuries-old way of life of the Walbiri tribe in the Northern Territory. Shows their skill at finding food and water and at making shelters. No ritual, only one short segment of chant.

People of the Australian Western Desert. AIAS. B/W. 150 min. Directed by Ian Dunlop.

In ten parts. "An attempt . . . to record something of the daily life and technology of the small family groups that still roam the desert." Stanley Hawes.

Primitive People. AIAS. B/W. 33 min. Produced by Gaumont British Instructional Films, Ltd. Peter Finch, narrator.

"A study of the nomadic Mewite people, aborigines of Arnhem Land, Australia. Principal sequences are of family groups, gathering food, building shelter, and funeral ceremonies." UCEMC. The last includes singing, dancing, and didjeridu playing.

Walbiri Ritual at Gunadjari. AIAS. Col. 28 min. Directed by Roger Sandall.

"Documents a three-day ceremony at a place where the lands of the Walbiri and Pintubi tribes join." Karl Heider.

Walbiri Ritual at Ngama. UCEMC, PSU(PAR). Col. 23 min. Directed by Roger Sandall.

A documentary of men's rituals before a sacred painted rock in the Northern Territory.

10. Music
South of the Sahara

Atta Annan Mensah

Awareness of old cultural links and the growth of new ones among the various countries of the African continent make regional divisions seem less and less meaningful. Close examination of differences between Arab music of the Maghreb and that of Egypt suggests a sub-Saharan African presence in the Maghreb (Crossley-Holland 1960:118–135; Hitti 1964:275), just as musical practices in the savanna belt north of the forest belt of West Africa suggest a North African presence. The occurrence of the one-string violin in North, East, West, and Central Africa is one of many connecting features that bind these regions together. These are some of the common bonds that African peoples prefer to emphasize today. On the other hand, dissimilarities in musical cultures in Africa point to a need for some division for the sake of convenience, and the one suggested by the title of this essay is well known to be convenient, even if no assumptions of uniformity can be made for the area within its confines. Resemblances and differences both occur in the old traditional music of sub-Saharan Africa as well as in the new, which has grown in stature and importance over the decades of the twentieth century.

Developments of the twentieth century have made it increasingly clear that students of African music should begin to reckon seriously with the music that takes its genesis from this century. For the growing amount of listening time and the growing proportion of young lovers of this music lead to the conclusion that it is the African music of the present and future. The first things young people do as soon as they can afford a collection is to acquire phonograph records with the latest African hits and pop music from the Western world. Radio disc jockeys, who usually belong to this group of collectors, serve listeners—old and young—with this new music on records in response to popular demand; the transistor radio excels its forerunner, the spring-driven phonograph, in bringing this music to the remotest ends of Africa's rural areas. In many parts of Africa, a young person's first homemade toys include musical instruments. Among these, the banjo, the guitar, and the snare and bass drums occur most frequently. This twentieth-century manifestation of interest and motivation is a result of the influence of Western pop music in Africa.

Another index of the growing importance of new African music may be seen in the proportion of press coverage given to it in sub-Saharan Africa. Nairobi's *Daily Nation* devotes a page every Saturday to current musical entertainment and adds lists of the Top Ten in African, Western, and Eastern (mainly Indian and Arab) pop music. In Accra, the *Daily Graphic* devotes a page in every Saturday issue to the same theme, and the important features and articles on this page are invariably about new pop music and pop bands.

The forces behind this trend have been strong and continue to grow in strength. One of these, urbanization, is by all accounts showing an upward trend. So are such change agents as the church, the school, and Western technology. The phonograph, the cinema, and the transistor radio all come to the city first and then spread to the rest of Africa. In the same way, the Western-type modern school has brought to Africa's youth new tastes, new ways of viewing their world, and techniques of implementing newly

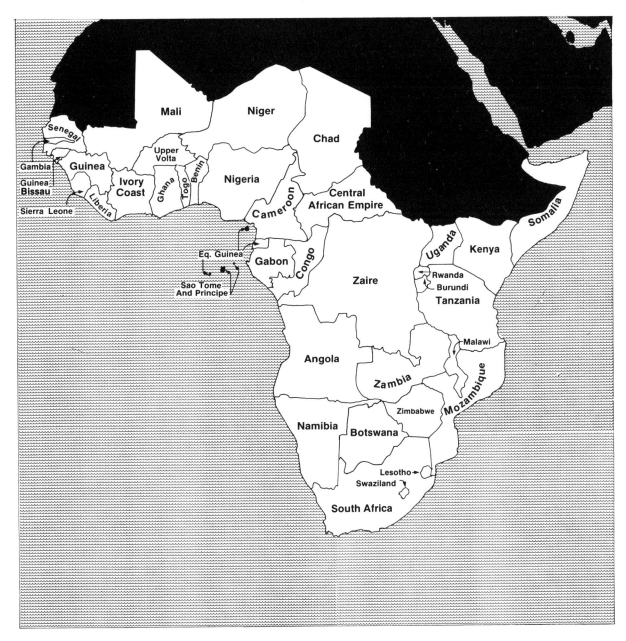

Sub-Saharan Africa

adopted ideas. The effects of these growing forces cannot be ignored in any serious study of music in sub-Saharan Africa, although the old traditional music still remains virile and is still regarded as the standard against which all value judgments should be made in music—new musical types of twentieth-century Africa still hold strong links with the old traditional music. What is this old traditional music? Where does it belong?

TRADITIONAL MUSIC

The great proportion of African traditional music is that occurring primarily in passage rites (birth, puberty, marriage, succession, and funeral ceremonies), worship, spirit possession rites, divining, and therapy. Some of this music is also the product of associations (hunters, warriors, secret societies) or serves as an aid to work. A fair number of monographs exist which stress the functional role of music in African life and there is no need to elaborate the point further (King 1961; Merriam 1957; Nketia 1955 and 1963*a*; and others), but it is important to note that traditional African societies also view their music as entertainment in other situations, calling it in many cases by a name approximating the meaning of the word *play* (e.g., the Bantu *ngoma* which also means "drum" or "drumming," and the Akan *agor* which also means "drumming" or "performance"). Thus there are types of music existing largely for purposes of amusement. But more interesting are instances that serve both as functional music and as entertainment. The *vimbuza* dance of the Tumbuka of the Eastern Province of Zambia is basically a spirit possession dance. But mediums of vimbuza spirits have often danced to delight village and town audiences, and the Zambia National Dance Troupe has benefited from the artistry of actual mediums without the difficulty or embarrassment of an actual possession ensuing.

FIGURE 10-2. *Kalimba*—An Nsenga (Zambia) hand piano (photographed by Zambia Cultural Services).

Instrumental Resources

Traditional African music draws on a variety of resources. There is a wide spectrum of musical instruments. Some are hard to classify, but all the four main acoustic classes are richly represented. Idiophones include a wide assortment of rattles, bells, concussed shells, xylophones, and hand pianos. The last-named instrument, called *sansa, mbira, likembe, budongo, kalimba*, and by many other names, is believed to have originated in Africa. The xylophone, which is also very widespread and exists in great variety in sub-Saharan Africa, has been variously ascribed to African and Indonesian origin. A controversy hangs over this issue. Those who cling to the African origin point out that an adopted instrument could not have been so widespread on such a vast continent and exist in such different degrees of complexity and sophistication.

Membranophones are undoubtedly the most widely diffused instruments in sub-Saharan Africa. Found in conical, cylindrical, barrel, hourglass, mortar, globular, and kettle shapes, double- and single-headed, they are played with sticks, hands, or a combination of both in various ways to obtain subtle varieties of sound. In some cases (friction drums) sound is produced by rubbing, with the aid of wet cloth, a stick inserted into the drum shell through the drumhead. The effect is that of a sustained low booming sound. The drum is often rubbed very fast to give the sound a percussive edge.

FIGURE 10-1. *Shijimba*—An Nkoya (Zambia) xylophone (photographed by A. A. Mensah).

FIGURE 10-3. *Nyanga*—A Nyangwe pan-pipe being played by Baba Chale Mafala (about 60 years) of Tete, Mozambique, photographed at his residence in Malawi by Maurice Djenda.

It is worth noting that a number of instruments called drums are not membranophones. The slit drum and the log drum consist of hollowed-out wood blocks or boxes played with sticks or fists. These are, strictly speaking, struck wooden gongs in the idiophone class. Likewise, pot drums (clay pots hit on the mouth with fanlike beaters to produce fluffy drumlike sounds) are not membranophones, but rather aerophones. All the above varieties of drum are widespread in East, West, Central, and southern Africa.

Chordophones are also widespread. There are board, trough, raft, and tube zithers, lyres, harps, and tube and shell bowed fiddles of various sizes. The same is true of aerophones, instruments from which sound (usually) is produced initially by encased vibrating air columns. Flutes in various sizes, those with notched mouthpieces, corked mouthpieces, whistle types, vertically and horizontally held flutes, as well as gourd and shell megaphones, oboe and clarinet types of wind instrument, and animal horn and wooden trumpets may be found in many places. Pot drum aerophones have already been mentioned under membranophones.

Ensembles

Sub-Saharan musical instruments are heard solo and in ensembles. Ensembles feature homogeneous and mixed instrumental groupings. Among the former may be mentioned drum ensembles, one-string violin ensembles, and ensembles of bells, trumpets, and flutes. In mixed ensembles, one type of instrument may predominate, with one or more instruments of different types added for specific coloring or other purposes. Thus the bell (*dawuru*) in Akan (Ghana) drum ensembles maintains an inexorable time line; the rattle in Kinyankole (Uganda/Kinyarwanda) ensembles contributes both color and a basic rhythm pattern; the flute (*endere*) brings countermelody, color, and added virtuosity to Kisoga and Kiganda (Uganda) drum and xylophone ensembles.

Ensembles range from a two-piece band to very large orchestras. In the Acholi (Uganda) *bwola* dance, one may hear as many as fifty or more drums, one carried by each dancer, in addition to a central core of a three-piece drum ensemble. A display of bwola for President Amin at Kitgum on December 18, 1971, featured over two hundred.

Musical instruments may be played by themselves, but more often they are used to accompany voices. Sometimes these instrumental ensembles function as the foundation of the music, however, and the voices assume the role of accompaniment. In the *ngolorombe* (panpipe) dance of the Chikunda of Zambia, panpipes and voices are pitched in equal dialogue. Vocal ensembles with only clapping in accompaniment also abound.

Rhythm

African musical instruments and vocal resources are organized in sonic time patterns that distinguish their idioms from those of other world regions, through the various scales, melody patterns, traditions of pitch clustering, and concurrent pitch lines, and rhythm. The paramountcy of rhythm in African music is widely recognized and generally regarded as the basis of the musical idiom. But there have been difficulties in explaining African rhythmic structure and its underlying principles. Most existing analyses seem to concern themselves with a search for one overriding basic principle governing all African rhythm and have resulted in the singling out of some striking feature which, no matter how important, should not, in view of other insistently striking features, be regarded as the dominant principle. From a comparative study of existing theories, it is indeed hard to rule out the possibility that African rhythm is governed by a combination of a number of regulative principles, not by merely one. Its full significance in all instances thus lies in a composite view that takes a number of factors into account, a view that may shift its emphasis from one element to another according to the situation. For instance, the overall steady duple effect of Akan drumming should be described on a different set of principles from those of the shifting entry points of Ndebele (Zimbabwe) and Zulu (South Africa) handclap patterns. The first exhibits layers of rhythmic lines of varying complexity with some amount of interplay of two against three pulses; the other two seem to exploit contrasting speeds of concurrent pulses. In both instances the presence of some regulative principle can be felt. Akan drumming, like many other types in sub-Saharan Africa, features a pivot line against which all other concurrent rhythmic lines are played. Though there is always one dominant rhythmic line in the drumming regarded as such, all other repetitive patterns may also serve as points of reference; players, dancers, and listeners derive enjoyment from shifting their attention from one rhythmic line to another within the full context of the other rhythms. In Ndebele and Zulu music, voices and handclapping are organized on the same principle of contrasting pulse values, although the actual rhythmic patterns are different.

Rhythm and pulse interplay is a frequent device in African music. But the individual rhythm lines also present characteristic devices which have generated a great deal of discussion. Some rhythm patterns are based on regular recurrent beats or their divisions and fall neatly into regular metrical divisions, but other patterns cannot be described in terms of beats and beat divisions and lie astride ordinary metrical divisions, this *adowa* (Akan) dance bell pattern, for instance:

EXAMPLE 10-1.

Some of these nondivisive patterns also feature alternate triple and duple divisions, such as this regulative claves pattern in popular bands:

EXAMPLE 10-2.

In the above instances some observers would regard the bar lines as a matter of convenience. This point is further discussed below. It should suffice here to note that the terms divisive, additive, and hemiola have been used as labels for the above types of African rhythm patterns.

Rhythm units often occur in exact repetition, though sometimes these repetitions are elaborated and varied. A master drummer's line may consist of wide recurring cycles of consecutive rhythm patterns which are continually reshuffled to heighten the interest and create a sense of variety. In full drum orchestras, this is often the main source of excitement, though not often the best aid to analysis. In contrast, the presence of rigorous order and periodicity has been readily recognized by observers and scholars, and various theories have been advanced to explain what goes on. Each of the theories has a basic validity. But growing experience with African rhythm justifies their further discussion.

Clash of rhythms. To observers, the simultaneous combination of different rhythm patterns has been by far the most striking aspect of sub-Saharan African music. In many traditions the concurrent rhythm lines result in a recurring main beat on which all the principal beats in the separate rhythm lines coincide. Between any two of these main beats the individual rhythm lines tend to retain their independence and the effect of multiple rhythm (or polyrhythm) is stressed. In some cases the main beats, the points at which the principal beats of the separate rhythms coincide, are so widely spaced that it is difficult for outsiders to feel their regular occurrence. One scholar speaks of a "clash of rhythms in which the beats never coincide" (Jones 1954:43 ff.). The principle of arithmetical ratio indicates that come together they must, however far between, if, as is the case in all sub-Saharan African music, pattern repetition exists and the component lines are not shifting their constituent beats all the time.

Polymeter. Time unit (meter) is an important aspect of rhythm. Although meter and rhythm are distinct musical qualities, the two elements have often been considered together by theorists, and the distinction has sometimes become blurred in the minds of students. In African music, when a number of independent rhythm lines occur simultaneously, they are often distinguished not only by the internal organization of their articulated time points

Notes:

Tsindonyi = Small drums played with light sticks.

Ingoma indini = Medium-sized drums played with both hands.

Ingoma ingulu or ikulu = Big drum played with stick or hand.

EXAMPLE 10-3.

(coinciding with the players' strokes) but also by their metrical organization or the number of beats that form a measure (or time unit). Observers have noted that the "parts" in an African ensemble are not always internally organized on the same metrical unit.

Example 10-3 was transcribed by the author from a *kadodi* band accompanying a group of dancing novices for circumcision rites in north Bugisu (Uganda). The small drums (*tsindonyi*) produce an unchanging time pattern in six-eight, while the medium size drums (*ngoma indini*) alternate straight compound duple bars and triplet hemiolic bars within a six-eight meter. The largest drum (*ngoma ingulu* or *ikulu*) produces a two-bar phrase articulated to depict compound duple and hemiolic bars followed by another two-bar phrase stressing a quadruple meter within two six-eight bars.

This is the master drum and it produces many alternates of this pattern; but the basic effect of

six followed by *three* in hemiola style and then by *four* is maintained by this drum throughout against a bustling overlay of compound duple meter.

However, the regulative effect of the pivot rhythm line and the resultant rhythm pattern impose overriding time divisions that govern the entire piece, even when some of the constituent parts seem to run counter to these time divisions. The principle of polymeter should therefore be only regarded as an analyst's guide in many instances. Burden texts describing some African drum orchestral patterns frequently express the resultant from the combination of the different parts and fall within one overall metric pattern, thus demonstrating that in the performer's view the ultimate reality of rhythm is isometric. For instance, the burden text for one Akan hourglass drum ensemble piece is repeated to learners within the rhythm pattern given above the following text:

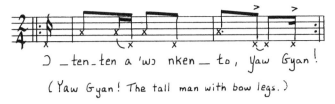

) _ ten _ ten a 'wɔ nken _ to, Yaw Gyan!

(Yaw Gyan! The tall man with bow legs.)

EXAMPLE 10-4.

The rhythm pattern to which the text is attached is really a combination of rhythm patterns and the last bar includes all the bit contributed by the *gyamadudu* (a large cylindrical double-headed drum):

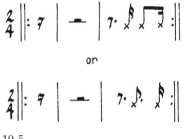

EXAMPLE 10-5.

EXAMPLE 10-6.

Heard in isolation this rhythm fragment may strike the analyst as falling within a triple bar, a small subjective adaption that would be likely to elude the inexperienced analyst. But repeated with the burden text, which spells out the resultant, the gyamadudu's part clearly falls within a duple measure with the rest of the combined rhythm patterns. In many other instances, the prevailing aesthetic norm is that all the rhythm lines making up the dance are regarded as different time organizations within one metrical pattern.

Metronome sense. Appreciation of music in sub-Saharan Africa often depends on the listener's (or the player's) ability to supply a subjective beat which enables him to orient himself to changing rhythmic activity in the music. This ability, subconsciously learned during child-

hood within the society, has been fully discussed by Richard Waterman under the label *metronome sense*. Though this ability cannot be included in the objective features of African rhythm, its importance cannot be overemphasized since it enables the listener (as well as the player) to enjoy the elaboration and sometimes shifting overlay of rhythmic network without straying (Waterman 1952:208–9).

Arsis and motor accent. Hornbostel precedes Waterman with a full discussion of an aspect of the subjective beat. In this discussion he draws attention to the twofold movement of the drummer's muscle. He concludes that the straining of the muscle during the act of beating (he calls this the arsis) and the audible motor accents are both significant aspects of the rhythmic reality. Hornbostel thought that the rhythmic unit begins on this silent beat. This duality of sub-Saharan African rhythm may be seen also in the bodily movement accompanying all other African instruments and singing (Hornbostel 1928: 25–26).

Rhythm definition. It should be noted that the element of stress (and intensity) does not appear to be the main device for defining rhythmic pattern or time unit. Contrast in drum beating is also obtained by pitch and timbre differentiation. These techniques are probably of equal importance in rhythm definition. Muffling the drumhead; beating on the center or near the rim of the drum; combining beating drumhead and beating on the drum shell; drubbing, patting, or bouncing the hand on the drumhead; striking it with the fingers or with open or cupped palm or fist, with or without stress—these constitute the main body of technical vocabulary of pitch and timbre definition and differentiation in drumming. A rhythm style may be defined by a selection from these and other techniques.

But it should be clear from what has already been said that rhythm is all-pervasive and is not restricted to drumming alone. The importance of pitch and timbre differentiation in African drumming should direct our attention to other media for rhythmic expression. Wind and stringed instruments, xylophones, and hand pianos are played in percussive style in order to define rhythm patterns more clearly. Nevertheless, certain specific practices in rhythmic organization seem to be largely restricted to particular types of ensemble. Metrical contrast is featured more within drum ensembles, where the main beat sometimes becomes elusive; in handclapping the main beats coincide more often and thus become more obvious; xylophone playing emphasizes resultant patterns from different pitch lines through the use of hocket style; in sung melody there are often offbeat entries.

To conclude, rhythm in African music may be described as patterns in time defined by lines or bands of differentiated pitched and timbral (or nonpitch) durational values, perceived against a background of regular pulsation that may be inwardly or acoustically expressed. A number of such differentiated lines or bands may be singly or concurrently expressed, with emphasis on internal bustle or periodicity, or both.

Timbre

Sub-Saharan African music is more than rhythm. Often, in fact, the aesthetic point of emphasis is not rhythm. Tonal coloring, interplay of pitch lines, and exploitation of sheer melodic beauty may be the main point of emphasis or an important element in a combination of aesthetic devices in a particular performance. Space restricts me to only brief notes on these elements, beginning with timbre.

Reference has been made to the great variety of tone quality in African drumming. Tone quality is in fact explored in many other ensembles. The use of different instruments, vocal styles, and various ensembles stresses the importance of this element, and in some instances it is clear that whole backgrounds of tone color are in reality supplied as settings for other musical elements. The provision of buzzer attachments to musical instruments, to an instrumentalist's wrist, or a dancer's calves or ankles is one of the usual devices used to build up this background. Sometimes this background is in the form of arabesque bands made up of fast-moving pitch lines in simultaneous motion or in hocket. Chopi xylophone orchestral sound furnishes a widely familiar example (Tracey

1948:5–7). Since this orchestral background and the parts running before it may or may not consist of sounds with definite pitch, it would be more accurate to speak of sonic color rather than tone color.

Vocal styles. The importance of sound quality in African music is often demonstrated by the human voice when it changes from natural singing to an imitation of a musical instrument, as illustrated by southern Masaba horn trumpet players in Uganda. But the human voice is used in its own right in the exploitation of tone color. In any particular locality the range of vocal styles may be limited; some areas may indeed have more than others. Thus the subdued two-part contrapuntal singing by priest and votary at the Brakune shrine in Ashanti, the open resonance of the singing at *adowa* social dances (Nketia 1963b:202, 203), and the loud and rapidly declaimed strains of the *Kwadwom* heroic court poetry, with nasalized alveolar phrase endings, can all be found in Ashanti traditional singing. Merriam refers to five vocal styles in the musical practices of the Bahutu (Rwanda) alone (1953:245–53). It would take a lot of space to describe all the known vocal styles. The following list of some of the more widely used types is offered by way of illustration.

Voice masking by high pitching and nasalizing is used in various places to symbolize royalty or the supernatural; but conch shell and gourd-and-mirliton trumpet ensembles that amplify some of these effects stress their aesthetic significance in music. In South Masaba (Bugisu District in Uganda) one hears wordless singing through ram or cow horn trumpet within the more usual embouchure technique. The practice of wordless singing is very diversified, embracing the use of vocables (with a special bias in favor of the vowel *e* pronounced as *a* in *nay*), yodel, and the more sustained vowel singing featured among the Bambuti of northeastern Zaire and other groups.

Pitch Combination

Pitch combination in African music has been studied under different names, and a number of conclusions have been put forward. One of these is that African music does not feature harmony, certainly not as an aspect of the *music makers'* musical conception. In cases where harmony has been conceded, its presence has been attributed to contacts with the Western world. In some cases the African has been credited with an original conception of harmony, but only as a manifestation of some early stage of human civilization long outmoded in Western Europe.

Richard Waterman, one of the first scholars to refute these conclusions, suggests that they are products of certain preconceptions about how the art of music has evolved among men (1952:208-9). There is also little doubt that such generalizations arose mainly from inadequate knowledge. Vasco da Gama's logbook of 1498 refers to evidence of simultaneous different pitches heard in southern and eastern Africa, and African systems are patchy and do not suggest a flow of musical wisdom from Europe. It seems therefore more correct to examine African traditions of pitch clustering and simultaneous pitch lines on their own terms and as indigenous developments. It is however an advantage, in order to communicate with a wider audience, to employ some of the familiar terms used by scholars, provided they are strictly confined to where they are really applicable.

Any simultaneous occurrence of two or more pitched sounds in African music may be regarded as a chord; the result may also be described as harmony. In sub-Saharan African music, pitched "voices" often act together and give rise to chordal effects. There are six ways in which these may occur:

Note: x in measure 3 indicates a downward slide.

EXAMPLE 10-7.

evidently established before the first European contacts occurred in these regions (Davidson 1964:122, 127). In all probability Vasco da Gama's log might have been describing what we now know as hocket, harmonic coloring by pitch couplings or clusterings, and simultaneous pitch lines. The arrival from Europe of such sophisticated devices, their diffusion and establishment by the fifteenth century, lies outside the realm of probability. Examination of other existing evidence (e.g., Bowdich 1819:368-69), including past and present examples of traditional African music, reveals practices of pitch combinations quite different from those of the days of diaphony, organum, and polyphony in Western Europe. Resemblances between European

1. In some choral singing, melody may be decorated by sporadic single-note couplings.

2. Sometimes melodic decoration is effected by concurrent fragments of melody added now and again to the main melody.

3. Harmony may occur at overlappings between cadence and openings of melodies during antiphony between voices, or voices and instruments. The above three instances are very widespread.

4. In some choral styles cadences are decorated by clusterings of voices. Cadential triadic clusters in Awutu *Sakumo* and Krobo *dipo* and *klama* ritual songs (Ghana) provide clear illustrations, as in example 10-7 (Mensah 1966:90).

5. Some instrumental styles, especially some

xylophone and some hand piano playing, produce pitch bands woven in hocket or arabesque styles which feature sporadic chords or continuous effects of broken chords. These can be illustrated from xylophone playing in Busoga (Uganda), Nkoya (Zambia), and Lobi (Ghana).

6. By far the most widely commented upon chordal effect is the occurrence of consistent simultaneous pitch lines in whole phrases or even longer passages (Crossley-Holland 1967:59–103). There are many varieties of this practice.

Melodies in parallel motion in thirds, fourths, and fifths have been noted in various places.

instances may feature vertical interval sequences of 7-5-3-3-3 . . ., or 5-4-3-3-3 . . ., or 4-3-3-3 . . ., or straight thirds all the way, etc. Imitative style with chord-producing overlappings may be found among the BaMbuti (northeastern Zaire), the Zulu/Swasi of southwest Africa, and some other groups. Ostinato accompaniment is a favorite musical device in many parts of sub-Saharan Africa and many instrumental and vocal accompaniments (e.g., the *cilapi* of the Cewa in Zambia and Malawi) are in this style. David Rycroft has noted a principle of nonsimultaneous entry in multipart singing among the

EXAMPLE 10-8. Example of "funnel-shaped" two-part extracted from a cadential chorus response to mukanda circumcision song from Lovale (Zambia).

EXAMPLE 10-9. Example of part singing from *cilapi* (hunters' song from Nsenga-Zambia).

Merriam notes significant stretches of contrary motion among the Bashi (1959:75). Oblique motion occurs in many traditions. Among the Luchazi and neighboring groups astride the Angolan-Zambian border, symmetrical combinations of similar and contrary motion of simultaneous melodies may be found which at times give rise to funnel-shaped melodic bands. Such

Ndebele of Zimbabwe. He describes the form as circular and notes the principles of chording (1967:88–103). Nguni groups in central and southern Africa also feature this style in some of their song traditions.

The question has often been posed as to whether pitch combination devices in sub-Saharan societies are viewed by their users as

FIGURE 10-4. *Chikunda*—A likishi in mask from a *mukanda* (circumcision camp) entering a Luchazi village, Zambia; women meet the likishi, believed to be one of several spirit characters which attend circumcision ritual and celebrations, with songs. This character is also known among the Chokwe as *Chikuta* where it is believed to have originated. (Photograph by Dr. Gerhard Kubik)

harmony, decoration, colored pitch bands, or sheer coincidence. David Rycroft has investigated whether the relationship between the parts in Ndebele singing is temporal, chordal, or contrapuntal (ibid. 102-3). Evidence of the isolated performer trying to sing accompanying parts while he had not ended the soloist's part stressed the importance of the accompaniment to the performer. A similar experience elsewhere reinforces this point. A Nsenga vocal group performed with a hand piano soloist. The next day the soloist was isolated and recorded alone. His items included some of the songs recorded with the vocal group during the previous night. It was observed that in his solo recordings he cut short some of his announcing phrases in order to bring in the responsive phrases (on his instrument). Asked

why he had made the cuts, he said he did so because they were there!

Among the Akans of Ghana, the word *inyiyim* or *inyiyiho*, meaning "decoration," is often applied to part singing. The sounding together of different notes at rest points and in melodic movement is enjoyed in Akan as in other African multipart musical traditions, and here emphasis may shift from the enjoyment of viewing the decorative part against the part decorated to the interplay or the blending in parallel motion. Looking at sub-Saharan Africa as a whole, parts may range from two to as many as six voices, according to the musical tradition and the resourcefulness of the performers, and in many instances stylistic procedures of chording and progressive pitch combinations are well defined. However, traditions of pitch combinations are by no means uniform and every instance calls for its own principles of analysis.

In concluding the discussion of this aspect of African music, it may be added that the notion held in certain quarters that tertiary chording goes with seven-note scales and quartal and quintal chording go with five-note scales is misleading. The Nsenga and the Tonga of Zambia and the Dagomba of Ghana, to cite three out of

notes d d^1 d^2 g g^1 and e^1 clearly lie on a sound network band or in a reticulate pattern. Broken chord effect can also be felt especially in the left-hand line.

Melody
The primary instrument of pitch combination in African music is melody. There is a very wide variety of African melodies and no theory exists that describes them all, but there are descrip-

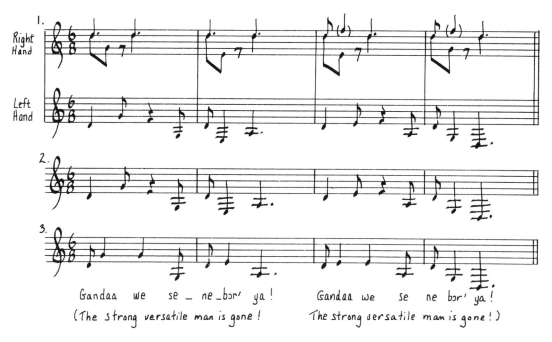

EXAMPLE 10-10.

several, use seven-note scales without tertiary harmony. The Tonga and Nsenga sometimes use parallel fourths and occasional fifths; the Dagomba prefer unison.

Broken chords and reticulate xylophone effect. In the Lobi example (ex. 10-10) from Ghana the top D's (on the upper staff) act alternately as junctions for a top and a middle part which are heard separately as well as together by the Lobi player. The left-hand Ds, the Gs, and the Es (on the lower staff) also combine with right-hand notes to form an inner line which the Lobi player also hears separately as shown in the song (see ex. 10-10, no. 3 below). Thus in the fragment the

tions that suggest some basic approaches to analysis (Merriam 1959a:66–67; Nettl 1965:140–44 [see May bibliography]; Nketia 1962a:44–51).

Shape. It has been observed that African melody generally follows a downward trend. Its shape has been likened to that of a ripsaw, beginning with a steep rise and then following a gradual slope. Instances have also been found with two levels, the first bit lying on a higher plane than the second, and some have been found which describe arcs.

Movement patterns. African melodies combine conjunct with disjunct movement. The latter form of melodic movement seems to suggest more character and has therefore received more attention from scholars. The descriptive terms *chasmatonic* or "wide stepped melody" (Brandel 1962:75–87) and *triadic split fifths* indicate some of the ways in which disjunct movement may be viewed. Pendular and interlocking (zigzag) forms of melodic movement have also been observed.

Other features of African melody include upward and downward slides frequently (but not always) used to provide emphasis or finality, especially those slides that terminate at pitchless, speechlike points. A piece of African melody may gravitate or play around some tonal center or carry configurations suggestive of modality.

Occasional melismas or more frequently the pace of rapid flow of syllables may constitute the main distinguishing feature of a melodic style. On the whole, sub-Saharan melodies are fast-moving.

Scale. Every melody can be reduced to a musical scale. There are different views on what a scale is, and discussions on African music reflect these differences. For this discussion a musical scale is conceived as an aggregate of all the constituent tones used within the octave in a melodic tradition arranged in an ascending or descending order of pitch. This series of pitch frequencies is normally usable at different octaves without change in the interval spacings (exceptions have been noted in some world cultures).

A variety of musical scales is used within sub-Saharan Africa, and some individual ethnic units are known to have more than one musical scale. The Lobi people, straddling the northeastern Ivory Coast border, use two xylophone tunings with different intervallic structures. The Acholi of Uganda have at least two scales, *larumu* and *laturi*, the latter regarded as easier for budding instrumentalists. In some parts of Acholi the laturi scale is also called *ogodo*, a tradition for simple songs. On the other hand, a wide distribution of similar scales can be found in sub-Saharan African music. For instance, the seven-note scale with the so-called "blue" notes (neutral seventh and sometimes a neutral third as well) is used by the Bemba of Zambia, the Luvale of Angola, the Baoule of Ivory Coast, the Chokosi of north Togo, and groups in other areas.

Research has not yet yielded clear, pronounced rules or evidence of standardization in African scale patterns. What is visible in African traditions, however, indicates precise conceptions of scale approached with varying margins of tolerance.

Instrumentalists go to great lengths to insure that their own particular instruments or ensembles are well in tune, but in many contexts distinct deviations are noticeable. Sometimes (especially in unison trumpet playing, as in the *amakondere* ensembles of Bunyori, Uganda), clearly audible beats occur—a pulsation effect produced by two notes nearly in tune when sounded together. This effect appears to be accepted by players and listeners. In one extreme, ensembles exist in Lozi (Zambia) in which xylophones in different tuning segments may be heard together with voices, each pursuing the melody concurrently at fixed intervals with the others and producing together with them an effect of polytonality.

Significance of Music

Sub-Saharan African music has been validly assessed from various viewpoints. This has been possible because of the varying emphasis placed on the ends it is employed to serve. As a vehicle of thought and a technique of dramatic expression, music takes its pride of place in storytelling where characters move and interact within a scene setting created in the minds of the audience by the storyteller. At some parts of the story members of the audience may rise up and enact portions of the scene with song and dance. In this sense and to varying extents in practically all instances, sub-Saharan music may be viewed as serving the scene with song and dance, and thus as serving the cause of drama. [The film *A Story A Story* illustrates this point.—ed.] Within contexts of ritual, music may provide a tonal world in which, as the belief goes, the spirit world can respond to the call of men, commune with men, and enable them to renew and revive their consciousness of safety and well-being in the hands of the gods and the ancestors. As such, music brings solace and uplift. On a mundane plane, men at work, at war, and in social groups have used music to express their identities, to seek inspiration, and to condition their minds and bodies for tasks ahead. Along with these may be considered music provided in situations of therapy. In all of these instances music is clearly viewed as functional and its full meaning and significance can only be seen within the contexts in which it occurs.

On many occasions, African musicians bearing props and costumes and dancing within specific settings, bring parts of the story of life home to everyone around. Here sculpture, metalwork, beadwork, basketry, weaving, music, dance, and elements of theater may be blended in the expression of ideas.

In all cases the elements of beauty and amusement are present, and it is clear that the resources of music are organized so that they may please the ear. In this process emphasis may be laid on the beauty of melody, of rhythm pattern, or of interaction between melodies or rhythmic patterns or both. In all cases music is viewed as a design in sound-time units in linear, reticulate, or band patterns, tinged with instrumental or vocal timbre. These patterns provide the effect of color, bustle, and drive in movement, which seems to be the African conception of the essence of life, and in combination with other arts within contextual settings they depict some of the rubrics of living together and reinforce the meaning and significance of life.

TWENTIETH-CENTURY DEVELOPMENTS

Aesthetic norms of music south of the Sahara derive from long ago. But in every region new influences are giving rise to some new kind of music.

Tarabu

To begin from the east coast, there is the *tarabu* or *tarab*, a type of popular music performed by a vocalist in Arab style, with or without a chorus, and accompanied by various instrumental combinations including some of the following instruments: the Arab *tabl*, the *'ud*, the Indian portable organ, the Western violin, the harmonica, sometimes the Spanish guitar, and African drums. In Dar es Salaam and other east coast cities, the tarabu also may be heard on occasions in dance bands with different setups. This east coast pop type, whose theme is almost invariably love, is believed to have been modeled on ensembles attached to the courts of sultanates and sheikhdoms in earlier times; it is said to have originated with east coast musicians who served their new music to gatherings at weddings, circumcision rites, and other social occasions. Tarabu music varies in style from almost pure Arab and Indian to highly jazzed flavors, with African drums at the other extreme. Its high point of popularity along the east coast, mainly in the cities, dates from the 1960s to the 1970s (the time of writing). The tarabu is also frequently broadcast on some radio stations in West and Central Africa.

Kwela

Kwela is a form of black South African pop music that became such a craze that in Johannesburg it was banned for disrupting traffic. Performers frequently played by the roadside and allegedly diverted the attention of motorists, some of whom pulled up to listen. But the kwela lived and spread among bands in Rhodesia, Zambia, Malawi, and other places in central and southern Africa, and many African radio stations have broadcast it across the continent.

The kwela, which is dance music, grew out of a number of popular dances that arose among black pop musicians in South Africa; the most prominent of these were the *phata-phata* and the *tsaba-tsaba*, in both of which a boy and a girl danced towards each other. These dances came just after the Second World War, when South African radio stations broadcast a stream of American pop music and jazz of the day. South African musicians took to this music and introduced many of its clichés into their own creations. The kwela is in fact often called "South African Jive." A typical kwela band consists of one or two penny whistles, a guitar, and two or more vocalists. But big bands with the usual jazz outfit also play the kwela. Kwela celebrities are penny whistle virtuosos; among the best known were Spokes Mashiyane and Lemmy Special of the 1960s.

Congolese

Congolese pop music has perhaps the widest circulation in sub-Saharan Africa. As its name implies, it originated in the Republics of Zaire and Congo (Brazzaville). Throughout the 1960s and up to the time of writing recordings of this music have dominated nightclubs, beer halls, and dance halls in Central and East Africa as well as those of its countries of origin and it is widely imitated by East and Central African dance bands in their own creations. "Congolese," also widely known as "Congolese rhumba," reflects influences from Latin America and carries the beat of Latin American, especially Cuban, forms. Its rise is generally ascribed to the influence of Radio Brazzaville which, during the Second World War, beamed a lot of Latin American music. A typical Congolese pop band consists of electric guitars (lead, rhythm, and harmony) and vocalists, although larger bands with trumpets, saxes, and trombones may be found.

Highlife

The oldest and perhaps most firmly established sub-Saharan African pop music type is the *highlife* of West Africa. Believed to have originated with marching bands formed by disbanded Ghanaian and West Indian soldiers before the turn of the century, it crystallized into a distinctive style and spread, incorporating contemporary practices in pop music and jazz from the Americans. The rest of the Ghanaian bands eventually caught up with it and by the end of the 1960s every resident hotel nightclub band had a few highlifes in its repertoire. The highlife is basically a catchy song repeated over and over with intervening solos (breaks) in which instrumentalist after instrumentalist may exhibit his skills in variations on the theme or some brief episodical material. Highlife bands have ranged from large fife and brass bands, orchestras with bowed strings, flutes, sousaphones, etc., through the swing band setup to the small combo, reflecting practices among jazz and calypso bands throughout their histories.

FACTORS IN THE SPREAD OF POP MUSIC

Of the factors leading to the rise of new African hybridized music, large-scale urbanization has been mentioned. Along with urbanization may be listed the coming of prosperity (in a small way, but nevertheless sufficient to generate new developments) to the ordinary African musician who was also included in the growing urbanized population. For the musician in town could afford to buy some Western musical instruments, or someone interested in his talent could buy one for him and hire him in his band. It is significant that for decades Ghana (formerly known as the Gold Coast), which had the highest per capita income in sub-Saharan Africa (Oliver and Fage 1962:216-25), also produced some of the earliest African pop music still performed.

The above précis of twentieth-century developments, which only attempts to outline the story of new pop music in sub-Saharan Africa, should not tempt the reader to the conclusion that new African music is all pop music. The importance of this music in providing linguae francae for large areas in Africa cannot be denied. Apart from being the most widely patronized, it has served as a source of inspiration for those working in other areas of African music. For instance, since the second decade of this century new theater traditions incorporating music have become established in various parts of Africa. Some of the top African pop hits have come from this source [see Professor Blacking's essay.—ed.].

Theater Music

But new African theater relies on a wider variety of music. Gibson Kente of South Africa, Byron Kawaddwa of Uganda, Hubert Ogunde of Nigeria, and Saka Acquaye of Ghana all make use of traditional choruses with drums and other traditional instruments. They also employ songs arranged in four-part harmony for S A T B as well as instrumental ensemble music combining African and Western musical elements.

Music on stage is essentially music presented by a group of performers to a nonparticipating audience. In this sense it emphasizes an aspect characteristic of much of the new African music. In the old African traditional way of life, music for sheer listening is confined to a few situations in which an individual (e.g., a *griot* in Senegal) or an ensemble performs to delight a royal court. Now, drawing inspiration from Western models, African composers write music for the listening audience only.

Christian Church Music

Music for Christian worship in Africa may also be related to the new music on stage and radio. From the early days of Christian churches in Africa converts have combed their own heritage to find music suitable to their new religion. Thus the Methodist Church in Ghana evolved and established the *ebibindwom* (popularly called Fanti lyric) which was entirely based on the musical idiom of the Akan ethnic group, especially the Fanti section. During the third decade of this century newly established churches in Zambia experimented with various forms of Bemba music. These were later abandoned, but during the 1960s Cajetan Lunsonga appeared with more viable experiments in the same idiom, and his Bemba church hymns were an immediate success (Pailloux 1969). Fr. Guido Haazened created the *Missa Luba* from traditional music, a source of inspiration for many others both before and after him.

* * *

Apart from incorporating some specific African elements, the new African music largely runs to basic aesthetic norms that derive ultimately from African traditional music. But the departures from the traditional music are also significant. For instance, it has been made clear in the preceding paragraphs that the new African music is not always designed to serve as an aspect of the dance, and that the inner responses of a listener who is not expected to participate physically in the performance are increasingly being relied on. The new music also derives from and relies on new social milieux for its relevance. The church, the school, the night-club, the cinema, the radio, and the theater or concert stage are foreign institutions that provide inspiration and a basis for much of Africa's new music south of the Sahara.

Glossary

adowa–A traditional social dance widespread in southern Ghana, especially Ashanti, where it is performed largely at funeral celebrations. The Ashanti adowa beat and step are becoming popular among Ghanaian nightclub bands.

agor (agoro)–A play; a musical ensemble; a musical performance in Akan (Ghana).

amakondere–Side-blown trumpets used in the *empango* royal dance ensemble in Bunyoro (Uganda). The ensemble also includes nine kettle-shaped drums. The trumpets are owned by specific clans, but the drums are kept in the royal palace in Bunyoro.

budongo–Hand piano; ensemble (or performance) of hand pianos. This name is used in Busoga and outlying districts of Uganda.

burden text–A line or phrase with a definite meaning employed as a memory aid to the sound and pattern of a rhythmic or melodic fragment.

bwola–An Acholi (Uganda) dance suite, with each dance of the suite characterized by specific figures, directional and floor patterns.

chasmatonic–Wide-skipped. The word is used to describe a melody characterized by disjunct movement or wide intervals.

cilapi–An anecdote; a commentary or lesson in the form of a short story, usually intoned over a ground provided by an accompanying voice. Found among Cewa societies in Zambia and Malawi.

Congolese–The term for current popular music developed by pop bands of Zaire, formerly the Belgian Congo, and bands of the neighboring Congo (Brazzaville).

dawuru (dawur)–A struck iron handbell.

ebibindwom–Literally, African song or songs; a type of African song sung in the early Fanti (Ghana) Methodist church, still used in Methodist churches in Fanti and other Akan-speaking areas of Ghana. Also referred to as "Fanti lyric."

endere–Ugandan reed flute.

griot–A praise singer found in some West African countries (e.g., Senegal, Gambia, Guinea). He usually accompanies himself on a drum or stringed instrument.

gymadudu-A cylindrical double-headed drum about 30cm in diameter and 75cm long played with a stick; it is the largest drum in the Akan royal orchestra, which consists mainly of hourglass drums (*donno*) in various sizes.

highlife-A popular dance style developed in West Africa and played by the latest pop bands. A typical highlife consists of a catchy tune of from 16 to 32 bars or more in the major mode, repeated over and over with intervening solo improvisations or breaks.

ikulu-Largest Ugandan drum, used by Bamasaba boys.

inyiyim (inyiyiho)-Embellishment, elaboration in accompaniment to a song or an instrumental piece; accompanying part.

Kwadwom-Heroic praise-singing in the Ashanti king's court, intoned with characteristic phrase endings. Ascribed to the royal courts of Denkyira (Ghana) during the eighteenth century, but probably from earlier times.

kwela-A type of popular dance piece developed by penny whistle players and guitarists in South Africa (especially Johannesburg). It consists of short phrases of melody repeated over and over with variation and bass accompaniment.

larumu-A type of tuning used in parts of Acholi (Uganda) by advanced players of the zither and hand piano.

laturi-A type of tuning used by players of medium ability of the zither and hand piano in Acholi. Laturi is also the name of a village.

likembe-A widespread name for the hand piano, e.g., in Acholi and Lovale (Zambia and Angola).

mbira-A widespread name for hand piano in Central and Southern Africa.

ngoma-Play; drum; performance. The word is widely used by East and Central African peoples.

ngoma indini-Medium size Ugandan drum.

ngoma inzulu-See *ikulu*.

ngolorombe-Chikunda (Zambia, Mozambique) panpipe ensemble; panpipes.

ogodo-An Acholi song type with the theme of love; also the name of a tuning for novices on the zither and the hand piano. In some parts of Acholi another name for *laturi* tuning.

phata-phata-A South African popular dance song type; one of the antecedents of the *kwela*.

sansa-Hand piano.

tabl-An Arab drum.

tsindonyi-Smallest Ugandan drum.

Bibliography

(A few duplicated references to the music of South Africa will be found in John Blacking's bibliography—ed.)

Blacking, John.
  1965. "Music in Uganda." *African Music*. 3:14-17.
  1969. "The Value of Music in Human Experience." In *Yearbook of the International Folk Music Council*, 1:33-71.

Boone, Olga.
  1936. *Les Xylophones du Congo Belge*. Tervuren: Annales du Musée du Congo Belge.
  1951. *Les Tambours du Congo Belge et du Ruanda-Urundi*.

Bowdich, T. E.
  1819. *Mission from Cape Coast Castle to Ashantee*. London: John Murray.

Brandel, Rose.
  1961. *The Music of Central Africa: An Ethnomusicological Study*. The Hague: Nijhoff.
  1962. "Types of Melodic Movement in Central Africa." *Ethnomusicology*, 6:75-87.

Crossley-Holland, Peter.
  1960. "The Arab World." In *The Pelican History of Music*, Vol. 1, edited by A. Robertson and D. Stevens, pp. 118-135. London: Penguin.

Crossley-Holland, Peter, ed.
  1967. *Journal of the International Folk Music Council*, 19:49-103. Contains five papers on African multi-part techniques by various scholars.

Darkwa, Asante.
  1974. "The New Musical Traditions in Ghana." Ph.D. dissertation, Wesleyan University.

Davidson, Basil.
  1964. *The African Past*. London: Longmans.

Dietz, Betty W., and M. B. Olatunji.
  1965. *Musical Instruments of Africa*. New York: John Day.

Dodgson, Stephen, ed.
  1966. *Composer*, No. 19. A series of papers on African music by J. H. Nketia, Fela Sowande, Hugh Tracey, A. A. Mensah, and others.

Euba, Akin.
  1967. "Multiple Pitch Lines in Yoruba Choral Music." *International Folk Music Journal*, 19:66-71.
  1970. "New Idioms of Music-Drama among the Yoruba: An Introductory Study." In *Yearbook of the International Folk Music Council*, 2:92-107.

Euba, Akin, ed.
   1974-1977. Ife Music Editions. Ile-Ife, Nigeria: University of Ife Press. Includes compositions by Ayo Bankole, Akin Euba, Anthony Okelo, and Ato Turkson.
Gaskin, L. J. P., comp.
   1971. *A Select Bibliography of Music in Africa*. Boston: Crescendo. Rev. rpt. of the 1965 edition.
Gwanga, Jonas, and E. John Miller Jr.
   1971. *African Song: Miriam Makeba*. Chicago: Quadrangle Books.
Hitti, P. K.
   1964. *History of the Arabs*. London: Macmillan.
Hornbostel, Erich M. von.
   1928. "African Negro Music." *Africa*, 1:30-62.
Ismail, Mahi.
   1972. "Musical Traditions in the Sudan." In *African Music*, pp. 94-98. Paris: UNESCO, *La Revue musicale*.
Jeffreys, M. D. W.
   1961. "Negro Influences on Indonesia." *African Music*, 2:10-16.
Jones, A. M.
   1949. *African Music in Northern Rhodesia and Some Other Places*. Livingstone's Zambia: Rhodes-Livingstone Museum.
   1954. "African Rhythm." *Africa*, 24:26-47.
   1959. *Studies in African Music*. 2 vols. London: Oxford University Press.
   1960. "Indonesia and Africa: The Xylophone as a Culture-Indicator." *African Music*, 2:36-47.
Kakoma, George.
   1969. *Songs from Buganda*. London: Oxford University Press.
   1972. "Musical Traditions of East Africa." In *African Music*, pp. 78-88. Paris: UNESCO, *La Revue musicale*.
King, A. M.
   1961. *Yoruba Sacred Music from Ekiti*. Ibadan, Nigeria: Ibadan University Press.
Kirby, Percival R.
   1934. *The Musical Instruments of the Native Races of South Africa*. London: Oxford University Press. Rpt. Johannesburg: Witwatersrand University Press, 1968.
Kubik, Gerhard.
   1960. "The Structure of Kiganda Xylophone Music." *African Music*, 2:6-30.
   1968. "Court Music in Uganda: Recordings of Xylophone Compositions Preserved in the Phonogramm Archiv of the Austrian Academy of Sciences, Vienna." *Bulletin of the International Committee on Urgent Anthropological and Ethnographical Research*, 10:41-51.

Kyagambiddwa, Joseph.
   1956. *African Music from the Source of the Nile*. London: Atlantic Press.
Laurentry, J. S.
   1960. *Les Cordophones du Congo Belge et du Ruanda-Urundi*. Tervuren: Annales du Musée Royal de Congo Belge.
Mapoma, Isaiah Mwesa.
   1969. "The Use of Folk Music among Some Bemba Church Congregations in Zambia." In *Yearbook of the International Folk Music Council*, 1:72-88.
Mbabi-Katana, S.
   1965. *Songs of East Africa*, Part I. London: Macmillan.
Mensah, A. A.
   1960. "The Akan Church Lyric." *International Review of Missions*, 49:183-88.
   1966a. "The Guans in Music." Master's thesis, University of Ghana, Legon.
   1966b. "The Impact of Western Music on the Musical Tradition of Ghana." *Composer*, 19:19-22.
   1972. "The Performing Arts in Zambia—Music and Dance." *Bulletin of the International Committee on Urgent Anthropological and Ethnographical Research*, Wien.
   1973. "Jazz the Round Trip." Wien: *Jazz Research*, 3/4:124-37.
Merriam, Alan P.
   1953. "African Music Re-examined in the Light of New Materials from the Belgian Congo and Ruanda-Urundi." *Zaire* 7:245-53.
   1957. *Africa South of the Sahara*. Album Notes for Folkways Record 4503.
   1959a. "African Music." In *Continuity and Change in African Culture*, edited by William R. Bascom and Melville J. Herskovitz, pp. 49-86. Chicago: University of Chicago Press.
   1959b. "Characteristics of African Music." *Journal of the International Folk Music Council*, 11:13-19.
   1962. "The African Idiom in Music." *Journal of American Folklore*, LXXV:120-30.
   1977. "Traditional Music of Black Africa." In *Africa*, edited by Phyllis M. Martin and Patrick O'Meara, pp. 243-58. Bloomington: Indiana University Press.
Nettl, Bruno.
   1965. *Folk and Traditional Music of the Western Continents* (See May bibliography).
   1975. "The Western Impact on World Music: Africa and the American Indians." In *Contemporary Music and Music Cultures*, by Charles Hamm, Bruno Nettl, and Ronald Byrnside, pp.

101-24. Englewood Cliffs: Prentice-Hall.

Nikiprowetsky, Tolia.
  1963. "The Griots of Senegal and Their Instruments." *International Folk Music Journal*, 15:79-82.

Nketia, J. H.
  1955. *Funeral Dirges of the Akan People*. Achimota: University College of the Gold Coast.
  1962*a*. "The Hocket Technique in African Music." *International Folk Music Journal*, 14:44-52.
  1962*b*. "The Problem of Meaning in African Music." *Ethnomusicology*, 6:1-7.
  1963*a*. *African Music in Ghana*. Evanston: Northwestern University Press.
  1963*b*. *Drumming in Akan Communities of Ghana*. Edinburgh: Thomas Nelson and Sons.
  1963*c*. *Folk Songs of Ghana*. Legon: University of Ghana.
  1974. *The Music of Africa*. New York: Norton.

Oliver, Roland, and J. D. Fage.
  1962. *A Short History of Africa*. London: Penguin.

Omibiyinyi, Mosunmola.
  1973. "The Task of the Music Educator in Africa." *The Black Perspective in Music*, 1:37-44.

Pailloux, R.
  1969. *St. Clement's Hymnal (Inyimbo Shipya)*. Mansa, Zambia: Saint Clement's Sec. School.

Rycroft, David.
  1967. "Nguni Vocal Polyphony." *Journal of the International Folk Music Council*, 19:88-103.

Serwadda, W. Moses.
  1974. *Songs and Stories from Uganda*. Transcribed and edited by Hewitt Pantaleoni. New York: Thomas W. Crowell.

Sowande, Fela.
  1967. *Six Papers on Aspects of Nigerian Music*. New York: Broadcasting Foundation of America.

Tracey, Hugh.
  1948. *Chopi Musicians: Their Music, Poetry and Instruments*. Rev. ed. London: Oxford University Press, 1970.

Turnbull, Colin M.
  1963. "The Lesson of the Pygmies." *Scientific American*, 208:28-37.

Wachsmann, Klaus P.
  1964. "Human Migration and African Harps." *Journal of the International Folk Music Council*, 16:84:88.

Wachsmann, Klaus, ed.
  1971. *Essays on Music and History in Africa*. Evanston: Northwestern University Press.

Wachsmann, K. P., and Margaret Trowell.
  1953. "The Sound Instruments." In *Tribal Crafts of Uganda*, edited by Margaret Trowell and K. P. Wachsmann, pp. 311-415. New York: Oxford University Press.

Waterman, Richard.
  1952. "African Influence on the Music of the Americas." In *Acculturation in the Americas*, edited by Sol Tax, pp. 208-9. Chicago: University of Chicago Press.

Discography

RESOURCES

Laade, Wolfgang. *Neue musik in Afrika, Asien und Ozeanien: Diskographie und historisch stilistischer Überblick*. Heidelberg: Selbstverlag, 1971.

Merriam, Alan P. *African Music on L.P.—An Annotated Discography*. Evanston: Northwestern University, 1970.

GENERAL TRADITIONAL MUSIC

Africa East and West. ier 6751.

Africa South of the Sahara. Folkways FE 503. Introduction and Notes by Alan P. Merriam.

The Music of Africa Series. Hugh Tracey. The International Library of African Music. Roodepoort.

No. 27	GALP	1322	Strings
No. 28	GALP	1323	Reeds (Mbira)
No. 29	GALP	1324	Drums
No. 30	GALP	1325	Flutes and Horns
No. 31	GALP	1326	Xylophones
No. 32	GALP	1327	Guitars
No. 36	GALP	1503	Guitars

Negro Folk Music of Africa and America. Folkways FE 4500. Harold Courlander. Foreword by Richard Alan Waterman.

Neue Musik in Afrika, Asien und Ozeanien: Diskographie und historisch-stilistischer Überblick. Wolfgang Laade. Heidelberg.

Sounds of Africa. Verve FTS 3021.

GENERAL: TWENTIETH CENTURY NEW AFRICAN MUSIC

Africa Speaks, America Answers. Decca DL 8446. Guy Warren with his Red Saunders Orchestra. Notes by Red Saunders.

Afrique. French Philips P08 672L (Voyage Autour du Monde series). Arranged music from Ghana, Nigeria, Mali, Senegal and Cameroon, on African musical instruments.

Angola: Victory is Certain: Songs of the Liberation Army of MPLA. Paredon 1002.

Concert pour un vieux masque: Pièces pour guitare.

French Philips P70 468L. Francis Bebey. Cover notes by Marcel Leclerc.

Geistliche Gesange der Mossi: Voltarepublik. Schwann Ams 12,018. Sung by Sisters of the Immaculate Conception.

"Kitumbiri" (Taarab). Saba-Saba 7-90. 45 rpm. Lucky Star Musical Club.

Marie-Lou. Phonogram Ltd. ASL 7-2038. 45 rpm. By Tabu Ley.

Missa des Piroguiers. Christophorus CLP 75,484. Composed and/or arranged by Elaine Barat.

Missa Shona. Schwann AMS 15,024. 45 rpm. Stefan Magwa Ponde.

Oba ko So. NCR 1-2. Ibadan: Institute of African Studies, University of Ibadan. Opera by Duro Ladipo. Edited by Wale Ogunyemi.

The Palmwine Drunkard. NCR 3-4. Ibadan: Institute of African Studies, University of Ibadan. Opera by 'Kola Ogunmola, based on a novel by Amos Tutnola.

Something New from Africa. Decca LK 4292.

Stars of West Africa: High Life Hits. Vols. 1 and 2. Decca WAL-1023.

Voices of Africa: High-Life and Other Popular Music by Saka Acquaye and His African Ensemble. Nonesuch H-72026. Edited by Kenneth S. Goldstein and Saka Acquaye.

CENTRAL AND SOUTHERN AFRICA: TRADITIONAL MUSIC

The African Mbira: Music of the Shona People of Rhodesia. Nonesuch H-72043. Played by Abraham Maraire.

African Story-Songs. University of Washington Press. Told and sung by Abraham Dumisani Maraire.

Ba-Benzele Pygmies. Bärenreiter BM30 L2303.

Burundi: musique traditionnelle. OCR 40.

"Koena" (Southern Sesotho). MD 36528. Lesotho, Basutoland: The Social Centre (P.O. Box 25, Roma, Lesotho).

Mbira Music of Rhodesia. University of Washington Press. Performed by Abraham Dumisani Maraire.

Music of Rhodesia. ILAM Series No. 26, GALP 1321.

Music from Rwanda. Bärenreiter BM30 L2302.

Musiques africaines: Chants et danses de la forêt centre-africaine. Harmonia Mundi HMO 30.733. Simkha Arom.

The Naked Prey. African Music (Nguni). Folkways FS 3854.

The Pygmies of the Ituri Forest. Folkways FE 4457.

Rhodesia (Roadside Songs). ILAM Series No. 19, GALP 1113.

Shona Liturgical Series. Gwelo, Southern Rhodesia: Manbo Press, P.O. Box 779. 29 small LP records.

EASTERN AFRICA: TRADITIONAL MUSIC

Ankole, West Uganda—Folk Music. No. 6 of a series of African music recordings issued by the Koninklijk Museum voor Midden-Afrika—Musée Royal de l'Afrique Central—Tervuren and by the Belgische Radio en Télévisie. Notes by Paul van Thiel, W.P.

Bantu Music from British East Africa, Vol. 10. Columbia World Library of Folk and Primitive Music KL 213.

Kenya Folk Songs. Asch 8503.

Music of Sudan: The Songs of Karim el Kably. Afrotone 500. Roxane C. Carlisle.

Music of Tanzania. ILAM No. 25, GALP 1320.

Music of Uganda. ILAM No. 24, GALP 1319.

WESTERN AFRICA: TRADITIONAL MUSIC

African Dances and Games. S&R 2000. Seth Kobla Ladzekpo and Alfred Kwashie Ladzekpo.

African Music. Folkways FW 8852.

Boorii Liturgy from Katsina (Nigeria). (A) A. V. King. The London Music Shop, Ltd.

De Teda uit Tibesti: Instrumentale Musiek. No. 4 of a series of African music recordings issued by the Koninklijk Museum voor Midden-Afrika—Musée Royal de l'Afrique Centrale—Tervuren and by the Belgische Radio en Télévisie. Notes by Monique Brandily.

Drums of the Yoruba of Nigeria. Folkways FE 4441.

The Fiery Drums of Africa: Songs and Dances of West Africa. Eurotone 124. Dinizulu and His Africans.

Folk Music of Ghana. Folkways FE 8859.

Kora par Soundioubou Sissoko: musique et chants traditionnels du Sénégal. FAN 9002. 45 rpm.

Luba-Shankadi: Vocale Muziek. No. 2 of a series of African music recordings issued by the Koninklijk Museum voor Midden-Afrika—Musée Royal de l'Afrique Centrale—Tervuren and by the Belgische Radio en Télévisie. Notes by Jos Gansemans.

Music from the Villages of Northeastern Nigeria. Asch Mankind Series AHM 4532, a-d.

The Music of the Dan. Bärenreiter BM30 L2301.

The Music of the Diola. Folkways FE 4323.

Music of the Jos Plateau and Other Regions of Nigeria. Folkways FE 4321.

Music of the Mende of Sierra Leone. Folkways FE 4322.

Music of the Northern Congo (Zaire). ILAM (Sudanic)

No. 22, GALP 1251; Bantu No. 23, GALP 1252.

Music of the Princes of Dahomey. Counterpoint/Esoteric 537.

Musique traditionelle. Ocora.

    Cameroun. OCR 25.

    Côte D'Ivoire. OCR 34.

    Dahomey. OCR 17.

    Gabon. OCR 41.

    Madagascar (Musique Malgacho). OCR 24.

    Madagascar (Valiha). OCR 18.

    Niger (La musique des griots). OCR 20.

    Niger (Nomades du Niger). OCR 29.

    Sénégal: la musique des griots. OCR 15.

    Togo. OCR 16.

    Zaire (Musique Kongo). OCR 35.

Muzick van de Mpangu. No. 5 of a series of African music recordings issued by the Koninklijk Museum voor Midden-Afrika—Musée Royal de l'Afrique Centrale—Tervuren and by the Belgische Radio en Télévisie. Notes by Gérard Ciparisse.

Nigeria—Hausa Music I & II: An Anthology of African Music. Bärenreiter BM30 L2306 and L2307.

Wolof Music of Senegal and Gambia. Folkways 4462.

Films

RESOURCES

Feld, Steven. *Filmography of the African Humanities.* Bloomington, Indiana: African Studies Program, Indiana University, 1972.

    Most of the 223 films in this annotated list are concerned with music or dance, or with both.

Films on Africa. Bloomington, Indiana: African Studies Program, Indiana University, 1971.

    Includes films on music and dance.

FILMS

An African Community: The Masai. BFA. Col. 16-1/4 min.

    Primarily a description of the way of life of a small group of the Masai in East Africa. Singing and dancing occur as they function in their living.

Annual Festival of the Dead. IFF and UC. Col. 14 min.

    "Members of the Dogon tribe of Mali . . . perform war games in the village square, to commemorate those who died during the past year. . . . Women bring offerings." CDF (Catalog of Dance-Films). African, Muslim, and Western dress are worn by participants in this obviously undirected record of important rites.

Atumpan. IE. Col. 42 min. Mantle Hood, producer.

    The construction, performance techniques, traditional and contemporary uses of a Ghanaian drum.

Bakuba—People of the Congo. AB. B/W. 19 min. Belgian direction (1957).

    Weaving, tattooing, dress ornamentation, dancing, and a Bakuba song. Western, but heavily African influenced musical score by André Souris.

Black African Heritage. WFD and UCLA. Col. 4 films, each about 60 min. Produced, written, and directed by Eliot Elisofon.

1. *The Congo.* Julian Bond, narrator.

    Among peoples shown are Watusi, pygmies, Wagenia, Bakuba, Bepende. Predominantly Western score, though some African dancing and singing. Many wooden sculptures from collections in the United States.

2. *The Bend in the Niger.* Ossie Davis, narrator.

    Pictures West African peoples living along the Niger: Bambaras, Borora, Moslem Hausa, Tauregs, Bozo, and Dendi. Shows music, dance, and sculpture of some of these peoples.

3. *The Slave Coast.* Maya Angelou, narrator.

    Ashanti of Ghana and Yoruba of Nigeria are visited. Miango, Dahomey, Dan dancers perform. Ancient Nok sculptures shown.

4. *Africa's Gift.* Gordon Parks, narrator.

    Comparison between music of the Senufo people of the Ivory Coast and that of the New World. Performers include Mongo Santamaria, "leading exponent of Afro-Cuban music," Lionel Hampton, and Randy Weston, "a leading exponent of modern jazz."

Chopi Africa. Maurice A. Machris Productions. Col. 53 min. Hugh Tracey, advisor.

    Photographed in Mozambique. Marriage and boys' puberty ceremonies, ritual dances, xylophone orchestra, singing. Other activities of daily life, including making a drum and bark cloth.

Discovering the Music of Africa. BFA. Col. 22 min. Sotirios Chianis, advisor.

    This film, made at UCLA's Institute of Ethnomusicology, under the direction of a master drummer from Ghana, demonstrates various drums from that country and their functions, as well as a polyrhythmic percussion ensemble. Study guide included.

Les Maîtres Fous. CF/MH. Col. 30 min.

    A documentary of the "newly formed Haouka sect" filmed in Ghana by Jean Rouch. African "ceremonial patterns are skillfully related to their colonial counterparts so that they form a demonic commentary on civilization."CF/MH.

Masked Dances, 3. PSU Col. 9 min. Silent.

"Masked dances by the Nuna people (Upper Volta, Africa) include dance of the ibis, the antelope, bucorous bird, horse-mask, monkey and the 'parvenu.'" CDF.

A Story A Story. Weston Wood. Col. 10 min. Directed by Gene Deitch.

Woodcut animation. Musical score on African instruments. Based on Caldecott award-winning book *Ananse the Spider: Tales from an Ashanti Village* by Pegg Appiah.

11. Trends in the Black Music of South Africa, 1959-1969

John Blacking

Listening to music without any verbal explanation is not only possible, it is positively desirable. If music does not "speak for itself," it cannot be considered successful as a special mode of nonverbal communication: all that can be said about a piece of music, and more, should be heard in the notes. Since the purpose of music is often to express feelings that are too precise for words, *writing* about South African music may seem both redundant and arrogant when intensive listening could provide more accurate information.

Yet I use language to introduce South African music, partly because an adequate course of listening would cost more and take longer than reading this essay, but chiefly because music is a social fact, and some verbal preparation for listening to it is therefore justified. As LeRoi Jones wrote in *Blues People*, music is "the result of certain attitudes, certain specific ways of thinking about the world, and only ultimately about the 'ways' in which music can be made" (1963:153).

Thus, when we hear new music, we will first select and interpret its sounds by means of acquired listening habits. This bias can be reduced if we know when, where, why, and how the unfamiliar sounds are produced. For example, we might first hear some African sounds as a drum pattern in 6/8 time, but after learning, and perhaps seeing, that they are produced by two players combining the same iambic motif in polymeter (ex. 11-1), and that different areas of the drumskin can be struck in different ways, so that variations in tonality become as important as the rhythm, then we realize that we must listen to the sounds in a new way if we are to understand even a little of what the music is about.

There is no harm in hearing all music in our own way, and it may be more realistic to admit that we can never hope to do more than that. But since both the makers of the different musics and their audiences have acquired their skills from others in the context of a particular social system, it should be possible for an outsider to understand the social system and to learn how to listen to the music in a similar way. He may not feel the music in exactly the same way as one brought up in the tradition, but neither will all who are brought up together have identical sensations, because each one has a unique social experience and correspondingly unique responses to the music associated with that experience. Nevertheless, because music is a shared experience about which there is at least some agreement within a given social group, there is a level at which its significance can always become known to an inquiring outsider. Through this knowledge, and especially its application in performance, it may be possible to hear and experience the sounds with more or less the same attitudes and ways of thinking that were involved in their creation.

It is hardly surprising that between 1959 and 1969 the sounds of music composed and performed around Durban and Johannesburg changed, because these were large cosmopolitan cities with a thriving record industry and

EXAMPLE 11-1. Reproduced with permission from John Blacking, *How Musical Is Man?* (Seattle: University of Washington Press, 1973).

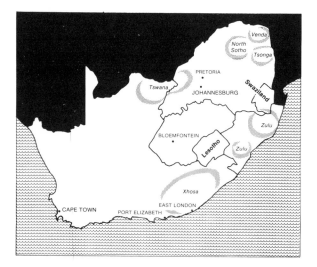

South Africa, showing locations of Bantu homelands.

listeners avid for the new sounds of Europe and America in the 1960s. But the change of sounds in South Africa was not so much a response to external influences as a reflection of the momentous political changes that were taking place. For this was the decade in which Black Consciousness and the idea of Black Power crystallized and came into the open, and in which blacks finally realized that they could not expect generosity or common sense from a dominant white minority, who deprived them of their land and of the right to vote and to move and sell their labor freely within their own country, and who maintained this dominance by spending the profits of the economy chiefly on benefits for whites and on police and military forces to control the blacks. The most striking change in the sounds of music between 1959 and 1969 was therefore the intrusion of a distinctly African idiom. As soon as we go beyond this simple observation, however, and the experience of hearing the changes, and attempt even a straightforward description of them, we come up against difficulties of interpretation that can only be resolved by viewing them in their sociopolitical context. For this reason an outline of the social and political background precedes a discussion of the music.

Between 1959 and 1969, the population of South Africa grew from 16 1/4 to 21 1/2 million, with the so-called Bantu and Coloured (of mixed descent) groups increasing at more than one and a half times the rate of the Whites. Thus the black/white ratio of the population changed from 66/21 to 70.5/17.5, with "Coloureds" (approx. 9.5%) and "Asians" of Indian and Chinese descent (approx. 2.5%) making up the remainder.

To many whites in South Africa the new sounds of music speak of increasing Europeanization, and the white musical experts often describe them as imitative. Even when such observations are intended as genuine compliments, they are not necessarily correct: for instance, a German Lutheran minister drew my attention to the way his church choir was singing "German" harmonies, but I was more aware of their deliberate Africanization of the hymn than of an attempt to copy the European original. Again, apparently technical explanations of Europeanization can misinterpret the musical intentions of the performers: for instance, it is often argued that melodies that do not follow the speechtone patterns of the indigenous language show a complete disregard for African tradition. But if the traditional relationship between patterns of speechtone and melody is such that in the solo section speechtone influences the patterns of melody while in the chorus musical forces take over, then hymns, urban wedding songs, and similar kinds of modern music may be the consequence not of "slavish imitation" of European models, but of their classification as *choruses*, in which the speechtone patterns of the words may be ignored.

White responses to modern African music are powerful evidence of the dangers of listening to a musical product without knowing something about its social and political context. The whites' ears deceive them, as a further careful hearing of this music would soon reveal: although they have been trained to listen critically, their appreciation of African sounds is blocked by their own perceptions of African cultures. They may hear imitations of their own culture instead of the signs of a creative process in which a growing concern for characteristically African themes and sounds has given birth to a modern music that is as truly African as the styles of the oral tradition. As the timbres and patterns of sound changed from the choral compositions of P. J. Simelane, J. P. Mohapeloa, and H. J. M. Masiza to Todd Matshikiza's jazz operas *King Kong* and *Mkhumbane*, Gibson Kente's *Sikalo*, and Jerry Mfusi's *Shaka*; from the music of Lo Six, the Manhattan Brothers, and Township Jazz to that of Gideon Nxumalo's International Jazz Band, Spokes Mashiyane, and the Malombo Jazz Makers, so the course of southern African music moved in a direction from which it is likely never to deviate.

There were indeed earlier composers who had used the African idiom effectively, such as Benjamin Tyamzashe (Hansen 1968:22), Michael M. Moerane, and John Knox Bokwe, and the black South African National Anthem, Enoch Sontonga's *Nkosi Sikilel'i Afrika*, is no more an imitation of a European hymn tune than the famous *Round Hymn* of Ntsikana (Bokwe 1910). Moreover, the hymns of Isaiah Shembe's church of the Nazarites, founded in 1911, were far more Zulu than European in style, and similarly syncretic sounds were used by other separatist churches. But the Africanness of these works was generally more accidental than self-conscious.

FIGURE 11-1. The competitors' stand at the 1963 jazz festival organized by Castle Beer, in Orlando Stadium, twelve miles from Johannesburg. Note that the leader of this band is wearing traditional Swazi dress. Photographs by John Blacking.

There had been a tendency in the urban areas to seek greater sophistication by adopting and adapting European and American styles, a tendency reinforced by increasing contacts between black and white musicians in the 1950s. This development culminated in the production of *King Kong* in 1959 (Glasser 1960), which led to the discovery of Miriam Makeba and to a substantial increase in professional musical activity. *King Kong* was a landmark in South African theater history because it was the first South African show to make a large profit. The achievement was even more remarkable in a racist state where increased profits are the hallmark of progress and whites are supposed to be "kulturally" superior, because the composer and performers were all blacks! But *King Kong* signaled both a climax of interracial cooperation and the end of the era during which black artists looked to European models. If the whites had the money and skills for promotion and production, it became clear that what audiences wanted was black music and artists. Furthermore, it did not escape the notice of some that one factor behind the lukewarm reception of *King Kong* in London may have been the "polishing up" of the "rougher" original version. The very next composition of Todd Matshikiza, *Mkhumbane*, began with an unaccompanied chorus, whose dramatically descending, gapped melody recalls the traditional Xhosa music that Matshikiza heard in his youth.

Changes in the form and content of music after *King Kong* were not isolated events in the history of South African music. They were the consequence of far-reaching political changes whose impact on music was inevitable, partly because music had been actively used in urban areas as an "agent of political expression" (Rhodes 1962) before and since the South African Freedom Songs of the early 1950s, and partly because music inevitably reflects political processes.

The political functions of music range from its use as an embellishment of political sentiments and as a quasi-totemic symbol of political groups, to its special function of establishing relationships among people through the performance and perception of humanly organized "forms in tonal motion." I call these two aspects of musical activity the political role of music and the politics of music, and shall discuss them later in the context of traditional music making. Willard Rhodes (1962) has drawn attention to the political importance of the words of the South African Freedom Songs, and it could be argued that the sounds of the music are unimportant except as a means of coordinating and focusing the activities of a group through rhythmical unity. But the music in itself had political significance, quite apart from its overt use in a political context. The combination of the triads and cadences of European hymn tunes and the rhythms and parallel movement of traditional African music expressed the new relationships and values of urban groups, who expected fuller participation in the social and political life of the community into which they had been drawn economically.

THE SOCIAL AND POLITICAL BACKGROUND

The political changes of the 1960s affected the musical life of South African cities in a number of ways. First, a severe tightening of apartheid legislation removed *King Kong's* threat to white theater by depriving blacks of the opportunity of performing to white audiences.

Second, intensification of the machinery of the police state insured that blacks who indulged in political talk or action would almost certainly go to prison, so that if music were to continue to be an agent of political expression it would have to be so in a more subtle way. Whites in South Africa rarely honor African cultures except when it suits them as an excuse for "separate development" and other forms of political oppression: thus, they were unlikely to accept the African convention that critics of authority should not be harmed as long as they "said it with music."

Third, political cooperation of blacks and whites became increasingly unsuccessful in the late 1950s and early 1960s, as the police state became more vigilant and sophisticated, and multiracialism became irrelevant in a context where to be political one must be antiwhite. As if in response to this, the Pan-Africanist Congress was formed in 1959, between the Treason Trial of 1956 and the arrest and imprisonment of black and white political activists in 1964, and ten months after its foundation its nationwide antipass campaign culminated in the massacre at Sharpeville on 21 March 1960 and the arrest of hundreds of blacks. The abortive political action of the early 1960s spelled out the futility of cooperation with white "liberals," most of whom could not help accepting the basic premises of apartheid, few of whom could accept the idea that blacks might be able to govern the country without their assistance and so had fundamentally different, corrosive views on political strategy, and all of whom had privileges that generally allowed them to be more safely outspoken and to escape the police network more easily than their black colleagues. The lesson was clear: just as the success of *King Kong* showed black musicians and composers that their source of strength was in Africa and not in Europe, so the failure of multiracial politics in a racist state exposed the ethnocentric position even of those whites who sincerely wanted to share power and showed blacks that their chief source of political weakness was cooperation with white South Africans.

The liberal argument was that industrialization, urbanization, and a common "Western" education had brought some unity to different ethnic groups, and that their political strength and future welfare lay in an expansion of this process of unification, especially through cooperation with whites in the management of the economy. But contrary to liberal predictions that the growth of the economy would break the barriers of apartheid as it had increased communication among ethnic groups, the growth of the economic surplus had allowed the white government to spend even more on the machinery of discrimination and the defense of white privilege. Politically, what was good for the South African economy was good for the rich whites, who could thereby maintain and even increase their social distance from the poorer blacks; what was bad for the economy was good for the blacks, who had much to gain from its collapse and very little to lose.

White rule may have brought some material, educational, and medical benefits to South Africa's indigenous black people, but it had also brought political slavery, starvation, and deficiency diseases to places that knew none of these before. It had not broken the spirit of the people, however; paradoxically, in its incidental and deliberate attempts to divide them it brought them together in common opposition to white domination.

Some musical consequences of these political changes were that blacks were thrown even more on their own resources for the development of their musical life; that they had to express political sentiments in the *sounds* of the music rather than in any words that might accompany it; and that the common characteris-

of South Africa brought some uniformity to the social and intellectual life of those who went to modern schools, but the cultural variety and the European rivalries of the missions added divisive elements: the Paris Evangelical and Roman Catholic missions divided Lesotho in a way that has had profound political consequences. The Roman Catholics, the Anglicans, and the Swedish Lutherans all left their mark on the Zulu; and the activities of the German Lutheran and Swiss missions among the Venda and the Shangana-Tsonga respectively were tantamount to introducing new ruling clans. The growth of African Separatist churches could have brought even greater division because they

	Approximate number	*Approximate percentage of African population*	
Xhosa	5,040,000	31.5	
Zulu	4,640,000	29.0	
Swazi	480,000	3.0	
Southern Ndebele	304,000	1.9	65.4
Northern Ndebele	96,000	0.6	
North Sotho	1,600,000	10.0	
South Sotho	1,616,000	10.1	
Tswana	1,280,000	8.0	28.7
Venda	400,000	2.5	2.5
Shangana-Tsonga	544,000	3.4	3.4
	16,000,000		100.0

tics of the music of ethnic groups became more pronounced than their differences. The political implication of these musical changes was that the differences between South African Bantu nations were not as fundamental as the South African whites claimed. The unity of different musical styles sprang not from common imitation of a single European musical tradition but from the realization of musical principles that are common to the different ethnic groups that constitute 71.2 percent of the total population.

The indigenous people, who numbered about sixteen million in 1959, have been subdivided as above, largely on the basis of geographical, linguistic, historical, and cultural variations.

The spread of Christianity to different parts

were recruited largely on ethnic grounds (Sundkler 1961), but on the contrary it tended to unite blacks in common opposition to white domination and to foster pride in traditional African beliefs, values, and institutions. In the end, European attempts to carve out spiritual empires in South Africa and to involve Africans in their own internecine struggles for power failed, partly because blacks were touched more by Christ's gospel of peace, social equality, and justice than by the European churches' record of religious wars, racism, bigotry, and injustice, and partly because very few white Christians practiced what they preached.

As an example of African unity, consider the African Christian church settlements of Shembe

FIGURE 11-2. A team of dancers from Johannesburg comes to Thengwe, in rural Venda, to perform *tshikona* at Easter 1958.

at Ekuphakameni and Lekganyane at Zion City, Moriah, outside Pietersburg. They are separated by nearly seven hundred miles, and the social organization, music, and ritual of the former are as unmistakably Zulu as those of the latter are Sotho. But they share a common concern for healing, prophecy, and an effective Christian brotherhood, and their social organization is modeled on that of the tribe, which was the most characteristic all-inclusive grouping in traditional society. Again, the Tswana living in Soweto and Johannesburg have large funerals whereas the Zulu have large weddings, probably because of contrasts in their systems of kinship and marriage. Also the urban wedding songs of the Zulu sound more solemn and serious than those of the Tswana. But both nations have in common a kin-based social network, in which bonds of descent, seniority of age, relationships by marriage, and belief in a continuity of existence between the living and the dead are crucial factors.

Changes in social and political life have often led to the paradoxical situation that some of the best performances of traditional South African communal music are to be found in contexts where the cultures and institutions that generated these styles have been destroyed or modified and many former social and political roles of music have become redundant or almost obsolete. Performance of music may have depended on certain social conditions, but their disappearance did not eliminate the music, which could in itself act as a catalyst for new kinds of social activity. For example, Venda migrant workers in urban areas formed teams of pipe dancers, and men accompanied them on the drums. Though deprived of chiefs and headmen and the normal situations for musicmaking, they developed a new economic and social framework for musical performance. By meeting on weekends, they probably play even more often than did their ancestors before the arrival of white missionaries in 1872; and their annual return to Venda in busloads at Eastertime brings, by common agreement, the finest performances of their national dance, *tshikona*, that can be heard today.

If migrants in mine, factory, and municipal compounds, and some residents of the townships outside every South African city, perform traditional music, it is not because they have been unaffected by cultural changes, but because the old music had a dynamic social base which has been transformed and adapted without losing its African character. In situations like this the music itself may become more politically significant than the events it accompanies, which was rarely the case in traditional society. A good example of such a development is provided by the dances performed by workers on the Witwatersrand Gold Mines in compounds during their leisure hours and to the public on Sunday mornings.

These mine dances reflect the synthesis of old and new that is the life of migrant laborers. Some dances, such as the Shangana-Tsonga *Makwaya* and the Bhaca gum boot dance, *Isicathulo*, were devised directly as a result of people's experiences of "Western" life. Some are modern versions of traditional dances, with new costumes and choreography; others have probably changed very little in style and basic structure over the last three or four centuries, though new melodies, rhythms, and dance steps have been introduced from time to time.

In all cases, the dances represent a dynamic tradition that still occupies much of the time of African peasants. Music and dancing lighten the load of communal labor; enhance weddings, funerals, initiations, and many kinds of celebration, ceremony, and religious rite; or soften the harshness of life and provide entertainment at a beer party. Although some of the songs and dances originate in the music performed by the age groups that certain tribes formed into military units, it would be quite incorrect to describe them as "war" songs and dances.

The dancers organize their teams carefully. There is always a manager, and there are directors both of the music and the dancing, each of whom usually has an assistant. A manager is responsible for arranging rehearsals, seeing that people attend regularly, and ensuring that there is beer to drink. He chooses the dance costumes, which are often provided by the mine officials. Managers do not necessarily take part in the dancing, and in some cases they may be seen standing by their teams during performances.

A director of music is responsible for starting and stopping each dance; choosing and often leading different songs and seeing that they are correctly performed; checking the tuning of instruments (which includes drums, because in a set of drums the tone of each one must be properly related to those of its fellows); and supervising the coordination of song and dance. Similarly, a director of dancing supervises the choice, variations, and performance of the dance steps. Just as the same dance steps may accompany different melodies, so a variety of steps may be used with the same melody. In many teams, the dance director blows a whistle to signal a change of step and calls out the name of the new step or demonstrates it himself.

The role of each functionary varies according to the style of the dance. In the Bhaca *Isicathulo* and the Xhosa *Amakwenkwe* dances, for example, even though the rhythm is enhanced and the dancers are encouraged by music on the guitar and concertina respectively, these players could hardly be called "directors of music."

Traditionally, several of the dances are performed by men and women together, so in some mine dances men wear costumes to indicate that they are playing women's roles. Moreover, instruments are allocated specifically to men or to women, and it is rare to find someone playing an instrument meant for the opposite sex. Drums are usually played by men, but notable exceptions to the rule are the Pedi, Lovedu, and Venda of the northern Transvaal, where even today, apart from the special case of their possession dances, only in urban teams of dancers will one see men playing the drums. In the rural setting, every ethnic group performs different dances, whose styles vary according to the form of the social events that they accompany. Many of those performed by mine workers might be called "national dances" in that they are sponsored by chiefs or headmen, accompany important rituals and ceremonies, and involve the largest numbers of men, women, and children.

The cultural variations that are crystallized in the different mine dances reflect contrasts generated by historical and ecological factors, rather than by social and cognitive processes. Local differences in the house-types, the rituals, and the social and political organization of the Zulu and the Southern Sotho, the Venda and the Tsonga, the Tswana and the Xhosa do not go deep enough to create fundamental divisions: long before the era of white domination, many Sotho were incorporated in the political structure of Swaziland and thousands of Zulu accepted the rule of Tswana chiefs. If they differ, Africans tend to align themselves more according to their position in the modern economy, on the basis of residence rather than tribal affiliation—a Zulu from Natal would support a Sotho from Natal, even as he quarreled with a Zulu from the Transvaal.

Even divisions among South African languages look more diverse than they are because Europeans devised different systems of orthography and word division on the basis of what they considered to be European equivalents. All are, in fact, classed together in the southeastern group of Bantu languages, although there is a distinct difference between the disyllabic prefixes of the Nguni languages (*umu-ntu, aba-ntu, ama-futha, ili-zwi*, etc.) and the monosyllabic prefixes of the Sotho languages (*mo-tho, ba-tho, ma-fura, le-ntsoe*, etc.) (Doke in Schapera 1950: 309-31), and a remarkable system of sound shifts makes speakers of the two types mutually unintelligible.

Although variations in the speechtone patterns of the different languages and in the syllabic structure of nouns and their corresponding noun concords may affect the rhythm and the line of melodies, it should be noted that music is more than embellished speech and that important elements such as prevailing meter, voice quality, tonality, and the composition of ensembles are all culturally determined. Moreover, not everything that sounds like music to European ears is necessarily regarded as music by Africans, and vice versa: the Zulu *izibongo* praise-poetry has melodic characteristics but is clearly distinguishable from song (Rycroft 1960:76-77)

and several Venda songs sound like spoken verse (Blacking 1967:48, 78, 91, 154, 155).

SOME COMMON ELEMENTS
OF THE MUSICAL SYSTEMS

Political events in the 1960s, particularly the emergence of black consciousness, gave new prominence to the use of the African idiom in modern music, but the process was possible only because of the adaptability and creativity of the "folk" tradition. Although in the sixteenth century Father André Fernandes reported hearing Chopi xylophone orchestras that may have sounded substantially the same as those playing in 1975 (Tracey 1970:145-46), it is inconceivable that southern African music remained static for several centuries until European influences affected it.

First, there is evidence of new compositions and change even within as highly structured an art form as the Chopi *ngodo* (Tracey 1970). Second, there are many cases of known musical diffusion where there is evidence of adaptive change and transformations of styles rather than straight imitation: for example, the Tswa adopted xylophones from the Chopi nearly a hundred years ago, but they have developed a style of playing and dancing that is very different. The Mpondo, the Mpondomise, the Bhaca, the Hlubi, the Nhlangwini, and the Swazi, have the *ndlamu* stamping dance commonly associated with the Zulu, but their tempi and their patterns of dance movement vary considerably. Third, because traveling and contact among different societies were common in southern Africa long before whites created an even larger area of discourse by recruiting migrant laborers to the diamond and gold mines, and because music has been both a factor in and a reflection of social and political processes, musical traditions have been dynamic and constantly changing (Blacking in Wachsmann 1971:185-212). Fourth, although orally transmitted music is supposed to be performed no less accurately than that which is written down, there are at least two constant variables in every performance that affect the way the music is realized on any particular occasion. These are the changing patterns of interaction of the per-

FIGURE 11-3. Members of a Chopi xylophone orchestra playing at a Mine Dance.

formers and the social context of performance, and no musical transcription is complete without reference to the range of variations that these variables may generate. In the case of ritual music, every performance may be almost identical; but more commonly the number of repeats of a section, a rhythm, or a variant may be the incidental musical consequence of social factors such as the number and the experience of dancers present and their current responses to one another and to members of the audience.

In most South African cultures, categories of music are distinguished according to their social function, and names given to different styles rarely indicate contrasts in music structure (e.g., Blacking 1965:29ff.). Although precise demarcations are not always made between music and nonmusic, regular metrical organization is generally essential for both, but melody is not (e.g., Blacking 1967:16ff.). Venda music, for ex-

ample, is a shared experience founded on a rhythmical stirring of the whole body of which singing is but one extension. Therefore, when we seem to hear a rest between two drumbeats, we must realize that for the player it is not a rest: each drumbeat is part of a total body movement in which the hand or a stick strikes the drumskin. As a system of socially accepted concepts and conventions, Venda music is obviously a shared experience, no matter how alone a performer may be; and although most music is composed by individuals whose names may not be known, it is modified by the collective during the course of trial performances and subsequent oral transmission. As a special kind of communion of bodies in space and time, the world of African music can also promote a shared experience of becoming, in which individuals venture into the reality of the world of the spirit through the collective consciousness of the

FIGURE 11-4. *Domba*, the dance of the Venda premarital initiation school.

community—they both experience and become the source of richer cultural forms (Blacking 1973:28ff.).

All South African peoples have a saying that expresses the philosophical basis of musical experience. The Zulu version (*umuntu ungumuntu ngabantu*) might be paraphrased, "Man can only become fully human through his relationships with his fellow men." It is a basic principle of African socialism, and its musical consequences are found all over sub-Saharan Africa whenever different parts are combined in polyrhythm and polyphony (see ex. 11-1). Such musical structures cannot be correctly performed unless each individual conducts himself and at the same time submits to the "invisible conductor" of the collective. Successful performance depends on the mutual interaction of players. Anyone who has performed in such ensembles will know just how the music generates a change of somatic state when all the players or singers of different parts "slot into" a common movement.

The principle may be applied "vertically" to distances between pitches, as well as "horizontally" to sequences in time. Since communal instrumental music is rare in South Africa, except in the subtropical parts of the Northern Transvaal, among the Northern Sotho, Venda, and Shangana-Tsonga peoples, it is not surprising that one of the most striking features of South African music is vocal polyphony. It may be produced by the overlap of solo and chorus parts in music whose form is responsorial (Rycroft 1967:93–95); by the addition of various parts in counterpoint to the basic melody (Blacking 1973:70–71); by straightforward harmonization with a blend of parallel motion and tonic-dominant progressions; or by the use of voices to produce a total pattern of sound from very short phrases, similar to an ensemble of drummers in polyrhythm. The last vocal technique is in fact used to provide a quasi-percussive accompaniment for the Bhaca ndlamu stamping dance (Tracey 1952:4-6, 51) and for the distinctive *khulo* music of Venda girls' initiations (Blacking 1970:56; 1973:83; see ex. 11-2*b*).

This treatment of voices is similar to the hocket technique employed in the "reed flute" ensembles (Kirby 1933:135-70) that are as notable a feature of South African communal music as vocal polyphony. The Venda have two different kinds of pipe music: their national dance tshikona is played on a set of twenty to twenty-four stopped pipes, each of which is named and tuned to one tone of a heptatonic scale (see ex. 11-2*a*; Blacking 1967:21, 26, and 177ff.); various dance tunes for young men are played on a different kind of stopped pipe made from the river reed and tuned to a pentatonic scale (ibid.

184). In playing the special music for each class of pipe, men dance round in a circle counter-clockwise, and women or girls play a set of drums in the center of the circle. (The circle dance is characteristic of the Venda and Northern Sotho, whereas among the Shangana-Tsonga, Southern Sotho, and Nguni peoples dancers are more commonly ranged in straight lines and the stamping of feet provides an important percussive element in the music.) The Pedi, Lovedu, and Ndebele have pentatonic ensembles, and the Lete of Botswana use a four-note "scale" that extends over five octaves (ex. 11-3). Analysis of Lete pipe melodies suggests that they are composed by combining different rhythmic figures blown according to the principles of polymeter. Thus, a variety of melodies can be produced by combining the same or different rhythmic patterns on different pipes: although the concept

EXAMPLE 11-2. Illustration of the transformation process by which *khulo* is related to *tshikona*, and summary of modes and basic chord sequence. (*a*) The upper tones of *tshikona*, transposed down a semitone. (*b*) The basic pattern of *khulo* for girls' voices. (*c*) Transposition of *tshikona* to the same pitch as *khulo*. Note the *f* natural and the position of the tritone. (*d*) Transformation of *tshikona*, rewriting d″ as *phala* instead of a″. Note how the position of the tritone differs from *tshikona* in (*c*) but agrees with *khulo* in (*b*). (*e*) The three modes used in *tshikona* and *khulo*, rewritten without accidentals. (*f*) The harmonic basis of *khulo*. The sequence of chords also fits the *tshikona* pattern, regardless of the different modes used. *Note*: the figures indicate the number of semitones in the intervals of the modes. Reprinted with permission from John Blacking, *How Musical Is Man?* (Seattle: University of Washington Press, 1973), p. 50.

underlying the music is rhythmic and similar to that of a drum ensemble, the musical result is melodic (Ballantine 1965:55ff.).

I have emphasized the word *scale* because although there is no doubt that all South African musical systems have "fixed stores of notes" on which melodies may be based, there do not seem to be words that are equivalent to *scale*. That the Venda system recognizes the interval of the octave is demonstrated by the fact that tones are called respectively *thakhula, phala, dangwe,* and *kholomo,* and so on, and the tones an octave higher are called *thakhulana, phalana, dangwana* and *kholomwana,* and so on, all of which are diminutives. But the nearest word for a scale does not refer to the intervals in an octave: *mu-*

common, and many songs are "hexatonic, resembling our own diatonic but without the seventh degree" (Rycroft in Wachsmann 1971: 216). There is, furthermore, no doubt that the semitone was widely used, though not in the position of leading note, long before South African music came under Western influence. Rycroft has suggested that one factor may have been "the unbraced musical bow, the classic Nguni instrument for solo song accompaniment. Among the Zulu and Swazi this is traditionally played in such a way as to yield an interval that roughly approximates a semitone" (ibid., 218).

The idea that the harmonics of the musical bow played a key role in generating some of the scales of South African vocal music was first

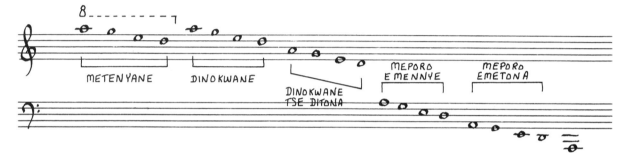

EXAMPLE 11-3. From Christopher Ballantine, "The Polyrhythmic Foundation of Tswana Pipe Melody," *African Music* (1965).

tavha may refer to the set of twenty-four heptatonic stopped pipes used for tshikona, the twelve pentatonic stopped pipes used for *givha* or *visa,* or a row of keys on the xylophone or *mbira* (the lamellaphone often referred to as a hand piano). Musical differences between the heptatonic and pentatonic sets of pipes are recognized, and they are not played together, but beyond saying that they "sound different" and "play different songs," the Venda do not talk about their contrasting musical features. Nor are there words to distinguish the different hexatonic and heptatonic modes used in songs, although their musical functions are discrete.

The Venda are the only South African society whose traditional music makes extensive use of heptatonic and hexatonic modes. Elsewhere, various types of pentatonic scale were and are

proposed by Kirby (1926), and it has many attractions, for musical bows of various types are widely distributed in central and southern Africa (Rycroft 1966; Kirby 1965:193ff.). Amplification of harmonics is an important feature of the playing technique, and the selection of resonated harmonics appears to influence the singer's choice of vocal scale. On the other hand, it can equally well be argued that in the quiet, personal style of bow-songs players select tunings and scales that are used in other areas of their musical system. Logically, it is easier to derive the organization of parts from the structure of the whole—as I have argued in the first part of this essay, we may expect systems of thought to be derived from social formations—but there is another feature of bow songs that appears so widely and in so many different transformations that it could hardly be derived from bow music, although the physical possibilities of bow playing make it a very obvious thing to do. This is the fluctuation of tonality up and down a semitone, a whole tone, or a minor third.

Tonal fluctuation is an essential feature of South African music (Blacking 1959; 1970) and many melodies seem to be derived from a conceptual framework of chords rather than single tones, so that a harmonized melody is the full realization of a sequence of "blocks" of sound and the single line of melody is in a sense incomplete. This is a consequence of the African social principle, mentioned earlier, that man reaches his fullness through interaction with others and that every individual presupposes a society. Fluctuations of tonality are often related to general movements of the body in dancing (forward/backward, left/right, up/down), and the different harmonic weights given to alternating tones may further be a consequence of social factors. For example, in the Venda national dance, tshikona (see ex. 11-2), two modes are generated by a pattern played on a single *mutavha* of stopped pipes. The pattern is formed by applying the *social* principle that each player should combine alternately with two different companions while at the same time applying the dance-generated, *spatial* principle that the tonality move away from a tone center (phala) towards the tone (thakhula) above phala which "lifts the melody" back on to the tone center. The continuous fluctuation of tonality between phala and thakhula gives the music a quality of perpetual motion; it corresponds with the raising, dipping, and turning of the body in each sequence of dance steps, and the changing patterns of interaction of the pipe players.

Example 11-4 shows how fluctuations in tonality are combined with the use of strong and weak chords to give the music movement: a tone is strongest when accompanied by its companion tone, a fifth below, so that the progression is from strong "tonic" (phala) to weak "leading note" (thakhula) to weak "tonic," strong "leading note," and back to strong "tonic." In tshikona, the strong "leading note" accompanies a lift and gathering of the body prior to its

FIGURE 11-5. A rural Venda plays one of the lowest tones in the *tshikona* melody on a pipe made from a piece of steel tubing.

"descent" on the first beat of the figure. This delayed movement from strong "tonic" to strong "leading note" is an elaboration of the more common fluctuation between two tones that have equal harmonic value.

Given a sequence of chords moving according to the requirements of tonal fluctuation (similar to the common tonic-subdominant-tonic-dominant-tonic sequence in much popular music), it follows that a variety of melodies can be derived

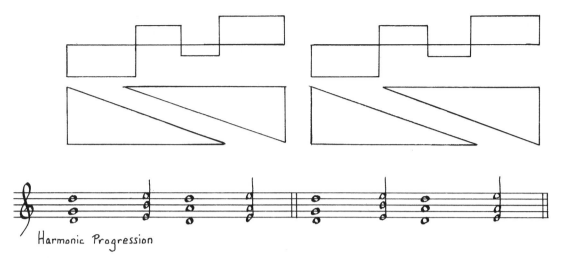

Harmonic Progression

EXAMPLE 11-4. Diagram of the harmonic and tonal progressions of *tshikona* and *khulo*, showing how the power of *phala* (d") and *thakhula* (e") alters as they change their companion tones. The rectangles symbolize shifts of tonality, and the changing thickness of the "wedges" illustrates the decrease and increase of the tonal power of *phala* and *thakhula*. Reprinted with permission from John Blacking, *How Musical Is Man?* (Seattle: University of Washington Press, 1973), p. 87.

EXAMPLE 11-5. "Venda Children's Song," from John Blacking, *How Musical Is Man?* (Seattle: University of Washington Press, 1973).

from them by extracting different sequences of tones from the chords. Since all such melodies are derived from the same set of chords, it follows that any one of them is "harmonically equivalent" to any other. When singers "fill out" a song with countermelodies, they must select tones from the chords that implicitly accompany the basic melody. Similarly, if changes in speechtone require an alteration in the pattern of an unaccompanied melody, the new tones must be "harmonically equivalent" to those that they replace (Blacking 1967:168ff.). This also accounts for the fact that two different melodies may be described as "the same," as in example 11-5: both versions of this Venda children's song (ibid., 102–3) are transformations of the same deep structure, which is essentially a sequence of chords given rhythmic impetus and contour by a string of words.

If "blocks" of harmony and tonality provide a basic force in much South African music, it is by building up patterns of tempo, meter, and rhythm that composers "chip away" at these "blocks" to capture force with form and produce melody. Apart from the music of the Shangana-Tsonga, and some Venda and Pedi music, the tempo of most South African music is slow, especially in comparison with the music of central Africa, where the same metric patterns may be found at twice the South African speed.

In South African music, apparent differences in tempo and meter may be reduced to one or two basic tempi and a few interrelated metrical patterns for all the music in a single society. The unity of tempi may be compared to a classical adagio, where the presence of thirty-second notes need not make its movement any faster or less relaxed. The interrelationship of metrical patterns is a consequence of the fact that they seem to be derived from a finite number of polymetric models, in much the same way that melodies are derived from harmonic models. Thus three quarter notes may occupy the same span of time as two dotted quarter notes, and

FIGURE 11-6. Venda children's game played at night. While a song is sung, someone in disguise comes out and dances.

vice versa; so a metrical pattern of four dotted quarter notes at ♩. = 90 is the same as six quarter notes at ♩ = 135, and several different patterns may be generated by adding or combining "units" of two or three that are linked by a single tempo, which may be implicit or explicit (see fig. 1 in Blacking 1970:8).

A common basic metrical unit in central African music, which is found in the northern Transvaal but does not seem to be much used farther south, is that of twelve eighth notes grouped as in example 11-6a. When one considers alternative arrangements of the same figure (ex. 11-6b), the relationship to an implicit 2:3 framework (ex. 11-6c) becomes clear.

Within the broader framework of the prevailing tempi and metrical patterns of each society's musical system, different melodies are created out of tonal and harmonic "blocks" by a

EXAMPLE 11-6.

variety of nonmusical processes that affect metric structures. The requirements of hoeing a field, threshing, grinding, pounding maize with pestle and mortar, or digging up a road with pickaxes (Rycroft 1967:93) all impose particular metric patterns on music, as do some of the symbolic movements of initiation songs (Blacking 1969:18–35; 1970:6). A fast, but metronomic tempo is essential in the possession music of the Shangana-Tsonga (Johnston 1971) and of the Venda, as I quickly discovered when I was dismissed as a drummer for hurrying the rhythm on one occasion (Blacking 1973:44–45). A similarly metronomic, but very slow, tempo is required for the religious dancing of the Nazarite church of Shembe.

Small but important variations in the shape and rhythm of melodies are generated by the different patterns of words chosen for each song. The basic principle in setting words to music is that one word syllable equals one tone, frequently given eighth-note duration in transcriptions, and that the nasals m̲ and n̲ usually count as separate syllables. Although the rhythm and speechtone patterns of the opening phrase of a song can establish the basic melody and harmonic structure of the whole song, so that further additions to the text are suggested as much by the initial *music* as by a logical continuation of the words (Blacking 1967:170–71), it does not always follow that there are consistent relationships between the number of eighth note "pulses" or quarter notes and dotted quarter notes in a musical phrase and the number of syllables of basic word phrases. The musical phrase generally contains more eighth note "pulses" than are required to contain all the syllables of a word phrase, so that there is room for flexibility in the creation of new words for an existing melody.

In an analysis of Venda initiation songs, I found that "the length of word phrases is not a relevant factor in the choice of meter. A pattern of words may suggest an appropriate meter, but more important factors in the composition of songs are the creation of total metrical patterns and the balance of rhythmical and tonal phrases within them" (Blacking 1970:7). Rycroft has observed that "of Nguni peoples it seems to be the Zulu who favor the most extreme forms of word distortion regarding syllable length and stress placement.... In song, the duration given to the longer and shorter syllables of spoken Zulu is frequently directly reversed, and stressed syllables are placed on off-beats" (Rycroft in Wachsmann 1971:237). Because regular meter is the basic criterion of music, it is not altogether surprising that in song the rhythms of speech are readily ignored.

Because pitch is a secondary musical criterion, the tonality of the languages is not as much affected as the rhythm by the transformation from speech into song. Thus, "a typical Nguni speech feature seems to persist in all their singing—whether traditional, missionized, or modern, and even when Nguni speakers sing in English. (It could perhaps be argued that the critical index is the semantic significance of speechtone rather than the relative musical importance of pitch and rhythm; but speechtone is not so crucial that incorrectly intoned speech is rendered unintelligible.) This is the pitch-lowering effect of most of their 'raised' consonants—*bh*, *d*, *g*, *z*, etc.—on higher notes or on high speechtones. High syllables that commence or end with such a consonant have a brief rising portamento on-glide, or a falling off-glide, respectively.... This feature, either in speech or in song, is not known to occur in any Bantu languages other than those of the Nguni group" (ibid., 1971:235–6; see also Rycroft 1957; 1960; and article in *South African Music Encyclopaedia*). In the Venda musical system the tone patterns of speech affect the structure of melodies chiefly in the first solo/call part of the melody. The rules (Blacking 1967:166–71) are assimilated by quite young children, who are able to distinguish between the correct Venda way of singing a melody (ex. 11-7*a*) and an incorrect version in which subtle changes of melody are ignored. Changes in patterns of speechtone may also affect the rhythmic structure of a song (ex. 11-7*b*).

Word-based melodies can influence the structures of purely instrumental music, and certainly of songs that are accompanied by instruments. Some instrumental soli are "transcriptions" of vocal pieces, and others are explorations of

EXAMPLE 11-7. Parts of two Venda children's songs, illustrating some effects of changing speechtones on the patterns of melody. Reprinted with permission from John Blacking, *How Musical Is Man?* (Seattle: University of Washington Press, 1973), p. 70.

the characteristics of the instruments, such as the distinctive layout of the keys on an mbira and the symmetrical movement of the thumbs in relation to them, or the melodic possibilities and limitations of overblowing on an open reed with notched embouchure or a closed, transverse flute with three holes. There are also songs, especially for the heptatonic xylophone and mbira of the Venda, in which the instrumental accompaniment consists of a set of variations on a ground that is structurally related to the song melody, and thus a musical structure that develops a life of its own.

Although the social context or accompanying words may influence the form of music and be important factors in its appreciation, there is abundant evidence of a special world of com-munication in which the rhythmic organization of tone is in itself highly valued. To recall the musical issues with which this essay began, we may refer to a description of some aspects of Nguni music in which different social groups have selected different *musical* characteristics both as an expression of the uniqueness of their cultures and as means of attaining the different worlds of experience that music seeks to create. "In ceremonial music and communal dance-songs an 'open' voice quality seems common to all Nguni, and there is a tendency among old men toward a tremulous vibrato. . . . But in young men's songs a tense voice quality is culti-vated, and sometimes an extremely low, forced bass. Young Swazi men employ portamento and sudden crescendi and diminuendi in their regimental chants and war cries (*izaga*). All Nguni employ portamento, but in different degrees. The Zulu probably use it the most extensively and the Xhosa the least" (Rycroft in Wachsmann 1971:217).

South African musical systems reflect both the different societies and the cultures in which they thrive, and they have a transcendental function: in the shared experience of music itself, of humanly significant form in tonal motion, there is the possibility of reaching beyond the constraints of words and social role and cultural time, by extending tonal and harmonic structures in a special world of musical time. Recent developments in South African music reflect the growth of a collective African consciousness. This should help to generate the energy and imagination required for black South Africans to transcend the confines of a white-dominated settler colony based on the values and institutions of an alien culture, and to build a new African state with the same confidence and ability that they have shown in creating their own black South African music.

Glossary

Amakwenkwe-A Xhosa word referring to the youths who perform the shaking dance, *Umteyo* (Tracey 1952:9, 151).

dangwe-The tone below the keynote (*phala*) in the Venda heptatonic scale.

givha-A Venda dance, the music of which is played by men and youths on sets of reed pipes tuned to a pentatonic scale, accompanied by women and girls on a set of drums.

Isicathulo-A Zulu word meaning "boots," given to the step dance, generally performed by Baca men, in which the dancers perform intricate clap rhythms that include slapping their Wellington boots.

izaga-A Zulu word referring to the characteristic cry originally associated with war.

izibongo-A Zulu word referring to praises intoned in honor of a person.

kholomo-A Venda word literally meaning "cattle," which in a musical context refers to the tone in the heptatonic scale two below the keynote *phala*.

khulo-A Venda word for a special type of singing by

women in which open vowels are used and only one, two, or three tones are used in sequence, in hocket style. The sound of khulo often resembles that of yodeling.

Makwaya-Derived from the English word "choir," this is the name given to a miming and group singing dance performed by the Shangana-Tsonga (Tracey 1952:16).

mutavha-A Venda word which refers to a complete set of divining dice, of metal amulets, or of reed pipes, and also to a row of keys on a xylophone or *mbira*.

ndlamu-A step dance characteristic of the Nguni peoples of southern Africa, usually performed by men in single or double lines. The tempo and the method of stamping the foot on the ground differ from one group to another (Tracey 1952:4-6).

ngodo-A word used by the Chopi of Mozambique to refer to their orchestral dance, the music of which is played on between ten and twenty xylophones, and divided into between nine and fifteen movements so that it may take as long as an hour to perform.

phala-The keynote of the Venda heptatonic scale (Blacking 1967:20-21; 1970:12-14).

thakula-A Venda word which literally means "the lifter." The last note in the Venda scale, a tone above *phala*, it leads a melody back to the keynote.

tshikona-The Venda national dance, played by men and youths on sets of from twenty to twenty-four reed pipes tuned to a heptatonic scale (each pipe producing a single tone), and accompanied by women and girls on a set of drums. The dance is performed in a circle, counterclockwise, with many different steps (Blacking 1965:25-26, 44-52).

visa-A Venda dance, similar to *givha* (above), but with a different rhythm and melodies played on the drums and pentatonic reed pipes. Like *givha*, it is danced in a circle, counterclockwise, with a variety of steps and sections in which individuals come out singly and dance with high leaps.

Bibliography

Adams, Charles R.
1980. "Basotho Music." In *Grove's Dictionary of Music and Musicians*. 6th ed. London: Macmillan.
Ballantine, Christopher.
1965. "The Polyrhythmic Foundation of Tswana Pipe Melody." *African Music* 3:52-67.

Blacking, John.

1959. "Problems of Pitch, Pattern and Harmony in the Ocarina Music of the Venda." *African Music* 2:15-23.

1962. "Musical Expeditions of the Venda." *African Music* 3:54-78.

1964. *Black Background*. New York: Abelard-Schuman.

1965. "The Role of Music in the Culture of the Venda of the Northern Transvaal." In *Studies in Ethnomusicology*, II, edited by M. Kolinski, pp. 20-53. New York: Oak Publications.

1967. *Venda Children's Songs*. Johannesburg: Witwatersrand University Press.

1969. "Songs, Dances, Mimes and Symbolism of Venda Girls' Initiation Schools." In *African Studies* 28, pts. 1-4.

1970. "Tonal Organization in the Music of Two Venda Initiation Schools." *Ethnomusicology* 14 (January), 1-56.

1973. *How Musical Is Man?* Seattle: University of Washington Press. 2d edition, Faber and Faber, 1976.

Bloom, Harry, and Pat Williams.

1961. *King Kong*. London: Fontana Books.

Bokwe, John Knox.

1910. *Amaculo ase Lovedale*. Lovedale, South Africa: Lovedale Mission Press.

Glasser, Mona.

1960. *King Kong: A Venture in the Theatre*. Cape Town: Norman Howell.

Hansen, Deirdre.

1968. *The Life and Work of Benjamin Tyamzashe*. Occasional Paper No. 11. Grahamstown: Institute of Social and Economic Research.

Huskisson, Yvonne.

1969. *The Bantu Composers of Southern Africa*. Johannesburg: South African Broadcasting Corporation.

Johnston, Thomas F.

1970. "Xizambi Friction-bow Music of the Shangana-Tsonga." *African Music* 4:81-95.

1971. "Shangana-Tsonga Drum and Bow Rhythms." *African Music* 5:59-72.

1972. "Possession Music of the Shangana-Tsonga." *African Music* 5:10-22.

1973a. "Musical Instruments and Practices of the Tsonga Beer-Drink." *Behavior Science Notes* 8:5-34.

1973b. "The Social Determinants of Tsonga Musical Behavior." *International Review of the Aesthetics and Sociology of Music* 4:108-30.

1973c. "Tsonga Children's Folksongs." *Journal of American Folklore* 86 (July-September), 225-42.

1973d. "Folk Dances of the Tsonga." *Viltis* 32:5-19.

Jones, LeRoi.

1963. *Blues People*. New York: William Morrow.

Kirby, Percival R.

1926. "Some Problems of Primitive Harmony and Polyphony." *South African Journal of Science* 33:951-70.

1933. "The Reed-Flute Ensembles of South Africa." *Journal of the Royal Anthropological Institute* 43 (July-December), 373-77.

1946. "The Musical Practices of the Native Races of South Africa." In I. Schapera, ed., *The Bantu-speaking Tribes of South Africa*, 271-89.

1965. *The Musical Instruments of the Native Races of South Africa*. 1934. Reprint. Johannesburg: Witwatersrand University Press.

Rhodes, Willard.

1962. "Music as an Agent of Political Expression." *Arts, Human Behavior and Africa, African Studies Bulletin* 5:14-22.

Rycroft, David.

1957a. "Linguistic and Melodic Interaction in Zulu Song." In *Akten des XXIV Internationalen Orientalisten Kongresses, München*, pp. 726-29. Wiesbaden: Deutsche Morgenländische Gesellschaft.

1957b. "Zulu Male Traditional Singing." *African Music* 1:33-35.

1960. "Melodic Features in Zulu Eulogistic Recitation." *African Language Studies* 1:60-78.

1962. "Zulu and Xhosa Praise Poetry and Song." *African Music* 3:79-85.

1966. "Friction Chordophones in South-Eastern Africa." *Galpin Society Journal* 19:84-100.

1967. "Nguni Vocal Polyphony." *Journal of the International Folk Music Council* 19:88-103.

Schapera, Isaac.

1950. *The Bantu-speaking Tribes of South Africa*. 1937. Reprint. Cape Town: Maskew Miller.

Sithole, E. Thamsanqa.

1979. "Ngoma Music among the Zulu." In *World Anthropology, Vol. 8: The Performing Arts*. Proceedings of the IXth International Congress of Anthropological and Ethnological Sciences, 1973. The Hague: Mouton.

Sundkler, B. G. M.

1961. *Bantu Prophets in South Africa*. 1948. Reprint. Oxford: International African Institute.

South African Music Encyclopedia.

Forthcoming. Articles on indigenous South African music by John Blacking, Yvonne Huskisson, Thomas Johnston, Percival R. Kirby, and David Rycroft. Pretoria: Human Sciences Research Council.

Tracey, Hugh.

1948. *Lalela Zulu: 100 Zulu Lyrics*. Johannesburg: African Music Society. Includes discography.

1952. *African Dances of the Witwatersrand Gold Mines*. Johannesburg: African Music Society. Includes photographs, discography, and glossary of terms.

1970. *Chopi Musicians: Their Music, Poetry, and Instruments*. 1948. Reprint. London: Oxford University Press.

Wachsmann, Klaus, ed.

1971. *Music and History in Africa*. Evanston, Ill.: Northwestern University Press. Articles by John Blacking ("Music and History in Vendaland"), Percival R. Kirby ("The Changing Face of African Music South of the Zambezi"), David Rycroft ("Stylistic Evidence in Nguni Song"), and others.

Discography

African Dances of the Witwatersrand Gold Mines. Music of Africa Series No. 12. GALP 1032/3. Also Decca LF 1254/5.

The African Music Society's Choice No. 2 Music of Africa Series No. 15. GALP 1019.

African Tribal Dances. CBS ALD-6624. Music performed in mine arenas by Mzingili, Pedi, Kwena, Lete, Hlubi, Tswa, Chopi, Shangana-Tsonga, Xhosa, Pondo, Baca, and Rotse.

Alibulali. HMV JP 2129. By Gideon Nxumalo, played by his International Jazz Band.

Bantu Choral Folk Songs. Folkways FW-6912.

Basutoland musique du fond des âges. Disques BAM (La Boîte à musique). LD 398.

Duke Ellington Presents the Dollar Brand Trio. Reprise R-6111.

Intsholo. GALP 1350. Compositions by African composers sung by The Johannesburg African Music Society, conducted by Ben Xatasi and Michael Rantho.

Izibongo zikaShaka and Izibongo zikaDingana. GE 967. By Mgadi. Praises of Shaka and Dingana.

King Kong. GALP 1040. Jazz Opera by Todd Matshikiza.

Miriam Makeba. RCA Victor LPM-2267. With the Belafonte Folk Singers.

Malombo Jazz Makers, Vol. 2. Continental 2B 8162. Modern African Jazz.

Mkhumbane. GALP 1103. Music by Todd Matshikiza, mostly for unaccompanied choir. Words by Alan Paton.

Music of Africa Series No. 18: Music from the Roadside, No. 1. GALP 1110. Selected South African music.

Music of the Baca and Sotho, including work songs. TR-64. International Library of African Music, Music of Africa series, includes recordings from all parts of South Africa.

Music of the Southern Sotho, including grinding songs. TR-104.

Music of the Tonga/Hlanganu of Moçambique, including women's pounding songs. TR-4.

Music of the Tswana, including threshing songs. TR-111.

Music of the Tswana (Kgatla), including threshing songs. TR-117.

Music of the Tswana (Lete), including a grinding song. TR-112.

Nkosi sikilel'i Afrika. CBS Columbia YE 117. By Enoch Sontonga.

Praises of Dinizulu. GE 1001.

Praises of Mpande and Cetshwayo. GE 998.

Separatist Hymns from the Zulu Church of Nazareth. TR-9.

Sikalo. CBS Columbia 33YE 1001. Musical by Gibson Kente.

Spokes of Africa. GALP 1049. Compositions by Spokes Mashiyane for penny whistle band.

Swazi Music and *Zulu, Swazi and Xhosa Instrumental and Vocal Music*, Nos. 1 and 3. Made by David Rycroft. Musée Royale de l'Afrique Centrale, Tervuren. Annotated recordings of African music.

Venda Music. Tape recorded by John Blacking. Published by the University of Washington Press in connection with *How Musical Is Man?*

The Voice of Africa: Miriam Makeba. RCA Victor LPM-2845.

The World of Miriam Makeba. RCA Victor LPM 2750.

Films

Bitter Melons. DER. Col. 30 min. Directed by John Marshall. Nicholas England, ethnomusicologist.

Filmed in Botswana, *Bitter Melons* emphasizes the search of the inhabitants of the Kalahari Desert for water. Throughout the film are heard the songs of an old man accompanying himself on a bow with an overturned enamel basin for a resonator. Children's games and game songs.

Dances of Southern Africa. Alfred G. Zantzinger. Col. 55 min. Commentary by Hugh and Andrew Tracey.

A great variety of dances from Rhodesia, South Africa, and Malawi. Some groups wear tribal, others Western dress.

Murudruni. UCB. Col. 60 min. Made by Derek Lamport.

Circumcision school of the Northern Sotho of the Transvaal. Shows the main rites, songs, and dances, with many musical recordings.

N / um Tchai: the Ceremonial Dance of the Kung Bushmen. DER. B/W. 22 min. Directed by John Marshall. Nicholas England, ethnomusicologist.

Filmed in Namibia, southwest Africa. Dance of Medicine Men, many of whom become frenzied and then go into deep trance.

12. Anlọ Eʋe Music in Anyako, Volta Region, Ghana

Alfred Kwashie Ladzekpo and Kọbla Ladzekpo[1]

Eʋe is spoken in southern Ghana and in the southern half of Togo and Dahomey. Along the coast it is heard as far east as Badagry in Nigeria (Westermann 1930). Ghanaian Eʋe are divided into two groups: northern and southern. The Anlọ Eʋe, the focus of this study, live in the extreme southeastern corner of Ghana and speak the Anlọ dialect of the Eʋe language. According to the Ghana government population census taken in 1960, they number more than 231,000 (*Gazetteer* 1962). In oral tradition, present-day Eʋe land is not the original home of all the Eʋe-speaking people. There are several accounts of their migration to the present land from various places such as the Sudan, Nigeria, Dahomey, and Togoland. In the different versions of the story, three places always appear: Oyo in present-day western Nigeria; Ketu in northern Dahomey; and Notsie in the Republic of Togo. Among these three places, Notsie is considered the Eʋe's last resting place in their journey to their present respective homes. In some respects Notsie is to the Eʋe as Egypt is to the Jews.

Migration of the Eʋe

The Eʋe are believed to have migrated from Notsie in the seventeenth century. We do not know how long they were there before. How-ever, we do know that they arrived in Notsie from Ketu during the reign of King Agọ Kọli I (ca. 1500), who was hospitable to them. This benevolent king died and his son Agọ Akọli II came to the throne. During the reign of the new king, things were not the same. Legends have it that the new ruler mistreated the Eʋe in many ways. For example, he ordered that all elderly people should be killed; but the Eʋe managed to keep one old man, Tegli, in hiding.

Because of the young king's repressive acts the Eʋe made a secret plan to escape. The city of Notsie was surrounded by a seventeen by thirty foot wall to protect its inhabitants from attack. Although this wall was a barrier to the Eʋe in planning their escape, they finally carried their plan through successfully.

After several consultations with Tegli at his hiding place, they drew up a master plan. They instructed the women to throw water against one spot on the wall while washing their clothes and dishes. When the elders found that the wall was wet enough, they implemented the final stage of their plan. They gathered all their people together near the wet wall and pretended to be entertaining themselves with music called *misego* ("tighten your belt").[2] There was a lot of jubilation in the Eʋe section of the city from late afternoon throughout the night. About midnight, while the rest of the people of Notsie went to bed and the music was going on, Tegli, the brain behind the plot, called a few people to the wet wall. He drew out the "Sword of Liberation" from its sheath, pointed it up, invoked the spirits of the gods and the ancestors and said a short prayer. Then he said, "O Mawuga Kitika-

---

1. This essay is part of an ongoing research project in which the authors have been engaged for some years on the subject of Anlọ Eʋe music and is dedicated to two people: the late Kofi Zate Ladzekpo, our father, and Husunu Adonu Afadi-Ladzekpo, our older brother. Father and son died in 1970 and 1969, respectively. They are the source of our knowledge, our "Encyclopedia Anlokana." Without them our knowledge of Anlọ folklore would be slight. For further information see K. Ladzekpo, "A Study Center at Anyako, Ghana."

2. Misego is still performed every November at Anlọgā to celebrate the Eʋe migration from Notsie.

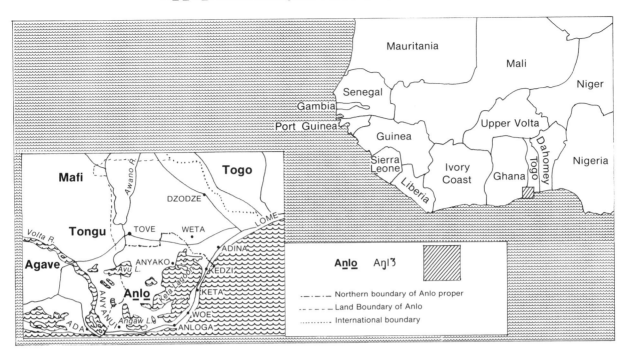

Volta Region of Africa

ta, W<u>uw</u>ona mi ne miadogo, az<u>o</u> adzo" (Oh great God Kitikata, open the door for us so that we walk through). With these words Tegli thrust the "Sword of Liberation" into the wet wall and bored a big hole through which the E<u>w</u>e escaped. Women, old men, and children left first, while some youths and middle-aged men stayed behind dancing to the misego music. After all the others had gone, the drummers and the few remaining dancers followed them. The last group[3] walked backward for two miles so that their footprints might not betray their whereabouts. The sword used by Tegli to bore the hole is said to be preserved to this day as part of the stool regalia of one of the chiefs of Ho, a town in northern E<u>w</u>eland.

From <u>N</u>otsie the E<u>w</u>e traveled together to a town that is now called Tsevie in the Republic of Togoland. It was there that they divided into different groups, of which one was the A<u>nl</u>o E<u>w</u>e. The A<u>nl</u>o traveled from Tsevie as one unit, but later divided into two under the leadership of <u>W</u>enya and his nephew Sri (Sr<u>o</u>e). After many discoveries and settlements, <u>W</u>enya's group crossed a sandbar where he informed his followers, "Mieva <u>d</u>o Kea ta," meaning they had reached the head or the tip of the sand. Subsequently the settlement there was named Keta (from *Kea ta*). When they reached what is now present-day A<u>nl</u>ogā, <u>W</u>enya was found to be aged and tiring. His followers asked him when they were going to leave, and he answered, "Nya amea me<u>nl</u>o afia <u>d</u>eke yiyi megale <u>n</u>unye o" (I am coiled, exhausted, and I can't go any farther). The name of this settlement was taken from the word *Me<u>nl</u>o* and was corrupted as *A<u>nl</u>o.* Since it was the capital of the whole A<u>nl</u>o nation, the adjective *ga* meaning "big" was added.

Another settlement of historical and cultural importance is the island town of Anyako, named for the leader Anya[4] who brought his people

3. There are two versions to this story: some people said the entire group walked backward, others said it was only the last group. By walking backward, their footprints would indicate that they were coming into the city. This would mislead any search party that the king might send after them.

4. The authors are descendents of Anya. This information was given to them by their late father. For a similar historical description, see H. Pantaleoni, "The Rhythm of Atsiã Dance Drumming among the A<u>nl</u>o (E<u>w</u>e) of Anyako." Ph.D. dissertation, Wesleyan University, 1972.

from Anlogã. This is our home and its musical customs are representative of the Anlo Ewe.

Occupations of Men and Women

Most men in Anyako are subsistence fishermen, weavers, farmers, and traders. The smuggling of European goods such as tobacco, liquor, perfumes, clothes, and other commodities from the nearby French-speaking countries is another major business for both men and women. Some men make their living by ferrying traders with their goods across the lagoon to Keta. With the development of motor roads, however, this business has declined considerably. Both men and women engage in livestock raising.

As in many other parts of West Africa, petty trading in Anyako is largely in the hands of women (Hodder and Ukwu 1969). Every fourth day is a big market day in Anyako and the surrounding areas including Keta, the commercial center. There are also "mid-market" or small market days in Anyako. Most women travel from one market to another selling their products and buying other things such as foodstuffs. They make short and long trading expeditions lasting from several days to months. Some women both young and old have kiosks or small stores attached to their houses where they sell all kinds of things. These stores are similar to grocery stores in the United States. Some women also run beer bars or liquor stores (Ladzekpo 1971:6, 7).

Religious Practices

The Anlo practice ancestor worship and Christianity, and many of them belong to cults that honor special deities. Although Christianity has a strong hold in Anyako, it has not discouraged the worship of *Afã*, god of divination, and *Yewe*, god of thunder and lightning.

Afã is the god of divination worshiped in West Africa among the Yoruba, the Dahomeans, and the Ewe of Togo and southern Ghana. Afã is also a cult, which originated in western Nigeria, where the god is called Ifa (he is called Fa in Dahomey).[5] The proof of the cult's Yoruba origin is the "unintelligible Yoruba language" that the Ewe employ in Afã worship (Nukun-

ya 1969:97). Membership in the cult is by individual decision. There is no forced membership as may sometimes be the case in the Yewe cult. On many occasions, usually before any great event, Afã is consulted for good luck or success. This apparently is not different from similar practices of the ancient Greeks to whom worship of the oracle of Delphi was a way of life. Most traditional Ewe communities in Dahomey, Togo, and Ghana often prelude their drumming and dancing performances with Afã music (Jones 1959, I:131, 134; Ladzekpo and Pantaleoni 1970:7, 15).

Yewe is the god of thunder and lightning. The Yewe cult originated in Dahomey and is widespread all over southern Eweland. It has a cult language, believed to be a Fon dialect, spoken by the members and their associates only. Yewe is a very exclusive cult and therefore often referred to in literature as a secret society (Jones 1959, I:93). The affairs of the society are so jealously guarded by its members that non-members are strictly forbidden to take part even in its music. To become a member of the Yewe cult, one has to go through an initiation ceremony. This is followed by a period of seclusion in the cult house which may last a little more or less than a year. There are many laws and taboos surrounding the Yewe cult which its members are obliged to observe. Offenders are severely punished in a public ceremony. Members can be expelled for contravening its laws, and as for nonmembers the punishment is more severe. The nature of the punishment may be either a fine, or forced membership in the society if one cannot pay the fine.

There are a number of Yewe cult houses or shrines in every town. These houses have some peculiar characteristics that distinguish them from ordinary houses.[6] It is an offense for a nonmember to enter the cult house. In front of each Yewe shrine, there is an open space where outdoor activities involving the cult are performed. The cult house is the center of most activities. Immediately after initiation the novices, *Husikpokpowo*, are kept here in total seclusion from one to three months. During this

---

5. See Bascom (1969) for a full description of Ifã divination in Yoruba; also Herskovitz (1938).

6. Two of these characteristics are the red, black, and indigo flag on the roof of the house, and the multi-colored dotted spots on the wall.

time they learn the cult language, the Yewe rules, and the taboos. After this they will be officially presented to the townspeople with drumming and dancing. The performance is known as "outdooring." During this time their cult names are announced. They are never again to be called by their former names. A fully graduated male member of the Yewe cult is called "*Husunu*" and a female "*Vodusi*." Despite all its laws and taboos, the Yewe cult can be said to be exoteric as well as esoteric, because its drumming and dancing are performed outside the cult house for the public to watch and its offenders are tried in public.

Music of Afã and Yewe

Both Afã and Yewe music are very popular in Anlo. At a performance of Afã drumming, one often finds nonmembers dancing with the full members of the cult. An initiated member or a noninitiated member may invite a friend from the audience into the dance area for a round or two of dancing together. It is a general practice in Anlo to use Afã drumming among a great number of secular dance clubs as a propitiatory prelude in order to invoke the blessing of the Afã deity for the success of the performance (Ladzekpo 1971:11; Jones 1959:134, 141).

Yewe music is considered to be one of the most developed forms of sacred music in Anlo. There are seven different drums in this music. As used here, drums do not connote the physical instruments of wood, pegs, and membrane, but rather in this context mean different rhythms, songs, clapping, and dance steps.[7] Unlike Afã music, Yewe music is restricted to Yewe festivities. As stated earlier, the affairs of Afã are

open, flexible, and inviting. Those of Yewe are completely exclusive, inflexible, and forbidden to nonmembers. By cult law nonmembers cannot take part in the music at all. But associate members may take part in the performance at a funeral of a deceased cult member. The activities of Yewe arouse feelings of awe and fear, and, as a result, of utter fascination in the minds and hearts of listeners, be they members or not.

THE DANCE CLUBS

Drumming and dancing in Anlo as a whole, and Anyako in particular, are organized in dance clubs (Ladzekpo 1971:6). The clubs function as a social outlet in the communities. That is to say, they are a form of entertainment, recreation (Nketia 1962:10), and ceremonial activity. Music making among Anlo Ewe-speaking people is not a frequent occurrence; it is occasional. The occasion may be to welcome a government official or a foreign visitor, to promote a political party, to inaugurate a new dance club, to install a new chief, or to perform at a funeral or some social gathering that might warrant a dance performance.

Membership in the Clubs

Anyako is divided into three wings reflecting the traditional military divisions of Anlo.[8] The center wing, Adotri, was subdivided after a bitter dispute, known as *halo*, an abusive song, in the late thirties. As a result of this subdivision, there are practically four divisions in the town of Anyako. However, on state occasions the two subdivisions group together again under the original name, Adotri.

Membership in the dance clubs is open to both sexes. The clubs are organized in age groups (Ladzekpo 1971:6; Pantaleoni 1972:10). In theory, every adult living in a particular vicinity is expected to belong to one of the dance clubs in his or her community. But in practice one sometimes finds people who do not belong to any. The

---

7. Jones writes: "The Yewe cult has seven dances: the word 'dance' includes not only the actual choreography, but the corpus of songs that belong to it in particular, together with its special drumming and orchestral accompaniment. Each dance is clearly distinguished by these features from any other dances" (1959:97). At the last day of the Yewe cult festival there is a special ritual called *wuxexle* meaning "counting the drums." This does not mean counting the drums numerically; it means playing the seven different styles of drumming that belong to the cult. At the beginning of the festival is an invocation of the deities and their presence throughout the length of the festivities. On the last day wuxexle or counting the different styles of drumming is done to honor all the deities that had been invoked before the festivities came to an end. Jones's usage is therefore not an accurate translation of this ritual.

8. Commentators on this subject include Jones 1959:120, 127; Ladzekpo 1971; Ladzekpo and Pantaleoni 1970; Nketia 1962:10-12; and Pantaleoni 1972:10. Jones writes, "Each town is divided into four To's (a military division). . . ." The military divisions are not four. Jones and his informant must have confused the subdivision of Anyako that makes the fourth division.

following chart lists some of the dance clubs in the three divisions of Anyako. Each club cultivates its own distinctive songs, but certain clubs share the same drumming music. Clubs marked with an asterisk (*) share a drumming known as *axatsewu*. Clubs marked with a double asterisk (**) share a drumming known as *akpewu*. Clubs not marked by asterisks bear the name of the drumming style they practice.[9]

member the repertoire of songs for the club, the music may last for years, as in the case of many of the dances still performed in Anyako. We know firsthand of several examples to substantiate this fact; but for our study here we shall cite only three.

1. *Adzomani.* When the Adzomani club was first started, the original composer, Tagbolo, had moved to Togo. He composed a few songs

Dance Clubs of Anyako

Lasibi (Left Wing)	Adotri (Center Wing)		Woe (Right Wing)
	Atigate	Afegame	
Atsiagbeko or Agbeko	Degbato**	Adzida*	Abuteni
Adzomani*	Kedzeanyi**	Cape Coast*	Adzidagā*
Abuteni	Kpomegbe**	Danger	Adzida evelia*
Agube	Mifetu*	Kete	Adzro
Bluku	Takada	Kpomegbe**	Alosogbe*
Britannia*	Woleke	Lagos*	Atsiā
Gadzo		Yelieho*	Dzado
Nobody*			Gahū
Yevavo*			Holland**
			Kedzeanyi**
			Kete
			Kinka
			Woleke

According to our informants, some of these dances are as old as the Anlo themselves. They were brought from Notsie or *hogbe*, the ancestral home.[10] The clubs listed on the chart were founded during the present century and although the original members of most of these clubs have died, the repertoires have been passed down through participant observation. The chief architect and the guiding force of the organization of the clubs is the poet/composer, the *heno*. Without him, chances are that the club will not last long. But if there are good singers who can play the role of precentor and re-

and taught them to one of his brothers to teach the group at Anyako. It did not take the group much time to learn the songs and they waited for new ones to come. When the new songs were not forthcoming, the newly formed club was threatened with an unexpected dilemma. Someone had to help save the situation. Kofi Zate Ladzekpo, who later became co-poet/composer (heno), began composing for the club. His first composition clearly states his philosophy: "Dzogbe dzoki be edu nu mesea menu dina wo o" (The savannah duiker [a kind of deer] says one does not know when he will have to run.) The dzoki lives in grassland. He is faced daily with all the hazards of living under such circumstances. He does not know when he will fall into a trap or become the prey of a hunter. So it is

9. Jones (1959:150) used one of the Adzidaga songs but failed to make the distinction between the two Adzidas.

10. The Ewe referred to Notsie as *hogbe*, the ancestral home.

said that he likes to run every now and then as practice against any eventual attack, so that when the time comes to run to save himself, it won't be too hard on him. Kofi Zate's taking over did save the situation until Tagbolo returned to join him and they became co-poet/composers until their deaths. This music is still performed and the songs of the co-poet/composers are still alive and contemporary.

2. *Yevavo.* Yevavo is a dance club that plays the axatsewu style of music. The club belonged to the late Husunu Adonu Afadi-Ladzekpo, son of Kofi Zate, and others of his age group. When the club was first started in the late thirties, there were three different men composing for the group. After a while these people ceased composing. One of them left Anyako for business reasons and the other two were no longer active. At this juncture, Husunu Adonu took over and became the poet-composer of the Ye-vavo club. Like those of his father's group, Adzomani, Husunu's songs for Yevavo have remained part of Lasibi's repertoire of songs.

3. *Adzidagã.* One of the oldest dance drumming clubs in the Woe division of Anyako is Adzidagã ("big Adzida"). It is called "big Adzida" to differentiate it from another Adzida club, formed by a younger group and called Adzida evelia ("second Adzida"). Some of the people actively performing Adzidagã now are children and grandchildren of the original members. Like their fathers, uncles, and older brothers, they have also learned the music and the dance movements through the method of participant observation.

Musical Styles

In Anlo music, drumming, dancing, singing, and handclapping are a single wholé, and if any part changes, the whole is changed. There are different styles of drumming and dancing in Anlo just as there are different clubs. Lack of knowledge of these differences always causes confusion among outside observers. Like many other people, the Anlo have their own aesthetic values in judging their art. If we were to make a taxonomy of American games and teams, we should wind up with three main games: football, basketball, and baseball. These games are

played by groups of people under different team names throughout the country. No matter what name they play under, and no matter what the color of their uniforms, the name of the game remains the same. Thus among the Anlo, two or three dance clubs with different names may perform the same style of Anlo music. In the details of the music, however, the styles of these two or three clubs will differ, just as the styles of Western composers differ though each may write what Westerners easily identify as the same kind of music—a fugue, a symphony, and so forth. People brought up in the tradition understand the music and know what to listen for. They know the intricacies that distinguish the work of different musicians and the broad features that distinguish the different kinds of music. The recreational dance music in Anyako may be classified according to its broad features in three groups: axatsewu, akpewu, and what may be called "specific style."

1. *Axatsewu.* Axatsewu is the generic term of a style of music which is dominated by rattles. *Axatse* means rattle and *wu* means drum. Axatsewu therefore literally means "rattle drum," because rattles are outstanding in this style of drumming. Axatsewu style is performed by different clubs under different names in all the three divisions of Anyako. They are Adzomani, Adzida, Alosogbe, Britannia, and so on. Though the general instrumental music for these groups is identical, there are diminutive differences from one section of town to another. Some of the differences are: (1) the introductory rhythm, (2) *hatsiãtsiã* and bell patterns (interlude music), and (3) the drum calls. These differ in all three sections.

2. *Akpewu.* Like axatsewu, akpewu is a combination of two words (akpe means to clap). Akpewu is the generic name of music dominated by handclapping or wooden clappers as opposed to rattles. In this music clapping is continuous throughout a performance. Akpewu is also performed by different clubs; for example, Kpomegbe and Holland among those in our chart. However, we know of a club in another town near Anyako which plays akpewu in the club called "Nobody," whereas in our chart Nobody Club plays axatsewu style.

Ideally every male member of an axatsewu club is supposed to be playing a rattle throughout the performance. But in practice this is not always so. However, twenty or more rattles are always being played during a performance. In akpewu the maximum number of rattles is four and they play a different pattern from that of axatsewu and in 4/4. The *gankogui* (double bell) (see fig. 12-2) continues to play the standard Anlo bell pattern of 12/8 but more slowly than in axatsewu (ex. 12-1). The drums used in both

men and the women.[11] The men are led by two male precentors who pace in the dance circle from one area to another. The leaders of the women, usually two men and a woman or two, stand close to the women. Sometimes the two women assisting the men move back and forth, passing each other, in between the first two rows of benches. In akpewu, on the other hand, both men and women sit together in one big circle. The front bench is occupied by the four rattle players. The song leaders, usually two men and a

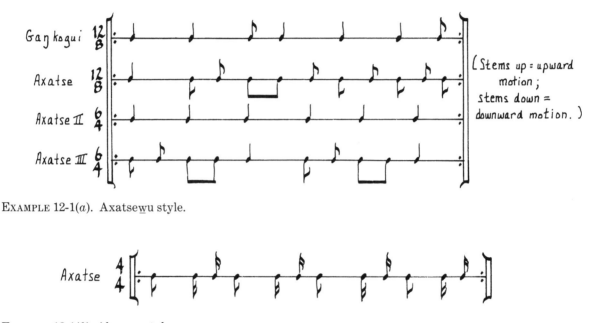

EXAMPLE 12-1(*a*). Axatsewu style.

EXAMPLE 12-1(*b*) Akpewu style.

styles are the standard Anlo combination: *atsimewu, sogo, kidi* and *kaganu* (fig. 12-3). At times a drum called *kloboto* (fig. 12-4) is added to sogo in some akpewu clubs. The sitting arrangements for both axatsewu and akpewu are similar with some minor differences. Usually the musicians in axatsewu will sit to the north of the dance area. In front of them as well as on their left and right are the rattle players.

To the south of the dance area the women, seated on benches, form two parallel rows. Two different songs are sung simultaneously by the

woman or two, also pace in the circle as they lead.

3. "Specific Style." In our chart there are a

11. According to Jones, "There are in Adzida some songs for men, in which case the male cantors start them, and some songs for women, which are likewise started by the women cantors. At times the woman cantor, in leading off one of the special Adzida songs, is helped by an extra male cantor, who leaves his place in the men's department and comes and stands in front of the women's forms" (1959:150). There are no "female cantors" as reported by Jones. In the men's song, the women's song is also led by male cantors. According to tradition, Adzida song leaders are always men, assisted by a woman or women. Jones's account is rather the opposite.

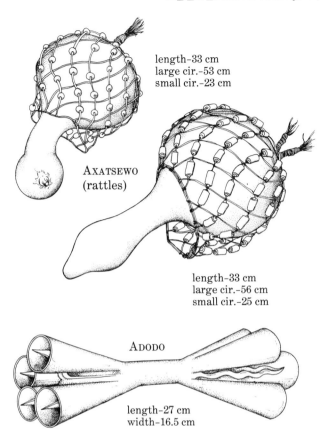

length-33 cm
large cir.-53 cm
small cir.-23 cm

AXATSEWO
(rattles)

length-33 cm
large cir.-56 cm
small cir.-25 cm

ADODO

length-27 cm
width-16.5 cm

FIGURE 12-1.

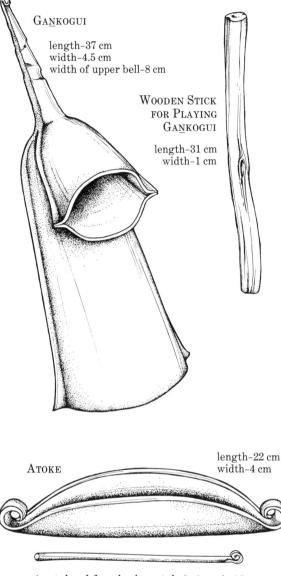

GA̱NKOGUI

length-37 cm
width-4.5 cm
width of upper bell-8 cm

WOODEN STICK
FOR PLAYING
GA̱NKOGUI

length-31 cm
width-1 cm

length-22 cm
width-4 cm

ATOKE

(metal rod for playing atoke)   length-16 cm

FIGURE 12-2.

number of examples of our third group, "specific styles," of which we shall discuss a selected few. What we mean by "specific style" is those dance clubs in which there are very distinctive styles of drumming and dancing different from those of the first two groups. In most cases, the names of these clubs are derived from the style of the music (for example, Taka̱da, Atsiãgbeko̱, Ga-hū, and Kete). In Taka̱da style the bell plays the same 12/8 as in the case of axatse̱wu and akpe̱wu, but in a medium tempo (♩=mm 120) (Ladzekpo and Pantaleoni 1970:1–31). Axatse plays a pattern different from both akpe̱wu and axatse̱wu (ex. 12-2). Another major characteristic is that the two lead drums, atsime̱wuwo, are played simultaneously in taka̱da, whereas in akpe̱wu and axatse̱wu the drummers play in turn. The drum patterns also differ in taka̱da from those of akpe̱wu and axatse̱wu. All the

three styles have interlude music, hatsiãtsiã. In hatsiãtsiã the drums are not used. The dancers and musicians move around the dance floor counterclockwise in a leisurely manner with gentle arm gestures, walking and singing in time with the bells. In taka̱da hatsiãtsiã bells are not used; instead of the bells, members carry rattles, tossing them into the air on every fourth

ATSIMEWU

height-124 cm
top width-22 cm
bottom width-25 cm

ATSIMEWUWO & WUDESTSI
(drums)   (stand)

SOGO

KAGANU

KIDI

height-55 cm
top width-14 cm
bottom width-11 cm

height-55 cm
top width-19 cm
bottom width-25 cm

height-67 cm
top width-22 cm
bottom width-30 cm

FIGURE 12-3.

beat. The sitting arrangement is the same as for akpewu, both men and women sitting together. The principal precentors are two or three women. As many rattles as possible are used.

Gahū is another style of drumming very popular in Anlo. It was brought to the area in the 1950s by some Anlo people who went on a fishing expedition in Badagry (western Nigeria). Gahū is a circle dance in which the dancers move in a four step movement, R, R, L, L, with their bodies leaning forward and flexing alternately one leg and then the other. (Axatsewu, akpewu, and takada are all performed in a mild crouching

by a group of people forming six to eight lines one behind the other, depending on the size of the group, with four to six abreast in each line.[12] There are many dance movements, all different from the Anlo "basic movement,"—the main dance movement in axatsewu and akpewu (Ladzekpo 1971:10). The "basic movement" is used especially by women and by some men who cannot do the main agbeko movement. As most of the men are doing the main agbeko movement, the women will be doing the "basic movement." One therefore sees a counterpoint of movement in agbeko performance. It is done

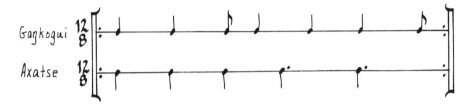

EXAMPLE 12-2. Takada style.

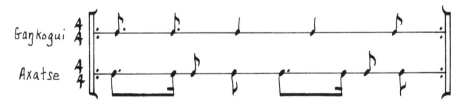

EXAMPLE 12-3. Gahū.

position. Dancers move onto the dance floor dancing in twos or threes. People even do solos at times if they feel like it.) In gahū all dance together on a signal from the lead drummer. The patterns for the rattles and the bell used in gahū differ from those in takada and have a different meter (ex. 12-3). The gahū lead drum, agboba, is built like a big oil barrel. It is not as tall as the standard Anlo drum, atsimewu, which is between four and a half and six feet high. Usually, the musicians and patrons in gahū will sit in the circle.

Atsiagbeko or Agbeko (these two names are interchangeable) is a platoon dance performed

in two tempos, slow and fast. The slow tempo is used for the processional while the fast one is for the main dance. However, in both cases the bell plays 12/8 and the rattle plays a steady four beats in the same manner (ex. 12-4). The dance with its drumming is by tradition so well organized and structured that no one today can call himself its choreographer.

Kete is a fast circle dance. It differs from all the other dances because of its game nature. The dancers form a big circle, facing in, doing one,

12. Jones (1959, VIII:60) refers to this as "the interesting and highly skilled Atsiagbeko dance" and calls it "a figure dance."

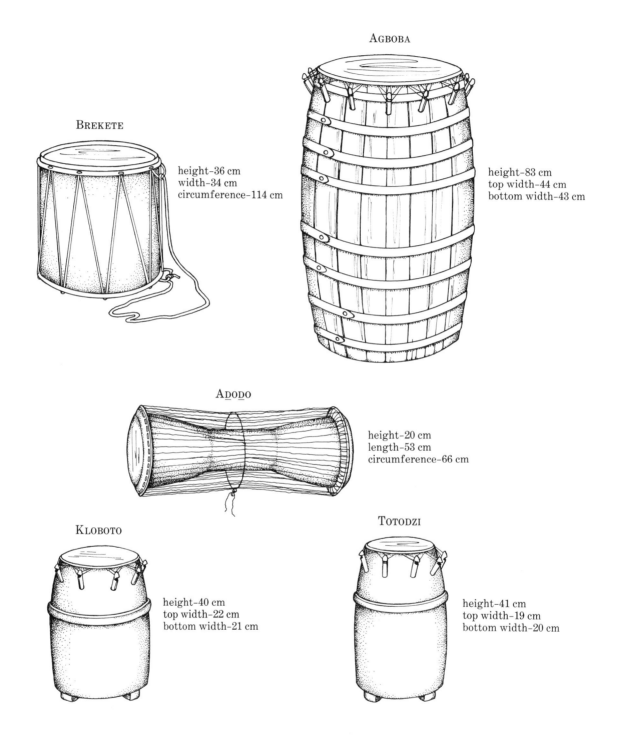

BREKETE

height-36 cm
width-34 cm
circumference-114 cm

AGBOBA

height-83 cm
top width-44 cm
bottom width-43 cm

ADODO

height-20 cm
length-53 cm
circumference-66 cm

KLOBOTO

height-40 cm
top width-22 cm
bottom width-21 cm

TOTODZI

height-41 cm
top width-19 cm
bottom width-20 cm

FIGURE 12-4.

two, or three steps in place. One dancer moves into the center of the circle and then dances toward someone of his or her choice. The person chosen will dance toward the soloist, sometimes meeting him or her halfway, both of them ending with a quick turn. The second person now becomes the new soloist and the first soloist takes his or her place in the circle. Here, too, you

take out their grief on the dance floor. One Adzomani song says, "Composer died and there was no music, *haye!* it is a disgrace." Good music at a funeral in A<u>nlo</u> therefore signifies the deepest expression of the loss of the beloved one; it is also a way of sharing with the deceased member of a group the music he had once enjoyed.

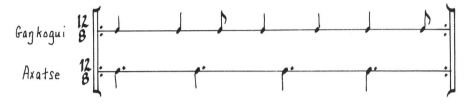

EXAMPLE 12-4. Agbek<u>o</u>.

occasionally see people doing the "basic movement" in trios or duets. Both the bell and the rattle play the 12/8 pattern, but at a fast tempo, (about ♩ = mm 132).

Performance Procedure

Each dance club chooses its own advisers, <u>*w*</u>*umegawo* (patrons) and *dadawo* (patronesses), as well as a name meaningful to the membership. Usually two men and two women advisers are chosen from the age group immediately above. Responsible for the well-being of the groups, the advisers also receive and inform the poet/composer(s), drummers, and a number of staunch members about invitations to perform. If the members agree, a convenient day will be set aside for the performance. About two or three days in advance of the performance, the patrons will hire a town crier to remind the members about their forthcoming event. A member who never shows up and never asks permission to be excused from performing will be fined.

Though death itself is a sorrowful event, people in Anyako, and in other A<u>nlo</u> communities, will refer to a funeral without music as "(what) a sad thing" (Ladzekpo 1971:6–8). Sitting around with little or nothing to do makes both the bereaved family and the mourners feel their grief more. But with music, the mourners can

INSTRUMENTAL MUSIC

A<u>nlo</u> E<u>we</u> music is largely dominated by two of the five classes of musical instruments defined by Curt Sachs (1940:454–67; see May bibliography): idiophones and membranophones. These two classes are of equal importance in our music and one cannot ignore either of them completely and still put on a complete program. There is some use of aerophones, but it is comparatively small.

Idiophones

We shall divide A<u>nlo</u> idiophones into three classes. They are bells, rattles, and clappers.

Bells: There are those with clappers called *a*<u>*w*</u>*aga*, and those without clappers; (1) *gankogui*, the ubiquitous African double bell; and (2) *atoke*, a boat-shaped bell laid on the open palm (see fig. 12-2). (This instrument has been nicknamed "taco bell" by American school children.)

Rattles: There are two kinds: (1) *axatse*, a hollow gourd with bamboo, wooden, or glass beads around it on a net. The rattling sound is made by the bamboo or beads (see fig. 12-1); (2) *adodo*, an iron cluster shaker, with bells at both ends of a central handle; this instrument is used mostly by members of the Ye<u>we</u> cult[13] (see fig. 12-1).

13. For similar descriptions see Jones 1959:96; also Pantaleoni 1972:378–79.

Clappers: (1) The human hand. The human hand plays a major part in Anlo instrumental music. We shall therefore classify it as part of our instrumentarium. (2) *Akpe (wo)*, wooden blocks struck together to reinforce the rhythms of handclapping. The usage of akpewo is a recent development that began in the 1950s.

Membranophones
Anlo drums are cylindrical or barrel-shaped; they are carved from a solid tree or made of wooden slats. Because of the scarcity of suitable woods in Anlo area nowadays, carved drums are on the verge of extinction. (Some youths do not even know of the existence of the carved drums of the past.) A traditional Anlo drum ensemble consists of atsimewu, sogo, kidi, kaganu, with rattles and bells. Atsimewu is a tall drum. It is between four and a half to six feet high and is open at the bottom. The open bottom is smaller than the top head in diameter. Atsimewu is always the lead drum and it is leaned against a special stand, *wudetsi*, when being played (see fig. 12-3). At times, two of them are used either simultaneously or alternately. Sogo is from two and a half to three feet tall; the bottom is closed and is wider than that of atsimewu. Sogo sometimes serves as second in command after atsimewu. It is used as a lead drum in dances such as agbadza, Afã and sogba.[14]

Kidi is similar to sogo but smaller in size and higher in pitch; kidi and sogo are used together as supporting drums. Unlike sogo, kidi is never used as a lead drum.

Kaganu is as tall as kidi but narrower in circumference and the head is tightened to produce a much higher pitch. It is open at the bottom. All three drums, sogo, kidi, and kaganu are supporting drums (see fig. 12-3). In those dances where the bell is not used, kaganu keeps the beat.[15]

Other drums found in traditional Anlo ensembles include the *agboba* (fig. 12-4), a large barrel drum about the height of sogo and about two and a half feet wide. It is closed at the bottom except for an opening of about six inches. This opening is used for putting water into the drum to wet the drumhead before tuning and to insure a tight seal among the slats. Kloboto and *totodzi* are two drums of almost equal size.[16] Open at the bottom, they are a little bit smaller than kidi, but almost as wide across. Kloboto is lower in pitch than totodzi and both of them are used as supporting drums in atsiagbeko, *atigo (Akpaluwu)*[17] and some other dances in akpewu style. Kloboto is used as lead drum in a dance called *kpegisu*[18] (see fig. 12-2).

The popular hourglass-shaped drum or pressure drum, called by various names in different parts of Africa, is also used to some extent. It is called *adodo* in Anlo. *Brekete* or *goeveme* is a double-headed drum between the size of kidi and sogo; the size of brekete depends on the kind of music for which it is used. It may be either cylindrical or wider in the middle and narrow at both ends. It is an Anlo version of an importation from northern Ghana along with a cult of brekete. All the drums we have described are played either by hand, with one stick, two sticks, or stick-and-hand technique. The stick or sticks may be either straight or curved as in the case of kloboto, totodzi, adodo, and brekete (see fig. 12-4).

Aerophones
Anlo aerophones include flutes carved out of wood; trumpets made from elephant tusks or bull's horns. (Trumpets are associated with the royal houses; they are not used in the club dances.) Whistles and bugles of European origin are used by some of the dance clubs to gather

14. Jones (1959:93–183) gives a full description of these dances. See also Ladzekpo (1971:10–11).

15. In a recreational drumming and dancing called *Ga* or *Gakpa*, the double clapperless bell, gankogui, is not used. Kaganu is used to keep the time. This dance has always been a favorite of old men.

16. Jones "The drum . . . called Klodzi or Kloboto is used for special dances and does not immediately concern us." He later on said, "It is used in the Atsiagebeko dance" (1959:57, 60).

17. Akpalu is a name of a famous Anlo poet/composer who used to compose in atigo style. His name, Akpalu, with its suffix, wu, meaning the drum or, in this usage, the music, has become synonymous with the music he created.

18. Presently there is no kpegisu dance club in Anlo that we know of. This music is only practiced by some families. According to Kwaku Kpogo Ladzekpo, a younger brother of Kofi Zate, it is very common to find that a music no longer performed by the whole community is still preserved in the families that were at one time composers and drummers for that particular music.

members together and to indicate a change of movement or to augment some rhythmic patterns or melodic lines.

VOCAL MUSIC

One of the major differences between the northern and southern styles of Ghanaian Ewe music is in their vocal music. According to Nketia (1962:34) two kinds of scales are in common use in Ghana: pentatonic and heptatonic (ex. 12-5). Northern Ewe music is based on the seven-tone diatonic scale, and its polyphony is

were performing Adzomani, and then happen to sing Britannia songs, they must go back to Adzomani songs before the end of the performance. But sometimes through forgetfulness this does not happen.

CONCLUSION

We have discussed three kinds of music in this essay; they are axatsewu, akpewu, and "specific styles." These kinds of music are very distinctive of the area of our concentration. Though some scholars think that African music

EXAMPLE 12-5. Pentatonic scale. Heptatonic scale.

based on the third as a harmonic interval. The Anlo Ewe use a five-tone scale; their harmony is based on parallel fourths. Comparatively, the Anlo sing in a very low range while their brothers in the north employ a very high tessitura.

Vocal music as practiced by the dance clubs in the south consists of three kinds of songs: processional, dance, and hatsiātsiā. Processional songs are those used by the clubs as they pass through the town or village before a performance. Dance songs are those sung during the drumming. Hatsiātsiā songs, as previously stated, are interlude songs. Dance songs for men are usually folk songs common to all the clubs in the area. Those for the women are specifically created by the composers in the various communities for their own groups. At a performance, the women may sing songs from other dance clubs in their own division, but not songs from dance clubs in other divisions. And when they do bring in the songs from another dance club, they are supposed to go back to one of the songs in the repertoire of the music they were first performing before the lead drummers bring the music to an end, that is to say if they

south of the Sahara is influenced by Islam, some elements of Anlo music have not been found elsewhere,[19] for example the two different songs that are sung simultaneously in axatsewu drumming.

Regardless of whether Anlo Ewe music, like many other African musics, is influenced by any other culture or not, the Anlo know that they left Notsie with a distinctive musical style. The music may be affected in certain ways due to many foreign contacts but the major elements that make it authentic Anlo music are still present. Anyako still retains its traditional military war wings and maintains its importance in educational, political, and cultural matters in Anlo; researchers and students of music have been going to Anyako every year since the early fifties to study. Though the traffic from the hinterland to Keta is not what it used to be, Anyako is still the landing stage for commerce en route to Keta, and the music still lives.

19. Jones (1947:4) "Knowing the remarkable imitative capacity of the African, we might invoke history to suggest that possibly he has acquired this culture (drumming, dancing, and singing) from outside influence from the powerful and widespread influence of Islam, for example."

Glossary

adodo-an iron cluster shaker, with bells at both ends of a central handle (used mostly by members of the Yewe cult).

adodo-hourglass-shaped or pressure drum.

Afã-a West African god of divination.

agboba-a large barrel drum.

Akpaluwu or atigo-music named for Akpalu (see footnote 17).

akpewu-an ensemble dominated by clapping.

atoke-A boat-shaped bell. Two *atokewo* and a *gankogui* or two form a choir of bells used in *hatsiãtsiã.*

atsiagbeko or *agbeko*-an offspring of an old war dance. It used to be called *atamgã* (*atam*, "oath" and *ga*, "great"). *Atamgã* means the "Great Oath."

atsimewu-the standard Anlo lead drum.

awaga-a bell with a clapper whose size may vary. It is used by most priests in invoking their deities.

axatse-a gourd rattle covered with netted beading.

axatsewu-a generic name for a musical ensemble largely dominated by rattles (*axatsewo*).

brekete or *goeveme*-literally the second name means "two sides." A double-headed drum of Islamic origin.

dadawo-patronesses and female leaders; sometimes the women as a whole are addressed this way just for courtesy.

gahã-an Anlo Ewe adaptation of Yoruba (Nigeria) dance.

ga or *gakpa*-a recreational music which has always been a favorite dance of old people.

gankogui-the ubiquitous African double bell that comes in different sizes. It keeps the timing for the musicians.

goeveme-see *brekete.*

halo-literally means "abusive song."

hatsiãtsiã-(interlude music) refers to solo and chorus songs accompanied usually by a choir of bells (or by rattles as in takada).

heno-a poet/composer, in Anlo a composer is responsible for the text of his songs as well as the melody.

hogbe-the ancestral home of the Ewe of Ghana.

husikpokpowo-the novices of the Yewe cult.

husunu-a fully graduated male member of the Yewe cult.

kaganu-the smallest drum in the Anlo drum set. It is as tall as *kidi* but narrower in circumference.

kete-a circle dance unique because of its game nature.

kidi-a drum similar to *sogo* in structure, but smaller and higher in pitch.

kloboto and *totodzi*-drums of almost equal size. Open at the bottom, they are a little bit smaller than *kidi.*

kpegisu-a dance club (see note 18).

misego-the full name is *misegodzi*, meaning "tighten your belt." But for brevity, it is called *misego.*

sogo-a medium-sized barrel-shaped drum. It is used as a lead drum in Afã drumming as well as in Yewe cult music.

takada-one of the musical ensembles under "specific style" (see chart).

totodzi-see Kloboto.

vodusi-a fully graduated female member of the Yewe cult.

wu-Any kind of Anlo membranophone. It also denotes the entire ensemble; i.e., drumming, dancing, and singing.

wudetsi-the stand for atsimewu.

wumegawo-patrons and elders of a dance club.

wuxexle-"counting the drums," it means playing the seven different styles of drumming that belong to the Yewe cult (see note 7).

Yewe-the god of thunder and lightning in southern Eweland.

Bibliography

Anyako, Studies of an Ewe Village.
    1971. U.S.T. Press, Occasional Report No. 14. Kumasi: University of Science and Technology, Department of Architecture.

Bascom, William.
    1969. *Ifa Divination, Communication between Gods and Men in West Africa.* Bloomington: Indiana University Press.

Gazetteer Population Census of Ghana.
    1962. 1:1960. Accra: The Government of Ghana.

Herskovitz, Melville J.
    1938. *Dahomey.* 2 vols. New York: Augustin.

Hodder, B. W., and U. Ukwu.
    1969. *Markets in West Africa.* Ibadan: Ibadan University Press.

von Hornbostel, Erich, and Curt Sachs.
    1961. "Classification of Musical Instruments." *Galpin Society Journal* 14:3-29.

Jones, A. M.
    1957. "Drums Down the Centuries." *African Music* 1, 4.

1959. *Studies in African Music* 2 vols. London: Oxford University Press.

Ladzekpo, Kobla, and Hewitt Pantaleoni.
1970. "Takada Drumming." *African Music* 4:6-31.

Nketia, Kwabena, J. H.
1963. *African Music in Ghana.* Evanston: Northwestern University Press.

Nukunya, A. K.
1969. *Kinship and Marriage Among the Anlo Ewe.* London: University of London, The Athlone Press.

Nutsuako, W. E.
1957. *A Short History of the Anyako Anlo Awoame Fia School, 1929-1932.* Cape Coast, Ghana: Mfantsiman Press.

Pantaleoni, Hewitt.
1972. "The Rhythm of Atsiã Dance Drumming Among the Anlo (Ewe) of Anyako." Ph.D. dissertation, Wesleyan University.

Sachs, Curt. 1944. *The History of Musical Instruments.* New York: W. W. Norton.

Westermann, Diedrich.
1930. *A Study of Ewe Language.* Translated by Aubrey Lewis Bickford-Smith. Oxford: Oxford University Press.

Discography

African Dances & Games S&R 2000. Seth Kobla Ladzekpo and Alfred Kwashie Ladzekpo.
Ewe Music of Ghana. AHM 4222, 1969. Recorded and edited by S. K. Ladzekpo.

Film

Discovering the Music of Africa BFA. Col. 22 min. Sotirios Chianis, advisor (see Mensah's film list).

13. The Music of Ethiopia

Cynthia Tse Kimberlin

Ethiopia is an enigma, still largely inaccessible and relatively unknown to the rest of the world. The mystery surrounding this part of East Africa has been enhanced by travelers' reports that have come down through the ages portraying the people with paradoxical characteristics (Reid 1968, Murphy 1968, Budge 1928, Mondon-Vidailhet 1922). Certainly the people are high-spirited and proud, but at the same time they are conservative and cautious. Having learned the lessons of war from centuries of invaders, the Ethiopians are also excellent soldiers. Ethiopia's bravery and past exploits have been celebrated in song, stirring the memories of the participants and instilling a sense of pride in those who have yet to take part. Until recently, Ethiopia was one of the last absolute monarchies on earth and nearly the poorest in terms of average income and gross national product. Because of current changes, however, it is uncertain which form of political system will emerge in the future. Nevertheless, Ethiopia remains rich in tradition and art.

Within its 457,000 square mile area Ethiopia contains over a hundred ethnic groups, each defined by the language or dialect spoken. The dominant group, the Amhara people, comprise about 35 percent of the total population of 25 million. Their language, Amharic, one of the two spoken languages also having a written tradition, is the national language and there are about 10 million people who speak it (Ghebremedhin 1972). Many of these Amharic speakers also speak one or more other languages or dialects. In this essay I will discuss the music of the Amharas, and in addition the music of the Adari, Dorze, Gurage, Oromo, Somali, and Tigre cultures, all of which can be found in Ethiopia and in Addis Ababa, the capital city.

Today Ethiopia has become a new interest among scholars of many disciplines. Philologists find Ethiopia's Semitic languages unique, for they are the result of continuous evolution over centuries (Leslau 1971). Geophysicists believe the Afar triangle, with its volcanoes and curiously shaped formations, has resulted from plate spreading, and is an incipient sea floor. They are eagerly studying the changes taking place there (Tazieff 1970). Archaeologists find much potential in Ethiopia, since there has been little prehistoric archaeological inquiry. Social anthropologists have a wealth of subjects for research or testing. Ethiopia is geographically in Africa, but for centuries its cultural affinities pointed toward Arabia and the Middle East, as well as toward Nubia. Christianity came to Ethiopia in the fourth century, probably through the efforts of Ezana who conquered Meroë, was bilingual in Greek and Gə'əz, the Ethiopian liturgical language, and ruled the Axumite empire (Doresse 1959:30-31, 62).

Ethiopians think of themselves as Africans but not as Negroes. This is understandable since the barriers to migration from the south are formidable. Such migrations did occur, but the deserts and then the Great Rift valley, includ-

This research was supported in part by a U.S. government grant under the Fulbright Hays Dissertation Research Fellowship program. I wish to thank the following who gave me invaluable assistance: Abdi Aidi, Alamu Aga, Alemayehu Fanta, Bariquicho Kadar, Camia Bedru, Gebrekal Negash, Girmai Biene, Kaful Asmaron, Jerome Kimberlin, Laq Mergata, Legassa Abdi, Mahey Sofa, Makonnen Haile, Mohammed Abdur Abman, Nasser, Dr. Richard Pankhurst, Sa'adu Ibrahim, Said Nuri, Sharafa Hussein, Sisay Gehbremedhin, Tsegaye Debalke, Bishop Paulos Tzadua, and Yasi Hasan.

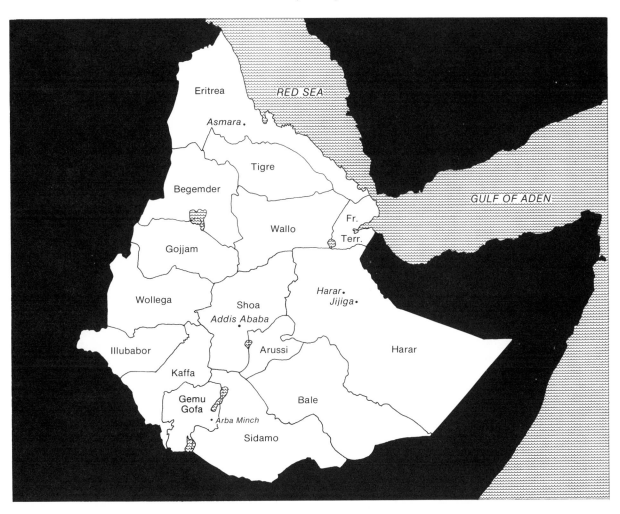

Ethiopia

ing its accompanying malaria, prevented large numbers of people from reaching the nucleus of today's Ethiopia, the highland plateau. Ethiopia is a crossroad, a Middle Eastern country in an African setting, and links two continents in a cultural synthesis that has produced a unique people in a unique place.

The enigma that is Ethiopia is reflected in the music of the people. Different scholars, at different times, have not lessened this mystery. Alan Merriam indirectly talks about Ethiopian music within the geographical framework of the African "East Horn":

> The music of the East Horn is clearly distinguishable from most of that of the East African

area by the intensity of the Islamic influence. Although there is considerable variation here, and within any one of these areas, the Islamic influence is dominant. [1959:78]

Debalke speaks about Ethiopian folk music in terms of a dominant music characteristic:

> In Ethiopian folk music *colour* is stressed more than either *progression* or *harmony*. [1967]

Michael Pound informs the researcher what to expect when he hears Ethiopian music:

> Finally, an investigator working on Ethiopian music should not expect to be rewarded with finding music of structural, harmonic, or rhythmic subtlety; but there is much else of great value and interest to be revealed—infinite melodic variation,

strongly emotive tunes and verses that spring directly from the volatile and eager spirits of the highlands, and links the past that may well prove to throw vital illumination on the cultures of other Middle Eastern peoples. [1968:125]

Sarosi marks Ethiopia's location as susceptible to many musical influences:

> Ethiopia is located so to speak at the very crossing point of the most important musical tendencies. Looking at the map, we can already gather that in this area the North-African arabesque chromatic style had to meet the more simple pentatonic, or even prepentatonic musical world of Central Africa. Indeed, the musical material reveals the fruitful junctore [*sic*] of the two different musical styles. And even more than that: surprising Central and East-Asian relations as well as the neighbourhood of Mediterranean Europe. [1970:281]

The diversity of peoples found in Ethiopia only adds to the confusion surrounding certain aspects of its music. The music has been described as primarily melodic with simple rhythmic accompaniment, yet it can be polyphonic and rhythmically complex. The vocal line is generally melismatic, but occasionally syllabic, and the instrumental accompaniment ranges from a single instrument to a whole battery. The voice quality can be high and nasal, but can also be low and mellow. Dances, sometimes quiet and demure, change and become loud and vigorous. There is no one kind of music that could truly represent the entire country, for how could a country with so many ethnic groups and languages, isolated by geographical, political, and cultural boundaries, produce homogeneous music?

Since very few scholarly publications exist specifically on Ethiopian music (Mondon-Vidailhet 1922; Wellesz 1920; Kebede 1967, 1969, 1971) and since the foundation on which Ethiopian music is based has not been dealt with adequately, I have chosen to discuss the sections on instruments and musical examples in specific rather than general terms. Musics from the seven cultural groups previously mentioned will be described in order to show the reader some of the extraordinary differences and similarities to be found among them. These musical traditions are important to Ethiopia's cultural life, al-

though not superior to other musical traditions contained within the Ethiopian political sphere. Ethiopia's provincial boundaries are politically determined. Lack of space, unfortunately, does not permit me to cover more of these interesting musical traditions and I hope that the interested reader will look further into the work of other scholars. In this study, words in Ethiopian languages are rendered in English transliteration according to the technique of Leslau (1968:1-7).

STATUS OF THE MUSICIAN

In general, the Ethiopian musician is known as *azmari* in the Amharic language (Kebede 1969:2). Hundreds of years ago the word meant "one who praises." This resulted from the fact that azmari were usually employed by noblemen who wished tales of warfare and good deeds made known to others in song (Mosley 1955: 177-79). Gradually the azmari came not only to praise his patron, but to sing poems of criticism against his patron's peers and enemies. Through the years azmari came to mean "one who criticizes" and then "one who defames." Today azmari connotes the latter meaning and is a pejorative term deplored by musicians. Amharas tend to call all musicians azmari simply because there is no other word in the language denoting a person who plays a musical instrument (Debalke 1972).

All Ethiopians make music during life cycle festivities. These lay musicians are not to be considered professional musicians although among some ethnic groups (principally Moslem) certain functions always demand a gifted lay musician as the music leader. These musicians do not earn a living from their musical abilities but may attend festivities far outside their own circle and may be treated well because of their musical ability and functional role.

In contrast to these lay musicians are the professionals. A number of instruments are played by professional musicians, but around the capital city only *masinqo* players and, to a much lesser extent, *krar* players can be found performing alone (see Musical Instruments below). As I have said, Amharas tend to call anyone who plays a musical instrument an azmari, but strictly speaking the word is not a collective term and only applies to masinqo players because of their traditional function (Tzadua 1972). Further research may show that the krar player could also be an azmari but at present this cannot be substantiated. Traditionally, krar players have not been thought of as retainers of noblemen but as those who entice others for immoral purposes (ibid.). Thus the krar is thought of as the instrument of pimps and prostitutes. Today it is difficult to find the krar being used for seduction; its usual purpose is the accompaniment of contemporary popular songs.

The azmari profession, a strictly male one, is not hereditary (Kimberlin 1972). Sons are forbidden by parents to take up the masinqo, although some do anyway, because being an azmari is to be in the lowest occupational status along with illiterates who are also blacksmiths, carpenters, servants, or have other jobs requiring use of the hands. These low-class jobs are thought to be low because they require only practice, with no thought or study. Some men become azmari because they have the ability to sing or are unsuited for other jobs open to them, but of these low-class jobs, azmari get the most money and have the most free time.

All Ethiopians learn songs (but not at school), and the incipient azmari will already know a number of songs by the time he decides to learn to play the masinqo. The masinqo itself is a difficult instrument to play, technically, and one must find a teacher. The teacher is usually another azmari who is willing to take on an apprentice, who then sometimes acts as a servant or in some other capacity to assist the teacher. The apprentice will remain with the teacher until he feels that he can learn no more or has learned enough to go out on his own.

The most common method of repertory building includes imitating the songs of other azmari as they work, songs played on the radio, or songs on recordings. The best azmari compose their own songs or at least their own words to be sung with a traditional melody—many azmari know very few melodies but several sets of words to sing with each melody. There are also certain well-known songs with which every azmari is familiar. Recently some Sudanese songs have enjoyed popularity on the radio, and some azmari have copied the melodies and style to use with Ethiopian ideas and language.

The azmari performs at weddings and parties but these jobs, although most desirable because of the money, are few unless the azmari is relatively famous. It is common to work at the *ṭäg bet*, a place where men go to talk and drink ṭäg (honey mead). An azmari frequently goes from one ṭäg bet to the next until he finds an owner willing to let him play for gratuities. Many azmari come to Addis Ababa because they have heard that there is more work there. One man told how he followed the coffee harvest for a few weeks each year, entertaining the employees and prospective coffee buyers. Another man was retained for three hundred and fifty dollars plus transportation to play a one-night stand at a wedding.

For those azmari who have their eyes set on even more popularity and wealth there are three avenues open: (1) to cut a record and hope it sells; (2) to join a performance group and hope it succeeds, and (3) to leave traditional instruments and take up Western ones, thus essentially ceasing to be azmari. The first two cases are self-explanatory. The third case, however, is relatively new in Ethiopia. The musician who plays Western instruments is not thought of as a low-status person. The establishments in which the Western-oriented group performs are prestige places such as the Hilton hotel, where exposure to the monied and tourist classes is assured. The Ethiopian playing Western instruments becomes sophisticated and a member of the emerging middle class. Although a musician cannot become a member of the nobility and still retain his musical profession, by becoming a Western-oriented musician—following the fad, so to speak—he can be assured that his status will not be that of the azmari.

Music within the Ethiopian Christian Orthodox and Roman Catholic churches is the concern of the *däbtära*. The däbtära functions in the church as a song leader and lay theologian. He leads all songs and many prayers of the Mass, but he is not a priest and cannot fulfill the holy offices. The education of priests is very different from that of däbtära. Many priests can barely read and write, so the däbtära is generally the carrier of knowledge in the church. This is not to say that the priest is always less educated than the däbtära. The priest can become a bishop, hold land, a title, and be wealthy, whereas the däbtära remains a teacher and assistant to the priest. The status of the däbtära as church musician is derived from his church position rather than from his musical function. Clergy, like the nobility, have high status in Ethiopian society.

Those people that become wealthy and/or educated outside of the sphere of religion change their perspective of music. Many wealthy Ethiopians find themselves courting the West as a necessary part of remaining wealthy. It is no wonder then that much of their entertaining involves Western-style music rather than the traditional Ethiopian style. On the other hand, wealthy people sometimes become more consciously Ethiopian, since they no longer have to struggle to live and have a chance to partake of the more "cultured" aspects of life. A rich person who has an inclination toward the aesthetic—art, philosophy, literature—frequently "discovers" the *bägänna*, the traditional musical instrument of the nobles and upper class (see Musical Instruments below).

One usually learns to play the bägänna for private aesthetic reasons, so the instrument is seldom played for an audience. Consequently it is difficult to determine how many people might play the instrument. Traditionally, once the decision to learn the art of the bägänna had been made, the problem arose of where to find a teacher. Prior to 1972 there was no bägänna teacher giving public lessons. Today, regularly scheduled classes are offered at the Yared Music School in Addis Ababa.

MUSICAL INSTRUMENTS

Many problems in Ethiopian organology have arisen because of semantics. The large number of languages and dialects in Ethiopia produce a great many different names for equivalent instruments. In addition, instruments are frequently misidentified by Ethiopians.

Generally, each Ethiopian ethnic group has a set of instruments, although the set for one ethnic group may include instruments from many other ethnic groups. Instruments of a group are partially geographically determined. For example, there will be no reed horns made where there are no reeds, no bamboo flutes where there is no bamboo, and no cedarwood instruments outside the ecological zone suitable for cedar trees. Instruments can also be culturally determined. For example, the Moslems in Ethiopia play drums, wood blocks, rattles, and tambourines, but seldom, if ever, will an orthodox Moslem play a stringed instrument. Another example exists in the Dorze ethnic group where the masinqo is nonexistent, but the krar is played.

Information exists on over fifty distinct instruments found in Ethiopia (Kimberlin 1972), but here I will give brief descriptions of only twelve. These twelve are illustrated further in the Music Examples section.

1. The Adari women of Harar use *käbəl*, a pair of rectangular wood blocks measuring about 15 cm. long, 7 cm. wide, and 3 cm. thick. One block is held in each hand, and they are struck together in an alternating up-down movement as a rhythmic accompaniment to songs.

height—26.5 cm
width—8.5 cm

FIGURE 13-1. *Şänaşəl*

2. *Mäqʷamyä*, a staff with a T-shaped metal head, is used in the Ethiopian Orthodox and Roman Catholic churches. The staff serves two purposes. Upon entering the church, one finds a number of staffs placed near the door. These are taken and used for support during the service if there are no seats. Also they are used by the däbtära as a rhythmic accompaniment to chanting and are sounded by striking the end against the floor with a vertical motion.

3. Another instrument used in the church is the ṣänaṣəl. "A legend ascribes its origin to Saint Yared who, upon hearing three birds sing in a tree, was reminded of the Trinity and thus constructed the instrument" (Ministry of Information booklet 1968:16). The ṣänaṣəl consists of a U-shaped metal frame with a wooden handle at the bottom. There are six disk rattles divided equally between two thick wires strung between the two-side frame members. The disks hit against one another and against the sides as the instrument is moved in an up-down motion produced primarily by slow wrist action. The frame sides are decorated with repeated perforated patterns in one or more designs.

4. *Dube* is the single-head bowl-shaped drum used by the Adari and Somali in Harar Province. The Somalis strike the drum with a wooden beater; the Adari use their hands. An Adari dube, one of the smaller sizes I saw, was 15 cm. high with a head diameter of 34 cm.

5. The typical cylindrical drum called *käbäro* in Amharic and *kärobo* by the Silti Gurage has two heads of equal diameter, comes in a number of sizes, and is usually carried with a shoulder strap. The Amhara and Tigre people use this drum for secular functions only. The Silti Gurage are Moslem and use it for religious and secular functions. A Tigre drum in my possession measures 34 cm. in height with a 29 cm. head diameter, but generally sizes of these drums today are determined by the sizes of old cylindrical metal containers. Popular sizes are one U.S. gallon for a small size, two and a half gallons for an average size, and five gallons for a large size. These drums have a rattling sound resulting from a few pebbles contained within.

6. The conical drum is also called käbäro. It has two heads of unequal diameter. The sides of the drum are curved but do not bulge out farther than the diameter of the larger head. The käbäro I have seen differ in size, an indication that drum making is not done within fixed guidelines. As these käbäro are only used for religious functions, they usually have decorated sides.

7. The *dəft*, used by the Adari, has a single membrane tacked onto a wooden frame ring. Metal disks are strung on metal bars which are inserted into the frame. The dəft I saw was imported from Japan, but the Adari also make their own (Bedru 1972). This instrument is known as the tambourine in the West.

8. The bägänna has already been mentioned as the instrument of the nobles. It is a ten-stringed plucked lyre with a trapezoidal sound box and measuring about 120 cm. in height. Although it has ten strings, only five need be tuned since the other five are used as finger rests; but if a plectrum is used, all strings must be tuned. The bägänna is made of wood, with the sound box covered with cowhide. Strings are made of sheep's gut. For a more complete discussion of the bägänna, its materials of construction, nomenclature, music, and texts see the article "The Bägänna of Ethiopia" (Kimberlin 1978).

9. The krar is a five- or six-stringed plucked lyre consisting of two upright pillars joined by a crossbar at the top, and held by the taut sound-box skin at the bottom to the front surface of the sound box. The sound box may be trapezoidal (Dorze style) or made from a wooden or metal bowl (Amhara and Tigre style). It can have five

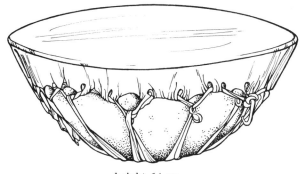

height–14 cm
diameter–45 cm

FIGURE 13-2. *Dube*

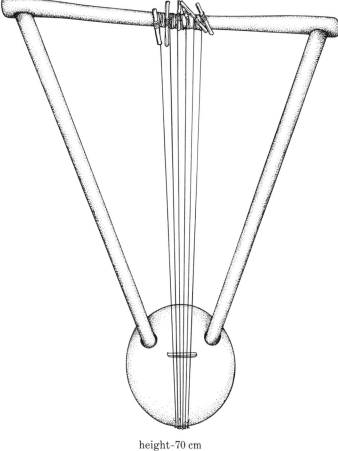

height–70 cm
width–57.7 cm

FIGURE 13-3. *Krar*

strings of gut (Dorze) or metal (Tigre) or six strings of gut, metal, or nylon (Amhara). The sound box is covered with goat skin. Kebede has described the Amhara krar in detail (Kebede 1967).

10. The masinqo, a single-stringed bowed spike fiddle with a diamond-shaped sound box, is the only Ethiopian bowed instrument. The materials used in making a masinqo are goatskin for the sound box covering, horsehair for the bow and spike strings, and wood for the rest of the instrument. Many types of wood are used depending on availability and strength. The strongest wood is used usually for the bridge and peg. The greatest physical distinction found among masinqo is the size of the sound box and

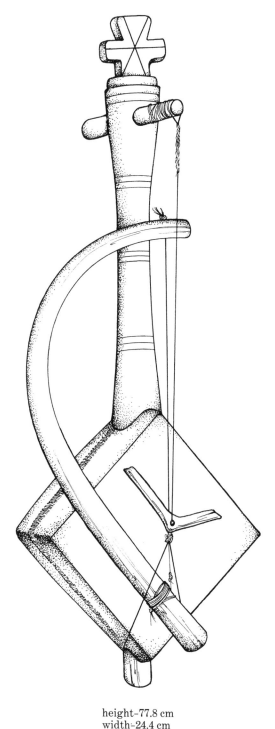

height–77.8 cm
width–24.4 cm

FIGURE 13-4. *Masinqo*

the shape and decoration of the spike head (Kimberlin 1972).

11. The *wašänt* is a hollow bamboo end-blown flute with four finger holes. Wašänt vary from 35 to 70 cm. in length depending upon the range of pitches desired. It is said that wašänt are made and played by shepherds and cowherds, but they are also played by others who have long

length–62.9 cm

FIGURE 13-5. *Wašänt*

hours to spend by themselves. Wašänt are usually made by using a hot wire or rod to burn out the bamboo segments and to pierce the finger holes.

12. *əmbilta* is a set of three end-blown flutes ranging from 75 cm. to 1.5 m. in length, with an inside diameter of about 3 cm. Material of construction varies. Formerly they were made of hollow reeds or bamboo of large diameter, but today one finds them made of thin-walled metal tubing having a 2.5 to 3 cm. inside diameter. Each of the three lengths of əmbilta has a different name and they differ from one another in length and finger holes. *Yima* is the longest, with no finger holes but a small slot on the underside close to the distal end. *Ora*, the middle size, has one finger hole and a small slot similar to yima. *Dəf* is the shortest flute and has no finger holes or slot. The ora produces three pitches; the other two have the same two pitches each, but an octave apart.

MUSIC EXAMPLES

Ethiopian music can be illustrated best by citing specific musical examples recorded by the author in 1972. Wherever different examples are played on the same type of instrument, a comparison of the instruments and their playing style is given. (Transcribed musical excerpts are given for some examples.) Relative pitches rather than actual pitches are notated, and to

give an idea of tempo the duration of each excerpt is indicated.

Qəñət is approximated by the English musical term *mode*. Though the exact meaning of qəñət has not been ascertained, the interval sequence is an important factor in its determination (Kimberlin 1976). Many qəñət exist but no study has been devoted to those of different ethnic groups except for the Amhara, for which there are at least four (Kebede 1967:159). Based on my studies of masinqo qəñət, the names of these pentatonic qəñət and their interval sequence calculated in cents are:

INTERVAL:	I	II	III	IV	V (octave)
Ančihoye	135	370	115	345	235
Təzəta	200	175	350	150	325
Ambasəl	115	345	235	135	370
Bati	325	200	175	350	150

Ančihoye and təzəta, supposedly the two oldest modes, mean "you are my love" and "my dearest one," respectively. Ambasəl and Bati are the names of two villages in Wallo Province. Ambasəl is derived from ančihoye and bati from təzəta (Kimberlin 1976). In the musical transcriptions the qəñət is identified by name; the pitch sequence is notated where the name is not known.

Musical instruments in the lyre class vary in their tuning sequence even when tuned to the same qəñət (see ex. 13-8 and Three Chordophones below for examples of bägänna and krar melodies in təzəta qəñət). Strings are not necessarily tuned from left to right but according to a specific melody or song (Kimberlin 1972).

In the examples: Slides and ornaments not clearly audible are notated with a straight line above or below the notes. Very rapid ornamentation that I would consider secondary to the main melody is notated with stems down (this applies only to the Amhara krar and Tigre masinqo transcriptions). An unstable or indeterminate pitch is written as "♩". Three transcriptions are marked with letters (A, B, C, etc.) indicating melodic divisions. A slight pause or cadence is indicated by "✸".

Throughout each example there is a strict underlying pulse, but I have refrained from inserting bar lines, rest marks, and time signatures in many cases for these insertions would only indicate an impression of rigidity and exactness that is not always the case.

To the Western ear, nothing in Ethiopian music seems fixed. Though two people may perform a song in the same qəñət, intervallic variances occur which are correct in terms of Ethiopian music but not necessarily so in Western terms. Rhythm is also difficult to assess since a number of rhythmic factors come into play simultaneously, as in the case of the masinqo player whose singing, instrumental accompaniment, body movements, and mood changes are all integrated into a single rhythmic complex. When notated on paper Ethiopian music appears frozen and bland, but what we actually hear is an unending variety of changes, fluctuations, and nuances difficult to capture on paper. Perhaps this is due to the fact that music in Ethiopia is an oral tradition, thus having no fixed written tradition (like the Western staff notation for example, which fixes pitch and rhythm) to cause rigidity.

Use of Instruments in the
Ethiopian Orthodox Church

The instrumental accompaniment to the chanting of the Ethiopian Orthodox and Catholic churches is shown in example 13-1. This accompaniment is a twenty-minute portion from the Ordinary and Proper preceding the sermon and was taken from the liturgy for the eighteenth Sunday after Pentecost in Addis Ababa. There were sixteen däbtära performing near the entrance of the church (where the music was recorded), singing and accompanying themselves on three instruments: ṣänaṣəl, käbäro, and mäq-^{w}amyä.

The instrumental accompaniment to the chanting is divided into five sections (Tzadua 1972). Each section is named for the manner in which the liturgy is to be performed and is distinguished by a particular rhythmic pattern and a different tempo, with each succeeding section increasing its tempo. Section 5 uses the same rhythmic pattern as section 4 except that the tempo is doubled. Section 1 is characterized by responsorial singing and only the mäq^{w}amyä

was used as instrumental accompaniment. The remaining sections are characterized by choral singing with no alternation of voices, plus the instrumental accompaniment of three käbäro and four ṣänaṣəl.

Three different sizes of käbäro were used: two large and one small. Each drum produced two tones of indeterminate pitch and was placed sideways on the floor in front of the player. The player sat on a low rectangular shaped stool and struck the drumheads with three parts of his hand: palm, fingertips, and flat of the hand. Sometimes one of the hands acted as a damper while the other hand struck the drumhead. Both hands were used as a damper when the sound was to cease.

The ṣänaṣəl was shaken with an up-down movement of the wrist. The mäq^{w}amyä was held in the middle by the right hand and the instrument outlined a four-beat unit, ending on beat four when the tip of the mäq^{w}amyä was hit on the floor. It took about seven seconds to complete one four-beat unit. According to Tzadua, the movement of the mäq^{w}amyä imitates the movement of grass blown gently by the wind (1972).

The instruments, as an accompaniment to the singing, provide a variety of contrast in sound, tempo, and rhythm (ex. 13-1).

Three Moslem Drum Styles

Drumming does not seem to be as predominant in Ethiopia as in other parts of Africa, particularly in Ghana and Nigeria. There are, however, three Moslem groups in Ethiopia which use the drum as their main instrument: the Silti Gurage, Adari, and Somali. I recorded the Silti Gurage in Addis Ababa where most of the Moslems earned their livelihood as common laborers. The Adari were living within the old walled city of Harar, and the Somali people were recorded in Jijiga northeast of Harar. None of these people were professional musicians, but they often performed at celebrations or parties for their friends.

Two basic drums were used: käbäro and dube. During a four-day wedding celebration in Harar, only the Adari women played the dube; the drum played by younger girls was the same but

1. ZƏMAME (ዘማሜ) The mäqᵂamyä was used to outline a repeated four-beat unit. Each four-beat unit lasted about seven seconds. On the fourth beat, the mäqᵂamyä was released slightly so that it dropped with its tip striking the ground.

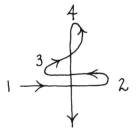

2. NƏUS MÄRÄGD (ንዑስ፡መረግድ) The käbäro and ṣänaṣəl played a repeated six-beat cycle. Time: 8 sec.

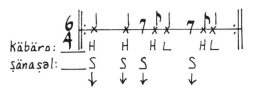

    H = high pitch tone.
    L = low pitch tone.
    S = ṣänaṣəl.
    ↑↓ = the upward or downward ṣänaṣəl motion.

3. ABIY MÄRÄGD (ዓቢይ፡መረግድ) The käbäro and ṣänaṣəl played four combinations of three basic rhythmic patterns which were repeated in varying sequences.

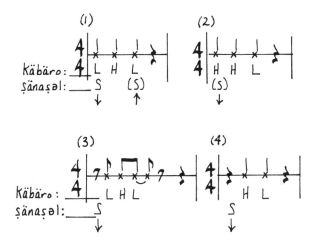

An excerpt using the above patterns (1,2,3,4) was performed as follows:

1111 4 11 3 1 4 11 3 1 3 11 3 11 3 11 4 1111 2 11 3 1 4 1111 3 1 3 11 3 11 4 11 4 1 3 111 4 11111

4. ṢƏFAT (ጸፋት) The käbäro and ṣänaṣəl played six combinations of two basic rhythmic patterns which were repeated in varying sequence.

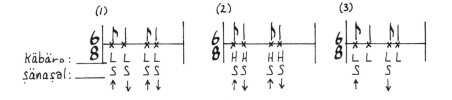

5. WÄRÄB (ወረብ) This section is like the ṣəfat except that the tempo is doubled (Tzadua 1972).

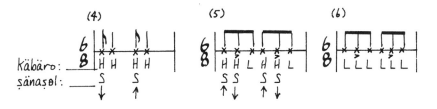

EXAMPLE 13-1. Instrumental accompaniment to church chanting.

smaller (Bedru 1972). Two drums were placed on the laps of women who were sitting on the ground just outside the groom's house. They struck the drum with both hands, using an open and damped technique of striking.

Somali women held the drum in the left hand at about eye level and struck it with a wooden beater. The performance I observed lasted about three hours with both men and women taking part in a social gathering.

The Silti Gurage used the käbäro to accompany their songs, which can include wedding, religious worship, and festive songs pertaining to other life-cycle events.

Clapping accompanied the drumming in all cases, and the Adari also used the käbәl. Adari women clapped and hit the wood blocks together with an alternate up-down movement. The Silti Gurage used a breathing in-out technique to accompany their drumming and clapping. They

clapped with a slight out-and-downward movement and the sound was sharp with the hands held tense. The Somali clapped with the flat of the hands, which were slightly relaxed. See example 13-2 for the relationship between the drum and other accompaniment.

Two Flutes: A Single and a Set
As previously stated, there are two flutes in Ethiopia called wašänt and әmbilta. The more versatile and talented wašänt players own between six and twelve wašänt, usually made by the owner. The player I recorded was a security guard and gardener by trade and played the wašänt for recreation. He had eight bamboo wašänt at the time and knew how to play in four qañət. He had four long and four short wašänt for each qañət, so that in choosing the appropriate length wašänt he could perform each qәñәt in a low or high pitch range. The two

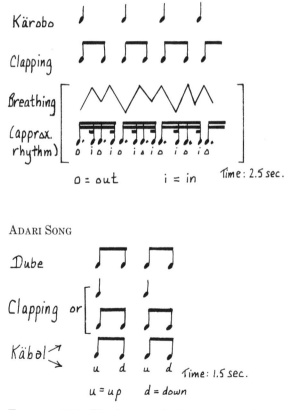

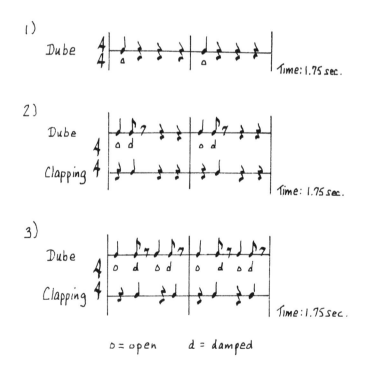

EXAMPLE 13-2. The drum and other accompaniment.

EXAMPLE 13-3. əmbilta melody. (Can be heard on the recording.)

wašänt tuned to the same qəñət overlapped in pitch rather than one wašänt being an extension of the other in range. Overblowing is common and so a wašänt usually has a range of two octaves.

The flute melody has an underlying pulse which the player taps out with his foot. The result is triple meter with some variation. He uses three basic melodic patterns which vary as they are repeated over and over. The melody itself is played in a very rapid but smooth style.

The əmbilta is found throughout Ethiopia. əmbilta found in Tigre and Eritrea Provinces are made of metal, whereas the əmbilta found farther south tend to be made of wood or bamboo (Lamma 1972). Three əmbilta of different lengths, when played together using a hocket technique, constitute one instrument set. Two play the same two pitches but an octave apart, and the third plays three pitches. Sometimes each player enters by himself, but simultaneous entry with one other player also occurs. The hocket form is such that the melody is continuous without a break from beginning to end, each player entering with his particular pattern on cue. I recorded a melody performed by three players who played metal instruments. They were professional musicians from Eritrea who were invited to play with a professional musical group headquartered in Addis Ababa (ibid.). The players danced around in a circle while performing. The melody, which is illustrated in example 13-3, is in triple time and their accompanying dance steps complemented this triple meter. Although əmbilta 2 and 3 share the same pitches an octave apart, each əmbilta emphasizes a different pitch—əmbilta 2 emphasizes C and əmbilta 3 emphasizes G. When pitches are sounded simultaneously, the most frequent intervals heard approximate a unison or octave, perfect fourth, perfect fifth, major third, and major sixth. əmbilta are primarily used for social gatherings and weddings and are not usually accompanied by other instruments.

Vocal: A Solo and a Duet

Two different styles of singing performed by a soloist in Addis Ababa and by two persons in Harar are examples of Ethiopia's vocal music. Women performed in these styles with the vocal aspect dominant and with secondary accompaniment such as the "Ah" exclamation sounded by the female chorus background during the

šəläla, and the dəft accompanying the duet. The solo šəläla was recorded in front of the Parliament building in Addis Ababa shortly before Emperor Haile Selassie gave his speech opening the Ethiopian Parliament for the 1973 session. The šəläla is a patriotic song used to inspire people on occasions of national celebrations or war. The duet was recorded in the company of guests in the evening on the third day of a four-day wedding celebration.

The text of the šəläla was presented in half-sung, half-spoken manner in speech rhythm; the pitches are approximated in example 13-4.

EXAMPLE 13-4.

The chorus sings "Ah" on e[1] intermittently. The song is such that it can last a few minutes or a few hours; this example lasted one and a half hours. The solo part is sung by two women, one taking over as the other rests.

The duet sung by the Adari women is an example of polyphony in which each singer repeats her own melodic pattern over and over. The singing is performed in an overlapping or dove-

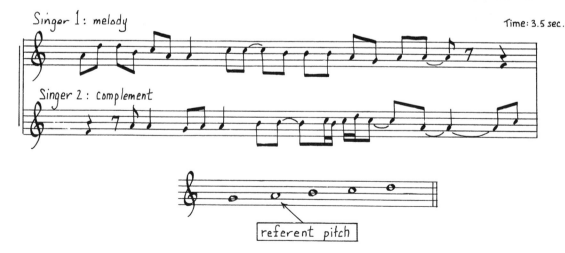

EXAMPLE 13-5. Adari vocal duet. (Can be heard on the recording.)

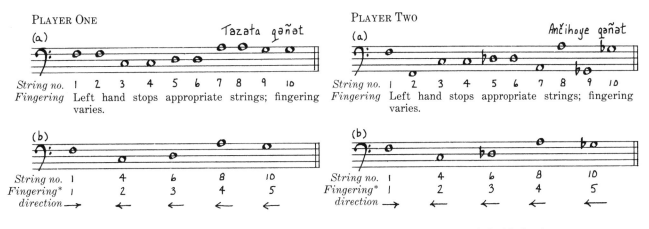

PLAYER ONE

(a) Tazata qañət

String no. 1 2 3 4 5 6 7 8 9 10
Fingering Left hand stops appropriate strings; fingering varies.

(b)

String no. 1 4 6 8 10
Fingering* 1 2 3 4 5
direction → ← ← ← ←

PLAYER TWO

(a) Ančihoye qañət

String no. 1 2 3 4 5 6 7 8 9 10
Fingering Left hand stops appropriate strings; fingering varies.

(b)

String no. 1 4 6 8 10
Fingering* 1 2 3 4 5
direction → ← ← ← ←

a) shows the pitches sounded with the plectrum.
b) shows the pitches sounded without the plectrum.
*Fingering: Refers to the left hand. Fingering #1 refers to the thumb.

a) shows the pitches sounded with the plectrum.
b) shows the pitches sounded without the plectrum.
  Sometimes player two choses to have the thumb move in the same direction as the other fingers instead of in the opposing direction.

EXAMPLE 13-6. Two bägänna tuning systems.

Bägänna fingering

Tazata qañət

2 3 1 5 1 5   1 5 1 5   1 1 3 1 1 3 2 4 2 3 1 5 1 5 1 5 1 5

Voice

A   A

1 1 3 1 1 3 2 4 2 3 1 5 1 3 1 3 1 1 3 2 4 2 4 5 2 3 1 1 1 3 1 1 3 2 4 2 2

B   B'

Time of entire song: 2 min. 16 sec.
Time of AABB': 17 sec.

Number of phrase pattern sets accompanying text	Voice (V) and/or bägänna (B)	Phrase pattern set	Number of phrase pattern sets accompanying text	Voice (V) and/or bägänna (B)	Phrase pattern set
1	B	A B	4	B	AA B B'
	BV	AA B↓		BV	AA B↓
2	B	B']	5	B	B']
	BV	AA B↓		BV	AA B↓
3	B	B']	6	B	B']
	BV	AA B↓		BV	AA B↓
	B	B']		B	B']

EXAMPLE 13-7. Bägänna melody.

EXAMPLE 13-8. Amhara krar melody.

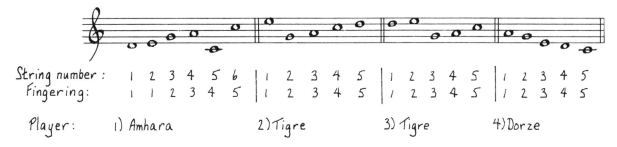

String number :   1 2 3 4 5 6 | 1 2 3 4 5 | 1 2 3 4 5 | 1 2 3 4 5
Fingering: 1 1 2 3 4 5 | 1 2 3 4 5 | 1 2 3 4 5 | 1 2 3 4 5

Player: 1) Amhara   2) Tigre   3) Tigre   4) Dorze

EXAMPLE 13-9.

Outline of main melody

Masinqo (Introduction)

Time: 14 sec.

EXAMPLE 13-10. Tigre masinqo melody. (Can be heard on the recording.)

tailing manner. The lead singer, who begins first, varies her melodic line more than the second woman, who sings with almost no noticeable variation. The lead woman in this case is considered a superior female singer in Harar and has the ability to vary a melodic pattern almost indefinitely, whereas the second woman, younger and less experienced, has a more limited skill. Example 13-5 shows the melodic relationship between the two singers. The melodic pattern is repeated twenty-five times; pitch a^1 is the referent pitch. The pace is fairly brisk, the style is characterized by much syncopation, and the repeated litany can continue indefinitely.

Three Chordophones: Two Plucked Lyres and One Bowed Fiddle

There are three types of chordophones, each different in appearance, function, and playing style: bägänna, krar, and masinqo.

Təzəta and ančihoye are the two bägänna qəñət. A player chooses one of the two qəñət for his music and then seldom changes to another. Example 13-6 shows the tuning systems of two

TABLE 13-1
Comparison of Three Krar

Parameter:	Dorze	Tigre	Amhara
Music participants	One; krar accompanies singing.	One; krar accompanies singing.	One; krar accompanies singing.
Text language:	Dorzinya.	Tygrinya.	Amharic.
Plectrum:	Leather.	Plastic.	None.
Number of strings:	Five.	Five.	Six.
Distinguishing krar characteristics	1) Strings wound around crossbar which acts as friction bar; 2) Pillars perpendicular to crossbar; 3) Sheep's gut strings.	1) Strings wound around friction pegs which are pushed through crossbar and rotated to adjust pitch; 2) Pillars form slight "V" shape; 3) Metal wire strings.	1) Strings wound around crossbar and peg levers; peg against crossbar and always perpendicular to it when rotated to adjust pitch; 2) Pillars form slight "V" shape; 3) Sheep's gut strings.
Playing style:	Right hand strums strings with plectrum while left hand stops/mutes strings.	Right hand strums strings with plectrum while left hand stops/mutes strings.	Left hand plucks strings.
Playing position:	Seated.	Seated.	Seated.
Qəñət:	Təzəta.	Təzəta.	Təzəta.
Tuning sequence:	See example 13-9.	See example 13-9.	See example 13-9.
Meter:	Duple.	Duple.	Triple.
Relationship between voice and krar:	Krar plays ostinato chordal melody while player sings independent melody.	Krar plays chordal accompaniment outlining basic melody of voice.	Krar plays a melodic, not chordal, part; krar and voice in heterophony.
Dominant krar characteristic:	Ostinato patterns with shifting accents.	Rhythmic patterns.	Melodic variation of vocal line.
Form:	Essentially strophic; instrumental introduction and interludes.	Strophic; instrumental introduction and interludes.	Strophic; instrumental introduction and interludes.
Continuity:	Sections blurred as voice enters intermittently; some vocal exclamations.	Fairly clearly defined sections; voice and instrument in heterophony.	Clear-cut sections; voice and instrument essentially in heterophony.
Approx. song length:	Seven minutes.	Five minutes.	Four minutes.

bägänna players. Note that player number one repeats his pitches in unison and player number two repeats his pitches both in unison and at the octave. There is no precise pitch range; the player's vocal range determines the instrumental range.

When a plectrum is used, then all the strings must be tuned. Otherwise only five of the strings are tuned and "the remaining strings are used for the finger rests or stops after the strings have been plucked. . . . In order for the sound to carry, the strings are placed into a U-shaped leather thong which is adjusted until a buzzing sound is heard" (Kimberlin 1978).

A transcription of a bägänna melody (performed without a plectrum) is shown in example 13-7. The form is essentially strophic with the voice and bägänna in heterophony, though the voice drops out while the bägänna finishes the phrase. The text concerns Emperor Theodore II, who committed suicide in 1868 during Napier's invasion of Ethiopia, and is titled "Death of the Left-handed Man":

The left handed died my bosom friend
Who gave me fat to eat and mead to drink.
Tatek is the horse and Kassa is the name
On Fridays there is unrest in Jerusalem.
One thousand black, one thousand grey horses of Shoa,
Everyone shivers when Theodore appears.
There is much crying on top of Magdala,
We do not know how many women died
But we know one man has died.

TABLE 13-2
COMPARISON OF THREE MASINQO

Parameter:	Amhara	Tigre	Oromo
Music participants:	One; masinqo accompanies singing.	One; masinqo accompanies singing.	One; masinqo accompanies singing.
Language:	Amharic.	Tygrinya.	Gallinya.
Distinguishing masinqo characteristic:	Box volume averages 2.2 to 4 liters.	Box volume averages 7.5 to 8.5 liters.	Box volume averages 1.8 to 2.2 liters.
Playing position:	Standing; masinqo supported by shoulder strap.	Seated; box placed between player's knees.	Seated; box placed between player's knees.
Qəñət:	Təzəta.	Essentially ambassal; shifts momentarily to təzəta.	Təzəta.
Meter:	Duple.	Triple.	Changing meters.
Form:	Strophic; instrumental introduction and interludes.	Strophic; instrumental introduction and interludes; at song's conclusion player hits box side with bow.	Strophic; instrumental introduction and interludes.
Relationship between masinqo and voice:	Essentially heterophony; intermittent vocal exclamations; short spoken section at end. Masinqo plays elaboration of vocal line.	Heterophony; masinqo plays some elaboration of vocal line.	Heterophony; masinqo plays elaboration of vocal line.
Distinguishing playing characteristics:	String bow pressure medium; melodic ornamentation not focused on particular pitches but rather on particular phrase—for example, ascending/descending runs common.	String bow pressure great; recurring rhythmic pulse; melodic ornamentation focused on particular pitches.	String bow pressure light; slight sliding of fingers of left hand resulting in blurring of many pitches in succession.
Approx. song length:	Five minutes.	Five minutes.	Six minutes.

Underestimating the king of Tigre,
Underestimating the king of Shoa,
You never killed a man except yourself.

They could not say "We killed him" for they found
    him dead,
They could not say "We captured him" for they
    have no captive in their hand,
What did the English say when they returned
    home?
We do not know for they are deceitful.
    [Bägänna text translated by Aga Alamu]
        (After Kimberlin 1978).

I have observed three types of krar: Amhara, Tigre, and Dorze, which had six, five, and five strings, respectively. A comparison of the three krar and an Amhara krar melody are given in table 13-1 and example 13-8. The descriptions are based on three krar players playing three particular songs. Only the Tigre player is a professional krar player; the Dorze is a weaver, and the Amhara is a masinqo teacher at a government school. There are individual preferences for the order of pitches in the tuning system. Example 13-9 shows examples of tuning systems of four krar players who each tuned his krar to the same qəñət, təzəta.

The masinqo is primarily played by the Amhara, Oromo, and Tigre ethnic groups. A comparison of three masinqo and a Tigre masinqo melody are given in table 13-2 and example 13-10. The Amhara song is a šəlälä and the Tigre text is about a notorious šəfta (outlaw) named Bašay Läma who was killed during one of his escapades. The sister of Bašay Läma subsequently became a šəfta, determined to avenge her brother's death (Ghebremedhin 1972).

CONCLUSION

Ethiopian music has similarities with that of other cultures. The ambassəl qəñət or mode seems to be found in Japan (Olsen 1973); the təzəta mode is found in China (Debalke 1972); the ṣänaṣəl or sistrum was used in Egypt (Mondon-Vidailhet 1922:3184); lyres resembling the krar are found in northeastern Africa (Kebede 1969:2). Whether or not these cultures were directly or indirectly influenced by Ethiopia, or vice versa, is only speculative. Ethiopian music has its own distinct identity in spite of internal differences or similarities with music of other countries, for Ethiopia's music—like its painting, pottery, sculpture, architecture, and dance —mirrors Ethiopian society and its people.

Glossary

abiy märägd-A division of church music performance.

ambasəl-One of the four known Ethiopian music modes.

ančihoye-One of the four known Ethiopian music modes.

azmari-A professional masinqo player.

bägänna-A ten-stringed plucked lyre.

bati-One of the four known Ethiopian music modes.

däbtära-A lay theologian and church musician.

dəft-A tambourine.

dube-A bowl-shaped drum.

əmbilta-An end-blown flute; three əmbilta of varying lengths constitute a set.

Gə'əz-The language of the Ethiopian liturgy.

käbäro (Kärobo)-A cylindrical or conical-shaped drum.

käbəl-A pair of wood blocks.

krar-A five- or six-stringed plucked lyre.

mäqʷamyä-An Ethiopian walking staff.

masinqo-A single-string, bowed spike fiddle.

nəus märägd-A division of Ethiopian church music performance.

qəñət-The Ethiopian approximate equivalent of Western "mode."

referent pitch-The basic pitch to which all other pitches relate.

ṣänaṣəl-A sistrum.

ṣəfat-A division of Ethiopian church music performance.

səfta-An outlaw.

šəläla-A song meant to arouse or prepare people for war.

ṭäg bet-A place where men go to talk and drink ṭäg or honey mead.

təzəta-One of the four known Ethiopian music modes.

wäräb-A division of Ethiopian church music performance.

wašänt-A four-hole end-blown flute of indefinite length.

zəmame-A division of Ethiopian church music performance.

Bibliography

Aga, Alamu.
  1972. Personal communication.
  1973. "The Baganna." *Yared Music School Annual*. Addis Ababa. Pp. 26-27.
Bedru, Camia.
  1972. Personal communication.
Budge, E. A.
  1928. *A History of Ethiopia*. 2 vols. London: Methuen.
Debalke, Tsegaye.
  1967. "Ethiopian Music and Musical Instruments." *Ethiopian Herald*. Addis Ababa. Nov. 5.
  1972. Personal communication.
Doresse, Jean.
  1959. *Ethiopia: Ancient Cities and Temples*. New York: G. P. Putnam.
Ghebremedhin, Sisay.
  1972. Personal communication.
Kebede, Ashanafi.
  1967. "The Krar." *Ethiopian Observer*. Addis Ababa. 11:154-61.
  1969a. *The Music of Ethiopia: Azmari Music of the Amharas*. Record notes, Anthology AST-6000, pp. 1-7.
  1969b. "Review of Ethiopian Musical Recordings." *The World of Music*, XI: 70-74.
  1971. "The Music of Ethiopia: Its Development and Cultural Setting." Ph.D. dissertation,

Wesleyan University. Available University Microfilms, Ann Arbor.

1977. "The Bowl-Lyre of Northeast Africa, *Krar*: The Devil's Instrument." *Ethnomusicology*, 21 (September), 379-95.

Kimberlin, Cynthia T.

1972. Unpublished field notes.

1974*a*. Record review of "Ethiopian Urban and Tribal Music," Vols. I and II, recorded by R. Johnson and R. Harrison, Lyrichord Stereo LLST 7243 and 7244, 1972; Vol. XVIII, No. 1 issue of *Ethnomusicology* (January), pp. 126-38.

1974*b*. Record review of "Ritual Music of Ethiopia," recorded and edited by L. Lerner and C. Wollner, Ethnic Folkways Records FE 4353, 1973; Vol. XVIII, No. 3 issue of *Ethnomusicology* (September), pp. 48-81.

1975. Record review of "Folk Music and Ceremonies of Ethiopia," recorded and edited by L. Lerner and C. Wollner, Ethnic Folkways Records FE 4354, 1974; Vol. XIX, No. 2 issue of *Ethnomusicology* (May), pp. 328-29.

1976. "Masinqo and the Nature of Qəñət." Ph.D. dissertation, University of California, Los Angeles. Available University Microfilms, Ann Arbor.

1978. "The Baganna of Ethiopia," *Ethiopianist Notes*, vol. 2, no. 2, pp. 13-29.

Lamma, Tasfaye.

1972. Personal communication.

Leslau, Wolf.

1968. *Amharic Textbook*. Berkeley and Los Angeles: University of California Press.

1971. Amharic Class Notes. Fall Quarter, University of California, Los Angeles.

Merriam, Alan P.

1959. "African Music." In *Continuity and Change in African Cultures*, edited by W. Bascom and M. Herskovits. Chicago: University of Chicago Press. Pp. 49-86.

Mosley, Leonard.

1955. *Haile Selassie*. Liverpool: Prescott.

Mondon-Vidailhet, F. M. C.

1922. "La musique éthiopienne." *Encyclopédie de la musique et dictionnaire du conservatoire*, edited by A. Lavignac and L. de la Laurencie, 1 ére partie, Paris: C. Delagrave. Pp. 3179-96.

Moorefield, Arthur A.

1975. "James Bruce: Ethnomusicologist or Abyssinian Lyre?" *Journal of the American Musicological Society*. 28:493-514.

Murphy, Dervia.

1968. *In Ethiopia with a Mule*. London: J. Murray.

Music, Dance, and Drama in Ethiopia.

1968. Addis Ababa: Ministry of Information.

Olsen, Dale.

1973. Personal communication.

Patterns of Progress: Music, Dance and Drama.

1968. Addis Ababa: Ministry of Information pamphlet. Vol. 9.

Pound, Michael.

1968. *Ethiopian Music: An Introduction*. London: Oxford University Press.

Reid, James M.

1968. *Traveller Extraordinary: The Life of James Bruce of Kinnaird*. New York: Norton.

Sarosi Balint.

1970. "Melodic Patterns in the Folk Music of the Ethiopian Peoples." *Proceedings of the Third International Conference of Ethiopian Studies*. Addis Ababa: Institute of Ethiopian Studies. No. 1, pp. 280-870.

Tazieff Haroun.

1970. "The Afar Triangle." *Scientific American*. 222:32-40.

Tzadua, Paulos.

1972. Personal communication.

Wellesz, Egon.

1920. "Studien zur aethiopischen Kirchenmusik." *Oriens Christianus*. n.s. 9, p. 74ff.

Discography

Drums for God. Epic BF 19044. Two selections from Ethiopia. Recording and notes by Robert Kauffman.

Ethiopia: I. Copts. Bärenreiter BM 30L 2304. Recording and notes by Jean Jenkins.

Ethiopia: II. Cushites. Bärenreiter BM 30L 2305. Recording and notes by Jean Jenkins.

Ethiopia: The Falasha and the Adjuran Tribe. Folkways FE 4355. Recording and notes by Lin Lerner and Chet Wollner.

Ethiopian Urban and Tribal Music: Mindanoo Mistiru: I. Lyrichord LLST 7243. Recording and notes by Ragnar Johnson.

Ethiopian Urban and Tribal Music: Gold from Wax: II. Lyrichord LLST 7244. Recording and notes by Ragnar Johnson.

Ethiopians. UNESCO AL 98/99. Recording and notes by J. Tubiana.

Ethiopie: polyphonies et techniques vocales. OCR 44. Recording and notes by Jean Jenkins.

Folk Music and Ceremonies of Ethiopia. Folkways FE 4354. Recording and notes by Lin Lerner and Chet Wollner.

Folk Music of Ethiopia. Folkways P 4405. Recording and notes by Harold Courlander.

Music of Eritrea: III. Tangent TGM 103. Recording and notes by Jean Jenkins.

The Music of Ethiopia: Azmari Music of the Amharas. Anthology AST 6000. Recording and notes by Ashanafi Kebede.

Music of the Central Highlands: I. Tangent TGM 101. Recordings and notes by Jean Jenkins.

Music of the Desert Nomads: II. Tangent TGM 102. Recording and notes by Jean Jenkins.

The Music of the Falashas. Folkways FE 4442. Recording and notes by Wolf Leslau.

Ritual Music of Ethiopia. Folkways FE 4353. Recording and notes by Chet Wollner and Lin Lerner.

Traditional Music of Ethiopia. Vogue CLVSX 164. Recording and notes by Jean Jenkins.

Films

Ethiopian Mosaic. CFMH. Col. 10 min.

A "teaser" showing very short glimpses of Ethiopian life with the use of jump cuts and no narration. Beautifully photographed. There are some ten- to fifteen-second film segments of the sound of sanza, flute, spike fiddle, drum, and sistrum. Intermittent background music played by a flute, plucked lyre, and drum ensemble.

The Falashas. ML. Col. ca. 30 min.

Depicts the life style of the Falashas, who live in northwestern Ethiopia, where they live according to Judaic Law and ritual.

The Nuer. FSC, CF/MH, UC. Col. 75 min.

The Nuer was filmed in Southwestern Ethiopia in Illubabor. The film does not focus on Nuer music but gives a general impression of the "rhythm and movement" of Nuer life.

14. Secular Classical Music in the Arabic Near East

Jozef M. Pacholczyk

The Near East, sometimes called the Middle East, is the large geographical area covering the western part of the continent of Asia and North Africa. This ethnically highly diversified area is inhabited by peoples speaking languages belonging to three different language families: Indo-European (Persians), Semito-Chamitic (Arabs), and Uralo-Altaic (Turks). For the last several millennia the Near East has been a cradle of great civilizations and cultures: Mesopotamian, Egyptian, Persian, and Islamic.

The Islamic civilization developed in the environment of the Islamic empire, a strong political power that emerged in the seventh century A.D. and soon dominated not only the entire Near East but even extended to Spain in the west and to north India and central Asia in the east. Two principal cultural elements unified this multinational empire: the religion, Islam, and (to a lesser extent) the language, Arabic. Arabic was accepted as a mother tongue in some areas; in others it became the language of administration and scholarly writings, in many ways functioning similarly to Latin in medieval Europe. It was primarily because of the language that the culture of this area was often superficially identified as Arabic.

The classical music of the Near East was developed in major centers of the Islamic empire, mainly in the capitals of the caliphates: Damascus, Baghdad, and Cordoba. It was rooted in the pre-Islamic musical tradition of the Arabs and enriched with elements from cultures of nations with which the Arabs came into contact through conquest. The present-day artistic music of the Near East is a descendant of this tradition and is rooted in the court music of the medieval Islamic empire. With the fall of the Islamic empire and growing decentralization, different styles of music emerged in various regions. I will discuss only a small segment of this tradition: the secular music of the classical tradition in the Arabic Near East, that is, in countries where Arabic is a primary language. Today this highly refined music is performed in Syria, Iraq, Lebanon, Jordan, Egypt, Libya, Tunisia, Algeria, and Morocco.

HISTORY

The history of music in the classical tradition of the Arabic Near East can be divided into four periods:

1. Pre-Islamic period of *Jāhilīya* ("ignorance"): until A.D. 622.
2. Period of Development: from the beginning of Islam (622) until the fall of Baghdad in the east (thirteenth century) and the fall of Granada in the west (fifteenth century).
3. Period of Conservation: thirteenth or fifteenth to nineteenth century.
4. Modern Period: end of nineteenth century to the present.

Pre-Islamic Period of Jāhilīya

Little is known about the music of the Arabs during the Jāhilīya period. The Arabic Peninsula was under the domain of the Mesopotamian civilization and developed as a part of the Semitic cultural area. Music was performed by the clan of *qaināt* ("singing girls") or, more rarely, by the *mughannī*, male musicians.

Music was primarily vocal and closely related to poetry. It was accompanied by instruments, the most common of which were the *duff* (tam-

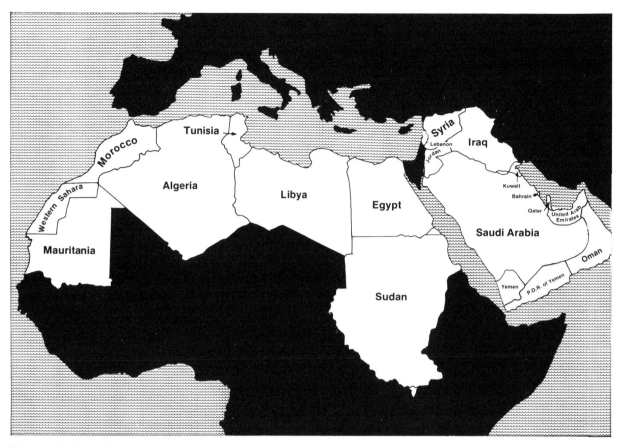

The Arabic Near East

bourine), *ṭabl* (drum), *ʿūd* (lute), *ṭunbūr* (long-necked lute), *nāy* (reed pipe), and *jank* (harp).

The oldest form of the chant is considered to be *ḥudā*, the caravan song, the rhythm of which was inspired by the camel's gait. From these songs developed other forms of the *ghinā'* ("chant"), *biqā'* ("lament"), *nawḥ* ("elegy"), and *naṣb* ("romance").

The music of the Arabs did not develop in isolation. They were in constant contact with neighboring peoples. Probably the most important associations were those with Sassanide Persia which developed toward the end of the Jāhilīya period in the centuries immediately preceding the advent of Islam.

Period of Development

Islam unified the Arab tribes of the peninsula and released a tremendous force that led to one of the most spectacular conquests in history.

Within less than a century the Arab armies had incorporated the vast areas from Spain through North Africa to Persia and central Asia into the powerful Islamic empire. This multitude of different cultures, brought together within a single political organization dominated by the Arabs and the Arabic language, merged and became the so-called Islamic culture. The principal contributors were Arabs, Persians, Byzantines, and Turks. The balance among their contributions in various areas is difficult to ascertain and often a subject of controversy.

The advent of Islam had a profound influence on the development of music. From the beginning, Islam held a negative attitude toward music and classified it as one of the *malāhī* ("forbidden pleasures"). The most probable cause of this attitude was the association of music with poetry. Poetry, which had its Golden Age in the years immediately preceding Islam, represented a system of values of the pre-Islam-ic "pagan" Arabs and thus did not correspond to the new moral system of Islam. Although the Qurʾān (the Holy Book of Islam) itself did not contain any statement against music, the nega-tive attitude toward music was developed by theologians on the basis of *Ḥadīth* ("tradition")[1] and was shared by all four legal schools of Islam: Hanafī, Hanbalī, Shafiʿī, and Mālikī.

During the reigns of the four so-called or-thodox caliphs[2] music did not find the most fa-vorable climate for development, yet during the following period of the first dynasty, the Umayyads (661-750), it began to flourish, and the court in Damascus became a center for de-velopment of the arts and sciences. The court became a meeting place in which different mu-sical concepts from all parts of the Umayyad Empire were entertained. Persian music be-came increasingly popular. A number of leading musicians of the time such as Ibn Misjah, Ibn Suraij, and Maʿbad traveled to Persia where they learned new melodies and concepts. Per-sian tunes and instruments were also imported by slaves. As Persian music became more and more popular in the Arabic central part of the caliphate, Arabic music made its way into Per-sia. But in spite of increasing contacts with neighboring cultures, music performed in the courts of the Umayyads was principally Arabic in character. This old Arabic music flourished during the early period of the following ʿAbbā-sid dynasty (750-1258), at the courts of such great caliphs as al-Mahdī, Hārūn al-Rašīd, and Maʾmūn. This period is considered the Golden Age of Islamic culture, when music reached its apogee.

From the famous *Kitāb al-Aghānī al-Kabīr (Great Book of Songs)*, by Abūʾl Faraj al-Iṣfahānī, we know the names of famous musicians of that time: Zalzal, Yaḥyā al-Makkī, Ibn Jāmiʿ, and above all Ibrāhīm and Isḥāq Mawsīlī, who were considered the greatest musicians of Islam.

They represented the old Arabic school. This school was opposed by the new Persian "roman-tic" school led by a relative of the caliph, Prince Ibrāhīm Ibn al-Mahdī (d. 839). The development of this school was a reflection of the increased Persianization of the court in Baghdad, the cap-ital of the ʿAbbāsid caliphate.

During the ʿAbbāsid period many branches of Islamic scholarship developed rapidly, among them medicine, astronomy, alchemy, geog-raphy, mathematics, and also music theory. This development was stimulated by the contact with ancient Greek writings which became available to Islamic scholars through transla-tions done in the Bait al-Ḥikma (House of Wis-dom), a library, astronomical observatory, and translation institute established in Baghdad by caliph al Maʾmūn.

A steady increase of separatist tendencies in various parts of the empire led to the establish-ment of a counter-caliphate in Spain with its center in Cordoba. After the excellent musician Abūʾl Ḥasan ʿAlī Ibn Nāfiʿ—called Ziryāb,[3] a student of Isḥāq al-Mawsīlī—arrived in Spain in 822 a new, distinct Andalusian style began to develop.

The eleventh century witnessed the increas-ing influence of Seljuk Turks in Baghdad and the political power of the empire weakened. Un-der the Fāṭimide dynasty Egypt separated herself from the empire and established an in-dependent caliphate. Political instability and decentralization affected the development of the arts: the local courts could not support mu-sicians to the same extent as in the past. How-ever, music was still developing. The work of one of the greatest music theorists, Ṣafī ad-Dīn ʿAbdʾ al-Muʾmin, coincides with the period of the collapse of the ʿAbbāsid caliphate and the destruction of Baghdad by the Mongol armies under Hulagu in 1258.

Period of Conservation

The fall of Baghdad and the collapse of the ʿAbbāsid caliphate initiated a period of cultural and intellectual stagnation in the Arabic Near East. The cultural centers moved eastward to

1. Ḥadīth ("tradition") is a body of short stories and information about Mohammed and his companions used in interpreting unclear passages of the Qurʾān.

2. Abū Bakr – 632-634
   ʿUmar – 634-644
   ʿUthmān – 644-656
   ʿAlī – 656-661

3. All Arabic names are very long. Usually one or two segments are used. Pseudonyms such as "Zalzal" and "Zir-yāb" are rare.

Persia and central Asia, to Bukhara and Samarkand, where culture and learning developed under the patronage of the Islamized Mongol rulers.

In Spain the position of the Moslems was threatened by the Christian *reconquista*. The expulsion of the last Moslems from Spain in 1492 brought to an end the golden period of Andalusian culture. Refugees from Spain settled in North Africa, Morocco, Algeria, and Tunisia, carrying with them their culture. But the environment in North Africa was far less favorable for the development of music than that of Spain. No new pieces were added to the Andalusian repertory, and the old compositions today are gradually being forgotten.

During this period the Turkish Ottoman domination over a large part of the Arabic Near East introduced some elements of Turkish music but generally failed to stimulate cultural and intellectual life.

The Modern Period

Napoleon's expedition to Egypt in 1798 had a tremendous impact on the Arabic Near East. It initiated an era of new contacts with Europe that were to bring substantial changes in all aspects of life.

The nineteenth century witnessed a *Nahḍa*— a political and cultural renaissance—that began in Egypt, Lebanon, and Syria. This renaissance was closely related to the development of the press and the establishment of modern universities and schools. In 1869 the first opera house in the Arabic world, Dār-al-Ūbīrā in Cairo, was opened. In the twentieth century a number of music academies and conservatories have been established throughout the Arabic world in which both classical-traditional and Western music are taught.

Reflecting the growing interest in music as a performing art and in musicology was the organization in 1932 of the Congress on Arabic Music in Cairo, with the participation of all the principal authorities on Arabic music from both the Arabic world and Europe—such as Alexis Chottin, Mahmūd Hefnī, Henry George Farmer, Rodolphe d'Erlanger, Raouf Yekta Bey, and Father Collangettes. One of the important accomplishments of the Congress was the issue of a large number of phonograph recordings by leading musicians of the contemporary Arab world. These recordings provide a priceless documentation of the music of this period.

The impact of Western culture, together with Western technology, changed the traditional system of values and caused a decline in the popularity of classical music. Few musicians today perform traditional forms in the traditional manner. A number of twentieth-century composers are trying to find new methods of composition, often by using certain devices borrowed from Western music.

After World War II, a new trend emerged in Egypt, and to some extent in Lebanon—a nationalist movement. Composers in this movement are attempting to create a new artistic music through the synthesis of both Arabic and European traditions.

HISTORY OF THEORY

From the eighth century on, we can observe the continuous effort of a number of scholars, philosophers, mathematicians, and virtuoso musicians of the Near East to observe and verbalize various aspects of music and to organize their knowledge in coherent systems. These theoretical systems were presented in numerous treatises. Two periods in the history of Near Eastern music theory can be distinguished: from the eighth to about the end of the eighteenth century, and from the end of the eighteenth century to the present.

In the first period the investigation of music was conducted by musicians and scholars of the Near East—the carriers of the culture—Arabs, Persians, or Turks. In the second period we find three principal kinds of writings: (1) by musicians and scholars educated in the East; (2) by the same educated in the West; and (3) by non-Arabs, mostly Europeans.

It seems, particularly in the first period, that music theory was developing rather independently from musical practice, and the relationship between the two was nominal. In the second period, the Western concept of objectivity prevailed in musical research and the theoretical system was in considerably closer relationship to the practice. It has to be understood, however, that theoretical writings are the source data for the development of various theoretical concepts rather than of the development of the music itself.

Three principal problems drew the attention of almost all theorists: (1) tonal material; (2) systems of melodic modes; and (3) systems of rhythmic modes.

The earliest theorist who attempted to describe and systemize Arabic modes of his time was Ibn Misjaḥ (d. 715). None of his original works has survived, and his system is known only from secondary sources.[4] This system consisted of eight modes called *Aṣābī* ("finger modes"). They were presented in the form of the fingering of the ʿūd, the favorite instrument among Near Eastern musicians.

Beginning in the ninth century, Greek music theory became available to Near Eastern scholars through the translation into Arabic of the works of such theorists as Aristoxenes, Cleonides, Nicomachus, Ptolemy, Aristides Quintilianus, and others. These translations were done in the Bait al-Ḥikma in Baghdad, as previously mentioned. The effect of this school of translators on the development of Islamic thinking cannot be overestimated. In music the Greek theoretical concepts were responsible for the development of the *ʿIlm al-Mūsīqī*, the science of music, and have had considerable influence on Near Eastern music theory until the present time.

The first theorist whose works bear signs of the strong influence of Greek musical theories is al-Kindī (Abū Yūsuf Yaʿqub Ibn Ishāq al-Kindī, ca. 790–874), of Arab descent. Only a few works by al-Kindī have survived. In these works the vocabulary of pitches obtainable from the five strings of the lute is given. The organization of these pitches is similar to the Greeks' Great Perfect System, a two-octave range divided into tetrachords.

Greek influence is also noticeable in his terminology, the Arabic terms being a close trans-

lation of the Greek. Al-Kindī mentioned only three melodic modes and presented them in the traditional manner according to fingering. He also presented eight rhythmic modes, *iqaʿāt* (sing. *iqaʿā*), as a cycle of beats repeated throughout a section of music. Al-Kindī was also interested in the problem of ethos, discussing the effect of music on human beings, the relationship between musical elements such as mode, melodic pattern or pitch, and cosmology and its association with moral and ethical qualities.

Another important figure in the music theory of the Near East is al-Fārābī (Abūʾ n-Naṣr Muḥammad Ibn Muḥammad Ibn Tarhān Ibn Uzlāgh al-Fārābī, 872-950). Together with al-Kindī he is the leading representative of the Oriental branch of the Arabic scholastic school. Of Turkish origin, he was born in Fārāb in Turkestan. In Baghdad he studied the Arabic language, philosophy, medicine, science, and music. He was one of the best ʿūd virtuosos of his time and a prolific writer. A number of his works have survived, which cover a broad range of topics representing nearly all areas of Islamic scholarship. A number of these works were later translated into Latin and made their way to Europe. The influence of his works on the development of both Islamic and European thought was profound. His major work on music, *Kitāb al-Mūsīqī al-Kabīr (The Great Book of Music)*, is the largest and one of the most important treatises on music in Near Eastern literature. It discusses the large array of problems relating to music. It consists of four parts, each containing two discourses, the first part being a philosophical treatise on the general theories of music. A considerable part of the work is concerned with tonal material, scales, and tetrachords—*jins* (pl. *ajnās*).

The scale system is similar to the Greek Great Perfect System. Although most of the ajnās are identifiable with the tetrachords described by various Greek theorists, they are not direct copies. The principal differences are in their organization and classification. It is quite possible that the similarities are the result of the adoption of certain mathematical procedures in computation of the intervals. The tetrachord

---

4. Principal sources are: Kitāb al-Aghānī al-Kabīr by Abu-'l-Faraj al-Isfahānī and the works of ʿAlī Ibn Yaḥya al-Munajjim an-Nadīm (d. 912) (see Owen Wright in bibliography).

system of al-Fārābī is very speculative, and it can be seriously doubted that all of the tetrachord forms were actually used in practice.

Al-Fārābī's approach to music theory had considerable influence on later music theorists. The most important of them was Abū ʿAlī al-Ḥusayn Ibn ʿAbduʾl-Lāh Ibn Sīnā (980-1037), known in the West as Avicenna, who was born in Afšanah in the district of Bukhara, of Persian origin. Avicenna was not himself a musician. His system did not constitute a major departure from the system of al-Fārābī.

It was not until the thirteenth century that a major step in the development of theory was taken. Ṣafī ad-Dīn (Abd al-Muʾmin Ibn Fākhir al-ʾUrmawī), who lived during the period of the final collapse of the Abbasid empire and the beginning of Mongol rule, developed a theory that was accepted and used until the nineteenth century. Some of the elements of this theory survived even in the twentieth century in the Turkish system of Raouf Yekta Bey.

Ṣafī ad-Dīn was the author of two works: *ar-Risāla aš-Šarafiya fī n-Nisab at-Taʾlīfiya (The Sharafian Treatise on Harmonic Relations)* and *Kitāb al-Adwār (Book of Cycles)*. By exploring the remaining possible mathematical permutations he organized and completed the scale and tetrachord system initiated and developed by the previous theorists and also developed an entirely new system, proposing the division of the octave into seventeen intervals of two sizes: limma (90 cents) and comma (24 cents).

The sequence of the intervals within an octave is as follows:

LLC   LLCL   LLC   LLC   LLCL
4th   2nd   4th

This can be called *an intermodal scale* and is a concept similar to that of the Western chromatic scale, the selected degrees of which constitute scales of particular modes. Alexander John Ellis (1814-1890), the well-known English writer on musical science, considered this scale the most perfect ever devised. From the number of possible modes Ṣafī ad-Dīn presents twelve fundamental modes, *šudūd*, and six secondary modes, *awazāt*.[5]

Besides the melodic modes, Ṣafī ad-Dīn presents eight principal rhythmic modes in the form of circles representing the cycles, as well as in the form of paradigms of the Arabic verb *faʿala* ("he did").

The works of this scholar contain the oldest Arabic music notation, consisting of very short fragments of melodies (fig. 14-1). The letters of the Arabic alphabet represent pitches and numbers under those letters indicate the rhythm. It is quite possible that this or a similar notation was employed by Near Eastern musicians occasionally even earlier than the thirteenth century, but it never became widely used. The fragments mentioned are basically the only ones known to us before the twentieth century, when, after some modifications, the Western type of notation was accepted—although this, even today, is not in popular use. Teaching by rote remains the most common method of transmitting the repertoire.

The impact of the theory of Ṣafī ad-Dīn was far-reaching. In the following centuries, many

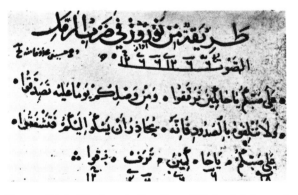

FIGURE 14-1. Music notation from Kitab-al-Adwar of Ṣafī ad-Dīn.

5. The *šudūd* are: ʿuššaq, nawā, abū salīik, rāst, ʿirāq, isfahān, zīrāfkand, buzurg, zangūla, rāhawī, husaynī, hijāzi. The *awazāt* are: kawāšt, kardānīya, salmak, naw-rūz, māya, šāh-nāz.

theorists and writers on music worked on refinements of the system; others incorporated it into their own or wrote commentaries on it.

The system that became the basis for the contemporary music of the Arabic Near East was developed at the beginning of the nineteenth century by the Lebanese musicologist Mikhā'īl Mašāqa in his work *ar-Risāla aš-Šihābiya (Treatise for Amir Shihab)*. Mašāqa devised a new type of intermodal scale. He divided an octave into twenty-four intervals of approximately a quarter tone (50 cents). This type of scale not only accommodates scales of modes containing the neutral third (Zalzalian third) but makes it possible to transpose these modes to any degree of this scale.

At the Cairo congress of 1932, several alternate quarter-tone scales were suggested, some constructed through mathematical computation, some obtained experimentally from the performance of individual musicians. The differences of opinion, both among the theorists and musicians as well as from recent research on the tonal structure of some forms of vocal music, indicate that none of these systems adequately reflects actual musical practice. However, they are convenient tools for descriptive and didactic purposes.

At the same conference an attempt was made to classify and codify the *maqāmāt* (sing. *maqām*), the modes as used in the Arabic Near East. They were described in terms of the scales (intervallic structure), ambitus, division into tetrachords, and the initial pitch. Subsequent research, in particular that of d'Erlanger, extended the definition of mode to include the hierarchy of pitches and melodic patterns.

There is no complete list of maqāmāt. The Cairo Congress presented a list of more than fifty maqāmāt from Egypt and Syria, some thirty-seven from Iraq (fifteen of them similar to those used in Egypt), and eighteen modes used in North Africa (Tunisia and Morocco). The scale of the maqām usually consists of seven pitches to the octave. The intervals between the degrees of the scale can be a quarter tone (rarely), a half-step, a three-quarter tone, or various forms of augmented tones such as 1-¼ or 1-½ tones.

The maqām is usually presented as a two-octave scale with indication of the tonic—*qarār*. Often the ascending and descending scales differ, indicating that in such cases the pitches vary according to the direction of the movement. Besides the tonic the maqām has other important structural degrees such as *ghammāz* (dominant, functioning as the central pitch of the climactic point of the melody) and *dhahīr* (subtonic, a kind of leading tone or group of tones that underline the cadential function of the tonic).

The maqām as a mode is an important generating force in Near Eastern music. It is the primary determinant of the form of improvisatory pieces exemplified by the *taqsīm* and *layālī*. At present, a modified Western system of music notation is used with the quarter-tone chromatic alterations. There are several signs used for this purpose:

$\sharp$	: half sharp
$\sharp$	: sharp
$\sharp$	: 3/4 sharp
$\flat$ or $\natural$	: half flat
$\flat$	: flat
$\flat$	: 3/4 flat

Music is notated from left to right. Since the Arabic language is written from right to left, writing the texts of the vocal pieces creates some problems. Usually the words are divided and written in reverse order in appropriate places.

In 1949 the French musicologist Rodolphe d'Erlanger, an authority on Arab music, compiled a list of 119 maqāmāt from eastern Arabic countries and 29 from Tunisia. Today, in the Oriental part of the Arabic Near East, the most commonly used maqāmāt are: ʿajam ʿušayrān, rāst, naqrīz, nihawand, ḥijāz-kar, ḥijāz-kar kurdī, bayātī, ḥusaynī, ḥijāzī, ṣabā, sah-gāh, and tšahār-gāh.

In Morocco the Andalusian music is performed in these modes: ʿuššaq, ʿirāq al-ʿajam, ḥjāzī' l-mšarqī, istihlāl, rasd, gharībat al-ḥusayn, māya, ḥjāzī' l-kabīr, isbihān, rasd adh-dhīl, and ramal al-māya.

The time aspect of the music of the Arabic Near East is organized in a system of rhythmic mode-periods, named *dawr* in Egypt, *ṭaqm* in Syria. Each period consists of a succession of beats (*naqarāt*, sing. *naqara*) of various timbres. It is repeated throughout the entire piece of music or a section of it. A large number of rhythmic modes are used in the Arabic Near East. In the Oriental part at least 111 are known, some of them very long, up to 176 beats and of complex structure. In Maghreb, to the contrary, relatively few are in use; in the Andalusian music of Morocco, only 5.

cultivated mainly in Egypt, Lebanon, Syria, and Iraq; Occidental music in Morocco, Algeria, and Tunisia (the countries carrying the tradition of Andalusia, Moorish Spain).

Eastern and Western styles vary considerably. In the Orient music was developed in the courts and remained strictly elitist. It is principally a vocal or instrumental solo or for a small ensemble, the number of musicians rarely exceeding five. It is mainly improvised and of virtuosic character.

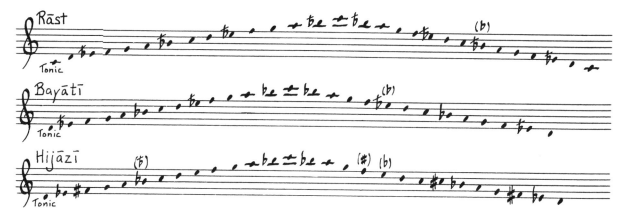

EXAMPLE 14-1. Three commonly used maqāmāt.

Drummers have the responsibility of supplying the rhythmic skeleton of a piece and of realizing the rhythmic mode. At their disposal is a large variety of beats, at least seven different timbres recognized by musicians.

FORMS

In general terms, the principal characteristics of the artistic music in the classical tradition of the Arabic Near East are: monophony and heterophony, a highly developed melodic line, the use of melodic and rhythmic modes, an association with the Arabic language and poetry, and the use of particular instruments. Presently we can distinguish two different musical styles, Oriental and Occidental, resulting from the different historical and cultural developments of Eastern and Western parts of the Arabic-speaking world. The Oriental artistic music is

The principal forms are solo instrumental taqsīm; vocal layālī; and (rarely today) *qasīda*, the form using as a text the classical, nonstrophic poetic form of the same name in classical Arabic. All these forms are improvisatory and in free rhythm. The principal organizational factor in the improvisation is the mode—maqām. A large number of maqāmāt are used, and modes with microtonal structure are very common. The ensemble pieces, performed by small ensembles of four or five musicians, are in large part composed although not written down. They often use complex rhythmic modes or cycles. Both rhythmic and melodic modes are understood as purely musical-technical concepts.

Occidental music developed in an atmosphere of political decentralization and instability. It extended from the courts to a larger audience and became more popular. Principally an ensemble music, it is performed by a group of some eight to twelve musicians performing instrumental (orchestral) and vocal (choral) parts. To a large extent it is composed, with improvisation playing a minor role. The vocal part is based on Andalusian strophic poetry—*muwaššaḥāt*, in correct literary Arabic. The number of modes is limited and those with microtones are less frequent than in Oriental music. The rhythmic modes are shorter; the melodic modes

The Oriental Nawba

The Oriental nawba as described at the Cairo conference consists of eight movements (pieces). The pieces are either instrumental or vocal with instrumental accompaniment, solo or ensemble, rhythmically free or measured. They are centered around a single maqām and ordered in a certain pattern (succession of rhythmic modes), with the most complex modes appearing at the beginning of a suite and the

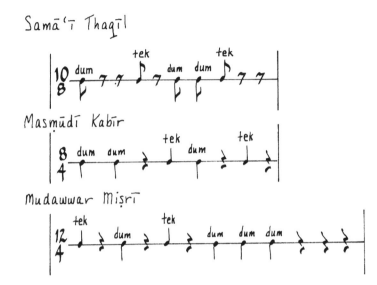

EXAMPLE 14-2. Three of the most common rhythmic modes in the Oriental part of the Arabic world, played on the drum. *Dum* indicates the primary beat, played in the center of the membrane of the drum. *Tek* denotes the secondary beat, played at the edge of the membrane.

are associated with complex mystical and musicotherapeutical concepts and organized in the symbolic *šajara aṭ-ṭubūʾ* ("tree of temperaments" or "tree of modes").

The principal form of artistic music of the classical tradition in the Arabic Near East is *nawba* (also called *waṣla* or *faṣl*). It is a suite of pieces—the movements are organized in a particular order and performed during a single performance. The idea of organizing the pieces into a suite can be traced back as far as the ʿAbbāsid period. At the present time, there are four different kinds of nawba, one belonging to the Oriental tradition and three to the Occidental.

simpler ones toward the end.

The Nawba is performed by the ensemble *takht*, consisting of the following instruments: ʿūd, *qanūn*, Western violin, nāy, duff, and sometimes *darabukka*.

ʿUd, lute (fig. 14-2) is the most widely used instrument in the Near East. It has a large pear-shaped wooden body with three, usually ornamented sound holes, short neck, five courses of double gut or nylon strings and is plucked with an eagle quill or plastic plectrum. It is a prototype of the European lute.

Qanūn (fig. 14-3) is a trapezoidal zither with twenty-four courses of triple gut or nylon strings stretched across the sound box. The sounding board is part wood and part skin. On each course of the strings there is a set of four moveable bridges that can shorten the string, raising the pitch by ¼, ½, and ¾ of a step. It is played with two plectra, one attached to each index finger.

Nāy (fig. 14-4) is a vertical cane flute with seven finger holes.

Duff is a single membrane frame drum with five sets of jingling plates. It is a prototype of the Basque tambourine.

Darabukka (fig. 14-5) is a single membrane goblet-shaped drum made of wood or clay (rarely metal).

The movements of the Oriental nawba are:

1. Taqāsīm (sing. taqsīm), the rhythmically free, improvised, solo instrumental preludes. The principal determinant of the form of taqsīm is maqām. The performer improvises passages in which he realizes structurally important degrees of the mode in a certain order particular to the chosen maqām.

2. *Bašraf*, an instrumental piece based on the relatively long and complex rhythmical mode.

3. *Samāʿī*, a piece of four or five sections. The first three (or four) sections are based on the quintuple rhythm named *samāʿī thaqīl*, and the last section on à ternary rhythm, *dārij samāʿī* or *sanguīn samāʿī*.

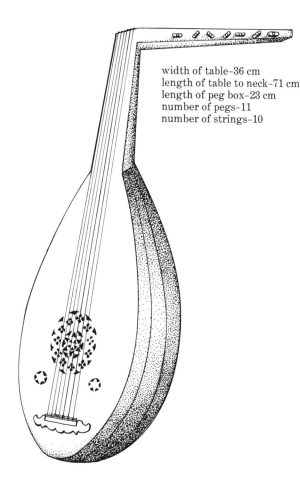

width of table-36 cm
length of table to neck-71 cm
length of peg box-23 cm
number of pegs-11
number of strings-10

FIGURE 14-2. *Ud*

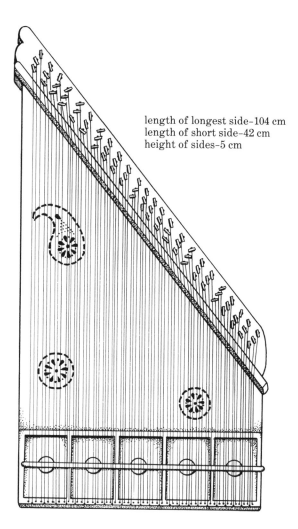

length of longest side-104 cm
length of short side-42 cm
height of sides-5 cm

FIGURE 14-3. *Qanūn*

4. A group of several *tawāsīḥ* (sing. *tawšīḥ*), composed vocal pieces with texts taken from the strophic poems of the same name, a genre developed in Andalusia and known in the entire area of the Arabic Near East. Tawāsīḥ (muwaš-šaḥāt) are sung in unison by the members of the ensemble.

5. Qaṣīda, an improvised solo vocal piece based on two, three, five, or seven verses of the classical Arabic poems of the same name and with the rhythmic scheme determined by the poetic meter of the text (its metric structure). Qaṣīda, a climactic form of the Oriental nawba, terminates the first "classical" section.

6. *Ṭahmīla*, an instrumental piece composed of alternate sections played by ensemble and solo instruments, opens the lighter and more popular part of the nawba. The ensemble sections, a kind of recurring coda, are composed. The solo sections played in turn by participating instrumentalists are to a considerable extent improvised from material in the ensemble coda.

7. Dawr, primarily an Egyptian vocal form based on *zajal*, a genre of popular poetry.

8. *Dārij*, a series of tawāsīḥ in short and fast rhythmic modes.

Since 1932 there have been many changes. Today the entire nawba is rarely heard and not a single recording of it is available in the West. The nawba as a whole has disintegrated, but some of the movements are performed as independent pieces. At private performances, the usual setting for classical music, one hears various pieces formerly belonging to the nawba, together with nonclassical or semiclassical pieces. Generally no modal unity is maintained.

The most important form is taqsīm. It is played on a number of instruments. In addition to the commonly used ʿūd, qanūn, violin, and nāy, one finds in Iraq the santūr, a trapezoidal zither; or in Lebanon the *buzūq*, as well as the *kamanja*, a bowed lute. Often, particularly in Egypt, the taqsīm consists of two sections: the first an improvisation in free rhythm, the second metered and in dance style, accompanied by a rhythmic instrument such as the darabukka or duff. The most frequently played instrumental ensemble pieces are samāʿī, tahmīla, and, to a lesser extent, bašraf.

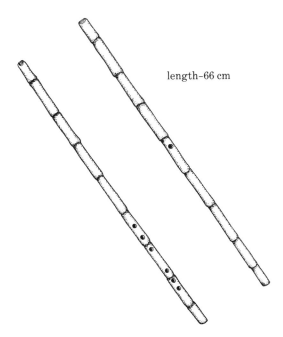

length-66 cm

FIGURE 14-4. *Nāy*

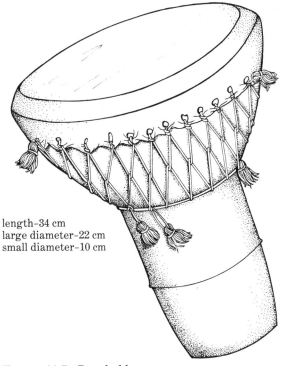

length-34 cm
large diameter-22 cm
small diameter-10 cm

FIGURE 14-5. *Darabukka*

EXAMPLE 14-3. Taqsīm in rāst (after d'Erlanger).

The most important vocal forms are layālī and tawšīḥ. Layālī is a solo improvisation, a kind of vocalise on the text *yā lail ya 'ainī* ("oh night, oh my eyes"), a form that permits the singer to display his or her virtuosity. It is often followed by *mawwāl*, also a solo improvisation on the popular poetic form of the same name. The popularity of the mawwāl is considerable.

The tawšīḥ is a composed piece with a text taken from the poetic genre of the same name. It was developed in Moorish Spain, and is popular throughout the Arabic Near East. Musically the tawāšīḥ from different parts of the Near East can vary considerably, since they depend on the poetic rather than the musical form.

This purely chamber music is usually performed for rather small audiences of selected listeners capable of appreciating the subtleties of the style in an atmosphere of intimate relationship between musician and audience. A beautifully rendered line of poetry, a masterfully improvised phrase, or a skillful modulation will be applauded immediately by the listeners, thus stimulating the performer to an even higher level of artistry.

The Occidental Nawba

The gradual Christian reconquest of Spain resulted in massive migrations of Moslems to North Africa. The earliest such migration (tenth to twelfth centuries) was from Seville to Tunis, a later (twelfth century) migration from Cordoba to Tlemcen (Algeria) and from Valencia to Fez (Morocco), and finally (fifteenth century) the last refugees from Granada settled in Fez and Tetuan (both in modern Morocco). As a result of these migrations three distinct schools of Andalusian music evolved, and today there are three different types of Andalusian nawba—Moroccan, Algerian, and Tunisian.

The immigrants in North Africa found themselves in an environment less favorable to the development of the arts. The original repertory of twenty-four nawbat was gradually forgotten.

The Moroccan Nawba. The Moroccan nawba is a suite of songs—*ṣanāᵓiᶜ* (sing. *ṣanᶜā*)—in a single melodic mode. It consists of five sections, *mīyāzen* (sing. *mizān*), each in one of the five rhythmic modes: *bsīṭ, qāim-u-nuṣf, bṭāīhī, quddām,* and *draj*. Each mizān is preceded by the orchestral introduction *tūšiya*. It follows an established pattern of acceleration that lends an element of variety to an otherwise modally unified structure. The gradual, nearly unnoticeable acceleration is present throughout the entire mizān. It becomes more rapid at two points, *el-qanṭraᵓ l-ūla* ("the first bridge") and *el-*

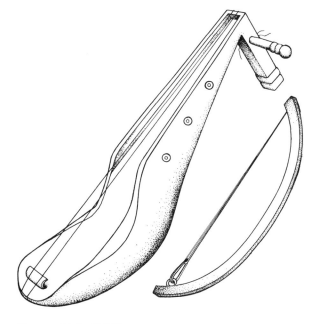

Figure 14-6. *Rebāb*

qanṭraᵓ th-thānia ("the second bridge"), and continues through the following section, *inṣirāf* ("the departure"), consisting of several songs leading to the final fast song, *qfel*, a sort of coda.

The individual nawbāt are associated with the particular times of the day most suitable for their performances. In present-day Morocco only eleven nawbāt are still remembered. Some parts of them, however, are said to be known to only one musician, Sidi Mohammad Ben Omar Jaidi, the royal court musician in Rabat.

The orchestra is usually composed of one rebāb (two-stringed bowed lute, fig. 14-6) played by the leader of the group, one small European violin held on the knee, two or three violas, two ᶜūd, the *tar* ("tambourine"), sometimes also a darabukka, and *ṭbilāt*, a pair of ceramic kettledrums. All members of the orchestra perform the choral part, the instrumentalists following the melodic line. Each part, however, is slightly different according to the idiom and function of the instrument. The result is a complex heterophony or quasi-polyphony.

Presently Andalusian music in Morocco is performed by professional musicians on all kinds of festive family occasions as well as on state occasions in the royal palace. It is customary for more prosperous families to hire an orchestra for wedding and circumcision parties. No entire nawbāt are performed any more. The usual performance, for example, at a party for males during a wedding celebration might consist of tūšiya in one melodic mode followed by several mīyāzen from different nawbāt in various modes, separated by elaborate free rhythm *inšād* performed by a solo singer, *munšid*.

The Algerian Nawba. The Algerian nawba consists of nine movements (after Rouanet):

1. *Ad-Dāᵓira*, a short instrumental or vocal prelude in free rhythm. The chanting is to the syllables *yā lā lan* or *yā leyl*.

2. *Mustakhbar aṣ-Ṣanᶜā*, a free-rhythm instrumental prelude performed in unison by the orchestra.

3. *A-Tūšiya*, instrumental overture in slow, binary rhythm.

4. *Al-Muṣaddarāt* (sing. *muṣaddar*), a suite of muwaššaḥāt in short rhythm.

5. *Al-Batayhiyāt* (sing. *al-Batāyhī*), a suite of muwaššaḥāt similar to muṣaddarāt.

6. *Al-Drajjāt* (sing. *al-Draj*), a suite of muwaššaḥāt in fast ternary rhythm, usually preceded by the instrumental prelude, *kursī*.

7. *Tūšiya al-Inṣirāfāt*, fast instrumental interlude.

8. *Al-Inṣirāfāt*, a suite of fast, light songs in ternary meter.

9. *Al-Makhlaṣ*, a very rapid melismatic vocal piece with muwaššāḥ text in ternary meter.

The Tunisian Nawba. The Tunisian nawba consists of ten movements (after d'Erlanger):

1. *Istiftāḥ*, the free-rhythm instrumental prelude performed in unison by the orchestra. There is only a limited number of these preludes, one in each mode.

2. *Al-Mṣaddar*, a measured instrumental overture played by the orchestra. It is a Tunisian equivalent of Oriental bašraf.

3. *Al-Abyāt* (sing. *al-bayt*), a vocal piece, based on a classical poem. It is the most refined part of the Tunisian nawba, the equivalent of the qaṣīda in the Oriental nawba.

4. *Al-Bṭāyhiyāt*, slow muwaššaḥāt in the meter of the same name.

5. *Al-Tūšiya*, an instrumental piece in quadruple meter.

6. *Al-Mšad*, an interlude by ʿūd and drum.

7. *Al-Barwal*, a muwaššaḥ preceded by an instrumental prelude.

8. *Al-Draj*, also a muwaššaḥ preceded by an instrumental prelude.

9. *Al-Khafīf*, a vocal piece of light character in the rhythmic mode of the same name.

10. *Al-Khatm*, the final vocal piece, fast, with rapid acceleration toward the end.

Since the performance of the Tunisian nawba is rather long and lasts from one and a half to two hours, the abbreviated nawba, *Mḥat*, is often performed.

Traditionally, training of classical musicians was done by rote in a master-student situation. No musical notation was used and improvisation was an important part of the instruction. As a result of twentieth-century westernization a number of music schools have been created in major centers of the Arab world. Some of these schools emphasize training in the classical Near East tradition, teaching both performance and music theory. Other schools offer training in both European as well as Near Eastern music. In both kinds of school, but to a great extent in the second one, a modified Western music notation is used.

The new type of music education has had a profound influence on the development of the music of the area. It produces musicians familiar with both Near Eastern and European musical systems, musicians seeking the synthesis of these two musical traditions through the adaptation to Near Eastern music of some of the elements of European music such as formal structure, harmony, counterpoint, and instrumentation.[6]

Principal Periods and Events in the History of the Arabic Near East from the Beginning of the Moslem Era to the Napoleonic Invasion.

A.D. 622 Beginning of the Moslem Era, Hijra, Establishment of the Islamic state.

A.D. 632 Death of Muhammad.

A.D. 632-661 Orthodox Caliphs.

A.D. 637 Conquest of Persia.

A.D. 661-750 Umayyad Caliphate, Capital in Damascus.

A.D. 711 Conquest of Spain.

A.D. 711-1492 Moslem Rule in Spain.

A.D. 750-1258 ʿAbbāsid Caliphate, Capital in Baghdad.

A.D. 1258 Fall of Baghdad under Mongol Armies.

A.D. 1250-1517 Mamluks in Egypt.

A.D. 1517-1924 Ottoman Empire.

A.D. 1798 Napoleonic Expedition in Egypt.

---

6. Few written musical examples of Near Eastern music have been included here because it is my conviction that even substantially modified Western musical notation inadequately represents the subtleties of Near Eastern intonation, ornaments, and intricacies of rhythm. Rather than presenting a misleading, oversimplified picture of this music, I suggest the reader refer to the original sound recordings.

Glossary

'*Abbāsid*-second dynasty of caliphs, A.D. 750-1258.

aṣābī-finger modes.

awazāt-secondary melodic modes.

bašraf-instrumental form.

biqā'-lament.

buzūq-long-necked plucked lute.

darabukka-goblet-shaped drum.

dhahīr-subtonic, degree of the mode.

duff-tambourine.

dum-primary beat.

Fāṭimide-dynasty in North Africa, A.D. 909-1171.

ghammāz-dominant, central pitch of the climactic point of the melody.

ghinā'-chant.

ḥadīth-tradition.

ḥudā'-caravan song.

inšād-solo vocal section in Moroccan nawba.

īqā'āt (sing. *iqā'a*)-rhythmic modes.

Jāhilīya-"ignorance," term used by the Arabs to refer to the period preceding the advent of Islam.

jins (pl. *ajnās*)-a concept similar to the tetrachord, a fourth divided into three intervals.

jank-harp.

kamanja-bowed lute.

layālī-vocal improvisatory form.

malāhī-forbidden pleasures.

maqām (pl. *maqāmāt*)-melodic mode.

mawwāl-poetic form, also vocal piece based on this form.

mḥat-abbreviated Tunisian nawba.

mizān- (pl. *mīyāzen*)-section of Moroccan nawba.

mughannī-male musicians.

muwaššaḥāt-Andalusian strophic poetry.

Naḥda-political and cultural renaissance of the Arab world.

naqarāt- (sing. *naqara*)-beat.

naṣb-romance.

nauḥ-elegy.

nawba (pl. *nawbāt*)-a suite of pieces (movements) performed during a single performance (also named *waṣla* or *faṣl*).

nāy-reed pipe, also flute.

qaināt-singing girls.

qanūn-trapezoidal plucked zither.

qarār-tonic.

qaṣīda-classical poetic form, also vocal improvisatory piece.

Qur'ān-Koran.

samā'ī-instrumental ensemble piece.

ṣan'ā (pl. *ṣanā'i'*)-songs in Moroccan nawba.

santūr-trapezoidal struck zither.

šudūd-fundamental melodic modes.

ṭabl (pl. *ṭubūl*)-drum.

taḥmīla-instrumental ensemble piece.

takht-ensemble consisting of '*ūd*, *qanūn*, *nāy*, violin, and *darabukka* or duff.

taqsīm-solo instrumental improvisatory piece.

tawšīḥ (pl. *tawāšīḥ*)-Andalusian strophic poetry, also vocal form based on this poetry.

ṭbilāt-a pair of ceramic kettledrums.

tek-secondary beat.

ṭunbūr-long-necked lute.

tūšiya-instrumental prelude.

'*ūd*-lute.

Umayyad-first dynasty of caliphs, A.D. 661-750.

Bibliography

Chottin, Alexis.

    1931. *Corpus de musique marocaine I, Nouba de Ochchâk*. Paris: Au Ménestrel, Hueugel.

    1939. *Tableau de la musique marocaine*. Paris: Paul Geuthner.

D'Erlanger, Rodolphe.

    1930-1959. *La Musique arabe*. Vols. 1-6. Paris: Paul Geuthner.

Farmer, Henry George.

    1929. *A History of Arabian Music to the XIIIth Century*. London: Luzak.

    1930. *Historical Facts for the Arabian Musical influence*. London: Reeves.

    1945. *The Minstrelsy of the Arabian Nights. A Study of the Music and Musicians in the Arabic "Alf Laila was Laila."* Bearsden, Scotland: issued privately.

    1957. "The Music of Islam." *New Oxford History of Music*, I: 421-77. London: Oxford University Press.

Lane, E. W.

    1836-1860. *An Account of the Manners and Customs of the Modern Egyptians*. 2 vols. London: Knight.

Pacholczyk, Jozef M.

    Forthcoming. "The Music of the Arabic Near East." In *Grove's Dictionary of Music and Musicians*, 6th ed. London: Macmillan.

Ribera, Julian.

    1929. *Music in Ancient Arabia and Spain*. Palo Alto: Stanford University Press.

Rouanet, Jules.

    1922-1931. "La musique arabe." *Encyclopédie de*

la musique et du conservatoire . . ., edited by A. Lavignac and L. de la Laurencie, prèmiere partie, V, pp. 2676-2939. Paris: C. Delagrave.

Shiloah, Amnon.
  1963. *Caractéristiques de l'art vocal arabe au moyen-âge*. Tel Aviv: Israel Music Institute.

Touma, Habib Hassan.
  1971. "The *Maqam* Phenomenon: An Improvisation Technique in the Music of the Middle East." *Ethnomusicology* 15 (January), 38-48.

Villoteau, G. A.
  1809-1826. "Description historique, technique, et litéraire des instrumens de musique des orientaux" and "De L'Etat actuel de l'art musical en Egypte." *Description de l'Egypte*. Vols. 10 and 14. Paris: Panckoucke.

Wright, Owen.
  1966. "Ibn al-Munajjim and the Early Arabian Modes." *Galpin Society Journal* 19 (April), 27-48.

Discography

The Andalusian Music of Morocco. Pachart Publishing House, Tucson, Arizona. Recorded in Morocco by Jozef Pacholczyk. Casette Tape.

Arab Music, Vol. 2. Lyrichord LLST 7198. Performed by the staff of the Institute of Arabic Music, Cairo.

Arabian Music: Maqam. Philips 6586 006. UNESCO collection, Musical Sources, edited for the International Music Council by the International Institute for Comparative Music Studies and Documentation, Berlin/Venice. Recorded by H. H. Touma, Baghdad Radio, and Jacques Cloavrec. Notes by H. H. Touma.

Iraq, Ud Classique Arabe par Munir Bashir. OCR 63.

Music for the Classical Oud. Folkways FW 8761. Played by Khamis el-Fino.

Music of Morocco. Library of Congress, Music Division, Recording Laboratory, AFSL63 and L.64.

From the Archive of Folksong, recorded and edited by Paul Bowles. Notes by Paul Bowles. (Andalus chorus [Fez] Record 2, Side B, Band 3.)

Musique Classique Algérienne—Noubas. Pathé PTX 40.908 XPTX 1508. Sung by Dahmane Ben Achour, Nouba Zidane, and Nouba Ghrib.

Nairo no Uta: Songs Along the Nile. Victor TL 70. Documentary report in "Sound of Egypt," compiled and supervised by Fumio Koizumi. Notes by Fumio Koizumi. Vol. 5, "Classical Music of Arab Tradition."

The Living Tradition, Music from the Middle East. Produced by Deben Bhattacharya. ARGO ZRG 532. (Mawwal and Andalusi Muwashshah, Side 1, Band 1.)

Taqsim ana Layali Cairo Tradition. Philips 6586010. UNESCO Collection, Musical Sources.

Tunisia, Vol. 1: The Classical Arab-Andalusian Music of Tunis. Folkways FW 8861. Recorded in Tunisia in 1960 by Wolfgang Laade.

Tunisian Music, UNESCO Collection—A Musical Anthology of the Orient. Bärenreiter Musicaphone, BM L2008. Edited by the International Music Council and the International Institute for Comparative Studies. Recordings and commentaries by Alain Daniélou.

Film

Discovering the Music of the Middle East. BFA. Col. 21 min. Sotirios Chianis, advisor. A Bernard Wilets Film.

  "In this film, the similarities of much of the music of the Middle East and Balkans are traced back to the spread of Mohammedanism. Such instruments as the oud, santur, qanun, cimbalum and dumbek are introduced and played. The concepts of highly ornamented melodic lines and asymmetrical rhythms are demonstrated. Finally, dance is combined with the music." BFA catalog.

15. Classical Iranian Music

Ella Zonis

Iran, country of desert and mountain, rugs and oil, what does it have in the world of music? If you were placed down suddenly in Tehran, the capital, what music would you have heard before the recent revolution? You would have thought you were in a Western city because most of what you immediately saw and heard was Western—a singer accompanied by a Western-style orchestra, a ballet, an opera, even Western symphonies. But if you stayed longer in Persia[1] you would discover five types of Iranian, not Western, music.

First would be folk music, found mostly outside of Tehran. In Iran there are many different tribes and numbers of non-Moslem peoples, each of whom have their own folk music and dances. Next would be Persianized popular music, which is still Iranian, using Iranian scales and language, but Westernized in the choice of instruments and rhythms. The music you hear only in Iran, or mainly here, would be a third group: the *Zur Khaneh* (House of Strength where gymnastics are performed), music heard in the House where the gymnasts perform, and the *nagarah khanah*, Persian tower music. Fourth would be classical music, the subject of this essay, and fifth is the music chanted in the mosques.

Religion is a difficult subject to discuss when dealing with Persian classical music, for Mohammed, the founder of Islam, was against "wine, woman, and song" (Omar Khayam). Actually he was only opposed to the licentiousness of the three and really had little to say about classical music. But strict Mohammedans, following the tradition dating from the seventh century, do not drink, the women wear veils, and there is practically no music among them. The rise and fall of a voice chanting the Koran (the book of prayer) is not considered music.

But the classical Persian music (from the seventh century to the present), *dastgah* (melody type) music, the art music, *is* religious. It is also grave and mournful. Classical music was considered the music of the court and of certain mystic orders (Sufi), to whom art music itself was religious. The music of Iran did not have, however, the patronage of the church which one can trace through the Western history of music. The art music of Iran is truly serious and sad. There are at least three reasons for this: the religion; the desolate mystique of the country, which is mostly desert and mountain; and Iran's history.

HISTORY

Persian history is important to its music for one specific reason: to explain its sadness. Foreign occupations not only influenced the theory and practice of the music itself as well as the musical instruments but also did much to mold the character and the attitudes of the people who create this music. The basic character of the Persian is, like his music, melancholy. The music has its happier moments, but it is not in general gay and unconcerned.

A helpful guide for Persian history is the following outline (Zonis 1973:20). In this table only four dynasties are Persian—those in italics. The rest (notice how long the periods lasted) are foreign.

ANCIENT PERIOD

Achaemenid Empire	6th to 4th c. B.C.
Greek conquest and cultural influence	4th c. B.C. to 2d c. A.D.
Sassanian Empire	3d to 7th c.

---

1. Iran is the true name of the country in Farsi, the national language; Persia is the Greek word. They may be used interchangeably.

MEDIEVAL

Arab conquest and cultural influence	7th-10th c.
Turkish and Mongolian conquests	11th-15th c.

RENAISSANCE

Safavid Kingdom	16th-18th c.

MODERN

Western political and cultural influence	19th c. to present
Pahlavi Empire	1925-1979 (?)

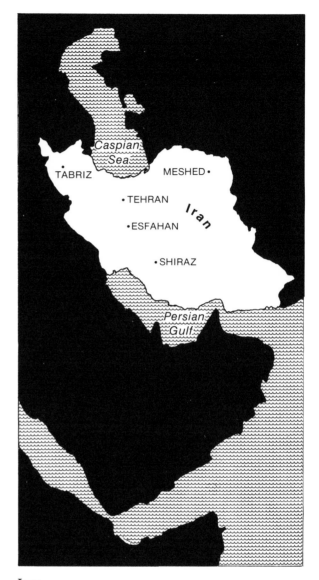

Iran

Of major importance in the history of Persian music is the long political and cultural contact between Persia and ancient Greece, which lasted from the fifth century B.C. well into the third century of the Christian era. The Persian expeditions into Greece were followed by Alexander the Great's decisive conquest of the Achaemenid Empire in 330 B.C., a century of Greek rule in Persia, and four centuries of continued Hellenic influence. During this time it is not unlikely that a significant musical interchange occurred. To the present day, Persian art music, composed by melody types, is still monophonic and organized in tetrachords. Further, Persian music theory is Greek in origin. The treatises of the medieval Islamic theorists were modeled after those of Euclid, Aristoxenos, Ptolemy, and others, which were translated into Arabic at Baghdad during the ninth century.

The earliest descriptions of Persian music appear in the writings of Greek historians, Herodotus and Xenophon among them. For the Sassanid period (A.D. 226-642) there are sources giving the names of musicians and their compositions, and players of instruments are included in the numerous bas-reliefs and engraved metal plates that survive from this artistic time. With the Arab conquest of Persia in the seventh century, there was such a blending of Persian and Arab music, instruments, and terminology that the question of which music more influenced the other is still debated. Many scientific treatises on music appeared as part of the extensive philosophical writings produced at Baghdad, an intellectual capital of the early medieval world. Of the great music theorists, two were Persian: Ibn Sina (Avicenna, 980-

1037), and Safi al-Din (d. 1294). Side by side with great activity in theory, however, was the Islamic disapproval of the practice of music that tended to discourage progress in both Persian and Arab music for at least a millennium.

During the Mongol and Timurid periods (1221-1501) the Persians discarded many aspects of Arab culture, and the musical treatises of Shirazi (d. 1310) and Ghaibi (d. 1435) were written in the Persian language. Although the next dynasty, the Safavid (1501-1736), brought forth a rebirth of Persian culture, the renewed religious fervor occasioned by adoption of the Shiʿa sect of Islam as the state religion again discouraged the practice of music. This antimusical atmosphere lasted until about 1900, when public concerts gradually became sanctioned and musicians were no longer considered socially inferior.

CLASSICAL IRANIAN MUSIC

The Ambience

Iranian classical music has its own very individual performance practice. In the past, and sometimes even now, the musician and his friends gathered in someone's living room or in the corner of the garden where they could play but where the neighbors would not hear. It was a music played only for friends and away from the public. In this setting the musician starts to play. The group also participates; upon verbal suggestions or glances from them, the musician will play in a certain way and develop certain ideas as they come to him. This is the kind of improvisation one finds in the classical art music of Iran, and Iranian music should be improvisatory.

So you are now very far from the Western music you first heard in Tehran. You are in someone's living room and a musician, or several musicians, has just entered. He chooses a dastgah, one of the twelve modes, and begins to play. Whenever the musician does something special, his friends will say something or look at him in a particular way that makes him happy. The player can go on for thirty to forty-five minutes in a single dastgah. Perhaps there may be a singer who will sing verses (*beyt*) from one of the great mystics. Now more musicians join in and a real musical evening takes place. All that was needed was a quiet place and some people.

That was dastgah music in its *traditional* setting. What happens when the performers are asked to play for radio or television, or to play for recordings? Well, the performer is told he has five or ten minutes to play. With that time limit, a player's incentive is partially gone. He has no time to warm up. Surprises do not come to him. And if he is playing for a large audience, or playing before a silent microphone, the subtleties of glances between the player and a small audience are lost. This is what has happened in the last twenty-five years in Iran.

Let us now turn back to an examination of the old classical music.

Theory

Persian music is presently organized into twelve systems called dastgah. Dastgah is a general word meaning apparatus, mechanism, scheme, or framework. Thus there are dastgah for weaving carpets, for conducting government operations, and for making music. When a musician performs, he plays in a certain dastgah for the length of the performance, which may last from five minutes to an hour. The dastgah in classical Persian music are also twelve in number. Transposed to start on C they are:

Mahur, Rast Panjgah	C	D	E	F	G	A	B	C
Shur, Dashti,	C	Dᵖ²	Eb	F	G	Ab	Bb	C
Abu Ata, Nava								
Bayat-e Tork	C	D	E	F	G	A	Bᵖ	C
Afshari	C	D	Eᵖ	F	G	A	Bb	C
Homayun	C	Dᵖ	E	F	G	Ab	Bb	C
Esfahan	C	D	Eb	F	G	Aᵖ	B(ᵖ)	C
*Sehgah*³	C	Dᵖ	Eᵖ	F	Gᵖ	A	Bᵖ	C
Chahargah	C	Dᵛ	E	F	G	Aᵖ	B	C

The dastgah is a collection of smaller units called *gusheh* in Persian and *maqām* in Arabic. A number of gusheh-ha, usually from three to fifteen, comprise a dastgah, the exact number depending on the performer's knowledge of the repertory and the length of time he wishes to play. Within each dastgah are several notes of special importance. One is the note where the dastgah stops, the *ist*. The second is the *shahed*, the note on which the melody centers. Third is the *moteghayer*, to be discussed later.

Diagram 15-1 illustrates the structure of the

---

2. This (ᵖ) is a *koron*, a three-quarter tone or one-quarter tone less than a whole step. There is also a microtone called *sori* (♯). These are not truly quarter tones, but it is easiest to think of them in this way. Thus in Persian music there are three possible divisions in a whole tone—for example, between C and D, in addition to our one, C♯ or D♭, these two: C C♯C♯ or D♭ D♭ D. So the Persian musician will select a scale having seven notes out of seventeen tones instead of twelve. For example, if he is playing Shur, he will select D♭ rather than D♭. This ♪ is a grace note, one note above (half or whole step depending on the context).

3. The tonic of Sehgah is not the lowest note, C, but the third, E♭.

dastgah. The bottom line represents the note that functions as a tonic, the upper line is the upper octave. Each rectangle is a gusheh. An important characteristic of this system is that each gusheh occupies a definite part of the octave. As in Indian music, the performance rises to the upper part of the range and then descends, ending where it began.

The dastgah, as a framework or an apparatus for making music, is relatively easy to understand: it is a collection of gusheh-ha. Each col-

dastgah. This is called *forud*, meaning descent, and it may be played between gusheh-ha, especially if the performance is quite long. (The forud is indicated by dotted lines on the diagram.)

The musician begins to play the *daramad*, the first section of the dastgah. After playing this section of the dastgah for a while (the while can be half an hour!), there is a slight pause in the music, and then something sounds different. The musician has changed gusheh. He has gone from the daramad into something else. This is called

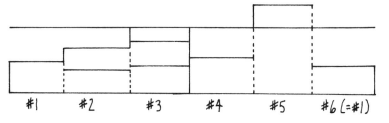

DIAGRAM 15-1. Dastgah as a collection of gusheh-ha.

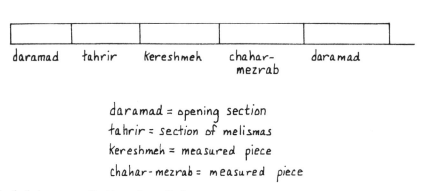

daramad = opening section
tahrir = section of melismas
kereshmeh = measured piece
chahar-mezrab = measured piece

DIAGRAM 15-2. Gusheh-ha as a collection of small pieces.

lection is unified in the following ways: all the gusheh-ha in a dastgah use the same scale degrees (or pitch collection) with, perhaps, the addition of one or two accidentals toward the middle of the performance. A dastgah performance usually begins and ends in the same tetrachord. Furthermore, the gusheh played at the opening is usually played at the end.

Yet another device for unifying a dastgah is a specific cadence pattern characteristic of each

the "maqām principle." The gusheh has, like the dastgah, an ist, usually different from the ist of the daramad, and it has a very different shahed. The gusheh may be further up the tetrachord, using, let us say, the fourth through the eighth notes of the scale. It always *sounds* different, be it in the melody, a rhythmic figure, or just the use of notes that differentiate that gusheh from any other. All gusheh-ha played by Iranian musicians are not the same, however; they are selected by each musician either beforehand or while he is playing.

So the musician has gone to a different gusheh and everyone knows where he has gone, for each gusheh contains a note called the moteghayer, which is not in the parent dastgah. Say, for example, the scale of the dastgah is the same as the Western melodic minor: C, D, E♭ F G A♭ B♭ C. This particular gusheh has A♮ as the moteghayer. So whenever you hear it, and the musician makes sure you do hear it, you know that this note is the moteghayer and you know he has gone to another gusheh. When he leaves this gusheh you will know the difference because you will once again hear A♭, not A♮, the moteghayer of the preceding gusheh.

Each gusheh has a title and tracing it can be fun. Some mean large, *bouzorg*, or small, *kouck-ek*. Some are the names of towns, Zabol and Ravandi; and some are names of people: Homayoun, Leyli, and Majnoun.

The total of all the gushehs in all twelve dastgahs is called the *radif*. There are several people who have notated their own radifs. The government of Iran printed the radif of Moussa Ma'ruffi,[4] which is now used in the National Conservatory, as a guide for learning the radif.

Rhythm
Rhythm in Persian music, unlike Arab and Indian music, is no longer systematized into the rhythmic modes (*iqa'at*) described by medieval Persian theorists. Most traditional art music is, in fact, unmeasured and performed in a free rubato manner. The strongest rhythmic factor in music of the radif comes from poetry, for, like the music of ancient Greece, Persian music is closely allied with poetry. Generally one couplet of classical verse is set to a single gusheh, with long melismatic sections and instrumental rhapsodizing between the various gusheh-ha. Thus the meter of the poetry imparts a kind of recurrent rhythmic structure to the otherwise unmeasured composition.

Although much of the classical music of Per-

sia is in free rhythm, the performer may also play pieces that have a definite beat: the *cha-har-mezrab* (four beats), *kereshmeh* where the rhythm goes , or just a *zar-bi* (measured). The progression to other gushehs can be compared to movements in a symphony, and they are quite like these.

Improvisation
A two-stage model may be constructed as an aid to exploring the process of improvisation. This can be stated as two questions: (1) What is the pattern or schema upon which improvisation is based? (2) How does the player transform this schema into an improvised composition? Our emphasis on defining the schema reminds me of an analogy made by the British musicologist Gerald Abraham, to the effect that "all music needs a framework as roses need a trellis" (1938: 38). Although one does not want to take this analogy too literally, the need for a framework for improvised music is even greater than for the composed music referred to by Abraham. In a music created more or less extemporaneously, where the composer-performer cannot go back and correct what he has just played, one is almost certain to find some kind of schema guiding his performance.

The schema used in Persian music bears no resemblance to the jazz model, for it is neither harmonic nor measured. It does, however, come quite close to an Indian raga. The Persian schema is not one fixed entity but falls along a melodic continuum that extends from an undefined melody, a mode, on one end to a definite melody on the other.

The part of the dastgah that forms the schema for improvisation in Persian music is the gusheh, the Persian version of a melody type. The *Harvard Dictionary* defines *melody types* as "a repertory of traditional melodies, melodic formulae, stereotyped figures, tonal progressions, ornamentations, rhythmic patterns, and so on, that serve as a model for the creation of new melodies" (Apel 1969:519; see May bibliography). This definition reminds me of a pot filled with musical materials that a musician can dip into, taking what he will to create an improvised performance. I prefer to take the mu-

4. The "Big Book," as the Ma'ruffi radif has come to be called, is an enormous collection of pieces in all the twelve dastgah. Musicians today will play from that collection rather than playing their own compositions.

sical materials out of the pot and arrange them along a continuum. On one end of the continuum, the right, the melody type is a schema that is quite definite—a specific melody or a tune. When a musician improvises on this schema, he plays the melody with only slight variations. The basic outline is preserved and is clearly recognized by the listener. The best example of a gusheh or melody type on this end of the continuum is a folk song. A genuine folk song performance is a kind of improvisation. No one person sings it exactly as it came down to him. One of the challenges of folk song research, of course, is to find all the variants of the tune and to try to trace the family relationships.

On the left side of the continuum is the melody type as a mode. Here the melody type is similar to a church mode: a scalar configuration with a preferential order of tones. Between these two poles—gusheh as a definite melody or tune and gusheh as a mode—is a range of possibilities. For example, working up from the pole that is gusheh as mode, the order of whole and half steps in the scale may suggest certain characteristic melodic patterns or motives. For instance, in pieces in the Phrygian mode ⌐(C D♭ E♭ F G A♭ B♭ C) where the interval between scale steps 2 and 1 is a half-step, the use of a descending upper leading tone (indicated by the bracket) is characteristic. Similarly, in the Persian gusheh of Shur when the scalar configuration is close to that of the Phrygian mode, the motive D -C becomes one of the most important characterizing features.[5]

Toward the middle of the continuum, a gusheh becomes more specified. It has a prominent melodic direction and a characteristic melodic contour; it may also have longer recognizable melodic particles, especially cadence formulas and specific rhythmic features. The closer we get to the pole where a melody type is a tune, the more definite and literal is the schema.

Thus the difference between gusheh as mode and gusheh as melody is a difference of degree rather than of kind. A mode, of course, is freer.

5. For a discussion of Persian intervals see Ella Zonis, *Classical Persian Music: An Introduction* (Cambridge, Mass.: Harvard University Press, 1973), pp. 52-8.

That is, a mode has inherent melodic possibilities rather than an inherent melodic shape.

Let us now examine two Persian gusheh-ha. They are from different dastgah and each is the opening section, or daramad. (The daramad is the most important gusheh and gives its name to the entire dastgah.) We will discuss the gusheh-ha of Shur and Chahargah.

Because we are dealing with an oral tradition, there is no single version of either gusheh. If you ask one musician to play Shur he will play one melody, and a second musician will play what initially sounds like a quite different tune. I use here versions belonging to one school of musicians in Iran, what might be called the Establishment School, because it has been widely recognized by the Ministry of Culture and has issued many publications. This is the school reputedly emanating from Mirza Abdullah as transmitted mainly through the Tehranian musicians of the first half of the twentieth century, Maʿruffi, Saba, and Borumand. This school does not represent the entire gusheh tradition in Iran, but merely one of its main branches. Hence one is left with the task of collecting as many versions as possible and distilling the essence of each to find the schema on which it is based.

In comparing the examples given for Chahargah and those for Shur (exs. 15-1 and 15-2), one will note a greater similarity among those of Chahargah. The goals and shapes of Chahargah melodies are the same: a rise from A♭ to C; a quick descent back to A♭; another rise, this time up to E; then a final cadence on C, usually with the third A♭ to C sounded again. There is even some agreement in the rhythmic configuration. This gusheh obviously is farther to the right along the continuum, where the melody is taken more literally than, say, the Indian rāga *riti-guala*.

The first four examples given for Shur, on the other hand, do not show a great agreement. Although the goals of the melody are the same, these goals are reached in different ways and in different times. Shur is thus closer to the concept of gusheh as mode; it is farther left along the continuum.

To grasp the pattern or schema for the gusheh of Chahargah one can, with a high degree of accuracy, simply play one of the melodies and say that *this* is Chahargah. For Shur, however, a single one of the melodies is not definite enough.

sheh melody as a framework for composition, a player improvises new *pieces*.

Carrying the analogy with genetics one step farther, just as genetic characteristics combine

	Shur	*Chahargah*
Pitch collection	(B♭) C D♭ E♭ F	(G) A♭ B C D♭ E F
Range	4th (with attached 2d)	6th (with attached 2d)
Most prominent interval	D♭ –C	A♭ –C
Hierarchy of pitches	7 only as a starting note	5 decorates 6
	1 most important pitch (shahed)	6 essential
	2 essential	7 barely touched
	3 important	1 most important pitch
	4 important	3 important secondary goal
	5 rare	4 barely touched
Predominant motion	descending	ascending
Final cadence pattern	no single pattern	

To discover the schema for Shur, we must find the basic structural characteristics from these examples. I would like to do this, giving, as it were, a recipe for Shur. As a contrast, I shall also give these parameters for Chahargah.

I now can summarize the first question: What is the pattern or schema upon which improvisation is based?

The basic schema for improvisation in classical Persian music is the gusheh. Gusheh-ha exist in various degrees of explicitness along a melodic continuum. At the pole of least definition, a gusheh is simply a collection of pitches with a preferential order and an inherent hierarchy. Moving along the continuum, a gusheh may have a characteristic contour, kind of motion between intervals, range, cadence pattern, kind of ornament, and so on until, at the end of maximum definition, it is a clearly defined melody.

When a writer calls a gusheh simply a melody, or when a native musician plays a melody to describe a gusheh, he means melody in a broader sense than melody as tune. I like to think of the word *melody* as used in *melody type* as a nuclear melody or as the genetic material for the creation of new melodies. Using the gu-

to produce an individual with a definite personality, so do the musical features I have outlined for these two gusheh-ha produce a specific character or personality associated with each. Shur is said to be mystical, noble, and sad; Chahargah, on the other hand, is joyful and vigorous. The concept of mood or ethos associated with each gusheh is found most clearly in the rāga system where each rāga even has its assigned time of day. It is also, of course, a feature of the Western modal system, where the character of each mode was described by theorists well into the sixteenth century.

I now can answer the second question: How does the performer use this schema to create an improvised composition? As I have mentioned, the schema always exists as some kind of melody. The recipe I abstracted for Shur and Chahargah is unknown to the practicing musician. Although modern players are more aware of theoretical considerations, older performers would never play a scale when asked to define a gusheh—they would always play a melody. (This would be like asking a Western musician what major is and getting a melody in reply.) Students learn gusheh-ha not by memorizing the scale and attendant features, but by memorizing melodies. The particular melody one learns may be quite short or it may already contain many of the elaborations of which I spoke. When the student becomes a performer and creates his own version of a gusheh, he alters and expands the melody he learned. He uses several processes. He can simply play what he learned, mak-

ing minor alterations. He can really improvise —this approaches centonization (the joining together of recognizable musical motives). He may also join several smaller pieces until the gusheh reaches major proportions.

Elaborations and extensions on the basic melodic framework of the gusheh are created through the use of three musical processes: ex-

EXAMPLE 15-1. Chahargah.

act and/or varied repetition, ornamentation, and centonization. We can see this by pointing to one of the short melodies of Shur as given in example 15-1, Vaziri, with an elaborated version in example 15-2, Borumand. Note first that the basic contours of the melody are preserved, or what can be described as the threefold structure: the stress on note C, the descents from the third and the fourth, E and F, and again emphasis on C. The techniques of repetition and ornamentation are also illustrated in this example (Zonis 1973:104–25).

The process of creating a composition through improvisation in Persian music also works on another level. This is the combining of a number of short pieces to create a longer section. The diagram for the gusheh (diagram 15-2) is similar to that for the dastgah (diagram 15-1). The number of pieces is also flexible, but they are usually in two styles, measured and unmeasured. The *un*measured style, called *avaz* in

Persian, is the more traditional, whereas the measured style, zarbi, is prevalent in newer music, perhaps reflecting the influence of Western music, or the current trend in Iran from improvised to composed music. In example 15-2, the Borumand illustrates the unmeasured style; the characteristic measured piece kereshmeh has a rhythmic pattern that always contains a hemiola.

To summarize the answer to the second question: The player uses the schema to create an improvised composition. First, he extends the nuclear melody by means of repetition, ornamentation, and centonization, thus creating a small piece. Next he plays a number of pieces, one after the other, until he feels that he has exhausted either his time or the melodic material of the gusheh.

An improvised composition in Persian music is not created during a single performance. Rather, it is built up over time. The work of a

EXAMPLE 15-2. Shur.

composer-performer is constantly changing. As he matures, gains added competence on his instrument, and especially as he hears other musicians, he changes his own performance. In classical Persian music, the feelings of the player and those of his audience are important determinants of what he plays, how long he plays, and how he plays.

An important stipulation for this kind of composition, however, is that the schema and its elaborations not be written down. Hence the melody is extended and varied in a less conscious, more intuitive, manner than in the kind of composition in which the process is controlled to a greater degree by notation. At the actual time of performance, the musician does not calculate the procedures that will guide his playing. Rather, he plays from a level of consciousness somewhat removed from the purely rational. Sometimes he may achieve a trancelike state,

Example 15-2. (continued)

FIGURE 15-1. The sehtar.

for a singer perhaps induced by the words, for an instrumentalist from the emotional connotations of the gusheh. Under these conditions, the player performs intuitively, where the dictates of the schema and of traditional procedures for improvising are integrated with his immediate mood and emotional needs.

INSTRUMENTS

Although Western instruments are widely used in Persia, some native instruments are favored for performances of classical music. The most popular plucked stringed instruments are the *sehtar* (fig. 15-1), a long-necked three-stringed lute with a pear-shaped wooden body, and its larger counterpart, the *tar* (fig. 15-2), which has a double belly, covered with a sheepskin membrane. The Persian dulcimer, the *santūr* (Arabic *santir*) (fig. 15-3), is also promi-

FIGURE 15-2. The tar.

nent. These three native instruments are comparable to the lute (*'ud*) and psaltery (*qanun*), the native instruments most often played today in Arab countries but used only rarely in Iran. The Persian *nay*, flute (fig. 15-4), and *kamanchay*, a spike fiddle held on the player's knee (fig. 15-5), still used in the provinces, have been replaced by their Western counterparts in the cities. The Persian drum is the *zarb* or *tombak* (fig. 15-6), held on the player's knee and struck with the palms and fingers of both hands.

CLASSICAL PERSIAN MUSIC TODAY

The issue facing those concerned with the future of classical Persian music is a vital one —how to keep it alive. In developing nations where the indigenous arts are often abandoned or changed radically during the process of westernization, music is particularly susceptible.

The popularity of Western music in Iran had two effects. First, it appeared that the better talents among Iranian composers and performers were attracted to Western music rather than to traditional Persian music. Western music seemed richer in possibilities—harmony, counterpoint, orchestration, the greater number of styles. Moreover, in a sociological sense, Western music seemed to offer a more direct road to fame and fortune. Second, Iranian composers often grafted features of Western music onto Persian music. The results in this area have not been successful.

But it was not only the attraction of Western music that threatened the existence of classical Persian music. A more important danger

FIGURE 15-3. The santūr.

FIGURE 15-4. The nāy.

existing within Persian music itself is the questionable relevance of this older music to Persian society in the second half of the twentieth century. Even those who are deeply attached and committed to classical Persian music must admit that this music is highly refined and limited in scope and appeal. Traditional Persian music is lyric, not dramatic; it is highly emotional, not intellectual; it is essentially decorative, graceful, soft, romantic; almost never harsh, forceful, loud, or dissonant. Classical Persian music is abstract; it is serious, sad, and mystical, much more often sacred than secular.

Added to these limitations in its character are limitations of a strictly musical nature such as the lack of measured rhythm, harmony, and counterpoint. Furthermore, the role of the artist in Persian music is to enrich or embellish the existing melody, to work on conventional material within an established framework—not to create his own material. To many musicians this compositional technique and its dependence upon tradition are too limiting. Finally, Persian music, like miniature painting, values the smallest detail; the tiny ornament, the small gradations of pitch and tone are crucial. This music does not work with the large blocks of sound (or noise) now in fashion among composers.

Classical Persian music is, however, being studied today in a special high school in Tehran and in Tehran University. In 1973 Persian performers were heard in the United States and Europe, and classical Persian music is now being taught in a dozen colleges across the United States. Perhaps this music *will* be kept alive.

FIGURE 15-5. The kamanchay.

FIGURE 15-6. The zarb (tombak).

Glossary

Abu Ata-one of the 12 melody types or modes, also one of the 5 secondary modes = C D♭ E♭ F G A♭ B♭ C; related to Shur.

Afshari-another one of the 12 modes, also one of the 5 secondary systems = C D E♭ F G A ( ) B♭ C; also related to Shur, but is most independent of its parent mode. (Among the Iranists, what, if anything, goes at the A is undecided.)

avaz-general term to indicate an unmeasured piece: classical poetry being used.

Bayat-e Tork-another secondary system from the total of 12 modes = C D E F G A B C.

beyt-a couplet in classical Persian poetry; each line of the pair ends with the same rhyme.

Chahargah-one of the 7 main modes of contemporary Persian music = C D E F G A B C; made up of 2 identical tetrachords.

chahar mezrab-meaning "four beats." One of the several measured virtuoso pieces, characterized by a rapid tempo, a recurring ostinato, and a pedal tone. It refers to a style of playing and not a form.

daramad-prelude to a performance of a piece of music in any of the modes.

dastgah (pl. dastgah-ha)-melody type or mode. There are 5 auxiliary ones and 7 main ones, altogether making 12. A musical scheme which composer-performers use as a basis for improvisation; has its own scale, hierarchy of scale degrees, and repertory of traditional melodies.

Dashti-one of the 5 subsidiary modes or melody types related to Shur, one of the 7 main ones: C D E F G A B♭ C. Often found in folk music of Persia.

Esfahan-one of the 5 subsidiary modes related to *Homayun*, one of the seven main ones = C D E♭ F G A♭ B C, a harmonic minor scale with the 6th raised a quarter tone.

forud-meaning "descent," a short melody frequently played at the conclusion of a melodic formula to connect it to a parent mode and reinforce the tonic.

gusheh (pl. gusheh-ha)-melodic formula used when a performer improvises. These short pieces have the range of a tetrachord or a pentachord. The gusheh is a melodic type, a traditional repertory of melodies, melodic formulae, tonal progressions, ornamentations, and rhythmic patterns that serve as a model for the creation of new melodies.

Homayun-name of another of the main modes or melody types = C D♭ E F G A♭ B♭ C.

iga⁢at-rhythmic mode; there are eight.

ist-the note of stopping, one of the important notes in a mode.

kamanchay-spiked fiddle (bowed). Has four strings, no frets, and is about the size of a viola. It is played resting upright on player's lap.

kereshmeh-an important measured piece found in many modes or melody types; always a strong hemiola effect throughout. Uses rhythmic pattern.

koron (♭)-indicates a microtone (quarter tone) below a note.

Mahur-one of the seven main modes or melody types = C D E F G A B C. Is distinct from the others in its happy ethos. One of the more popular modes today. Dominant and supertonic are important scale degrees.

maqam-an Arabian musical system or mode.

moteghayer-"changeable"; comparable to an accidental in Western music, a note outside of the scale or mode.

Nava-one of the seven principal modes or melody types related to Shur = C D E♭ F G A♭ B♭ C. One of the less popular and least performed modes.

nay-Persian vertical flute; simplest and oldest instrument here. Made of cane with metal mouthpiece; six finger holes in front and one at the back. Has two different mouth positions. Important folk instrument.

radif-entire collection of melodies in all the 12 modes or melody types.

Rast Pangjah-"fifth place"—similar to Western major scale; one of the seven main modes or melody types = C D E F G A B C.

santur-trapezoidal, struck dulcimer, popular in Iran. Has seventy-two strings arranged in groups of four. Strings are strung from left to right. Today it is tuned so that there is only one group of strings for each of the seven notes of the octave.

Sehgah-one of the seven main modes or melody types = C D♭ E♭ F G♭ A♭ B♭ C.

sehtar (setar)-long-necked, four-stringed lute with pear-shaped wooden body. Has frets like the *tar*—no plectrum is used. Used as solo instrument.

shahed-the note of stress or emphasis in the hierarchy of notes found in a melodic formula used in improvisations.

Shur-one of the seven main modes or melody types = C D♭ E♭ F G A♭ B♭ C. It has the greatest number of melodic formulas (gusheh-ha). Considered a parent mode to four subsidiary ones.

sori(♯)-indicates that a note is a microtone interval above the lower tone.

tahrir-vocal trill (ornamentation in songs).

tar-another plucked, long-necked lute with double

belly, covered with sheepskin membrane. It has six strings, tuned in pairs, and twenty-six movable gut frets. Used as solo instrument and to accompany singers.

tasnif-a measured, composed song or ballad, the most popular form in Persian cities today. Poetry for each type of singing is different—occasionally quotes single lines from classics but uses contemporary poetry or topical subjects.

tekke-ha-pieces with individual names and a special style, usually having strict metric regularity. May be in any of the twelve modes as they have no modal identity.

zarb (tombak)-a goblet-shaped drum carved of a single block of wood, open at the lower end.

Bibliography

Abraham, Gerald.
 1938. *A Hundred Years of Music*. London: Duckworth.
Barkechli, Mehdi.
 1960. "La musique iranniene." In *L'Histoire de la musique*, edited by Roland Manuel. *Encyclopédie de la pléiade*, 9, 1. Paris.
Caron, Nelly, and Dariouche Safvate.
 1966. *Iran, les traditions musicales*. Collection de l'Institut International d'Etudes Comparatives de la Musique publiée sous le patronage du Conseil International de la Musique. Paris: Buchet/Chastel.
Farhat, Hormoz.
 1965. "The Dastgah Concept in Persian Music." Ph.D. dissertation, University of California, Los Angeles. University Microfilms, Ann Arbor, Michigan, 1966.
Gerson-Kiwi, Edith.
 1963. *The Persian Doctrine of Dastga-Composition*. Tel-Aviv: Israel Music Institute.
Khatchi, Khatchi.
 1962. *Der Dastgah*. Regensbury: Bosse.
Nettl, Bruno.
 1970. "Attitudes toward Persian Music in Tehran." *Musical Quarterly* 56 (April), 183-97.
 1974. "Aspects of Form of the Instrumental Āvāz." *Ethnomusicology* 18 (September), 405-14.
 1975. "The Role of Music in Culture: Iran, A Recently Developed Nation." In *Contemporary Music and Music Cultures*, by Charles Hamm, Bruno Nettl, and Ronald Byrnside, pp. 71-100. Englewood Cliffs, N.J.: Prentice-Hall.
Porte, Jacques.
 1968. "Musique musulmane." *Encyclopédie des musiques sacrées* 1:387-466.
Spector, Johanna.
 1967. "Musical Tradition and Innovation." In *Central Asia: A Century of Russian Rule*, edited by Edward Allworth, pp. 434-84. New York: Columbia University Press.
Tsuge, Gen'ichi.
 1970. "Rhythmic Aspects of the Âvâz in Persian Music." *Ethnomusicology* 14 (May), 205-27.
Wilkens, Eckart.
 1967. *Künstler und Amateure im persischen Santurspiel*. Studien zum Gestaltungsvermögen in der iranischen Musik. Regensburg: Bosse.
Zonis, Ella.
 1973. *Classical Persian Music*. Cambridge, Mass.: Harvard University Press.

Discography

Classical Music of Iran, Dastgah Systems. Folkways FW 8831, 8832. Compiled and edited by Ella Zonis.
Folk Songs and Dances of Iran. Folkways FW 8858. Notes written by Anthony Byan Shay.
Kurdish Folk Music from Western Iran. Ethnic Folkways Library FE 4103. Recorded by Dieter and Nerthus Christensen, notes by Dieter Christensen, edited by Frank Gillis.
The Middle East: Modes and Melodies of the Middle East. Lloyd Miller, East-West Records EWI.
Music for the Classical Oud. Folkways FW 8761.
Music of Iran: Santur Recital. Nasser Rastegar-Najad. 3 vols. Lyrichord LL 135, 165, 166, LLST 7135, 7165, 7166.
Music of Iran, the Tar. Lyrichord LL 201, LLST 7201. Bijan Samandar.
Music of the Russian Middle East. Ethnic Folkways Library FE 4416. Notes by Henry Cowell.
A Musical Anthology of the Orient: Iran I and II. Bärenreiter-Musicaphon, UNESCO Collection, BM 30 L 2004, 2005. Recordings and commentaries by Alain Daniélou.
Near and Far East. Lloyd Miller, East-West Records.
Santur, Tunbuk, and Tar: Music and Drum Rhythms from Iran. Limelight Stereo, LS 86057. Edited by Deben Bhattacharya.

16. On Jewish Music

Abraham A. Schwadron

At the time of this writing Jewish history has been marked by 5740 years of continuous heritage, identification, and development. From common roots in the Tigris-Euphrates valley of the ancient Near East, the Hebrew people are to be found today in North America, Central and South America, Europe, Asia, Australia, New Zealand, and Africa—settled in almost one hundred different countries in populations ranging from several hundred in the Philippine Islands to millions in the United States.

Given such global and cultural diffusion, it might well be asked whether, and on what grounds, one can properly conceive of Jewish music. Indeed, considering that the study of music in the lives of Hebrew (Jewish) people is encumbered by the complexities of ethnic, religious, social, cultural, and national determinants—an intricate web of enculturation and acculturation—the question has merit. What makes music "Jewish"? The musical materials? The Jewishness of the composer? The connotative or denotative contextual message? Is there a locus of agreement on all these questions for those who would inquire?

Difficulties of differentiation aside, the results of recent scholarly research—notably during this century in the studies of Idelsohn, Gerson-Kiwi, Gradenwitz, Rosowsky, Sendrey, Werner, and Yasser—are indicative not only of a conceptual validity but also of a growing fund of diverse and convincing musical information and materials. The collective significance of the research emerges in two important ways. First, it is representative of music identified with and performed by Jews in a variety of geographical areas. Second, it functions as a critical focal point for comparative analysis in the search for substantive reliability, particularly in relating one culture group with another and in analyzing and synthesizing that which is with that which was (or may have been).

In approaching answers to the questions raised, it should be helpful to consider some ideas intrinsic to two key terms. The first term, which serves both the layman and the scholar in understanding the Jew and his music, is—as Tevye in *Fiddler on the Roof* so vividly puts it—*tradition.* The term requires an empathic view of Jewish history, ideals, beliefs, aspirations, and achievements, as well as of confrontation, exile, and martyrdom. Jews have had to bow to superior strength for almost 2,000 years, but have managed to survive and still maintain their individuality. Such individuality is threefold: (1) it is reflective, ritually and spiritually bound to the biblical past; (2) it is adaptive to the particular culture in which the Jew finds himself; and (3) it is unifying, in that the Jew, regardless of his cultural domicile, identifies certain commonalities with Jewish brethren worldwide.

There is no completely satisfactory answer to the problem of what is a Jew, in an anthropological sense. Attempts to point up racial, national, ethnic, cultural, ethical, moral, and/or religious characteristics in systematic fashion have been attempted, but all these fall short of that complex whole in which particulars function to defy sweeping generalizations.

The problem invites this question: What is shared by the Falasha (Jews of Ethiopia), Sephardim (Spanish-Portuguese Jews), Yemenites (Jews of Yemen in Arabia), the Jews of Cochin, India, the polyethnic admixture of Jews in modern Israel, the black-American Jews, and the Orthodox, Conservative, and Reform postures that characterize contemporary world Jewry? On the strength of both objective and subjective evidence we are drawn to the hypothesis that commonalities shared are primarily the biblical heritage; and secondarily (on the weight of this and historical circumstance) the spiritual-humanistic affiliation of one Jew with another regardless of national origin. The Torah (the Pentateuch or Five Books of Moses), the Haftorah (Prophets), the talmudic sources, commentaries and codes (*Mishna, Gemara, Midrash, Shulchan Aruch, Pirke Avoth*), and the host of *Ketubim* (holy writings, to include the Psalms, Proverbs, etc.) serve collectively as a powerful fulcrum for the cultural cohesion (and philosophical disputation) of Jewish thought and expression—on ethics and aesthetics, on permanence and change, on the sacred and the profane, on ritual and festival, and on abstract monotheism.[1] There is substance to the statement that the Jews are a "people of books."

Tradition suggests, in retrospect, common Semitic-Oriental origins, a basically common set of sacred beliefs, history, books, and language and a sense of common destiny. Hebrew remains the traditional sacred language and is the common spoken tongue in Israel today.

Conversely, we must also consider those particulars that qualify (and sometimes defy) tradition and point up variety within unity. For example, aside from the many traditional laws governing the selection, preparation, and consumption of food, one is hard put to specify "universals" about Jewish cooking. This is at best a synthesis of cuisine reflecting the many countries to which Jews have wandered. (There are exceptions, such as the use of matzoh—unleavened bread—used in the course of the *Pesach Seder*, the Passover domestic ceremony recalling the exodus from Egypt. Matzoh is ritually traditional to this festival and common to Jews everywhere, as is the ritual observance of the occasion.) Beyond the diversity of culinary

tastes (albeit governed by religious restrictions) other differences—in vernacular language, Hebrew pronunciation, liturgical and ritualistic custom, in folk as well as in synagogue music—are notable. Notwithstanding the complex of cultural factors characterizing the Jew globally, there are shared roots in basic historical and religious traditions.

The second key term that appears necessary in understanding the Jew and his music is a very sensitive one—*compromise*. The term implies both the need for adaptation and the desire to maintain individuality under assimilated and often adverse conditions. Further, the term remains as timely for the modern Jew as it was for his biblical ancestors.

The ability of the Jew to survive and thrive in the face of the vicissitudes of apostasy, profanity, the medieval Crusades, the German-Polish-Russian pogroms, the Spanish Inquisition, and the Nazi holocaust, on the one hand, and his constant struggle between rationalism and mysticism,[2] on the other, points up the significance, however controversial, of compromise. The exiled Babylonian psalmist who, under the yoke of Nebuchadnezzar, poignantly upheld the religious tenet of the ethical loftiness of temple music during the glorious days of David and Solomon, proclaimed it well: "How shall we sing the Lord's song in a foreign land?"

There are no firm geographical boundaries to which the ethnomusicologist can confine himself for any universal conclusions about Jewish music. Rather, its dynamics and diversities suggest that geographical limitations must be transcended by broader, comparative attitudes and methods of inquiry rooted in Jewish consciousness—a matter of both tradition and compromise. Although Idelsohn's massive study and compilation of Hebrew-Oriental melodies (Near and Middle East, 1914 to 1932) constitute a prime musicological contribution, they remain incomplete. The music of the Jews in Peru, in Australia, in Japan, in Burma, in Kenya awaits

---

1. The central doctrine of Judaic monotheism is expressed in the ancient prayer: *Shema Yisroel Adonoi Elohenu Adonoi Echod* (Hear, O Israel, the Lord thy God, the Lord is One).

2. During the *Haskalah* (Enlightenment) movement, late nineteenth to the early twentieth century, modern secular thought on art, philosophy, and science posed bold challenges against traditional Jewish views.

further comparative research, for which studies like those of Lachmann (1940) on the Jews of Djerba, Katz (1972, 1975) on the Judeo-Spanish ballad, and Spector (1973) on the Cochin Jews are exemplary.

Compromise and tradition involve a cross-current of influences from which adaptation and selection merge into that which the Jew himself would consider Jewish music. The process is often complicated by factors of assimilation, parochialism, subjective preference, and Jewish "awareness." To unravel this web some understanding of the history of Jewish music is necessary. Unfortunately, space limitations permit only a cursory, capsule view here; but the bibliography and discography following this essay include works that cover the subject more thoroughly.

Probably the most important musical contribution of the ancient Hebrews was the elevation of the status of liturgical music in union with ritual ceremonies. What is known of music in the Temple of Solomon and in the second Temple (rebuilt, after the Babylonian exile, under the benevolent reign of Darius, King of Persia, c. 516 B.C.E.) is indicative of a high degree of musico-liturgical organization. From descriptive accounts of Solomon's Temple, for example, we learn that 24 choral groups consisting of 288 musicians were utilized in some 21 weekly services. The lack of any precise provision in Mosaic Law for music and the biblical dictum forbidding "graven images" inhibited precise written accounts and illustrations. Since actual sounds are not available and musical notation was nonexistent, we are obliged to speculate, albeit confidently, from secondary literary sources as to the aural splendor of the sound in context.

We know of the instruments used: the lyre (*kinnor, azor*), the silver trumpets (*hatsot-serot*), the harp (*nebel*), the woodwinds (*halib, abug, ugab*), the hand drums (*tof*), the metal cymbals (*meziltayim* or *zelzelim*), the shaking instruments of metal frame, rods, and attached loose rings (*shalishim* and *menaanim*), the small golden bells worn on the high priest's garment (*paamonim*), and the ram's horn (shofar) (see fig. 16-1). All these cannot be successfully separated from various environmental influences—Phoenician, Egyptian, Assyrian, and Greek—either in terms of instrumental construction or sound production. It would be accurate to state that however compromised by selective borrowing, it is in the particular uses of music—sacred and secular, ethical and aesthetical—that ancient Jewish music made a unique contribution. To this point, Sendrey and Norton (1964:227) observe that "to an almost unparalleled degree the Hebrews throughout history had been quick to accept from other cultures whatever features were compatible with their own religious institutions."

The music of ancient Israel represents almost fourteen centuries of change, roughly from 1300 B.C.E. to C.E. 70,[3] the date of Titus's siege of Jerusalem, the destruction of the second Temple, the collapse of the Hebrew nation, and the beginning of a large geographical dispersal of the Jews. Later, with the establishment of the Holy Roman Empire (eighth century) under Charlemagne, Jews had migrated en masse to Spain, Italy, the Rhineland, and to many other areas. The Diaspora (dispersion or exile, the Hebrew equivalent is *galut*) motivated necessary compromise within the bosom of tradition: the synagogue replaced the destroyed Temple; new orders of liturgical service, prayers, and rabbinical writings were prepared; and, in national mourning for not only the loss of the Temple but also freedom, instrumental music—sacred and secular—was banned and consequently lost. Only the shofar remains today; it is held in the Jewish subconscious in symbolic messianic significance. In the vocal tradition, remnants of the biblical cantillations still prevail—a subject of musicological speculation because of the pitfalls of aural tradition and acculturation. Only gradually, undoubtedly in response to felt aesthetic and sociocultural needs, were restrictions on instrumental music lifted, as for joyous occasions like weddings. To this time, however, the censorship of instrumental mu-

---

3. According to Jewish history, this time span would bridge the period before the exodus to the first century of the "common era" (C.E.). (Religious precepts prevent the acceptance of the implication of anno Domini [A.D.].) In the Jewish calendar the decline of Jewish national life (and music) is marked by the destruction of the Temple at Jerusalem in the month of *Ab*, 3830 (A.D. 70).

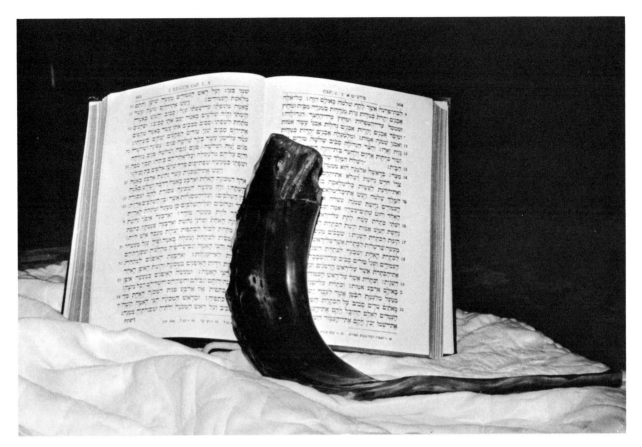

FIGURE 16-1. Shofar. (Courtesy Temple Beth-El, Providence, Rhode Island. Photograph by Terry Schwadron, Providence Journal-Bulletin.)

sic (aside from the selective use of the shofar) is maintained in Orthodox worship. The intensity of this general mourning is expressed in the final hopeful (and now paradoxical) phrase of the *Hagadah* (the domestic reading at Passover); *L'shonoh habah b'Yerushalayim* (Next year in Jerusalem).

Although the Diaspora should be viewed properly from a global point of view, it has been studied from two broad classifications—Oriental/Middle East and Occidental. The inbred resistance to change of the people of the Oriental Diaspora provides singular paths of research into what may be close to the authentic music of the traditional past. The music of the Yemenite Jews, for example, who have lived in comparative isolation since the destruction of Solomon's Temple, is considered highly representative of ancient practices. The Middle East continues to

be, therefore, a lucrative area for the studies of Jewish musical antiquity.

The developmental history of Occidental Jews, in contrast, is a drama of adaptation, assimilation (or near-assimilation), and survival in which the Jew was obliged to thrust his desire to maintain cultural identity against the mainstream of Western thought and change. In general, European Jews have been classified either as Sephardim or Ashkenazim.

The Sephardic (Spanish-Portuguese) Jews were those who settled on the Iberian Peninsula. Their history from the fourth century A.D., replete with periods of peaceful coexistence, religious persecution and exile, climaxed in 1492 during the Spanish Inquisition with the expulsion of some 300,000 people who refused conversion to Christianity. (Of interest here are the *Marranos*—crypto-Jews—who were baptized, but practiced Judaism secretly. They too suffered the fate of identification under the Inquisition.) Refugees fled to Palestine, Egypt, Syria, North Africa, the Balkans, to other countries in western Europe and, eventually, to the New World.

The Ashkenazic (Hebrew for "German") Jews colonized in central and eastern Europe as well as in Greece and Turkey. After the Crusades an orgy of religious persecution drove German Jews eastward. By the fifteenth century large numbers had settled in Poland and Russia.

Although Hebrew remained the common liturgical language, folk languages other than the particular national tongue developed. For example, *Malayali* evolved among the Cochin Jews; *Ladino* (an old Castilian dialect mixed with Hebrew) was employed by the Sephardim; *Yiddish* ("Jewish"), by the Ashkenazim. The last of these can be traced to fragmented German, Flemish, and Netherlandish dialects of the Middle Ages, but as a functional Jewish language of communication its German-Slavic-Hebrew derivation (c. seventeenth century) is most characteristic. Malayali, Ladino, Yiddish, and the others, are intrinsically related to the musics of these respective subcultures.[4]

The development of Jewish music can be considered in terms of various movements, which are listed below with concomitant events in the sociocultural history of European Jewry.

1. The *piyutim* movement—climaxing in the Spanish-Arabic school, tenth to twelfth centuries. Piyutim are poetic, religious prayers, of which the earliest forms remain anonymous. From the eleventh through the fifteenth century melodic settings, particularly for the Sabbath (see ex. 16-2) and High Holy Days, were developed in both Sephardic and Ashkenazic traditions by *paytanim*, composers who were themselves professional precentors.

2. The *chazzanic* movement—extending from the Middle Ages through the nineteenth century in Europe. The *chazzanim* (cantors) were professional precentors whose improvisations on the piyutim merged with the traditional cantillations and resulted in freely created cantorial melodies (*chazzanut*). The movement rose to brilliant artistic heights, stylistically characterized by improvised song, coloratura and ornately embellished passages, and vocal gymnastics. Schools of admiring followers soon formed.

An influential compromise in bridging tradition and the prevailing Western styles was brought about by the Viennese cantor, Salomon Sulzer (1835-1876). In effect, he is considered responsible for the foundations of modern synagogue music. Further, he restored the position of cantorate from that of itinerant Jewish "minstrel" to that of a trained, organized office, musically and spiritually.

3. The Renaissance movement—during which certain Jews, under restrictive conditions, entered musical life outside the confines of the ghetto. In Mantua, during the late sixteenth and early seventeenth century, some Jewish musicians not only participated in the mainstream of European music, but also attempted reforms in synagogue music, such as the introduction of choirs and harmony. Most notable among these musicians was Salomone Rossi, a talented composer, singer, and violinist favored at the royal court. Although some of his music was published and sung in some Italian synagogues, it was short-lived.[5] Among Conservative and Reform Jews today there has been a renewed interest in the modern transcription, publication, and performance of Rossi's music in both liturgical and nonliturgical contexts.

4. The *chassidic* movement—from developments in the early eighteenth century. The *chassidim* constituted a pietist sect originating in the Pale (an area in Poland-Russia), for whom music was a prime means of ecstatic divine

---

4. Any gap between eastern Ashkenazim and those who remained in Germany was broadened not only by the latter's "worldliness" but also by the fact that the German Jew considered Yiddish a guttural jargon, not worthy of serious attention or association with the Jew of "high bearing." The point here is simply that the folk language—Yiddish (from the German *Jüdisch*, "Jewish")—is not, as some may assume, universal among Jews, Occidental or Oriental.

5. With the capture of Mantua by the Austrians in 1630, close to 2,000 Jews were expelled. Those who remained regressed to extreme traditional postures. (See the facsimile of Rossi's music reproduced in Idelsohn's *Jewish Music in Its Historical Development* [1967], p. 200, for an interesting observation: the music in typical Renaissance notation runs left to right while the Hebrew text—a mourner's prayer—is printed right to left letterwise, but left to right wordwise. Musically, the Italian Renaissance secular style prevails.)

communication. A singular characteristic of chassidic song (*nigun*) is an intentional lack of text, a factor that heightens the aesthetic quality of pure vocalization by means of a reiterated neutral and itself meaningless syllable. The songs and spontaneous dances suggest the mystical and cabalistic search of man's spiritual-physical yearning for closeness to his God. The music, varying stylistically from modes of free recitative to those of marked rhythmic vitality, bears resemblance to both synagogue and secular melodies. The latter were "compromised" from Oriental predilections in Slavic and Ukranian folk song, dances, and marches (see ex. 16-8).

5. The Reform movement—following the French Revolution. Nurtured by German-Jewish progressivists and neo-humanists, traditional Judaism was charged with the need for change. Proponents of the Reform movement sought to introduce the vernacular (German), to remodel the worship service and religious education, and to discard what remained of Semitic-Oriental song.

The first Reform Temple in Europe, in which the ritual and the music (including the use of an organ) were rearranged, was established in Seesen, Westphalia, in 1810. Idelsohn describes the scope of the change:

> He [Israel Jacobson (1768-1828), an advocate of reform] provided the Temple with a bell which, according to Christian custom, should announce the time of prayer. Jacobson's program for the service was this: Alongside of the Hebrew texts of the prayers, which at the beginning he did not touch, he introduced German hymns to the tunes of Christian chorales. He abolished the chanting of the Pentateuch and Prophets according to the traditional modes, and together with these he discarded the *chazzan*. He himself read the service without any chant, according to the manner of reading the Bible text and prayers in the Protestant Church. He brought to the Temple the gown of the Church. He also introduced the confirmation of boys and girls (1811). [1967:235-36][6]

Such ultrareform motivated other modifications toward moderate-reform. Conservatives,

6. A musical facsimile of the German choral melody with Hebrew text (both music *and* words running right to left) from Jacobson's Hymnal is included by Idelsohn on p. 237. Among the most recent modern counterparts to this reformed hymnal is *The Union Songster*, cited in the bibliography.

for example, sought to maintain desirable aspects of traditional song and ritual in the light of acculturation. Indeed, the existence today of Reform, Conservative, and Orthodox houses of Jewish worship indicates that issues of tradition and compromise are still at loggerheads.

6. The *Haskalah* movement—a philosophical struggle between rationalism and mysticism. At stake in this undercurrent of reform were (as suggested above) cultural attitudes of broad political and social significance—of assimilation, of Zionism, of idealism, as well as of passivism.

One important musical outgrowth occurred in the Pale—an area constituting approximately 4 percent of the entire Russian territory in which 94 percent of the Jewish (Yiddish-speaking) population were settled in meager living conditions. (*Fiddler on the Roof* is dramatically and musically nostalgic of this.) In seeking to nurture a national Jewish musical art, Russo-Jewish composers "received legal permission" near the close of the nineteenth century to form a Society for Jewish Folk Music. Aside from the collective results in publications from 1901 to 1918, the Society represents the first modern gathering dedicated to the tasks of research and creative synthesis of a Jewish musical art.

The Jewish folk music collected by the Society is inclusive of broad national differentiation, of sociofunctional categories, of Yiddish, Hebrew, and vernacular linguistic influences and admixtures, of chassidic melodies (nigunim) and *zemiroth* (see exs. 16-5 and 16-10) (semireligious domestic chants and recitations), and of the various dance musics played by *klesmorim* (itinerant folk musicians)—*tantzes* (see ex. 16-7), *shers*, *freilachs* (see ex. 16-9) and even the Near Eastern hora.

Beyond the mere collecting and transcribing of materials, composers in the Society (Rubinstein, Halévy, Goldmark, Krein, and others) used these Jewish folk songs in various creative arrangements and compositions employing Western harmonies, piano accompaniments, and a host of settings for vocal and instrumental groups. The net results—particularly in view of the tradition-compromise posture—continue to remain important to ethnomusicologists, in general, and to Jewish folklorists, in particular.

7. Contemporary movements—trends toward

a modern musical renaissance. From about 1880 to the recent past, many European Jews found respite from persecution by migrating to other lands. Some musical developments in the United States and Israel where vast numbers settled are illustrative of the problems of tradition and compromise. In both nations a remarkable renaissance of Jewish music-consciousness has emerged.

With the establishment of the State of Israel in 1948 came the attendant problems of unifying polyethnic mixtures (principally Asian, African, and European) in national, social, and cultural ways. The role played by music is admirable. One need only consider the fine Israel Philharmonic Orchestra, the Gadna Israel National Youth Orchestra, the numerous choral groups and chamber ensembles, as well as the strongly spirited desire for and admirable accomplishments in both new folk and "serious" music.

The Israeli Composers' League fosters creativity toward a unified Jewish musical identity. The music of this national school is an interesting blend of the old and the new, of religious and biblical themes in perspectives of secular style. The result is an interesting eclecticism that includes Middle Eastern melody and irregular rhythms with Western harmonies; post-Webern serialism, electronic, aleatoric, and other avantgarde tendencies; Hebraic phonic patterns and heterophony; and traditional Eastern and Western instrumental sound sources.

Apropos to Israel and to the United States is the statement: "There are many mansions in the house of Jewish music." In major cities of the United States the heritage of Ashkenazic and Sephardic music, sacred and secular, is still evident. Orthodox, Conservative, and Reform congregations remain, however, as persistent reminders of the tradition-compromise dilemma.[7] Eastern European immigration reinforced

orthodoxy, the cantorial art, and folk song. Under the aegis of democratic spirit and new opportunities, however, other creative channels opened. The Yiddish theater introduced a composed folk song blending the Old and New Worlds in both text and music. Many of these tunes, and others, stylistically similar, progressed via Tin Pan Alley to the popular hit parades.[8] (The social treatment of these topics by Irving Howe [1976] is highly recommended to the reader.)

Composition for both liturgical purposes and the concert hall has also been encouraged. Arguments of Jewish "authenticity" notwithstanding, the creative output is not without significance. At odds is the delicate, artistic task of striking effectively into the depths of the Jewish experience and expressing this essence with creative musical uniqueness. Given the "many mansions," the dynamics of the musical mainstream, and the highly charged host of subjective preferences, the contemporary composer is confronted with the dilemma of assuming some posture relative to both tradition and compromise. Among the outstanding composers who have contributed (however contentious as "Jewish music" their works may be) are Samuel Adler, Arthur Berger, Leonard Bernstein, Marc Blitzstein, Ernest Bloch, Henry Brandt, Mario Castelnuovo-Tedesco, Aaron Copland, David Diamond, Herbert Fromm, Isadore Freed, Lukas Foss, Bernard Rogers, Arnold Schoenberg, William Schuman, and Ernst Toch. The list is far from inclusive. It does not account for the many composers, performers, conductors, educators, scholars, and social agencies (such as the National Jewish Music Council) involved directly or

---

7. Orthodox congregations maintain the term synagogue (*shul*, from central European ghetto-Yiddish jargon). The Touro Synagogue in Newport, R.I., originally Sephardic and active during the American Revolution, still functioning as a house of worship, has been proclaimed a national historical landmark. (At the time of this writing, its congrega-

tion is largely Ashkenazic; its spiritual leader, an Irish-Jewish rabbi.)

The first Reform congregation (1845), Temple Emanu-El in New York City, introduced the choir, organ, and the participation of women. The service followed German-Protestant, Anglo-American patterns; the music included adaptations of Mozart, Mendelssohn, Beethoven, Baptist revival hymns, and even operatic arias.

8. Among such "pop" tunes as "Bei Mir Bist Du Schoen" are such older Yiddish songs as "Tum Balalaika," and also the folk songs of the Israeli kibbutz—"Hava Negillah," "Tsena, Tsena," and others.

indirectly in this contemporary renaissance—a creative movement to express anew the spirit of Judaism through music.[9] I have suggested by way of this brief sociohistorical survey that the questions What is a Jew and What is Jewish music are intrinsically involved with the complexities of tradition and compromise. In the final analysis, both questions, however defensible as particular probes into Jewish music, remain moot.

For the Jew, his music is quite alive. He might argue for it nostalgically; he might argue over matters of authenticity; he might base solutions on nonmusical grounds (such as spiritual or contextual references); or he might rationalize liberally, contending that if one "feels" that it is Jewish, then who can possibly claim that it is not? (Indeed, it is traditional in talmudic inquiry that when given one problem and two perceptive Jews, three or more defensible answers are likely to emerge.)

It has been argued, for example, that Bloch's *Schelomo* is "more Jewish" than Bernstein's *Kaddish Symphony*; that both lack the Jewish "content" of Fromm's *Adath Israel*; that all of these, as well as Schoenberg's *Kol Nidre*, Diamond's *Psalms for Orchestra*, and Schuman's ballet *Judith*, are less "Jewish" than the folk songs of Israel, or the tunes of the chassidim: and, finally, that none of these is *really* representative of primary sources or of the authentic music of the ancient Hebrews. What further disputes are liable to occur over the composition of "Jewish music" by non-Jewish composers—Marcello, Ravel, Prokofiev?

A precise definition, devoid of contention, cannot be formed, but I can submit that what is sought may be contained in the Yiddish word, *Yiddishkeit* ("Jewishness"). In essence, the term points up commonalities expressive of an illusive sense of "felt-knowing"—that universal idea embracing all beliefs, postures, and practices identified fundamentally with Judaism—however defiant of sheer logic.[10]

Are there musical characteristics of Yiddishkeit? The question is rhetorical but worthy of examination. I shall amend the question slightly to point up those categories of Jewish music most evident today.

The oldest surviving musical remnant is biblical chant, usually referred to as cantillation. Traditionally transmitted orally, cantillation is a product of Hebrew prosodic structure and compromised Oriental concepts of music. Its musical system differs somewhat from that of Occidental music in rhythmic, melodic, and stylistic particulars: in tonal intervals, accents, sound qualities, forms, and artistic interpretations; in the absence of precise notation, harmony, or chords; and in Western concepts of entertainment, scalar structures, performance practices, sound sources, ethics, and fidelity to the "composer's" intention.

Akin to Oriental music, the Hebrew vocal cantillations are structured on "melodicles": tropes, self-contained melodic formulas or tonal groups called in Hebrew *neginot* (strings, or melodies).[11] From ancient hand-finger gestures that served to indicate melodic rise-fall, the felt need to "fix" the tradition gave rise (in the sixth to ninth centuries) to systems of hieroglyphic (ecphonetic) symbols or neumes placed above and below words. These *ta'amim* (signs) bear both musical and grammatical significance by suggesting the melodic manner of rendering the

9. It should be stressed again that even arguments over the purity of music in "closed" Jewish settlements, over the problems of change in oral traditions, over ethnic purity in folk song, and over concomitant problems, e.g., interpretations of the musical renditions of the Psalms, still stand in need of musicological study. (Certain parallels, for example those linking the biblical cantillations to early Christian psalmody, have been confirmed by A. Idelsohn and P. Wagner, thus identifying common aspects in the Judeo-Christian tradition.)

10. Yiddishkeit has a counterpart in what contemporary black Americans have promulgated as "soul." Both are scientifically nebulous, yet empirically defensible. The old saws about jazz are analogous: "If you have to ask what Jazz is, you'll never know"; and "New Orleans Dixieland is *real* Jazz."

11. The relationship of neginot to the Arabic-Persian maqām and the Hindu rāga is notable. In common are the uses of "melodicles" and the combining of such motives by considerations of mood, accentual pattern, sequence, ethical context, and a variety of coloristic embellishments. All these give rise to the uniqueness of interpretation, mosaically related to the original framework, but artistically rendered in an inventive diversity of improvised decorations—melismas, free rhythms, microtones, interpolations, portamentos, runs, shakes, trills, etc.

word or phrase and also the word accent. While the ta'amim lack a melodic-rhythmic preciseness, their particular, derived names imply the desired musical motion. Some examples of the twenty-eight signs are presented in figure 16-2. Their function—to intensify the spiritual import of the text—is enhanced by a monodic, unaccompanied style relatively free in improvisation and elaboration. (For comprehensive and detailed treatments of Ashkenazic biblical cantillations see Rosowsky [1957] and Binder [1959]. For comparative information see Idelsohn [1967:35-71].)

Aside from their origin, the manner of ren-

dition, melodic selection, and function of ta'amim and neginot are unique to the Jew in the chanting of the Torah and Haftorah. To this day they reflect Jewish expression in spirit and practice to all Jews, in spite of difficulties posed by different ethnic and oral traditions. Even though in Reform practices the ta'amim and neginot are often realized in Western notation for the purpose of preparing the thirteen-year-old for bar mitzvah (at which time the initiate chants an appropriate Torah and Haftorah portion from the sacred scrolls), in large part the chants are still transmitted by rote.

A portion from Exodus 21:1-7 illustrates the

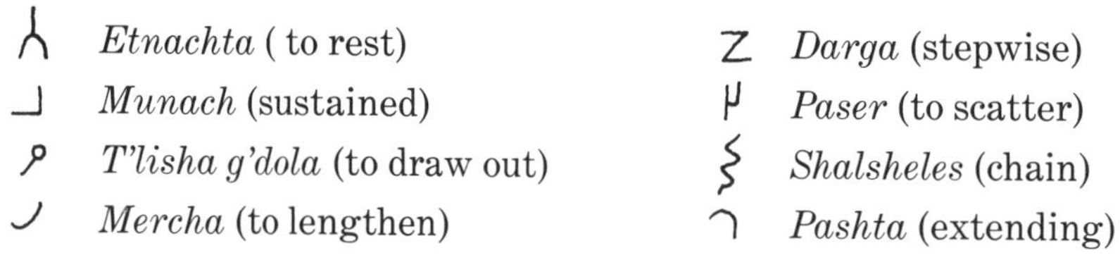

Λ *Etnachta* (to rest)

$\lrcorner$ *Munach* (sustained)

$\wp$ *T'lisha g'dola* (to draw out)

$\smile$ *Mercha* (to lengthen)

Z *Darga* (stepwise)

$\mathsf{\mu}$ *Paser* (to scatter)

$\lessgtr$ *Shalsheles* (chain)

$\cap$ *Pashta* (extending)

FIGURE 16-2. Some examples of ta'amim.

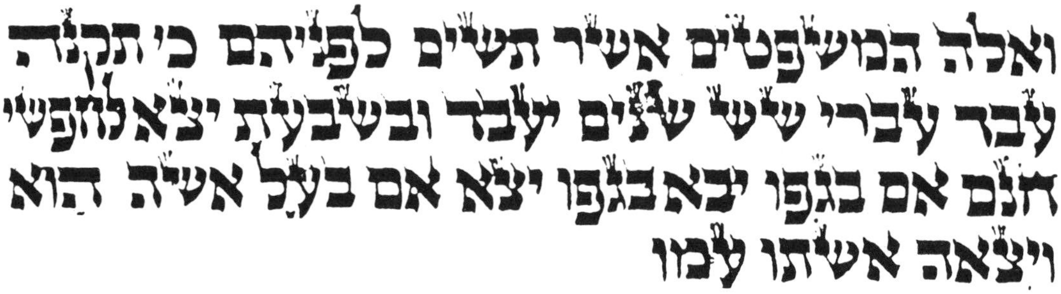

וְאֵלֶּה הַמִּשְׁפָּטִים אֲשֶׁר תָּשִׂים לִפְנֵיהֶם כִּי תִקְנֶה
עֶבֶד עִבְרִי שֵׁשׁ שָׁנִים יַעֲבֹד וּבַשְּׁבִעִת יֵצֵא לַחָפְשִׁי
חִנָּם אִם בְּגַפּוֹ יָבֹא בְּגַפּוֹ יֵצֵא אִם בַּעַל אִשָּׁה הוּא
וְיָצְאָה אִשְׁתּוֹ עִמּוֹ

FIGURE 16-3. From the Torah without vowels and ta'amim.

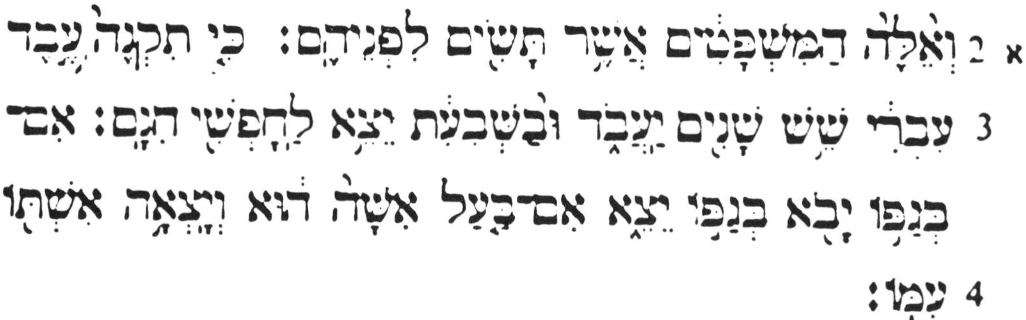

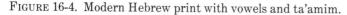

2 וְאֵלֶּה הַמִּשְׁפָּטִים אֲשֶׁר תָּשִׂים לִפְנֵיהֶם: כִּי תִקְנֶה עֶבֶד א

3 עִבְרִי שֵׁשׁ שָׁנִים יַעֲבֹד וּבַשְּׁבִעִת יֵצֵא לַחָפְשִׁי חִנָּם: אִם

בְּגַפּוֹ יָבֹא בְּגַפּוֹ יֵצֵא אִם בַּעַל אִשָּׁה הוּא וְיָצְאָה אִשְׁתּוֹ

4 עִמּוֹ:

FIGURE 16-4. Modern Hebrew print with vowels and ta'amim.

practice as realized in Ashkenazic tradition. The Hebrew text is indicated first as it appears in the Torah (fig. 16-3); then with modern Hebrew characters to include vowel markings and the ta'amim as these are printed above and below the text (fig. 16-4). (Hebrew is to be read right to left.)

In example 16-1 the Roman transliteration and Western musical notation show a basic realization of an actual rendition (the bar mitzvah of the writer's son) in 1967. Only the first two sentences of the portion from Exodus (figs. 16-3 and 16-4) are treated here. The double diamondlike markings (⧫) conform to sentence endings as indicated in figure 16-4.

The chanting of prayers (piyutim) both by laymen and professional cantors constitutes another genre of existing Jewish music. The music for these liturgical and semiliturgical poems was often borrowed and adapted from the popular melodies of the peoples in whose midst the Jews lived. They are sung on occasions appropriate to daily prayers, Sabbath services (ex. 16-2), and other minor and major festivals; the structural, modal, and general stylistic characteristics differ with the particular religio-contextual ethos.

Since differentiation in tonal (pitch) systems developed culturally between Oriental (microtone) and Occidental (semitone) practices, variations among the musics of Ashkenazic, Sephardic, Yemenite, Moroccan, Tunisian, and other Jews are still evident. Classification of all piyutim in Western modal (scalar) systems would be a problem. To be sure one can recognize semblances of older modes such as Mixolydian, Phrygian, Dorian, Aeolian, Ionian, with both mixtures and alterations of these. However, the Western-conditioned ear will sometimes consider that music to be out of tune which stylistical-

EXAMPLE 16-1. Western notation of Ashkenazic biblical cantillation.

EXAMPLE 16-2. Adon Olam (Lord of the World) Sabbath hymn, Ashkenazic.

ly derives its very character from other tuning systems (or indeed, may be a kind of subconscious compromise reflecting the Oriental past).

According to Idelsohn (1967:35–89) some of the ancient modes identified with the general evolvement of piyutim might be earmarked historically. Two are present in chanting of the Pentateuch (Phrygian and Lydian); one in Prophets (Dorian or Aeolian); one in Job (Ionian); and one evolved from the influx of Mongolian Tartaric tribes into Asian Minor, Syria, the Ukraine, Palestine, and Egypt. The last of these (the *Ahavoh-Rabboh* mode) was to assume a significant role in various secular forms of Jewish music (ex. 16-3).

EXAMPLE 16-3. Ahavoh-Rabboh mode.

This mode (Ahavoh-Rabboh, after a prayer used in the morning ritual) gradually made its way through Hungary, Russia, and Poland. Its musico-aesthetic quality, characterized musically by the interval of the augmented second and associated psychologically with romantic-religious fervor, was considered most appropriate not only for parts of the Sabbath and High Holy Day services (namely, Kol Nidre) but for folk music as well. The layman can sense the "flavor" of the augmented second in the familiar song "Hava Negillah," or by singing the *chalutz* (pioneer) song (ex. 16-4) and noting the quality of the interval in brackets. The translation of the Hebrew text is as follows: "Behold how good and delightful it is to dwell together with brothers."

But Jewish folk song is yet another category in which "Hineh Mah Tov" is just one example. Here, in contrast to the cantillations and piyutim, one is likely to find a variety of languages, mixtures, and even the lack of text. Further, it is often difficult to differentiate the religious from the secular context, since the songs do reflect the Judaic spirit, but in a manner uninhibited by liturgy and ritual. Humor, sadness, love, family,

nostalgia, social plight, work, riddles and nonsense, education and philosophy, lullabies and laments—all become descriptively expressive in the folk song.

This is not to suggest that differences are not to be discerned. Surely one can contrast the semireligious Ashkenazic zemirot with the folk poetry of the Judeo-Spanish (Ladino) songs. "Eliyohu Hanovi" (Elijah, the Prophet) is illustrative of the former (ex. 16-5). It is considered a religious domestic folk song to be sung at the close of the Sabbath, commenting on the advent of the Messiah. The secular Ladino folk song "Mama Si Yo" (ex. 16-6) expresses the feelings of a young, lovesick girl who would prefer to have her lover and twelve boyfriends at her funeral procession rather than the official services of chazzanim.[12]

The "Broiges Tanz" (Angry Dance) is a wedding dance-song with Yiddish text suggesting that love is the means to repair marital spats. The opening verse (ex. 16-7) can be translated loosely: "Are you angry with me? I don't know why. All day long you've had a long face." The refrain includes a reiterated, meaningless syllable characteristic of chassidic song; and the ongoing verse-refrain pattern, with changing text for each verse, provides also for characteristic expression in folk dancing.

Where the biblical cantillations are purely vocal and the piyutim subject to Orthodox-Reform preferences, the folk song is generally accompanied. Such accompaniment may be provided by stamping-clapping (body sounds), simple improvised or complex folk instruments, piano, small vocal or instrumental ensembles, or even full orchestra. These songs, whether fast or slow, are usually rhythmically incisive and characterized further by regularity of tempo and meter and possibly by some syncopation. Dances are commonly included whenever appropriate. Nor are passages and even entire songs in more rubato, contemplative, recitative-like styles, excluded.

That many Jewish folk songs are in minor

12. See the discography (*Ladino Folk Songs*) for a recorded example of "Mami Si Yo." Aside from this and "Un Cavritico" all other musical examples in this essay are derived from the writer's personal Ashkenazic background.

modes does not presume any associated notion of sadness. In fact, many modes are used in many contexts without any necessary cause-effect relationship (unlike the biblical cantillations). Example 16-5 is in harmonic minor and example 16-6 (seemingly of Greek-Turkish origin) is in the Dorian mode, with neither qualifying the text in any particular way. One need only compare two familiar Israeli folk tunes to note similarities of context and spirit, but differences in musical mode: "Tsena, Tsena" in major and "Shalom Alechem" in natural minor. Furthermore, rhythm, tempo, and performance style would also be inaccurate yardsticks by

EXAMPLE 16-4. "Hineh Mah Tov" (Behold How Good).

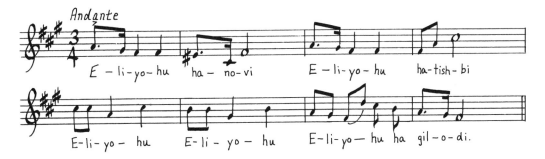

EXAMPLE 16-5. "Eliyohu Hanovi" (Elijah the Prophet).

EXAMPLE 16-6. "Mama Si Yo."

EXAMPLE 16-7. "Broiges Tanz" (Angry Dance, Yiddish).

EXAMPLE 16-8. "Nigun Bialik."

which one might attempt concrete syntheses of music, text, and purpose.

Some selected musical examples are included to supplement the discussion. Example 16-8 is a well-known chassidic nigun attributed to the rabbi-poet Bialik. The melody is sung on such textless syllables as la, lu, ra, la-ra, bi, dai, and so on. Notable are the minor-major sections, repetitions, syncopations as well as the dancelike character. A number of chassidic songs with and without words are included in Idelsohn's *Thesaurus* (1914-32), Vinaver's *Anthology* (1950), and Pasternak's *Songs* (1973).

Freilachs, generally textless dance tunes, were often borrowed, adapted, or invented by Yiddish musical bands (klezmorim) in the Jewish village (*shtetl*) for festive occasions such as weddings. The music in example 16-9 involves mixed modes—major and mixolydian. In actual performance considerable ornamentation, occasional heterophony, and expressive dissonance (by way of "pitch wailing") are characteristic. The reiterated rhythmic ostinato figure notated

above the melody is also characteristic for accompaniment.

Like the song "Eliyohu Hanovi" there are other zemirot (domestic songs) sung for the Sabbath and special occasions. Among these is a semiliturgical poem (fifteenth to sixteenth centuries, originally set in Aramaic) sung at Passover—"Chad Gadyo" (One Kid). The particular melody and Aramaic text (ex. 16-10) are traditional to the writer's family, Ashkenazic Jews from Galicia.

The text is cumulative (universally there are similar poetic structures, for example, "The House that Jack Built"). For many Jews it takes on allegorical and symbolic meanings directed to intrinsic concerns of Jewishness—past, present and future. As a parable the biblical idea of *lex talionis*, the law of retaliation, is often posed as the central theme. Allegorically, among several interpretations, the kid is symbolized as Israel (at large); the two coins, as the two tablets of the Ten Commandments (to others, as Moses and Aaron); the cat, as ancient Assyria, and so

EXAMPLE 16-9. "Freilach" (Yiddish Dance).

forth. Thus, this song (like many others of its kind) has a didactic value unique to the occasion celebrating liberation from bondage.

The translated text for the final verse-chorus (there are ten) follows:

> Then came the Holy One, Blessed be He,
> and slew the angel of death,
> who killed the *Schochet* (ritual slaughterer)
> who slaughtered the ox,
> which drank the water,
> which extinguished the fire,
> which burned the staff,
> which beat the dog,
> which bit the cat,
> which devoured the kid,
> which my father bought for two zuzeem,
> One kid, one kid.

The writer's current research interests are in the "Chad Gadyo," its numerous musical versions and variants both published and unpublished. The problems are compounded by illusive matters of global migration, philosophy (for instance, some Western Sephardim will not sing this song—the reasons remain speculative), linguistics, function, available documentation, and a host of open-ended paths of inquiry.

The appearance of the augmented second interval in the opening part of example 16-10 may suggest a similarity to the Ahavoh-Rabboh mode, but in this case the interval is located between the third and fourth steps (ex. 16-11*a*). It will also be noted that the interval becomes "natural" in the chorus section, so that the scale

EXAMPLE 16-10. "Chad Gadyo" (One Kid) [Translation: One kid, one kid, which my father bought for two *zuzeem* (ancient coins). Then came a cat and devoured the kid which my father bought for two zuzeem; etc.].

changes (ex. 16-11*b*). While both (11*a* and 11*b*) are minor modes, such mixing is not unusual. Indeed, in this case the musical structure functions to highlight formal divisions (verse-chorus) and to treat factors of changing tension-release in the text, both in play while the central minor tonality is maintained.

EXAMPLE 16-11*a*-*b*. Scales for "Chad Gadyo" (ex. 10).

Idelsohn (1967:184-85) identifies the initial scale (ex. 16-11*a*) with Ukranian folk song and the Arabic *Hedjaz* scale. Just how it was shaped into the particular melody sung by my father at the conclusion of the Passover Seder is unknown. Collectively the augmented second, the embel-

lishments (*dreylach*, in Yiddish), the free recitative sections (often performed with pious fervor and further musical improvisation) the portamenti, the overall minor quality—all reflect the Semitic-Oriental past.

The last example is a Sephardic version of the "Chad Gadyo" (in Ladino, "Un Cavritico") recorded and transcribed by the writer in 1976 (ex. 16-12). The informant, now residing in Salisbury, Rhodesia, learned this version (still sung by him) as a child on the island of Rhodes. Contrasts, musically and textually, with example 16-10 are self-evident.

To summarize, the characteristics of Jewish music rest fundamentally on a sensitive understanding of the historical roots and the complexities of the Jewish Diaspora. Beyond lies the intriguing play of traditional idealism and selective cultural compromise—the means, however controversial, by which Jewish identity has been maintained. Musically, whatever was borrowed was remolded into unique shapes expressive of the essential inner character of Judaism—a continuous, Janus-faced process of gleaning from the past in hopeful view of the future.

EXAMPLE 16-12. *Un Cavritico.*

Glossary

Ashkenazim-Jews who lived in Germanic lands during the Middle Ages and later migrated to other locations in Eastern and Western Europe.

bar mitzvah-Literally, "son of the commandment"; ritual service wherein the thirteen-year-old male (or female [bas or bat mitzvah] in Reform views) demonstrates by intoning the biblical cantillations his understanding of and faith in the Jewish heritage.

Chassidim-Pious Jews of the Russian-Polish Pale for whom the religious folk song (see *nigun*) had particularly ecstatic meaning.

chazzanim-Professional cantors who functioned as precentors and were well known for improvisations on prayer motives and freely created melodies.

chazzanut-Freely created cantorial melodies.

Falashas-Jews of Ethiopia, said to have migrated to this area after the destruction of Solomon's Temple.

Haftorah-Biblical writings of the prophets, including Isaiah, Samuel, Jeremiah, Kings, Ezekiel.

hagadah-The domestic reading at the Passover feast (see *seder*).

haskalah-Movement of "Jewish Enlightenment" in Europe from the end of the nineteenth to the early twentieth century.

hora-Near Eastern line dance, comparable to the Russian *sher*, Jewish *freilach*.

klesmorim-Itinerant Jewish folk musicians of the Russian Pale.

Kol Nidre-Prayer for Day of Atonement probably dating from the Marranos of Spain and Portugal.

ladino-The Sephardic folk language, a synthesis of old Castilian and Hebrew.

malayali-A dialect evolved by the Cochin Jews.

marranos-Baptized Spanish or Portuguese Jews who practiced Judaism secretly.

matzoh-The unleavened bread associated with the Passover meal commemorating the hasty departure from bondage in ancient Egypt.

neginot-Melodic formulas, tonal groups, or "melodicles" collectively structuring the vocal cantillations utilized in biblical chanting.

nigun-A chassidic song, usually textless, sung on a one-syllable reiterated vocable.

paytanim-Precentors who set popular verse into prayers, climaxing in the 10th-12th century Spanish-Arabic school.

Pesach-Passover, the ancient historical festival recalling the Egyptian bondage of the Israelites and their deliverance by God (see *matzoh, seder*).

piyutim-Poetic prayers comprising the paytanic literature (see *paytanim*).

seder-The Passover domestic "order," or agenda of service—symbolic ritual, reading, feasting—in memory of the exodus from Egypt as set forth in the Bible.

Sephardim-Jews who settled in Spain and Portugal following the Diaspora.

shofar-Ram's horn, the sole remaining musical instrument from Jewish antiquity, in contemporary use only on the High Holy Days.

synagogue-In ancient Israel a praying assembly of Jews, located in those provinces removed from the Jerusalem Temple. In modern use the term usually refers to an Orthodox house of worship.

ta'amim-Visual symbols (signs) indicating musical and grammatical motion and accent.

Talmud-Rabbinical works (composed of *Mishna* and *Gemara*) interpreting and commenting on Mosaic law, dating from 100 B.C.E. to C.E. 500.

temple-In ancient Israel the singular reference to the house of worship in Jerusalem (the Temple of David and Solomon destroyed c. 606 B.C.E., rebuilt c. 536 B.C.E.). In the modern meaning the term may refer to Conservative or Reform houses of worship.

Torah—Body of law and teaching comprised of the five books of Moses, the Pentateuch (Genesis, Exodus, Leviticus, Numbers, Deuteronomy).

Yiddish (Jewish)-A polyglot folk language said to have originated when Ashkenazim settled en masse in Slavic territory. In common reference the terms Yiddish, Jewish, Hebrew, Israelite are synonymous.

zemirot-Domestic folk songs of both a religious and secular nature.

Bibliography

SOURCE READINGS ON JUDAISM

Angel, Mark D.
1974. *The Sephardim of the United States: An Exploratory Study*. New York: Union of Sephardic Congregations.

Ausubel, Nathan.
1974. *The Book of Jewish Knowledge*. Sixth printing. New York: Crown Publishers, Inc. An encyclopedic treatment of Judaism and the Jewish people indicated by 10,000 entries of key terms.

Birmingham, Stephen.

1967. *Our Crowd.* New York: Harper and Row. An account of the social life and customs of German Jews who settled in the United States.

1971. *The Grandees: America's Sephardic Elite.* New York: Harper and Row.

Code of Jewish Law (Kitzur Schulchan Aruch).

1927. Compiled by Rabbi S. Ganzfried, translated by N. E. Goldin. New York: Hebrew Publishing Co. Traditional Orthodox reference for laws governing rituals, morals, ethics, dietary, hygienic, etc., observances.

Hertz, H. H., ed.

1965. *The Pentateuch and Haftorahs.* London: Soncino Press. Hebrew text, English translation and commentary (the Holy Scriptures) for synagogue, school, and home in a one-volume authoritative edition; see the *ta'amim* and suggested *neginot* (pp. 1045-1048)—the comparative cantillations (proper names and symbols) in Western notation—for chanting the Torah (Pentateuch) and Haftorah (Prophets). For another notated variation of cantillations see Rabbi Simon Glazer, ed. *The Five Books of Moses,* New York: Ktav Publishing House, 1935. Pp. 1098-1100.

Howe, Irving.

1976. *World of our Fathers.* New York: Harcourt Brace Jovanovich. "The journey of the east European Jews to America and the life they found and made"; an account of four decades of Jewish migration and settlement beginning in the 1880s centering on the trials of adjusting Yiddish culture to the new American society. The author concentrated on classic patterns in New York City.

Katz, Jacob.

1961. *Tradition and Crisis: Jewish Society at the End of the Middle Ages.* New York: Schocken Books. Sociocultural background to the rise of the Jewish Enlightenment movement.

Manners, Ande.

1972. *Poor Cousins.* New York: Coward, McCann and Geoghan. A descriptive account of the Americanization of Jewish emigrants from the Russian Pale.

Roth, Cecil.

1974. *A History of the Marranos.* Fourth edition, with a new introduction by Herman P. Salomon, New York: Hermon Press.

Rudavsky, David.

1975. "Yiddish, Ladino, Hebrew." *The Alliance Review,* 26 (Fall), 13-20. A critical discussion of the roots and uses of Yiddish and Ladino dialects in relation to Hebrew, deemed the traditionally essential holy language of Judaism.

Sachar, Abram L.

1967. *A History of the Jews.* New York: Alfred A. Knopf.

Trachtenburg, Joshua.

1970. *Jewish Magic and Superstition: A Study in Folk Religion.* New York: Atheneum. Beliefs and practices in traditional folk Judaism coupling mysticism and faith.

Wigoder, Geoffrey, ed. in chief.

1973. *Encyclopaedia Judaica.* 16 vols. 2d (corrected) printing. Jerusalem: Macmillan.

SOURCE READINGS ON JEWISH MUSIC

Avenary, Hanoch.

1971*a.* "The Concept of Mode in European Synogogue Chant." *Yuval.* Jerusalem. 2:11-21.

1971*b. Hebrew Hymn Tunes: The Rise and Development of a Musical Tradition.* Tel Aviv: Israel Music Institute. Hebrew and English.

Bibliography of Publications and Other Resources on Jewish Music.

1969. Compiled by Albert Weisser. New York: National Jewish Music Council. Extension and revision of a similar compilation by J. Yasser in 1953. Contains over 1000 entries available only in English from 1955 to 1968 including pamphlets, articles, newspapers, proceedings, symposia, encyclopedias, dictionaries, theses, bibliographies, reviews, and world sources of library materials.

Binder, A. W.

1959. *Biblical Chant.* New York: Philosophical Library. A textbook for students using the Ashkenazic system of cantillation.

1971. *Studies in Jewish Music.* Edited by Irene Heskes. New York: Bloch Publishing. Collected writings and bibliographical articles by P. Gradenwitz, J. Yasser, I. Heskes, and A. Binder.

Cohon, Baruch J.

1950. "The Structure of the Synagogue Prayer-Chant." *Journal of the American Musicological Society,* 3:17-32.

Gerson-Kiwi, Edith.

1950. "Wedding Dances and Songs of the Jews of Bokhara." *Journal of the International Folk Music Council* 2:17.

1957. "Musique dans la Bible." In *Dictionnaire de la Bible.* Suppl. vol. 5. Paris.

1973. "Le musicien dans la société d'Orient et d'Occident." *Cultures,* 1:175-204.

Ginsburg, Saul, and S. Marek.

  1901. *Jewish Folksongs in Russia.* St. Petersburg: Voskhod. One of the publications stemming from the Russian Society for the Study of Jewish Folk Music.

Gradenwitz, Peter.

  1949. *The Music of Israel: Its Rise and Growth through 5000 Years.* New York: Norton.

Idelsohn, Abraham Z.

  1967a. *Jewish Liturgy and Its Development.* 1932. Reprint. New York: Schocken Books.

  1967b. *Jewish Music: In Its Historical Development.* 1929. Reprint. New York: Schocken Books. Classical, scholarly treatment includes musical facsimiles as well as numerous examples of synagogue and folk song in many traditions.

Katz, Israel J.

  1972, 1976. *Judeo-Spanish Traditional Ballads from Jerusalem.* New York: *The Institute of Medieval Music, No. 23.* 2 vols: no. 1, 1972; no. 2, 1976. Scholarly, ethnomusicological study of the Sephardic-Castilian *Romancero.* Volume 1 treats the topic in a critical analysis; volume 2 includes transcriptions and one recording.

  1973. "The 'Myth' of the Sephardic Music Legacy from Spain." *Proceedings in the Fifth World Congress of Jewish Studies*, vol. 4, pp. 237-43. Jerusalem: World Union of Jewish Studies.

Kirshenblatt-Gimblett, Barbara.

  1974. "Yiddish Folk Songs in Europe and America." *Balkan-Arts Traditions*, New York: New York Folk Festival.

Kraeling, Carl H.' and Lucella Mowry.

  1957. "Music in the Bible." *The New Oxford Dictionary of Music: Ancient and Oriental Music*, 1:283-312. Edited by Egon Wellesz. London: Oxford University Press.

Lachmann, Robert.

  1940. *Jewish Cantillation and Song in the Isle of Djerba.* Jerusalem: Hebrew University. Important discussion of Jewish music on this North African island, particularly of the song-dances of women, and domestic and musical analysis.

Nulman, Macy.

  1975. *Concise Encyclopedia of Jewish Music.* New York: McGraw-Hill.

Rabinovitch, Israel.

  1952. *Of Jewish Music; Ancient and Modern.* Montreal: The Book Center.

Rosowsky, Salomon.

  1957. *The Cantillation of the Bible: The Five Books of Moses.* New York: The Reconstructionist Press. A monumental work establishing a landmark in Jewish musicological research; collection and comparative synthesis toward a restoration of traditional chant. The author founded the Jerusalem Conservatory of Music and conducted his research in Palestine. He was also one of the founders of the Russian Society for Jewish Folk Music in 1908.

Rothmüller, Aron M.

  1960. *The Music of the Jews: An Historical Appreciation.* Perpetua Edition, New York: A. S. Barnes and Co. Comprehensive review of history and genre including sections on the twentieth century—composers, research, the question of "Jewish music," etc. See chapters 14-17, pp. 139-237.

Rubin, Ruth.

  1974. *Voices of a People: The Story of Yiddish Folksong.* 2nd ed. New York: McGraw-Hill.

Sachs, Curt.

  1940. *The History of Musical Instruments* (see May bibliography). Detailed treatment of instruments of ancient Israel; physical and socio-liturgical descriptions. See pp. 67-68, 72, 83, 102, 105-127, 141.

  1943. *The Rise of Music in the Ancient World, East and West.* New York: Norton. Musical styles, instruments, and systems of the Orient and the Occident from ancient to medieval times. See the section on Jewish music, pp. 79-96.

  1946. *The Commonwealth of Art: Style in the Fine Arts, Music and the Dance.* New York: Norton. See discussion on "Jewish Music in Biblical Times," pp. 47-48.

Schwadron, Abraham A.

  1970. "On Religion, Music, and Education." *Journal of Research in Music Education*, 18 (Summer), 157-66. Discussion of some critical issues relevant to the use of sacred music in the public schools.

Sendrey, Alfred.

  1969. *Music in Ancient Israel.* New York: Philosophical Library.

Sendrey, Alfred, and Mildred Norton.

  1964. *David's Harp: The Story of Music in Biblical Times.* New York: New American Library. Particularly interesting treatment of Oriental heritage, problems in musical interpretation of the Psalms, dance, superstition, ethics, aesthetics, and Western views—all in chronological organization.

Sephardic Liturgy.

  1959. E. Avinum and J. Papo, chant collaboration; F. Reizenstein, introductory notes; O. Camhy, chant performance. London: Vallentine, Mitchell for World Sephardic Organization. Hebrew text and English translation based on prayer books of the late Rev. David Aaron de Sola, Spanish-Portuguese Congregation of London.

Soltes, Abraham.
1970. *Off the Willows: The Rebirth of Modern Jewish Music.* New York: Bloch Publishing. A description of the renaissance of Jewish music during the past two generations: new synagogue music, role of the cantor, Jewish composition, etc.

Spector, Johanna.
1973. "Jewish Songs from Cochin, India: With Special Reference to Cantillation and Shingli Tunes." *Proceedings of the Fifth World Congress of Jewish Studies,* 4:245-65. Jerusalem, World Union of Jewish Studies.

Weisser, Albert.
1954. *The Modern Renaissance Jewish Music.* New York: Bloch Publishing. Traces roots of past 100 years in eastern Europe and America, including publications and activities of the Russian Society for the Study of Jewish Folk Music.

Werner, Eric.
1959. *The Sacred Bridge.* New York: Columbia University. Study of comparative liturgical music interrelating church and synagogue.
1976. *A Voice Still Heard: Sacred Song of the Ashkenazic Jews.* University Park, Penn.: Pennsylvania State University Press.

Wulstan, David.
1973. "The Sounding of the Shofar." *Journal of the Galpin Society,* January, pp. 29-46.

Yasser, Joseph.
1970. *Selected Writings and Lectures.* Compiled by Albert Weisser. New York: The Jewish Liturgical Musical Society of America.

SELECTED MUSICAL COLLECTIONS

Adler, Israel, ed.
1965. *Compositions from the Repertoire of the Portuguese Jewish Community of Amsterdam.* Tel Aviv: Israeli Music Publications.

Binder, Abraham W., comp. and ed.
1942. *Pioneer Songs of Palestine (Shire' Chalutzim).* New York: Edward B. Marks Music Corp. Hebrew with English transliterations, piano accompaniment.

Cahan, I. L.
1920. *Yiddish Folksongs.* New York: Yiddish Literary Publishing Co.

Eisenstein, Judith F.
1972. *Heritage of Music: The Music of the Jewish People.* New York: Union of American Hebrew Congregations.

Ephros, Gershon, ed.
1929-1953. *Cantorial Anthology.* Vols. 1-4. New York: Bloch Publishing. Eclectic musical pluralism from Salomone Rossi to Bloch and Achron.

Hast, Marcus.
1910. *Liturgy and Ritual: A Complete Edition of Traditional and Original Compositions of Synagogue Music.* London: Bibliophile Press. Hebrew with English transliteration, vocal score and accompaniment.

Idelsohn, Abraham.
1914-1932. *Thesaurus of Hebrew-Oriental Melodies.* 10 vols. Leipzig: Breitkopf and Haertel. Reprint, New York: Ktav Publishing House, 1973. 10 vols. in 4. An outstanding landmark of Jewish musicological research treating, in order of volumes, musical collections of Yemenites, Babylonians, Persians (including Bokharans and Daghastans), Oriental Sephardim (and survey of Arab music), Moroccans, German Ashkenazim, South German Jews, East European and Chazzanim, East European folk song and Chassidic songs. Published in Hebrew, German, and English; treats musical analysis, historical details, texts, pronunciation, comparative study, etc.
1951. *The Jewish Song Book,* edited by B. J. Cohon. Cincinnati: Cincinnati Publications for Judaism. Compendium of music for the complete Jewish religious year; piano accompaniments.

Jewish Melodies of the Italian Rite (Canti Liturgici Ebraica Rito Italiano).
1967. Transcriptions and comments by Elio Piattelli. Rome: Edition De Santis. Synagogue melodies and chants; Hebrew-Italian-English texts.

Larrea, Arcadio de, ed.
1954. *Canciones Rituales Hispano-Judías.* Madrid: Instituto de Estudios Africanos. Songs in the Sephardic traditional ritual.

Lefkowitch, Henry.
1952. *A Treasury of Jewish Folk Songs.* New York: Schocken Books.

Levy, Isaac, ed.
1965, 1974, 1977. *Anthology of Judeo-Spanish Liturgy.* Vols. 1-4, 1965; vols. 5-6, 1974; vols. 7, 8, 9, 1977. Jerusalem: Mavan Book Mfg. Hebrew and Spanish text with the former transliterated; Sephardic ritual music.

Nadel, Arno, comp. and ed.
1937. *Songs of the Sabbath (Zmiroth Shabbot).*

Berlin: Schocken Books. Hebrew text with transliteration; part unaccompanied, part with piano accompaniment; domestic Sabbath songs.

Nathanson, Moshe.
1974. *Zamru Lo*, vol. 3. New York: Cantors Assembly. Congregational melodies for the Shalosh R'galim and the High Holidays.

Pasternak, Velvel.
1973. *Rejoice!: Songs in Modern Hassidic Style.* New York: Tara Publications. An edited collection of traditional and composed hassidic songs, sacred and secular, in the American musical idiom.

Rabinowitch, I.
1940. *Musik bei Yiden (Jewish Music).* Montreal: Eagle Publishing.

Rubin, Ruth, comp. and ed.
1965. *Jewish Folk Songs.* New York: Oak Publications. Forty-eight songs in English transliteration and adapted English texts including 10 by known composers (appendix contains text in Yiddish script). Preface and foreword treat historical background; guitar accompaniments (harmonic indications) by E. Raim included for each song.

1967, ed. *A Treasury of Jewish Folksong.* New York: Schocken. Children's songs, work songs, holiday songs, partisan songs, and songs of Israel. Texts in Hebrew or Yiddish with English translation.

Sephardi Melodies.
1931. London: Oxford University Press. Music of Spanish-Portuguese Jews' Congregation in London. Part I, photographic reproductions of original ancient scores; Part 2, synagogue songs from c. 1880, including some harmonized melodies.

Synagogue Music by Contemporary Composers.
1952. New York: G. Schirmer. Compositions by L. Bernstein, D. Diamond, A. Berger, M. Gould, etc.; controversial as to association with musical tradition.

Union Songster.
1960. New York: The Central Conference of American Rabbis. Songs and prayers for Jewish youth for daily, holiday, festival, and special services; accompaniments, part-singing, traditional and composed. Reform view.

Vinaver, Chemjo, comp. and ed.
1950. *Anthology of Jewish Music.* New York: Edward B. Marks Music Corp. Sacred chant and religious folk song of the eastern European Jew; includes some sacred synagogue composition by Arnold Schoenberg.

Zilberts, Zavel.
1951. *Music for the Synagogue.* New York: Board of American Hazan-Ministers. Reflective of Reconstructionist movement in Conservative congregations.

Discography

*Indicates recommended sections for listening

Call of the Shofar. Folkways Religious Series FR 8922. Notes by D. Hausdoff.

Cantorials. Folkways Religious Series Vol. I, FR 8916, Cantor Y. Kaefsky; Vol. II, FR 8923, Cantor A. Brun; Vol. III, FR 8924, Cantor A. Brun; Vol. IV, FW 6940, Cantor A. Brun. Selections of cantorial liturgical melodies in traditional style.

Die Musik der Bibel: In der Tradition althebräischer Melodien. Schwann AMS 8. Collection and notes by Edith Gerson-Kiwi. Cantillations of Pentateuch, Psalms, Prophets, Esther; shofar, folk songs and hymns—Tunis, Yemen, Persia, Egypt, Syria, Turkey, Iraq, Italy, Afghanistan, Morocco, Kurdistan. Comparative approach, materials from editor's studies and archives in Israel. Descriptive information (ta'amim, neginot, etc.) in German. *Comparative cantillations of Psalm 92 and first lines of Genesis.

Encyclopédie des musiques sacrées. Éditions Labergerie, Paris; Erata LDEV 511, Vol. I, traditions juives. Notes by Leon Abromowicz. Scholarly collection of cantillations (Pentateuch and Prophets), piyutim, chassidic chant, and shofar; Ashkenazic and Sephardic—six items from various geographical areas.

Ethiopia: The Falasha and the Adjuran Tribe. Folkways FE 4355. Recording and commentary by Lin Lerner and Chad Wollner.

Friday Night Services. Folkways FR 8917. Cantor Joseph Kenfsky, soloist.

Hebrew Folk Songs. Folkways 6928.

History of Music in Sound. Vol. I, "Ancient and Oriental Music," RCA Victor LM 6057. Egon Wellesz, editor; Gerald Abraham, general editor. *"Jewish Music" (Psalms 8, 137; hymn: *Hasha'na Rabba*, Cantor J. Goldstein).

In Israel Today. Westminster WF 9805-6, 9810-11 (4 Vols.). Field recordings, notes, and photographs by Deben Bhattacharya under auspices of UNESCO, 1960. Songs, dances of Israeli Jews from Bukhara, Uzbekistan, Cochin, Morocco, Yemen, Atlas

Mountains, Tunisia, Spain, and eastern Europe; sacred and secular; folk, liturgical, ceremonial, and vocal with indigenous instruments.

Israel Symphony. E. Bloch, Vanguard VRS 423.

Israeli Folk Dances. Minute Man + − 24. Dvora Lapson, consultant.

Issacher Miron: Prothalamia Hebraica. The wedding celebration in contemporary Israeli Sephardic idiom. Musical Heritage Society, MHS 1948. Cover notes by P. Kwartin.

Jewish Folksongs. Folkways FW 8740. Ruth Rubin, vocalist; settings by R. Neuman. Yiddish.

Kabbalistiche und Chassidische Musik. Lumen 109. Cantor Chaim Storosum, director, Collegium Musicum Judaicum, Amsterdam. Instrumental and vocal arrangements of traditional melodies by Cantor Storosum.

Karmon Israeli Group: The Best of Karmon Israeli. Two discs. Vanguard VSD 51. Israeli folk music with Hebrew text.

Ladino Folk Songs. Collectors Guild CGL 605. Judeo-Spanish ballads and songs of love sung by Raphael Yair El Nadav. *Mama Si Yo, Side B, No. 6.

Music of the Falashas. See Kimberlin discography.

Music of the Spanish and Portuguese Synagogue. Folkways Religious Series 8961. Notes by John Levy.

Musical Sources: UNESCO Collection. Philips 6586001. Religious Psalmody, Vol. IV-1, "Jewish Music." Editor, A. Daniélou; notes, A. Shiloach. Collection for the International Music Council for International Institute for Comparative Studies: sacred and secular music of eleven different communities; cantillations, prayers (Sabbath and other Holy Days); psalms, and *shofar (Moroccan—High Holy Days, side 1, band i).

Niloh Service: Concluding Service for Yom Kippur. Folkways FR 8927. Descriptive notes on the performer (Cantor Abraham Brun) and text (Hebrew, with English translations).

Romancero-Judeo Español: Anthology of Sephardic Liturgy and Romance. Peters Int., CBS S63245. Y. Gaon, Y. Banal, and R. Samsonov, soloists.

Sacred Service for the Sabbath Morning. D. Milhaud. Westminster XWN 19052. Scored for baritone, narrator, mixed choir, orchestra or organ.

Schelomo. E. Bloch, Columbia MS-6253. Rhapsody for violoncello and orchestra.

Sederavond (Songs of the Passover Seder). KKL 6810939, 1976. Hans and Asher Bloemendal with instrumental arrangements by A. Krelage on the occasion of the 75th anniversary of the Jewish National Fund (KKL).

Sephardic Folk Songs. Folkways FW 8737. Notes by M. J. Bebardete.

Songs of the Gerer Hassidim. Aderet 105. *Ani Maamin (I believe) partisan folk song (Vol. 2). Hebrew.

Symphony No. 3 ("Kaddish"). L. Bernstein. Columbia KS 6605. For speaker, mezzo-soprano, mixed choir, boys' choir, and orchestra.

The Music of Arnold Schoenberg. Columbia M2L 309, M2S 709. Notes by Claudio Spies. *Kol Nidre, Dreimal Tausend Jahre, Vol. III.

The Music of Salomone Rossi, Hebreo of Mantua. Columbia ML 5204. Notes by Joel Newman.

Two Thousand Years of Music. Folkways 3700. Notes by Curt Sachs. *"Jewish Music": Kaddish (Song of Praise) and Avodoh (for Day of Atonement).

Yemenite and Other Israeli Folksongs. Folkways 8735.

Yemenite Passover. Folkways Religious Series FR 8921. The reading and chanting of the traditional Passover Service (*Hagadah*). Yemenites, recorded in Israel, notes by T. H. Gaster.

Films

Bar Mitzvah. NFBC. B/W. 14 min.

A portrayal of the bar mitzvah ceremony, with its cantillation, preceded by a glimpse of the requisite training.

The Cantor's Son. AB. B/W. 90 min.

The story of a Jewish boy who leaves his native village of Belz, Poland, to make his name and fame in the U.S.A., then returns to Belz. Featured is the great cantor, Moishe Oysher, who sings both cantorial music and Yiddish folk songs. In Yiddish with English subtitles.

The Dybbuk. AB. Color. 95 min.

A tragedy of the possession of a young girl's spirit by the *Dybbuk*, whose exorcism brings the climax of the play. Much Jewish ritual.

The Falashas. See essay on music of Ethiopia, films section.

Gestures of Sand. UCLA. B/W. 18 min. Allegra Fuller Snyder, director.

A contemporary interpretation by dancer Margalit Oved, who "explores the patterns of music, movement, ritual and myth which were integrally a part of the life of the Jews of Aden." UCLA Media Center Catalogue, 1972.

The Ghetto Pillow. CF/MH. Color. 21 min.

A portrayal of life in an old European village

through the watercolors of the artist, Samuel Rothbort. Ritual and ceremonies, as well as daily life, are depicted. Cantorial singing by Cantor Louis Danto.

Shalom. AB. Color. 74 min.

"Story of Israel from its beginnings to the present. . . . Actual photographs and movie footage depict the early Zionists, the plight of refugee European Jews after World War II, and the proclamation of the State of Israel in 1948." One sees Haifa, Bethlehem, Nazareth, Tel Aviv, the Negev desert, Gaza, Jerusalem. The film "concentrates on the many problems faced by Israel's people, espe-cially the constant need to be alert for possible war and the difficulty in solving the plight of the Arab refugees." AB Catalogue.

Sighet, Sighet. CF/MH. B/W. 27 min.

"A survivor of the town of Sighet . . . from which 10,000 Jews were deported to the ovens of Auschwitz, returns unknown and unseen, a silent witness to the town where he was born and grew up. . . . The film is a personal and poetic treatment of the great tragedy of the Nazi persecution of the Jews. . . . Written and narrated by Elie Wiesel, music composed and performed by Jimmy Giuffre." CF/MH Catalogue.

17. North American Native Music

David P. McAllester

For at least 20,000 years descendants of migrants from East Asia to the Western Hemisphere have been developing the unique complex of cultures known today as "American Indian." The ways of life evolved by these first settlers in the New World ranged from agricultural city-states to small hunting bands. Integral in these many cultures were varied and sophisticated developments in the arts, of which music was, and still is, a vital part. This essay will survey the most striking features of the music as it is now performed among the native peoples of North America.

Though Indian music falls into a number of regional styles, there are some overall similarities as well. Nearly all is vocal, sung by choruses, usually male, in robust "outdoor" voices. There are often strong emphases, sharp attacks at beginnings of phrases; sometimes shouts and even animal calls lend excitement to the melodies. With exceptions, noted below, song texts contain a large proportion of nonsense syllables or vocables such as the "Yu-waw, yu-waw, hi hi hi, yu-wah hi!" with which example 17-1 begins.

Melodic structures are made up of short phrases organized in clear-cut patterns with heavy weight on the tonic. Tone systems vary from several kinds of pentatonic to diatonic and even occasional chromatic scales. Melodies are almost always monophonic; steady duple or single meters are characteristic. The instrumental music is one of the most specialized in the world. Except for a few kinds of flutes and whistles it is almost entirely confined to percussive accompaniment for the voice by a wide variety of drums, rattles, and rasps. All American Indian drumming is done with a single drumstick for each player. In the case of certain large drums there may be several players beating the accompaniment together. Some instruments, such as the flageolet with external wind channel of the Plains, the water drum of the Southwest and Eastern Woodlands, and the multiple wooden whistles of the Northwest Coast, are unique to the New World.

Most American Indian music is closely tied to religion. Even game songs and dance songs may be part of rituals that are concerned with thanksgiving, the growing of crops, the healing of sickness, or the search for sacred power to help meet many of life's crises.

Within the frame of overall similarities sketched above, Indian singers recognize a large number of regional styles. It is usually possible for a knowledgeable listener to identify the vocal techniques and melodic patterns even of a particular tribe, just as local styles can be identified in the other arts as well. Certain tribal musics are closely enough related to each other to permit their inclusion in larger groupings. Some of these regional musical styles and certain intertribal genres of song are described here in an attempt to suggest, in the small space of one essay, the complexity of native American music.

THE EASTERN WOODLANDS

Before Europeans came to North America, the greatest development of Woodlands culture was in the south where agricultural towns grew large enough to support an aristocracy. Earthwork pyramids were built with temples at the top; great mounds of many different shapes were used for burials and other religious purposes. The remains of these may still be seen from Ohio south to Georgia and Tennessee. To

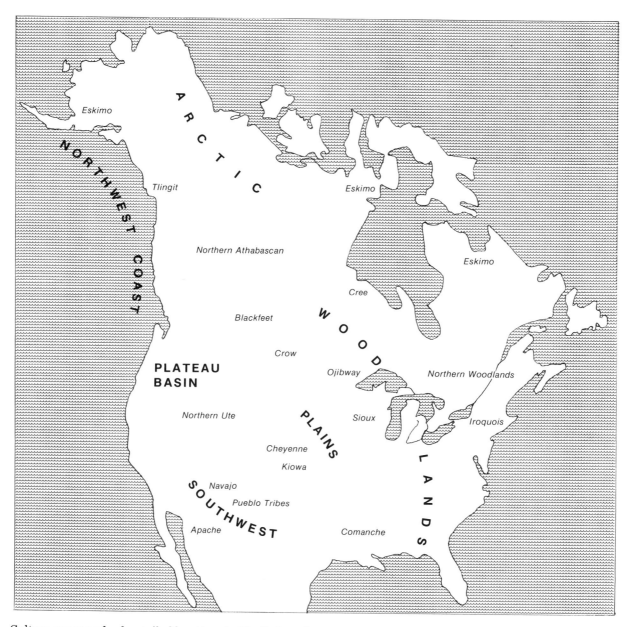

Culture areas and a few tribal locations in North America

the north and east, farms and villages were smaller and, in addition to agriculture, a good part of the economy was based on hunting. Still farther north, in what is now Canada, there was little or no farming, and hunting played a major part in the struggle for existence.

Throughout this area, religion focused on giving thanks to plants and animals for the food they provided. Hunters expressed their respect and gratitude to the game they caught, and the farming communities gave ritual expression to their dependence on corn, beans, and squash, called by the Iroquois the "three life-giving sisters." In these rituals there were dance, prayer, and always music.

The music of the Woodlands has certain qual-

FIGURE 17-1. Iroquois rattles of cow-horn (above) and elm and hickory bark (below). Photograph by Carol Reck

FIGURE 17-2. Northwest coast rattle of cedar-wood carved and painted to represent the raven. Decorated with cedar-bark. Photograph courtesy of Daniel W. Gómez-Ibáñez

ities that strike the ear immediately. It is sung in an open, relaxed style rather like that of the ballad singers of northern Europe. Many songs are antiphonal, or call and response, in pattern: a leader starts and a chorus comes in after him. The two parts may continue to take turns throughout the song. The Cherokee Stomp Dance (ex. 17-1) shows the responsorial structure and also another feature of some kinds of Woodlands music: rather long, complex melodic phrases. The text is made up entirely of vocables.

The Stomp Dance

The Stomp Dance is performed widely in the Eastern Woodlands area. The leader conducts the dance as well as the song. As he improvises the calls he leads a line of dancers in a fast prancing step in time to the music. On the principle of follow-the-leader, when the leader crouches all the others do so too; if he turns in place and then goes on, all the other dancers do the same one after another so the turn moves down the line. At times the dancers fall into a walk in order to rest. Then the leader starts the fast "stomp" step again and the others follow him. A good leader knows many vocable patterns for the song and can introduce a variety of entertaining variations on the dance steps.

Other Woodlands genres include popular songs that may be used on any social occasion, social dance songs like the Stomp Dance, and sacred songs and dances like the Drum Dance of the Ojibwa. There are ceremonial songs that do not include dances where the focus is on ritual texts, as in the religious society songs of the Iroquois and the Midewiwin cycle of the Ojibwa, in which poems of epic length may be performed

EXAMPLE 17-1. Cherokee Stomp Dance. Rhodes, *Indian Songs of Today*, AAFS L36, band B6, transcribed by McAllester.

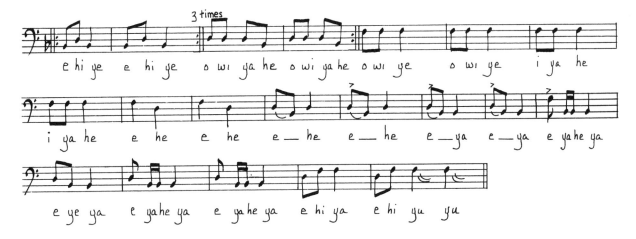

3 times

e hi ye   e hi ye   o wi ya he   o wi ya he   o wi ye   o wi ye   i ya he

i ya he   e he   e he   e — he   e — he   e — ya   e — ya   e ya he ya

e ye ya   e ya he ya   e ya he ya   e hi ya   e hi yu   yu

EXAMPLE 17-1. (continued)

for hours or even over a number of days. Here, of course, there are long meaningful texts instead of the vocables mentioned above. A few lines from a Midewiwin song will convey its emphasis on the spiritual power of the forces of nature.

Song of Initiation
to the Third Degree
of the Midewiwin

Let us be a spirit,
Let the spirit come from the mouth.
I own this lodge
Through which I pass.
Mother is having it over again.
(The Earth Mother
Is repeating the great medicine.)
Friends, I am afraid,
I am afraid, friends,
Of the spirits sitting around me.
I am going,
With medicine bag,
To the lodge.
We are still
Sitting in a circle.

[Hoffman 1891: 246-47.
Arranged and with
explanatory parentheses
by D. P. McA.]

THE PLAINS

Extending over a huge area in the west-central United States and up into Canada are the rolling, open grasslands known as the Plains. The Indians of this region lived the kind of life most often shown in films and on television. These were the horseback warriors and buffalo hunters. Their graceful, conical tipis are among the most efficient movable homes ever invented and their magnificent eagle-feather warbonnets are the symbol of the American Indian all over the world.

The different language stocks in the Plains area give evidence of the diverse origins of the tribal communities found there. Efficient hunting of enormous herds of bison, made possible when Spanish conquistadores introduced the horse from Europe, led to the flowering of a vigorous exploitation of the seemingly limitless Plains. Horse raiding and constant warfare over choice hunting grounds produced an ethic of dashing bravery and self-discipline and a religion based on individual visions leading to success in warfare and hunting. Dependence on the bison for food, shelter, and clothing resulted in a deep reverence for this life-supporting animal. Whatever their origin, the tribes that moved out into the Plains shared the tipi, the costume, and the way of life that seemed best adapted to their new home.

Plains music is higher and more piercing in vocal style than that of the Woodlands peoples. It is often sung in a powerful falsetto and the songs tend to start at the upper limit of the singer's range. The melodic line then sweeps down in successively lower arcs to an ending heavily weighted on the tonic after which the whole pattern is repeated again and again. The first few notes are often sung by a leader or a small group; then other male singers join in and finally so do women singers, whose voices soar an octave over those of the men. The most common Plains drum is a single-headed tambourine type played with a padded stick, but the marching band bass drum has been adopted for occasions such as powwows and some other kinds of singing and dancing. Example 17-2, Sioux Rabbit Dance, is a characteristic Plains song. Comparison with example 17-1 gives an idea of the differences between the song styles of the Plains and Woodlands regions—the Stomp Dance song is undulating in melodic direction; the Rabbit Dance song shows the strong downward tendency just described. The former has a drumbeat solidly tied to the meter of the vocal part, whereas the drum in the latter never seems quite to coincide with the vocal pulse, thus creating the dynamic interplay between voice and accompaniment that is often part of the Plains style. Yet in both songs there is the percussion accompaniment, the use of vocables, shouts, and cries providing musical ornamentation and the monophonic vocal orientation of the melody that characterizes most native American music.

Plains music is of many kinds. There are individual songs given in a dream or a vision by a spirit helper who will aid the dreamer at the difficult points in his life. There are group songs of the religious societies such as the Soldier Society of the Blackfeet or the Medicine Society of the Comanches. There are many types of dance songs, some of them with profound religious significance, such as the Sun Dance, and others with largely social functions, such as the songs of the Grass Dance, the Forty-nine Dance, the War Dance, and the Fancy Dance.

The social dances last mentioned have a special place in the overall view of American Indian music, since many of these songs have been adopted by Indian groups outside the Plains area. In the powwows described below Plains songs and costumes are much used. These powwows take place all over the country, often in large cities like New York and Chicago where there are good-sized Indian populations.

The songs of the Plains Indians usually have brief meaningful texts in a setting of vocable patterns. Two examples follow:

Song of the Antelope Ceremony (Kiowa)
A haiya he ya- ya,
A haiya he ya- ya,
A haiya he ya- ya,
A haiya he ya- ya,
A haiya, a-hai-ya, ai ya he,
Heya- a- a- ha.
A haiya he ya- ya,
A haiya he ya- ya.

My grandmother punished me,
I wept until I fell asleep,
In dream came a holy power, wonderful,
Mighty to win food.

He- ye- ye-.

[Curtis 1907:236-37]

Morning Song (Cheyenne)
Ai- heya- hi, ai-
Ai- heya- hi,
Ai- heya- hi,

Ahe, yahe, he-
Yu- heyu-.

He, our Father,
He hath shown His mercy unto me,
In peace I walk the straight road.

Ahe, ahe, hi-
Yu- heyu-.

[Ibid. 172-73]

The American Indian Powwow

The powwow has evolved from various kinds of social gatherings in the past and from the tribal fairs and rodeos of recent times. Powwows take place in nearly every part of the country and sometimes as often as every month in large cities where there are Indian populations. A newsletter, *Powwow Trails*, gives listings of the major gatherings of this kind. *American Indian News* is another newsletter that lists powwows along with other information of special interest to Indians.

A powwow is essentially an occasion for singing and dancing to which the zest of competition is often added. Prizes are offered for best costumes, best performance in a number of dance events, and, when the occasion is held

EXAMPLE 17-2. Sioux Rabbit Dance. Rhodes, *Music of the Sioux and the Navajo*, Folkways 4401, transcribed by McAllester. Sung by Benjamin Sitting Up (leader), Lucy Randall, Paul High Horse, Oliver Standing Bear, James Quiver.

out-of-doors on a campground, for the best made and most beautifully decorated tipi. The proceedings usually start with a Flag Song in salute to the United States flag. Then the dance competitions and other events are announced. Food concessions serve Indian foods, and traders are there to sell Indian handicrafts or items for costume making such as buckskins, beads, feathers, and even hanks of sinew thread similar to those the old-time Indians used for their sewing.

At times the regular events will be interrupted for a "giveaway." This is a Plains Indian custom of showing appreciation and respect for people who have come a very long way to be present or who have done an extra amount of work to make the powwow a success. It will be announced that a certain person will make a giveaway in honor of so-and-so. There will be drumbeating to signal each gift and an announcer will often say what it is: "A handsome Pendleton blanket is presented by John Smith to Henry Eagle in honor of the long trip he made all the way from South Dakota to be at this powwow!"

Then the dancing and the contests will resume and the day passes with interludes for rest and for picnicking and visiting. In the evening there are likely to be bonfires and special exhibitions and still more dancing and singing contests. The larger powwows may continue for a whole weekend. Like the Caledonian Games of the Scots, these are times when people can forget their everyday jobs and get together for good times and the remembrance of their cultural heritage.

The Plains War Dance

This dance has now become the favorite exhibition dance at powwows, Indian fairs, Indian shows, and even Boy Scout Jamborees. The basic step is a step-pat with one foot, then the same thing with the other foot. The body is held straight from the hips up and the head is high. There is usually something held in the right hand such as a decorated stick or a feather fan. The swinging of ribbons and leather fringes and the graceful waving of feathers are very much part of the dance.

The variations in body and head posture and the developments on the basic step are almost infinite. The dancer crouches, sways, nods his head, dances in circles, turns figure-eights, always with a dignified, remote expression. He must know the musical style so well that he can stop exactly as the singing ends. One extra step, like one extra drumbeat by an inexperienced drummer, will spoil the effect.

THE SOUTHWEST

Two cultural and musical styles predominate in the Southwest. In this region of deserts, arid plateaus, and towering mountain ranges with forests on their flanks are two major contrasting Indian cultures. One is that of the pueblos. From east to west these include such villages as Taos, San Juan, Cochiti, Laguna, Zuni, Oraibi, and Hotevilla, nearly thirty in all, ranging from eastern New Mexico to central Arizona. The other is that of the Navajos and the Apaches, closely related tribes who were formerly hunters and raiders and who now combine a little farming with raising livestock to support themselves. The ways of life and the musics of these two groups are so different, even though they have lived for centuries in the same region, that they will be discussed separately here.

The Pueblos

The Pueblo (Spanish for "town") Indians lived in villages surrounded by small farms for well over a thousand years before the Spanish colonists settled in this part of the New World. Spanish rule was imposed in the sixteenth century and today nearly every Pueblo has a Catholic church and Pueblo Indians have Spanish names as well as their native ones. In spite of their conversion they also continue to practice their traditional religion. Ceremonies are largely focused on their agricultural needs: prayers and rituals beseech the supernatural powers for rain and for successful crops. One of the most characteristic sights and sounds in the Pueblos is a long line of masked and costumed dancers singing with deep strong voices to their deities of rain and fertility. The Corn People Gatzina Song in example 17-3 illustrates this kind of music. The drum accompaniment, the use of vocables throughout, and the religious context of this song are all "Indian," but the tremolo drumming in the introduction, the strongly patterned pauses in the otherwise steady single-pulse accompaniment, and the long cadential phrases on the tonic set the song apart as "Pueblo." Like some kinds of Woodlands music, Pueblo songs make use of long developments of musical ideas. Although this song has only three really different phrases (X, A, and B), many Pueblo songs may have a dozen or more and require four or five pages for a complete nota-

FIGURE 17-3. Navajo water-drum: clay pot with buckskin cover. Photograph by Carol Reck

EXAMPLE 17-3. Corn People Gatzina Song (Acoma). Recorded and transcribed by Natalie Curtis. *The Indians' Book*, Dover, New York (1907:451-52).

EXAMPLE 17-3. (continued)

tion. The feature that strikes the ear most strongly in Pueblo singing is the deep pitch and the precision of the choral performance.

A Zuni Harvest Dance
This dance, performed by two couples standing side by side, gives an idea of the restrained figures of Pueblo dancing. As a large chorus sings about the blessed corn, the dancers step lightly from one foot to the other without moving from position. A special drummer provides the accompaniment on a large double-headed barrel drum with a single padded drumstick. At certain points in the song the dancers turn around, still standing in the same spot, until they are facing the way they were in the beginning. When the drumming and singing slow down the dance steps slow down also, and at the breaks, when the drumming stops for a moment, the dancing stops too in perfect unison with the music.

The Navajos and Apaches
The Navajos and Apaches seem to have come to the Southwest as one tribe, as recently as A.D. 1200-1300, hundreds of years after the Pueblo Indians had established their farming communities there. These newcomers moved down from the north and we can still find a clue to their origin among the Indian tribes of northwest Canada where languages related to Navajo and Apache are also spoken.

Today the Navajos inhabit 16 million acres in Arizona, New Mexico, and Utah—the largest Indian reservation. More Navajos than Apaches have become farmers or sheepherders, perhaps because of their closer associations with some of the Pueblo peoples. The Navajo population is now more than 150,000, whereas the Apaches are scattered to the east and south of them in about a dozen tribes of a few thousand each. Culturally the Navajos and Apaches are similar. Their religion concentrates especially on healing the sick. In dramatic ceremonies sometimes lasting as long as nine days and nights, art, theater, and music are brought together to bring supernatural power to the aid of some person in need of help. The long chants invoke deities such as Changing Woman, Enemy Slayer, and Talking God to restore harmony in the life of an individual by bringing him into balance with the world of nature and the gods.

The songs of the Apaches and Navajos include short topical melodies sung for entertainment, highly melodious popular songs drawn from the public parts of certain ceremonies, very sacred prayer songs, and the chanted strophes of such ceremonials as Mountainway and Shootingway. The musical style is illustrated here with an example of social dance music from each tribe.

Apache Social Dance Song
This kind of song is used by the Apaches for an informal occasion when people are simply having a good time and feel like singing and dancing. The lively rhythm, the vital pulsing voice, the high nasal register with subtle ornamentations, and the characteristic vocables all give the listener the impression of an idiosyncratic style. A large water drum made of an iron kettle with a tanned buckskin drumhead is used, played

with a slender drumstick about twelve inches long and bent in a hoop about four inches in diameter at the distal end. The steady soft booming accompaniment is distinct from that of any other American Indian drumming. Like many Apache and Navajo songs the tone system is based on the open triad. In this case the melody is limited to the triad on F except for an occasional passing movement on G. Except for a few dotted quarters the note values are all quarters and eighths.

The text of example 17-4 is given in transcription of the Apache. In the translation, given here, one can observe the common Indian form of a few meaningful lines set off by an elaborate pattern of vocables.[1]

Weya yeya, 'Aweniya hiyo'aweniya hiyo
    Nehyaŋa 'ayo 'awe ne yaha 'anae
      neyeya,
    'Aweniyo hiyo'aweniya heyo
    Nehyaŋa 'ayo 'awe ne yaha 'anae ne

In Deshiko, by the water,
The girls go two together.
    Nehyaja 'ayo 'awe ne yaha 'anae
      neyeya,

    'Aweniya hiya'aweniya hiyo
    Nehyaja 'ayo 'awe ne yaha 'anae
      neyeya,

In Deshiko the girls go in pairs,
With curly hair they go in pairs,
    Nehyaŋa 'ayo 'awe ne yaha 'anae
      neyeya.

The dance is performed by a short line of people with their arms linked. They move forward, four light steps, and then back again. This may be done in a large irregular circle made up of several such lines, all facing in. At night there is usually a bonfire in the center of the circle and the dancers move in toward the fire and then back out again. The movement back is also obliquely to the left so that the overall movement of the circle is around the fire, clockwise. Another

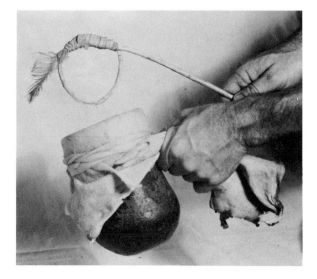

FIGURE 17-4. Navajo water-drum showing looped stick drum-beater. Photograph courtesy of Daniel W. Gómez-Ibáñez

form of this dance is performed in double lines, one of women and the other of men. As the two lines face each other the women dance forward four steps while the men step back; then the figure is reversed and the women go back while the men advance. *Tułpai* in the name of the song means "grey water" and refers to a home brew of fermented corn sprouts which is also a part of such occasions.

Navajo Circle Dance Song

In the Enemyway ceremony there is public dancing to commemorate the return of Navajo warriors from a mythical war party. Though most of the ceremony is closed to outsiders, the dancing provides the occasion for young people to meet while their parents have a chance to exchange news, eat and drink, and enjoy themselves watching or participating in the dancing. The Circle Dance is one of several kinds of public dance during the three-day ceremony. A circle of men hold hands and move sidewise with a step-drag figure. At the end of the song they stop and start the movement in the other direction as they sing a new song.

As in Apache social singing the vocal style is high, tense, and nasal with subtle inflections ornamenting the melodic line. The melodies are

---

1. For the reader who would like to be able to pronounce the texts examples of 17-4 and 17-5, vowels have "continental" values and consonants are as in English except: ŋ, like the ng in "long ago"; ', like the glottal catch in "oh-oh"; ł, like Polish ł or ll in Welsh "Flloyd," unvoiced, with breath coming out on both sides of tongue in "l" position; ą, nasalized, as in French "Jean"; aa, and other doubled vowels indicate long vowels; ′ over vowels, indicates high tone as in Chinese speech tones.

EXAMPLE 17-4. Apache Tuɫpai Song. Recorded and transcribed by McAllester in Cibecue, Arizona, 1955. Sung by Arden Dazen, James Patterson.

bold and acrobatic with occasional leaps of as much as an octave. The tone system in this case is pentatonic rather than triadic—in fact the third degree is missing altogether. Here, too, the accompaniment is on a water drum, but instead of the big iron kettle of the Apaches, the Navajos make theirs of a clay pot about six inches high and four inches across. Its soft thump is barely audible in a large singing group. Although many Navajo social songs have texts made up entirely of vocables, example 17-5 shows a few lines in a vocable setting.

The main purpose of the Enemyway ceremony is to counteract the dangerous effects of going to war, especially by protecting the warrior and his family from the spirits of slain enemies. The songs of the public dances, however, do not deal with ghosts or warfare except indirectly. When there are meaningful texts they deal, in a jocular way, with girlfriends and social situations. Here is a translation of the Circle Dance text in example 17-5:

> He-, neya-, my cousin [sweetheart]
> Really together, together,
> Together we will go.
>
> 'Eye, ne-ye, yo-he, ne-ya,
> My cousin,
> Really together, together,
> Together we will go,
> Heya, nahi ya-, 'a-, 'eyo-, hi ne-ya.

Ceremonial Music

The "classic" music of the Navajos and Apaches is found in the long sacred chants already mentioned. Here a dedicated male chorus sits all night following the lead of the priest or ceremonial practitioner who holds thousands of lines

FIGURE 17-5. Iroquois flageolet. Photograph courtesy of Daniel W. Gómez-Ibáñez

of ritual poetry in his memory. The music unfolds in a sequence of song cycles in which melody alternates with chant. Songs begin with a chorus of vocables, settle into a recitation of long texts, and then end with another chorus,

FIGURE 17-6. Water-drum for the peyote ceremony: pottery, with buckskin cover. Photograph courtesy of Daniel W. Gómez-Ibáñez

usually a repetition of the one at the beginning. In Navajo chanting, the instrumental accompaniment may be with several kinds of rattles or a shallow basket turned over on the ground and thumped with a special drumstick woven of yucca leaves. Apache ceremonial music may be accompanied by the large kettledrum, various rattles, and, for certain specific songs, a rasp made of notched manzanita.

The poetry in these songs tells the story of the creation of the world. The particular episodes may be chosen for their appropriateness to the trouble of the one who is ill, the "one-sung-over." If the sickness has to do with snakes, for instance, the ceremony chosen might be Shootingway, which treats of the sojourn of one of the deities with the snake people. By a dramatic reenactment of this sojourn in the ceremony, the one-sung-over is thought to assume snake power and thus return to a state of harmony with the snake beings of this world.

A short example of text follows, illustrating the kinds of imagery used. The description is of the procedures of the ritual bath taught to mankind when the world began.

♩=104

He ___ ne _ ya ___ shi ze di ___ t'aa ɬadot' aa ɬa doo' t'aa ɬa
My cousin really together together to-

doo ___ ni ki diit' a-shi la 'e ye ne ___ 'e yo ___ he ne-
gether we will go (two)

ya shi ya he ya na hi ya ___ 'a ___ 'a _ 'e yo—

hi ne ___ ya t'aa ɬa do _ t'aa ɬa do t'aa ɬa do ___ ni

ki diit' a-shi la - 'e ye ne _ 'e yo ___ hi ne ___ ya

t'áá : just, really
ɬa'í : one
Dóó (doolееɬ): will be
nihi diit' ash : we (two) will go
ɬá : it so happens

EXAMPLE 17-5. Navajo Circle Dance Song. Recorded and transcribed by McAllester in Sodona, Arizona, 1957. Sung by Albert G. Sandoval, Jr., and Ray Winnie of Lukachukai, Arizona.

Bathing Song from the Red Antway Ceremony
'e ne ya-a-a,

Beautifully he placed it, beautifully he placed it,
Beautifully he placed it, golaghei.

Now the Emergence Place, exactly at its rim he
    placed it,
First Man's home, in the very center he placed it,
Pollen of a smoothed place, exactly on top he
    placed it,
A turquoise basket he placed,
Dark soaproot, he placed it,
Now its dew, he placed it,
Its pollen he placed it,

Beautifully he placed it, beautifully he placed it,

Beautifully he placed it, golaghei.
[Wyman 1965: 194-95]

THE PLATEAU AND GREAT BASIN AREA

Extending from southern California, western Utah, western Colorado and Nevada (the Basin) northward across Idaho, eastern Oregon, eastern Washington and into Canada (Plateau), this huge area has a general aridity and poverty of natural resources that made farming impossible for the native inhabitants and led them to live in small, nomadic hunting and gathering bands. Much of their subsistence was on seeds,

FIGURE 17-8. Northwest coast cedar rattle. Photograph by Carol Reck

FIGURE 17-7. Peyote drum with drum-stick and gourd rattle. Photograph courtesy of Daniel W. Gómez-Ibáñez

roots, and other wild plants supplemented by game such as rabbits and antelope, and extensive fishing in that part of the Plateau traversed by large rivers.

Extraordinary knowledge of natural history and animal behavior was necessary for survival. The religion was based on dreams that led to healing powers or special leadership in the hunt. Mat weaving and basketry were highly developed skills. Many of the house forms were variations on a basic brush shelter covered with tule mats. The old nomadic life style is gone today and the Indians live on small reservations or on the edge of towns or ranches as part-time laborers. Among the features of their culture that still persist is a style of music unique to this region.

This music is notable for its open, relaxed vocal style. The melodies are brief in duration and narrow in compass. They make frequent use of paired phrases. Example 17-6 of Northern Ute music, the Bear Dance, illustrates these features. This song style is of particular interest because of an extensive religious and musical influence that spread from the Great Basin to a wide area of the Plains. This influence is described below in a brief account of the Ghost Dance religion.

Ghost Dance Music: A Special Song Style
The Ghost Dance religion arose among the Paiute Indians of Nevada in 1870 and again in 1890, at which time it had a phenomenal spread among the Plains Indians who sought religious help now that their military resistance was at an end. A prophet named Wovoka dreamed that dance and prayer would cause the European invaders to disappear. The Ghost Dance was performed in a large circle to the music of plaintive songs of suffering and pleas for help. Many of the participants went into a state of trance in which they saw visions of their dead relatives restored to life and of a happier time

ahead when the buffalo would return and the white man would be gone forever.

The songs, no matter where they were sung, had an unusual uniformity of style. They were similar to the music of the Great Basin and had developed the feature of paired phrasing to the point where each new phrase was sung twice in what Herzog has described as "paired progression" (Herzog 1935:404). This special intertribal song style is shown in example 17-7.

Music of the Native American Church:
A Special Song Style
Another special song style that has an intertribal circulation among native Americans, espe-

The music, however, does not follow the tense, high vocal style of the Plains but is sung in a quieter, almost hymnlike voice. Peyote songs have a relatively narrow range and are restricted like Navajo and Apache music to only quarter and eighth-note values. The tempo is moderately fast, the melodic profile is moderately downward and shows a marked attraction to the tonic in the concluding phrases. Here again the water drum is used. Its provenance has been noted among the Navajos and Apaches: it is one of the clues for a possible Apache origin of Peyote music. A few words should be said about this unique instrument. It differs from most of the drums of the world in that it has a

EXAMPLE 17-6. Ute Bear Dance. Recorded and transcribed by Densmore, *Northern Ute Music* (1922:59). Sung by Nikavari at White Rocks, Utah, 1914.

cially in the western United States, is that of the Native American or Peyote Church. Starting in the late nineteenth century, a religion based on sacred visions, all-night worship, prayer, and singing spread into Oklahoma from Mexico and Texas and from Oklahoma has moved west as far as California and north as far as Canada.

Because of its long-established base in Oklahoma, especially among the Kiowa and Comanche people, the graphic art of the Native American Church has taken the geometric forms of the Plains Indians. The sacred dwelling in which the ceremony ideally takes place is the Plains tipi even though the worshippers may be Navajos or Menominis who use the tipi for no other purpose.

membrane of tanned leather, often buckskin, instead of the usual dry, untanned leather or rawhide. The body of the drum is made of wood, clay, or metal in the shape of a pot, kettle, or keg, and is partly filled with water, usually a third to a half full. The single drumhead is stretched at high tension over the mouth of the pot or the open end of the barrel. The tanned leather shrinks even tighter when moistened, whereas wet rawhide would loosen and lose its resonance.

The drum is shaken now and then, between songs, to keep the drumhead wet. Often a fine spray is thrown up from the drumhead by the intense beat of the unpadded drumstick. This stick is also a unique feature: everywhere else in North America the sticks used with dry drums

EXAMPLE 17-7. Teton Sioux Ghost Dance Song. Recorded and transcribed by Natalie Curtis, *The Indians' Book*, Dover, New York (1907:66). Sung by Tatanka-Ptecila at Rosebud, South Dakota.

are padded to soften the impact a bare stick makes on the rawhide, which dries to an almost metallic hardness.

The water inside the drum serves other functions besides keeping the drumhead wet. It has symbolic connotations of rain and is also thought to produce a special resonance since the water inside the drum is in constant motion complementary to the vibrations of the drumhead. There may be special ceremonial observances in connection with the water. In the case of the Peyote drum, for example, four live coals, said to represent lightning, are dropped into the water and, at the conclusion of the ceremony, when the drum is unlaced, the water is poured along a crescent-shaped earthen altar.

The texts of the Peyote songs are largely vocables, but may contain brief poetic phrases describing visions, the beauty of the coming dawn, or addressing the peyote plant, a small cactus which is eaten as a sacrament and which helps to induce the visions. As characteristic as the "Amen" at the end of a Christian hymn is the phrase "he ne yo wa" or some variation of it, which concludes most Peyote songs.

THE NORTHWEST COAST

The carved and painted masks, boxes, canoes, and other woodwork of the Indians of the Northwest Coast are found in museums and art

EXAMPLE 17-8. Comanche Peyote Song. Recorded and transcribed by McAllester, *Peyote Music*, Viking Fund Publication in *Anthropology* no. 13 (1949:119). Sung by Tekwak'l at Indiahoma, Oklahoma, 1940.

collections all over the world. The art style, with its bold stylization and gleaming shell insets, is more like that of the Polynesian Maoris of New Zealand than that of any of the other North American Indians. The high development of this art and the society that supported it was based on the salmon runs in the coastal rivers of what is now Washington, Oregon, and British Columbia. Though the Indians of the region did not practice agriculture, the salmon provided the reliable food supply ordinarily guaranteed only by farming.

Out of this abundance developed an elaborate social organization with nobles, commoners, and slaves, wars of conquest, and villages of big plank houses decorated with painted family crests that were also often carved on "totem poles" sometimes over sixty feet high. Important families maintained their status by ac-

cumulating wealth through warfare, their own labor, and that of their slaves, and by elaborate gift exchanges known as potlatches. The idea of private property and income based on the accumulation of interest was highly developed. Exclusive ownership extended to such seeming intangibles as names, rank, totemic designs, and music.

Northwest Coast Music

Nowhere else in North America was the idea so strongly developed that songs belonged legally only to one family or even to one person. Religion, the subject of much of the music, was also a private matter since much of the supernatural power available to an individual was passed down to him in his family inheritance. There were also individual dream songs and a large literature of personal songs addressed to members of the family. Group observances such as the Spirit Dance appealed to ancestral spirits, and there were thanksgiving ceremonies honoring the spirits of salmon and other gifts of nature. Much of this tradition continues today: potlatch songs, love songs, and spirit songs are still performed. A new syncretistic religion, the Shaker Church, combines Christian ideas with important ideas of the old Spirit Dance.

The musical instruments of the Northwest Coast require special mention. The rich inventory of rattles and drums, present here as elsewhere in North America, has the special feature of carved and painted rattles in the shape of birds, especially the mythical Raven. In addition there are wooden whistles, flutes, and horns in great variety, some of them played on the bagpipe principle by squeezing an attached fish bladder full of air. A double reed cedarwood "horn" is the only instance of this member of the aerophone family noted for North America. Some of the whistles are carved in such a way that a single oblong wooden instrument produces four different pitches when blown at each of its four corners.

The vocal style, less intense than that of the Plains or the Athabascans of the Southwest, is reminiscent of the eastern Woodlands. The singing is often highly emotional. Songs dedicated to particular members of the family bring back overpowering personal memories. The moods range from playfulness to deep melan-

choly, and the melodies seem to reflect these moods in ways recognizable even to listeners from outside the tradition.

Example 17-9 illustrates the playful side of Northwest Coast music. It is about the trickster deity, Raven, who was given whiskey by a friendly Russian sea captain and began to feel happy. The event is celebrated in a dance song that would be suitable for guests to sing after a potlatch. The words are simple:

> Raven was drinking;
> He didn't care about anything.
> The wolf says, "Take pity."

This song is downward in its general melodic direction but not in the plunging arclike manner of Plains music. The first long phrase is undulating in its movement and so is most of the second. The tonic is reached in the third phrase, but the melody bounds upward again and a strong definition of the tonic is only achieved in the last few measures of the song. The outstanding features are the comic words and the strongly syncopated rhythmic structure. The interplay between the leaping, offbeat vocal part and the strong, steady drumming seems to fit the playful character of the song as a whole.

In general, other outstanding features of Northwest Coast music are close-knit melodies (stepwise and even chromatic progressions), extended melodic development resulting in long phrases, and sometimes an unusual number of different phrases before a repeat. There is a tendency, found also in Eskimo music [see essay on Eskimo music in this volume], for the melody as a whole to rise in pitch so that by the end of the song the tonic may be as much as a third higher than it was at the beginning.

NEW NATIVE MUSIC AND MUSICAL INTERESTS

Although elements of Western influence are apparent in some of the musics discussed above (powwow music, Northwest Coast music), many styles of new music, in English, with guitars, can be heard on the reservations and in Native American communities in such large cities as Los Angeles, San Diego, and Chicago.

There are between twenty and thirty radio stations that devote air time to Native Ameri-

FIGURE 17-9. Apache fiddle of hollowed-out century plant stalk. Fiddle and bow string are both of horsehair. Photograph courtesy of Daniel W. Gómez-Ibáñez

EXAMPLE 17-9. Funny Dance Song: How Raven Became Drunk on Whiskey. De Laguna, *Under Mt. St. Elias* (1972:1268–70), transcribed by McAllester. Sung by Charley White, Jack Reed, Jenny White, Minnie Johnson at Yakutat Bay, Alaska, 1952.

can listeners. This may range from a few hours a day on a commercial station to the Public Service radio KTDB-FM in Ramah, New Mexico, which broadcasts to Navajos, mostly in their own language, for eighteen hours a day, seven days a week. The music requests received by such programs indicate the tastes and interests of the radio-listening segment of the Native American population. Some traditional Native music is requested but the favorites are non-Native stars of country and western music such as Glen Campbell and Don Williams. There are numerous Navajo, Zuni, Hopi, and Hualapi country and western bands. "The Fenders"

(Navajo) have been making personal appearances and selling their records for fifteen years. "The Sundowners" (also Navajo) are currently the most commercially successful. "Xit" and "Redbone" are rock bands made up, in large part, of urban Indians in Albuquerque and Los Angeles, respectively. They have a large following of Native and non-Native fans across the country.

Several styles of religious music are high on the request lists, including country gospel and inspirational Indian music from the Mormon Church. The latter makes some use of Native languages and traditional vocables, but the po-

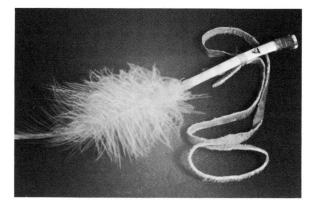

FIGURE 17-10. Eagle-bone whistle used in the Plains Sun dance. Decorated with sacred eagle down. Photograph courtesy of Daniel W. Gómez-Ibáñez

pular appeal comes from the Nashville-style melody and backup orchestra.

Although traditional music retains much of its former function and vitality, many new sounds have been added to the repertory, especially in the last twenty years. The new music shows a continuation of the strong religious orientation mentioned earlier in this essay, a highly articulate "red consciousness," aimed at both the Native American and the non-Native American worlds, an identification with a country and western ethos, and an impressive skill in performing Euro-Afro-American popular musical styles in which are expressed both Native and non-Native American ideas.

* * *

There are inevitable limits in any discourse on music by words alone. This is particularly true in the case of Native American music, much of which is inseparable from social or religious dance. In actual performance, costume and movement are an essential part of the whole, especially when the costume may include bells, deer-hoof or shell jingles, or other sound-making elements.

To all this should be added the light of campfires, the pungent smell of woodsmoke, and the fragrance of Indian cooking. Until one has experienced it one can only guess at the social excitement of a powwow or the solemn power of

a religious ceremonial. Today we must also consider such elements as the tape recorder, the transistor radio, and the overwhelming effect of a group such as "The Sundowners," highly amplified, performing for an audience of hundreds of Navajo teenagers at the Civic Center at Tuba City, or Window Rock, Arizona. It is the cultural context of any music that conveys its ultimate meaning.

Bibliography

GENERAL

Bibliographies
The American Indian in Graduate Studies, a Bibliography of Theses and Dissertations, Contributions from the Museum of the American Indian.
   1957. Vol. 15. New York: Heye Foundation. 13,684 items, 40 under "music."
Murdock, George Peter.
   1960. *Ethnographic Bibliography of North America.* New Haven: Human Relations Area Files.

Textbooks on the American Indian
Driver, Harold.
   1961. *Indians of North America.* Chicago: University of Chicago Press.
Indians of the Americas.
   1955. Washington, D.C.: National Geographic Society. A "color-illustrated record."
Leacock, Eleanor B., and Nancy O. Lurie, eds.
   1971. *North American Indians in Historical Perspective.* New York: Random House.
Spencer, Robert F. et al.
   1965. *The Native Americans.* New York: Harper and Row.
Underhill, Ruth M.
   1953. *Red Man's America.* Chicago: University of Chicago Press.
Walker, Deward E., Jr.
   1972. *The Emergent Native Americans, a Reader in Culture Contact.* Boston: Little, Brown.

Books on the Contemporary Scene
Cahn, Edgar S.
   1969. *Our Brother's Keeper: The Indian in White America.* New York: World Publishers.

Deloria, Vine, Jr.
    1969. *Custer Died for Your Sins.* New York: Macmillan.

De Laguna, Frederica.
    1972. *Under Mt. St. Elias: The History and Culture of the Yakutat Tlingit.* Smithsonian Contributions to Anthropology, vol. 7, part 3. Washington, D.C.: Smithsonian Institution Press.

McNickle, D'Arcy.
    1962. *The Indian Tribes of the United States: Ethnic and Cultural Survival.* New York: Oxford University Press.

Steiner, Stan.
    1968. *The New Indians.* New York: Harper and Row.

Textbooks and the American Indians.
    1970. San Francisco: Indian Historian Press.

Waddell, Jack O., and O. Michael Watson.
    1971. *The American Indian in Urban Society.* Boston: Little, Brown.

Wyman, Leland C.
    1965. *The Red Antway of the Navajo.* Santa Fe, N.M.: Museum of Navajo Ceremonial Art.

AMERICAN INDIAN NEWSLETTERS

Akwesasne Notes.
    Mohawk Nation, via Rooseveltown, N.Y. 13683.

The Navajo Times.
    P.O. Box 310, Window Rock, Arizona 86515.

AMERICAN INDIAN MUSIC

Bibliographies

Frances Densmore and American Indian Music.
    1968. Compiled and edited by Charles Hofmann. New York: New York Museum of the American Indian, Heye Foundation. Lists 175 of her books and articles on American Indian music, 7 recordings, 8 completed, unpublished Mss.

"Special Bibliography, Gertrude Prokosch Kurath."
    1970. Compiled by Joann W. Kealiinohomuku and Frank J. Gillis. *Ethnomusicology* 14 (January), 114-28.

Books and Articles

Curtis, Natalie.
    1968. *The Indians' Book.* New York: Harper, 1907; rev. ed., 1923; Dover paperback, 1968. Contains many excellent transcriptions from 19 tribes across the country.

Densmore, Frances.
    1910. *Chippewa Music.* Bulletin 45. Washington, D.C.: Bureau of American Ethnology.
    1913. *Chippewa Music II.* Bulletin 53. Bureau of American Ethnology.
    1918. *Teton Sioux Music.* Bulletin 61. Bureau of American Ethnology.
        These are the outstanding ones. Others in the BAE series are: *Mandan and Hidatsa,* 80; *Menominee,* 102; *British Columbia,* 136; *Nootka and Quileute,* 124; *Northern Ute,* 75; *Papago,* 90; *Pawnee,* 93; *Yuman and Yaqui,* 110.

Fletcher, Alice C.
    1893. *A Study of Omaha Indian Music.* Cambridge, Mass.: Harvard University Press.
    1904. *The Hako.* 22nd Annual Report, Part 2. Washington, D.C.: Bureau of American Ethnology.

Fletcher, Alice C., and Francis LaFlesche.
    1911. *The Omaha Tribe.* 27th Annual Report, No. 27 (1906). Washington, D.C.: Bureau of American Ethnology.

Garfield, Viola, Paul S. Wingert, and Marius Barbeau.
    1952. *The Tsimshian: Their Arts and Music.* No. 18. New York: American Ethnology Society.

Herzog, George.
    1935. "Plains Ghost Dance and Great Basin Music." *American Anthropologist* 37 (July), 403-19.
    1936. "A Comparison of Pueblo and Pima Musical styles." *Journal of American Folklore* 49, 283-417.

Hoffman, W.J.
    1891. "The Midewiwin or 'Grand Medicine Society' of the Ojibwa." In *Seventh Annual Report of the Bureau of Ethnology, 1855-1886,* pp. 149-300. Washington, D.C.: Government Printing Office.

Kurath, Gertrude P.
    1968. *Dance and Song Rituals of Six Nations Reserve, Ontario.* Bulletin 220. Ottawa: National Museum of Canada.

Kurath, Gertrude P., with Antonio Garcia.
    1970. *Music and Dance of the Tewa Pueblos.* Museum of New Mexico Research Records, No. 8. Santa Fe: Museum of New Mexico Press.

McAllester, David P.
    1949. *Peyote Music.* New York: Viking Fund Publications in Anthropology.
    1952. "Menomini Peyote Music." In *Menomini Peyote,* edited by J. S. Slotkin, pp. 681-700.

Transactions of the American Philosophical Society, vol. 42, part 4.

1954. *Enemy Way Music.* Papers of Peabody Museum, vol. 41, no. 3. Cambridge, Mass.: Harvard University Press.

1961. *Indian Music of the Southwest.* Colorado Springs: Taylor Museum.

Merriam, Alan P.

1967. *Ethnomusicology of the Flathead Indians.* Chicago: Aldine Press.

Nettl, Bruno.

1954. *North American Indian Musical Styles.* Philadelphia: American Folklore Society.

1969. "Musical Areas Reconsidered: A Critique of North American Indian Research." In *Essays in Musicology in Honor of Bragan Plamenac on His 70th Birthday*, edited by Gustave Reese and Robert J. Snow, pp. 181-89. Pittsburgh: University of Pittsburgh Press.

Roberts, Helen.

1933. *Form in Primitive Music.* New York: Norton. With 30 transcriptions of Southern California songs.

1936. *Musical Areas in Aboriginal North America*, No. 12. New Haven: Yale University Publications in Anthropology.

Roberts, Helen, with Morris Swadesh.

1955. *Songs of the Nootka Indians of Western Vancouver Island.* Transactions of the American Philosophical Society, vol. 45, part 3.

Speck, Frank G.

1911. *Ceremonial Songs of the Creek and Yuchi Indians*, II. Philadelphia: University of Pennsylvania Publications in Anthropology. 120 transcriptions.

1940. *Penobscot Man.* Philadelphia: University of Pennsylvania Press. 40 transcriptions by Edward Sapir.

1942. *The Tutelo Spirit Adoption Ceremony.* Harrisburg, Penn.: Pennsylvania Historical Commission. 24 transcriptions by George Herzog.

Discography

General

Indian Songs of Today. AAFS L36. recorded and edited by Willard Rhodes.

Songs of Earth, Water, Fire, and Sky: Music of the American Indians. New World 246. Recorded and edited by Charlotte Heth.

Woodlands

Creek-Seminole Native Gospel Songs. Soundchief 401.

Delaware, Cherokee, Choctaw, Creek. AAFS L37. Recorded and edited by Willard Rhodes.

Iroquois Social Dance Songs (3 records). Irocrafts. Notes by William Guy Spittal.

Menomini. Soundchief 300.

Seneca Songs from Coldspring Longhouse. AAFS L17. Recorded and edited by William N. Fenton in cooperation with the Smithsonian Institution.

Songs and Dances of Great Lakes Indians. Folkways 4003. Recorded by Gertrude P. Kurath.

Plains

Comanche, Cheyenne, Kiowa, Caddo, Wichita, Pawnee. AAFS L39. Recorded and edited by Willard Rhodes.

Handgames of the Kiowa, Kiowa Apache, and Comanche. Indian House 2501. Recording and notes by Tony Isaacs.

Indian Music of the Canadian Plains. Folkways 4464. Recorded by Kenneth Peacock.

Kiowa. AAFS L35. Recorded and edited by Willard Rhodes.

Music of the Sioux and the Navajo. Folkways 4401. Recorded by Willard Rhodes.

Sioux. AAFS L40. Recorded and edited by Willard Rhodes.

War Songs of the Ponca (2 records). Indian House 2001-2002. Recording and notes by Tony Isaacs.

Southwest

Apache. AAFS L42. Recorded and edited by Willard Rhodes.

Music of the American Indians of the Southwest. Folkways 4420. Recorded by Willard Rhodes in cooperation with U.S. Bureau of Indian Affairs.

Navajo. AAFS L41. Recorded and edited by Willard Rhodes.

Navajo Skip, Dance, and Two-Step Songs. Indian House 1503. Recording and notes by Tony Isaacs.

Night and Daylight Yeibichai (Navajo). Indian House 1502. Recording and notes by Tony Isaacs.

Pueblo, Apache, Navajo. Taylor Museum. Recorded by David P. McAllester, edited by Donald N. Brown.

Pueblo: Taos, San Ildefonso, Zuni, Hopi. AAFS L43. Recorded and edited by Willard Rhodes.

Round Dance Songs of Taos Pueblo. Indian House 1001. Recording and notes by Tony Isaacs.

Songs of the Papago. AAFS L31. Recorded and edited by Frances Densmore.

Great Basin

Great Basin: Paiute, Washo, Ute, Bannock, Shoshone. AAFS L38. Recorded and edited by Willard Rhodes.

Northwest Coast
Northwest (Puget Sound). AAFS L34. Recorded and edited by Willard Rhodes.
Songs of the Nootka and Quileute. AAFS L32. Recorded and edited by Frances Densmore.

California
Songs of Love, Luck, Animals, and Magic: Songs of Yurok and Tolowa Indians. New World 297. Recorded and edited by Charlotte Heth.

Films

Resource
A Filmography for American Indian Education.
Prepared for Carroll Warner Williams and Gloria Bird. Santa Fe: Zia Ciné, 1973. With the support of Research and Cultural Studies Development Section, Santa Fe, Bureau of Indian Affairs, United States Department of the Interior. In addition to films on the Indians of North America, includes films on the Eskimo and the Indians of Mexico, Central and South America.

The Exiles. UCLA. B/W. 72 min. Directed by Kent Mackenzie.
"A sensitive and accurate picture of urban Indian life portraying the difficulties of resettlement from the reservation to a big city. A few scenes showing contemporary powwow music are included and a brief example of traditional music on the reservation." D. P. McAllester.

Washoe. WAAC. B/W. 56 min. Directed by Veronica Pataky.
"A picture of the life of the Washoe Indians of Nevada focused on traditional ceremonies such as the Pine Nut Ceremony and the girls' Puberty Ritual. A handgame is also shown with singing and drumming on boards." D. P. McAllester.

18. Music of the Alaskan Eskimos

Lorraine D. Koranda

The sounds of Eskimo music are heard along the top of the world in the arctic regions of North America and Asia. Although there are distinctly "Eskimo" characteristics in all the music, each geographical area and each group of people within an area have their own variations and styles. For instance, the Canadian Eskimos share most of the folklore (for texts), musical structure, instruments, and dances with other Eskimos; however, since they tend to be more nomadic than most, they have more limited art forms. There is generally less ceremonial purpose to their music and a more active dancing style; individual Canadian groups will vary as to whether the music is performed indoors or out, the manner of playing a drum, or how the dancers are arranged in a particular song. This essay focuses on the style and performing traditions of the Alaskan Eskimo—since I have conducted most of my field study and research, recording and documentation, in this part of the Eskimo's arctic—but illustrates the basic characteristics of all Eskimo music.

Eskimo music and performing practices are derivatives of the natural and social environment of the musician. The Eskimo's survival has depended until recent times on his ability as a hunter and his ingenuity in providing the basic needs of shelter, food, and clothing. To assure success in these tasks frequent appeals were made to the *inua* (spirits) of animals or to the spirit of the atmosphere, *sila* (exs. 18-1 and 18-2). The appeal was made primarily through the medium of drum songs sung by the hunter himself or through an intermediary, the *angakok* or shaman. Rituals and festivals involving singing, dancing, mime, feats of magic, story-telling, and sporting competition were celebrated to honor the spirits. The singing of traditional songs was an important activity connected with the traditional rituals. For each celebration new songs were composed, and participants performed personal and family songs. From these celebrations evolved a wealth of Eskimo song literature that adds immeasurably to our understanding of Eskimo culture as a whole.

Eskimo songs refer to every facet of life. By far the most numerous are the hunting power songs, which relate hunting incidents or are connected with stories of courageous hunting feats. Included in this category are the hunting songs for good fortune. Composed by the hunter or by an angakok, the power songs were used sparingly, only for the purpose intended, and formerly were never sung solely as entertainment, though they may be today.[1]

Power songs could be purchased; but if the purchaser failed to pay, he would forget the words. "It happened every time," claimed one knowledgeable informant (Koranda 1962:Field Notes).

The angakok's hunting power songs include boat launching songs, gut parka songs for whale hunting success, special songs for placing the final stitches in the umiak (open skin boat), harpoon power songs, songs to weaken a whale after it was harpooned, and whale hunting ceremonial songs. In addition, there are power

---

1. An informant told of singing a song in the presence of his mother, who demanded to know where he had learned it. When he told her that he had heard his father sing it while they were seal hunting, she ordered her son never to sing it again. It was his father's seal hunting power song. To sing it for any purpose other than the hunt would dissipate its power.

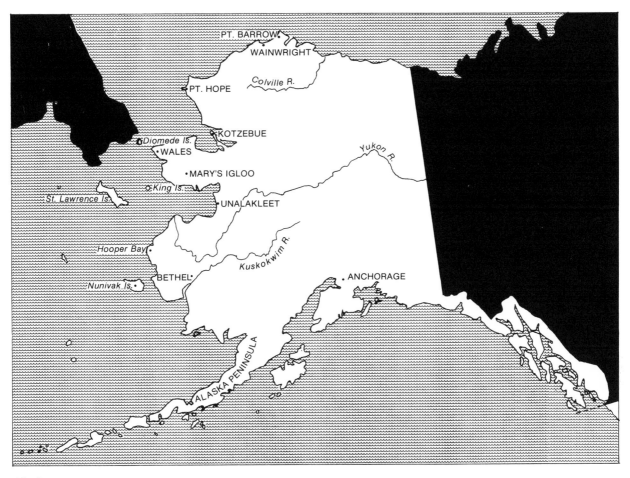

Alaska

songs composed to honor spirits of the animals, such as seals, whale, caribou, reindeer, wolves, foxes, and birds. There are relatively few polar bear songs, few walrus songs, and very few fishing songs.

Power songs also were sung to transport the singer, by means of self-hypnosis and through a trancelike state of mind, to a world apart.[2] An

interesting ritual game song composed for the whale hunt celebration (*nelukatuk*) is the *nelukataun*, or Blanket Toss Song. Other games, such as the making of "cat's cradle" string

2. Relative to such experiences is an account that illustrates a contemporary Eskimo's attitude toward shamanism. Field investigation included asking informants to relate the first musical experience they could recall. An informant, whose family had included several angakoks, told of awakening one night when he was so small that he "couldn't sit up because the diaper was too big." His mother was no longer in bed, but was seated on the floor singing and drumming. The scene remained in his memory, and several years later he asked his mother what she had been doing that night. She told him that she had become very lonesome for the subject's older brother, who was then at an arctic

whaling camp near Herschel Island. So she sang a power song to transport herself to the camp. Arriving at the camp, the mother saw that her son's mukluks needed mending, so she picked them up, but was startled by the sound of the boy's tent companions awakening. Hastily running out of the tent to prevent their seeing her spirit-self, she accidentally kicked over the chamber pot and dropped her son's mukluks.

When the son returned home, his mother asked him if anything unusual had happened at the whaling camp. "Yes," he replied. "One night I put my mukluks by my bedroll; but when I awoke, one was outside the tent, and the other was wet because the pot was dumped over." The informant clearly indicated that he believed his mother had visited the brother by means of the power song and drumming. He and many other informants believe, however, that such power probably is not possible today, or necessary.

Yahng ah ah ahng ah-ah s'mit kuk ah ah-ah ah-ahng puh mahng ah ah-ah

yahng eh yahng eh un-gey-hah i ka yo ung ah ah yeh yah ah ah——ah

ung ah eh s'lyah ee-yah-eh s'lya mo kah ung ah yah nitkahtchuk mo——

ung oh it-tchu-uk oh nah ah nee l'yahng ah ay yung eh eh eh

EXAMPLE 18-1. Weather Power Song, Kotzebue.

1. Text fragmentary, with several recognizable words, among them "Sila," and meaningless syllables. Five ascending slurred note patterns, two descending; remainder of text syllabic.
2. Scale pentatonic, M2, M2, m3, M2. Pitch center and final cadence E. Repeated notes mark half cadence and final cadence.
3. Meter varied and chantlike.
4. Range M6, except for one B that extends it to an octave. Sung octave lower.
5. Phrase rhythm comparatively ornate. Rhythmic figure 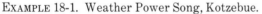 marks end of measures 4, 8, and 9. Some syncopation. "Sila" pattern marked by grace note. Rhythmic repetition, measures 1 and 2; repeated figures, measures 5, 6, and 7.

figures, juggling beach rocks, and jumping rope, also are accompanied by special songs.

Three of the most important festivals, the Messenger Feast, the Bladder Festival, and the Great Feast to the Dead were marked by complicated musico-dramatic performances; for the Trading Festival there were competitive dances and the performance of personal and family songs (Lantis 66:53–74).

Fortune songs other than those composed for hunting power are also known. The Top Spinning Fortune Songs from Point Hope and the personal fortune songs from the St. Michael area are examples of these.

At Point Hope, a unique set of fortune songs accompanies the spinning of a top. This top spinning performance was reported in 1927 by Rasmussen, who had witnessed it in connection with a Great Thanksgiving Festival to the souls of dead whales (Rasmussen 1927:332–33). These songs and the spinning of the top are now part of the Point Hope festivities at Christmas. The top, about a foot tall, is adorned with feathers so fastened that they fly off as the top is spun and

EXAMPLE 18-2. Shaman's Hunting Power Song, Hooper Bay.

1. Text indistinct, but begins with "Sila." Except for several two-pitch slurs, the text is syllabic.
2. Scale essentially pentatonic. Song begins and ends on Bᵇ, the pitch center. Sections and final cadence, Bᵇ.
3. Meter alternates 4/4 and 3/4.
4. Range M7, although the highest pitch (G) is heard only once.

fortune songs are sung (ex. 18-3). If the top does not spin well, bad luck is indicated for the singer. Puppets are associated with the top spinning performance. Puppet rowing songs are performed to accompany the action of toy figures seated in an umiak. Although such performances are rare today, one such puppet rowing song has been collected by the author.

Since the old angakok songs or power songs were learned by relatively few singers, were not sung very often lest their power abate, and may have included archaic words or the angakok's secret language, the transcription and translation of their texts is difficult. A contemporary singer may have forgotten the words of these and other very old songs; song texts may be quite fragmentary. Therefore it is imperative to have the singer give a translation of the song and discuss its meaning. Some discrepancies in actual text and interpretation will be noted. Literal translations leave much doubt as to the meaning of the text and suggest fascinating areas for future study. An example here serves to emphasize this point. An old angakok's song

EXAMPLE 18-3. Top Spinning Fortune Song, Point Hope.

1. Text somewhat indistinct, but consists of meaningful words and meaningless syllables.
2. Scale six tones. Melody consists of M3, A-F and M3, F-D♭. C is introduced by a skip of m3 just preceding the final cadence. Both M3 intervals have stepwise closures.
3. Meter 6/8. Phrase rhythm has some syncopation.
4. Range M6.
5. Intonation on pitch that will be tonic, but is not introduced into the melodic line until measure 12.
6. Drum accompaniment ♩♫ throughout. Drum ends before song ends.

(ex. 18-4) whose subject is the finding of a rock with a hole in it to use for a magic amulet has this literal text:

> The lamp's whale oil
> In the land back up there
> As I search for a hole.

It is essential that the informant explain the meaning of this song, for otherwise it is evanescent and could be interpreted in several ways. The song means that the angakok was roaming the beach at night looking for a special amulet—a rock with a hole in it to wear on a string around his neck. The translators suggested that the hole might represent the idea of escape, the use of self-hypnosis to induce the trancelike state which would enable the angakok to free his mind from his body and travel to a distant land under the sea, to the moon, or to another part of the known world.

A similar problem of translation was encountered in one of the old string game songs, of which many are extant. This one is sung by an elderly informant from Wainwright. The "Song for Unwinding String" is known to be very old, and the performer, whose knowledge of traditions is extensive, professes not to know what the words mean. The text includes archaic or meaningless words. This is what remains:

> The bearded seal's ?
> A hole there on its front
> (words unknown)
> Whose 'person' is this that comes?
> Let me do it her?
> Do it, Hey!

[Reed 1972]

EXAMPLE 18-4. Shaman's Amulet Song, King Island.
1. Text fragmentary, with numerous meaningless syllables, and predominantly syllabic.
2. Scale essentially six pitches, but scalewise progressions are limited to three adjacent pitches (measures 2, 4, 7, 9). Extended cadence on F. Pitch center seems to be E♭, since the melodic figures descend to it regularly.
3. Meter alternates 6/8 with 9/8. Note a possible shift, measures 5 and 6.
4. Range M7, but the highest pitch (D) is heard only once.
5. Phrase rhythm complex, with syncopation, dotted note figures, ties, and slurs. Singer intones introduction rhythmically related to the song.
6. Drum accompaniment regular. Note cross-rhythm at final cadence.

Many myths relate the transformation of sea mammals into human beings who would sometimes mate with men in order to populate an area. This may be a song related to such a story (Reed 1972).

Along the entire coast of Alaska north of the Kuskokwim, juggling songs, which accompanied a women's game of juggling beach rocks, are known.[3] These songs, being extremely old, have some archaic words or meaningless syllables, and the sentences are fragmentary (ex. 18-5). The text is invariably indelicate, treating the subject of a woman's lack of physical attraction for her husband or alluding to sexual intercourse.[4] It is difficult to persuade a Christianized Eskimo woman to sing the song in its entirety. Modesty forbids the singing of some of the words, so the singer may substitute meaningless syllables. Some of the songs are so old that the meaning of the fragmentary word groups is lost.

There are numerous versions of these juggling songs, some containing melodic figures borrowed from others (ex. 18-6). There are also contextual relationships between some songs, as illustrated in the translations that follow:

Unalakleet Juggling Song

I am juggling like a seagull
Parallel-juggling like a seagull
Going faster like a hawk flies
On the island where the birds nest
On a sandy point on the island
On a place where loose sand . . .
Ikitaar (name of young bride)

3. Today, women of the Kuskokwim area know the juggling game, but profess not to know the songs.
4. Murdoch, observing a performance of the juggling song and game, wrote: "I never succeeded in catching the words of this chant, which are uttered with considerable rapidity, and do not appear to be ordinary words. . . . Some of the words are certainly indelicate to judge from the unequivocal gestures by which I once saw them accompanied" (1892:384).

EXAMPLE 18-5. Juggling Song, Unalakleet.

1. Text predominantly syllabic, unusually complete, and poetically complex.
2. Scale pentatonic to measure 25. Measures 26-45 use six pitches. A seventh pitch is introduced in measure 46. Measures 9 and 11 contain a portamento. The pitch center is G♯.
3. Meter alternates 2/4 with 3/4.
4. Range M7.
5. Melodic organization inventive. The song "radiates" from m3 (measures 1 and 5) to P4 (measures 25 and 29) to P5 (measures 33 and 35). Then the design is reversed (measures 41 and 46), and the song ends with an M2 cadence. Much repetition of phrases or measures.

EXAMPLE 18-7. Joking Song, Point Hope.

1. Text is indistinct, except for joking partner's name. Meaningless syllables employed.
2. Scale pentatonic. Pitch center probably C♯. Unusual repetition of tonic C♯, dominant G♯, and final cadence supertonic D♯. This song seems harmonically based, yet it retains the chantlike motion, the supertonic cadence, and the gapped scale of older examples.
3. Meter varied, irregular.
4. Range very wide, octave plus m3. Personal song; reflects singer's vocal skill. Sung an octave lower.
5. Singer intones introduction without reference to the rhythmic patterns in the song. One repeated melodic design, measures 6, 7 and 8, 9.

up there?") The informant translates this, "Why is that raven hollering over on the bank?" The meaning, according to the informant, is that the contestant being tossed on the walrus-hide blanket must look out toward the horizon, not at his feet, or he will lose his balance and fall. Rude and humorous insults were hurled at the contestant in the blanket in an attempt to cause the player such embarrassment that he would fall. A nelukataun that illustrates this has a text translated as: "See that woman in the blanket. She thinks she knows my husband." The Eskimo women interpret "knows" to mean "has intimate knowledge," and consider the song very amusing.

Joking Partner Songs, another type of ridicule song, were very common in the past (ex. 18-7). A few may still be heard, but several of the renowned joking partnerships have been dissolved by death, so the song type is quite rare.

It seems to have bound together in a special friendship cousins or chosen unrelated partners who resided in separate villages.[6] The best examples of joking songs extant are by men partners, but several women's joking songs indicate that women also engaged in this activity. Several joking song texts are:

> I call my reindeer Milligrok.

The singer had an especially close relationship with his partner, whose name he gave to his reindeer.

> I wish to see my cousin from Shungnak.
> I will dance to his songs.

The singer is anxious to hear from his cousin through song.

> See how that man walks! [He limps.]
> I wouldn't want to be seen walking like that!

The singer is ridiculing one who "walks funny," but is not crippled.

> Diomede girls are without eyebrows, without
>   chins, and have big mustaches.

After extolling the virtues of girls from Noorvik, Selawik, Kobuk, and Kotzebue, the singer insulted the Diomede girls, and his Diomede Joking Partner took offense. The partnership was ended.

In order to send a song to one's joking partner in another village, it was necessary to teach the song to someone who was going to that village. The messenger would then "deliver" this song to the joking partner and learn his reply song to take back to the home village. These partnerships also existed for the exchange of material gifts as well as for song. The gift exchange between partners was part of the Trading Festival and the Messenger Feast.

Traditional songs were sung for the Messenger Feast, a hunting festival similar to the potlatch of the Northwest Indians, which was known in every part of Eskimo Alaska (Lantis

66:62). The feast usually took place during the winter, although it may have been given in spring or summer. The *umealik* (headman) of the village extended an invitation to the headman of a neighboring village to attend a feast and gift exchange. The host was privileged to indicate the kinds of gifts he expected, and in return gave generously of food and material gifts. The festival lasted for several days. Chosen runners sang the Invitation Songs. Welcome Songs were sung when the guests arrived. There were many competition songs, dances, races, and games.

Some songs were composed especially for the Messenger Feast, and during the course of the festivities many family and personal songs were performed. The traditional Wolf Dances, accompanied by box drum, originally had been composed and taught to the participants by the angakok (Koranda 72:15-18).

Texts for the Messenger Feast Invitation Songs are not known today, although a few tunes are sung haltingly and recalled with difficulty. This may be because the runner or messenger learned the song for the occasion, but once its function had been served the song was not likely to be added to the village repertoire. On the other hand, Welcome Songs have been retained in memory more successfully—perhaps because they were learned by a group and were, in some instances, passed along to succeeding generations.

A few Box Drum Songs are still recalled. Their texts are surprising. One of the best known says, "I never before saw a white man. This one carried a two-handled saw" (or "a saw with handles on both ends of it"). The song commemorates the coming of the first white man to Kotzebue Sound (ex. 18-8*a*, 18-8*b*). Such an event was considered worthy of remembrance in the celebration of the most important ritual in that area.

Another of the Wolf Dance Songs has the fragmentary text *anili taumna*, which means "Let it go out, that one." The Eskimos who knew the ritual interpret this to mean "Let us go out into the darkness," because this was the text of a farewell song to the honored headmen at the conclusion of the Feast. The same refrain is used

---

6. There is some disagreement between this statement and the analysis of joking partner relationships made by Spencer. The joking song from Kotzebue made for a cousin seems to indicate that occasionally relatives engaged in this kind of activity. See Spencer 1959:167-77, and Van Stone 1962:98-99.

EXAMPLE 18-9. Challenge Song, King Island.

1. Text complete poetic idea. Words are in phonetic transcription.
2. Scale essentially four tones. A fifth pitch (C) appears in measures 8 and 9 as the final cadence is approached. This characteristic also is found in ritual music for the Messenger Feast.
3. Meter alternates between 4/4 and 3/4. Rhythm and pitch combine to give a distinctive quality to the melodic line (P5 interval in sixteenths). Ascending intervals of P5, M3, and M2 all in six-teenths, with a final sixteenth on a unison, give further evidence of rhythmic and intervallic organization.
4. Range one octave.
5. Pitch center D. The melody is closely "anchored" to this pitch. Every measure but one contains it.
6. Accent on penultimate eighth in drum accompaniment often coincides with tied figure in vocal line to create interesting counter rhythm. Drum ceases before final two cadences pulses in voice line.

three songs had been perfected by one group, the rival kasigi was notified by loud banging on the floor. This marked the beginning of the celebration to honor the bladders. The ceremony concluded with the bladders being placed under the sea ice.[7] Some of the songs composed for the

Bladder Festival were used also for the Festival to the Dead (Koranda 72:18–20).

There are no war songs in Alaskan Eskimo musical literature. Tales of violence and blood revenge are told, and several blood revenge songs relating incidents of violence are known, but only one song even hints at an organized attack or defense (ex. 18-9). It is a challenge song from a King Island chief to the Siberians.

7. Songs and recollections of the Bladder Festival by Eskimos of Hooper Bay are to be found in *Alaskan Eskimo Songs and Stories* (Koranda, 1972).

The text says:

> I am strong
> I am healthy
> I will protect my people
> Come over
> I alone challenge you
> I have killed many Siberians
> Come over

"Bow and Arrow Fight Song" from Wainwright tells of a fight between an Eskimo and a white whaler over a woman. "Samururuk's Tobacco Song" relates an unfair trading incident that ended in violence long ago at Point Hope. Violence was not a common way, however, of settling disputes. In the past Eskimos preferred to settle disputes by means of ridicule song contests. The person who had a grievance challenged the offender to a song contest of ridicule and invective. The loser in this musical battle of wits suffered great shame, perhaps so great that he chose to leave the village. At times ridicule songs were sung at a social gathering to "punish" one who had offended the community.

Eskimo love songs range in emotional expression from simple statements of friendship to expressions of desire to mate. An example of the latter is "Kakiyana's Love Song" from Point Hope, a highly poetic old family song.

> What has cooled my house?
> The sun couldn't keep this house warm.
> Who is she?
> A young woman
> With a child in her parka.
> What has happened to my cold house?
> When she takes the child out,
> We are going to make love.

There is no need in the Eskimo culture for lullabies. A baby being bounced in the hood of its mother's parka as she goes about her daily chores will probably be quite content with the warmth and motion of the mother's body and will fall asleep to whatever tune she hums. But there are many songs composed for children, most of which exhibit the Eskimos' delightful sense of humor. Frequently Eskimo informants explain that the purpose of a song is to quiet the children "when they are noising too much" (Koranda 1953:Field Notes). Many string games and their accompanying songs are for children;

there are numerous stories with songs that are sung by animal characters, contain animal calls, and are used for social training. Children were relatively undisciplined (and still are) in Eskimo communities,[8] but frightening them by means of spirit performances in the kasigi and teasing them through song were quite common methods of discipline.

Songs were composed to commemorate first occasions.[9] The following text illustrates a teasing attitude toward a boy's first haircut (ex. 18-10), which now makes him look like a white man (*kassak*):

Bethel: Haircut Song

tanrumauligmi aŋ utŋ urteliniuq
tanrumauligmi caiyaqanriliniuq
qarelekumanrilŋ urnek
qaralelerluku
asmixteliniuatni
pacexluku ayaxluku
aa aa aa aa
Before I see him, he looks like a big man.
Before I see him, he is growing up.
He puts a different color on his head.
They cut hair, back of his head.
It looks like a kassak.

Another song, composed by the informant's grandmother in about 1900, had a text that asked, "Where can I find a father for this baby in my parka?" It is significant that many non-Eskimo women tend to interpret the text to mean that the child is probably illegitimate; but Eskimo women, upon hearing the song, question the fate of the child's father, saying, "Did he have an accident while hunting?" "Was he drowned?" "He must be dead."

There are numerous myths, legends, and folk stories, many of which include songs. The common themes in these are the orphaned child who lives with a grandmother, the lady shaman who plays evil tricks, the animal or bird that takes human form, the human who becomes animal,

8. Permissiveness in disciplining children is mentioned by Boas (1964 reprint:158-72) and commented on by Van Stone (1962:84-86).

9. A boy's hair was cut for the first time after he had killed his first bird or seal. In areas where the Bladder Festival was celebrated, the bladder of the bird or animal was saved for display during the ceremonies. A food treat might be given as a commemoration of this important event.

EXAMPLE 18-12. Song from "The Sea Gull," Point Hope.

1. Text syllabic with translatable words and archaic or untranslatable language.
2. Scale essentially pentatonic. A sixth pitch (A) occurs only once. B and B♭, marking the two outer limits of the range, occur only once each.
3. Meter 4/4 throughout.
4. Melody is sectional. In measures 1-4 G is the key center, with an m3 above and below. Measures 5 and 6 are repeated in 7 and 8. M2 refrain ends this section. E becomes new key center. The design encompasses a P4 above and a P4 below the new center. The final cadence is the M2 refrain. Final F♯.
5. Range dim octave.

Contemporary songs may refer to contemporary mechanical devices—an electric light placed in the dance hall, an Evinrude motor, or a low-flying plane observed while fishing. Others comment on contemporary events, such as the selection of a queen to reign over the community winter festival, Joe Louis's boxing victories, or a "Republican Stump Dance."[11]

In general, Eskimos tend to lack interest in national or international affairs unless these events touch their lives. During World War II they became extremely concerned at Little Diomede Island over contact with Soviet nationals from Big Diomede Island, which lies only two miles away. They still speak of the contact episode and, when singing songs learned from Siberian Eskimos, explain the source and manner of obtaining such songs. Incidentally, one of the favorite contemporary Siberian Eskimo songs says, "Where can I get a drink of whiskey? If I had some whiskey I could sing better."

Vast numbers of songs were composed to ac-company dancing, which is categorized either as ceremonial or for social purposes of entertainment. The dances were usually done in the kasigi, though in good weather they might also have been performed on the beach, with the drummers seated near the upturned umiak. Today the dances are most often performed in the community hall. The mimic dances that depict hunting scenes or activities such as the building of a sod house or icehouse are called "Acting Dances" at Barrow and Wainwright, and "Motion Dances" from Point Hope south. These dances are choreographed; all of the dancers do the same motions simultaneously. "Common Dances" or "Muscle Dances" are those in which anyone may dance using whatever motions he wishes. The term "Muscle Dance" may have referred at an earlier time to the actual rippling of arm and shoulder muscles and the rhythmically controlled contortions of the head and neck.

Eskimo dancers use only very limited floor space in executing their steps.[12] The women take

11. A few contemporary composers interpolate phrases of well-known community songs, such as "Long Way to Tipperary" or "Irish Washerwoman," into the Eskimo-style composition.

12. Exceptions to this spacial limitation are the Loon Dances of Point Barrow, in which the dancer imitates the loon's flight, and the line dances of the Messenger Feast and Bladder Festival.

EXAMPLE 18-13. Two Contemporary Songs.

a. Lonesome Song, Colville River.

1. Text is a combination of meaningful words and meaningless syllables, predominantly syllabic.
2. Scale is essentially pentatonic, although the sixth pitch (C) occurs twice prominently. It is avoided in measure 8, where the descending Eskimo theme (bracketed) emphasizes the gap.
3. Meter varied.
4. Range M6.
5. The melodic curve of descending P5 in the first four measures, followed by a narrowing into M3, the upward arc formed by sequential P4ths, and the narrowing or tightening process toward the end is an elaboration of the usual downward trend of the melodies. Measure 7 seems atypical in its sequential ascending P4ths. Phrase rhythm is complex. Extended repeated note cadence on A♭ pitch center, as in older Eskimo songs.
6. Drum accompaniment on pulse and regular throughout.

very short, shuffling steps, or remain in place while bending their knees, swaying, and moving their arms in a most graceful manner. As they dance, women invariably keep their eyes downward in deference to the men. The men dance boldly with very vigorous, exaggeratedly masculine motions. They, too, move very little from their dance positions, but shift their weight from one foot to the other and make percussive stamping sounds. The men hold their heads high; their faces reflect the enjoyment, excitement, or humor of the occasion. They may make animalistic sounds, such as seal barks, or be encouraged in their dancing by such calls from the drummers and singers. The dance usually starts quietly as the song is sung the first time, but upon its repetition the motions become very energetic (Lomax 68:226–27).

Dancers always wear or carry gloves. Ornamental dance mitts or gauntlet gloves are desirable, but ordinary cotton workman's gloves or woolen mittens are acceptable and commonly used. Eskimos cannot give a reason for this custom; but after much consideration, numbers of informants have expressed the idea that, since all dancing was at one time ceremonial for the purpose of pleasing the spirits, covering the hands that did menial tasks and which might touch ritual paraphernalia was required. They liken this to the non-Eskimo ceremonial practice of covering one's head in church or in the presence of the Holy Spirit. Another theory is that the gloves protected one, in the past, from evil spirits. Covering the hands was of such importance that dance gloves were never removed while dancing, even though women might strip to the waist and men dance nearly naked. Today the dance gloves are sometimes held symbolically rather than worn, but this is rare.

Eskimo dancers never touch hands while dancing or dance in closed position. Amused by Western dance styles, they often include in their contemporary dance programs satirical imitations of ballroom dancing—without touching their partners. One dance group also performs the "Eskimo Virginia Reel."

A style of dance that originated on Diomede Island is popular at Wales, and is imitated

FIGURE 18-1. Large carved wooden mask. Anthropomorphic face with peg teeth. Bands around the face and board, lips, and pegged-in teeth are red. The forehead is blue-black. On the reverse side eyes, nose, and mouth are rimmed with red. Height: 36.2 cm. ca. 1895. Courtesy of Dr. Frank Norick, Lowie Museum of Anthropology. Photograph by Dr. John Koranda.

dance gloves with percussive amulets are still in use, as previously stated. Although the Eskimos used bows and arrows in hunting and fighting, this did not inspire them to use the bow principle to develop a stringed instrument, although a few Eskimos have constructed one-string fiddles for personal use. Bones were never utilized for flutes, but in very early times they were used as clappers. Now they are rarely seen. Bone was used at times as a beater for the box drum. It is apparent that voice and keylowtik satisfied the Eskimos' musical needs.

The keylowtik or tchauyuk, which accompanies all dance performances, is a hoop of spruce or alder about two feet in diameter, covered on one side with a membrane from the whale's liver, walrus stomach membrane, or fawn skin. If these cover materials are not available, plastic may be substituted. Also in private performance a dustpan or garbage can lid will suffice if a keylowtik is not readily available. This membrane is stretched taut and secured with the sinew, which is wrapped around the drum frame. A short bone or wooden handle, sometimes carved ornamentally, is attached to the frame. The drum is held at about the height of the drummer's face and may be moved in a gently swaying motion or twirled at the conclusion of the performance. It is beaten with a slender, flexible willow or spruce stick, which may touch only the drum frame to produce a light tap, or strike both frame and drumhead, producing a resonant vibration of the membrane and a sharp accompanying tap. The frame and the drumhead are often struck alternately. On the north coast of Alaska the drum is struck from underneath, but in the area near the mouth of the Yukon and the Kuskokwim rivers it is generally struck on the upper surface, especially for the ceremonial dances.

The drum is usually played by men, but women are not excluded from playing it. Both men and women informants have stated that women may play the drum, but it is a rare experience to see one doing so.[13]

The drums are not tuned. Before and during a performance, however, the drummer dampens the drumhead with water to make it more resilient and less likely to break. The water does affect the pitch slightly and thus, although it is not applied with any particular intent to affect the pitch, the process is sometimes referred to as "tuning" the drum.

The drummer must know the song and the dance motions, and must provide a strongly rhythmic beat for the dancers. A talent for drumming is highly praised and widely recognized. The drummers of King Island are considered to be exceptionally talented, as are the Point Hope drummers, who have contributed a stylistic feature imitated at times by drummers from other villages. The Point Hopers usually end the drumming several pulses before the end of the song.

The ritual box drum (kaylukuk) was a box shape, open at both ends, to which a striking post was attached. The top of the box was shaped with five points on each side, and a simple design was painted around the top. Eagle

13. Exchange of men's and women's roles, including drumming, was noted by several investigators (Petrof, Curtis, and Lantis) and was reported by a King Island informant in 1962 (Koranda 1962:Field Notes).

FIGURE 18-2. Finger mask with anthropomorphic face and two finger holes. Lower Yukon River. Courtesy of Dr. Frank Norick, Lowie Museum of Anthropology. Photograph by Dr. John Koranda.

feathers, signifying the giver of the Messenger Feast ceremony to the Eskimos, decorated the top corners of the drum and the top of the beater. Eagle claws or baleen lacings were used as a design on the front panel. The drum was suspended from a tripod or from the kasigi ceiling pole. A drummer was selected for the honor of beating this ceremonial drum. His introductory drumbeat for the Wolf Dances was a rapid tattoo in imitation of the eagle's heartbeat. Box drums are used by several contemporary dance groups in concert performance.

The preferred voice quality for public performance is strident, loud, harsh, and without obvious variation in dynamic levels except for stress or accent. Crescendo and decrescendo are not generally employed in the shaping of a phrase. The language is particularly guttural, with several postvelar sounds that give a raspy effect to the vocal tone (Milan 58:52-58). The melodic contours are marked by a grating abrasiveness imparted to the tone by the language.[14] The songs are sung in unison or unison at the octave between men's and women's voices.

The drummers, usually men, are traditionally seated on the floor in a row facing the audience, and the chorus, usually women, is seated on the

14. The northern inyupiaq language is somewhat harsher than the west coastal language (yupik), which gives a more mellifluous sound quality to the vocal sound.

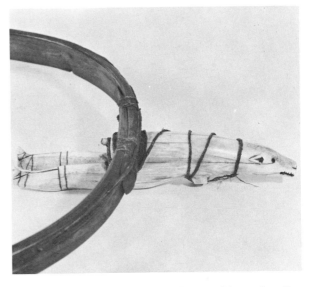

FIGURE 18-4. *Tchauyuk*, or *keylowtik* hoop frame drum. Wood handle represents long-beaked bird head with seal-like tail; drum head is seal or walrus bladder. Design of man with arms outstretched. Fish design between the forearms. Pre-1898. Courtesy of Dr. Frank Norick, Lowie Museum of Anthropology. Photograph by Dr. John Koranda.

FIGURE 18-5. Drum frame with carved ivory handle. The handle is a composite of polar bear, walrus, and human legs, which dangle separately. Pre-1898. Photograph by Dr. John Koranda.

of meaningless syllables or words, are repeated. Meaningless syllables used as a song text must be sung as meticulously as words. Therefore it is to be assumed that they are not entirely "meaningless," but might better be called "neutral." As previously stated, the texts are often fragmentary; since the songs have been passed along, orally, from generation to generation, the words may have been forgotten and nonsense syllables interpolated. There are sometimes archaic words or a language that now defies translation. It is evident, also, that the listener is expected to know to what event the song refers. The text is elliptical because more is not required for understanding.

The texts are predominantly syllabic, with few slurs. Word accent may vary from the speech accent; dance accent seems to take precedence over normal speech accent. The majority of songs are sung at a moderate tempo and are very brief, requiring less than one minute performing time per stanza. Exceptions to this are

the game songs, particularly the women's juggling songs, and some of the personal and family songs.

The musical material is commonly restricted to four or five pitches, although some songs may employ as many as six tones, or as few as two or three. From this limited material, several types of scale can be organized (ex. 18-15).

Final cadences are marked by repeated notes, sometimes several measures in duration. Repeated notes may also mark the end of a section or phrase. The cadence note invariably lies low in the scale. It is not necessarily the pitch that has been established by its frequency as the pitch center or tonic. The cadence is sometimes sung as a throbbing, repetitious pulsation. As in all unaccompanied singing, there are pitch discrepancies in the intonation. With the Point Hope singers this seems to be a deliberate alteration of tone downward, or flatting. On the whole, singers from other areas tend to sing "in tune" with no obviously deliberate deviation from European vocal intonation.

The melodic line may be embellished with grace notes, especially in power songs and ritual melodies. Repetition of melodic figures is heard,

FIGURE 18-6. Box Drum. Collected by Knud Rasmussen. Photograph provided by The National Museum, Copenhagen, Denmark. Courtesy of Dr. Helge Larsen.

but phrase repetition is rare. Exceptions are to be found in the game songs. There are sequence patterns, or "incipient" sequences, often at the interval of the fourth. Strings of successive thirds are evident; and the filling of interval gaps of fourths, fifths, or octave with combinations of descending thirds and seconds has produced a thematic figure so often heard that it can be termed an "Eskimo theme."

The widest intervals are heard early in the melodic structure, the melody tending to tighten into small intervals toward the final cadence, a characteristic to be observed in much of the aboriginal music of North America (McAllester 1949:71-73). The most interesting of such tightening processes is to be heard in an old juggling song, which starts with intervals of a third, progresses to skips of the fourth, then to a fifth, its widest interval. Then the pattern reverses, creating an arc not unlike the arc of a tossed pebble (ex. 18-5).

Portamenti in the melodic line are rare, but there are a few instances of their use. They are probably "borrowed" from Indian songs of adjacent areas.

The singer sometimes intones several pulses on one or two pitches to start the song (exs. 18-3, 18-4, 18-8*a*, 18-8*b*, 18-9). The intonation pattern may or may not share a rhythmic or thematic idea with the song. Its purpose is to settle the tonality of the song and its vocal placement. It is usually heard only once; but there are examples of very old songs from King Island being performed with an intonation at the beginning of each stanza of the song. The rhythm is generally free in the manner of a chant; the meter in many songs varies freely. However, keeping in mind that the bar lines are arbitrarily placed by the transcriber of the songs, the metric organization is at times astonishing.

Alternating duple (or compound duple) meter with triple (or compound triple) meter is common. Dance motions sometimes dictate a unique combination of metric patterns; for example, one women's dance song from Wainwright is organized into patterns of 5 pulses, 12, 5, 11, 9, 14 (5 plus 9), 5, 11, 9, 14 (5 plus 9), 11, 5, 2. If the dance motion requires it, a metrical pattern of 3/4 may be extended in an occasional measure by the addition of a single eighth note, resulting in a measure of 7/8. Similar extensions are made in what appears to be duple meter.

There are songs of course that are metrically

EXAMPLE 18-15. Scales and Vocal Range in Alaskan Eskimo Songs.

regular throughout, and there are several examples extant of songs that have an actual refrain marked by a metric change that continues throughout the final section. Having no concern for harmonic progression, the Eskimo is not bound by European systems of meter.

Although it is not a commonly used device, a few songs contain musical representation of the text, for example, a limping pattern in a ridicule song referring to a man's awkward gait, an angakok's laughter in a masked dance, complex phrase rhythms to imitate the loon's movements, a wide ascending interval in a blanket toss song, and animal sounds, such as walrus puffing, seal barks, wolf howls, and bird calls.

The Eskimo has had limited material with which to achieve his survival; the rigors of his life have required careful husbanding of this material. Economy of means is characteristic of his life and of his art forms. Except for those instances of the performance of a single power song or, as in the Messenger Feast ritual, the invitation song sung by the messenger, Eskimo songs seem to have been intended to be heard as parts of a whole—a series of auditory experiences. Through listening to a number of Eskimo songs, one perceives these qualities that distinguish Eskimo musical composition.

The old rituals are no longer performed in Alaska, but there has been very recently a revival of interest in the traditional Eskimo arts, which is being encouraged by the Alaska Festival of Music, the University of Alaska, and the Alaska Council of the Arts. Performing groups are active in the major cities and villages of Alaska, and native young people are becoming interested in the musical, dramatic, and practical arts and crafts of their own culture.

Glossary

angakok-shaman.
atun-among Canadian Eskimo, song and drum accompaniment to a dance.
deyoomiet-(literally) something held in the hand, dance fans.
inupiaq-Eskimo language from Seward Peninsula to Greenland.
inua-soul; spirit.

karigi, kasigi, kashim-ceremonial house, communal house.
kassak-white man.
kaylukok, kaylukuk-box drum.
keylowtik, kilaut-hoop frame drum.
mukluk-Eskimo fur boot.
nelukatuk-blanket (skin) toss, the whale ceremonial.
nelukataun-blanket toss song.
pisik-among Canadian Eskimo, a song with dance and drum accompaniment by the singer.
sauyit-hoop frame drum.
Sedna-in Eskimo mythology, "the woman who controls the sea."
sila-spirit of the atmosphere; spirit of weather.
tchauyuk-hoop frame drum.
umealik, umialik-headman or wealthy man; (literally) the boat owner.
umiak-open skin boat.
yupik-Eskimo language of the west coast of Alaska, south of the Yukon River, St. Lawrence Island, and the Siberian Eskimos.

Bibliography

Alaskan Eskimo
Anderson, H. Dewey, and Walter Crosby Eells.
   1935. *Alaska Natives: A Survey of Their Sociological and Educational Status.* Palo Alto: Stanford University Press.
Balikci, Asen.
   1970. *The Netsilik Eskimo.* Garden City, N. Y.: The Natural History Press. Pp. 134-44, 197-238.
Bandi, Hans-Georg.
   1964. *Eskimo Prehistory.* College: University of Alaska Press.
Barbeau, Marius, and Viola E. Garfield.
   1951. *The Tsimshian: Their Arts and Music.* New York: J. J. Augustin.
Birket-Smith, Kaj.
   1935. *The Eskimo.* New York: E. P. Dutton.
Boas, Franz.
   1888. *The Central Eskimos.* Report to the Smithsonian Institution. Reprinted. Lincoln: University of Nebraska Press, 1964.
   1901, 1907. *The Eskimo of Baffin Land and Hudson Bay.* Vol. 15, part 1 (1901), vol. 15, part 2 (1907). American Museum of Natural History.
Cavanaugh, Beverley.
   1972. "Annotated Bibliography: Eskimo Music." *Ethnomusicology* 16 (September), 479-87. This whole issue is the Canadian issue of *Ethnomusicology.*

Dall, William.
    1873. "Explorations on the Western Coast of North America." *Annual Report, Smithsonian Institution, 1873.* Washington: Government Printing Office, 1874.

Giddings, J. L., Jr.
    1956. *Forest Eskimos.* Philadelphia: University Museum Press.
    1961. *Kobuk River People.* Studies of Northern Peoples No. 1. College: University of Alaska Press.

Gubser, Nicholas J.
    1965. *The Nunamiut Eskimos, Hunters of Caribou.* New Haven: Yale University Press.

Hawkes, Ernest William.
    1913. *The "Inviting-In" Feast of the Alaskan Eskimo.* Department of Mines, memoir 45, no. 3. Ottawa: Government Printing Bureau.
    1914. *The Dance Festivals of the Alaskan Eskimos.* University of Pennsylvania Anthropological Publications, vol. 6, no. 2.

Hughes, Charles Campbell.
    1959. "Translation of I. K. Voblov's 'Eskimo Ceremonies.'" *Anthropological Papers* 7:71-90. College, Alaska: University of Alaska.

Hughes, Charles Campbell, with Jane M. Hughes.
    1960. *An Eskimo Village in the Modern World.* Ithaca: Cornell University Press.

Ingstad, Helge.
    1954. *Nunamiut: Among Alaska's Inland Eskimos.* New York: Norton. Pp. 238-50.

Jenness, Diamond.
    1922. *The Life of the Copper Eskimos. Report of the Canadian Arctic Expedition, 1913-1918.* Ottawa: F. A. Acland. 12:179-225.
    1924. *Eskimo Folklore. Report of the Canadian Arctic Expedition, 1913-1918,* Ottawa: F. A. Acland. Vol. 13.
    1959. *The People of the Twilight.* Chicago: University of Chicago Press.

Johnston, Thomas F.
    1976a. *Eskimo Music by Region, a Circumpolar Comparative Study.* Ottawa: National Museums of Canada, Canadian Ethnology Services. Paper 32. P. 222.
    1976b. "The Eskimo Songs of Northwestern Alaska." *Arctic* 29:7-19.
    1976c. "Eskimo music from King Island, Alaska." *Tennessee Folklore Society Bulletin* (Murfreesboro), 42:167-71.
    1976d. "The social background of Eskimo music in Northwest Alaska." *Journal of American Folklore,* 89:438-48.

Koranda, Lorraine D.
    1964. "Some Traditional Songs of the Alaskan Eskimos." *Anthropological Papers* 12:17-32. College: University of Alaska.
    1968. "Three Songs for the Bladder Festival, Hooper Bay." *Anthropological Papers* 14:27-31. College: University of Alaska.
    1970a. "Eskimo Music: The Songs and the Instruments." *Cross-Cultural Arts in Alaska. Alaska Review,* pp. 75-80. Anchorage: Alaska Methodist University.
    1970b. "Not a Lately Song." *University Review,* pp. 110-14. Kansas City: University of Missouri.
    1972. *Alaskan Eskimo Songs and Stories.* Seattle: University of Washington Press.

Lantis, Margaret.
    1947. *Alaskan Eskimo Ceremonialism.* American Ethnological Society Monograph 11. Reissue. Seattle: University of Washington Press, 1966.
    1953. "Nunivak Eskimo Personality As Revealed in the Mythology." *Anthropological Papers* 2:109-74. College: University of Alaska.
    1959. "Folk Medicine and Hygiene." *Anthropological Papers* vol. 8 no. 1. College: University of Alaska.
    1960. *Eskimo Childhood and Interpersonal Relationships.* Seattle: University of Washington Press.

Lommel, Andreas.
    1967. *Shamanism, The Beginnings of Art.* New York: McGraw-Hill.

Lomax, Alan.
    1968. *Folk Song Style and Culture.* No. 88. Washington: American Association for the Advancement of Science.

Lucier, Charles.
    1951-52. Field Notes.
    1958. "Noatagmiut Eskimo Myths." *Anthropological Papers* vol. 6, no. 2. College: University of Alaska.

McAllester, David.
    1949. *Peyote Music.* New York: Viking Fund Publications in Anthropology, no. 13.

McKennan, Robert A.
    1959. *The Upper Tanana Indians.* New Haven: Yale University Press.

Menager, Francis J., S.J.
    1962. *The Kingdom of the Seal.* Chicago: Loyola University Press.

Milan, Frederick.
    1958. *Observations on the Contemporary Eskimo of Wainwright, Alaska.* Technical Report 57-114. Fairbanks: Arctic Aeromedical Laboratory.

Murdoch, John.
    1892. *Ethnological Results of the Point Barrow Expedition.* Ninth Annual Report, Bureau of American Ethnology. Washington: Government Printing Office.
Nansen, Fridtjof.
    1893. *Eskimo Life.* Translated by William Archer. London: Longmans, Green.
Nelson, Edward William.
    1899. *The Eskimo about Bering Strait.* Eighteenth Annual Report, Bureau of Ethnology, Smithsonian Institution. Washington: Government Printing Office.
Nettl, Bruno.
    1953. "American Indian Music North of Mexico: Its Styles and Areas." Ph.D. dissertation, University of Michigan.
Oswalt, Wendell H.
    1963. *Napaskiak, An Alaskan Eskimo Community.* Tucson: University of Arizona Press.
Rasmussen, Knud.
    1927. *Across Arctic America.* Narrative of the Fifth Thule Expedition. New York: G. P. Putnam's Sons.
    1932. *The Eagle's Gift.* New York: Doubleday, Doran.
Ray, Dorothy Jean.
    1967. *Eskimo Masks: Art and Ceremony.* Photographs by Alfred Blaker. Seattle: University of Washington Press.
Ray, Patrick H.
    1885. *Report on the International Polar Expedition to Point Barrow.* Washington: Government Printing Office.
Reed, Irene.
    1972. Personal Communication.
Roberts, Helen H.
    1936. *Musical Areas in Aboriginal North America.* Yale University Publications in Anthropology, no. 12. New Haven: Yale University Press.
Roberts, Helen H., and Diamond Jenness.
    1925. *Songs of the Copper Eskimos,* Report of the Canadian Arctic Expedition, 1913-1918, vol. 14. Ottawa: F. A. Acland.
Rudenko, S. I.
    1961. *The Ancient Culture of the Bering Sea and the Eskimo Problem.* Translated by Paul Tolstoy. Toronto: University of Toronto Press.
Spencer, Robert.
    1959. *The North Alaskan Eskimo, A Study in Ecology and Society.* Bulletin 171. Washington: Smithsonian Institution, Bureau of Ethnology.

Stefansson, Vilhjalmur.
    1924. *My Life with the Eskimo.* New York: Macmillan.
VanStone, James W.
    1958. "An Eskimo Community and the Outside World." *Anthropological Papers,* vol. 7, no. 1. College: University of Alaska.
    1962. *Point Hope: An Eskimo Village in Transition.* Seattle: University of Washington Press.
Van Valin, William B.
    1941. *Eskimoland Speaks.* Caldwell, Idaho: Caxton Printers.
Weyer, Edward Moffat, Jr.
    1932. *The Eskimos, Their Environment and Folkways.* New Haven: Yale University Press.
Wymper, Frederick.
    1869. *Travels and Adventure in the Territory of Alaska.* New York: Harper and Bros.

Canadian Eskimo
Balikci, Asen.
    1970. *The Netsilik Eskimo,* pp. 139-44; 197-238. Garden City: The Natural History Press.
Beclard-d'Harcourt, Marguerite.
    1928. "Le système pentaphone dans les chants des Copper Eskimos." Proceedings of the 22nd Session of the International Congress of Americanists 2:15-23.
Birket-Smith, Kaj.
    1929. "The Caribou Eskimo: Material and Social Life," vol. 5, parts 1 and 2. Report of the Fifth Thule Expedition. Copenhagen.
Boas, Franz.
    1888. *The Central Eskimo,* pp. 240-250. Washington: Smithsonian Institute, Sixth Annual Report of the Bureau of American Ethnology. *The Central Eskimo,* intro. Henry B. Collins. Lincoln: University of Nebraska Press.
    1894. "Eskimo Tales and Songs." *Journal of American Folklore* 7:45-50.
    1897. "Eskimo Tales and Songs." *Journal of American Folklore* 10:109-15.
    1901. *The Eskimos of Baffin Land and Hudson Bay,* vol. 15. American Museum of Natural History.
    1907. *The Eskimo of Baffin Land and Hudson Bay,* vol. 15, part 2. American Museum of Natural History.
Boas, Franz, and Henry Rink.
    1889. "Eskimo Tales and Songs." *Journal of American Folklore* 2:123-31.
Department of Northern Affairs and National Re-

sources.

1959. *Canadian Eskimos.* Ottawa: Queen's Printer.

Cavanaugh, Beverley.

1972. "Annotated Bibliography: Eskimo Music." *Ethnomusicology* 6 (September), 479-87.

DeNevi, Don.

1969. "Essays in musical retribalization: Hudson Bay." *Music Educator's Journal* 56 (September), 66-68.

Esteicher, Zygmunt.

1948. "La Musique des Esquimaux-Caribous." *Bulletin de la Société Neuchateloise de Géographie* 5(1):1-54.

1950. "Die Musik der Eskimos: Eine vergleichende Studie." *Anthropos* 45:659-720.

1956. "Cinq Chants des Esquimaux Ahearmiut," in Geert van den Steenhoven, *Research Report on Caribou Eskimo Law.* The Hague: Canada Department of Northern Affairs and Natural Resources.

(N.D.) "The Music of the Caribou Eskimos," prepared for V. Stefansson, ed., *Encyclopedia Arctica*, vol. 2.

(N.D.) "Zur Polyrhythmik in der Musik der Eskimos." *Schweizerische Musikzeitung* 87:411-15.

Freuchen, Peter.

1961. *Book of the Eskimos*, pp. 202-10. Cleveland: World Publishing Co.

Jenness, Diamond.

1922. "The Life of the Copper Eskimos," 12: 179-225. Report of the Canadian Arctic Expedition, 1913-1918. Ottawa: F. A. Acland.

Leden, Christian.

1929. *Uber Kiwatins Eisfelder*, pp. 272-77. Leipzig: Brockhaus.

Rasmussen, Knud.

1929. "Intellectual Culture of the Copper Eskimos," vol. 7, part 1; part 2, 1930. Copenhagen: Thule Report.

1931. "The Netsilik Eskimos," 8. Copenhagen: Thule Report.

Roberts, Helen, and Diamond Jenness.

1925. "Songs of the Copper Eskimos," vol. 14. Report of the Canadian Arctic Expedition, 1913-1918. Ottawa: F. A. Acland.

Rousseliere, Guy Mary.

1959. "Innusivut: Our Way of Living." *Beaver* 289:29-36.

Speck, Franck G.

1935. "Labrador Eskimo mask and clown." *University of Pennsylvania General Magazine and Historical Chronicle* 37(2):159-73.

Steenhoven, Geert van den.

1959. "Songs and Dances: Characteristic life expression of the Eskimo." *Eskimo* 50 (March), 3-6.

Discography

Catalogue

Songs and Legends. Alaska Library Network Catalogue 2. Anchorage: Alaska Library Association, 1974. Cassette catalogue of Alaskan Eskimo and Indian music and folklore.

Alaskan Eskimo Songs and Stories. Seattle: University of Washington Press. Compiled and recorded by Lorraine D. Koranda. One disc with illustrated booklet documenting 42 songs and stories recorded in the field by Eskimo informants.

The Eskimos of Hudson Bay and Alaska. Folkways 4444. Recording and notes by Laura Boulton. One disc with accompanying notes.

Words Rise Up. Washington: Curriculum Development Associates, Inc. Netsilik Eskimo folk tales and legends translated and told by non-Eskimos. Two discs.

Films

Eskimo Sea Hunters—Northwestern Alaska. UWF. B/W. 20 min.

Narrated by a Point Hope Eskimo boy. Activities that include hunting, using products of the hunt for food and clothing, trading artifacts, and dancing provide a realistic portrayal of Arctic life thirty years ago. In the drum dance, the drummers play in Alaskan Eskimo style, striking the wooden frame of the drum from below. Several children are shown joining in the dance. Recommended by Doreen Binnington.

Legend of the Raven. NFBC. Col. 13 min.

An ancient legend from Baffin Island told by means of stone carvings. In the background are heard a drum dance and a power song.

The Living Stone. NFBC. Col. 30 min.

Centers around Eskimo stone carving and the struggle for existence in the Arctic. One Eskimo song. Attractive contemporary background music. Resembles *Nanook of the North.*

Netsilik Eskimo Series. EDC and NFBC.

Filming supervised by Asen Balikci. Except for rare snatches of song or drum, there is no music.

At the Autumn River Camp, Parts I and II. Col. 60 min.

At the Winter Sea Ice Camp, Parts I-IV. Col. 137 min.

Parts of a series of films depicting the traditional way of life of the Netsilik Eskimo. Other films in the series are *At the Caribou Crossing Place, Stalking Seal on the Spring Ice, Group Hunting on the Spring Ice, Building a Kayak, Fishing at the Stone Weir, Jigging for Lake Trout.*

Eskimo Artist—Kenjuak. NFBC. Col. 20 min.

A blend of the old and new ways of life.

Angotee, Story of an Eskimo Boy. NFBC. Col. and B/W. 31 min.

The growth of a modern Eskimo hunter from birth to maturity.

Unless otherwise indicated all of these films recommended by L. K.

19. Symbol and Function in South American Indian Music

Dale A. Olsen

Perhaps no musical culture has been so misunderstood and so dismissed as that of the native inhabitants of South America. From the Spanish conquest until the present their music has either been called "monotonous," "noisy," "primitive," "out of tune," or been disregarded altogether. Like any other non-Western music, however, it must be approached from the viewpoint of its culture, and seen this way it takes on new dimensions. Most South American Indians traditionally view their music as having supernatural qualities. Consequently, much of it is filled with symbolism. In many instances they themselves have described the function, symbolism, and meaning of their music and musical instruments. It is with their eyes that we should try to view their varied musical traditions.

Since the European conquest of South America beginning in the fifteenth century, many of the American Indian's traditions have been absorbed by the dominant culture, and many have disappeared altogether. The number of indigenous languages spoken in pre-Columbian times has been estimated at 1,492 (Loukotka 1968:17); today perhaps 300 or 400 languages are spoken (Sorensen 1973:313). The famous linguist Joseph Greenberg has placed South American speakers of indigenous languages into four all-embracing groups, called phyla: the Macro-Chibchan, the Andean-Equatorial, the Ge-Pano-Carib, and the Hokan (Steward and Faron 1959:22-23). More conclusive research will have to be done before scholars can agree on any one classification of native South American languages.

Cultural classification of South American Indians has also been an area of disagreement among anthropologists. The most useful because of its conciseness is the classification by Steward as it appears in the *Handbook of South American Indians* (1949, V:674). Steward includes four cultural types: the Tropical Forest, the Andean, the Circum-Caribbean, and the Marginal (for a summary of the many classifications see Galvão 1967:167-80). According to him the Marginal cultures, Paleo-Indian, were the earliest, and were pushed into the less desirable areas of South America by the later, more developed cultures, the Meso- and Neo-Indians. Research has shown that very possibly at least two large migrations of people came from Asia across the Bering Strait during two periods of the Wisconsin glaciation, somewhere between 50,000 to 35,000 years ago, and again between approximately 25,000 to 12,000 years ago, when a land bridge supporting a tundra vegetation existed (Wilbert 1966:17-18).

The racial origin of the Amerindians possibly involved a hybridization of two elements, the Caucasoid and the Mongoloid, the former being the first immigrants into the New World, and the latter the second wave (ibid., 18). Varying mixtures of these early people, and possibly others, created a racial diversity among the native Americans. Just as it is not possible to speak of one South American Indian language, culture, or race, neither is it possible to speak of one South American Indian musical style, but rather one must speak of the musical style of individual cultures. No attempt has yet been made to determine a classification of musical styles for native South America, and if one did exist it would be at least as controversial as the linguistic and cultural classifications, especially because of the difficulty of recording the important ritualistic

1. Sinu
2. Tairona
3. Manabí (Esmeraldas)
4. Moche (Mochica)
5. Chancay
6. Recuay
7. Nazca
8. Tiawanacu
9. Quechua (Inca, Q'ero)
10. Aymara
11. Araucanian (Mapuche)
12. Selk'nam (Ona)
13. Yahgan
14. Alacaluf
15. Cuna
16. Kogi
17. Goajiro
18. Yupa (Motilon)
19. Barí (Motilon)
20. Tunebo
21. Cubeo
22. Tukano (Desana)
23. Witoto
24. Jívaro (Shuar)
25. Warao
26. Piaroa
27. Yekuaná (Makiritare)
28. Yanomamö
29. Taulipang (Pemón)
30. Makushi
31. Cashanhua
32. Sharanahua
33. Campa
34. Cayabi
35. Suya
36. Camayura
37. Chavante
38. Trumai
39. Karaja
40. Javahé
41. Kraho
42. Yaulapiti
43. Guaraní
44. Apapocuva
45. Mojo
46. Sirionó
47. Tucuna
48. Arawak
49. Carib
50. Kuikuru

Alphabetic List of cultures, with corresponding numbers, that appear on Map.

Alacaluf, 14
Apapocuva, 44
Araucanian, 11 (Mapuche)
Arawak, 48
Aymara, 10
Barí, 19 (Motilon)
Camayura, 36
Campa, 33
Carib, 49
Cashanhua, 31
Cayabi, 34
Chancay, 5
Chavante, 37

Cubeo, 21
Cuna, 15
Goajiro, 17
Guaraní, 43
Javahé, 40
Jívaro, 24 (Shuar)
Karaja, 39
Kogi, 16
Kraho, 41
Kuikuru, 50
Makushi, 30
Manabí, 3 (Esmeraldas)
Moche, 4 (Mochica)

Mojo, 45
Nazca, 7
Piaroa, 26
Quechua, 9 (Inca, Q'ero)
Recuay, 6
Selk'nam, 12 (Ona)
Sharanahua, 32
Sinu, 1
Sirionó, 46
Suya, 35
Tairona, 2
Taulipang, 29 (Pemón)
Tiawanacu, 8

Trumai, 38
Tucuna, 47
Tukano, 22 (Desana)
Tunebo, 20
Warao, 25
Witoto, 23
Yahgan, 13
Yanomamö, 28
Yaulapiti, 42
Yekuaná, 27 (Makiritare)
Yupa, 18 (Motilon)

Locations of selected South American Indian cultures. © 1975 by Dale Olsen.

musics. Often early travelers, explorers, missionaries, and ethnologists observed that a particular tribe was so "primitive" that it possessed neither musical instruments nor song, when in reality the indigenes probably had no desire to share their sacred flutes, bull-roarers, or supernatural songs with the strange, bearded, white foreigners. Several writers of this century, however, have attempted distribution maps (Nordenskiöld 1919) or charts (Izikowitz 1935) of native South American musical instruments.

MUSICAL CHARACTERISTICS

In spite of the great diversity of musical styles, a few general functions and characteristics of South American Indian music can be mentioned. A translation of the very word *music* does not exist among many American Indian cultures. Often terms for musical instruments have meanings that indirectly include their instrumental sounds as well. The word for *sing* often means "recite" (among the Cuna), to "use the mouth or lips" (among the Warao), or "falling into trance" (among the Selk'nam). Because often no word expresses the concept of music as Westerners employ it, it can be assumed that its use is functional and thus vital and central to the culture. In its most traditional form, music probably did not exist for its own sake, but was possibly always used for supernatural supplication in varying degrees. Most musical instruments were, and still are, in many cultures carefully fashioned and preserved and often elaborately designed, befitting their ritualistic functions. Generally, melodies and words are inseparable, and the very power of the song depends on their proper union. Yet there is a paradox in that many words of the most sacred songs are no longer understood. Overall the meaning is clear, but individually the words are not translatable; they are frozen into the ritualistic song, a remnant of an archaic language. The singer knows they are correct only because they have always been sung that way, and that is how he learned them. Since they are the words of the time-honored tribal ancestors, and were perhaps originally the gift of a particular spirit, their power continues unchanged. Occasionally pure melody is used, with the performer humming, whistling, or simply singing one or two words. Among the Jívaro (Harner 1972:71-72) and the Warao, songs are even "sung" mentally, that is, silently. The spirits are, after all, capable of such forms of nonaural and very personal communication. Voice masking occurs during songs where direct spirit communication takes place between a shaman and his (or her) otherworldly contact. This altering of the voice can be achieved with the vocal cords alone or by external means such as cupping the hands, coating the throat and vocal cords by inhaling the vapor of a resin that has been applied to the tip of the shamanic cigar, as among the Warao, or singing into a special small clay pot after drinking the hallucinogenic *ayahuasca* contained therein, as among the Sharanahua (Siskind 1973:36).

Most of the melodies consist of fairly short musical motives placed in descending order and characterized by a slight decrescendo (recorded ex. 6.2). There are, however, exceptions to this. For example, although the *hoarotu* shaman among the Warao adheres consistently to a descending pattern with a decrescendo while curing (ex. 19-1), he does the opposite in his inflicting role (ex. 19-2). It appears then that specific melodies exist for specific functions. This fact is also apparent among the Jívaro, who often symbolically relate the structure of their melodies with social function (List 1965:150). Concerning the fragmentary quality of much native American music von Hornbostel (Karsten 1935:501) writes that many similar musical units are joined together "in the same way as pearls are strung into a necklace" (exs. 19-3 and 19-4). The melodic range of these musical units varies from culture to culture, and even from function to function. For example, among many marginal cultures (belonging neither to Andean nor Tropical Forest cultural areas), such as the Fuegians of Tierra del Fuego, the melodic units often consist of only two notes at the approximate distance of a whole tone (von Hornbostel 1948:68). This limited range, however, also occurs among a few shamanistic songs of the Warao, a more advanced Tropical Forest culture, although the majority of Warao melodies employ a more extensive gamut of from three to five or more pitches. It is difficult, therefore, to

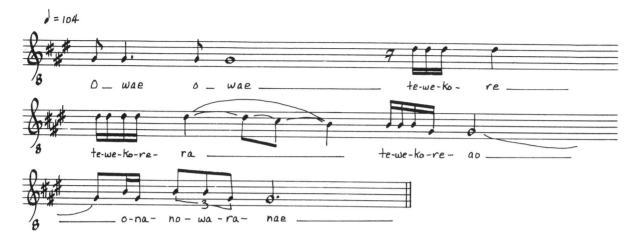

EXAMPLE 19-1. Warao hoarotu shaman curing song excerpt. Source: Dale A. Olsen.

EXAMPLE 19-2. Warao hoarotu shaman inflicting song excerpt. Source: Dale A. Olsen.

make a correlation between breadth of melody and cultural level, as some writers have maintained (von Hornbostel 1936:364 and Sachs 1965:59).

The intervals chosen for these melodic units also vary according to culture. The preconception that South American Indian music is pentatonic is rather simplistic. Pentatonicism does occur, but its use has been widely overstressed and too "exotically" linked with the great Andean civilizations, evoking many romantic impressions such as the "melancholic state of the Indians." Since the Spanish conquest (which probably produced the Indians' melancholy),

native Andean melodies have been adapted to the tuning system of the West, more than likely causing an overpredominance of a pentatonic tuning that matches the black keys of the piano. However, analysis of the scales of ancient coastal Peruvian musical instruments, such as those of the Nazca (Stevenson 1968:248-49), Moche, and Chancay cultures (ex. 19-5), and of the pitches selected by the more unacculturated Indian groups of Peru, such as the Andean Q'eros (ex. 19-6), indicates a use of microtones, pitches that do not correspond to Western tuning. Among other native South American cultures as well, microtones play an important role in the

EXAMPLE 19-3. Sanema shamanistic curing song. Source: Walter Coppens.

construction of intervals that only approximate those of Western music. Many supernatural songs correspond quite closely to modal music as found in the early Western Christian Church. Certainly much Amerindian music was influenced by Catholic missionaries, but most of the shamanistic songs are traditional, probably completely indigenous, and very ancient in origin (ex. 19-7).

Concerning texture, the majority of South American Indian music is monophonic, although music of more than one melodic line does exist. When it occurs, multipart music has various forms; the most common constructions for vocal music are a freestyle round or canon (recorded ex. 6.2), and parallelism, similar to Western medieval organum. The rhythm of native South American music varies according to function. Some songs where spirit communication or healing is being conducted are in a slow free rhythm (ex. 19-8); other ceremonial musics are fast and measured, at times displaying metric changes similar to Western medieval and contemporary music (exs. 19-9 and 19-10). Often, measured music is associated with dance, a very important medium among land-oriented cultures (as opposed to water- or canoe-oriented). Dance, which is almost always ceremonial, is usually a group affair, with a shaman or another leader officiating. It may be done in absolute silence as occasionally among the Kogi of Columbia (Reichel-Dolmatoff 1951, II:138), with the rhythm of handclapping, foot-stamping, rattle-shaking, or to the accompaniment of elaborate musical instruments such as panpipes, vertical flutes, bamboo clarinets, staff rattles, stamping tubes, and/or other sound makers. These, then, are the most important general characteristics of native South American music.

SYMBOLISM AND MEANING

Now let us examine specific examples of symbolism and function in native South American music, beginning with the theurgical vocal music. The most common term used to describe magical, religious, or ceremonial song is *chanting*. Defined as "the intoning of words for supernatural purposes," the resulting song, or chant, has a power unimagined in our present Western culture. Living in a world surrounded by good and evil spirits in which most animate or inanimate objects are believed to have supernatural qualities, the Indians use chant as a means of averting impending danger, inflicting illness or causing destruction, curing illness or relieving pain, calling spirits and conversing with them, giving thanks, casting love spells, and so forth. According to mythology, chants were given to mortals by powerful spirits. Among the now extinct Ona (Selk'nam) there was a myth about the origin of chanting in which an ancestor spirit, the creator of chanting, was able to kill a whale and land it single-hand-

EXAMPLE 19-4. Warao nonshamanistic birth complication curing song excerpt. Source: Dale A. Olsen.

edly with the supernatural help of song (Métraux 1949:583). According to the creation myth of the Tukano of Colombia, the sun is one of the most important sources of supernatural songs (Reichel-Dolmatoff 1971:29, 36). Certain animals are also used as song sources because they are messengers of the gods. In the same Tukano creation myth a bird teaches a new mother how to sing chants that will protect her from the animals, thus enabling her and all future Tukano mothers to go to the river and bathe after childbirth (ibid., 31). The special power attributed to birds in native South American mythology is often carried over into the music. The bird is one of the most important magical animals because it can traverse two worlds, heaven and earth. For this reason many flutes are constructed from bird bones, many rattles are adorned with bird feathers, and the aid of bird spirits is often solicited by the shaman through song. Women as well as men sing chants, and in many agricultural cultures the women attend to matters of planting and harvesting by singing to the Earth Mother and

other helpful spirits. The majority of the supernatural songs, however, are the property of certain men because of the masculine role usually associated with being a shaman, priest, chief, or other important tribal leader. There are a few exceptions, however, as among the Araucanians, where women are the shamans.

Perhaps the single most important function of song is associated with shamanism. A shaman is an individual who, through supernatural powers acquired during apprenticeship, is believed capable of contacting spirits in cosmological flights of ecstasy, primarily for curing but occasionally for causing illness. In some cultures there are distinct types of shamans, each derived from the portion of the supernatural universe in which the practitioner conducts his business, and each shamanic office has its particular songs. Song, among shamans, is the most important tool for reaching ecstasy, except in certain cultures which use hallucinogenic drugs for achieving trance. According to Mircea Eliade (1972:401), trance achieved without hallucinogens is "pure trance," whereas ecstasy

EXAMPLE 19-5. Nazca panpipe. Source: Dale A. Olsen.

EXAMPLE 19-6. Q'ero panpipe melody. Source: *Mountain Music of Peru*, Folkways FE 4539.

achieved with drugs or other intoxicants, such as tobacco, is decadent. Even when hallucinogenic drugs are employed, singing still has very important functions: (1) it enables those in trance to see the proper visions; (2) the speed of the music regulates the speed of the vision; and (3) the melodies alleviate nausea (Katz and Dobkin de Rios 1971:326). Among the Sharanahua of the Peruvian jungle, for example, the shamans sing while they drink the hallucinogenic ayahuasca, claiming that without calling the proper visions through song, only visions of snakes would appear (Siskind 1973:32). How does music alone cause a trance? Von Hornbostel writes the following concerning the now extinct Fuegians:

> Hypnotising through the incessant and monotonous repetition of one short motive, with speed and strength ever increased by forceful accents and abrupt movements and accompanied by violent rhythmic movement of the whole body, song is the only means of intoxication known by earliest cultures. [1948:85]

Drumming is another ecstasy-inducing musical device, as among the Araucanian Indians of the southern Andes, where the female shaman puts herself into a trance by drumming upon her kettledrum. These states of ecstasy, and others like them, are induced by cultural conditioning for which music acts as a catalyst. Through cultural conditioning the Araucanian shaman knows that her drum is the symbol of power, or rather that it *is* power. Made from a section of a tree that may symbolize the central pole (the center of the universe) the shaman, by drumming on the tree, believes herself to ascend into the cosmos. The use of horsehide for the skin of the Araucanian shaman's drum may also be symbolic, for in that culture the horse is a supernatural creature that carries the shaman to the center of the sky, much like the bird in other cultures. It is perhaps also significant that during the Araucanian harvest ceremony the long bamboo trumpet, which is covered with horse gut, plays a rhythm imitative of a horse galloping while the shaman sings and beats her drum.

Song also plays an important part in one's learning to become a shaman. Often a youth receives the calling by singing in his sleep (von Hornbostel 1948:86), or by hearing a song in his dreams (Wilbert 1974:49). The Fuegians and the pa tribe often knows as many as sixty songs, and his method of remembering them is unique. Each song has a particular mnemonic symbol which is copied onto a small wooden block, thus aiding his memory (Wilbert 1974:49).

The most important function of the shaman is curing illness. All illnesses are believed to be caused supernaturally, either directly by the spirits, such as the grotesquely playful ancestor spirits or the deadly spirits living in the westernmost part of the cosmos, or by a malevolent

EXAMPLE 19-7. Pemon shamanistic curing song excerpt. Source: Cesareo de Armellada.

Apapocuva-Guaraní believed that these songs were given to the sleeping potential initiate by a deceased ancestor (Métraux 1949:589). According to Wilbert, if a Yupa dream recipient is able to reproduce his song exactly as it appeared in his dream, it is considered a true supernatural calling. It is necessary for him to receive various songs in this manner to be considered a serious candidate. Among other cultures, such as the Tukano (Reichel-Dolmatoff 1971:154) and the Warao, shamanistic songs are learned during apprenticeship, either in a group or individually. During his learning period, the neophyte usually takes care to reproduce his teacher's songs and shamanic sounds without alteration, but in actual practice the new shaman will elaborate upon them in the form of a personal conversation with the spirits. Remembering ceremonial songs is a special talent of the shaman, and a Warao hoarotu shaman (one of three types) told me he knew five hundred songs. Another Warao shaman, a *bahanarotu*, sang every song he knew, and the number totaled seventy-two, a more likely figure. The leading shaman of a Yu-

shaman, who has solicited aid from the spirits to kill or cause illness either for personal reasons or because he has a calling to feed the gods. Even illnesses inflicted by so-called natural means, such as snakebites, scorpion stings, machete wounds, and abscessed teeth, are believed to be caused indirectly by spirits that have either enticed the animal or object into doing damage or have possessed it completely. The curing of such nonshamanistic inflictions among the Warao requires the singing of a prayerful, soothing chant, rather than the more involved shamanic songs which are accompanied by trance. The more serious shamanistic illnesses are of three types among South American Indians: (1) intrusion of the spiritual *essence* of an object, an animal, or any portion of either, or of a spirit itself, into the victim's body; (2) soul loss; and (3) improper balance with nature. Among the Warao Indians, who recognize only the first type of illness, the hoarotu shaman employs mental song for causing sickness, death, or destruction. This malevolent shaman, usually upon receiving the message that the Supreme Hoa spirit in the

EXAMPLE 19-8. Tariana shamanistic curing song. Source: E. Biocca, *Viaggi Tra Gli Indi*, Vol. 4, Record 15B.

EXAMPLE 19-9. Sanema shamanistic curing song. Source: Walter Coppens.

EXAMPLE 19-10. Kogi shamanistic rainmaking song. Source: Manuel Benavides.

westernmost part of the cosmos needs human food, will sit within view of his victim and stare at him while blowing tobacco smoke toward him, all the while mentally singing his inflicting song. He is soliciting the aid of the Hoa spirits and naming the proper essence to be sent via magical arrows into his victim. His behavior has a tremendous psychological effect upon the victim, and it may, even within a few hours,

> lead to a decrease in the volume of blood and a concomitant drop in blood pressure, which result in irreparable damage to the circulatory organs. The rejection of food and drink, frequent among patients in the throes of intense anxiety, precipitates this process; dehydration acts as a stimulus to the sympathetic nervous system, and the de-

crease in blood volume is accentuated by the growing permeability of the capillary vessels . . . death results, yet the autopsy reveals no lesions. [Lévi-Strauss 1963:168]

Symbolism plays a very important role in the curing of intrusion illnesses because of the necessity of naming. It is the function of the curing shaman, along with his helping spirits, to decipher and name the illness-causing spirit essence. The most powerful element of his cure is song, and among the Jívaro Indians of Ecuador shamanistic curing is called literally "to cure sickness by singing" (Karsten 1935:414). Shamans in numerous cultures partake of hallucinogens to aid in elucidating the supernatural cause of the illness through visions; however, the cure itself is accomplished by singing. Naming the illness-causing spirit essence in song is a difficult task because of the innumerable object, animal, spirit, or intangible essences that may have been sent through the air as magical arrows. As native cultures become more acculturated the number of nameable items increases, including such objects as outboard motors, airplanes, radios, and even the white man's God. The shaman, however, has clues that are furnished knowingly or unknowingly by the patient. Among the Sharanahua, for example, the dream of the patient and the symptoms of the malady offer clues to the cause (Siskind 1973:32). When the patient reports a particular image that occurred to him or her in a dream, the shaman then sings a song about that image. Among the Warao the shaman also names certain things in song that are symbolized by the symptoms. If the patient, for example, has a high fever, the shaman names the sun as the intrusive essence; if he has the chills, the coldness of the Orinoco River is named; if the victim has trouble breathing, an object symbolizing suffocation, such as a bone or metal collar, is named; if his speech is incoherent, a stuttering foreigner or a group of chattering birds is named; if the patient is silent, the silence of twilight is named (Olsen, Dale 1973:147–54). The Carib-speaking Taulipáng (Taurepän, Pemon), another native Venezuelan culture, have a similar symbolic phenomenon in their curing techniques. If, for example, a patient is suffering from a swelling caused by eating deer flesh, a jaguar is named in song because jaguars feed on deer. Likewise, if someone suffers from a sore throat, a song is sung that names the howler monkey because of its good voice (Métraux 1949:583). Among the Warao, when the shaman has successfully named the illness-causing essence through song, the inflicted part of the victim's body vibrates. Then the shaman removes the essence by either suction or massage.

Illnesses caused by soul loss require a different type of cure than intrusion illnesses. Song, however, is just as important. Among the Cuna, for example, the shaman's chant takes the patient on a supernatural journey to the underworld, and it describes to the patient how the

shaman's spirit helpers retrieve the lost soul after countless battles (McCosker 1974:16).

The singing style of a curing shaman varies from culture to culture and function to function. Among the Warao each of the three shamans (*wisiratu*, bahanarotu, and hoarotu) sings differently, some employing voice masking and some not. The wisiratu shaman, the most common religious practitioner and also the most loved, cures, with his large rattle, illnesses caused by ancestor spirits. His song cycle consists of three parts with three separate melodies, each with a different function. They are contact and conversation with helping spirits, naming the illness-causing spirit, and dialogue with evil spirits. Prior to his trance, which is culturally induced by song and tobacco smoke, the wisiratu makes numerous nonmusical grunts and belches that are actually releasing his helping spirits from within his body. In other cultures, such as the Jívaro, musical sections also occur, but whistling is added to the presung sections and has the important function of alerting the helping spirits (Harner 1973:23). The whistle of the Jívaro shaman is also in two parts: the first is the actual curing melody, the second a nonmusical signal. Whistling is also prominent among the Indians and their descendents in Iquitos, Peru, where it is believed that during the ayahuasca healing sessions, whistling is the means by which the nature spirits and the guardian spirit of the ayahuasca vine are conjured up (Katz and Dobkin de Rios 1971:324). As the helping and other spirits are evoked by the shaman, voice masking is often used. The Warao believe that this altered raspy voice does not symbolize the spirit's voice, but that it *is* the supernatural itself. They also believe that when the voice masking ceases and the shaman continues singing, now in a natural voice, it is the voice of the transformed shaman who is no longer like other Warao, but who is himself a supernatural being. The Fuegians believe that as soon as the evoked spirit enters the shaman, it borrows the shaman's voice and sings (von Hornbostel 1948:86), while the Campa of Peru believe that the good spirits come in bodily form (clearly seen only by the shaman), singing, dancing, and in full ceremonial dress (Weiss

1973:44). They also believe that when the sha- man sings, he is singing along with the spirits and thus repeating what they sing. In some cultures the shaman, often in a drug-induced trance state, encounters animals that he must subdue. During such scenes, as among the Yanomamö of Venezuela, the shaman's song takes on characteristics of a wild beast, with the shaman singing wildly, buzzing his lips, and creating a frenzied atmosphere. In contrast, the Jívaro shaman at times sings softly, while the giant butterfly sings to him with his wings (Harner 1973:15). Shamanic curing songs, then, employ and are permeated with a variety of symbols, largely understood only by the sha- mans (and the spirits) themselves.

Hunting is another important function for which a shaman is frequently, although not al- ways, employed. Among the Tukano the sha- man's most important function is to be an intermediary between the hunter and the su- pernatural Master of the Game Animals (Rei- chel-Dolmatoff 1971:15). Through song, and while in trance, the shaman may visit the Mas- ter at his spiritual abode, where the animals are hanging from the ceiling, to ask for permission to hunt. Or the shaman may go in reality into the forest where preparations for the hunt are car- ried out, always with song and tobacco as his faithful companions. During his sacred songs, the shaman never speaks about killing the an- imals nor about food, but rather about "mak- ing love, caressing, and other erotic acts" in a symbolic sense between the hunters and the Master of the Game Animals (ibid., 224). Among the Cuna farther north, however, praise songs are sung to the animals telling them that their purpose is to provide food and that they should thus make themselves easy to catch (McCosker 1974:15). In Jívaro society the women play an important part in religious life because of their ability to communicate with and draw power from the Earth Mother. Consequently, a Jívaro nonshaman hunter often takes a wife with him, not only to tend to the hunting dog, but more importantly to sing to the Earth Mother and solicit her help for a successful hunt (Harner 1972:75). Because silence is of utmost impor- tance in hunting, the wife usually sings men- tally.

Women play another important role in the supernatural beliefs of most native South Americans, and song is again the power ele- ment. Planting and harvesting are usually the duties of the women, especially among the Jívaro, who sing the following song to the Earth Mother:

> Nungüi, mother, help us in our work!
> Make my sowing flourish,
> remove the weeds from my field,
> make the leaves of the plant strong,
> make the root big like the *sikímuro* (big root,
>   resembling the manioc)!
> Fertilize my field,
> multiply my crop of manioc,
> multiply my crop of camote (sweet potato),
> multiply my crop of earth-nuts! [Karsten 1935:199]

During the manioc-planting ceremony the wom- en sing to the manioc stems, which are believed to be the souls of the plants (List 1965:138). As the women sing to the Earth Mother, so the men sing to the Earth Mother's husband for the cultivation of the plantain (ibid., 139). It is interesting to observe the possible sexual dis- tinction between the manioc, a food grown in the womb of mother earth and sung to by the women, and the plantain, grown above the earth, in a phallic shape, and sung to by the men. The husband of the Earth Mother is also ad- dressed in song by the Jívaro men as they begin to chop down a large tree. Here is a portion of the text:

> Shakaëma, man in the earth,
> come and help us in our work!
> May you cut down the trees,
> send away the soul from the stems,
> remove the trunks from the fields! [Karsten 1935:199]

The Warao also have a song to help the men cut down a large tree for building a canoe. The song begins by telling how in a dream the singer, a young man, received a calling to build a canoe. The entire process of cutting down the tree and making the canoe, which is the topic of the song text, is symbolic of sexual intercourse between the man and the female spirit of the forest. If the youth is successful in making a good canoe, he has become a man.

Most of the supernatural song texts of native South Americans emphasize one very important element for proper spirit propitiation and solicitation: naming. This act, as we have seen, is at the very center of shamanistic inflicting and curing, and it also occurs in the nonshamanistic songs. The naming often does not consist of simply one general identification of the subject, but goes through a very detailed process of naming its minute parts which eventually lead up to the precise name. A Warao inflicting song of a hoarotu shaman, for example, names a small species of alligator (*baba*) as the object whose spirit essence will be sent through the air via magical arrows. But, before the baba itself can be precisely named, the shaman must first name its tail, waist, skin, scales, and neck, as well as the sound that it produces with its scales. Similarly, in a hoarotu curing song certain items must also be prefatory to the naming of the precise essence. Among the Jívaro a similar type of naming occurs in songs sung by men and women to aid in the fermentation of the *chonta* palm beer. They must review the entire history of the palm, from the time it is first planted until it is full grown with ripened fruits ready for the fermentation of the brew (ibid., 499). The same phenomenon occurs during the wedding ceremony, when all the fruits cultivated by the women, plus the entire history of the growth of the manioc, the most important crop, are mentioned in their song (ibid., 199). Naming in this way also exists in Tunebo culture in a song to insure that the hills will not crumble and that the sun will not disappear bringing darkness and the ultimate end of the world. In this song the Tunebos sing "the names of all the peaks from east to west, which God sang to them when he appeared" (Stoddart 1962:150).

Another area where supernatural songs are extremely important among South American Indians is for protection against evil spirits and animals that have transformed themselves into horrible beasts, capable of eating humans as they travel through the jungle or on the rivers. It might be possible to escape such awesome creatures by running, but often there is no time. Spirits usually announce their approach by whistling, by making cracking noises, or by imitating sounds like a tree falling or teeth gnashing, but these warnings are often too late, and the only way to protect oneself is by singing a magical protection song. Among the Warao it

is the protection song itself which has the power; it is not for conjuring up supernatural help. The Warao believe that when walking in the jungle it is not necessary to carry a gun if one knows the proper song; even the most fearful jaguar will fall dead when its doom song is sung and the singer hits the animal with a stick that has been musically loaded with a magical charm. Likewise among the Peruvian Cashinahua, while in trance magical songs are used as protection against animal apparitions: "One large female snake tried to swallow me, but since I was chanting she couldn't succeed" (Kensinger 1973:9).

Other songs are protection against mortal enemies, as among the feuding Jívaro. In order to protect her household from enemies that may be lurking in the family garden, the woman, with the power of Earth Mother, sings to the manioc plants that are believed to have the desire and ability to suck the blood from anybody who touches them. In her song she also asks that the manioc not attack members of her family, but only the enemy:

> Don't suck the blood of my husband
> And also don't suck the blood of my daughter.
> When you want to suck blood,
> Suck the blood of my enemies.
> When my husband comes,
> He will look very beautiful and very clear.
> But when our enemies come,
> They will come very pale
> And in the form of demons [demons lack blood].
> And you will know
> Who will die . . .
> And when they enter this garden,
> They will have their blood sucked. [Harner 1972:76]

Many other types of supernatural songs exist among South American Indians, for just about every activity. The Jívaro had magical songs associated with their rather unusual practice of making shrunken heads, plus others sung during the Victory Feast for increasing the magical power of the trophy. One of the final songs was directed to the shrunken head by the women after it had served its magical purpose. This song's function was to send the murdered man's soul, trapped inside the head, back to its original village. They sang:

> Now, now, go back to your house where you lived.
> Your wife is there calling you from your house.

You have come here to make us happy.
Finally we have finished.
So return. [Ibid., 146]

Magical love songs are very common throughout indigenous South America, and through them women are bewitched to love a man. In the Warao version a man sings and names all the parts of a woman from her feet to the hair on her head, creating in her uncontrollable sexual desires for the singer. Instrumental melodies on either the flute or the musical bow provide love magic as well, but these are almost always instrumental versions of songs, though the musician often has words in his head as he plays.

Songs for the dead usually have a deeper meaning than just communication of sadness. Among the Cuna, for example, an official singer's song acts as a musical psychopomp; that is, it functions to guide the body and soul of the deceased to the burial grounds, and then it protects the soul as it journeys to the underworld (McCosker 1974:18). Wailing for the dead, on the other hand, always done in a stylized sobbing fashion and usually by the women, expresses bereavement.

Songs which would, from a non-Indian point of view, be thought of as strictly secular, such as lullabies, often have a deeper meaning. Many of the Warao lullabies, for example, have supernatural content that seems to have the educational function of familiarizing the child with the dangers of wild animals and hostile spirits. The texts relate the idea of "go to sleep child, or else . . . ," and some of the consequences are that the child's crying may attract animals, such as a toothless deer, or a hungry jaguar who thinks the crying sound is a deer, or spirits, such as a mythological jaguar whose boneless head is pure flesh, and who has the ability to learn and speak Warao, or the evil spirit made of bones who is capable of eating the Warao from within (Olsen, Dale 1975:29). The lullabies of the Cuna Indians also have an educational function. Theirs, however, are addressed to social and economic education; they describe to the female child her future role in their matriarchal society, and to the male child they describe working conditions at home and in the white man's world, which he may enter as an adult (McCosker 1974:26).

SOCIAL FUNCTION

Native South American vocal music also has a social function. Social music is often used to accompany dance and the drinking of homemade beer, resulting occasionally in promiscuous sexual behavior and fighting, as among the Jívaro (Harner 1972:108-110). The Mapuche Indians of Chile, a subtribe of the Araucanians, have an altogether different type of social gathering where music functions to call attention to and correct social misbehavior. These improvised "assembly songs" give the individual an opportunity to relieve inner tension as well as to call attention to complaints about a person of a tribal or family nature (Titiev 1949:2). Symbolism is an important aspect of the song texts. In one song, for example, a woman told the group how she dreamed of a fox, and that it was bad for her. The Mapuche interpretation of this is that the wife realizes that her husband has become accustomed to stealing and general wrongdoing. At that point the group tells the husband to shape up, and he, without anger, sings in a reply that he will mend his ways (Titiev 1949:8). Farther south, among the native inhabitants of Tierra del Fuego, all songs, including the profane ones, were connected somehow with superstitions about origins. Today among the Cuna, at the opposite end of the continent, village political meetings include songs about Cuna heritage, about God, the Earth Mother, and the creation of the world (McCosker 1974: 19). These songs are followed by an interpretive lecture that applies the meanings of the song texts to current problems.

MUSICAL INSTRUMENTS

Nowhere is symbolism more pronounced than in the musical instruments of the native South Americans. Not only are their shapes and designs filled with symbolism, but also, and even more importantly, are the sounds they produce. Certain musical instruments generally have sexual roles and even taboos associated with them. It is almost universal among South American Indians that the flute, a phallic symbol, is an instrument restricted to male use while the container rattle and the drum, as vaginal symbols, are often for female use, although not restricted exclusively to them. The conch shell trumpet is an instrument whose construction makes it very female, although it is used by males, an interesting paradox. Painted or incised designs are important additions on many musical instruments. The Tukano paint their large slit drum with diamonds and stripes, representing the mythical snake that brought the first men to this world (Reichel-Dolmatoff 1971:119). Often designs have shamanistic importance and add power to the instrument, but, like the ritual words in song texts, their precise meaning may be lost while the general significance remains. It is within the area of sound, however, that the most important symbolism often exists. Several cultures in the Amazon Basin have been studied in detail with reference to sound symbolism (Lévi-Strauss 1973:331–36; Reichel-Dolmatoff 1971:115–16). Among the Tukano, for example, three levels of sound—whistling, vibration, and percussion—constitute a symbolic taxonomy of musical instruments. The whistling sound is produced by the flute, and it symbolizes sexual invitation. The association of love with the flute is indeed a universal among most native South Americans of meso- and neo-Indian cultural development. The opposite sound is vibration—buzzing or humming—which symbolizes the aggressive male principle as a warning or threat. This sound is associated with hummingbirds, dragonflies, bees, wasps, hornets, horseflies, and other insects that buzz when they fly, and is represented by such instruments as the indigenous clarinet, the bull-roarer, and other buzzing sound makers. The percussion sound falls between the whistling and vibration categories, and its "staccato of realization" represents "a synthesis of opposites . . . an act of creation in which male and female energy have united" (Reichel-Dolmatoff 1971:116). The instruments in this group include the drum, the gourd or calabash rattle, and the anklet rattles of dancers.

Judging from their numbers, musical instruments were extremely important in the ancient civilizations of northwestern and western South America, from as far north as the Sinu and Tairona cultures of present northern Colombia (fig. 19-1) to the great middle coastal and Andean cultures of Manabí, Moche, Chancay, Nazca, Ica, and Tiahuanacu in present Ecuador, Peru, and Bolivia. Although it is musicologically dangerous to make conclusions from playing these musical instruments, since we have no precise ideas of fingering and blowing techniques, their designs and depictions in iconographical sources indicate a high degree of religiosity associated with them (fig. 19-2). Often pottery depicts entire scenes of shamans or priests using musical instruments in their rituals. Even today musical and other ancient artifacts are used by shamans as powerful objects, and with an ancient Moche ocarina (globular flute) a Peruvian shaman, who is a descendant of the Moche people, can still call both the spirits of the mountains and of the sea for aid in curing illnesses.

With such power invested in musical instruments, it is easier to understand, but not forgive, how colonial ecclesiastical authorities tried to destroy all musical instruments of the Indians. In the seventeenth century, for example, a Jesuit missionary reported how he had personally destroyed 4,023 drums and flutes in the Peruvian villages, and in 1614 those native Americans in the bishopric of Lima who even possessed such "pagan" objects were subject to three hundred lashes in the public square (Slonimsky 1946:47). Unfortunately, this intolerant attitude still persists in many parts of South America.

The most important of the sacred musical instruments is an idiophone, the gourd or calabash shamanic rattle. Its very sound, usually produced by quartz pebbles striking the inside of the container, is considered by most Amerindian cultures to be the voice of a spirit, while by other cultures to call the spirits. The shape of the rattle often has anthropomorphic symbolism. Among the Warao, for example, the large shamanic rattle is considered a head spirit, with the handle, the calabash, the slits, and the feathers on top representing the neck, the head, the mouth, and the hair of the spirit (fig. 19-3). The

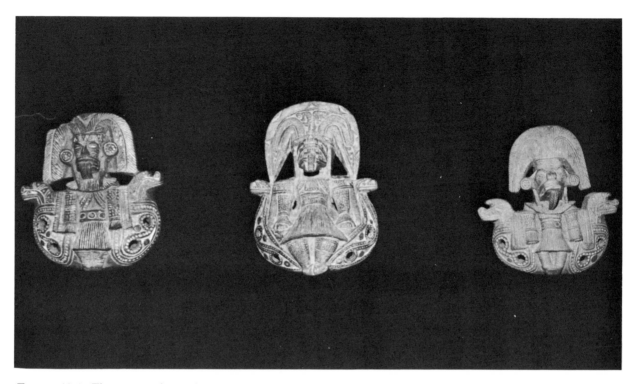

FIGURE 19-1. Three ceramic ocarinas or globular flutes from the Tairona culture of the Sierra Nevada of Santa Marta, Colombia (ca. A.D. 500–1500), from the private collection of Guillermo Cano, Bogotá. Each instrument has four finger holes (sixteen fingering possibilities) with a fipple-type mouthpiece extending from the top of the headdress to the back of the head. The richly ornate and highly stylized anthropomorphic figure sits on a double-headed serpent throne or boat. The figures are approximately four inches tall.

Tukano have a shamanic rattle whose red handle symbolizes the penis and the terrestrial world, the yellow feather decoration at the top of the handle represents the sun's fertility, and the gourd body symbolizes the uterus (Reichel-Dolmatoff 1971:114). One can perhaps understand this sexual symbolism in the light of rebirth, as the patient or the initiate reemerges from his old into his new state. A unique type of gourd rattle is used among the Kuikuru of the Upper Xingú region of Brazil. The gourd body is slightly loose on the handle, and when rolled along the forearm a squeaking sound, the voice of a spirit, is produced (Dole 1973:298). Occasionally, perhaps where gourds or calabashes are not available, substitutes are used for the container rattle. Among the Taulipáng and the Jívaro the shaman shakes a bundle of leaves during curing rituals. The Jívaro consider the points of the leaves, taken from a special plant with magical properties, as the tongues of the sorcerer who caused the illness (Karsten 1935: 417). Thus the curing shaman has extra power to remove the intrusion. Some hunting and gathering cultures often have rattle archetypes, such as the Selk'nam of Tierra del Fuego who create a rustling sound by vigorously shaking their skin mantles (von Hornbostel 1948: 89), and the Yanomamö who have an imaginary rattle capable of flying through the air (Wilbert, personal communication).

Another very symbolic idiophone is the hollowed log slit drum. It was once used as a signal instrument by the Jívaro, Tukano, Witoto, and other jungle cultures, but today it is less common (Harner 1972:206). Often used in pairs and representing male and female, among the Witoto the appropriate sexual organs are carved

FIGURE 19-2. Ceramic iconographic vessel from the Recuay culture of the north highlands in Perú (ca. 400 B.C.–A.D. 800), from the John and Mary Carter Collection, The Florida State University, Tallahassee, Florida. This artifact, in white and red with geometric design done in black resist painting, depicts a priestly flutist surrounded by five small figures (one broken) holding cups. This reflects the importance of music, possibly used by the shaman-priest to reach ecstatic flight (Olsen, Diane 1978:104). The vessel stands seven inches high.

into each drum, and the female drum has two breasts inside (Radin 1942:126). The Tukano slit drum represents the Snake-Canoe in which humanity arrived. It also symbolizes a uterus, the slits represent a vagina, and the drumstick a phallus (Reichel-Dolmatoff 1971:114). This drum (female) and drumstick (male) symbolism is universal among native South Americans, and for that reason drums played with two drumsticks are known to be the result of acculturation.

Membranophones are common among native South Americans. Sometimes they are the result of Western or African influence. Numerous icons from the ancient Pacific coast depict shamanic, priestly, or death figures playing on a small drum with one stick, possibly symbolizing shamanic ecstasy and the death-rebirth element of shamanism. The large double-headed drum, known as the *bombo* in the Andes, was brought by the Spanish, but is possibly Turkish in origin. Often these instruments are used during Andean religious festivals, and indigenous tradition continues as the native inhabitants and their descendants adorn them with colored bands, place garlic and red pepper inside them, breathe tobacco smoke into them, and pour drops of liquor over them, thus assuring the life of the sounding powers that reside in them (Jimenez Borja 1951:5).

One of the most common aerophones is the panpipe (see Olsen, "Folk music..."). Numerous examples exist from ancient America, as well as icons that depict them as priestly instruments, often played in pairs. The practice today among the Aymará is to play them in hocket; with each instrument capable of playing only half the pitches, a set of two is required to play the complete scale in an interlocking fashion. Not only is this technique more practical (each player has only half the notes to play), but it was probably spiritual at one time because of the magical significance of dualism. Today, however, a solo player may perform on a set of two panpipes by himself by placing them back-to-back and blowing each tube as the melody requires. Among the Tukano the number of tubes depends on the age of the male performer and the consequent development of his sexual or-

gans. Thus boys between five and nine years of age play panpipes that have only three tubes, while adult men play instruments that have from eight to nine (Reichel-Dolmatoff 1971:111).

Flutes with finger holes were probably developed later than panpipes. Again numerous examples of bone, clay, and cane have been excavated from pre-Columbian tombs. Some individual burial sites have contained dozens of bone

FIGURE 19-3. The sacred shamanistic rattle of the Warao Indians of the Orinoco Delta in Venezuela. This instrument, called *hebu-mataro*, was collected from the Winikina area in 1954, and is the property of the museum of the Fundación La Salle in Caracas, Venezuela. The slits of the rattle (the mouths of the head spirit) have sexual distinction: the vertical slits are placed over a female patient, and the horizontal over a male.

flutes, and early writers explained these as graves of early flute makers. It is probably more likely that such burial techniques were used for important persons, priests or shamans perhaps, the belief being that the flutes (phallic symbols) placed in the earth (the womb of mother earth) would assure life after death. These flutes, with a notched mouthpiece, are called *kenas* (Aymará *kena-kena*) throughout the Andes and were sometimes made from human bones. Playing human tibias gave warring Indians power over their enemies, provided that they were enemy bones. Performing on a human bone flute was also a way of showing bereavement. One Incan legend, for example, relates how the sister-bride of one of the slain Incan kings went into the dead man's tomb, made a flute from his shin bone, and played a mournful melody on it. The type of bone for present flute use is either deer or bird. Both are shamanistic because of their elusive nature, and in the case of the bird, its ability to fly. Multinote flutes are capable of transmitting messages to the supernatural, the animal, and the human world. Concerning the last, for example, hunters and fishers in the Amazon Basin play melodies that announce their return and success (Lévi-Strauss 1973: 324-26). Large aerophones of the recorder type, called flageolets by some, are common sacred flutes of Amazon Indians. Among the Camayurá of Brazil they are thought to embody powerful spirits and are believed to have been gifts of the sun. The Cubeo of the northwest Amazon believe that the sound of the sacred flutes, "ta tara ta tara," is that of the butterfly (Goldman 1963:272), also a shamanistic animal because of its metamorphosis from a lowly larva. These sacred flutes are played in pairs, representing male and female.

Large sacred bamboo or bark trumpets are also a part of many traditional Amazon and Orinoco basin cultures. These often represented the vegetation demons or ancestors and, under penalty of death, were hidden from the women and children (Métraux 1949:576). The characteristic sound is buzzing, and among the Cubeo they are called "dragonfly," although on another occasion they are referred to as "grandmother" (Goldman 1963:219, 241).

A chordophone, the musical bow, is found very infrequently in traditional South American culture. Many writers on the subject claim an African derivation for its existence, and it is possible that some native cultures borrowed the instrument from African slaves. There are, however, possible autochthonous examples of musical bows in various parts of native South America, namely among the Araucanians, who had a double musical bow (perhaps symbolic of dualism), the Jívaro, and the Yupa. Among the Jívaro the instrument is shamanic and is capable of conjuring up spirits and casting magical love spells on the women. Also among the Yupa it is used by both men and women as an instrument to entice the opposite sex. The sexual symbolism is evident because of the shape of the bow and the use of a small stick for bowing purposes. Most often the musical bow of native South Americans is a mouth bow and it is almost always bowed with a stick, although among the Jívaro it is usually struck, perhaps an African-derived technique. The sound of the unusual Araucanian double bow, however, is produced by passing the hair of one bow over the hair of the other.

Many more types of musical instruments, and indeed many other vocal forms, are found within the diverse cultures of the native South Americans, most of them symbolic expressions of the supernatural, or at least of the sociological and economic attitudes of the Indians. Unfortunately, perhaps very little of the traditional musical cultures will withstand the great acculturative trends of this century. These last musical frontiers are easily destroyed by the road-building bulldozers, the oil-seeking conglomerates, and the wave of those who follow with their transistor radios, guitars, and Western harmony. Perhaps new forms will appear which, to the Indians themselves, will be acceptable expressions of their Indianness, such as the *Hallelujah* of the Guinea Highlands or the brass bands of the Andes, both worthy of study and, much more importantly, meaningful modes of expression for them, the native inhabitants of South America.

Glossary

ayahuasca-Quechua: "vine of the dead." A liquid hallucinogenic mixture made from a plant of the species Banisteriopsis. Known by this name in Ecuador and Peru, called *yagé* or *yajé* in Colombia, and *caapi* in Brazil.

bahanarotu-Warao: "owner of bahana." The "white" shaman of Warao culture, associated with light and the easternmost part of the cosmos.

Fuegians-The native inhabitants of Tierra del Fuego, including the Yahgan and the Selk'nam or Ona.

hoarotu-Warao: "owner of hoa." The "black" shaman of Warao culture, associated with the supernatural abode of the dead in the westernmost part of the cosmos.

kena (also *quena, kena-kena, quena-quena*)-Aymará The common term for the notched end-blown flute of the Andes, made today from cane, bamboo, plastic, or copper tubing, and in ancient times from cane, bone, clay, and possibly stone and gold or silver.

voice masking-An alteration of the voice, usually by constricting the vocal cords, for spirit communication.

wisiratu-Warao: "owner of pains." The priest shaman of Warao culture, associated with ancestor spirits and user of the large rattle called *hebumataro*.

Bibliography

Aretz, Isabel.
    1952. "Músicas Pentatónicas en Sudamérica." *Archivos Venezolanos de Folklore*, 1:283-309.
    1970. "Cantos Araucanos de Mujeres." *Revista Venezolana de Folklore* 3:73-104.

Arguedas, José María.
    1957. *The Singing Mountaineers*. Austin: University of Texas Press.

Baltasar de Matallana, R. P.
    1939. *La Música Indígena Taurepán*. Caracas: Editorial Venezuela.

Biocca, Ettore.
    1966. *Viaggi Tra Gli Indi*. Vol. 4. Roma: Consiglio Nazionale Delle Ricerche.

Collaer, Paul.
    1970. *Music of the Americas*. London and Dublin: Curzon Press Ltd.

Dole, Gertrude E.
    1973. "Shamanism and Political Control among the Kuikuru." In D. R. Gross, ed. *Peoples and Cultures of Native South America*, Garden City, N.Y.: Doubleday/The Natural History Press.

Eliade, Mircea.
    1972. *Shamanism: Archaic Techniques of Ecstasy*. Bollingen Series 76. Princeton: Princeton University Press.

Galvão, Eduardo.
    1967. "Indigenous Culture Areas of Brazil, 1900-1959." In J. H. Hopper, ed. *Indians of Brazil in the Twentieth Century*, Washington, D.C.: Institute for Cross-Cultural Research.

Goldman, Irving.
    1963. *The Cubeo, Indians of the Northwest Amazon*. Illinois Studies in Anthropology No. 2. Urbana: The University of Illinois Press.

d'Harcourt, R., and M. d'Harcourt.
    1925. *La Musique des Incas et ses survivances*. 2 vols. Paris: Librairie Orientaliste Paul Geuthner.
    1959. *La Musique des Aymara sur les hauts plateaux boliviens*. Paris: Société des Américanistes, Musée de l'Homme.

Harner, Michael J.
    1972. *The Jívaro: People of the Sacred Waterfalls*. Garden City, N.Y.: Doubleday/Natural History Press.
    1973. "The Sound of Rushing Water." In Michael J. Harner, ed. *Hallucinogens and Shamanism*, London: Oxford University Press.

Hornbostel, Erich M. von.
    1936. "Fuegian Songs." *American Anthropologist* 38:357-67.
    1948. "The Music of the Fuegians." *Ethnos* 3-4:61-102.
    1955-1956. "La Música de los Makuschí, Taulipáng y Yekuaná." *Archivos Venezolanos de Folklore*, año 4-5, tomo 3, no. 1, pp. 137-58.

Isamitt, Carlos.
    1937. "Cuatro Instrumentos Musicales Araucanos." *Boletín Latino Americano de Música* 3:55-66.
    1938. "Los Instrumentos Araucanos." *Boletín Latino Americano de Música* 4:306-12.

Izikowitz, Karl Gustav.
    1935. *Musical and Other Sound Instruments of the South American Indians*. Göteborg: Elanders Boktryckeri Aktiebolag.

Jimenez Borja, Arturo.
    1951. *Instrumentos Musicales del Perú*. Lima: Museo de la Cultura.

Karsten, Rafael.
    1935. *The Head-hunters of Western Amazonas.*

Commentationes Humanarum Litterarum, 7, 1. Helsingfors: Societas Scientiarum Fennica.

Katz, Fred, and Marlene Dobkin de Rios.
  1971. "Hallucinogenic Music: An Analysis of the Role of Whistling in Peruvian Ayahuasca Healing Sessions." *Journal of American Folklore* 84:320-27.

Kensinger, Kenneth M.
  1973. "Banisteriopsis Usage Among the Peruvian Cashinahua." In Michael J. Harner, ed. *Hallucinogens and Shamanism*, London: Oxford University Press.

Key, Mary.
  1963. "Music of the Sirionó (Guaranían)." *Journal of the Society for Ethnomusicology* 7:17-21.

Kloos, Peter.
  1968. "Becoming a Pïyei: Variability and Similarity in Carib Shamanism." *Anthropológica* 24:3-25.

Lavin, Carlos.
  1961. "La Música de los Araucanos." *Anuario Musical*, pp. 201-15.

Lévi-Strauss, Claude.
  1961. *Tristes Tropiques*. New York: Criterion Books.
  1963. *Structural Anthropology*. New York: Basic Books.
  1973. *From Honey to Ashes*. London: Jonathan Cape.

List, George.
  1965. "Music in the Culture of the Jibaro Indians of the Ecuadorian Montaña." *Primera Conferencia Interamericana de Etnomusicología*. Washington, D.C.: Union Panamericana, Secretaría General de la Organización de los Estados Americanos.

Loukotka, Čestmír.
  1968. *Classification of South American Indian Languages*. Los Angeles: Latin American Center, University of California.

Lucas, Theodore D.
  1971. "Songs of the Shipibo of the Upper Amazon." *Anuario, Yearbook for Inter-American Musical Research* 7:59-81.

McCosker, Sandra Smith.
  1974. *The Lullabies of the San Blas Cuna Indians of Panama*. Etnologiska Studier 33. Göteborg: Etnografiska Museum, 1974.

Métraux, Alfred.
  1949. "Religion and Shamanism." In Julian H. Steward, ed. *Handbook of South American Indians*, 5. Washington, D.C.: United States Printing Office.

Moreno, Segundo Luis.
  1972. *Historia de la música en el Ecuador*. Quito: Editorial casa de la cultura ecuatoriana.

Murdock, G. P.
  1951. *Outline of South American Cultures*. Vol. 2. New Haven: Human Relations Area Files, Inc.

Nordenskiöld, Erland.
  1919. *An Ethno-Geographical Analysis of the Material Culture of Two Indian Tribes in the Gran Chaco*. Comparative Ethnographical Studies 1. Göteborg: Elanders Boktryckeri Aktiebolag.
  1920. *The Changes in the Material Culture of Two Indian Tribes under the Influence of New Surroundings*. Comparative Ethnographical Studies 2. Göteborg: Elanders Boktryckeri Aktiebolag.

Olsen, Dale A.
  1973. "Music and Shamanism of the Winikina-Warao Indians of Venezuela: Music for Curing and Other Theurgy." Ph.D. dissertation, University of California, Los Angeles. Ann Arbor: University Microfilms.
  1974. "The Function of Naming in the Curing Songs of the Warao Indians of Venezuela." *Anuario, Yearbook for Inter-American Musical Research* 10:88-122.
  1975. "Music-Induced Altered States of Consciousness among Warao Shamans." *Journal of Latin American Lore*, 1:19-33.

Olsen, Diane.
  1978. *Precolumbian Exhibition: The John and Mary Carter Collection*. Tallahassee: The Florida State University Office of Publications.

Orrego-Salas, Juan A.
  1966. "Araucanian Indian Instruments." *Journal of the Society for Ethnomusicology* 10:48-57.

Radin, Paul.
  1942. *Indians of South America*. Garden City, N.Y.: Doubleday, Doran.

Ramón y Rivera, Luis Felipe.
  1966. "Music of the Motilone Indians." *Journal of the Society for Ethnomusicology* 10:18-27.
  1969. "Formaciones Escalísticas en la Etnomúsica Latinoamericana." *Yearbook, International Folkmusic Council*, pp. 201-25.

Reichel-Dolmatoff, Gerardo.
  1945. "Los Indios Motilones: Etnografía y Lingüística." *Revista del Instituto Etnológico Nacional* (Bogotá) 2:15-115.
  1951. *Los Kogi: Una Tribu de la Sierra Nevada de Santa Marta, Colombia*. Vol. 2. Bogotá: Editorial Iqueima.

1971. *Amazonian Cosmos: The Sexual and Religious Symbolism of the Tukano Indians.* Chicago: The University of Chicago Press.

Sharon, Douglas.
1972. "The San Pedro Cactus in Peruvian Folk Healing." In Peter T. Furst, ed. *Flesh of the Gods.* New York: Praeger.

Siskind, Janet.
1973. "Visions and Cures Among the Sharanahua." In Michael J. Harner, ed. *Hallucinogens and Shamanism.* London: Oxford University Press.

Slonimsky, Nicolas.
1945. *Music of Latin America.* New York: Thomas Y. Crowell.

Sorensen, Arthur P., Jr.
1973. "South American Indian Linguistics at the Turn of the Seventies." In Daniel R. Gross, ed. *Peoples and Cultures of Native South America.* Garden City, N.Y.: Doubleday/The Natural History Press.

Stevenson, Robert.
1968. *Music in Aztec & Inca Territory.* Berkeley and Los Angeles: University of California Press.

Steward, Julian H., ed.
1949. *Handbook of South American Indians.* 5 vols. Washington, D.C.: United States Printing Office.

Steward, Julian H., and Louis C. Faron.
1959. *Native Peoples of South America.* New York: McGraw-Hill.

Stoddart, D. R.
1962. "Myth and Ceremonial among the Tunebo Indians of Eastern Colombia." *Journal of American Folklore* 75:147-52.

Titiev, Mischa.
1949. "Social Singing among the Mapuche." *Anthropological Papers,* Museum of Anthropology, University of Michigan, no. 2. Ann Arbor: University of Michigan Press.

Vega, Garcilaso de la.
1961. *The Royal Commentaries of the Inca.* New York: Avon Books, The Orion Press.

Villas Boas, Orlando, and Claudio Villas Boas.
1973. *Xingu: The Indians, Their Myths.* New York: Farrar, Straus and Giroux.

Weiss, Gerald.
1973. "Shamanism and Priesthood in the Light of the Campa *Ayahuasca* Ceremony." In Michael J. Harner, ed. *Hallucinogens and Shamanism.* London: Oxford University Press.

Whiffen, Thomas.
1915. *The North-West Amazons.* New York: Duffield.

Wilbert, Johannes.
1972a. *Survivors of Eldorado.* New York: Praeger.
1972b. "Tobacco and Shamanistic Ecstasy among the Warao Indians of Venezuela." In Peter T. Furst, ed. *Flesh of the Gods.* New York: Praeger.
1974. *Yupa Folktales.* Los Angeles: Latin American Center, University of California.

Discography

Amerindian Ceremonial Music from Chile. UNESCO. Philips 6586 #O26.

Anthology of Brazilian Indian Music. Folkways FE 4311.

Aspectos de la Cultura Indigena. Fray Javier Montoya Sanchez, ETHNIA. Discos Orbe Ltda., Bogotá, Colombia (Colombia).

Brésil—Musique indienne. Vol. 1. Collection du musée de l'homme. Vogue Contrepoint MC 20.137 (Brazil).

Chicha Maya, Folklore de la Guajira Venezolana. Folklore de Venezuela. Vol. 4. Sonido Laffer, Caracas, Venezuela.

Fiestas of Peru, Music of the High Andes. Nonesuch Explorer Series H-72045.

Indians of Matto Grosso. Folkways FE 4446.

Indiens d'Amazonie. Ethnologie Vivante. Le chant du Monde. LDX 7450l. Gravure Universelle.

Indians of the Upper Amazon. Folkways FE 4458 (Brazil, Colombia).

Instruments and Music of Bolivia. Folkways, FM 4012.

Kingdom of the Sun, Peru's Inca Heritage. Nonesuch Explorer Series H-72029.

Mountain Music of Peru. Folkways FE 4539.

Música indígena Makiritare. Fundación La Salle, Caracas, Venezuela (Venezuela).

Música indígena Venezolana. Vol. 1. Música guajira. Editado por el Ministerio de Justicia, Comisión Indigenista, Caracas, Venezuela.

Music of Peru. Folkways FE 4415.

The Music of Some Indian Tribes of Colombia. Anglo-Colombian Recording Expedition 1960-61 (Moser-Tayler Collection). The British Institute of Recorded Sound, Brian Moser and Donald Tayler 1972, 29 Exhibition Road, London SW7.

Music of the Upper Amazon. The Iawa and Bora Indians. Olympic Records, the Atlas Collection 6116.

Music of the Venezuelan Yekuana Indians. Folkways Ethnic Records FE 4104.

Musiques du Pérou. Paucartambo, Indiens Q'eros. Disques Ocora OCR 30.

Primitive Music of the World. Selected and edited by Henry Cowell. Folkways FE 4581 (Panamá, Perú).

Selk'nam Chants of Tierra del Fuego, Argentina. Ethnic Folkways, FE 4176.

Tamunanque y Mosaicos del Folklore Venezolano. Sonido Laffer. Caracas, Venezuela.

Traditional Music of Peru. Folkways FE 4456.

Venezuela. The Columbia World Library of Folk and Primitive Music. Vol. 9. Collected by Juan Liscano, edited by Alan Lomax. Col. SL-212.

Viaggi Tragli Indi. Ettore Biocca. Vol. 4. Dischi. Rome, Italy (Venezuela, Colombia).

Xingú: Cantos e ritmos. Philips 6349 022 (Brazil).

Films

Ebena: Hallucinogenic Ecstasy among the Indians. LAC. Col. 23 min. Made by Inga Steinvorth-Goetz.

Filmed among the Yanoama Indians of Venezuela. Considerable singing and/or chanting by the shaman under the influence of a drug made from acacia and other vegetable matter.

Imajinero. IR. Col. 52 min. Made by Jorge Preloran. English version by Robert Gardner.

"The story of an Indian folk artist living in the barren country of Northwest Argentina . . . at a place where Inca and Spanish traditions meet . . . This film goes well beyond ethnographic descriptions of the obvious kind. It is essentially a reflection on the universality of the human condition." Asen Balikci. Little, if any, music.

Journey to Chinale. CF/MG. Col. 25 min.

About Carib-speaking Oyana Indians, who migrate from Brazil to Surinam. Important for "comprehensive footage on the feast and ritual ordeal of the Maraké in which huge, stinging ants are pressed against the bodies of the initiates." CFMG. Western score except for a few native flute sounds.

Poisons and Drugs in the Amazon Jungle. LAC. Col. 29 min. Directed (?) by Georg J. Seitz.

Documentation includes limited use of singing during the curing ritual (Yanomamö and Tukano).

Rituelle Tänze. Institut für den Wissenschaftlichen Film. Col. 5 min. Silent. Lewis T. Laffer, photographer.

A documentary about the Warao Indians of Venezuela, showing their daily life. Includes ritualistic curing music. "Authentic documentation on representative parts of several ritual dances, such as 'najanamo,' 'jabisanuka,' 'jubakaia-moni.' " Peter Kennedy.

Tanzfest. Institut für den Wissenschaftlichen Film. Col. 9 min. Silent. Meinhard Schuster, photographer.

"Authentic documentation on proceedings during the Makiritare animal dance festival [on the upper Orinoco]. Reed instruments and drums accompany a round-dance." Peter Kennedy.

The Warao. LAC. Col. 58 min. Made by Jorge Preloran.

A documentary about the Warao Indians of Venezuela, showing their daily life. Includes ritualistic curing music.

Woodwinds and Dance. IFF. Col. 10 min.

Part of a series of eight films entitled *Indians of the Orinoco: The Makiritare*, who live in mountainous jungles of Venezuela and Brazil. In this film the Indians make long wooden instruments resembling clarinets, play them, and dance.

20. Folk Music of South America—A Musical Mosaic

Dale A. Olsen

Few continents display such racial, cultural, political, and musical diversity as does South America. In less than five hundred years nearly all the races of the world have mingled on this great land mass. In addition, many of the world's belief systems, ranging from ancient Amerindian shamanism and an African pantheon of gods, through Christianity, Judaism, and Hinduism, to the more recent Tenrikyo, Hallelujah, and atheistic Marxist ideologies, plus other cultural differences, all form the substance for the musical expressions of the South American folk—elements for a "musical mosaic."

In the vast body of music in the oral tradition of South America one can make two very large divisions: between the music of the Native Americans and that of the immigrants to South America within the past five hundred years. The emphasis here is the music in the oral tradition of the South American folk that has been either European, African, or Amerindian derived, or is any mixture of the three.

Politically, historians of South America have made a distinction among countries where the Indian predominates (Bolivia, Ecuador, and Peru), where Negro background is an important characteristic (Brazil, Colombia, and Venezuela), where European blood predominates (Argentina and Uruguay), and, finally, where the mestizo is most common (Brazil, Chile, Colombia, Paraguay, and Venezuela) (Herring 1968: 16). There is, of course, much overlap in this kind of breakdown because racial groups do not necessarily remain in a particular country. In addition, the percentage of genes determining the difference between Indian, European, and African on the one hand and mestizo (literally "mixed blood," but in South America it usually refers to mixed Spanish and Indian), mulatto (mixed black and white), criollo (creole, especially in Venezuela, born in Venezuela of black or white descent but often mixed), and zambo (mixed black and Indian) on the other has not been determined. Musically, as well as racially, distinctions are very difficult to categorize. It is perhaps best to think of the folk music of South America as a mestizo phenomenon that is culturally rather than racially determined. The typical South American of today, like the descendant of any immigrant, is no longer Spanish, African, or Italian (even though his blood may be "pure"); he is a South American, a new breed which has adapted to a new culture. By redefining the term *mestizo* as a cultural mixture it would be possible to think of South American folk music in varying degrees of "mestization" or hybridization, from the most pure to the most mixed.

It will be appropriate to begin with European-derived folk music, followed by African-derived, Amerindian, and concluding with the most mixed forms of our musical mosaic.

EUROPEAN-DERIVED FOLK MUSIC

Many songs throughout portions of South America have a Spanish or Portuguese air about them. Yet few writers have actually pinpointed Iberian songs that may have served as sources, the reason being that most of the songs of European origin have long since died out in their native country while being preserved in obscure pockets in South America. The same situation is true with certain ancient English ballads that are still sung in the mountain regions of the

South America. Approximate areas where slaves were situated during the colonial time are indicated by dots. Most of these areas, with the exception of Chile, have a sizeable black population today.

United States, yet have disappeared in the British Isles.

The earliest arrivals from Europe to make a lasting impression on South America were the conquistadores, the conquerors, hungry for gold. They and the immigrants to follow were mostly from the low social classes of the Iberian peninsula, and their music was the popular music of the common people, diffused throughout many portions of the New World by minstrels who came, vihuela and guitar in hand, with the conquering armies (Grebe 1967:338). Other musical carriers were the missionaries, who applied their refined religious poetry to simple Hispanic secular melodies. Some of this early Spanish sung poetry has been preserved in Chile, for example, which has always been an isolated part of the world (until air travel) because of the extremely arid Atacama desert on the north, the awesome Andes to the east, and the vast Pacific on the west (ibid., 337). The long span between arrivals of ships from the motherland was another kind of isolation, and musicians clung to old traditions with their instruments and songs long after they had disappeared from the mother countries (Hague 1934:62).

Another area of preservation is in the Chocó of Colombia, a *departamento* or state located in the dense rain forest of the northern Pacific littoral, a virtual no-man's-land, where certain Spanish-derived songs, including *alabaos*, salves, and villancicos have been sustained (Abadía 1970:118). It is not unusual for these songs to be religious or somewhat spiritual in nature, since music associated with the supernatural tends to resist change the most. The alabao (also called alabado and *alabanza*), for example, is a song of religious exaltation dedicated to the saints, which today occasionally takes on a profane air. Although it is at times still sung unaccompanied, it is often performed with percussion, for the majority of the inhabitants of the Chocó are of African descent. The alabao is also sung at wakes, when friends come from the surrounding rural areas to say their last farewells to the deceased, to express condolences to the family, to make sure the subject is really dead (an important consideration in a locale where modern funerary practices are not available), and to recite the deceased's life history. The salve, an unaccompanied sung prayer dedicated to the Virgin, is also used during funeral rites. In Spain the term *villancico* literally means a "rustic song" (Chase 1959:40), while in South America it is basically a Christmas song. In the Chocó many of the texts have been taken from the oral tradition, even though the villancico still retains its Christmas function. The word is not used everywhere in South America; nevertheless, many of the Christmas melodies are of the villancico type, meaning that they are basically solo songs with instrumental accompaniment (in the style of sixteenth-century Spain), featuring a simplicity of melody, rhythm, and structure with a simple and uniform accompaniment (Ramón y Rivera 1969: 123). A more common type of Christmas song throughout South America is the aguinaldo, which literally means "New Year's gift," or "Christmas box." Aguinaldos are generally performed by large groups that go from house to house and sing under the windows of those visited, in a manner similar to the caroling that takes place at Christmas time in England and the United States. Melodically, aguinaldos are related to the older villancicos; however, in Venezuela for example, they employ syncopation and a freer style of performance including glissandos (Aretz 1965:81).

Other typical Iberian-derived folk songs are unaccompanied lullabies, called *arrullos* (literally "cooing") or *arrorrós*, and *canciones de cuna* ("cradle songs"). The rural black population is responsible for the preservation of many Spanish- and Portuguese-derived lullabies. Although most of the melodies become altered over the centuries, generally owing to their simplicity (a phenomenon of the oral tradition in folk music), often the text retains identifiable characteristics. George List (1973:75) points out a minor but very interesting alteration between the Spanish and the Colombian texts of lullabies he collected on the Caribbean coast (also called the Atlantic littoral) of Colombia. This change is between the familiar command form *duérmete* ("sleep thee") used in Spain, and the formal *duérmase* ("sleep you") used in Colombia. As List explains, the slave or servant was not allowed to speak or even sing to the child in the familiar. Today the formal usage continues in some rural Colombian communities, even though the person singing the lullaby is usually the mother. With regard to melodies, however, no similarities could be found with the Spanish repertoire of lullabies (ibid., 81), so much had the Colombian examples changed. Often, common melodies will be adapted for the lullaby text; for example, in Venezuela a number of Spanish-derived lullabies are based on the melody of the first eight bars of the Venezuelan national

American music, and it is most often found in the genres mentioned above as well as in children's songs (Grebe 1967:327). Where the musical inspiration is religious in nature (i.e., Catholic), the use of modality is not infrequent, as in example 20-2, an excerpt of a Catholic vesper service for St. Michael, recorded in the small Christianized Mojo Indian community known as San Miguel de Isiboro, Bolivia.

Although an Indian community, the inhabitants of San Miguel de Isiboro have been missionized by the Jesuits since possibly the seven-

EXAMPLE 20-1. Canción de Cuna, Chile (Antología del Folklore Musical Chilena, Vol. IV, RCA Victor CML 2295-X, Side A, Band 5). Transcribed by Dale A. Olsen, with permission.

anthem, a familiar tune in Venezuelan households (Ramón y Rivera 1969:13). Lullabies are almost always sung unaccompanied because of their function of soothing and lulling the child to sleep. Example 20-1, a Chilean lullaby, demonstrates the melodic simplicity and the syllabic text. The dotted rhythm creates a lilting and hypnotic effect.

There are also isolated regions in Brazil where Portuguese-derived material has been preserved. In the dry northeast of Brazil, in the *sertão* or backlands, another no-man's-land, very little racial and consequent musical mixture has taken place. As a result, many romances or ballads that still have modal characteristics typical of the Renaissance continue there, whereas they have vanished from their Iberian sources (Martins Lamas 1955:28).

Modality is one of the traditional Renaissance musical characteristics that can be used as a determinant of European archaism in South

teenth century, and this type of Catholic music may be typical in very isolated areas regardless of the racial composition of the people. The music is in the oral tradition, yet such archaisms as the Aeolian mode are employed with a raised sixth (indicated by brackets) in the organumlike response. In the Middle Ages and the Renaissance this technique was called *musica ficta* and was used to eliminate the tritone, the "diabolus in musica."

Narrative forms of solo songs with guitar or similar accompaniment also show a direct relationship to Spanish modal archetypes. The similarity, however, is more in function than in melody, except for indications of modal features. The popular Iberian Renaissance ballad form known as the *romance* achieved a certain popularity in South America in various forms and under various names. The most common names besides romance are *corrido*, a term used in the southern provinces of Spain as well as in

Mexico, Venezuela, Colombia, Chile, and even the Philippine Islands (Duran 1950:60), and *décima*, a term that refers to the ten-line stanzas of its text. In Latin America, as in Spain, this ballad form is used to tell of historical and current events. Another sung poetic type, perhaps related to the romance, is the Chilean *verso*, a ritual rural folksong based on archaic texts of the seventeenth-century Spanish court, and classified according to subject matter as *a lo divino* ("of the divine"), or *a lo humano* ("of humanity") (Grebe 1967:327). Occasionally folk songs show a few characteristics that indicate possible romance derivation, such as melodic simplicity emphasizing the importance of the text rather than the music, repetition, and a lack of chromaticism. These traits appear in the Argentinian and Uruguayan milonga, and more rarely in a few examples of the *vidala, estilo*,

tono, and tonada (Aretz 1952:95, 157). These few general characteristics, however, are not sufficient evidence for assuming a Spanish romance derivation. Robert Stevenson (1968:312), for example, in discussing a printed Peruvian romance from the seventeenth century, points out that the Spanish Renaissance romance form requires, in addition to the above, repetition of the melody with every four poetic lines, no refrain, no modulation, rhythmic simplicity and regularity, no cadential leaps, and a use of fermatas at phrase endings, suggesting that the usual New World romance, "though poured into a vintage bottle, is new wine of the seventeenth century." The reason for this musical freedom of the South American romance and its variants is that it was not customary to print the music in the sixteenth and seventeenth century Spanish *Romanceros* (romance songbooks), and the oral

EXAMPLE 20-2. Catholic vesper service for St. Michael, San Miguel de Isiboro, Bolivia, recorded September 1968. Collection of Dori Reeks and Dale A. Olsen.

tradition prevailed in America as in Spain (Chase 1959:45).

Often the romance is sung in the usual syllabic manner, but with two voices singing in parallel thirds rather than as a solo, always with the ubiquitous guitar or its like. In central Brazil the *moda da viola* is a rural song, accompanied by the *viola* (a small guitar), that shows affinity with the Iberian romance (Béhague 1973:185), although it is not strictly folkloric because many are written and composed by a well-known popular poet (Martins Lamas 1955:28).

The *copla* ("couplet," a stanza of four lines, the second and fourth rhyming), another Spanish poetic form set to music, is also found in South America, especially in Colombia. Many of the texts in the Andean region of that country resemble those found in Spain (List 1967:118). Copla texts are, in fact, similar throughout South America, and some versions display certain regional or nationalistic features so characteristic in folklore. For example, the following copla from the northern Argentinian mountain province of Catamarca shows a very close identity to a copla from the mountain provinces of Cundinamarca and Boyacá in Colombia:

> *Argentina:* La cajita que yo tengo
> tiene boca y sabe hablar;
> si tuviera también ojos
> me acompañara a llorar.
>
> The *cajita* [drum] that I have
> Has a mouth and knows how to talk;
> If it also had eyes
> It would accompany me to cry.
>
> *Colombia:* Este tiple tiene boca
> corazón y sabe hablar,
> solo le faltan los ojos
> para ayudarme a llorar.
>
> This *tiple* [guitar type] has a mouth,
> A heart, and knows how to talk,
> It only lacks eyes
> To help me to cry.
> [Piñeros Corpas:23; my translation]

Also, in the Atlantic littoral region of Colombia, copla texts are used in cattle-herding songs known as *vaquerías* (List 1967:118). The cattle herders or Colombian cowboys sing copla stanzas back and forth to each other to keep the herd moving. In the *llanos* or plains region of Vene-

zuela the *llaneros* or cowboys also sing coplas to quiet the cattle and to keep them together (Ramón y Rivera 1969:23).

Another genre employing a type of narration is the competition song, known in Spain by the name of *desafío* (literally "challenge" or "duel"). In Renaissance Europe, such improvised singing duels took place between minstrels on subjects ranging from religion and cosmology to history or geography (Bastide 1972:186). The desafío, though rare today in Europe, is still found in the Spanish provinces of Galicia and Asturias (Romeu 1948:149), but is perhaps more common in parts of South America. Accompanied by the guitar, or a similar portable string instrument, the genre is known in Brazil as *cantoría* (earlier it was also desafío), in Venezuela as *porfías* (literally "quarrels") or *polo en porfías*, and in Argentina as contrapunto or *payas*. In Chile, the *canto a lo pueta* serves as the medium for the song debate, although this "singing in the style of the poet" is normally an epic-lyric genre, sung by men accompanied by the guitar or *guitarrón* (a large 25-string guitar), to a group of four décimas (Dannemann and Sheehy 1975). As a musical genre requiring fast, spontaneous melodic and textual improvisation, the desafío is unrivaled. In a typical situation that I happened to witness in the small Venezuelan town of Suapire during the summer of 1974, a rather poorly attired peasant in his late fifties appeared at the main section of town where several younger men were singing and playing the *cuatro* (a small four-stringed guitar). He began announcing in song who he was, challenging a younger singer to a musical duel. After about thirty minutes of antiphonal song, and numerous hesitations by the less experienced singer, the younger man conceded, shook the older man's hand, and the crowd that had gathered applauded the contest. This style of performance continued for several hours more, as other men tried their turn at outdoing the older man. In Brazil, especially in the sertão, opponents would warm themselves up by shouting abuses to each other. Often these improvised battles would be between a black and a white man, which gave the Negro, in the good humor of a game, the opportunity to release his innermost feelings toward his one-time master (Bastide 1972:186). Because of the wit of the Negro, he often outdid his Caucasian opponent, as in the following excerpt of a text where a black contestant was mocked because of his color and he replied:

> White paper is worthless in itself
> But write on it
> With black ink
> And it's worth millions. [*ibid.*]

Lyrical, accompanied folk songs of Iberian origin, based on amorous themes, are also common throughout South America. The most common names are canción (song) and tonada (tune) in Chile and Argentina, estilo (literally "style") in Argentina and Uruguay, and *toada* (Portuguese for tonada) in Brazil, the four being virtually the same in function and sentiment. The tonada is one of the most important folk song types in rural central Chile, and its musical characteristics are typically Spanish. Perhaps the most important Iberian element is the use of dual meter, manifested in either or both of two ways: *a*) 6/8 in voice part against 3/4 in accompaniment (one meter against another is called *bimeter*); and *b*) alternation between 6/8 and 3/4 in either the vocal part or both lines. Slonimsky (1946:55) calls the former concept the "Colonial rhythm," and Aretz (1967:14) refers to the latter as *sesquiáltera*. Both concepts are prevalent in most Spanish-derived dance forms. The melody of the tonada is two-part or binary, and the intervals seldom exceed a fifth. Harmonically it is nearly always in major, with tonic, subdominant, and dominant (I, IV, V) chords prevailing. In Chile the interpreters are nearly always women, and the guitar is the most important accompanying instrument, although the accordion is becoming increasingly popular. Example 20-3 demonstrates all of the above characteristics plus the technique of *rasqueado*, or strumming on the guitar to the rhythm ♫♫♫ (the "x" indicates a downward motion of the hand, stopping all the strings with the palm while at the same time the fingernails sweep the string, thereby creating a sound of undetermined pitch). Other tonada strums are ♫♫♫ and ♫♫♫♫ .

Another Chilean lyrical folk song style is the *parabién* ("congratulation"), whose name is derived from its original function of congratulating newlyweds. Today the form is used in any song context, with the rhythm, a lilting 3/4, determining the style. The guitar accompaniment usually alternates between strumming the rhythm ♫♫♫ and picking (*punteado*) the bass, the countermelody, and the melody lines (only the punteado is indicated in the notation of example 20-4. The melodic elements of the vocal part are very similar to those of the tonada; the alternation between triple (3/4) and duple meter (2/4 in this case, but 4/4 in others) is a characteristic of the parabién. Example 20-4 is typical of this class of songs.

A lyrical song style of Brazil that can be considered in the folk song category only by virtue of its assimilation and adoption by the people is the *modinha*. Originally they were composed salon songs in the Italian operatic tradition; here, however, modinhas may be an urban outgrowth of the rural modas da viola. Because of their beauty, often amorous topics, and omnipresent *saudade* ("nostalgia," a typical Brazilian characteristic) many of these popular songs are in the oral tradition and are favorites of the Brazilian people.

In the area of dance music some European forms have been preserved. Again in the Colombian Chocó, the ancient dances known as the danza, the *contradanza*, the polka, the jota, and the mazurka have been kept alive by Negro groups (Abadía 1970:119). The first two of these are Hispanic variants of the English country dance. They had a major role in the development of the Cuban habanera and later the Argentinean tango (Slonimsky 1946:56). In Chile the contradanza style still can be found in the dance forms *cielito* and *pericona* (Dannemann and Sheehy 1975). The polka and the mazurka also indicate northern European influence, although their existence as pure forms is for the most part historical. They have, however, merged with other forms creating, for example in Argentina, the *gato polqueado* (combined with the Argentinian *gato*) and the *ranchera* (Aretz 1952:103). A relatively recent and pure form of the polka, however, is performed in central

EXAMPLE 20-3. *El Pajarito*—Tonada, Colchagua province, Department of San Fernando, Chile, August 1967. Collection of Dale A. Olsen.

Chile. Called *polka alemana*, it is danced by German immigrants and their descendants in the southern provinces of Valdivia, Osorno, and Llanquihue (Dannemann and Sheehy 1975). The jota is a Spanish form still to be found in various pockets of South America, such as in central Argentina. It and the many mestizo forms derived from it are characterized especially by the use of zapateo ("shoe tapping") so familiar in much male Spanish dancing. In Venezuela the jota has been used with the malagueña, also Spanish in origin, as the music for the religious *velorios* (from *vela*, "candle") of the cross (Ramón y Rivera 1969:60). Another Venezuelan and also Colombian dance of Spanish origin, stemming perhaps from the fandango, is the joropo. It is likewise characterized by zapateo, and its melody often includes melismas similar to Spanish cante jondo (Abadía 1970:101).

Spanish- and Portuguese-derived instrumental music emphasizes string instruments of the lute or guitar and harp types. In the northern countries of Venezuela and Colombia, numerous small guitarlike instruments whose names derive from the number of strings they have are in common usage. These are the *cuatro* (four strings), *cinco* (five), *seis* (six), *cuatro y medio* (four strings with one resonance string), and *cinco y medio* (five strings with one resonance string). Other guitar types include the tiple (literally "treble," it has four orders of double and triple strings in Venezuela and four orders of triple strings in Colombia), *requinto* (a small-sized tiple with the first and fourth order of strings doubled rather than tripled; called "first guitar" in Venezuela), *bandola* (mandolin-type consisting of four orders of triple and two orders of double strings, played with a plectrum), *ban-*

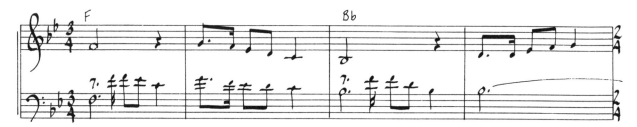

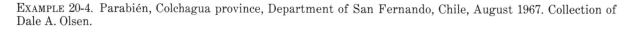

EXAMPLE 20-4. Parabién, Colchagua province, Department of San Fernando, Chile, August 1967. Collection of Dale A. Olsen.

FIGURE 20-1: *a*, *b*, *c*. Three views of three different types of charangos from the Andean region. Charango *a*, from Cuzco, Peru, is in the shape of a small guitar with a flat back. Charango *b*, from Cochabamba, Bolivia, has its neck and resonating chamber carved from one piece of wood. Charango *c*, from Cuzco, Peru, uses a hairy armadillo shell for its resonating body. The instruments are approximately two feet in length.

FIGURE 20-2: *a*, *b*, *c*.

dolina (a small-scale bandola), and of course the guitar (called the "large guitar" in Venezuela). Argentina and Uruguay boast the guitar and on rare occasions the requinto; central Chile, in addition to the guitar, occasionally makes use of the *bandurría* (a pear-shaped instrument with six orders of double strings), bandola (teardrop shape, four orders of double and two orders of triple strings), and the guitarrón (five orders of multiple strings totaling twenty-one with four additional resonance strings called "little devils") of possible Italian Renaissance origin. In portions of Brazil, in addition to the guitar called *violão* three other string instruments of the guitar type may be found: the viola (derived perhaps from a thirteenth-century Iberian instrument called *viola de mão*; today it comes in various sizes with five or six orders of double strings), *côcho* (a viola with five gut strings used in the Mato Grosso), and *cavaquinho* (a small viola, also known by the names of *cavaco*, *machete*, and *machetinho*, with four strings). Many other guitarlike instruments abound throughout South America with many different regional names. Perhaps the best known after the guitar is the Andean charango, a five-course, double-stringed Indian version of the Spanish bandurría (Stevenson 1968:291; figs. 20-1, 20-2, 20-3). Its unique construction feature is the often used armadillo shell back, but the construction of what is generically called charango today may vary in number of strings and in material. I have seen "charangos" made from turtle shells, gourds, carved wood, cut wood like a guitar, and hairy and hairless armadillo shells. When the instrument is used in mestizo music its tuning can be in A-minor or E-minor (example 20-5). In other situations the tuning varies, and in Aymara rituals it is often strummed and used as a noisemaker, perhaps as a replacement for a rattle, with apparently little concern for Western tuning.

Example 20-6, a guitar solo from rural Chile, serves as an example of peasant solo guitar music. The style uses punteado throughout, except

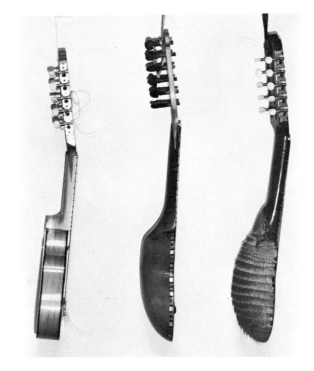

FIGURE 20-3: *a, b, c.*

FIGURE 20-4. A blind Peruvian harpist near Cuzco, Peru, playing for a wedding celebration.

on the last chord. The two-line simplicity is enriched and complicated by the use of bimeter, in this case duple against triple in the form of 2/4 for the melody and 6/8 for the accompaniment. The form is binary, consisting of six measures of "A" and eight measures of "B," each repeated twice with slight variations.

The folk harps found in Venezuela, Colombia, Peru, Chile, Argentina, and Paraguay are diatonic instruments without pedals (fig. 20-4). One Peruvian harp is played in an unusual manner during festivals—it is hoisted up and played upside down on the harpist's shoulder. An example of harp music is shown in example 20-15.

AFRICAN-DERIVED FOLK MUSIC

Europeans began bringing African slaves to the New World only a few years after its discovery, and from that time a major process of musical syncretism began. Changes in the music of the African descendants since the early sixteenth century range from the minute to the overwhelming. Unlike the attitude of most North American slave owners, who sought to

destroy the cultural identity of the Negro, the South American masters realized that a more productive and reproductive slave was one who was allowed to dance, make music, and adhere to many of his traditional ways (Bastide 1972:172), even though he was often forcibly baptized into the Catholic Church (Herring 1968:112). This "conversion," however, the white man's justification for enslaving the black, did little to stop the continuance of the African's native religious beliefs. It was, in fact, a substitution rather than a conversion, for many of the Catholic saints in Brazil and elsewhere are but new names and faces for African deities.

In those areas where African religions flourished (especially in the jungle of Surinam, where the Dutch-owned slaves escaped to establish their own nations), music, dance, and other African traditions thrived and very possibly continue to exist today. Through the secrecy of the African-derived religions found in and around Bahia, Brazil, music and dance also continued, although as far back as the 1930s Ramos (1939:94) wrote "It is difficult to identify in the present day Brazil exactly those elements in folklore which can be traced back to the African." More recently, Gérard Béhague (1973:221) explains that among certain Bahian cults, new

portant Afro-American music cultures and those for which written and sound material is commercially available within a broad perspective. Thus, beginning on our continuum from the "most African" river cultures of Surinam through the blacks of Bahia, either the Town Negroes of Surinam, the blacks of the Barlovento region of Venezuela, or the Negroes of the Pacific littoral of Colombia would be next. The black cultures of Rio de Janeiro and sur-

EXAMPLE 20-5.

material derived from carnival and other musics are inserted into the possession songs during the performance of rituals. In spite of the differences between the blacks of the Surinam river cultures (also called Bush Negroes), and the blacks of Bahia, their culture and folklore are usually classified together by scholars who like to categorize. Bastide (1972:171), for example, outlines three strata of folklore in black America: 1) African, or the pure and traditional core; 2) Negro or Creole, which evolved in America; and 3) white, which shows a borrowing either from white to black for assimilation and social acceptance, or black to white. John Storm Roberts (1974:19) also categorizes the music of black Americans into Neo-African (preservation aspect) and Afro-American (cultural blending). I prefer to think of the music and its cultural aspects on a scale from that which has preserved the most to that which has fewest African characteristics, based on recent evidence. The purpose here is not to start any chauvinistic battles over which music is more distinctly African-derived, region A or region B. I am more concerned with placing the more im-

rounding areas, the Negroes in the vicinity of Lake Maracaibo in Venezuela, and the pockets of African descendants in the Atlantic littoral of Colombia could follow. Next could be the urban black musical cultures found in such cities as Caracas, Cali, and Montevideo, followed by the isolated Negro settlements up and down the coast around Lima, Peru. Last on the scale could possibly be the blacks of Chalguayaco in Ecuador. Before discussing several of these cultures in some detail, it is important to mention the most prominent Africanisms and African remnants in South American music and dance.

Perhaps the most important vocal characteristic of African-derived music in South America is the use of call and response, or responsorial technique. The 1941–1942 recordings of Afro-Bahian religious music by Herskovits demonstrate this phenomenon in nearly all the ritual songs. Generally the call is sung by a male leader, which is answered by a female chorus singing in unison. The calls vary, but for the most part they are high-pitched, long, and ornate, with equally long responses. Often the leader will alter his solo during the repetitions,

EXAMPLE 20-6. Guitar solo, Colchagua province, Department of San Fernando, Chile, August 1967. Collection of Dale A. Olsen.

EXAMPLE 20-6. (continued)

and at times he will enter early, creating a harmonic overlap with the response. In a recent recording of Bahian ritual music, the choral response is sung in thirds, with the upper note of the pair dominating. In an old recording of semireligious music of Venezuela, the call and response technique also features unison in the response one time and heterophony in another. However, in some recordings of basically non-ritual music of Bahia and the Pacific littoral of Colombia the responses are again in parallel thirds, and the responses in the Colombian examples clearly outline a dominant tonic harmony, with the call outlining the tonic. A modern (1974) personal recording (ex. 20-9) of semireligious music in Curiepe, Venezuela, demonstrates a unison response. Thus, many varieties of texture exist in conjunction with the call and response technique, and all are found today in Africa (Nketia 1974:140-46).

Scale forms used in South American Negro music also have their counterparts in Africa. Modal forms, diatonic scales in either major or minor, and pentatonic scales are all characteristic. Occasionally a blue third can be heard, especially in the leader's solo during responsorial songs.

Percussion is the most important overall characteristic of Afro-South American music, and in Bahia singing is considered an accompaniment to drumming (Herskovits 1971:1-2). The drums themselves display numerous Africanisms that have nearly identical counterparts in portions of West Africa. As there are regional differences in drum construction in West Africa, so differences exist in South America. Most of the drums of the New World were originally constructed from hollowed-out logs, but today in Brazil they are most commonly constructed from barrel staves (ibid., 11). Hollowed log drums vary in shape from the conical *conuno* of Western Colombia, to the goblet-shaped *nanda* of the Bush Negroes, to the cylindrical *mina* of Venezuela; in length from several to as much as eight feet for the Surinam Town Negro *agida*; and in design from the roughhewn tripod foot *curbata* of Venezuela, to the beautifully carved *apinti* of Surinam. Most of the drums are single-headed, with the exception of the Venezue-lan round drums, which are double-headed. More important are the ways in which the heads are fastened and consequently tuned. The majority are lashed around pegs that, when driven into the drum, tighten the head and raise the pitch. Other drums have wedges that increase the tension on a hoop and consequently tighten the drumhead. Still others have tacked on heads, such as the curious double-headed round drum of Venezuela, which, although completely cylindrical on the outside, has a partition with a small hole in the inside, making it function as an hourglass drum (Max Brandt, personal communication). Such are only a few of the many drums belonging to the descendants of African slaves in South America.

The playing techniques are fairly consistent since all of the drums are floor- rather than hand-held. The usual position for a long drum is to place it between the legs, or to prop it up on an *X* formation of sticks; the smaller drums are placed directly on the floor or ground. By tipping the smaller drums the resonance can be altered, thus creating a difference, if not in pitch, at least in sound. Pitch (but not tuning) can be altered while playing by striking the head near the edge rather than in the middle. Hands are perhaps the most common beaters; however, two sticks, and also one stick and one hand, are frequent, the choice in ritual music often depending on the spirit with whom one is communicating. Sticks are also used as rhythm makers by a second and even a third player striking on the side of a tilted long drum, as is the case with the Venezuelan mina.

Other percussion instruments abound, such as double metal bells in Brazil, "iron against iron" (a makeshift idiophone) and a wooden bench among the Surinam river cultures, stamping tubes in Venezuela, and bamboo rattles in Western Colombia.

In the usual three-drum ensemble the most characteristic rhythm played on the principal, nonimprovising drum is short-long-short (♫). Although this rhythm is not a common drum pattern for solo drum in Africa, it does occur frequently in ensembles as well as in vocal lines. A Brazilian musicologist once tried to explain this typical Afro-Hispanic rhythm by suggesting it developed as an adulterated form of the Iberian 6/8 meter when played against the African 2/4. His analysis is shown in example 20-7, and to my knowledge no one has refuted his theory.

EXAMPLE 20-7.

One of the most important spiritual expressions is the dance, and in South American Negro dancing of religious or secular nature many Africanisms can be seen. Some of these characteristics include: (1) collective ring or circle dancing (although Andean and other Amerindian cultures often employ a circle), the dancers often being only women; (2) one person dancing solo in the center of a circle of spectators who accompany the drum rhythm by handclapping; (3) the dancers half raising their arms; (4) dancing in a slightly bent posture; (5) during a couple dance the man and woman beginning by facing each other and continuing by receding and approaching, at times singing with the chorus on the response (Tompkins 1973:60 citing Romero 1946:96); and (6) the *umbigada* or navel to navel contact, often called "belly-blow" (Bastide 1972:180).

A closer look at some of the important Afro-American musical cultures of South America should be of interest. The runaway slaves of Surinam, basically of Yoruba extraction, began to inhabit the bush (jungle in Surinam) from 1667 on, when the British traded this small area to the Dutch for New York. For the next hundred years refugee slaves expanded the jungle settlements that were so similar in climate to their African homes, until about 1772, when they obtained their independence (Dark 1970:3). One of the most interesting aspects

of the Bush Negro is his supernatural beliefs about his drums and other musical instruments. His particular skill in handling the supernatural earned him the name *Djuka* by the Town Negroes, the freedmen who remained in the city after emancipation. According to Kolinski (1936:520), the Djuka's drums have three functions: (1) they conjure up ancestor spirits and deities, (2) they speak the messages of the spirits once they are conjured up, and (3) they facilitate the spirits' return after each ceremonial function. The voice of the drum is believed to be the voice of the spirit that has been called; while dancing, the dancers must face the drums out of respect for the voices of the spirits within the instruments. The apinti drum invokes the sky gods, the agida invokes the snake deities, and the *tumao* the spirits of the bush. Their sounds are so powerful that immediately upon hearing a drum the believer can become possessed. No woman is allowed to play or even to touch a drum, without bringing about physical changes, such as elongation of the breasts (ibid., 523). The women's role within the Bush Negro's musical culture is to sing during most of the songs, to accompany them with handclapping, and occasionally to play the *saka-sake* or gourd rattle and the *kwakwa* or low bench idiophone. Communications to the living from their ancestors are often transmitted via a possessed participant who sings the message.

The most African-derived religious forms involving music in Brazil are more difficult to identify than those of Surinam, owing to the large number of African descendants, the vast areas they inhabit, and the various African localities from which the Portuguese obtained their slaves (West Africa, including the Yorubas, Ewes, Fantis, Ashantis; West Sudanese area, including the Hausas, Tapas, Mandingos and Fulah; and southwest Angola, the Congo, and Mozambique, including the Bantu cultures [Ramos 1939:81]). Many of the musico-religious structures are syncretic combinations of the beliefs of these various nations often combined with Christianity. They are the *macumba* in Rio de Janeiro, the *candomblé* in Bahia, the *shangô* and *catimbo* in the northeast, and the *pagelanca* in the north where African and Amerindian

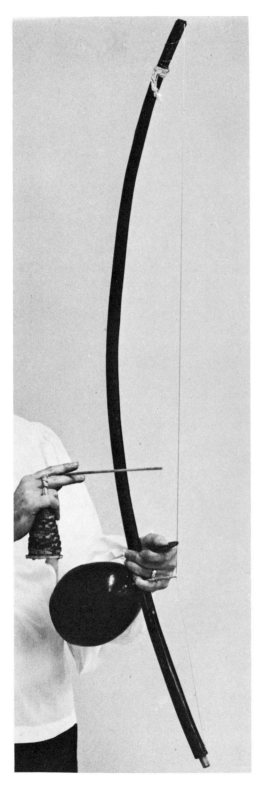

have mixed, forming part of the caboclo culture. The terms *candomblé* and *macumba* originally referred to a dance with accompaniment by certain musical instruments, but today they mean the ritual itself (ibid., 82). The ritual drumming and dancing of the candomblé is called *batucada* or *batuque*, which at times uses the following syncopated drum patterns: (Duran 1950:22). However, the individual traits of the many candomblé rituals in Bahia (there were more than six hundred candomblé groups counted in 1956 [Amado 1966:172]) perhaps generate many unique rhythmic nuances. Each Bahian deity has his own drum rhythm. These rhythms, combined with the songs of praise, are the primary musical languages. The drummer is naturally the most important musician because he makes the sacred drums speak. He is held in highest esteem when he can also lead the singing.

Another Bahian musical and dance genre that shows African derivation is the *capoeira*, an artistic sport from the days when African slaves wore shackles on their wrists. I was informed by a Bahian capoeira instructor that the only method of self-defense for such an unfortunate was to bend down and kick his oppressor. Today capoeira has developed into a striking art form in which two opponents attempt to give each other blows with their feet while doing cartwheels and making other body movements. The origin of the word apparently comes from the name for chicken coop (capoeira), where fugitive slaves hid from their masters. Because they resisted with such violent and agile movements when caught, they were given the name capoeira (Almeida 1961:125-26). The principal musical instrument for the present sport is the *berimbau* or *urucungo*, a musical bow, in its original form from Angola (fig. 20-5). The instru-

FIGURE 20-5. The *berimbau* or musical bow from Bahia, Brazil. The right hand shakes the wicker rattle known as the *caxixi* while the stick strikes the metal string. The left hand operates a washer or similar metal object that touches the string, thereby raising the pitch. The open end of the calabash creates a "wa-wa" effect when moved to and from the player's stomach.

ment resembles a hunter's bow and is approximately four feet in length. It has one metal string and a calabash resonator and is struck with a stick by the right hand while the left holds the instrument and also holds, between thumb and index finger, a large washer or other metal object that is pressed against the string to raise the pitch. The player holds in his right hand a wicker basket rattle called *caxixí* (pronounced kasheshé). He can alter the instrument's sound by placing the open end of the calabash resonator against his stomach, creating a "wa-wa" sound; hence, it is often called the *berimbau de barriga*, or "berimbau of the belly" (Ta-

vares de Lima 1965:213). The rhythms played on this instrument vary, but several of the most typical are shown in example 20-8. Several berimbaus are used in a performance, along with other percussion instruments, especially the tambourine and several African-derived drums. The performers play and also sing in responsorial fashion until one of the capoeiristas scores a blow on his opponent.

Next on the continuum are the black inhabitants of the Barlovento region of northeastern Venezuela. Each year on the eve of June 23, African descendants of the town of Curiepe begin their two-day celebration of the Festival of

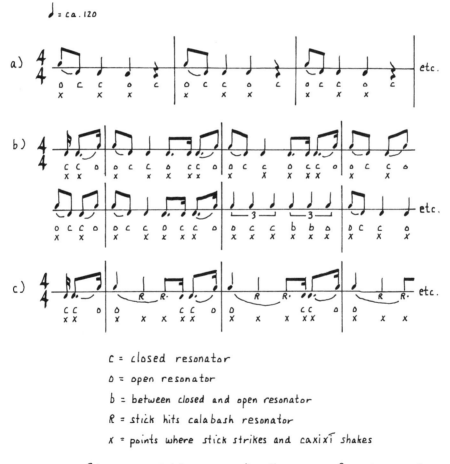

EXAMPLE 20-8. Berimbau rhythms. Collection of Dale A. Olsen.

FIGURE 20-6. The *curbata* drum, used by African descendants during the Saint John festival in Curiepe, Venezuela (Barlovento region). This drum maintains the steady beat of the drum ensemble. Its tripod foot rests over one of the poles that forms the X formation of the mina drum stand.

St. John. This has become a major tourist attraction, and much of the African dancing has been infiltrated by modern popular dance techniques. Nevertheless, especially on side streets, it is still possible to hear traditional performances on the curbata (fig. 20-6) and mina (fig. 20-7) drums. Although only two drummers participate in the dance of the "big drum," this duo is augmented to a trio and more often a quartet of players by adding the *laures* (fig. 20-7) or rhythm sticks, whose players perform on the side of the mina. The percussion is accompanied by singers participating in the usual responsorial fashion. Example 20-9, an excerpt from a typical performance recorded in 1974, indicates

how the small drum, the curbata, plays the basic rhythm ♫ which is also so common in Brazil. The large drum, the mina, and the laures are free to improvise their patterns. Bastide (1972: 175) writes that this festival in honor of St. John the Baptist and the festival of St. Benedict the Moor, a Negro saint, contain dances of Bantu origin.

Another traditional African-derived musical culture is found in the Pacific littoral of Colombia, centering in the city of Buenaventura. Here the important African instrument is the marimba (fig. 20-8), a twenty-one-keyed xylophone (some have between eighteen and twenty-six) that, in Colombia, is suspended from the ceiling of a marimba house and is usually played by two players, one on each side of the instrument, using two rubber knobbed mallets apiece. The most important musical form associated with the marimba is the *currulao*, or marimba dance, which, according to Bastide (1972:175), mimes a couple's first amorous approaches. Along with the marimba, the currulao is accompanied by a pair of traditional drums, the conuno (called male and female instruments), a *bombo* (a large double headed drum of European derivation), a *guasá* (a tubular rattle made from a section of bamboo with pebbles or seeds within and a number of nails driven through the sides into the chamber), and maracas (Amerindian or possibly African-derived rattles). Variants of the currulao include the *bunde*, a musical song and dance derived from the African *wunde* from Sierra Leone, and the bambuco, a dance which possibly borrows its name from an African tribe called Bambouk (Abadía 1970:111), although it may also be derived from indigenous American sources. As a song form, the bambuco is part of the national repertoire of Colombia and is a mestizo development.

Continuing on the Africanism scale of South American music brings us back to Brazil, where perhaps the most common form of typically Afro-Brazilian music is the samba. Samba, however, means different things throughout portions of Brazil. For example, in the north it refers to the place where any type of dance is held; around Bahia it means the batuque; in the

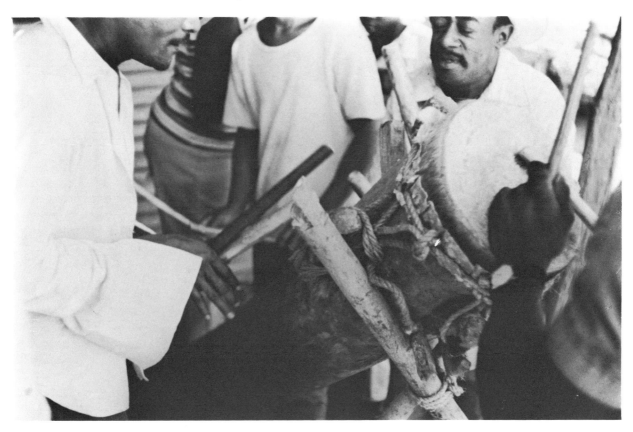

FIGURE 20-7. The *mina* drum used by African descendants in Curiepe, Venezuela (Barlovento region), during the festival of Saint John. The drummer improvises, as do the players of the *laures* or beaters on the side of the mina.

sertão it distinguishes music in duple rhythm devoid of typical Negro syncopation; and in Rio de Janeiro it stands for that rhythmical genre of popular dance music associated with carnival (Martins Lamas 1955:27). The Bahia and the Rio de Janeiro sambas will be discussed here. The first type is loosely called the "rural samba," a generic term for circle dance music of Bantu derivation (Béhague 1973:195), of which the *samba da roda* ("of the circle") is a variety. Although often identified with the batuque and probably derived from the music and dancing of candomblé, it is somewhat milder in tempo with fewer accents than its prototype. The technique of responsorial singing continues in the rural samba, and syncopation is employed. The instrumentation of the Bahian samba occasionally

FIGURE 20-8. A 21-keyed *marimba* used by African descendants in the Pacific littoral of Colombia.

EXAMPLE 20-9. Big drum ensemble, Festival of San Juan, Curiepe, Venezuela, recorded June 24, 1974. Collection of Dale A. Olsen.

EXAMPLE 20-9. (continued)

includes instruments a step away from the more African batuque, such as the *pandeiro* (tambourine), *violão* or guitar, a rattle, and at times the berimbau (Roberts 1974:77). The Rio de Janeiro variety is called the "urban samba," and it exists in two forms, the *samba de morro* ("of the hill") and the "downtown samba." The former is the genre associated with the inhabitants of the *favelas* or slums of Rio (located on the hills overlooking the commercial and middle to upper class residential areas), who each year prior to carnival learn the new sambas and *marchas* (marches) in the *escolas de samba* (samba schools). During the typical meetings of the escola de samba, a dance and music master teaches the new movements and songs for that year's carnival, while the percussion section provides the dance rhythms. The melodies are usually sung in unison chorus by all the dancers after the song leader sings a verse (the style is not responsorial). They are strikingly European, or more correctly, Brazilian European, but not African in their contour, although they are syncopated. The rhythms of the percussion, however, are very complex and extremely sonorous with the added use of double bells, rattles, tambourines, and the *puíta*, a friction drum. Many of the other drums are Western military side drums. The samba of the "elite," the so-called downtown samba, is popular music. The songs, sung in unison chorus, are arrangements accompanied by a typical salon orchestra of brasses and reeds, with a trap drummer providing rhythms that only occasionally demonstrate Africanisms. With this type of music, and others like it farther down the African heritage scale, the point is reached where it is nearly impossible to see the derivations.

A final form of black and white religious and musical syncretism includes a large body of folklore that centers around what Bastide (1972:184) calls "folk Catholicism." These religious folk festivals are called *autos* in many parts of South America, and are known as *congos* among Brazilian blacks. Autos are popular religious dramatizations found throughout the Iberian peninsula, and were a tool used by the Jesuits for the purpose of converting Indians and Negroes in the New World, while congos in Bahia, after the beginning of the seventeenth century, were "dramatized representations of the coronation of Negro kings in Africa" (Ramos 1939:96). They contain dances in duple meter with occasional African-derived musical characteristics such as the responsorial technique and drumming (Béhague 1973:187).

AMERINDIAN-DERIVED AND -INFLUENCED MUSICAL FOLKLORE

Through the centuries the Amerindian tradition has permeated the music of Bolivia, Peru, Ecuador, portions of northern Chile and Argentina, and sections of southern Colombia. These are areas that were under the dominance of the vast Inca civilization which stretched from just north of present-day Quito, Ecuador, to central

Chile. The Inca[1] themselves have left few if any archaeological examples of musical instruments, perhaps because they were more involved in military conquests, but music was important in their religious and everyday life. These rulers in the royal city of Cuzco were in fact so interested in music that certain subjugated peoples particularly skilled in that art were brought in to perform and possibly to teach—the Inca capital had the first schools of music in the Americas (Stevenson 1968:274). The musical skills of some of the pre-Inca peoples, such as the Nazca, the Moche, the Chancay, and the Chimú, whose descendants may have been among those brought to Cuzco, were outstanding, judging from the elaborate and varied musical instruments and iconography that remain. It is no surprise, then, that the early Spanish missionaries found the Andean Indians able to adapt almost immediately to the polyphonic traditions of Renaissance Europe (ibid., 277).

The realm of folk music, as opposed to Catholic sacred music, however, is where the most interesting changes took place. Rather than superimposing a completely foreign musical tradition on the native Andeans as the Catholic Church did, and even more so the Protestants, the nonliturgical folk music was created by a blend of Spanish and indigenous musical elements whose complexity has not yet been understood. In trying to comprehend the music of the Inca (present Quechua Indians) and the Aymara (present Indians of highland Bolivia and Peruvian Lake Titicaca region), the famous and prolific French musicologist d'Harcourt lists the pentatonic scale as the basis for the music of Andean natives (Slonimsky 1945:50). He continues his evolutionary tracing by explaining that hybridization or mestization of this Indian scale with the European scale resulted in a mestizo gamut that is the same as the European major or minor. The third step in his understanding this process is half-step elaboration that results in chromaticism. A study, however,

of the tones of pre-Columbian instruments, and of the music of less acculturated Indian tribes on the eastern slopes of the Andes [see Olsen, "Symbol and Function," this volume] reveals that the pentatonic scale is not necessarily the basic one. In addition, analysis of Andean music collected in recent years by Peruvian musicologists (Holzmann 1964, 1968; Pagaza Galdo 1967) suggests that another musical system, the so-called tritonic scale (three notes), is more basic than the pentatonic. Another basic tuning system is the tetratonic (four notes), which does not occur very often in the Andean plateau region, although it does occur among the Q'eros (descendants of the Inca perhaps) and other tribes east of the Andes. However, a bitonic system (in this instance, two tones at the interval of a fourth) also occurs among the Q'eros, indicating that their culture, like that of tropical forest tribes, has certain tuning systems that may be associated with certain functions. The frequency with which scales other than the pentatonic occur in the highland region of the Andes may indicate that they are archaic survivals of the ancient past. The pentatonic scale, however, is certainly the most common today, and seems to have been since recording techniques began to be used with such studies as d'Harcourt's *La Musique des Incas et ses survivances*, published in 1925. There are two possible explanations for the persistent use of the pentatonic scale in the Andes: (1) it may have been associated with a particular nonreligious type of music, and thus survived the conquest and resultant religious conversion that tried to eradicate anything "pagan," including music that the Indians associated with their religious beliefs; or more likely (2) the pentatonic scale itself has been created via hybridization. The more basic tritonic scale, for example, occurring mostly in the Peruvian states of Ayacucho, Apurimac, and Junín, is found in two versions, as shown in example 20-10 (the beginning note chosen is arbitrary). By adding several passing tones, and there are examples from the repertoire that include them, the pentatonic scales Mode A and Mode B (according to d'Harcourt 1925:134 and 1959:38) are created (ex. 20-11). To carry this one step further by adding two more passing tones

---

1. The term *Inca* is used collectively for the Quechua speakers who built their capital in Cuzco, Peru, and spread out from there. Inca, correctly, means only the royalty, or those who descended directly from the Sun, according to their belief.

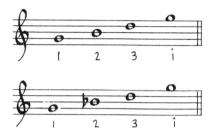

EXAMPLE 20-10.

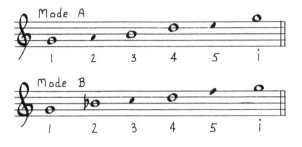

EXAMPLE 20-11.

EXAMPLE 20-12.

to the original scales, the major and the natural minor scale are created (ex. 20-12).

Often the sixth and seventh degrees of the natural minor scale are altered by using E-natural and F-sharp ascending and F-natural and E-flat descending, creating the melodic minor scale. Numerous examples exist that use only a few of the above passing tones, creating scales that might be termed "incomplete" by the Western theorist. There are, for example, folk songs that are melodically based on a "pentatonic" Mode A scale without the fifth degree (or is this a tritonic scale with an added pitch between the second and third degrees?), others

similar to the natural minor scale but without the sixth, and still others resembling the melodic minor without the second. These are perhaps indications of the evolutionary process of hybridization. It is especially revealing to see how these various scales are used within their cultural context. Two folk pieces, one tritonic and the other major (from Holzmann 1964:Numbers 10 and 16), reveal unlike functions. The first is a typical song from Ayacucho that is sung during a cattle marking ritual with pre-Columbian indigenous roots and the second is a dance melody of the Nativity, called "Adoration of the Baby Jesus." Because of the great mixture or hybridization that has occurred in Andean music since the sixteenth century and because of regional differences in culture, language, religion, and so on, such evidence of evolutionary processes in musical scales is rare.

Several rhythmic patterns are also characteristic of Andean music, especially of the *wayno* (*huayno, huaino, huaiño*), a two-step type of dance of Indian origin that is in addition a narrative song form used to transmit historical and current events. The rhythms are ♫♪ and ♫♪♫♪ , syncopations not unlike those found in African vocal music and African-derived music in South America. However, the origin of these rhythms in Inca territory is not African, but Amerindian, perhaps stemming from the breath attack required in playing the panpipes, an important folk instrument today, with preconquest origins. The accents and articulations of these rhythms differ from the African interpretations of them as shown in example 20-13.

EXAMPLE 20-13.

Many of the musical instruments used throughout the Andean highlands are Indian-derived or influenced, such as the panpipes (*antara* in Peru, *sicu* in Bolivia, *zampoña* in Chile, *rondador* in Ecuador), vertical fipple flutes (*pincuyllo, tarka*), trumpets (*pututu*, "conch"; *waqra puku*, "horn"), and the drum (*tinya*). The principal instrument, however, is the notched flute called the *quena* (*kena*), an Aymara name (originally *kena-kena*). Although usually a solo instrument, two diatonic quenas occasionally combine with the charango, mandolin or guitar, violin, and harp to form an ensemble for carnival and other celebrations. Many of the ensembles that at one time included the indigenous-derived quenas and panpipes are today made up of Western woodwinds and brasses. One of the

most typical orchestras of this type can be found in Huancayo, Peru. Its instrumentation consists completely of Western instruments, including approximately four saxophones, several clarinets, a violin, and a harp. The music, however, alternating between full orchestra, harp and violin, and saxophone duet, contains melodies based on the pentatonic scale that has been reinforced with several passing tones, creating a near minor modality. Example 20-14 is a section of the "Farewell for Santiago" (St. James), an event that occurred in the coliseum of Huancayo. Performers on an alto and a tenor saxophone played this duet in which they ornamented the melody much as the quena players did in past years. The improvised tags at the ends of two of the musical phrases are Western-jazz-influenced.

The European-derived diatonic harp of Peru, in addition to its ensemble role, is a beautiful solo instrument. Harpists very frequently play Indian-derived music such as the *yaraví*, a slow and expressive song perhaps associated with love, followed by a fast fuga (fugue) or wayno. Example 20-15 demonstrates the harp style in an interpretation of the music of Cuzco, with its pentatonic scale over minor harmony and typical rhythms.

Certain festivals of patron saints or of the Holy Virgin, especially in northern and central Chile, are also characterized by cultural and musical blending with strong Indian flavor. In Chile a very rich musical folklore is presented in one of two ways, depending on the geographic location. Many festivals of central Chile include a minimal amount of dancing with much of the music performed by vertical flutes that are capable of producing only one note (two groups of instruments alternate in hocket) and drums. The emphasis here is on verbal proclamations of faith directed toward a saint or the Virgin. The musicians and dancers, usually one and the same, are called *chinos*, with no reference to the Chinese, but possibly to a Quechua word meaning "humble servant" (Urrutia 1968:59). The sounds of these central Chilean flutes are very similar to the notes produced on the Araucanian *pifilka*, from which the chino flutes may be derived since central Chile was inhabited by the Araucanian Indians during pre-Inca times.

EXAMPLE 20-14. Saxophone duet, Despedida de Santiago, Huancayo, Dept. de Junín, August 1974. Collection of Dale A. Olsen.

EXAMPLE 20-15. Harp solo, music from Cuzco, Sr. Navarro, harpist, Huancayo, Peru, August 1974. Collection of Dale A. Olsen.

EXAMPLE 20-15. (continued)

etc.

EXAMPLE 20-15. (continued)

These flutes are made with a widening at their proximal end in the form of an elongated *V*. This shape is called "butterfly wings" by the players (Pumarino and Sangüeza 1968:21), a term that may refer to the shamanistic associations with that insect [see Olsen, "Symbol and Function," this volume] as well as its shape (fig. 20-9).

In contrast to central Chile, the north features many dancing groups, accompanied by panpipe players, fifers and drummers (fig. 20-10) or brass bands, with the emphasis placed here on the dancing as a physical confirmation of faith. The music of the northern festivals is characterized by the typical Andean rhythm ♫♩ and by scales varying from the tritonic to the melodic minor, as seen in examples 20-16 and 20-17 from the festival of La Tirana.

The origin of these festivals is pre-Columbian, possibly associated with harvest, crops, rain, and performed by the tributaries of the Sun. The Spanish conquest and domination put a Catholic seal on the indigenous expression and transformed it into a syncretic ceremony. Today it is difficult to separate the two, and in trying to do so I am constantly reminded of the Catholic priest at the festival of Aiquina in northern

Chile who announced over the loudspeaker, "Faithful followers, be sure to hold your candles in your right hands and not your left, for to do the latter is pagan."

An Indian-influenced religious festival is also found in Brazil with the autos of the caboclos (in Brazil, mixed Indian and Portuguese; the dancers are called *cabocolinhos* or *caboclinhos*). Their drama occurs during carnival in the northeast of Brazil, especially in Recife, when basically they proclaim their submission and conversion to Roman Catholic Christianity. The undertones of their proclamation, however, are often endowed with protest, as when the queen, for example, says: "We, here, in this forest, lived peacefully. What motive does one race have to come and make trouble with another?" (Almeida 1961:42; my translation). During the parade maneuvers of the cabocolinhos some of the musicians perform an accented and syncopated rhythm on a common European side drum and a *caracaxá* (scraped idiophone), while a flutist plays a fast, highly repetitive Western type melody in the major mode on his flute of indigenous dimensions. The cabocolinhos themselves are attired in breechcloths and feathered skirts, feather headdresses and feather brace-

EXAMPLE 20-16. Brass band and bass drums, Festival of Nuestra Señora del Carmen, Virgin of La Tirana, northern Chile, July 16, 1968. Collection of Dale A. Olsen.

EXAMPLE 20-17. Band of fifes, drums, and rachets, Festival of Nuestra Señora del Carmen, Virgin of La Tirana, northern Chile, July 16, 1968. Collection of Dale A. Olsen.

lets, brandishing arrows and hatchets in their hands. The melodies of much caboclo music show a trace of modality, owing perhaps to the isolation of this territory (Corrêa de Azevedo 1948:55).

Native American and Protestant religious expressions have also been joined to form a new and syncretic religion in the Guinea Highlands of Guyana and Venezuela. This religious cult and its corresponding music are called *Hallelujah*. The song leader or prophet, often a converted shaman, frequently draws his musical

FIGURE 20-9. A "chino" dancing group during the 1967 festival of Andacollo, in the Norte Chico region of north central Chile. The dancing participants are paying their *mandas* or promises to the Virgin of Andacollo. The chino flutists dance while playing their alternating notes.

language from an older body of popular Irish and Scottish songs (von Hornbostel 1955-56:153). Many of these melodies, however, descend in a typical native American fashion. The function of the songs is prayer, through which contact with God is attained (Butt Colson 1971:53). Dance, accompanied by song, is also an important means in Hallelujah of mass communication with God (ibid.).

MUSICAL SYNTHESIS—THE CENTER OF THE MOSAIC

A certain large segment of South American folk music consists of such a unique blend of musical styles that much of it is generally associated with the nationalistic pride of a particular country or countries. Its unique musical feature is precisely this blend, which makes it difficult to readily distinguish its musical derivations. Gilbert Chase (cited in Tompkins 1973:24) has ex-

plained how after independence underdeveloped countries felt a need to create a national folklore in order to achieve self-confidence. Thus many countries extracted elements from their Negro and Indian traditions for the creation of new South American song and dance genres. The most typical of these musical styles are couple dance forms, perhaps because of the happy, carefree, and amorous associations with dance.

A dance form known all the way from Mexico and California to Chile and Argentina was developed in Peru during colonial times. It is known by a variety of names, including cueca in Chile and Bolivia, marinera in Peru (so named in honor of the sailors who lost their lives in the late nineteenth-century War of the Pacific with Chile), *zamba* in Argentina, *ecuadór* in Ecuador, *cueca Chilena* or just *Chilena* in Mexico, and

FIGURE 20-10. Fifers playing a dance accompaniment during the 1968 Festival of Aiquina, in northern Chile. Each flutist blows into a plastic mouthpiece attached to the tin fifes, making each instrument a kind of fipple blown horizontal flute. A painting of John and Jacqueline Kennedy adorns the head of the bass drum.

zambacueca or zamacueca throughout colonial South America. In Peru this popular dance was African in style and was at times accompanied by the Spanish harp, guitar, and the indigenous pincuyllo (Romero, cited in Tompkins 1973:19). A number of scholars have supported an African derivation for this dance with semantic evidence: zamba equals *semba*, Bantu for "greeting," and cueca comes from *cuque*, Bantu meaning "dance" (Nicomedes Santa Cruz, cited by Tompkins 1973:55). Other evidence points to the term *cueca* as meaning the clucking of a hen, and many of the mestizo dances throughout South America have sexual overtones of conquest and submission, often symbolically interpreted as a rooster conquering a hen. There are comparable African dances. Additional writers suggest a Spanish and Moorish origin, based on other semantic evidence and the style of dancing. Whatever the derivation, the zamacueca achieved a great popularity and spread through-

out Chile, Bolivia, Ecuador, Paraguay, Argentina, and Uruguay in the nineteenth century, and was even danced in California during the days of the gold rush. In Chile and Peru the cueca and marinera respectively have become national dances in which many historical and political events are described in the texts. Thus, in many cases they are similar in function to the corrido and ballad. Musically the most identifiable traits are the continuous fast 6/8 meter in the accompaniment, the alternation of the melody between 6/8 and 3/4, and the preference for the third as a cadential note rather than the tonic. The dance characteristics include the use of a handkerchief or scarf, the seductive nature, shoe tapping by the male, and straight body posture.

In Colombia the most characteristic songs and dances are the *cumbia* and bambuco. Both reveal an almost indistinguishable blend of elements from various ethnic backgrounds. The cumbia, for example, the most popular folk dance of the Atlantic littoral, is very possibly of mixed Indian and African descent. Like the southern zamacueca and its variants, the choreography of the cumbia is erotic, with male conquest of the female as the characteristic theme. The cultural blend of this dance includes an African-derived style of drumming, Indian-derived aerophones, and costumes and song style of Spanish background (Zapata Olivella, Delia 1962:190). The bambuco, on the other hand, shows no African influence except possibly for its name, as mentioned earlier. However, another source for its name may be a group of native Americans in the Pacific littoral known as the Bambas (Abadía 1970:84). Musically the bambuco is a blend of indigenous American melodic styles, Spanish 6/8 rhythms possibly of Basque origin (ibid.), and conceivably Negro syncopations. Its most usual instrumentation is the Spanish-derived tiple accompanying a vocal duet style. Its characteristic choreographic theme is again pursuit of the woman by the man, terminating with the former's timid consent.

Another musically synthesized dance form, on a par with the "elite" urban samba of Rio de Janeiro, is the Argentinian tango. Once the rage of World War I America and Europe, the tango reveals African influence in its name and choreography, English origin in its relationship to the habanera which can be traced to the country dance of seventeenth-century Britain, Spanish background with its similarity to the Andalusian tango, and most important, Argentinian sentiment with the texts often emphasizing aspects of life in that country. In spite of its great popularity, negative attitudes were common, ranging from condemnation by such political leaders as the Queen of England and the Kaiser of Germany to damnation by the Pope and a certain Dr. Morgan who, at the 1914 Bible Conference held in Atlanta, Georgia, "declared that the Tango is a reversion to the ape, and a confirmation of the Darwin theory" (Slonimsky 1946:60–61).

In the latter part of our twentieth century the musical mosaic is continuing to expand, becoming more and more elaborate. On the one hand is

the new protest song movement led by Victor Jara, which began in Chile with the Parra family and reached its peak with Jara's death during the Chilean revolution. Currently several excellent musical groups devoted to the new song movement are living in exile in Mexico and Europe. On the other hand is the folk Mass movement in which the Catholic Church is reaching out with new folkloric interpretations of its old liturgical forms. Some of these vernacular folk Masses are the *Misa Incaica* in Quechua and the *Misa Criolla* in Spanish. In the realm of popular music, such jazz-rock musicians as Sergio Mendes, Gato Barbieri, Aierto, and Paulinho da Costa have done much to introduce Latin American folk elements to other parts of the world. Even the multimillion dollar business of Muzak was influenced by South American folk music at one time as the condor passed through and beyond that realm into the nightclubs of Paris.[2] Indeed, throughout much of the Western world certain new and well-polished segments of South America's musical mosaic are becoming ever more important contemporary expressions.

The majority of South America's folk music, however, remains almost a hidden art to the rest of the world. It is a rarely heard expression because it belongs to a people with whom most outsiders have never become acquainted. These songs of everyday life will probably always remain (and perhaps even die) as a sincere, humble, simple, and paradoxically complex music, much like the people who create and perform them.

Glossary

agida–A large goblet-shaped single-headed drum of the Surinam river cultures (Bush Negroes). The instrument is usually ornamented with carved snake designs, and its function is to invoke the snake deities.

2. Reference here is made to the Peruvian folk song *El Condor Pasa*, made popular in the United States of America by the American folk-rock duo of Simon and Garfunkel in the 1970s. This song became one of the most popular and most recorded of all South American folk songs.

alabao (alabado, alabanza)-Religious song of praise dedicated to the saints; of Iberian origin and found throughout Latin America.

apinti-A long cylindrical single-headed drum of the Surinam Town Negroes.

arrullo (arrorró)-Literally "cooing"; a type of lullaby in South America.

bandola-A mandolin type of chordophone of Iberian origin, usually teardrop shape, with six orders of multiple strings, played with a plectrum.

bandolina-A small-scale bandola.

berimbau-A Brazilian musical bow with a calabash resonator, derived from Angola.

bombo-A large double-headed drum of European derivation found throughout Spanish South America.

bunde-A musical song and dance of the Pacific littoral of Colombia and a variant of the currulao, possibly derived from Sierra Leone.

cabocolinho (caboclinho)-Mixed Indian and Portuguese (caboclos) dancers in the autos of northeast Brazil.

cajita-A small Spanish-American double-headed drum of European origin; also the name given to a box or drawer that is struck with the hands in Peru as an accompaniment for the marinera.

canción de cuna-A cradle song or lullaby in Spanish America.

canto a lo pueta-An epic-lyric song genre of central Chile, sung by men to the accompaniment of the guitar or guitarrón, and also used as the medium for song debate.

cantoría-An improvised singing duel in Brazil, once known as *desafío*.

caracaxá-A scraped idiophone used by the cabocolinhos of northeastern Brazil during the autos of the caboclos.

catimbo-A syncretic religious ritual in the northeast of Brazil, similar in function to the candomblé and macumba of central coastal Brazil.

cavaca-A small guitar-type with four strings, found in sections of Brazil.

caxixi-A small wicker basket rattle used in the right hand of the berimbau player in Brazil.

Chilena (cueca Chilena)-The name given to the Chilean-derived cueca in Mexico.

cielito-A Chilean dance form similar and possibly derived from the Spanish contradanza that in turn came from the English country-dance.

côcho-A small guitar-type instrument with five gut strings in the Brazilian state of Mato Grosso.

contradanza-The English-derived country-dance as found in Spain and portions of Latin America.

conuno-A conical hollowed log single-headed drum from the Pacific littoral of Colombia derived from Africa.

copla-A "couplet," a stanza of four lines, the second and fourth rhyming, set to music; a Spanish poetic form with music.

corrido-A popular Latin American and Spanish ballad form.

cuatro-A small four-stringed guitar-type found in Venezuela and Colombia.

cumbia-A Colombian song and dance form showing cultural blending.

curbata-A medium-sized, hollowed-log, single-headed drum with a tripod base used by African descendants in northeast coastal Venezuela.

currulao-A dance accompanied by the marimba and other percussive instruments in the Pacific littoral of Colombia.

décima-A Spanish and Latin American ballad form with ten-line stanzas in its text.

desafío-Literally "challenge," "duel"; in portions of Spain and possibly Brazil this is an improvised singing duel of Renaissance origin. Known as cantoría today in Brazil.

ecuadór-The name given the cueca in Ecuador, a fast couples dance.

escolas de samba-Literally "samba schools" in Brazil, especially in Rio de Janeiro, where for months prior to carnival many Brazilians practice the song and dance routines that will be performed during this important event.

estilo-A lyrical accompanied folk song type of Iberian origin found in Argentina and Uruguay.

gato polqueado-An Argentinian song and dance form that shows a mixture of Spanish-derived and northern European-derived music, the gato and the polka respectively.

guasá-A tubular rattle from the Pacific littoral of Colombia; made from a section of bamboo, with pebbles or seeds inside it, and a number of nails driven through its sides and into the chamber.

guitarrón-A large 25-string guitar type from central Chile, of possible Italian Renaissance origin.

Hallelujah-A syncretic religious cult of some native Americans in the Guinea Highlands of Guyana and Venezuela.

kwakwa-A low wooden bench struck as an idiophone during religious rituals of the Surinam river cultures.

laures-Rhythm sticks played against the side of the large mina drum during the festival of Saint John in northeastern coastal Venezuela.

machete-A small Brazilian guitar-type with four strings.

machetinho-A small Brazilian guitar-type with four strings.

mina-A large cylindrical drum with one head; played during the festival of Saint John in northeastern coastal Venezuela; African-derived.

moda da viola-A rural Brazilian song type, similar to the romance and accompanied by the viola, a small guitar-type.

modinha-A Brazilian popular song type showing Italian operatic influence.

nanda-A goblet-shaped single-headed drum of the Surinam river cultures.

pagelanca-A syncretic religious ritual in the north of Brazil where African and Amerindian have mixed.

parabién-Literally "congratulation," a Chilean lyrical folk song style whose name is derived from its original function of congratulating newlyweds.

payas-The name given in Argentina for musical duels between two singers, similar to the desafío or cantoría in Brazil.

pericona-A Chilean dance form that shows a similarity to the Spanish contradanza.

pifilka-A one- or two-tubed vertical flute without finger holes of Chile's Araucanian Indians.

pincuyllo-A Quechua Indian term for flute which today refers to a Peruvian vertical plug or fipple flute, similar in mouthpiece construction to the European recorder.

polka alemana-The German polka as found among Chile's German population in the south-central portion of that country.

porfías-Literally "quarrels"; the name given in Venezuela for musical duels between two singers, similar to the desafío in Brazil.

puíta-A friction membranophone used in Brazil during carnival by the musicians in the samba schools.

punteado-Picking on the guitar in South America.

pututu-A Quechua Indian term for the conch shell trumpet in Peru.

*quena (*also *kena)*-The notched end-blown flute of the Andes (see glossary in Olsen, "Symbol and Function," this volume).

ranchera-An Argentinian song and dance form, a blend of northern European and Spanish styles.

requinto-A small guitar-type of Venezuela, similar to but smaller than the Colombian tiple.

romancero-In Spain, a collection of romances in book form.

rondador-The panpipe in Ecuador.

saka-sake-A gourd rattle used by the people of the Surinam river cultures during their religious rituals.

salve-A Spanish-American unaccompanied sung prayer dedicated to the Virgin.

samba da roda-A variety of the circle dance and its music, possibly of Bantu derivation, found in the region of Bahia, Brazil.

samba de morro-Literally "samba of the hill"; a variety of the urban samba of Rio de Janeiro, Brazil, and associated with the slum dwellers living on the hills of that city.

tarka-A wooden vertical plug or fipple flute of Peru and Bolivia, whose construction much resembles a baroque organ pipe.

tinya-A small, hand-held, double-headed drum of pre-Colombian origin, belonging to the indigenous population of Peru and Bolivia.

tiple-Literally "treble"; a guitar-type found in Venezuela and especially in Colombia, with four orders of multiple strings.

toada-Portuguese for tonada, literally "tune"; a Brazilian song type.

tono-An Argentinian song form.

tumao-A single-headed drum of the Surinam river cultures; it has the power to invoke the spirits of the bush.

urucungo-Another name for the berimbau, the musical bow among Brazilian blacks.

vaquería-A cattle-herding song in the Atlantic littoral region of Colombia.

velorio-A religious song in South America whose name is derived from the use of candles (*velas*) during the ceremony; of Iberian origin.

verso-A ritual rural folksong found in Chile and elsewhere in Iberian-influenced America, based on archaic texts of the seventeenth-century Spanish court.

vidala-An Argentinian song form.

vihuela-A Brazilian guitar-type of European Renaissance origin.

villancico-Literally "rustic song"; an Iberian-derived song form, often associated with Christmas in South America.

viola-A small Brazilian guitar-type.

viola de mão-A small thirteenth-century Iberian guitar-type from which several guitar forms are derived in Brazil.

violão-The Portuguese term for guitar in Brazil.

waqra puka-A Quechua Indian term for the spiral-shaped horn trumpet in Peru.

wayno (huayno, huaino, huaiño)-A two-step dance genre of Indian origin that occasionally functions as a narrative song form used to transmit historical and current events in the Andean region of central South America.

yaraví (harahui, harawi)-A slow song or instrumental genre of Indian origin that often precedes the fast wayno in the Andean region of central South America.

zamba-An Argentinian dance and song form that possibly developed from the Chilean cueca and the earlier zamacueca.

zambacueca-A common name, along with *zamacueca*, for a fast couple dance that originated in Peru during colonial times.

zampoña-A Spanish name for the panpipe found in northern Chile.

Bibliography

Abadía M., Guillermo.
   1970. *Compendio General de Folklore Colombiano.* Suplemento No. 1. Bogotá: Instituto Colombiano de Cultura, Instituto Colombiano de Antropología, Revista Colombiana de Folclor.

Allende, Humberto.
   1941. "Chilean Folk Music." *Bulletin of the Pan American Union* 65 (September), 917-24.

Almeida, Renato.
   1961. *Tablado Folclórico.* São Paulo, Ricordi Brazileira.

Amado, Jorge.
   1966. *Bahia de Todos os Santos.* São Paulo: Livraria Martins Editôra.

Andrade, Mário de.
   1964. *Modinhas Imperiais.* São Paulo: Livraria Martins Editôra.

Aretz, Isabel.
   1952. *El Folklore Musical Argentino.* Buenos Aires: Ricordi Americana.
   1965. "Cantos Navideños en el Folklore Venezolano." In *Primera Conferencia Interamericana de Etnomusicología,* pp. 75-86. Washington, D.C.: Union Panamericana, Secretaria General de la Organización de los Estados Americanos.
   1967a. *Instrumentos Musicales de Venezuela.* Cumaná: Universidad de Oriente, Colección la Heredad.
   1967b. "Raices Europeas de la Música Folklórica de Venezuela. El Aporte Indígena." In *Music in the Americas,* pp. 7-17. The Hague, The Netherlands: Indiana University Research Center in Anthropology, Folklore, and Linguistics.
   1970. *El Tamunangue.* Barquisimento, Venezuela: Universidad Centro-Occidental.

Ayestarán, Lauro.
   1967. *El Folklore Musical Uruguayo.* Montevideo: Arca Editorial.

Bastide, Roger.
   1972. *African Civilizations in the New World.* New York: Harper and Row, Harper Torchbooks.

Béhague, Gerard.
   1973. "Latin American Folk Music" (see May bibliography).

Bermúdez Silva, Jesús y Guillermo Abadía M.
   1970. *Aires Musicales de los Indios Guambiano del Cauca (Colombia).* Bogotá: Imprenta Nacional.

Boettner, Juan Max.
   N. D. *Música y Músicos del Paraguay.* Asunción: Edición de Autores Paraguayos Asociados.

Butt Colson, Audrey.
   1971. "Hallelujah Among the Patamona Indians." In *Antropológica* no. 28, pp. 25-58.

Cancionero Popular Americano.
   1950. Washington, D.C.: Union Panamericana.

Carvalho, José Jorge de.
   1975. "Formas Narrativas do Noroeste Brasileiro." *Revista INIDEF.* Venezuela 1 (April), 33-68.

Carvalho Neto, Paulo de.
   1962. "The Candombe, a Dramatic Dance from Afro-Uruguayan Folklore." *Journal of the Society for Ethnomusicology* 6: 164-74.

Chase, Gilbert.
   1959. *The Music of Spain.* 2d ed. New York: Dover.
   1962. *A Guide to the Music of Latin America.* 2d ed. Washington, D.C.: Pan American Union.

Corrêa de Azevedo, Luiz Heitor.
   1948. *Brief History of Music in Brazil.* Washington, D.C.: Pan American Union.
   1967. "Vissungos, Negro Work Songs of the Diamond District in Minas Gerais, Brazil." In *Music in the Americas,* pp. 64-67. The Hague, The Netherlands: Indiana University Research Center in Anthropology, Folklore, and Linguistics.

Dannemann, Manuel, and Daniel Sheehy.
   1975. Record liner notes to *Traditional Music of Chile,* ABC Records Inc.—Command COMS-9003.

Dark, Philip J. C.
   1970. *Bush Negro Art.* London: Alec Tiranti.

Domínguez, Luis Arturo y Adolfo Salazar Quijada.
   1969. *Fiestas y Danzas Folklóricas de Venezuela.* Caracas: Monte Avila Editores, C.A.

Duran, Gustavo.
   1950. *Recordings of Latin American Songs and*

Dances. Washington, D.C.: Pan American Union.

Echevarría Bravo, Pedro.
1951. *Cancionero Musical Popular Manchego*. Madrid: La Sociedad General de Autores de España.

Figueiredo Filho, J. de.
1962. *O Folclore no Cariri*. Fortaleza, Brazil: Imprensa Universitária do Ceará.

Folk Songs and Dances of the Americas.
1967, 1969. Washington, D.C.: Pan American Union, 1967 (no. 2), 1969 (no. 1).

Grebe, María-Ester.
1967. "Modality in Spanish Renaissance Vihuela Music and Archaic Chilean Folksongs: A Comparative Study." *Journal of the Society for Ethnomusicology* 11:326-42.

Hague, Eleanor.
1934. *Latin American Music*. Santa Ana, Calif.: The Fine Arts Press.

d'Harcourt, R., and M. d'Harcourt.
1925. *La Musique des Incas et ses survivances*. 2 vols. Paris: Librairie Orientaliste Paul Geuthner.
1959. *La Musique des Aymara sur les hauts plateaux boliviens*. Paris: Société des Americanistes, Musée de l'Homme.

Herring, Hubert.
1968. *A History of Latin America*. 3d ed. New York: Knopf.

Herskovits, Melville J.
1936. *Suriname Folk-lore*. Columbia University Contributions to Anthropology, Vol. 27. New York: Columbia University Press.
1944. "Drums and Drummers in Afro-Brazilian Cult Life." *Musical Quarterly* 30:447-92.

Herskovits, Melville J., and Frances S. Herskovits.
1971. "Afro-Bahian Religious Songs." *Folk Music of Brazil*, from the Archive of Folk Song, Album L-13.

Holzmann, Rodolfo.
1964. *"Panorama de la Música Tradicional del Perú."* Ministerio de Educación Pública, Escuela Nacional de Música y Danzas Folklóricas, Servicio Musicológico. Lima: Casa Mozart.
1968. "De la Trifonía a la Heptafonía en la Música Tradicional Peruana." Reprinted from the Revista *San Marcos*, 1968. Lima: Comité de Extensión Universitaria de la Universidad Nacional Mayor de San Marcos.

Izurieta Goya, Clemente.
N. D. *Instrumentos Folklorico-musicales, Usados en Chile*. Santiago: INDAP Difusion.

Kolinski, M.
1936. "Suriname Music." In *Suriname Folk-lore*, edited by Melville J. Herskovits and Frances S. Herskovits. Columbia University Contributions to Anthropology, Vol. 27. New York: Columbia University Press.

Lavín, Carlos.
1950. "La Tirana. Fiesta ritual de la provincia de Tarapacá." *Revista Musical Chilena* (Santiago), year 6, no. 37, (Autumn), pp. 12-36.

List, George.
1956. "The Musical Bow at Palenque." *Journal of the International Folk Music Council* 18:36-49.
1967. "The Folk Music of the Atlantic Littoral of Colombia, an Introduction." In *Music in the Americas*, pp. 115-22. The Hague: Indiana University Research Center in Anthropology, Folklore, and Linguistics.
1973. "A Comparison of Certain Aspects of Colombian and Spanish Folksong." *Yearbook of the International Folk Music Council* 5:72-84.

Lloyd, A. L., and Isabel Aretz de Ramón y Rivera.
1966. *Folk Songs of the Americas*. New York: Oak Publications.

Mata Machade Filho, Aires da.
1964. *O Negro e o Garimpo em Minas Gerais*. Retratos do Brazil, Vol. 26. Rio de Janeiro: Editõra Civilizacão Brasileira, S.A.

Martínez Terrero, S.J., José.
1973. *Cancionero Musical Venezolano*. Vol. 1. Caracas: Centro de Communicación Social "J.M. Pellin."

Martins Lamas, Dulce.
1955. "Folk Music and Popular Music in Brazil." *Journal of the International Folk Music Council* 7:27-29.

Merriam, Alan P.
1956. "Songs of the Ketu Cult of Bahia, Brazil." *African Music* 1:53-82.

Music in Latin America, A Brief Survey.
1942. Vol. 3 of the Series on Literature, Art, Music; Club and Study Series No. 3. Washington, D.C.: Pan American Union.

Nketia, J. H. Kwabena.
1974. *The Music of Africa*. New York: Norton.

Pagaza Galdo, Consuelo.
1967. *Cancionero Andino Sur*. Ministerio de Educación Pública, Escuela Nacional de Música y Danzas Folklóricas, Servicio Musicológico. Lima: Casa Mozart.

Pedrell, Felipe.
1922. *Cancionero Musical Popular Español*. 4 vols. Barcelona: Casa Editorial de Música, Boileau.

Pendle, George.
    1963. *A History of Latin America*. Baltimore: Penguin.
Piñeros Corpas, Joaquin.
    N. D. *Introducción al Cancionero Noble de Colombia*. Bogotá: Edición especial de la Universidad de los Andes, Autorizada por el Ministerio de Educación Nacional. Record notes to three discs manufactured in Colombia by Industrias Fonoton Ltda.
Plath, Oreste.
    1966. *Folklore Religioso Chileno*. Santiago: Ediciones PlaTur.
Pumarino V., Ramón and Arturo Sangüeza.
    1968. *Los Bailes Chinos en Aconcagua y Valparaiso*. Santiago, Chile: Consejería Nacional de Promoción Popular.
Ramón y Rivera, Luis Felipe.
    1962. "Rhythmic and Melodic Elements in Negro Music of Venezuela." *Journal of the International Folk Music Council* 14:56-60.
    1965. "Cantos Negros de la Fiesta de San Juan." In *Primera Conferencia Interamericana de Etnomusicología*, pp. 155-75. Washington, D.C.: Unión Panamericana, Secretaría General de la Organización de los Estados Americanos.
    1967*a*. "El Mestizaje de la Música Afro-Venezolana." In *Music in the Americas*, pp. 176-82. The Hague: Indiana University Research Center in Anthropology, Folklore, and Linguistics.
    1967*b*. *Música Indígena Folklorica y Popular de Venezuela*. Buenos Aires: Ricordi Americana, Sociedad Anónima Editorial y Comercial.
    1969. *La Música Folklórica de Venezuela*. Caracas: Monte Avila Editores, C.A.
    1971. *La Música Afrovenezolana*. Caracas: Universidad Central de Venezuela, Imprenta Universitaria.
    1972. *La Canción Venezolana*. Maracaibo, Venezuela: Universidad del Zulia, Dirección de cultura.
Ramos, Arthur.
    1939. *The Negro in Brazil*. Washington, D.C.: The Associated Publishers, Inc.
Roberts, John Storm.
    1974. *Black Music of Two Worlds*. New York: William Morrow.
Romeu, José.
    1948. "El canto dialogado en la canción popular. Los cantares a desafío." *Anuario Musical* (Barcelona) 3:133-61.
Serrano Redonnet, Ana.
    1964. *Cancionero Musical Argentino*. Buenos Aires: Ediciones Culturales Argentinas.
Slonimsky, Nicolas.
    1946. *Music of Latin America*. New York: Thomas Y. Crowell Co.
Stevenson, Robert.
    1968*a*. "The Afro-American Musical Legacy to 1800." *The Musical Quarterly* 54 (October), 475-502.
    1968*b*. *Music in Aztec & Inca Territory*. Berkeley and Los Angeles: University of California Press.
Tavares de Lima, Rossini.
    1965. "Música Folclorica e Instrumentos Musicais do Brasil." In *Primera Conferencia Interamericana de Etnomusicología*, pp. 205-24. Washington, D.C.: Unión Panamericana, Secretaría General de la Organización de los Estados Americanos.
Teixeira d'Assumpcão.
    1967. *Curso de Folclore Musical Brasileiro*. Rio de Janeiro: Livraría Freitas Bastos S.A.
Tolosa Cataldo, Bernardo.
    1967. *Cantos y Leyendas Regionals*. Antofagasta, Chile.
Tompkins, William David.
    1973. "The Marinera. A Historical and Analytical Study of the National Dance of Peru." Master's thesis, University of California at Los Angeles.
Urrutia Blondel, Jorge.
    1968. "Danzas rituales en la provincia de Santiago." *Revista Musical Chilena*, año 22, no. 103, pp. 43-76.
Vega, Carlos.
    1967. "Las especies homónimas y afines de 'Los orígenes del Tango argentino." *Revista Musical Chilena*, año 21, no. 101, pp. 49-65.
West, Robert C.
    1957. *The Pacific Lowlands of Colombia*. Baton Rouge: Louisiana State University Press.
Zapata Olivella, Delia.
    1962. "La cumbia, síntesis musical de la Nación colombiana. Reseña histórica y coreográfica." *Revista Colombiana de Folclor* 3:187-204.
Zapata Olivella, Manuel.
    1962. "Cantos religiosos de los negros de Palenque." *Revista Colombiana de Folclor* 3: 205-11.

Discography

African & Afro-American Drums. Ethnic Folkways Library FE 4502. Edited by Harold Courlander.

Contains examples of Surinam Bush Negro and Bahian drumming.

Afro-Brazilian Religious Songs. Lyrichord LLST 7315.

Afro-Hispanic Music from Western Colombia and Ecuador. Ethnic Folkways Library FE 4376. Recorded, edited, and with notes by Norman E. Whitten.

Amazonia. Cult Music of northern Brazil. Lyrichord LLST 7300.

Amer[n]dian Music of Chile: Aymara Qawashqar Patuche. Folkways FE 4054.

Antología de Folklore Musical Chileno, Vol. 1. RCA Victor CML-2043. Universidad de Chile, Instituto de Investigaciones Musicales, Facultad de Ciencias y Artes Musicales.

Antología de Folklore Musical Chileno, Vol. 2, RCA Victor CML-2085. Universidad de Chile, Instituto de Investigaciones Musicales, Facultad de Ciencias y Artes Musicales.

Antología de Folklore Musical Chileno, Vol. 3. RCA Victor CML-2190. Universidad de Chile, Instituto de Investigaciones Musicales, Facultad de Ciencias y Artes Musicales.

Antología de Folklore Musical Chileno, Vol. 4. RCA Victor CML-2295. Universidad de Chile, Instituto de Investigaciones Musicales, Facultad de Ciencias y Artes Musicales.

Anthology of Spanish Folklore Music. Everest 3286/4. Produced in conjunction with UNESCO.

Argentina: The Indians of the Gran Chaco. Lyrichord LLST 7295.

Argentine Folk Songs. Folkways Records & Service Corp., N.Y. FW 6810. Sung by Octavio Corvalan with Guitar.

Bahia. Sound Image, vol. 3. Traditional music and moments of Brazil.

Batucada Fantastica. Musidisc MLP-7057. Fábrica Venezolana de Discos C.A. Os Rítmistas Brasileiros dir. por Luciano Perrone. Brazilian rhythms by professional ensemble.

Bolivia Tropical. Piray LPP-1003. Banda Oriental de "Pan de Arroz." Folk music from Bolivian jungle.

Brazil: Songs of Protest. Monitor MFS 717. Zelia Barbosa sings of the Sertão & Favela, the dry northeast and the slums.

Canción Protesta: Protest song of Latin America. Paredon P1001. Recorded in Cuba; various Latin American folk groups.

Caymmi Visita Tom. ME-17. Bossa Nova music from Bahia, Brazil, with Tom Jobim. Elenco, de Aloysio de Oliveira.

Chile. The Siege of Santa Maria de Iquique. Paredon P-1019. A "People's Cantata" of the Chilean nitrate miners. Composed by Luis Advis, performed by Quilapayún. Protest music from Chile.

Chile Vencerá! An Anthology of Chilean New Song 1962-1973. Rounder Records. Protest music.

Chimbanguelero, Folklore del Estado Mérida. Vol. 2. Folklore de Venezuela Vol. 3, Laffer; Negro and European influenced folk music from the state of Mérida.

Como yo lo siento. Orfeo. ULP 2768. Santiago Chalar. An Uruguayan guitarist and folksinger.

Curacas. Promecin records; instrumental folk music from Argentina, Bolivia, Peru, and Chile performed by a Chilean folklore group.

Ecuador, The Cry of Freedom! El Grito de Libertad! Paredon P-1034. Protest music of South America performed by Jatari, a folkloric ensemble from Ecuador.

Fiestas of Peru, Music of the High Andes. Nonesuch Explorer Series H-72045. Recorded by David Lewiston in the field.

Folklore. Campo LPC-1002. Bolivian folk music performed by a folkloric group. Domínguez, Favre y Cavour.

Folklore musical y música folklórica Argentina. 6 vols. Qualiton QF-3001. Recorded by Jorge Novati and Irma Ruiz; an extensive anthology.

Folk Music of Brazil. AFS L13. Edited by Melville J. Herskovits and Frances S. Herskovits.

Folk Music of Venezuela. AFS L15. Edited by Juan Liscano and Charles Seeger.

In Praise of Oxalá and Other Gods, Black Music of South America. Nonesuch Explorer Series H-72036. Recorded by David Lewiston in Brazil, Colombia, and Ecuador.

Instruments and Music of Bolivia. Ethnic Folkways Library FM 4012. Recorded by Bernard Keiler; indigenous music of highlands.

Introducción al cancionero noble de colombia (Introduction to the Noble Song Book of Colombia). Edición especial de la Universidad de los Andes. Antares Ltda. Joaquin Piñeros Corpas. Anthology of Colombian folkmusic.

Jaime Guardia y su Charango. Lider, IEMPSA LD-1590. Peruvian folksinger and charango virtuoso.

Javanese Music from Surinam. Lyrichord LLST 7317.

Kingdom of the Sun, Peru's Inca Heritage. Nonesuch Explorer Series H-72029. Recorded by David Lewiston in the field.

Lamento de Quenas. Lider, IEMPSA LD-1604. Los Indios del Perú. Peruvian folklore group featuring the quena flutes.

La Peña de los Parra. Demon LPD-015. Featuring Isabel and Angel Parra and other Chilean folklorists.

La Peña de los Parra, Vol. 2. Arena LPD-054. Isabel

and Angel Parra and other Chilean folklorists.

Las Ultimas Composiciones de Violeta Parra. RCA Victor CML-2456. Famous Chilean folklorist, mother of Isabel and Angel Parra.

Los Cóndores de Uyuni. Lauro CDLR 2216; 45 rpm. A Bolivian panpipe ensemble.

Machu Picchu. Sono Radio L.P.L. 1088, S.E. 8031. Peruvian folklore ensemble.

Misa a la Chilena. Odeon LDC-36521. Vicente Bianchi. Chilean folk mass.

Misa Chilena. RCA Victor CML-2255. Raúl de Ramón. Chilean folk mass.

Misa Criolla. Philips 82039PL. Ariel Ramírez. Argentine folk mass.

Misa Incaica. Odeon LD 1441. A Bolivian and Peruvian folk mass, sung in Quechua.

Misa Intermisional Colombiana. Sello Vergara SV LP-225. A Colombian folk mass.

Mountain Music of Peru. Folkways FE 4539. Recorded by John Cohen. Anthology of Peruvian music from the Andes.

Música Folklorica de Venezuela. International Folk Music Council. Anthologie de la musique populaire. Disques Ocora OCR 78, RTF.

Music from Mato Grosso. Ethnic Folkways FE 4446. Recorded by Edward M. Weyer, Jr. Several examples of Caboclo music from the Mato Grosso, Brazil.

Music of Colombia. Folkways FW 6804. Recorded by A. H. Whiteford.

Music of Peru. Folkways FE 4415.

Musiques du Pérou. OCR 30. Recorded by Pierre Allard. Indian-derived music from Peru.

Negro Folk Music of Africa and America. Ethnic Folkways FE 4500. African-derived music from Brazil and Colombia.

Oratorio Para el Pueblo. Demon LPD-012. Angel Parra. A folk mass by a Chilean folklorist.

Peru: Music from the Land of Macchu Picchu. Lyrichord LLST 7294.

Quilapayún. Odeon LDC-36614. Chilean folklore ensemble, with Víctor Jara.

Recuerdos de Chile. RCA Victor CML-2001. Chilean folksongs recorded by various folklore groups of nightclub caliber.

Songs and Dances of Bolivia. Folkways FW 6871.

Songs and Dances of Brazil. Folkways FW 6953.

Songs of Brazil. Westminster Collectors Series W-9807. Clara Petraglia. Portuguese and African-derived songs sung by a Brazilian folklorist.

Songs of Chile. Folkways FW 8817. Martina and Maria Diaz. Traditional Chilean folksongs sung by Chilean folksingers.

Songs of the Guiana Jungle. Request Records RLP 8039. Ramjohn Hold and the Potaro Porknockers.

Folkmusic from Guyana.

Tamunangue y Mosaicos del Folklore Venezolano. Sonido Laffer. Spanish-, African-, and Indian- derived music of Venezuela.

The Columbia World Library of Folk and Primitive Music: Venezuela. Vol. 9. Columbia Masterworks SL-212. Collected by Alan Lomax. Spanish-, African-, and Indian-derived music of Venezuela.

The Piñata Party Presents Music of Peru. Folkways FW 8749. Peruvian folk music recorded in the field and by a folkloric group.

Traditional Chilean Songs. Folkways FW 8748. Rolando Alarcon. Chilean folklorist.

Traditional Music of Chile. ABC Records-Command COMS-9003. Recorded in the field by the University of Chile—University of California Cooperative Program.

Traditional Music of Peru. Ethnic Folkways Library FE 4456. Recorded by Babs Brown and Samuel Martí.

Uruguay: ¡A Desalambrar! Tear Down the Fences! Paredon P-1011. Daniel Viglietti. Protest music from Uruguay sung by Uruguayan folklorist.

Víctor Jara. Demon LPD-034-X. Martyred Chilean folklorist, leader of new protest song movement.

Viracocha: Legendary Music of the Andes. Lyrichord LLST 7264.

Films

A Valparaiso. CF/MH. B/W (a little color). 30 min. Directed by Jonis Ivens. In French, with English subtitles.

A kaleidoscope of the poorer section of this oceanside city built on steep hills, where life stops when the funicular does. One shot of the cueca.

Berimbau. NYF. Col. 12 min. Filmed in Brazil by Tony Talbot.

"Documents the playing of . . . the 'berimbau,' derived from the hunting bow of Angola peoples. . . . The performer, Nana, is a nationally recognized musician." Paul Vigoros.

Bolivian Boy. CF/MH. Col. 15 min.

A picture of rural life at 13,000 feet. Also some shots of La Paz. Indian flutes and some guitar music.

Flavio. CF/MH. B/W. 12 min.

The miserable life of an impoverished family in a tenement area high on a hill in Rio de Janeiro is depicted through the eyes of a twelve-year-old boy through a combination of stills and motion. Score by Carlos Surinach.

Index

Additions to the Bibliographies, 1982

Chapter 2: Evolution and Revolution in Chinese Music

"China" and "Taiwan." In *The New Grove Dictionary of Music and Musicians*. 1980. London: Macmillan.
Han Kuo-huang.
1978. "The Chinese Concept of Program Music." *Asian Music*, vol. X, No. 1:7–38.
1979. "The Modern Chinese Orchestra." *Asian Music*, Vol. XI, No. 1:1–40.
Kaufmann, Walter.
1976. *Musical References in the Chinese Classics*. Detroit: Information Coordinators, Inc. (Detroit Monographs in Musicology, 5.)
Thrasher, Alan R.
1981. "The Sociology of Chinese Music: An Introduction." *Asian Music*, Vol. XII, No. 2:17–53.
Wu Zuguang, Huang Zuolin and Mei Shaowu.
1981. *Peking Opera and Mei Lanfang: A Guide to China's Traditional Theatre and the Art of Its Great Master*. Peking: New World Press.
Yang Yin-liu.
1981. *Chung-kuo Yin-yüeh Shi-kao* (Draft History of Chinese Music). 2 vols. Peking: Yin-yüeh Ch'u-pan-she.

Chapter 6: Some Principles of Indian Classical Music

Powers, Harold, Nazir Jairazbhoy, Regula Qreshi, Robert Simon, Bonnie Wade, and Kapila Vatsyayan.
1980. "India: subcontinent of" (seven articles). In *The New Grove Dictionary of Music and Musicians*. London: Macmillan.

Chapter 7: Musical Strata in Sumatra, Java, and Bali

Sumatra
Kartomi, Margaret J.
1981. "Dualism in Unity: the Ceremonial Music of the

Mandailing Raja Tradition." *Asian Music* XII: 2, 74–108.
Java
Becker, Judith O.
1979. "Time and Tune in Java." *The Imagination of Reality: Essays in Southeast Asian Coherence Systems*. Edited by A. L. Becker and A. Yengoyan. Norwood, N.J.: Ablex Publishing Co.
1980. "A Southeast Asian Musical Process: Thai *Thaw* and Javanese *Irama*." *Ethnomusicology* XXIV (3): 453–464.

Chapter 9: The Traditional Music of the Australian Aborigines

Ellis, Catherine J.
1980. "Australia. Folk Music 3. Aboriginal Music and Dance in Southern Australia." *The New Grove Dictionary of Music and Musicians*, I: 722–728. London: Macmillan.
Jones, Trevor A.
1980. "Australia. Folk Music 1. General." *The New Grove Dictionary of Music and Musicians*, I: 711–713. London: Macmillan.
1980. "Didjeridu." *The New Grove Dictionary of Music and Musicians*, V: 461–462. London: Macmillan.
In press. "Australia, Folk Music of." *Oxford Companion to Music* (new edition). Oxford: Oxford University Press.
Kartomi, Margaret J.
1980. "Childlikeness in Playsongs: A Case Study Among the Pitjintjara at Yalata, South Australia." *Miscellanea Musicologica*, No. 11: 172–214.
Moyle, Alice M.
1974. "Pitch and Loudness Ambits in Some North Australian Songs." *Selected Reports in Ethnomusicology* 2(1): 17–30.
1977. "Aborigines: Music, Song and Dance." In *The

Australian Encyclopedia, 3rd ed., I: 37-40. Sydney: Grolier Society.

1980. "Corroboree." *The New Grove Dictionary of Music and Musicians*, IV: 804-805. London: Macmillan.

1980. "Australia. Folk Music 2. Aboriginal Music and Dance in Northern Australia." *The New Grove Dictionary of Music and Musicians*, I: 713-722. London: Macmillan.

1981. "The Australian Didjeridu: A Late Musical Intrusion." *World Archaeology* XII, No. 3: 321-331.

Moyle, Richard M.

1979. *Songs of the Pintupi. Musical Life in a Central Australian Society.* Canberra: Australian Institute of Aboriginal Studies.

Pritan, Prabhu (Antony McCardell).

1980. "Aspects of Musical Structure in Australian Aboriginal Songs of the South-West of the Western Desert." *Studies in Music*, No. 14: 9-44.

Stubington, Jill.

1979. "North Australian Aboriginal Music." In J. Isaacs (ed.), *Australian Aboriginal Music*, 7-19. Sydney: Aboriginal Artists Agency.

Chapter 12: Anlo Ewe Music in Anyako, Volta Region, Ghana

Ladzekpo, Kobla.

1971. "Social Mechanics of Good Music." *African Music* 5, 1:6-22.

1973. "A Study Center at Anyako, Ghana." SEM *Newsletter* 7, 5 (September-October), [6]-[7].

Chapter 13: The Music of Ethiopia

Doresse, Jean.

1959. *Ethiopia.* New York: G. P. Putnam's Sons.

Haberland, Eike, et al.

1963. *Galla Süd-Äthiopiens.* Stuttgart: W. Kohlhammer.

Hallpike, Christopher R.

1972. *The Konso of Ethiopia: A Study of the Values of a Cushitic People.* Oxford: The Clarendon Press.

Jensen, A. E., et al.

1959. *Altvölker Süd-Äthiopiens.* Stuttgart: W. Kohlhammer.

Kebede, Ashenafi.

[c. 1977]. *Secular Verse and Poetry in Ethiopian Traditional Music.* International Institute for African Music.

1980. "The Sacred Chant of Ethiopian Monotheistic Churches: Music in Black Jewish and Christian Communities." *Black Perspective in Music*, 8(1):21-34.

Kimberlin, Cynthia Tse and J. Kimberlin.

In press. "Masingo Organology, or the Morphology of Ethiopia's Bowed Spike Fiddle." *Selected Reports in Ethnomusicology.*

Legesse, Asmarom.

1973. *Gada: Three Approaches to the Study of African Society.* New York: Free Press.

Leslau, Wolf.

1969. *Falasha Anthology.* New York: Schocken Books. First published 1951.

Levine, Donald N.

1965. *Wax and Gold: Tradition and Innovation in Ethiopian Culture.* Chicago: University of Chicago Press.

1974. *Greater Ethiopia: The Evolution of a Multiethnic Society.* Chicago: University of Chicago Press.

Lewis, Herbert S.

1965. *Galla Monarchy: Jimma Abba Jifar, Ethiopia, 1830-1932.* Madison: University of Wisconsin Press.

Lipsky, G. A. et al.

1962. *Ethiopia.* New Haven: Human Relations Area File.

Perham, Marjery.

1969. *The Government of Ethiopia.* Evanston: Northwestern University Press. First published 1948.

Shack, William S.

1966. *The Gurage: A People of the Ensete Culture.* London: Oxford University Press.

1974. *Amhara, Tigrina, and Related Peoples.* Ethnographic Survey of Africa Series, International Publications Service.

Shelemay, Kay Kaufman.

1977. "The Liturgical Music of the Falasha of Ethopia." Ph.D. dissertation, University of Michigan. Available from University Microfilms, Ann Arbor.

1978a. "A Quarter-Century in the Life of a Falasha Prayer." *Yearbook of the International Folk Music Council*, X: 83-108.

1979b. "Rethinking Falasha Liturgical History." *Proceedings of the Fifth International Conference on Ethiopian Studies at the University of Chicago.* Chicago: University of Illinois Press.

1980c. "'Historical Ethnomusicology': Reconstructing Falasha Liturgical History." *Ethnomusicology*, 24(2): 233-258.

Simoons, Frederick.

1960. *Northwest Ethiopia.* Madison: University of Wisconsin Press.

Trimingham, J. Spencer.

1965. *Islam in Ethiopia.* London: Frank Cass Co.

Ullendorff, Edward.

1960. *The Ethiopians.* London: Oxford University Press.

Chapter 16: On Jewish Music

Armstead, S., I. V. Katz, and J. Silverman.

1981. "Sobre la antigua discografiá sefadri y el romancero." *La Córonica*, Vol. 11, No. 2, Spring: 138-144.

Avenary, Hanoch.

1979. *Encounters of East and West in Music: Selected Writings.* Tel Aviv: Faculty of Visual and Performing Arts, Tel Aviv University.

Fromm, Herbert.

1978. *On Jewish Music: A Composer's View.* New York: Bloch Publishing Co., Inc.

Gerson-Kiwi, Edith.

1980. *Migrations and Mutations of the Music in East-West: Selected Writings.* Tel Aviv: Department of Musicology, Tel Aviv University.

Israel Studies in Musicology.

1978-82. Jerusalem: Israel Musicological Society.

Koskoff, Ellen.

1979. "Contemporary Nigun Composition in an American Hasidic Community." *Selected Reports in Ethnomusicology*, Vol. 3, No. 1: 153-173.

Musica Judaica.

1975-81. 3 vols. New York: American Society for Jewish Music.

National Council for Culture and Art.

1980. *Aspects of Music in Israel.* Tel Aviv: Israel Composer's League.

Saminsky, Lazare.

1980. *Voices of a People. The Story of Yiddish Folk Song.* Reprint of 1934 ed. New York: AMS Press.

Schwadron, Abraham A.
    1982. "Chad Gadya: A Domestic Song for Passover." *Selected Reports in Ethnomusicology*, Festschrift edition, Vol. IV, No. 1, in press.
Shelemay, Kay Kaufman.
    1980. "Historical Musicology Reconstructing Falasha Liturgical History." *Ethnomusicology*, Vol. 24, No. 2, May: 233-258.
Shiloah, Amnon.
    1978. "The Symbolism of Music in the Kabbalistic Tradition." *The World of Music*, Vol. 22, No. 3: 56-65.
Slobin, Mark.
    1976. "A Survey of Early Jewish American Sheet Music (1898-1921)." *Working Papers in Yiddish and Eastern European Jewish Studies*, No. 17. New York: Max Weinrich Center for Advanced Studies of the YIVO Institute for Jewish Research.
Weich-Shanak, Susana.
    1978. "The Wedding Songs of the Bulgarian-Sephardi Jews: A Preliminary Study." *Assaph: Studies in the Arts* (Section A, Orbis Musicae), No. 6: 81-107.
Werner, Eric.
    1981. "Traces of Jewish Hagiolatry." *Hebrew Union College Annual*, Vol. 51: 39-60.
Yuval Monograph Series.
    1974-78. Seven monographs. Jewish Music Research Centre, Hebrew University. Jerusalem: Magnes Press.

Chapter 18: Music of the Alaskan Eskimos

Alaskan Eskimo

Hauser, Michael.
    1977. "Formal Structure in Polar Eskimo Drum Songs." *Ethnomusicology* 21(January): 33-53.
Johnston, Thomas F.
    1975. "Songs and Dances of the Alaskan Eskimo." *Viltis Folklore* 33:68.

Canadian Eskimo

Cavanaugh, Beverly Anne.
    1979. *Music of the Netsilik Eskimo.* Toronto: University of Toronto. Doctoral dissertation.
Hoffman, Charles.
    1974. *Drum Dance: Legends, Ceremonies, Dances, and Songs of the Eskimos.* Toronto: Gage.
O'Connell, Sheldon.
    1979. "Music of the Inuit." *The Beaver* (Autumn): 12-17.

Chapter 19: Symbol and Function in South American Indian Music

Aytai, Desidério.
    1981. "A Música Instrumental Xavante." *Latin American Music Review* 2:103-129.
Baumann, Max Peter.
    1981. "Music, Dance, and Song of the Chipayas (Bolivia)." *Latin American Music Review* 2:171-222.
Coba Andrade, Carlos A.
    1978. "Estudio Sobre el *Tumank o Tsayantur*, Arco Musical del Ecuador." *Folklore Americano* 25:79-100.
Grebe, María Ester.
    1973. "El kultrún mapuche: un microcosmo simbólico." *Revista Musical Chilena* 123-124:3-42.
    1974a. "La música alacalufe: aculturación y cambio estilístico." *Revista Musical Chilena* 126-127:47-79.
    1974b. "Presencia del dualismo en la cultura y música mapuche." *Revista Musical Chilena* 126-127:80-111.
Halmos, István.
    1974. "Preliminary Report on a Field Work among Piaroa Indians." *Revista Venezolana de Folklore* 5:58-73.
Hawberli, Joerg.
    1979. "Twelve Nasca Panpipes: A Study." *Journal of the Society for Ethnomusicology* 23:57-74.
Hill, Jonathan.
    1979. "Kamayura Flute Music." *Journal of the Society for Ethnomusicology* 23:417-432.
Holzmann, Rodolfo.
    1980. "Cuatro Ejemplos de Música Q'ero (Cuzco, Perú)." *Latin American Music Review* 1:74-91.
Juarez Toledo, J. Manuel.
    1978. "Música Tradicional de los Yucpa-Irapa del Estado Zulia, Venezuela." *Folklore Americano* 26:59-81.
Menezes Bastos, Rafael José de.
    1978. *A Musicológica Kamayurá.* Brasilia: Fundação Nacional do Indio.
Merino, Luis.
    1974. "Instrumentos musicales, cultura mapuche y el *Cautiverio feliz* del Maestre de Campo Francisco Núñez y Bascuñan." *Revista Musical Chilena* 128: 56-95.
Olsen, Dale A.
    1979. "Musical Instruments of the Native Peoples of the Orinoco Delta, the Caribbean and Beyond." *Revista/Review Interamericana* 8:577-613.
    1980. "Magical Protection Songs of the Warao Indians—Part I: Animals." *Latin American Music Review* 1:131-161.
    1981. "Magical Protection Songs of the Warao Indians—Part II: Spirits." *Latin American Music Review* 2:1-10.
Robertson, Carol E.
    1979. "Pulling the Ancestors: Performance Practice and Praxis in Mapuche Ordering." *Journal of the Society for Ethnomusicology* 23:395-416.
Schechter, John M.
    1979. "The Inca *Cantar Historico*: A Lexico-Historical Elaboration on Two Cultural Themes." *Journal of the Society for Ethnomusicology* 23:191-204.
Seeger, Anthony.
    1979. "What Can We Learn When They Sing? Vocal Genres of the Suya Indians of Central Brazil." *Journal of the Society for Ethnomusicology* 23:373-394.
    1980. "Sing For Your Sister: The Structure and Performance of Suya *Akia*." In Norma McLeod and Marcia Herndon, eds., *The Ethnography of Musical Performance.* Norwood, Pa.: Norwood Editions.
Seitz, Barbara J.
    1981a. "Power Songs of the Sacha Huarmi (Jungle Woman): As Transformational Communication Acts." In *Discourse in Ethnomusicology II. A Tribute to Alan P. Merriam.* Bloomington, Indiana: Ethnomusicology Publications Group.
    1981b. "Quichua Songs to Sadden the Heart: Music in a Communication Event." *Latin American Music Review* 2:223-251.
Stocks, Anthony.
    1979. "Tendiendo un Puente Entre el Cielo y la Tierra en Alas de la Canción." *Amazonia Peruana* 2, no. 4:71-100.
Valencia Ch., Americo.
    1980a. "Los Sikuris de la Isla de Taquile: Part 1." *Boletín*

de Lima 8:52-60.
1980b. "Los Sikuris de la Isla de Taquile: Conclusion."
Boletín de Lima 9:62-75.
1981a. "Los Chiriguanos de Huanacané: Part 1." *Boletín de Lima* 12:35-43.
1981b. "Los Chiriguanos de Huancané: Part 2." *Boletín de Lima* 13:46-56.
1981c. "Los Chiriguanos de Huancané: Conclusion." *Boletín de Lima* 14:23-29.
Wilbert, Johannes.
1974. "The Calabash of the Ruffled Feathers." *Artscanada*, December 1973/January 1974:90-93.

Chapter 20: Folk Music of South America—A Musical Mosaic

Alvarez, Cristina and María Ester Grebe.
1974. "La trifonía atacameña y sus perspectivas interculturales." *Revista Musical Chilena* 126-127:21-46.
Aretz, Isabel and Luís Filipe Ramón y Rivera.
1976. "Areas musicales de tradición oral en América latina." *Revista Musical Chilena* 134:9-55.
Carpio Muñoz, Juan Guillermo.
1976. *El Yaraví Arequipeña*. Arequipa, Peru: Los Talleres La Colmena.
Gushiken, Jose J.
1979. *El Violín de Isua*. Lima, Peru: Universidad Nacional Mayor de San Marcos.
Kazadi wa Mukuna.
n.d. *Contribuicão Bantu na Música Popular Brasileira*. São Paulo: Global Editora e Distribuidora Ltda.
List, George.
1973. "El Conjunto de Gaitas de Colombia: la herencia de tres culturas." *Revista Musical Chilena* 123-124:43-62.
1980. "African Influences in the Rhythmic and Metric Organization of Colombian Costeño Folksong and Folk Music." *Latin American Music Review* 1:6-17.
Mendoza de Arce, Daniel.
1981. "A Structural Approach to the Rural Society and Music of the Rio de la Plata and Southern Brazil."

Latin American Music Review 2:66-90.
Menezes Bastos, Rafael José de.
1974. "Las músicas tradicionales del Brasil." *Revista Musical Chilena* 125:21-77.
Olsen, Dale A.
1976. "Música vesperal Mojo en San Miguel de Isiboro, Bolovia." *Revista Musical Chilena* 133:28-46.
1980. "Japanese Music in Peru." *Journal of the Society for Asian Music* 11, 2:41-51.
Polak, A.
1974. "Influencia de los cultos afroamericanos en Venezuela." *Revista Venezolana de Folklore* 5:83-88.
Price, Sally and Richard.
1980. *Afro-American Arts of the Suriname Rain Forest*. Berkeley and Los Angeles: University of California Press.
Santa Cruz Gamarra, César.
1977. *El Waltz y el valse criollo*. Lima, Peru: Instituto Nacional de Cultura.
Tinhorão, José Ramos.
1978. *Pequena História da Música Popular*. Petropolis, Brazil: Editora Vozes Ltda.
Vale, Flausino Rodrigues.
1978. *Elementos de Folclore Musical Brasileiro*. São Paulo: Companhia Editora Nacional. *Brasiliana*, Vol. 57.
Vega, Carlos.
1946. *Los Instrumentos Musicales Aborígenes y Criollos de la Argentina*. Bueons Aires: Ediciones Centurion.
Waddey, Ralph C.
1980. "Viola de Samba and Samba de Viola in the Reconcavo of Bahia (Brazil)." *Latin American Music Review* 1:196-212.
1981. "Viola de Samba and Samba de Viola in the Reconcavo of Bahia (Brazil). Part II: Samba de Viola." *Latin American Music Review* 2:252-279.
Whitten, Jr., Norman E.
1975. "Musical Contexts in the Pacific Lowlands of Colombia and Ecuador." In *Cultural and Social Anthropology*, Peter B. Hammond, ed. New York: Macmillan Publishing Co., Inc.

Additions to the Discographies, 1982

Chapter 2: Evolution and Revolution in Chinese Music

46. *Vocal Music of Contemporary China*, Vol. I, the Han People; Vol. II, the National Minorities. Folkways FE-4091-2. (Selected and annotated by Han Kuo-huang.)
47. *West Meets East.* Asian Music Ensemble, Northern Illinois University. Folkways FSS-37455.
48. *Phases of the Moon: Traditional Chinese Music.* CBS M-36705.

Chapter 7: Musical Strata in Sumatra, Java, and Bali

Java: Music of Mystical Enchantment. Lyrichord Stereo LLST 7301 (ES 1042).
Music of Mandailing, Sumatra. Bärenreiter (in press). Edited by Hans Oesch. Series: An Anthology of Southeast Asian Music. Recorded by H. and M. J. Kartomi.
Music of Angkola, Sumatra. Bärenreiter (in press). Edited by Hans Oesch. Series: An Anthology of Southeast Asian Music. Recorded by H. and M.J. Kartomi.

Scintillating Sounds of Bali. Lyrichord Stereo LLST 7305 (ES 1041).
Street Music of Central Java. Lyrichord Stereo LLST 7310 (ES 1040).
Javanese Music from Surinam. Lyrichord Stereo LLST 7317 (ES 1039).

Chapter 9: The Traditional Music of the Australian Aborigines

Aboriginal Music from Australia. UNESCO Collection. Musical Sources, Philips 6586-034. Alice M. Moyle.
Aboriginal Sound Instruments. Australian Institute of Aboriginal Studies, AIAS/14. Alice M. Moyle. (Companion booklet available separately.)
Bamyili Corroboree: Songs of Djoli Laiwanga: Didjeridu, Sticks and Singers. Grevillea Records GRV1030. Douglas Myers.
The Bora of the Pascoe River, Cape York Peninsula, North-

east Australia. Ethnic Folkways (U.S.) FE4211. Wolfgang Laade.

Djambidj. An Aboriginal song series from northern Australia. Australian Institute of Aboriginal Studies, AIAS/16. Bryan Butler and Stephen Wild. (Companion booklet available separately.)

The First Australians. Aboriginal Artists Agency, AAA-04.

Modern Music of Torres Strait. Australian Institute of Aboriginal Studies, AIAS/15. Jeremy Becket. (Companion booklet available separately.)

Music of Aboriginal Australia. Aboriginal Theatre Foundation. South Pacific Festival of the Arts. Adventures in Sound, Hibiscus, HLS-48.

Songs of Bamyili. Aboriginal Artists Agency, AAA-01.

Songs from the Kimberleys. Australian Institute of Aboriginal Studies, AIAS/13. Alice M. Moyle. (Companion booklet available separately.)

Songs from North Queensland. Australian Institute of Aboriginal Studies, AIAS/12. Alice M. Moyle. (Companion booklet available separately.)

Songs of the Tiwi. Aboriginal Artists Agency, AAA-02.

Songs of Torres Strait. Aboriginal Artists Agency, AAA-03.

Traditional Songs of the Western Torres Straits, South Pacific. Ethnic Folkways (U.S.) FE4025. Wolfgang Laade.

Wandjuk Marika in Port Moresby: Didjeridu Solo. Larrikin Records, LPE-014. Frederick Duvelle and Jennifer Isaacs.

Chapter 13: The Music of Ethiopia

Ethiopie; polyphonies des Dorze. Le Chant du Monde LDX 74646. Recordings and commentary by Bernard Lortat-Jacob.

Südäthiopian. Musik de Hamar. Museum für Völkerkunde, West Berlin. MC 6. Recordings and commentary by Ivo Strecker.

Chapter 16: On Jewish Music

A Centennial of Jewish Music. Tambur Records, Cedarhurst, New York; TR-593. One 12″ LP disc, 1977.

Cantares de Safarad. La Coramusa, Buenos Aires; E-027. Sung by Eleonora Noga Alberti. Oné 12″ LP disc, 1980.

Chad Gadya (Only One Kid.) Folkways FR-8920. Compiled and edited by A. Schwadron. 1982.

Greek-Jewish Musical Traditions. Ethnic Folkways Records, FE-4205. Recordings and notes by Amnon Shiloah. One 12″ LP disc, 1978.

Hasidic Tunes of Dancing and Rejoicing. RCA, Jerusalem, Hebrew University; YJRL-029. Edited by A. Hajdu and Y. Mazor.

Ich Benk noch dem Nigun: A Collection of Yiddish Songs. Tara Publications, Cedarhurst, New York. One 12″ LP disc, 1979.

Israël: Traditional Liturgiques des Communautes Juives. 1. les jours de Kippour. Radio France, Paris; OCORA-558529. One 12″ LP disc, 1977.

Judeo-Baroque Music. Harmonia Mundi, Paris: HM-1021, Boston Camerata. One 12″ LP disc, 1979.

Kelzmer Music (1910–1942). Folkways FSS-34021. Compiled by H. Sapoznik. Notes by H. Sapoznik, W. Z. Feldman, and A. Statman; YIVO Institute for Jewish Research. One 12″ disc, 1980.

Modzitzer Favorites, Volume 4. Israel, Neginah NRS-1206. Two 12″ LP discs, 1975.

Morasha; Traditional Musical Heritage. Folkways FE-

4203. Recorded and annotated by Amnon Shiloah, Israel. Two 12″ LP discs, 1978.

Sefarad. The Sephardic Tradition in Ladino Song. Tambur Records, Cedarhurst, New York; TR-590. One 12″ LP disc, 1977.

Sefardi Songs from the Balkans. Anthology of Musical Traditions in Israel, Jerusalem, Hebrew University, Jewish Music Research Centre; AMTL-8001. Recordings and commentaries by Susana Weich-Shanak. One 12″ LP disc, 1980.

Synagogal Art Music, XIIth-XVIIIth Centuries. Religious Poems, Cantatas, and Choral Works. Eastronics, Ltd., Jerusalem: AMTI-7901. One 12″ LP disc, 1978.

The Music of Salamone Rossi, Hebreo of Mantua. Reissue by Odyssey Y-35226, New York Pro Musica. One 12″ LP disc, 1980.

The Russian Jewish Composers. Musique International, Chicago; Vol. I, M-7501-A, 1976; Vol. II, M-7501-9, 1977; Vol. IV, M-7504-A, 1977.

The Yiddish Art Song. University of Washington Press, Seattle; OLY-105. One 12″ LP disc, 1976.

Chapter 19: Symbol and Function in South American Indian Music

Argentina. The Indians of the Gran Chaco. Lyrichord Stereo LLST 7295.

Argentine Folk Music, the Chaquenos in song and dance, magic rituals of the Chacos. Lyrichord Stereo LLST 7254.

HEKURA, Yanomamö Shamanism from Southern Venezuela. Quartz 004.

Música Indígena Guajibo. Fundación La Salle / Instituto Interamericano de Etnomusicología y Folklore (Venezuela).

Music of the Haut Oyapok, Oyampi and Emerillon Indian Tribes, French Guiana, South America. Ethnic Folkways Records FE 4235.

Musique des Indiens Bora et Witoto d'Amazonie colombienne. Collection C.N.R.S./Musée de l'Homme, Archives d'Ethnomusicologie. AEM 01.

Sacred and Profane Music of the IKA. (Colombia). Ethnic Folkways Records FE 4055.

Soul Vine Shaman. Sinchi Yachaj: Powerful Shaman of the Napo River. (Ecuador). Sacha Runa Research Foundation.

Wayãpí Guyane. (French Guiana). Office de la Recherche Scientifique et Technique Outre-mer Société d'Études Linguistiques et Anthropologiques de France. Selaf Orstom CETO 792.

Yanoama. Techniche 1 Vocali Sciamanismo. (Venezuela). I Suoni. Musica di Tradizione Orale. CETRA / SU 5003.

Chapter 20: Folk Music of South America—A Musical Mosaic

Agrupación Con Convenezuela: Música Popular y Folklórica Venezolana, Vol. 1. YVLP-009.

Antología del Vals Peruano. Los Morochucos. Lider, IEMPSA ELD-1518.

Ayacucho. (Peruvian guitar of Raúl García Z.) Sono Radio LPL 2105.

Argentina: The Guitar of the Pampas. Lyrichord Stereo LLST 7253.

Atahualpa Yupanqui. Pa' Alumbrar los Corazones. (Argentina). Discos Latin International DLIS-6021.

Atahualpa Yupanqui. La Canción, el Poeta y el Hombre. (Argentina). Discos Latin International DLIS-5009.

Banda Santa Lucía de Moche. (Peru). VIRREY VIR 946.

Black Orpheus (*Orfeu Negro*). The Original Sound Track of the Movie. (Brazil). Epic LN 3672.

Cantares Huaracinos. (Peru). Lider, IEMPSA ELD 02.06.681.

Cantos Costeños. Folksongs of the Atlantic Coastal Region of Colombia. Ethnosound, Anthology Record and Tape Corp. EST-8003.

Cumanana. Nicomedes Santa Cruz. (Peru). Philips P 6350 001 – P 6350 002.

Danzas y Cantos Afrovenezolanos. (Venezuela). Oswaldo Lares, Caracas.

El Arpa de Florencio Coronado. Bajo el Cielo del Perú. Sono Radio L.P.L. 2348.

Flute Music of the Andes. The Atlas Series. 6112.

Harp Music of the Andes. (Actually Paraguay). The Atlas Series. 6124.

Inti-illimani. Música y Canto de los Pueblos Andinos. (Chilean group in exile). Alerce ALP-218.

la Pampa y la Puna. (Peruvian guitar of Dr. Raúl García Z.). Sono Radio S.E.-9423.

Música de Venezuela. Cantos y Danzas de la Costa Central. Vol. 1. Oswaldo Lares, Caracas.

Música de Venezuela. Popular-Folklorica. (Indio Figueredo). Oswaldo Lares, Caracas.

Música Venezolana. (Serenata Guayanesa y Hernan Gamboa). Fundación Gran Marischal de Ayacucho.

Music From Saramaka. A Dynamic Afro-American Tradition. Ethnic Folkways Records FE 4225.

Music of the Incas. Ayllu Sulca. Lyrichord Stereo LLST 7348.

Nordeste e Violas. (Song and viola music from Northeast Brazil). Discos Continental, Musicolor 1-04-405-150.

Quilapayun. Les Flutes Chiliennes. (Chilean group in exile). Sounds Superb 2M 048 52157.

Quilapayun. Patria. (Chilean group in exile). DICAP Pathe Marconi C 068-98285.

Sentimiento Juajino. (Central Peruvian orchestra Lira Jaujina). Virrey VIR-910.

Socabón. Nicomedes Santa Cruz. (Peru). Virrey VIR-0000948.9-0000949.9.

Viva La Marinera. (Peru). Odeon IEMPSA ELD 02.01.561.

Additions to the Filmographies, 1982

Chapter 9: The Traditional Music of the Australian Aborigines

A Walbiri Fire Ceremony: Ngatjakula. AIAS. Col. 21 min. Directed by Roger Sandall.

Goodbye Old Man. AIAS. Col. 70 min. Directed by David MacDougall.

Mourning for Mangatopi. AIAS. Col. 56 min. Directed by Curtis Levy.

Chapter 13: The Music of Ethiopia

Ethiopian Dances. Hungarian Academy of Sciences, Folk Music Research Group. B/W. 24 min.

Harvest: 3,000 Years. UNI Films, UCLA. B/W. 137 min.

Nyangatom: Yellow Rifles. UNI Films, UCLA. Col. 90 min.

Rivers of Sand. UCEMC. Col. 83 min.

Chapter 16: On Jewish Music

About the Jews of India. Col. 40 min. 1979. Jewish Media Service, Jewish Welfare Board, New York City.

Image before My Eyes. Col. 90 min. 1980. YIVO Institute for Jewish Research, New York City.

Song of Radauti. B/W. 25 min. 1978. Jewish Media Service, Jewish Welfare Board, New York City.

The Arab Jews. Col. 28 min. 1976. Jewish Media Service, Jewish Welfare Board, New York City.

This Year in Russia. B/W. 13 min. 1976. United Jewish Appeal, c/o Alden Films, Brooklyn, New York.